DIAGHILEV

About Diaghilev

'One of the most interesting and characteristic figures of our fatherland, uniting in his person the boundless charm and indomitable strength of Russian culture.' *Alexandre Benois*

'Everything about Diaghilev is terrible and significant.' *Aleksandr Blok*

'That ogre, that sacred monster, [...] that Russian prince to whom life was tolerable only to the extent to which he could summon up marvels.' *Jean Cocteau*

'Diaghilev, that terrible and charming man, who could make stones dance.' *Claude Debussy*

'Diaghilev is Louis XIV.' *Henri Matisse*

'Diaghilev, the irreplaceable Diaghilev was a wizard, a sorcerer.' *François Poulenc*

'A giant, undoubtedly the only one whose dimensions increase the more he recedes into the distance.' *Sergey Prokofiev*

'Diaghilev's an amiable sort, but he's an awful person.' *Erik Satie*

'We must create a breakthrough, we must amaze and not be afraid to amaze, we must make our entrance all at once, display our every facet, all the merits and shortcomings of our national identity.' Sergey Diaghilev

DIAGHILEV

· A LIFE ·

Sjeng Scheijen

Translated by Jane Hedley-Prôle and S. J. Leinbach

P

PROFILE BOOKS

First published in Great Britain in 2009 by
PROFILE BOOKS LTD
3A Exmouth House
Pine Street
London ECIR OJH
www.profilebooks.com

First published in 2009 as *Sergej Diaghilev: Een leven voor de kunst*
by Uitgeverij Bert Bakker, Amsterdam

English-language publication has been made possible with the financial support of the
Foundation for the Production and Translation of Dutch Literature

1 3 5 7 9 10 8 6 4 2

Typeset in Caslon by MacGuru Ltd
info@macguru.org.uk
Designed by Sue Lamble

Printed and bound in Great Britain by
T. J. International

A CIP catalogue record for this book is available from the British Library.

ISBN 978 1 84668 141 7
eISBN 978 1 84765 245 4

Contents

CONTENTS

· TRANSLATORS' NOTE ·

THE EXCHANGE RATES for the rouble were stable in the early years
of the twentieth century, and those given for the 1914 edition of Baedeker's
Russia are just over £10 (or $50) for 100 roubles.

The translations from the Russian were made by Peter Carson and are the
copyright of Profile Books. During our lengthy collaboration Peter proved to
be the perfect editor: efficient, unflappable and a source of unfailing support.
We would like to take this opportunity to thank him.

Jane Hedley-Prôle and S. J. Leinbach

· INTRODUCTION: DEATH IN VENICE ·

ON 21 AUGUST 1929 a funeral barge set off from the Grand Hotel on the Lido for the little island of San Michele, where the city of Venice has buried its dead since the beginning of the nineteenth century. The body in the barge, bound for the Greek Orthodox section of the cemetery, was that of Sergey Pavlovich Diaghilev, founder and leader of the Ballets Russes and one of the most influential pioneers of modern art in the twentieth century. In the course of a twenty-three-year career Diaghilev had made his mark in Europe and the Americas, and in this relatively short space of time he transformed the world of dance, theatre, music and the visual arts as no one had ever done before (or has done since).

From 1896 he was active in Russia as a critic, exhibition organiser, publisher and art historian. Through his journal *Mir iskusstva* and exhibitions he brought Russian art out of years of stagnation, championed international symbolism, art nouveau, the Arts and Crafts Movement and Russian neo-nationalism, and revived forgotten aspects of Russia's artistic past. He set up a travelling, privately financed ballet troupe that performed in Europe's and America's most famous venues, and for nearly quarter of a century it would be the world's leading dance company. Its early productions fed the craze for Slavic and oriental exoticism, catapulting the Ballets Russes to instant fame. Shortly before the First World War, Diaghilev reinvented his company as a laboratory and platform for the avant-garde, working with artists such as Picasso, Cocteau, Derain, Braque and Matisse, as well as Russian modernists such as Larionov, Goncharova and Naum Gabo. His ventures, which often met with strong resistance from those closest to him, entailed huge personal and financial risks. Diaghilev's company did more for the prestige and scope of the European avant-garde than any other single entity.[1]

Diaghilev achieved all this with an improvised organisation that had no official headquarters for the first ten years of its existence and, even more incredibly, no regular funding. He himself had no home and almost no possessions. He roamed the world with his manservant and a couple of suitcases, staying at expensive hotels (which he sometimes left without paying the bill). He oversaw programming, contracts, publicity and casting, and assumed creative responsibility for his productions, many of which bear his artistic stamp. Financial crises were the leitmotif of his life. He often teetered on the brink of ruin, and on at least one occasion he actually had to flee his creditors. Yet at the same time he was the fêted guest of kings, noblemen and captains of industry.

Diaghilev spent his infancy in St Petersburg and his youth in Perm, at the foot of the northern Urals, where his family had their roots. No one who knew him failed to say how Russian he was, and how attached he was to his homeland, from which he was effectively exiled by the First World War. Even after fifteen years of uninterrupted residence in western Europe, at a time when his company was hiring more and more foreigners, his inner circle was almost exclusively Russian. Diaghilev's separation from Russia may well have been the greatest sorrow of his life. Yet it was not just the result of forces beyond his control; his European exile was also a very conscious choice.

Diaghilev saw the promotion of Russian art in Europe as his mission in life, and the West's acceptance of Russia, at the beginning of the twentieth century, as a major European cultural nation, is in large part his personal achievement. His friend Alexandre Benois, a renowned Russian intellectual, called him 'one of the most interesting and characteristic figures of our fatherland, uniting in his person the boundless charm and indomitable strength of Russian culture'.[2]

Despite this, his relationship with the Russian establishment was a troubled one. The courtiers of Tsar Nicolas II frequently tried to frustrate and sabotage Diaghilev's success in Western Europe. By the time of the Soviet regime Diaghilev was regarded as a has-been, and ultimately as an enemy of the state. Yet in Europe and America his death was front-page news, and in the wake of his passing the papers were full of reminiscences and necrologies.

In his own country his death merited only a solitary mention: a brief obituary on page fifteen of the Red Panorama, a journal of art and literature.

Diaghilev's tomb is engraved with the words *Venise, inspiratrice éternelle de nos apaisements*. The impresario had a long, intense love affair with the city on the lagoon where, for many years, he spent his summer holidays. He first went there at the age of eighteen and was to return again and again. To Diaghilev, Venice represented the ultimate work of art, an exquisite construct of the imagination. It was a place where the chaos of nature had been surmounted by feats of artifice. The city was a product of human imagination, a fantastic and mythological place. Like others before him, Diaghilev fancied Venice a mirage, or a giant stage on which countless extras performed amid ever-changing decors. It was also the city in which Wagner, the idol of his youth, had died. His hero-worship of the composer undoubtedly inspired his dramatic prediction, in a letter to his stepmother in 1902, that he would die in Venice:

> You ask if I love Venice, and why we've come here. As to the second question I'll say it's not a matter of why. We've simply come, for it's so good and calming for the nerves here, and life is so little like life in general; besides in Venice one can't 'live' – one can only 'be' ... I never could understand the point of having shops and stock exchanges and soldiers here! You can't take any of that seriously here. Does the Doges' Palace exist, and San Marco and the evening sea air? All this forms a truth so delicious that I feel that I can emulate Wagner in one way and will come to Venice to die. Wasn't that a masterstroke on Wagner's part? In the age of Romanticism young ladies sobbed over the death of Chopin in the Canary Islands,[3] but how feeble that was by comparison with the great man of Bayreuth! If Nietzsche crucified himself with his madness, Wagner too made himself like God, when having composed Parsifal he came to die in la Vendramini. It's such a cold and awesome palace, not the playful Gothic of the Ca d'Oro but like a Renaissance coffin, one grand enough to hold within itself the great spirit of the little monster from Bayreuth.
>
> And so I am convinced I will end my days here, where there's nowhere to hurry to, where one needn't make any effort to live; and that's our main problem, all of us don't just live; we strive terribly to live as if without those efforts our life would come to an end.[4]

It has been suggested that Diaghilev modelled his 'death in Venice' on that of Gustav Aschenbach, the protagonist of Thomas Mann's eponymous novella. Diaghilev knew the book well, but it is quite clear that it is not the fictional writer Aschenbach (based on the composer Gustav Mahler) but Wagner whom Diaghilev took as his example.

Diaghilev was tormented by morbid fantasies throughout his life: many friends and associates noted his fearful obsession with death. He was terrified of contagious diseases and ever on the alert for 'bad omens'; he tried to ward off evil with amulets and rituals. He dealt with his fears by turning death into an act in the theatrical spectacle of his life. According to Diaghilev, it was a stroke of genius on Wagner's part to go to Venice to die, because by so doing he transformed his own life into a work of art, thereby negating the ultimate chaos of death. Diaghilev, too, wanted to die there, in the hope of giving meaning to his passing, of linking annihilation with an act of creativity.

In many ways, Venice provides the key to understanding Diaghilev's complex and hidden self. It was a place of peace, where he could withdraw and dream away his time. A man with no home of his own and no private life, who lived in the public eye, in theatres, hotels and restaurants, must have needed at least one bolt-hole to which he could return every year. Moreover, Diaghilev was someone who kept his most intimate feelings hidden, perhaps because his visibility made him vulnerable. These secretive tendencies were exacerbated by the difficulty of living an openly homosexual lifestyle at a time when 'sexual deviancy' was considered an illness. He only shared his doubts, fears and private feelings with his closest friends and, as he grew older, not even with them. An artist who knew him well noted that, even during the early days in St Petersburg, Diaghilev rarely issued spontaneous invitations or dropped in on friends just for a chat.[5] The death of his father shortly before the war, and of his beloved stepmother shortly after, were kept secret from nearly all his friends and even his lover. He regularly shut himself up in archives in search of old scores, just as he had once scoured the Petersburg archives for forgotten eighteenth-century artists. Venice was the place where he gave free rein to his inner life, a life of idle thoughts and daydreams, in which he could rediscover his creativity and forget practical cares. He once described such a moment to his stepmother:

God created dreams and gave us the ability to dream. From that comes all mysticism and all poetry. But one fairytale does exist in reality and not in a dream. It doesn't belong to *The Thousand and One Nights*, for it is more magical in its mixture of enchantment and waking reality. In Venice that borderline is as shrouded in mist as the outlines of her palaces and the shores of the lagoons. Venice secretes a poison, and that poison lies in the way all that is real and can be sensed is in constant contact with magic and mystery; one loses the consciousness of reality and forgets the past [illegible]. So you must know that for ten days I've forgotten who I am, whether my life has work, desires, thoughts – all that has been left behind over there in the land of men; here there is something else, always present, always illusory and always to be cherished. A uniquely precious, uniquely free state of mind, one of constantly drunken and insatiably expectant intoxication. It's all astonishing and quite unexpected and therefore strange. Nothing concrete, everything calm, in truth just like a graveyard; maybe life does only exist where concepts are blurred and death stands alongside inspiration and vitality, just as a night is only good when dreams are born and the impossibility of life is fulfilled in the real images of dreams. That's what I think of when I look at the green water of the Canale Grande, playing in the rays of the burning October sun.[6]

Venice also symbolised something else to Diaghilev: the grandeur of European culture. He idolised Renaissance art and possessed an encyclopaedic knowledge of the architecture and music of that period. Europe's past was forever on his mind, and he measured even his most daring experiments against the canonical works of the Western tradition.

Diaghilev was not always an innovator. In his early years as editor of the journal *Mir iskusstva* he was downright conservative, at least by European standards:

In music you can't go further than Richard Wagner, just as in painting you can't be more 'stripped down' than Zorn or Manet. The road is not a sure one. Art, at least the art of man, isn't simply birdsong. Above all it's work. A thing must be well made … To go forward we can't pin all our wellbeing on the audacity of the new.[7]

When Diaghilev wrote these words, Van Gogh had been dead for nearly ten years. Such a statement from the progenitor of pivotal modernist works such as *Le Sacre du printemps*, *Parade*, *Les Noces* and *Le Pas d'acier* may seem surprising, but to some extent he never quite lost his earliest convictions. His love of craftsmanship, of the 'thing well made', remained with him throughout his career, and he transmitted it to the young artists with whom he worked. Just after the end of the First World War Diaghilev played a significant part in the emergence of neoclassicism in France, a movement that sought to halt the unbridled experimentation of the early modernists. He encouraged 'his' artists, composers and choreographers to look to the past, even at the risk of inhibiting their creative intuition. That nostalgia could stifle artistic inspiration was something of which Diaghilev was well aware. In 1902, while in Venice, he witnessed the collapse of the Campanile, an event that impressed him deeply and which provided him with a lasting insight:

> The culture of twenty centuries, pressing down on our shoulders, prevents us from creating, and if along with S. Marco's Campanile the whole of our beloved Venice tumbled down, we would go mad with grief, but ... for men of the future there would be one serious obstacle the less.[8]

Diaghilev was aware that to be truly innovative, an artist has to be an iconoclast, to break with the past. Yet at the same time, he loved the old Europe unconditionally. It is this paradox that inspired his productions, and the resultant dynamic was a source of energy.

Diaghilev's dedication to the arts was complete; moderation was out of the question. Without total commitment there could be no art; indeed, life itself would be incomplete. A dream had to be pursued with unflagging devotion; there could be no bourgeois distinction between work and leisure, between the business of breadwinning and the life of the mind and soul. As far as he was concerned, life was work, interspersed with brief intervals of rest. Work allowed him to make his mark on the intransigent continuum of time, to transform life into something manageable and meaningful. He squeezed every last drop out of life, living in the eye of a whirlwind of joy and sorrow, conflict and reconciliation, a personal cloud of turbulence that left those around him breathless.

To Diaghilev, true beauty was energising and ambivalent. It plumbed the depths of human experience and feeling, and thus by its very nature provoked extreme reactions and emotions. And here lies the essence of his identity. If we look beyond the conflicts, the legendary charm, the dictatorial tendencies, the unparalleled eye for talent, the cunning and deceitfulness, the self-assurance and prophetic gifts, we see a man driven by an overpowering need to explore the mystery of human creativity in its highest form. While his father and grandfather were content, as so many other Russians had been before them, to live a life for the tsar in the army and the civil service, Diaghilev resolved to transform his age and consecrated his life to the cult of beauty.

· I ·

A Big Head
1872–1880

THERE IS NO CORRELATION between the durability of a story and its veracity.

One of the most persistent myths about Diaghilev concerns his large head and the role it supposedly played in his birth. Sergey, the son of Pavel Diaghilev, entered the world on 19 March 1872 in the little village of Selishchi in the province of Novgorod, close to the barracks where his father was stationed.[1] According to some sources his mother died in labour;[2] according to others, her death occurred 'a few days later'.[3] As the story would have it, the cause was not a breech birth or other complications, or even the lack of good medical care (hardly inconceivable at the close of the nineteenth-century in rural Russia) – but rather the gigantic dimensions of baby Sergey's head.[4]

The story originated with Diaghilev himself,[5] and it was accepted by nearly all his biographers and the various memoirists who knew him. Diaghilev's first biographer, Arnold Haskell, describes it as a 'head [that] is too large for the body ... [with] a magnificent expanse of noble forehead'.[6] It was often said that Sergey was tormented by a lifelong feeling of guilt for causing his mother's premature death 'owing to the inordinate size of [his] head'.[7]

In reality the birth was not the least bit traumatic, and Yevgeniya Diaghileva (née Yevreynova) passed away a good three months after the arrival of young Sergey, who had a perfectly normal-sized head.[8] Pavel Pavlovich wrote to his mother that his wife was up and about ten days after the delivery and that the doctor had assured them that everything was fine.[9] A month later she fell ill and was confined to her bed. The family called in a second doctor, who diagnosed her with peritonitis. On 5 May Pavel wrote to his mother that the situation had taken a sharp turn for the worse. In all likelihood Yevgenia had contracted puerperal fever. Caused by the bacterium *Streptococcus pyogenes*, this disease claimed the lives of one in five women in Europe before 1879. The infection was so devastating because it was spread by the very people that women relied on for medical care. As early as the 1860s the Hungarian physician Ignaz Semmelweis discovered that mortality rates for puerperal fever fell dramatically if midwives and doctors thoroughly washed their hands before performing internal examinations or assisting in deliveries. Unfortunately this valuable knowledge had not reached Novgorod by 1872.[10]

Sergey's father, Pavel Pavlovich, was twenty-five when he lost his wife and gained a son. Pavel was a colonel in the cavalry at the time of Sergey's birth and would eventually rise to the rank of major-general.[11] The Diaghilev family belonged to the landed nobility and were fairly well off, owning a number of distilleries on the outskirts of Perm, a provincial town at the foot of the Urals. In the second half of the nineteenth century the Russian gentry were in a precarious position, and the Diaghilevs were certainly no exception. The gradual encroachment of Western capitalism undermined age-old social relationships and spurred the rise of a new middle class. This process of transformation increased mobility and production, and both enriched and impoverished large segments of society. After the emancipation of the serfs in 1861, many rural aristocrats struggled to stay afloat. The fortunes of the Diaghilevs were intertwined with the modernisation of Russian society in the decade that followed. In 1810 the family had acquired a country estate in Bikbarda, where they produced vodka and other spirits at their distillery.[12] Vodka production was in the hands of government-sanctioned regional monopolies, which paid rent to the state in return for the privilege. The Diaghilevs owed their wealth to just such a monopoly, which in this case covered Perm and the surrounding territory.

In the first half of the nineteenth century the Diaghilevs edged their way up Perm's social ladder, and in time they became one of the richest and most powerful families in the region. The regular income from the distillery gave them the freedom to take up various social and intellectual pursuits, and thus the Diaghilevs set their sights on St Petersburg, the epicentre of tsarist society, which had everything an imperial capital could offer: power, higher education, art, entertainment and comfort. A world away from the wilds of the Urals.

The established method for staking out a position in the city's pecking order was to join the army, and it was in this way that the Diaghilevs, like so many other provincial families, secured their place in the rapidly growing capital. The credit for this upward mobility goes to Sergey's grandfather, Pavel Dmitriyevich. Pavel began his career in the military, where he distinguished himself in several wars, eventually becoming a high-ranking official at the Ministry of Finance. After leaving the civil service he returned to Perm, where he renovated and enlarged the vodka distillery in Bikbarda. In 1851 he bought a second distillery in the village of Nikolayevskoye,[13] where he also built a large church. A number of his children, including Sergey's father, stayed behind in St Petersburg. The family owned a house in the capital, on chic Furshtatskaya Street, where Diaghilev's grandmother, who detested provincial life, continued to live for many years after her husband had moved back home. After returning to Perm, Pavel Dmitriyevich threw himself into various religious and cultural charity projects, including funding the Kamsko-Beryozovsky monastery a few dozen miles outside the city. He was also the second largest sponsor behind the construction of the Perm opera house.[14]

Diaghilev's grandfather had a reputation as a deeply pious man. There are all sorts of fantastic stories about the extent of his religious mania, most of which – like the tale that he once devoured several wooden crosses[15] – are less than credible. We do know that he must have been a brilliant, energetic, enterprising and colourful figure, who was ahead of his time in many respects. When serfdom was abolished, Pavel Dmitriyevich was instrumental in the construction of the Church of the Resurrection in the centre of the town, to commemorate 'the liberation of the peasants'.[16] The Diaghilevs, it should be mentioned, owned no serfs themselves, a fact that goes some way to explaining their enthusiasm for the new order. Two years later Tsar Alexander also liberalised the system of vodka monopolies and introduced alcohol duties, thereby opening the door to private initiative. It can be assumed that the family was less thrilled about this development.[17] Yet in the 1860s there seemed to be few problems on the horizon for Pavel Dmitriyevich, even as competitors began creeping into the lucrative vodka market.

The crowning glory of his social attainments was his offspring's alliances: several of his nine children married partners from older, better-situated St Petersburg families. His daughters were more successful in this respect than his sons, possibly because he was able to offer his future in-laws a generous dowry of 25,000 roubles. Two of his daughters, Anna and Julia, married highly ambitious men, one of whom would become a senator and the other a government minister, respectively. In the early 1870s almost all his children were living in the better neighbourhoods of St Petersburg, and by pursuing careers in the imperial bureaucracy and the army they rose to the highest echelons of tsarist society.[18] The Diaghilevs, who had lived as landed nobles in the wilderness of Siberia and the Urals, took full advantage of the new social movements of the nineteenth century, forging a future for themselves that promised cultivation, status and wealth.

Sergey's father carried on the family tradition, after a fashion. In the army he rose above his father in rank, but as a businessman he was notably less successful. Pavel Pavlovich was a romantic and bon vivant and, like his father and son, a keen amateur musician and a great music lover in general. He married Sergey's mother at a young age and lived a fairly carefree existence, confident that the distilleries in Perm would continue to generate wealth into perpetuity. He was constantly running up large debts with a blithe disregard for how they might be paid off.

Shortly before Sergey's birth, Pavel's sister, Maria Koribut-Kubitovich, had lost her husband, and she and her three children, Yury, Pavel (Pavka) and Natalia, came to live with him. After his wife died, Pavel's financial outlook was downright bleak. Four children and his sister were now dependent on him, and there was no way he could support them on what he earned. But despite that, the Diaghilev home was a happy one. Brother and sister, widower and widow, were a great comfort to each other and they were determined to stay together. Whenever Pavel couldn't sleep, which was often the case in the first few months after his wife's death, he and his sister would take long nightly walks along the chilly, windswept river banks of St Petersburg.[19] And with Maria in the house, young Sergey did not want for maternal attention and care. Sergey grew close to his cousin, Pavel Koribut, who would later become a member of the great man's entourage. In fact, he would be the only relative to attend Diaghilev's funeral. Sergey's father was given an apartment at an officers' barracks on Shpalernaya Street in St Petersburg, where his sister and the children could stay if he was stationed out of town. Shpalernaya Street was located in a new, upmarket neighbourhood, popular with the bourgeois elite. Pavel's eldest sister Anna lived on nearby Furshtatskaya Street, a stone's throw from the family home.

Anna, eleven years Pavel's senior, was well known in Russia as an activist for the rights of women and the poor. She was typical of the generation to come of age in the 1860s: liberal, reform-minded, active and socially engaged. She was married to Vladimir Filosofov, procurator-general of the military courts, member of the imperial Council of State and, it was said, a personal friend of Tsar Alexander II. It seems clear that some of Anna Filosofova's qualities – an unusual mix of upper-class gentility and liberal progressive-ness – rubbed off on the other members of the family, even though there was plainly some distance between the eldest sister and the other children, including Diaghilev's father.

But whatever the exact nature of the familial relationships, with his sister Maria at home and his sister Anna round the corner, Pavel had no reason to feel lonely. In his second wife's memoirs Pavel comes across as a cheerful, energetic, happy-go-lucky man who appreciated the joys of family life and did not brood on setbacks. To judge by the evidence, he was not the type to fret about monetary matters: there was always the mansion in Perm, the estate in Bikbarda, a set of wealthy in-laws (the Filosofovs) and the distill-eries to fall back on.

By this time the Diaghilevs and Filosofovs had largely shaken off their provincial roots and had become true metropolitans. Like so many members of the landed nobility who settled in the capital, they adopted a lifestyle that was largely indistinguishable from that of the local bourgeoisie. Old patriar-chal customs made way for careerism and self-fulfilment. Family life revolved around art, education and holidays, the aim being to cultivate their minds, elevate their social status and improve their quality of life. It was people like the Diaghilevs – a small, but rapidly growing group of not only urbanised merchants and industrialists, but also emancipated members of the landed nobility – who would become the driving force behind the great cultural revival that swept over Russia around the turn of the century and would later come to influence Europe as a whole.

A few months after his wife's death, Pavel Diaghilev began to rekindle his social life. He was regularly deployed to encampments along the railway line to Warsaw. On one of his train journeys he struck up an acquaintance with the Panayev family from Peterhof, the imperial palace complex a few miles outside St Petersburg. The Panayevs were a cultured family who embraced the ideals of education and cultivation that were coming into vogue in Petersburg. Three of their children were named Achilles, Plato and Yelena (Helen). Pavel Diaghilev was invited to the balls they hosted and would also visit their home in the evening. He was one of the few unmarried men to be granted that privilege, because the dour master of the house knew very well that most male guests were only after the hand of his daughter. But Diaghilev 'sat down at the piano and started singing gipsy and Russian songs. Father always loved them,' wrote Yelena. 'He became emotional and asked for an aria in which the singer hit a high C … That was how Pavel Pavlovich unconsciously won an unexpected and difficult victory thanks to his tenor voice and his cheerful nature.'[20]

He was invited over on several occasions to sing at musical soirées. After a time the family asked him if he would consider staging a small opera at their home, with a role, of course, for their daughter Yelena. The Panayevs had taken a liking to Pavel Diaghilev, and they were not averse to giving love a helping hand.

The two rehearsed together, honing their singing and acting, and a few months later they announced their engagement. Yelena was happy with Pavel's proposal, but before consenting, she first wanted to meet Sergey. She later wrote about that first meeting:

> I so well remember little Seryozha twelve years ago. You were almost three when I saw you for the first time. I was betrothed then and I felt I absolutely had to see you before the wedding. You represented then for me almost a matter of life and death as I had secretly decided that, for all my love for your father, I wouldn't marry him unless I felt I could love you too … As we came nearer to Romanshchino I was overcome by a painful emotion which became almost intolerable when we began to approach the house. I'll never forget those moments. How could I? I could see from a distance that people were standing and waiting for us on the porch. We drove up. Polenka jumped off the box where he was sitting because my

Yelena Valerianovna Diaghileva

father was with me in the carriage. We climbed the three steps. Marisha was standing there holding a child in a bright blue dress with a sailor collar decorated with gold anchors. It was you – a helpless small boy who held my fate in his little hands.

I just managed to say, 'It's Seryozha ...' And in fear and trembling I held out my arms to you. Then a miracle happened ... I took it to be a miracle then, as God's answer to my agonising questions to him, and I think the same today. It was a miracle.

Without a moment's hesitation, without a second's pause in front of a face you didn't know at all, you stretched out your little hands to me, leaned in toward me, and when in amazement I took you from Marisha, you hugged my neck so tightly with both arms and pressed your head to my cheek.

From that moment you became mine. My first motherly feelings were for you.[21]

The couple were married on 14 October 1874. There were more than 200 guests at the wedding banquet, including Pavel's entire regiment. After the wedding the young family – Pavel, Yelena and Sergey – moved into the cavalry barracks on Galernaya Street. Maria and her children moved to an apartment a few hundred yards away, at the corner of Furstatskaya and Voskresenskaya Streets, but the two families stayed close and saw each other every day.[22]

Nine months after the wedding a second son, Valentin, was born, followed three years later by a third, Yury. Yelena Diaghileva doted on her three boys. There is no evidence that she gave Sergey any less attention than her own children. Indeed, it would seem that Pavel's first child was her favourite. Yelena raised her three boys to love and appreciate the arts. Her memoirs give no cause to suspect that she possessed an uncommonly sharp or critical intellect, though they do offer a unique glimpse into the world where Diaghilev grew up. In her reminiscences she comes across as a dreamy, good-hearted and loving woman, with great respect for intellectual authority. Possibly the most striking aspect of her personality was her boundless optimism: adversity and misfortune were brushed aside, forgotten or simply overlooked. Although she has been described as a strong woman, her outlook on life was dreamy and idealised, coloured by a poetic, warm-blooded disposition and an abiding ignorance of anything to do with business or material concerns. The last of these was a trait she shared to a large degree with her husband.

This is not to say, however, that she couldn't be strict or demanding with her children. According to Diaghilev's trusted friend Walter 'Valechka' Nouvel, it was she who shaped young Sergey's character, especially his extraordinary willpower, which was his defining characteristic. 'He often told me that his mother (he used no other name for her) taught him never to use the words "I can't". "You must forget that phrase," she used to say to him. "When people want to, they can."'[23]

In her memoirs Yelena described the two families' first Christmas together:

I didn't want Seryozha to suspect anything about even the preparations for the Christmas tree, and in this I was extremely successful. He was told that the ventilation windows were open in the drawing room and so he couldn't go in there. When the candles were lit, the doors were opened and Seryozha went into the drawing room; I ran forward to see him coming in and to watch his first impression. I can see his small figure now, in a little blue suit with shorts to the knee, in short socks and little shoes, with his tummy sticking out and his hands behind his back. He stopped in that

Sergey Diaghilev and his stepmother

pose almost at the door, gravely inspected the tree with its glittering lights, glanced at the toys placed around it and said quietly, 'Not bad ...'[24]

Pavel Diaghilev now had a large family to look after: three children of his own, plus Maria and her three little ones. The family spent the winters in St Petersburg or abroad. In the winter of 1875–6 they travelled to France, where they visited Paris and Nice and rented a summer house in Menton.

In Paris, Yelena met Ivan Turgenev at the home of his great love, the singer Pauline Viardot, and even had a brief conversation with the writer, an encounter she never forgot.

It was the last time that Diaghilev's parents would set foot outside the Russian empire.

Summers were spent on the family estate in Bikbarda, about 190 miles from Perm. The whole family would gather there (at the height of the season there could be as many as fifty people at the property), and they would make music, put on plays, give poetry readings, and eat and drink. They lived in rather grand style in both Petersburg and Bikbarda, with long excursions, servants (at the bare minimum a governess, a nanny, a scullery maid and a footman) and a dim-witted doctor who expressed concern about young Sergey's development. According to Yelena:

> From the very first time we went to him for some trivial illness of Seryozha's, [this doctor] had warned me that we must look after the child very carefully, especially till he was seven … He told me not to speed up his development, and I even remember [the doctor] telling me later to hold him back as he didn't like my stories of Seryozha's inquisitiveness and powers of observation. When I asked what I should do about that, he said, 'Simply don't answer his questions … Just say nothing … That's much better than inventing something or giving muddled explanations.'[25]

But maintaining a house full of servants and engaging the services of a personal physician, not to mention the many trips and parties, cost well in excess of Pavel's income from the vodka distilleries, and his army pay was meagre, to say the least. According to Yelena, during his whole career as an officer Pavel was paid a salary just once: the princely sum of three roubles.[26] With his extensive network of social contacts he could have easily carved out a career for himself in the imperial bureaucracy, but that was not his style. 'Only Germans worry about their careers,' Pavel maintained.[27]

The Diaghilevs' financial problems became more serious after 1878, eventually forcing them to return to Perm, far from the socially demanding (and expensive) St Petersburg. They must also have felt that life would be much cheaper if the whole family lived together. Around this time they were visited by a whole series of financial crises. In the late 1870s grandfather Pavel Dmitriyevich found himself in dire straits, thanks to his many lavish charitable projects and a diminishing income from the vodka distillery. Competitors from Ekaterinburg, the other major town in the Urals, were eating into his profits. In 1878, in an effort to escape his obligations, he attempted to file for bankruptcy, but the judge refused to grant his petition.[28]

As a result of the trouble brewing in Perm, Pavel Pavlovich soon had his own army of creditors to contend with back in St Petersburg. Perhaps some members of the family hoped Pavel would take more of an active interest in the languishing family business, now that his father was getting on in years and was clearly unable to respond to the new dynamics of the vodka market. The departure was postponed several times, first because of the birth of their third son, Yury, then because of the difficulty of finding a new position in the army in Perm. Eventually Pavel managed to find a job with the infantry – a degrading comedown for a cavalry officer – and the family was able to make the move.

In the summer of 1879 a last glimmer of hope appeared. Pavel's brother-in-law, Pyotr Parensov, was unexpectedly appointed Russia's Minister of War in Bulgaria, and there was talk that he would take Pavel with him to Bulgaria as head of his cavalry guard. Buoyed by this turn of events, Pavel met with his creditors one last time, hoping they would grant him a final stay of payment. But these hopes vanished, and the family had no choice but to pull up sticks and head back to the remote, inhospitable region at the foot of the Urals.[29]

By 1879 the Diaghilevs were back in Perm, their attempt to secure a new life in St Petersburg officially a failure.

· 2 ·

The Fruits of Enlightenment
1879–1890

'EUROPE'S SUN RISES IN PERM.' Or so goes an old saying in this city, perched on the continent's easternmost rim. In Diaghilev's day, Perm was the administrative centre of an area roughly twice the size of the Netherlands, but the town itself was sparsely populated, with only a few streets of stone houses. These were in the neoclassical style favoured by Catherine the Great, who sought to add a touch of grandeur to the provincial capitals during her reign. There was little industry; the oil that now gives the town a degree of prosperity had yet to be discovered.

In this gateway to Siberia, transport and distribution formed the pillars of the economy. The 'goods' that were transported included prisoners. Every convict in the Russian empire destined for Siberia passed through Perm's town gates. Diaghilev's grandmother used to say of Perm, 'The only people you ever see are prisoners in chains.'[1] The contrast with the vibrant atmosphere of St Petersburg could not have been greater.

The journey from the capital to Perm (870 miles as the crow flies – about the distance from London to Cracow) took many days. The train only went as far as Nizhny Novgorod, some 300 miles east of Moscow. From there, travellers continued by steamer down the Volga and Kama rivers to Perm, and Diaghilev thus became used to long-distance travel from a very early age.

The Diaghilevs' dining room, Perm

On arrival in Perm, Pavel's family moved into the 'old house' on Siberia Street, the home of Diaghilev's grandfather. There Sergey contracted scarlet fever and diphtheria. The nearest doctor was over sixty miles away, but fortunately he managed to arrive in time to cure Seryozha. After a few weeks Pavel returned to St Petersburg for further negotiations with his creditors.

The Diaghilevs enjoyed a much higher social standing in Perm than in St Petersburg. Despite their financial difficulties, they lived like kings. Aristocrats were thin on the ground in Perm; the elite (such as it was) consisted mainly of merchants. The old house served as the family headquarters. It was situated on the city's main thoroughfare, which also happened to be the chief artery for prisoner transports. Among those who had passed by in rattling chains on their way to exile were the Decembrists and Fyodor Dostoyevsky. The house had exactly twenty rooms,[2] with a separate schoolroom for the children. Of the servants, only a governess and the nanny Dunya lived in.

Every effort was made to transplant the music-filled life of St Petersburg to Perm. During their time in the capital Yelena and Pavel had held musical soirées every other Thursday, in which thirty or so professional and amateur musicians took part. Yelena's sister Alexandra 'Tatusha' Panayeva-Kartseva, a celebrated singer who often performed in France and Italy, was a regular at these affairs. Her admirers included Tchaikovsky, who dedicated his song cycle op. 47 to her.[3] Tatusha married a nephew of the composer, making Diaghilev and Tchaikovsky distant cousins by marriage. That was why the Diaghilevs always called Tchaikovsky 'Dyadya [Uncle] Petya'. In later life Diaghilev used to relate how, as a child, he had visited Tchaikovsky at his estate in Klin on a number of occasions.[4] Yelena does not mention these visits, but it is a fact that Diaghilev was very well acquainted with Tchaikovsky's two younger brothers, the twins Modest and Anatol.[5]

Mussorgsky is said to have been another regular at the Thursday soirées, and Diaghilev claimed to have met him several times as a child. During his lifetime almost no one took Mussorgsky seriously as a composer, and the Diaghilevs were no exception. As Diaghilev wrote, 'My aunt ... would announce, "I'm singing tonight. Don't forget to send Mussorgsky." What a line – it's forever engraved in my memory.'[6]

Even if the family was not progressive or perceptive enough to recognise Mussorgsky's talent, their music-making in St Petersburg was a serious and passionate business. Excerpts were performed from operas by Tchaikovsky (*The Oprichnik*), Glinka (*A Life for the Tsar*) and Gounod (*Faust*). Wagner was also on the bill, though the a capella performance of the overture from *Tannhäuser* described by Yelena in her diary sounds a rather dubious undertaking.[7] Though these amateurish affairs might not seem very impressive, it should be remembered that Russia's professional music culture was still in its infancy; scores were hard to come by, and performers had to arrange and copy the various parts themselves. Moreover, the works in question were often advanced and had seldom been heard. The Diaghilevs performed Tchaikovsky's *Oprichnik* only two years after its premiere; their production of *Faust* was probably the first time the French original had been heard in Russia (two years earlier, the Imperial Opera had staged a Russian version at the Mariinsky Theatre).[8] Both Gounod and Tchaikovsky were to remain among Diaghilev's favourite composers.[9]

In Perm, the family tried to breathe new life into the torpid musical soirées of the local aristocrats' club. Diaghilev's uncle Ivan, a creditable cellist, was put in charge of the little orchestra formed for these occasions; the choir was entrusted to Eduard Eduardovich Dennemark, a stray German who tutored the young Diaghilevs and taught German at the boys' grammar school. Just as in St Petersburg, a great many arias were sung, mainly in Italian (Verdi) and Russian (mostly works by Tchaikovsky and Glinka). Nearly all chroniclers report that Diaghilev's father was a great fan of Glinka, and knew his entire opera *Ruslan and Lyudmila* by heart. In the words of one of Diaghilev's classmates, 'The Diaghilev home was one of the most brilliant and intellectual in Perm. Indeed, it was the Athens of Perm.'[10]

Sergey was given piano and singing lessons, and displayed an exceptional talent for music at an early age. He also tried his hand at composing. His first known piece is a brief romance in the style of Glinka, entitled 'Ty pomnish li, Maria?' (Do you remember, Maria?), to a famous lyric by Aleksey Tolstoy, composed at the age of fifteen to mark his parents' wedding anniversary. His mother carefully preserved the calligraphed score; it is Diaghilev's only surviving composition.

For the many who lived in remote towns and villages, amateur dramatics, music-making, sketching, reading and writing were a welcome distraction, especially during the endless winter months. Both Yelena's memoirs and Sergey's childhood letters vividly convey the joy of such pastimes. The memoirs describing family life in Bikbarda, and the letters sent from Bikbarda to Perm, portray the warm and creative atmosphere of those long summer days in the village at the foot of the Urals. Bikbarda was the site of the distillery, a stone mansion and a number of wooden houses belonging to the family, including the house with the veranda that Yelena Diaghileva described in great detail:

> Our veranda was the usual kind: a wooden Russian one with columns and a roof; it stretched along the whole southern façade of the single-storeyed wooden house and even beyond the façade, ending in a big rotunda coming out from the corner of the house and over the garden railings onto the road which ran along the ravine. Beyond the ravine were the factory, the village and the great forest, boundless as the sea. We usually took tea in the evenings in the rotunda and watched the sunset … Part of the veranda, at the opposite end from the rotunda, served as a dining room in summer, and up to fifty could easily sit down at table there. In another part next to the rotunda were divans, armchairs and stools.[11]

To the east of the village was a small lake in which the children would swim in summer. At its edge was a hill whose lofty summit commanded a

Yury, Sergey and Valentin Diaghilev

view of the surrounding area. As befitted an 'Athenian' family, they called it Parnassus. The Diaghilevs had a church built in the village. Under the communists it was converted into a cinema; under the capitalists into a discotheque. It has since fallen into ruin, and today it serves only as a nesting place for crows.

Sergey's father joined the rest of the party for only a few weeks in midsummer. Sometimes the children would go there by themselves, without their mother, accompanied solely by their nanny and their tutor. Their grandmother and Uncle Vanya (Ivan Diaghilev) lived in Bikbarda all year round. While there, Sergey wrote regularly to his parents in Perm:

> Today we're all going for a walk ... At lunch they gave us most delicious cold roast beef with zhile [he meant en gelée], then there was very delicious kvas. Uncle Vanya said, 'Oh Alyona, Alyona, what a pity she isn't here, she'd have had some.' I was sorry too. When they gave the beef to Linchik [his half-brother Valentin] he said, 'The slices of beef are really Spanish,' and Granny asked, 'Why Spanish?' and he said, 'Because all Spaniards are thin like these slices of beef and only Germans are fat, like our new brewer.' Everyone laughed a lot. After the roast beef, they gave us beef with horseradish and Linchik put a huge amount of horseradish on a bit of beef and made a big face. Then Uncle Vanya said, 'Aha! Now you're in a pickle!' After that Granny told a very very funny story about pickles ...[12]

> Lina kisses your little arm with the bracelet and kisses Aunt Tatusia all over. He wants her told he is taking the medicines every day. Yura kisses you a million million times. But I kiss you only once but a trillion times harder than all the above put together.
> Sergun, your black-eyed piglet, the son of your heart, your 11-year-old grandfather, your little friend,
> Seryozha[13]

Music, literature and drama were not only central to the children's education; they were the glue that held the family together.

In Bikbarda a choir was set up, consisting of members of the family and of the church choir, and of course they sang Glinka's *A Life for the Tsar*. The deacon's father, who had a fine bass voice but was not officially allowed to sing in a secular choir, was persuaded to perform in an al fresco concert in which he 'hid from view behind some pine trees'.[14]

The children performed plays, recited poetry and made music:

> The day after you went away we did a play ... *Sleeping Beauty*, I was the prince who kissed Beauty's hand and she woke up. We loved doing the play.[15]

Diaghilev in his school uniform

Yesterday, the 27th July, we gave Granny a concert … Sezya recited some fables of Krylov's, 'The Pig under the Oak' and 'The Swan, the Crab and the Pike' … Linchik did Lermontov's 'Ship of the Air'. George did 'Why are you Neighing, My Restless Steed?', also with a lot of feeling and meaning and with long pauses during which he snorted and bellowed.

I played a duet of Mendelssohn's 'Songs without Words' with M. Nussbaum, then one or two things from the music you sent me. We all got terrific applause and I had to play two more solos … Granny is spoiling me terribly: we are having one book sent after another. I just finished reading *The Silver Prince* and now I'm reading *Ivanhoe*, which I'm devouring as much as *The Silver Prince* … Well, darling Mama, now you can't write me that I write you too little: I've written to you about everything down to the tiniest detail. Oh, except this. Murka has had babies, as pretty as she is. There were 5 but 2 we had to throw in the river since she can only feed 3.[16]

The arts also featured prominently at the boys' grammar school that Diaghilev attended in Perm. On 4 February 1888 Sergey performed at a school concert, playing a Chopin waltz and a song by Rubinstein and singing a few popular romances.[17] The classmate who had called the Diaghilevs' house the 'Athens of Perm' remembered Diaghilev as

> a strapping boy, heavily built for his age with a head conspicuous for its size, and an expressive face. He was cultured and mature for his age and for his grade at school. He knew about things that we, his contemporaries in the same class, had no conception of – Russian and foreign literature, the theatre and music. He spoke French and German fluently and well, he played music …
>
> He used to come to class completely unprepared for the lessons and at once began to prepare them with the help of the best students. No one refused him help and when the lesson started and he was suddenly called on there started an energetic system of 'prompts' and various signs. During the written lessons he used to get notes and cribs in good time.
>
> Thanks to this help and his own adroitness, resourcefulness and in part sheer coolness, Seryozha Diaghilev usually came out of all critical situations the absolute winner.[18]

During his last years at the grammar school he immersed himself ever more deeply in music. He composed scenes for an opera based on Pushkin's drama *Boris Godunov* and gamely took piano lessons, even though he found them somewhat tedious. He overcame technical difficulties easily, having naturally mobile fingers, and he sight-read with great ease, laying the foundations of a wide knowledge of written music.[19]

On 7 February 1890 Sergey played the solo in the first movement of Schumann's Piano Concerto at a school concert, earning himself a mention in the local paper.[20] It was his first public performance.

In Perm Diaghilev excelled easily, having no rivals. But in St Petersburg, where he later attended university, he would encounter competition for the first time, and soon lose his privileged position. No wonder he wrote to his stepmother in his first year:

> I so often think back on my time at the summer school with a lump in my throat, especially the later years. Of course I don't want to relive them, but my memories of that time conjure up such a special intimacy that I'm sure I shall never encounter its like again …[21]

The Diaghilev family: left to right, Valentin, Pavel Pavlovich, Yury, Yelena, Sergey

The serenity of the Diaghilevs' family home stood in sharp contrast to the violence of daily life in Russia – a violence that was as visible in the streets as it was in politics. On 1 March 1881 Tsar Alexander II was assassinated in a bomb attack.[22] The government proclaimed a state of emergency, which was to remain in force until the revolution of 1917. It effectively turned Russia into a police state, though the grip of the police and the secret service on public life had been tightening since 1878, in response to the first terrorist acts. The security services were given ever greater powers and ever more public funding. The secret service, in particular, became an independent force in Russian society, increasingly contemptuous of existing bureaucratic and social hierarchies.

A prime illustration of this high-handedness is the arrest and exile of Anna Filosofova-Diaghileva, Diaghilev's Aunt Nona, despite her own and her husband's social prominence. But she was also an influential lobbyist for women's rights and a pioneer of women's higher education. One of her alleged crimes was to have given her husband's greatcoat to a prisoner shuffling past on his way to Siberia.[23]

The rise of terrorism and the assassination of Alexander marked the end of an era in Russian society. Those who came of age in the 1870s and 1880s – with Diaghilev as a typical representative – would violently oppose the previous reformist generation, partly because of increased government oppression, and partly because of a genuine aversion to the idealism of their predecessors. It was typical that Vladimir Stasov, one of the intellectual leaders of the 'progressives' and a close friend of Aunt Nona's, would eventually become Diaghilev's arch enemy.

Unlike the Filosofovs, the Diaghilevs were very well aware that reforms could threaten established interests. They were therefore less progressive than their in-laws, but in principle espoused the same political and social ideals. Aunt Nona's banishment in 1878 must have been just as much of a shock to the family as the tsar's murder three years later. Filosofova was in fact able to return to St Petersburg shortly after the coronation of Alexander III, thanks to intercession on her behalf, but the authorities had made it very clear that political involvement had its limits.

In the late 1880s Diaghilev read Goncharov's novel *The Precipice*, an ambitious attempt to portray the whole spectrum of Russian society and politics. Sergey discussed the book with his stepmother in three long letters, which shed more light on political opinions within the family. Diaghilev shows some sympathy for Mark, the book's nihilist: 'Last time I forgot to write to you about Mark. And I'm afraid my view won't be very accurate. He's a clever man but a nihilist, and I don't think one can say all nihilists are stupid (we had a big argument about this with Aunt and now Uncle Bob sometimes calls me a liberal and thinks I'm a nihilist, but you know me, my darling).'[24]

The correspondence between mother and stepson became more and more intimate as Sergey grew up. Their closeness was not affected even after Sergey learned from his father that Yelena was not his real mother. The letter she wrote to him after this revelation shows Yelena at her most touching:

My little Seryozha. Yesterday a new era began for you and for me: you left my care and went under your father's masculine eye, and I said goodbye to your childhood. The time has come which I have always dreaded, even though it always seemed so far off; the time when a son begins to recognise the man in himself. With this he crosses a threshold where I have to stop. Yesterday's talk with your father was a final break. I don't think you will ever forget that talk because it has made a powerful impression on you. Seryozha, it was the first conversation of yours at which I couldn't be present. So – it's over ... My part in your education is complete. How quickly these twelve years have gone by. How frightening to think that what is done is done and that nothing can be changed. It's such an important thing. Now there will come the results, the consequences. Lord, have mercy and bless us. I took on a great responsibility – so bravely, so confidently; I've brought up a man and now he is gently freeing his hand from mine and wants to walk on, although he is still next to me, not alone. And it's time. Nature has its signs: he is taller than me, his voice has broken, there is dark fluff on his upper lip ... Goodbye, little Seryozha ...[25]

Diaghilev had a troubled relationship with his father. It appears that Pavel did not concern himself very much with the boy's upbringing, and when he did, his methods were old-fashioned. In contrast to the stream of letters Diaghilev penned to his stepmother, he wrote no more than around ten addressed exclusively to his father (to judge by the surviving correspondence), and these were almost all superficial. According to Walter Nouvel, the two treated one another with indifference.[26]

However, around Diaghilev's seventeenth birthday, Pavel did take his son's upbringing in hand in at least one respect. Sergey was taken to a prostitute to be relieved of his virginity, a practice that was not unusual among the nobility. In the past, this task often fell to a female serf (and the practice probably endured for a while in rural areas), but after the abolition of serfdom the gentry turned to urban prostitutes. The phenomenon has been described by various writers, including Tolstoy and Turgenev. It is even said that Igor Stravinsky took his adolescent sons to French prostitutes in the 1920s, to prepare them for the act of love.[27]

But for the young Diaghilev, who was undoubtedly already aware of his homosexuality, the whole exercise must have been deeply distressing and degrading. It was probably the first and only time he slept with a woman. In a tragicomic turn of fate, the encounter left him with a venereal disease.[28]

According to Serge Lifar, his last premier danseur and one of his biographers, the business with the prostitute was the cause of Diaghilev's often tortured relationships with women. This appears far-fetched, however. Diaghilev was perfectly capable of close, emotional attachments to women, though always to women like his bosom friend Misia Sert and the dancer Tamara Karsavina, who were devoted to him and indeed more or less worshipped him. His craving for female devotion more probably reflected the relationships he had with women in his youth – his stepmother and his nanny – which were themselves tied to his patriarchal position as the eldest son. Again, the Diaghilevs' emancipated liberalism seems to sit uneasily with their patriarchal instincts, as evidenced by the upbringing of their eldest son and their treatment of servants.

Next to his stepmother, Diaghilev's nanny was by far the most important woman in his early life. She was his carer in the period between his mother's death and Pavel's remarriage, and would continue to play a major role in his upbringing for many years. Later, when Diaghilev went to St Petersburg to study, she accompanied him as a live-in companion. Diaghilev's manservant, Vasily Zuikov, also was to follow him around the world. He was roughly the same age as Diaghilev, and was in his service from the early 1890s.

In 1879, after his failed attempt to file for bankruptcy, Diaghilev's grandfather had given an overseer called Afanasy Pavlovich Eskin power of attorney over his estate.[29] Pavel Diaghilev could have taken over as manager that same year, but preferred to leave everything in Eskin's hands. When Diaghilev's grandfather died in 1883, the estate passed to his widow. Pavel and Uncle Vanya agreed that the latter should take over the estate but he, too, was content to leave its day-to-day management to Eskin.[30]

The Diaghilevs' ignorance of their own business affairs became painfully clear the following year. Yelena Diaghileva wrote in her diary in 1884: 'Eskin killed himself in the night of 4 February, after butchering four people. His death revealed that the business is in a terrible state. Dreadful troubles.'[31] On 8 February the scandal also reached the pages of the Perm Government Gazette. Apparently, Eskin became deranged and killed his sister and two other people with a sword before turning the weapon on his wife and himself. Both died of their injuries a few days later.[32] The paper speculated that Eskin had acted in a fit of insanity. Although a few more items on the murders appeared over the following fortnight, no new facts were reported.[33] The Diaghilevs managed to keep their connection to Eskin out of the papers, but the consequences of his financial mismanagement could not be so easily concealed: Pavel Pavlovich had to find 50,000 roubles without delay. This was an enormous sum, and it testifies to the Diaghilevs' wealth and social standing (and the trust of those prepared to advance them money) that Pavel Pavlovich was able to raise the full amount.

Yelena Diaghileva's lengthy diary entries reveal nothing more about this quadruple killing. What lay behind it? What effect did these events have on the general operation of the estate and the distilleries? Were the children told what had happened and, if so, how did they react? It seems that in those days the people of Perm were lucky to die peacefully in their beds. A casual glance through the newspapers of 1882 reveals new murders and 'unnatural deaths' almost every month. A few weeks after the bloodbath, the paper reported that the body of a young man had been found in front of the Diaghilevs' house.[34] In all likelihood he had drunk too much and died of exposure. The children must have come into contact with violent death from an early age, but the Eskin murders were shocking and brutal even by the standards of the times. Sergey must have heard about them, and he probably knew Eskin and his family well, but no further information seems to exist.

The financial side of the whole affair is equally obscure. Did the 50,000 roubles cover just the debts incurred by Eskin, or did it also include damages or bribes (to keep the family name out of the papers, for instance)? Pavel could not, of course, raise this sum without incurring new debts. A solution had to be found. About a year after the murder, Pavel took out a five-year mortgage of 125,000 roubles on his entire property (the distilleries plus all the houses and their contents) from his closest competitor, Alfons Poklovsky-Kozell.[35] The conditions of the mortgage were simple. The entire amount had to be repaid within five years, otherwise the property would be forfeit.

New creditors were forever appearing to badger Pavel, as Yelena's diary notes with increasing frequency, and by the end of 1889 the situation had become hopeless. On 23 May 1890 Poklovsky-Kozell went to court to demand a public auction of Pavel's property.[36] Diaghilev's father was given some four months to meet his obligations.

· 3 ·
Rise and Fall
1890–1891

AS EVENTS IN BIKBARDA spiralled towards their grim climax, Sergey headed off to the capital to enrol at the university as a law student. He then continued on to Bogdanovskoye, the Filosofovs' estate (near Pskov), where he would meet the young man who was to become his first great love: Dmitry 'Dima' Filosofov, Anna Filosofova's son. The cousins had already been corresponding for some time, and the boys' parents decided that the time had come for them to set off together on their grand tour, the extended journey through the great cultural capitals of Europe which was then de rigueur for young men from the upper classes. After that they would return, to begin their studies.

There were only two ways for aristocrats to secure or strengthen their position in the capital's hierarchy: joining the army (as Diaghilev's father and grandfather had done) or entering the civil service. Sergey was plainly not army material, and thus it was decided, probably without much discussion, that he would pursue a career in the imperial bureaucracy. The best preparation for such a career was to study law. It seems safe to assume that government bureaucrat was not the eighteen-year-old Sergey's dream job, but it was hardly the worst option open to him. Apart from the steady income (or at least a more favourable tax bracket), government work opened a number of social doors, conferring a certain status and various privileges. Even for men with artistic ambitions, the civil service was by no means an unusual career choice. A great many of the composers Diaghilev admired – Mussorgsky, Rimsky-Korsakov, Cui, Borodin – earned a living as public officials, either in the government bureaucracy or the army, without sacrificing their artistic aspirations.

The grand tour that Sergey and Dima were now planning at Bogdanovskoye would be their last spell of freedom before they set out on their predetermined career paths. At the Filosofovs' estate life was much as it had been in Bikbarda, though slightly less family oriented. Being much closer to the capital, the house was populated not only by relatives, but also by a steady stream of friends, acquaintances, colleagues and kindred spirits. Alexandre Benois, a good friend of Dima's who was a regular visitor, gives a lively account of life at Bogdanovskoye:

> The Filosofovs entertained often and for any reason. Masses of people came, old and young; generals, admirals and officials sat down to play cards with venerable ladies; cousins and cousins of cousins (and younger uncles) fooled around like small children, played games, argued, organised charades. The evening almost always culminated in dancing and on those occasions the piano which was usually in Dima's room was put in the biggest room of the flat, the State Councillor's imposing, slightly gloomy study. Either Valechka or I would spiritedly play our drawing-room repertoire – waltzes, polkas, mazurkas and quadrilles. We liked it less when Anna Pavlovna got the famous lawyer Gerard to recite poetry. His speciality was Alfred de Musset but his affected French accent reduced his audience to painful fits of barely contained laughter.[1]

On the face of it, Dima was the polar opposite of his theatrical, exuberant, sensuous and at times almost boorish cousin. Filosofov was cerebral, phlegmatic and philosophical, and blessed with a mordant wit. A slender, elegant and rather sickly young urbanite, he could be arrogant at times, but he was always courteous to a fault.[2] According to a peer, Dima was 'born into opulence and idleness and always dressed like a London dandy. He read Oscar Wilde and, not surprisingly, became an aesthete.'[3] Filosofov was a great lover of literature and secretly dreamt of becoming a writer himself. Diaghilev undoubtedly profited a great deal from his cousin's expertise on this subject. Dima, for his part, learned about music from Sergey, while Sergey made good use of Dima's great knowledge of the theatre. During his last few years of grammar school the latter kept a notebook in which he recorded every performance he attended. A year before his final exams, there were fifty-nine listings in the notebook, including plays by the Meiningen company, which visited St Petersburg in 1885 and 1890 and was to have such a defining influence on Stanislavsky.[4]

The cousins hit it off from the start. 'I spend most of my time with Dima,' Diaghilev wrote to his stepmother. 'We chat a lot. He's clever and interesting. And we have so much in common.'[5] Filosofov and Diaghilev would soon become lovers, but it is unclear when the relationship turned romantic. In any case it was after their European tour.[6]

Benois suggested that Dima was already having homosexual dalliances with his school friends, most notably the future artist Konstantin 'Kostya' Somov, later a prominent figure in Diaghilev's circle.[7] Dima became a writer, as he had hoped, concentrating on 'weighty' subjects like philosophy and literary criticism. Though somewhat insipid, his later essays always exhibited great precision and insight. That mix of the bland and the precise is characteristic of even his earliest writings. His diaries, for example, stand in stark contrast to Diaghilev's letters, which are always highly emotional, even hysterical in their theatricality, full of hyperbole and ungrammatical outbursts. All things considered, it's a wonder the two got along together as well as they did.

We know a great deal about the grand tour since both wrote copiously on the subject: Diaghilev in letters to his stepmother, Filosofov in his diary. He described Diaghilev's arrival at the estate as follows:

> Sergey arrived at the end of June. He was noisy and full of joie de vivre. He brought to Bogdanovskoye 'the Diaghilev touch'. Seryozha soon won everyone's hearts. He teased Mama and she laughed till she was exhausted. Seryozha guffawed himself, showing his strong teeth. It was interesting to watch Papa's reaction to Seryozha. He didn't talk much to him, he observed. But every time Seryozha guffawed, he laughed himself and said, 'He has an amazingly attractive laugh.'[8]

Others, too, were struck by his boisterous laugh. 'Every time he laughed,' wrote Benois, 'the hinges of his jaw dropped open, exposing a vast interior vista. And Sergey laughed constantly.'[9] Many years later Jean Cocteau would describe Diaghilev's laugh as that of 'a very young crocodile'.[10]

On their way back to St Petersburg they stopped at Pushkin's tomb. The great author was buried not far from Bogdanovskoye, and there Diaghilev removed his hat 'with genuine reverence'. They took a train from St Petersburg to Warsaw and then travelled on to Vienna. According to Dima, their days were filled with laughter.[11] Despite their crippling financial problems the Diaghilevs felt they had to give their son 1,000 roubles for the journey, while the much wealthier Filosofov had to make do with half that amount.[12]

It was in Vienna that Sergey first visited a major theatre. The two eighteen-year-olds attended a number of performances at the Vienna Opera, including Mozart's *Marriage of Figaro*, Rossini's *Barber of Seville*, Wagner's *Lohengrin* and *Der fliegende Holländer* and Verdi's *Aida*. It was also there that Sergey saw his first ballet: *Die Puppenfee* (The Fairy Doll). 'Oh, my darling mother, you mustn't laugh at me for being so delighted by everything. It really is all so delightful!!'[13]

From there they continued on to Trieste, where they stayed for a few days before taking a steamboat to Venice. On arrival, Diaghilev wrote to his stepmother. It was his first letter from the city that would play such a defining role in his life:

> We didn't take a gondola the first day but went everywhere we could on foot. We took a guide and tramped over the whole city. Among other things we climbed the campanile of S. Marco. It was only in the evening as there was a lovely moon we went for a boat ride … I only then really understood what a magic kingdom I had entered. You know what I'm like! It's impossible for someone who hasn't been to Venice to describe all her enchantments.[14]

> The next day we devoted to looking at churches and palaces, all wonderfully beautiful and splendid but surprisingly dead and lifeless. The heat was hellish. Venice makes a strange impression: sometimes it's so beautiful you want to lie down and die, sometimes it's so gloomy and stinking you just want to get away. In short, it's a marvellous but slightly depressing little city.[15]

One morning Diaghilev saw on a poster that the 'illustrious baritone' Antonio Cotogni would be giving a concert in Recoaro, a small town near Venice. When Dima refused to go, Diaghilev made the eight-hour trek on his own, arriving just in time to get a ticket. In the meantime Dima travelled on to Milan. Sergey wrote to his mother that

> Cotogni's singing was so astonishingly good that it was all I could do to keep from throwing my arms around his neck …
>
> After the concert I went straight back. It meant a three-hour drive through the mountains by horse-drawn cab. I hired a cab and set off, but then such a storm broke out in the mountains that I shook like an autumn leaf. Lord above, the terrors of a storm high up in the mountains! Somehow we got to the station and at two in the afternoon I was in Milan. It turned out that Dima had already looked at Milan and had gone off to Bellaggio three hours before. I went to have a quick look at Milan and hurried to catch up with him.[16]

It is hard to know what is more remarkable: that Diaghilev should have made such a Herculean effort to attend the concert, or that he had heard of Cotogni in the first place.[17] A few years later the very same Cotogni would move to St Petersburg and set up shop as a singing teacher, taking the young Diaghilev under his wing. It is one of the many bizarre coincidences that crop up again and again in Diaghilev's life.

In Padua he was deeply moved by the grandeur of the churches and the Catholic Mass. While there, he dropped in on a service dedicated to St Francis. He later wrote to his mother, 'Oh God, what a marvellous sight. Really and truly, Mama, I'm thinking about converting to Catholicism.'[18]

Diaghilev wrote very little about the art he saw in Venice and Padua, although it must have made an impression on him. The young student-to-be had seen very few works of art of any note. Perm had no museum or any other significant collection of art, either public or private. In the 'old house' on Siberia Street there were a few paintings by local artists, and Diaghilev's father had a collection of reproductions of engravings by Rembrandt and Raphael, among others.[19] Yet all things considered, Sergey Diaghilev, a defining figure in the history of Russian art and one of its most important chroniclers, had seen very little art of any significance before coming to Italy.

Sometime in the beginning of August, Diaghilev arrived in Bellaggio. There, on 6 or 7 August, he received a letter from his stepmother. That letter is now lost, but it is not difficult to reconstruct its content. It contained news of the dreaded event that everyone had seen coming. All hope was now lost and bankruptcy imminent. Diaghilev wrote back to his stepmother:

> Darling,
> However hard and sad the things you write about the whole affair, the scandals and troubles, still none of it would matter and I wouldn't have to be so upset about it all if you hadn't written how all this is affecting our dear, beloved, only Papa. I so want to hug him tightly – so tightly, to assure him how strongly I feel, how much I love him and bless him, in order to help him, he's so dear, so good. Really, Mama, for all of my 'egotism' as you say, I have so much instinctive love for him, it sometimes can be hidden but it's always there and will not cease to be and to reflect everything he is going through.[20]

From Bellaggio they took a ferry, travelling on to Lugano and Lake Maggiore by carriage, and from there to Lake Geneva via the Simplon Pass (which reminded him of the Caucasus). They stayed in Vevey, 'in the countryside', which they used as a base for excursions to Geneva. Although they had planned on spending only a few hours there, a music competition featuring thousands of participants caused them to extend their stay by a few days. From Geneva they went to Lucerne via Interlaken, where they met the Somovs and a number of other Russian families spending the summer there.

After a week in Lucerne they took a coach to Frankfurt, passing through Zürich, Basel and Strasbourg. They decided to leave Paris for another time. Sergey wanted to see Berlin, by way of Prague, Leipzig and Dresden, but in the end they elected to take a direct train from Frankfurt to Berlin. According to Filosofov they travelled 'with the utmost economy, in third class, only splashing out on second class for long-distance journeys. We ate only one meal a day, hoarding our scanty reserves for opera tickets.'[21] Sergey described Berlin as a 'frightful dump', and the opera was 'an even more vile mess than we'd expected'.[22] From Berlin they headed back to St Petersburg via Warsaw, arriving sometime in August.

Diaghilev had written to his stepmother that he wanted to come back to Perm as soon as he returned to Russia, but he was probably advised to stay in St Petersburg for a time. The magnitude of the disaster hanging over the family gradually became clear. The 7 October 1890 issue of the Perm Government Gazette ran the following notice: 'In the year 1890, 9 October, Colonel Pavel Pavlovich Diaghilev was declared a bankrupt debtor of non-commercial status by decision of Perm Magistrates Court.'[23] All movable and immovable property located in the district was confiscated. Any other creditors or anyone in possession of goods given as collateral by the bankrupt debtor was asked to make themselves known to the authorities.

In the days that followed, all of Pavel Pavlovich Diaghilev's property – and that of his two brothers, whom he had dragged down into bankruptcy with him – was auctioned off piecemeal. The house in Perm, the estate and distillery in Bikbarda, the pianos, the art, the mirrors and the carriage – everything had to go. Every auction, six in total, was reported in the Government Gazette, complete with inventory lists. Prior to the auctions, the value of the whole estate was appraised at 143,296 roubles, though it was probably sold for less than that.[24] All their possessions in Bikbarda went to the Poklovsky-Kozells, while the distillery in Nikolayevskoye was bought by the 'farmer Sibiryakov'.[25]

Returning to Perm was now out of the question. It was as if Diaghilev's entire childhood had been wiped out in the blink of an eye. It was soon decided that he would move in with the Filosofovs, who would see to it that he had a smooth transition to university life.

The Diaghilevs' reaction to this calamity was one of utter resignation. In her memoirs Yelena Diaghileva devotes only a few words to the loss of all her worldly possessions, and the subject comes up only occasionally in Diaghilev's letters. While the estate, the distilleries and the mansion were being auctioned and his parents were forced to stay with acquaintances, Diaghilev wrote to ask them how the weather was, whether it was cold enough for skating and whether his nanny had already made her jam.[26] This sang-froid in the face of financial ruin would prove to be a useful trait for the adult Diaghilev.[27]

It is not exactly clear how the Diaghilevs managed to eke out an existence in Perm. The only bright side to the bankruptcy was that Pavel Diaghilev could finally start off with a clean slate again. And even now, the family was far from destitute; in all likelihood they were supported by relatives in St Petersburg. Perhaps the Filosofovs, the Panayevs or the Koributs helped them out. It is also possible that Pavel managed to hang on to a small portion of his property. We know for certain that at least one category of asset was spared: part of the inheritance from Pavel's first wife belonged to Sergey personally (and thus lay beyond the reach of his father's creditors). This gave rise to a peculiar state of affairs in which the eldest son, who was barely eighteen, was the only member of the family with any property.

In any case the crisis mobilised family, friends and acquaintances. The Diaghilevs may have been bankrupt vodka distillers from the provinces, but they were also part of a clan: a small, yet close-knit clan of landed Russian aristocrats. Within six months Pavel Diaghilev could look forward to a new position in the army, even securing himself a promotion in the process. As a major-general he would head a regiment stationed in Peterhof. Yet for Pavel's two youngest sons the future was less rosy. There was no money left to send Valentin and Yury to university; they had no choice but to join the army. They were duly sent to St Petersburg, where they reported to the cavalry regiment in which their father had served.

For the time being, Diaghilev would continue to live with the Filosofovs. In their house on chic Galernaya Street, he and Dima shared a room for a year. 'Dima and I have become very close,' he wrote to his stepmother a few months later.[28] Almost a year passed before he returned to Perm for the last time, in the early summer of 1891. On the steamboat *Mikhail*, which brought him to Kazan, he read *Les rois en exil* by Alphonse Daudet, a book that reminded him of his own situation: 'Aren't we actually kings in exile too?'[29]

· 4 ·

Student Years: A Visit to Tolstoy

1891–1893

THROWN ENTIRELY ON HIS OWN RESOURCES, the young Diaghilev now had to prove himself in Petersburg society. The crème de la crème comprised some 7,500 persons, including the Diaghilevs, according to *Velikosvetsky ezhegodnik*, an annual social register. In such a small world, the bankruptcies of prominent families could not be hushed up, and the Diaghilevs' situation must have been common knowledge. Sergey struggled to make ends meet, with some help from the Filosofovs, meanwhile attempting to get his hands on the money he had inherited from his mother.

Around the autumn of 1891 he succeeded, at least in part, and was able to move into a five-room apartment at 28 Galernaya Street.[1] His two half-brothers, Valentin and Yury, joined different army corps in the capital, lodging with him whenever they were on leave. The household was swelled by the arrival of his old nanny, who had lost her place at Perm after the bankruptcy. Diaghilev now had to feed four people on the precarious income from his inheritance. Not only that, but he was also responsible for bringing up his half-brothers: no small task, as Yury, the youngest, had been only thirteen when they set up house together. He took in a lodger, a fellow student by the name of Misha Andreyev. Yet money was still very tight. His full inheritance was not yet forthcoming, and he was in the difficult position of a man with ample assets and no cash. He had little contact with his late mother's family, the Yevreynovs, though they were undoubtedly involved in the settlement of the estate.[2]

Yelena must have suffered terribly at having to give up her boys, but Diaghilev wrote to his stepmother regularly to let her know how Valentin and Yury were faring. He usually went to great lengths to reassure her, though on other occasions he spoke openly of his money problems. Once, Diaghilev told her that they were going hungry. The younger boys also kept up a stream of letters to their mother, affectionately nicknamed 'Lepus'.

After a few months the situation improved, and Sergey was able to invest some of his financial reserves. His correspondence also shows that he began sending money to his parents with some regularity. Yet his money management was erratic. Sometimes large sums were spent; at other times there was no money for food. This was a pattern that would persist for the rest of his life.

> I sometimes have a bit of a battle with Nyanya [nanny]. Her favourite theme of attack is my treatment of my brothers. That they have no separate rooms, that I economise on lunch when they come etc. Meanwhile the other day when they were at home, on Nyanya's and Misha's advice we had the following for lunch: 1. ham; 2. skoblyonka [a rich dish of veal, pork, potatoes, onion and cheese]; 3. cheese omelette; 4. fruit dumplings.
>
> When I remarked that such lunches weren't healthy, since having eaten our fill of them, both I and the boys became just like animals and couldn't do any work for at least three hours after all this, Nyanya made such a row: the boys had been starving for a week, one's not allowed to feed them even on a holiday etc. But today I've been much more restrained and am not taking all this so much to heart.[3]

But Yury wrote to 'dear Lepus' that Seryozha had been looking after him like a mother.[4]

During these first years on his own, Diaghilev's main social contacts were with his family. Besides Dima, whom he saw almost daily, he was often in the company of his cousins Pavka Koribut and Kolya Diaghilev. Kolya was a talented cellist, and the two often made music together. Pavka had long been Diaghilev's faithful companion, spending the summers with him at Bikbarda.

Diaghilev as a university student

But his company was no longer congenial to Diaghilev, who complained in letters to his stepmother that he was 'tiresome', 'irritating' and 'no longer sympathetic'. Dima had even less patience with Pavka, speaking openly of his revulsion for him. But Pavka – a slightly older, fatter and slower version of Diaghilev – proved to be the kind of man who refused to take a hint. He turned up cheerily at parties given by Diaghilev and Filosofov to which he had not been invited.[5] Writing about Pavka, Benois observed: 'He was very attractive in his affectionateness, in his readiness to agree and to enjoy himself with you and when it was needed to sympathise and grieve … For all that it was difficult to get to know Pavka properly. He didn't let you in to the inmost recesses of his being; he didn't trust you completely.'[6]

Diaghilev attended university lectures together with Dima. He sent detailed accounts to his stepmother of his daily routine:

How do I spend my day? I get up about 10 and go to university about 11. I always lunch at home and very often friends have lunch with us, coming here from the university. After lunch I either pay calls or go shopping, or go somewhere on business, or read, or sing (most often of all) or play duets (very often).

I have made the following decision: (I don't know if you'll like my decision) to go to university very regularly, to listen attentively to lectures, to furnish my room in spartan fashion, so that it's just comfortable enough to live in, thus saving me money, and after university to read or play the piano or pay visits if essential, to have dinner with friends and to spend all my money on opera or concerts.

A little later he added, 'University amazes and terrifies me, and I love it …'[7]

According to Dima, that love was a fickle one. He wrote in his diary: 'We went to the university as a gang but I think I was the only one to take it seriously. Diaghilev, Nouvel and Benois went there only occasionally, when they needed to. They had to do something … Really for Seryozha the university didn't exist. I don't even understand why he went there … He loathed taking the examination.'[8]

Dima did, however, influence his cousin's reading. Diaghilev would never be a bookworm – he was too mercurial for that – but in his early student years he often referred to novels and plays that he had read: 'Mainly reading Ibsen and Zola.'[9]

I am reading and working. I've read Maeterlinck – rubbish … I've read Ibsen's new play, *An Enemy of the People* – a very interesting piece. We're all generally very keen on Ibsen – a very good and interesting writer. I am now reading a new book *La Guerre de 1870* [by Helmuth von Moltke]. It's a most interesting and serious book on which I must work. I am sitting like an officer of the general staff, surrounded by maps, dictionaries etc. And at the same time I'm reading [Zola's] *La Joie de vivre*.[10]

He also read a lot of Dostoyevsky, Tolstoy and Maupassant. His preference for realists is striking at a time when his friends (and Russians in general) were devouring works by Romantic novelists such as E. T. A. Hoffmann and Edgar Allan Poe.

At a certain point he and Dima hatched a plan to visit Leo Tolstoy at his estate Yasnaya Polyana. On a whim they travelled to Moscow, where, to their amazement, they managed to obtain an audience with the great writer. Both had seen the premiere of his play *The Fruits of Enlightenment* and had fallen under his spell. In the 1890s he was at the height of his fame. No churchman, politician or intellectual leader even approached Tolstoy's status, and many a commentator remarked that he was mightier than the tsar.

Diaghilev, too, was impressed by Tolstoy's ethical and philosophical teachings, and he consulted them whenever he was troubled by existential questions. His struggle to make sense of things was hardly surprising, given the stress caused by separation from his family and the weighty responsibility of looking after his young half-brothers.[11]

He wrote a long letter to his stepmother, giving every detail of his and Dima's conversation with Tolstoy. The letter is more carefully constructed than his other correspondence. It undoubtedly took him a long time to compose, and he may have been helped a little by Dima.[12] It is an important document, being the first piece of prose in which Diaghilev adopts a high-flown style and seeks to describe an occasion in a writerly fashion. His detailed descriptions of interiors are a fair imitation of the great Russian Romantic authors (note the detail about the stolen boots at the coaching inn). Although Diaghilev and Filosofov plainly had trouble distinguishing between essentials and trivia (in print, the letter would run to ten pages), they are extremely observant, not least of their own behaviour. Diaghilev is strikingly candid, admitting that their excuse for calling on Tolstoy was just a ruse. They had scraped together a few roubles on the pretext of contributing to his latest charitable project. When the great man asked what brought them to Moscow they invented a story on the spot; clearly they had no scruples about lying to their hero. They were also surprisingly upset to spot a couple of students' caps hanging in the hallway. Though desperate to talk to Tolstoy, the thought of doing so in the presence of plebeian students was unbearable. Complete candour about one's faults – such as arrogance or mendacity – can have a certain charm. It is a trick Diaghilev puts to good use here, and one that became something of a stock in trade.

18 February [1892, St Petersburg]
A conversation with Lev Nikolayevich Tolstoy.

… Tolstoy was staying in a private house in Khamovniki, a remote part of the city. About 6 p.m. we drove up to a typical large Moscow gentleman's house, all lit up, single-storeyed and free-standing, with a big mezzanine, built between garden and courtyard … We went into the entry and at first were going to ring but the door turned out not to be locked. We went into the hall. It was a big room. On the left, directly opposite us, was a big wooden staircase going upstairs. Next to the staircase was a corridor

leading into the depths of the house, and further to the right an open door
into the dining room, where we could see the corner of a laid table. We
could hear lively sounds and voices in the house. There was a coat-stand
with a lot of fur coats, and a table in front of a mirror on which there were
several student caps. We were a bit embarrassed by that, we had no desire
to speak to Tolstoy in front of others, especially students. In the middle of
the hall stood a footman in white gloves and tails, seeing off someone who
was leaving. We asked him whether Lev Nikolayevich was at home. 'The
Count is at home, he's about to eat.' 'We have some business with him just
for five minutes.' 'But it would be better if you came back at seven, then
the Count'll be free and you can sit with him as long as you want.' At that
point some young ladies came downstairs, they must have been L.N.'s
daughters. We backed away a bit and went out with the firm resolve of
returning in an hour. It was a long way to go back home, it was too cold to
wait on the street. The cabby told us he knew an excellent inn 'near by on
Golubyatnoye' where we could sit and have some tea. We agreed and he
took us to a big, dirty, cabmen's tavern. We asked for tea and newspapers
and began to wait. Time dragged slowly by. Pedlars were walking about the
place, carrying all kinds of rubbish, and right by us in the room there was a
terrible cry – someone's boots had been stolen. We felt soiled in spirit. Our
energy began to drain. The trip to L.N. seemed stupid and impertinent.
One wanted to get it over with as quickly as possible. At quarter to seven
we decided to go ...

Again the door wasn't locked, again there appeared the same footman
in tails and asked how to announce us. We asked him simply to say that
two Petersburg students wanted to see Lev Nikolayevich. First he ran
off upstairs, then came downstairs and finally led us down the corridor.
We could see the table in the dining room hadn't been cleared. Upstairs
they were playing some Schumann on the piano and everywhere was the
sound of voices. In the corridor we met a couple of grammar-school boys
who bowed to us politely. We went up into a small room which must
have belonged to one of Tolstoy's elder sons. Above the desk hung an
oleograph of Repin's painting of 'Lev Tolstoy Out Hunting'. On the desk
were his visiting cards, decanters and a book lying open, *Lettres de Marie
Bashkirtzeff*. The furniture was just a hard bed with one pillow covered with
an old grey blanket, a hard armchair, a trunk, a chair and a bookcase with
some books. I sat on the chair; Dima was tempted by the trunk on which
some men's clothes had been thrown. We stayed waiting like that for about

five minutes which seemed like years. We shook at every movement in the corridor.

Finally, we heard footsteps and the coughing of an elderly man, and Lev Nikolayevich came in. He wore a black cloth blouse, loose black trousers, boots, and a strap as a belt … What particularly struck me about him was the combination of peasant's working clothes and a gentlemanly way of behaving and speaking. Nothing in his person or his clothes or his voice or his behaviour or his conversation could have given offence, not the tiniest detail. His whole person moved one, being a peculiar embodiment of truth and naturalness. He spoke in a bass voice and quite loudly …

Having greeted us he asked, 'How can I help you?' I stammered out the sentence I had prepared: 'Lev Nikolayevich, we are Petersburg students who wanted to send you the contributions we'd scraped together, but learning you were in Moscow we decided to give them to you in person.' Tolstoy: 'Very nice. And what brings you to Moscow?'

(Here Dima allowed himself a small lie; it was somehow terribly awkward to confess we had come to Moscow to have a good time.) Dima: 'We have things to do here.' Tolstoy: 'Oh, the university …' Dima: 'No, my father sent us.' T: 'Aha, and have you come for long?'

The conversation proceeds somewhat awkwardly for several more pages. Tolstoy speaks at length about the need for soup kitchens. He also expands on the subject of charity, by analogy with the parable of Zacchaeus from the book of Matthew. At length, Diaghilev continues:

T: 'Well, you must excuse me, I'd very much like to talk to you more but I have guests.'

(Then, when he held out his hand to us, Dima couldn't contain himself.) D: 'Lev Nikolayevich, may we kiss you?'

Lev Nikolayevich embraced him first, next he gave me a couple of kisses, and then he opened the door into the corridor for us. We hastened to pass through and as we were leaving we heard his quiet footsteps moving away behind us …

When we got out onto the street, our first words were exclamations: 'But he's a saint, he's really a saint!' We were so moved we almost wept. There was something inexpressibly sincere, touching and holy in the whole person of this great man. It's funny that we could smell his beard for a long time, which we had touched as we embraced him …

Hoping for a memento of their visit, Diaghilev wrote to Tolstoy's daughter, Tatyana Lvovna, enclosing a photograph of Tolstoy with a request for an autograph, which they received.

About three days after our visit to Tolstoy our cousin Biryukov went to see him. Among other things Lev Nikolayevich had asked him: 'Who was it who was talking to me the other day about your wife?'
Biryukov: 'Oh, a couple of students, Filosofov and Diaghilev.'
T: 'Yes, yes. I was talking to them. Tell me, the Diaghilevs were very rich, didn't they go bust recently? Were they utterly ruined?'
B: 'Yes, but this Diaghilev has something to live on from his dead mother.'
T: 'They were nice young men, so enthusiastic. And are they your wife's cousins in a family sense or are they cousins in spirit?'
B: 'No, it's a very close family and they all love one another.'
    Hearing these few sentences pleased us so much: it meant Tolstoy hadn't completely forgotten us …
    That was my meeting and correspondence with Tolstoy. I don't know if I'll ever again in my life meet or write to him. I hope so with all my heart because moments and impressions like that remain in one's heart for ever like bright points of light. No one has ever made such an unusual and strange impression on me. After seeing him I understood that on the road to achieving perfection a man can acquire moral sanctity; I understood that the prophets and saints we read about in the Scriptures aren't just impossible myth. I learned that today too there can be holy warriors who seek out the truth and spread the word. I know that when I re-read these lines in thirty years they will seem quite ridiculous to me. This enthusiasm and passion will pass but why conceal them when the passion is begging to be released?[13]

After returning to St Petersburg, Diaghilev wrote three more letters to Tolstoy. Ilya Zilbershteyn, Russia's leading authority on Diaghilev, saw the letters in the 1960s or 1970s and quoted an excerpt from one written on 15 April 1892, about two months after the visit to Moscow. Diaghilev is clearly replying to a letter from Tolstoy: 'You wrote to me,' he reminded him, 'that you had liked me, and these weren't just words: I can't believe you would ever say or write what you didn't feel. This word of affection has given me some small right to turn to you again and to make my confession to you about a subject on which I must have your counsel; and to whom should I turn for counsel but to you?'[14]

Nothing is known about the remainder of this letter, or the two that immediately followed. On the last occasion Diaghilev wrote to Tolstoy on 19 March 1893 – his twenty-first birthday – with a question about 'the eternal question of the meaning of life'.[15] In that letter he states, 'The dream and purpose of my life are to work creatively in the realm of the arts.'[16]

To some extent Diaghilev was like any other star-struck youth, seeking to get close to a great man by writing to him. Nevertheless, the fact that Tolstoy replied several times (and did so personally, rather than through his secretary) shows that he took Diaghilev's letters with a modicum of seriousness. Looking back, we can say that this brief correspondence with Tolstoy marks a new stage in Diaghilev's development. On reaching the age of twenty-one, he gradually distanced himself from the ideology of his elders, the idealists of the 1860s and 1870s, of whom Tolstoy was the most radical exponent. And though Diaghilev would always write about Tolstoy with deep admiration and respect, when years later he presented his own ideas to the world in his exhibitions and his journal *Mir iskusstva* (World of Art), he and his former hero were on opposite sides of an aesthetic divide.

· 5 ·

Student Years: Alexandre Benois

1890–1894

BY FAR THE MOST IMPORTANT new face to appear during Diaghilev's first years in St Petersburg was Alexandre Benois ('Shura' to his friends). A friend and former classmate of Dima's, Benois came from a family of famous architects and artists of French and Venetian extraction. Alexandre's father was a much sought-after architect, as were his maternal grandfather and his brother Nikolay. Another brother, Albert, was a well-known watercolourist. The members of the Benois family dominated the artistic life of the capital. They could be found at the imperial court (one of Alexandre's forebears had been Tsar Paul's chef), at the art academy (where a number of them taught) and in all manner of organisations, from artists' societies to cultural heritage associations.

But it was not only the visual arts that interested Alexandre's family; they were also active in the world of music and theatre. The children were given drawing and music lessons at the highest level and challenged to excel in the arts. The house was full of art; besides the many pieces by family members, there were various Italian and German works, including pastels by Guardi. The Benoises even owned a painting by Leonardo da Vinci. One of the last pieces by the Italian master in private hands, it now hangs in the Hermitage under the title the 'Benois Madonna'.

No history of twentieth-century Russian culture, however cursory, would

Benois: self-portrait

be complete without a mention of this illustrious family's most famous son. Alexandre was an astonishingly productive painter and graphic artist, a celebrated set and costume designer, illustrator, book designer and publisher. On top of all that he was an influential and prolific critic. He began publishing as a young man and remained active into very old age (he lived to be ninety). As an art historian he was entirely self-taught, but that did not prevent him from writing a great many books on art history, including a three-volume *History of Russian Art* and a twenty-volume *History of Art of All Nations and All Periods.* Alexandre maintained contact with an extensive network of artists, art historians and critics throughout Europe by means of a steady stream of long, painstakingly composed letters. His epistolary legacy is immense, and even today little of it has been catalogued. For most of his life he kept a meticulous record of his activities in diaries, lists (books read, performances attended) and sketchbooks filled with people and scenes from his own life. The Benois archive – manuscripts, drawings, paintings – in the depots of the Russian Museum in St Petersburg comprises literally thousands of items, and even this is a mere fraction of his total output.[1] In the turbulent years following the 1917 Revolution, Benois was also instrumental in preserving and protecting Russia's art treasures. This led to his reluctantly accepting the post of head curator of the Hermitage, a position he held from 1918 until he left the Soviet Union for good in 1926.

Everything Benois produced in his lifetime was made with care and dedication. Nothing in his output, whether artistic or literary, was slapdash, superficial or ungrammatical. He was not the type of man to go in for cheap effects or easy successes. Yet despite all this, he lacked any great artistic talent. He found his own style and stance early on and would never stray from them for the rest of his life. He had little interest in new trends or indeed in anything beyond his own narrow horizon. He repeated himself again and again, dismissing the whole of modern art as so much hot air, snobbery and fraud. He called futurism 'a cult of emptiness, of gloom, of the "nothing" of the black square in the white frame […]',[2] while cubism was 'that grimace of our time'.[3] While undeniably erudite, eloquent and passionate, his writings on art history lack true insight into the complexity of artistic phenomena. Few would now take issue with John Bowlt's final verdict on Benois: 'Nowadays the name of Alexandre Benois means comparatively little to the Western art historian – and perhaps, ultimately, there is no particular reason why it should.'[4] Yet it is impossible to dismiss him completely, if only because of the role he played in the life and career of a man he regarded alternately as his best friend and his greatest tormentor: Sergey Diaghilev.

Diaghilev met Benois in 1890, shortly before his first trip abroad, in the company of another of Dima's friends, Walter Nouvel. Later, looking back on this meeting, Benois would write: 'This cousin was nothing like the thin and pale Dima … What struck us was how robust he looked. He had full rosy cheeks and sparkling white teeth in two even rows between bright crimson lips.'[5]

Sergey was treated with all the matter-of-fact, cruel disdain that an urbane youth of nineteen or twenty feels towards a slightly younger lad from the provinces. Benois wrote:

It was generally obvious that he was extremely excited at being in the capital, at the same time he was happy to meet his cousin's closest friends … To sum up the impression Seryozha made, I would say we thought him a nice boy, a good solid provincial, perhaps not too bright, a bit earth-bound, a bit primitive, but generally likeable. If Valechka and I then at once decided to welcome him into our group, it was purely a matter of kinship – his being a cousin of Dima's.[6]

Filosofov could also clearly recall that first meeting between Sergey and his friends:

> I remember as if it were yesterday Sergey Diaghilev's first meeting (in the autumn of 1890) with a key member of Shura Benois's circle, V. F. or rather Valechka Nouvel. A pretty caustic character and a good musician, who liked to 'épater les bourgeois' more than any of us, he decided then and there to make the provincial twit feel awkward. Having just read Nietzsche's articles attacking Wagner, he mocked Wagner and Borodin and praised Carmen. In short he stirred things up like a metropolitan. But the provincial wasn't put out.[7]

Benois, Filosofov and Nouvel formed a clique that first took shape at the Karl von May Academy on Vasilevsky Island, the largest island in the Neva delta. This private boys' grammar school was a modern, liberal institution attended by the sons of the intelligentsia. According to Shura the place was run with Teutonic rigour, and many subjects were even taught in German.[8] The school's liberal outlook was evident from its policy of accepting not only the children of doctors, artists, architects and lawyers, but also the 'children of the kitchen maid'.[9] In an effort to play down class differences, the school authorities prohibited parents from dropping off their children in a coach or car. This resulted in chaotic scenes every morning around the corner from the school.

The contrast could not have been greater between the May Academy and the grammar school in Perm, where little lord Diaghilev had been regarded in awe by his classmates and given preferential treatment by his teachers in the hope of currying favour with his parents.

The artist Konstantin 'Kostya' Somov had also attended the May Academy, and even though he had left early to go to art school, he and his old school chums saw each other quite regularly. Shortly before they met Diaghilev, the group would be joined by the artist Lev 'Lyovushka' Rozenberg, who would change his surname to Bakst not long thereafter. Benois tried to give the club a more official status, to combine their artistic and intellectual interests with the romantic allure of a secret society. In his memoirs Benois writes that the friends gave themselves names like the Society for Self-Study and the Nevsky Pickwickians, but the latter designation is mentioned neither in any contemporary sources nor in the reminiscences of Nouvel or Filosofov. It is quite possible that Benois was romanticising his school days and simply dreamt up the name sometime in the 1930s or 1940s, when he was composing his memoirs.

Diaghilev wrote to his stepmother on a number of occasions about his visits to what he always called the Mayevtsy (the May crowd):

> At university we're a very close group, all the Mayevtsy are very decent fellows, I'm already on ty ['thou', i.e. intimate] terms with several of them. I go to Benois's, where about five of us have formed a little club, and once a week we each give a lecture on the history of art. There've been three now. Benois on 'The development of art in Germany', Kalin (another student) on 'Modern criticism', Nouvel on 'The history of opera'. I'm going to give a lecture on the Karamazovs and then do something about music.[10]

Yet the relationship between Sergey and the others in the group remained strained, mainly because the former had little time for what he perceived as their arrogance, refusing to kowtow to their supposed authority. The following scene took place in 1891, when Diaghilev and Benois were on their way back to Bogdanovskoye together. To Benois, who never forgot the moment, it took on the status of 'an important symbol' of their relationship.[11]

> Having come back from Bogdanovskoye earlier than the others, Seryozha wanted to go with me and visit Valechka, who was then staying with his mother at a dacha in Pargolovo. But we didn't find Valechka at home, he'd gone for a walk and so we set off to look for him, rather at random. It was oppressively hot and we soon began to sweat, got tired and had an overwhelming desire to lie down. We chose a dry spot and stretched out on the grass. Lying on my back and gazing at the cloudless sky, I resolved to use this opportunity and get to know our new friend more systematically ... I had to find out how much he suited us, whether he was hopelessly far removed from us, in sum whether he was worth bothering with ... And now this serious conversation was interrupted in the most childish way. Lying on my back I couldn't see what Seryozha was doing and so I was completely taken by surprise when he fell on me and started to punch me, wanting me to fight and roaring with laughter. Our group didn't do things like that; we were all 'well-brought-up mother's boys' and

averse to all forms of physical exercise, especially fighting. I quickly realised as well that I was no match for the stout, muscly Seryozha. The elder risked being the loser. I had to resort to guile – I gave a piercing cry, 'You've broken my arm.' Seryozha didn't stop at once; I could see in his eyes the thrill of victory and his desire to enjoy it to the last drop. However, meeting no more resistance and only hearing my groans and cries, he stopped the silly game, jumped to his feet and even helped me to get up. To be more convincing I went on rubbing my arm although I didn't in fact feel any especial pain.[12]

The relationship between the two boys would be a stormy one right from the start. Benois's claim that he acted as a sort of mentor to Diaghilev in those early years is an exaggeration at best, and it is clear that Diaghilev's get-togethers with Benois's circle were just one aspect of his busy social calendar. In the very first year Sergey wrote to his stepmother about an argument he had had with Benois that cast a pall over the friendship, at least for a time:

> As far as our lectures are concerned I can tell you that they are still taking place, although I seldom go to them because I have quarrelled with Benois, the founder of our society. However, I'm not the only one to have done so; his friends' ardour for him has also cooled. Although everyone, Dima foremost, says that he is a very clever and talented man, his hidden talents, which for a stranger are absolutely invisible, are not enough to forgive his huge faults – boorishness, affectations, various childish tricks and bad behaviour. And one fine day when we were coming back from the theatre and he was behaving badly in the street, jumping about, yelling and God knows what else, I quarrelled with him and told him that I didn't want to go around with such a boor.[13]

At least as important to his future development was his progress in music during those first years in St Petersburg. To start with, he took lessons from his Aunt Tatusha ('Just imagine, Auntie managed to coax a very good voice out of me'),[14] but he also sought out other teachers. He took singing lessons with a Professor Gabel, who taught at the conservatory. He spoke of the lessons in a letter to his stepmother, with his customary lack of modesty: 'He's very pleased with me and said … that I have a good voice, but that I have many faults which he is sure he'll correct, he being such an intelligent and musical pupil. I am having lessons twice a week. I'll begin to study theory on 1 November, although I don't yet know definitely with whom.'[15]

Not everyone was thrilled by his desire to enrol at the conservatory. Anna Filosofova, who tried to make sure her nephew followed the right path in life (that is to say the progressive path), told him a few home truths: 'She [Filosofova] says that I'm being selfish and that we don't need people to write symphonies but to help the masses.'[16] For a time Diaghilev did set aside his plans to enter the conservatory, though he went on looking for a suitable composition teacher. In any case, we know that during those years he received instruction from the composers Nikolay Solovyov and Nikolay Sokolov, both professors at the conservatory.[17]

One day Diaghilev was invited to a musical gathering at the home of Platon Vaksel, the influential music critic of the *Journal de St Petersbourg*, and from that point on he became a regular member of his circle.[18] A year later he would also begin attending the soirées held by Alexandra Molas, Nikolay Rimsky-Korsakov's sister-in-law and a fervent supporter of the group of composers collectively known as 'Kuchka' (typically rendered as 'the Five' or 'the Mighty Handful' in English).* On these occasions he would meet Balakirev, Cui and Rimsky.[19] These composers advocated a progressive, anti-academic, nationalist programme, allied to the principles espoused by the Peredvizhniki school of painting (also known as the Itinerants). They aspired to be the musical manifestation of the ideals of the 1860s and 1870s and hoped that they could hasten the dawn of a national consciousness by forging a native Russian musical idiom and spicing up their music with 'authentic' folk tunes. It is in no small measure due to the Five's energy and zest for innovation, their quest for identity and their aversion to 'Western' clichés that Russian music flourished in the second half of the nineteenth century.

In attending Vaksel's and Molas's soirées, Diaghilev found himself at the heart of the Petersburg music scene as early as 1893. This is highly significant because the work of the Five would come to occupy a prominent place in the repertoire of the Ballets Russes up until the First World War. The soirées gave the twenty-one-year-old Diaghilev a unique chance to become acquainted

....

*The five men in question were Mily Balakirev, Alexander Borodin, César Cui, Modest Mussorgsky and Rimsky-Korsakov himself.

with their repertoire. He also established contacts that would enable him to hobnob with the composers many years later.

During this period, another significant trait emerged. Even at this young age, Diaghilev's tastes and preferences were developing independently of his social surroundings. Despite the disapproval of his much older associates, the lad from the provinces developed a passion for the music of Wagner, a man who was treated more like a foreign disease than an artist, by both Vaksel's circle and the Five (with the exception of Rimsky-Korsakov).[20]

Diaghilev would later be reluctant to own up to his youthful flirtation with Wagner. From 1914 (if not before), he was a confirmed defender of Franco-Russian modernism and thus deeply opposed to German music, with its expressionist tendencies. Despite his later protestations to the contrary, Diaghilev was a dyed-in-the-wool Wagnerian up until his conquest of the Paris art world. He saw his first two Wagner productions in Vienna in 1890, but it is unclear if this marked the start of his Wagner phase. It is not inconceivable that Alexandre Benois fanned young Sergey's budding interest in the composer. As early as 1889 Benois attended the first performance of the *Ring* cycle in Russia, which made a deep impression on him and precipitated his own conversion to Wagnerism. Yet Benois is also partly responsible for the smokescreen that hangs over this phase of Diaghilev's artistic development. The former's memoirs represent Diaghilev as a typical aficionado of the Russian repertoire (Tchaikovsky, Mussorgsky) and a man with little or no appreciation for foreign music, a portrayal that was in keeping with Benois's attempt to depict the Diaghilev of the early 1890s as a provincial naïf.

But by 1892 Diaghilev was an ardent 'Wagner fanatic', as he wrote to his stepmother.[21] He sang and played Wagner with his friends, and longed to visit Germany to see more performances. He asked a relative to send a letter of recommendation to Giuseppe Kaschmann, an Italian baritone who performed frequently in Petersburg and Moscow, but who that season would be singing at the Festspielhaus in Bayreuth.[22]

With the coveted letter in hand, Diaghilev left in early July on his second big trip abroad, this time on his own. His principal destination: Germany; his principal goal: to meet as many famous people as possible. He wrote regular letters to his stepmother, for example this one from Nuremberg on 14 July 1892:

I went to Ischl to see the famous Brahms who lives there. As soon as I got there, I went to see him but he had gone for a walk and I only saw him in the evening. Brahms turned out to be a lively little German who doesn't speak French. He at once agreed to my request for an autograph and signed a visiting card. I sat with him for about quarter of an hour but the conversation was laboured, as we had difficulty in understanding each other. At every word of mine, for example that I'd come to Ischl in order to see him, he fidgeted and went red. In Germany he's terribly neglected. His apartment is like an old tavern. Such a talent and in such surroundings. But just think, Beethoven too was a poor German, and deaf as well. Better to imagine them than to see them. But I am still glad that I could give him a heart-felt handshake – *une cordiale poignée de main*. Then I went to Salzburg. I saluted Mozart and came to Nuremberg. It's an astonishing town, a museum from end to end, you feel you're in the 17th century, surrounded by Fausts and Gretchens. Pure delight. Well, yesterday I was in Bayreuth and went to the *Meistersinger von Nürnberg*. Until I've heard all four operas I won't write you my impressions in any detail. I'll only say this: I am certain that people who are disappointed in themselves and their lives, and see no point in living, people who have been put in a difficult situation by life's misfortunes and finally people who despair to the point of bringing their life to an artificial end – all of them should come here.[23]

Wagner as a panacea for all the young Werthers of the world. When Diaghilev later tried to describe the music to his stepmother, he did not fixate on the Sturm und Drang element, but instead set out – perhaps for the very first time – his belief in aestheticism, the superiority of art to life:

The noise grew, it became a tempest, louder and louder, a tornado of noise, more, more, more, thunder in the heavens, then torrents of rain, then whole forests of noise – darkness! And suddenly paradise, the melodies of the Muses playing on their lyres. Everything is here: pettiness, intrigues, grief, anger, love, jealousy, tenderness, cries, groans – all of this goes on until eventually the whole of it mingles to present life as it flows on for each of us, and above it all triumphs the truth of beauty …

So tell everybody, go there, there is something there which can't be found anywhere else. Darling, I'll tell you later in detail when I see all the operas.[24]

I think this journey of mine will be useful for me for practising my German. It turns out I have to speak German much more than I imagined, and I make myself understood. But all the same Russian society is the most cultivated; I speak French terribly but up till now I haven't met one German who spoke French even like me. They all speak their Yiddish tongue, and the Austrian yokels especially are rogues. You see, I pay Russia her due.[25]

On 27 July he wrote to his stepmother again, this time from Munich. He had seen seven operas in Bayreuth, which did nothing to dampen his enthusiasm for Wagner. He had spoken with Kaschmann and sung for him. According to Diaghilev, Kaschmann would later tell Vaksel that the young Russian had *'une belle voix'*.[26] Diaghilev was less taken by the staging of the opera, and in another letter to his stepmother the future director of the Ballets Russes discussed his preference for cuts, foreshadowing a practice he would later adopt as an impresario:

> About the music itself I'll say its only fault is the occasional longueur, but it depends on the director, in this case Mme Wagner, making appropriate cuts, and she so reveres her husband's music that she won't allow a single note to be cut. Heavens above! In Shakespeare, Beethoven, Glinka etc. masses of cuts are made. I do understand that one shouldn't insert one's own material, but to cut out what is antiquated and boring is to improve a piece. The fault is Mme Cosima's.[27]

By September Diaghilev was back in St Petersburg, fully determined to dedicate the rest of his life to music. He composed at a furious pace, producing a number of works that he performed at intimate recitals. Nevertheless, the decision caused him great unease, and from time to time he openly doubted his abilities. And doubt was a state of mind with which Diaghilev had great difficulty coping. Tellingly, it is around this time that his letters begin to speak of various crises, major and minor. These letters lay bare Diaghilev's dramatic mood swings, in sometimes painful detail. On 14 October 1892 he wrote to his stepmother:

> My mood is now going through a Lazarus period into *joie de vivre*. I don't know if this happens to everyone or if it's solely due to my nerves. It's this

mass of insoluble problems and my continual pursuit by the inevitability, incomprehensibility and momentousness of death, in short the whole aim of life, you'll understand me. Do you remember you and I spoke about this last summer? During those long autumn evenings in the country I was led by everything to this never-ending train of thought. This last month in the midst of city life I have felt better and these painful attacks have been less frequent. I really seriously want to be treated for nerves.[28]

But most of the time Diaghilev is the very picture of self-confidence, ready for a life of distinction:

Yes, I am beginning to feel strength in myself and to realise that, damn it, I am not a completely ordinary man (!!!). That's rather arrogant, but I don't care. One thing frightens me, that I was born in the century when there is neither a public nor 'experts nor judges'. Good God, I despair when I see that I understand music better than anyone, no, seriously no one understands anything, but everyone judges, forms his opinion in two minutes and then speaks his mind.[29]

By mid-1894 he feels strong enough to engage in a more serious confrontation:

As for my own compositions, they're all the same or very nearly so, apart from something I'm doing at the moment and which I mean to dedicate to you. But for the time being, however curious you are to know, I'm going to have to keep you in the dark. That's the way it is! Fat Lepus, that's very annoying for you; you'll just have to be a little annoyed for a bit … Now I'm coming to the matter which recently has been bothering me most – my visit to Rimsky-Korsakov.[30]

When Sergey wrote these lines to his stepmother, the appointment had already been made with Rimsky-Korsakov, whom he had undoubtedly spoken to occasionally at the Petersburg musical soirées. On 18 September 1894 his brother Yury wrote to his mother, 'On Wednesday, Seryozha is going to show his work to Rimsky-Korsakov.'[31]

At that time, in the wake of Tchaikovsky's death, Rimsky was Russia's greatest living composer and a celebrated educator. He was not only the most powerful man at the St Petersburg conservatory, he was also highly active in what was essentially the only progressive musical society, the Belyayev circle. And an important detail for Diaghilev: he was virtually the only composer in Russia who took Wagner seriously. All things considered, Rimsky was an understandable choice, though given Diaghilev's options, 'Hobson's choice' might have been nearer the mark.

· 6 ·

'The Serge Diaguileff Museum': St Petersburg, Rome, Genoa, Paris
1894–1896

BY THE TIME HE VISITED Rimsky-Korsakov with samples of his work, Diaghilev had quite an oeuvre to choose from, most of it dating from the previous year. On 14 August 1893 Diaghilev and other musicians gave a concert at Bogdanovskoye, where he performed three of his own works – a piano composition entitled 'Mélodie' and two romances: *David the Psalmist* and *The Maiden and the Sun*. He also sang Amfortas' monologue from Wagner's *Parsifal* and played a piano duet (an arrangement of the overture from *Lohengrin*) with a Mrs Kamenetskaya.[1] A year later he had, as he informed his stepmother in a letter, 'once again composed a deathless work, *Romance pour violoncello et piano* ... a vulgar specimen of salon frippery, though at the same time a charming and melodic little piece'.[2]

In 1893 he was hard at work on a violin sonata, conceived as a much more serious piece, but he was having difficulty in making it coalesce. Then a theme suddenly presented itself – the unexpected death, on 25 October, of Pyotr Ilyich Tchaikovsky, whom Diaghilev and his friends worshipped: 'We're all deeply shaken by the death of Tchaikovsky. I simply sobbed during the whole *panikhida* [the requiem service held in the home of the deceased immediately after the death]. It was especially awful after we had just seen him conduct [his Sixth Symphony], a man full of strength. Of course I had a role in the funeral and was the first to lay a wreath.'[3]

Many years later Diaghilev noted down his memories of the day he learned of Tchaikovsky's death, apparently only for his own purposes, though with an unexpected twist:

> Without knowing what I was doing I jumped up and although I knew he had died of cholera I went to Malaya Morskaya to Pyotr Ilyich's flat. When I entered the house all the doors were open wide and no one greeted me. There was disorder in the rooms, on a table I saw an abandoned orchestral score of the Sixth Symphony and on a sofa P.I.'s famous brown camelhair cap which he never took off. In the next room there were voices. I went in and saw P.I. still lying on a divan, dressed in a black coat. Around him the sailor N. Rimsky Korsakov [he had been in the navy] and the singer N. Figner were busy arranging the table. We picked up P.I.'s body – I held his feet – carried it across the room and put it on the table. Apart from us there was nobody in the flat (everyone who had been with him at the time of death had gone off …). I found P.I. little changed and just as young as he was before the end. I ran to get some flowers and the whole of the first day there was only my wreath lying on his feet.[4]

This story, however incredible, is not necessarily a fabrication. Diaghilev knew Tchaikovsky well enough to walk in during the preparations for the *panikhida*, and newspaper reports confirm that Diaghilev was indeed the first to lay a wreath.[5]

That same day Diaghilev resumed work on his sonata, now intended to convey his feelings about Tchaikovsky's death. It was finished two and a half weeks later.

> My sonata is definitely finished, albeit clumsily, in any case it's steeped in feeling and true tonality, it's entirely [illegible text] in a minor key, and if I were to give it a name, it would be something like this: 'The death of Tchaikovsky in particular and the death of all people in general'. Of course, this sonata doesn't illustrate this sentence, because to illustrate it I would need to write something stronger, but it is a perfect description of my mood, especially in the second part, written on the day of Tchaikovsky's death, and at the end of the first.[6]

That winter, Diaghilev and Dima Filosofov again left for a long trip abroad, this time to Italy and France. Diaghilev had already written to his stepmother in the autumn to say that he wished to become better acquainted with the French repertoire. He mentioned Massenet and Saint-Saëns, whom he claimed were unknown in St Petersburg, and expressed his hope of being allowed to study harmony with them. But the French composer to whom he first submitted his work in the spring of 1894 was in fact a more logical choice: Emmanuel Chabrier. Chabrier was France's most fervent Wagnerian. In an incident that epitomised fin-de-siècle Wagnermania, he famously burst into tears on hearing the cellos intone the opening 'A' in a production of *Tristan* in Munich in March 1880. Chabrier was a cult figure among the French modernists – Manet painted his portrait no fewer than three times – but he had great difficulty in getting his work performed. His opera *Gwendoline* (1877–85) had to wait eight years for its premiere; when Diaghilev visited him in December 1893, rehearsals were finally under way.

Diaghilev had originally intended to stay in Paris for only three days but prolonged his visit to attend a performance of *Die Walküre*. Hearing that *Gwendoline* would have its premiere a few days later, he again postponed his departure, and went to great lengths to secure an invitation to the dress rehearsal: 'Yesterday morning I went to get a definite answer from the composer in person – from Chabrier. I am let in by a little old man who promptly embraces me. He takes me into his study, calls his wife, chatters away without stopping, shows me his picture gallery, and gives me a wonderful place for rehearsing ...'[7]

Excited as ever, he wrote to his stepmother that he had heard Chabrier's music in the company of the writers Zola and Dumas *fils*, and the composers Massenet and Vincent d'Indy. He promised to send some of his pieces to Chabrier and to correspond with him, apparently unaware that the composer was terminally ill, afflicted by a form of paralysis (which was probably syphilitic in nature). A few days after meeting Diaghilev, Chabrier suffered a stroke at the premiere of *Gwendoline* and was unable to recognise the music he heard as his own.[8]

Diaghilev then travelled via Genoa to Nice, where he endeavoured to shake Verdi's hand. At the time of the encounter, Verdi was just leaving his house for the opera. 'Picture me gawping at him through my pince-nez – I was in danger of forgetting my manners entirely.'[9]

At Valrose, the estate of the recently deceased Baron Paul von Derwies, Diaghilev continued his composing. A Russian industrialist and patron of the arts, von Derwies had taken up residence on the Côte d'Azur. He had two chateaux built on his massive estate, as well as a 400-seat concert hall. There was even a Valrose Orchestra. Its repertoire contained many Russian works, but the ensemble was best known for promoting the music of Wagner, causing the estate to be nicknamed the 'Bayreuth of Nice'. On a trip to Menton in the 1870s Diaghilev's parents had been given a warm welcome by the baron, and they had played music together. Von Derwies had even asked Pavel Diaghilev to sing in a performance of Glinka's *A Life for the Tsar* to be staged in 1879 (probably the first time the opera was heard outside Russia), but Pavel, perhaps doubting his abilities, politely declined the offer.[10]

In any case, the relationship between von Derwies and the Diaghilevs had been sufficiently cordial to ensure that their son was welcomed with open arms and given full use of the Steinway. He wrote to his stepmother that he had started on yet another violin sonata and was busy composing a '*poème* to a text by Baudelaire'. It is unclear whether the violin sonata was an entirely new work or a reworking of the one composed in the spring of 1893, lamenting the death of Tchaikovsky. The choice of author was probably inspired by Filosofov or Benois, though Diaghilev would certainly have been aware of Baudelaire's status as the most prominent French intellectual to champion Wagner, following his article 'Richard Wagner et Tannhäuser à Paris'.

When Diaghilev finally returned to St Petersburg in the summer of 1894, after his longest foreign trip ever, he continued to beaver away at his sonata. On 28 August he was able to write to his stepmother that he had composed the last note and that he was 'not dissatisfied'. From someone so little troubled by false modesty, this verdict sounds curiously hesitant. Diaghilev clearly wanted to write a piece that would find favour with Chabrier, or that at least sounded modern and European. But he wrote, 'I just can't rid myself of a Russian spirit. All the themes have a kind of Russian flavour that I'm not at all happy with.'[11] We do not know whether he sent his work to Paris in the end, but it is immaterial, because Chabrier was by then in the last stages of his illness (he would die that December).

Chabrier's death robbed Diaghilev of the hope of studying composition in France. Even with that avenue closed, he remained convinced of his future as a composer and decided to submit his work to Rimsky-Korsakov, confident that the latter would be prepared to teach him music theory.

Diaghilev visited Rimsky-Korsakov on 22 September. A number of accounts of that visit have been preserved, but the most detailed is to be found in the journal of Vasily Yastrebtsev, who had been close friends with Rimsky-Korsakov and his wife for sixteen years. His entry for the day of Diaghilev's visit includes the following:

> Nikolay Andreyevich gave an account of a curious visit he had had from some young man named Diaghilev, who fancies himself a great composer but, nevertheless, would like to study theory with Nikolay Andreyevich. His compositions proved to be absurd, and Nikolay Andreyevich told him so bluntly, whereupon he became offended and, on leaving, declared arrogantly that nevertheless he believes in himself and his gifts; that he will never forget this day and that some day Rimsky-Korsakov's opinion will occupy a shameful place in his (Rimsky-Korsakov's) biography and make him regret his rash words, but then it will be too late …
>
> Apropos of this, I recalled Lombroso's theory about the existence of a certain type of deranged person who, though undoubtedly gifted, never creates anything that is not bizarre, inane and even downright stupid.[12]

Rimsky-Korsakov's dismissal of Diaghilev appears in various other sources, including slightly varying accounts by Pavka Koribut and Walter Nouvel. According to the latter, Diaghilev gave the following parting shot on leaving Rimsky-Korsakov's study, 'History will show which of us was the greater!'[13] The reliability of Yastrebtsev's account is debatable. The reference to Lombroso sounds oddly forced. It is moreover strange that Rimsky-Korsakov acted as if he didn't know Diaghilev, even though they had undoubtedly met, if not at Molas's house then at Vaksel's. The date of publication of Yastrebtsev's journal – March 1917 – may be indicative. By 1917 Diaghilev was world famous and, in the wake of the February Revolution, he was being put forward by various factions as Russia's new Minister of Culture, a proposal that found favour with Prime Minister Alexander Kerensky. But Rimsky-Korsakov's heirs loathed him for his cavalier treatment of the *Schéhérazade* suite and Rimsky's orchestration of Mussorgsky's *Khovanshchina*. It seems very probable that Yastrebtsev – who was a member of Kerensky's Kadet

Party – sought to drive a wedge between Kerensky and his intended culture minister with his heavy-handed remarks about Lombroso.

But in September 1894 Diaghilev was still a young man with a broken dream and no idea about what to do with his life. Rimsky-Korsakov's rejection must have been devastating. For over two years he had focused all his energy and creativity on becoming a composer, and the outcome had been disastrous. For the first time in his life he was confronted with his own limitations, and with the narrow-mindedness and uniformity of the Petersburg music scene. Rimsky-Korsakov and his school reigned supreme in the realm of contemporary music, and there was little room for a young composer, either at the conservatory or at one of the few venues where new music was performed. Moscow might have offered possibilities, but moving there was out of the question for social, cultural and financial reasons.

In the meantime, his friends had been energetically pursuing their own careers. The year before, Alexandre Benois had shot to fame overnight as the author of the chapter on Russian art in Richard Muther's *Geschichte der Malerei im 19. Jahrhundert* (one of the first serious overviews of European art history). It was quite a coup for the twenty-two-year-old law student. He had simply written to Muther offering his services, though had somewhat inflated his qualifications, to say the least. After receiving a vague go-ahead he had thrown himself into the task with all the blind ambition of youth. Kostya Somov, the most talented artist in Benois's circle, had made his public debut in 1894. He worked tirelessly to develop his technique, soon finding an individual voice. Lev Bakst studied in the ateliers of Jean-Léon Gérôme and Albert Edelfelt, doing what Sergey had wanted to do: train as an artist in Paris, the epicentre of the European art world. Only Diaghilev, the yokel from Perm, had yet to achieve anything.

Benois, Filosofov and Nouvel prepared to finish their studies the following summer, but Sergey, who was now a year behind, had no prospect of graduating before the summer of 1896. His absences, particularly his last long trip, had left him with a lot of catching up to do. Russia was by then a police state, and students wishing to travel abroad needed permission from the dean of their university to obtain a passport. Diaghilev secured his by deceit, claiming he had to visit family abroad. But to justify his much longer 1893–4 trip he needed a better excuse. In exchange for a bribe, a doctor issued him with a certificate stating that he urgently needed to travel to a warm climate to alleviate 'chronic pain'.[14]

But although events had dented his ego, Diaghilev may also have felt some slight relief. Despite a burning ambition to become a composer, he regarded his compositions with a degree of irony, even displaying a rare flash of self-criticism. He never doubted his talent as a critic, but it was that very talent that all too often reminded him of his own creative shortcomings. His failure as a composer helped him realise that his genius lay not in artistic creation, but in perceiving the genius of others.

As he redefined his life's ambition, more humdrum affairs clamoured to be dealt with. There were exams to be sat and friendships to be rekindled. His two half-brothers had been neglected, and claimed his attention. Valentin and Yury, by now nineteen and seventeen years old, were still dependent on their older brother, even though they were on the verge of careers in the military. Yury, in particular, had difficulty coping with the demands of army training, and his future was uncertain. Both boys still lived with him when they were not staying at their barracks, and cousin Pavka continued to drop by as the spirit moved him. His father, too, spent the night with him whenever army duties required him to be in St Petersburg. The relationship between father and son remained tense: 'I so wanted Papa to be sweet and nice ... Everything depends on that, especially when you're dealing with a trombone like Pavka and a hothouse plant like Dima.'[15]

As regards the latter, although very little is known about Diaghilev's precise relationship with his cousin, they were inseparable at this time, and the pattern of their relationship, with Diaghilev leading and Dima following, had been set. The Russian nobility were extremely tolerant of youthful homosexual dalliances, provided the youths in question married a member of the opposite sex at some point. Poor Sergey had few prospects on that front: there were scarcely any women of his age in his direct circle. Most of his closest friends, Filosofov, Somov, Nouvel and probably Pavka, were homosexual, so he remained in a relentlessly male world.

Given Diaghilev's volatile nature, he must have gone through some dark nights of the soul during this period. On 11 December that year, after a fairly protracted silence, he wrote a long letter to his stepmother. It conveys his great bewilderment and the apparent impossibility of being candid about his problems.

Several times I've been meaning to write to you to get a little closer to you again, my dear friend from whom I've become so distant – though I don't know why, and don't want to be. I find I can't write what I want to say, and maybe I don't even know what I want to say.

I am now fairly calm, but all autumn I've been in a state of complete intoxication, something unusual for me and not really in harmony with the ethos of my age or with my deeply buried convictions. This intoxication has taken me away from life, having taken over my own. Husbanding my strength, time, energy – everything is out of kilter. Moreover, everything's become slippery and superficial – and that's bad too.

I've now become a human being again, I'm back to working a lot. I'd be glad to see you, but I'll tell you the truth – I'm afraid.

I recommend everyone to do everything in secret as much as possible, even if it involves deceit. All my life I've done the opposite, I've lost all my secrets and now I'm sorry. At all events I am writing to you not to tell you *le dernier cri* [the last word of fashion] but to send you a word of love, to get closer to you, because life drives people apart.[16]

Yelena Diaghileva must have been worried to receive this confused letter, but by now she was used to the sombre moods that could afflict her stepson, and she was probably also aware of certain factors that made his life so complicated: his thwarted ambitions, his difficulty in relating to women and his intense devotion to his cousin Dima. But by now she also knew how quickly his mood could change when he found a new outlet for his boundless energy and ambition. The recovery was not slow in coming; in the spring of 1895, Diaghilev suddenly became absorbed by a new passion – one which came as a surprise even to those who knew him: the visual arts.

Around that time he moved to a new apartment closer to the city centre, at 45 Liteyny Prospekt, nowadays a noisy, grimy thoroughfare but at the time a modern, wide boulevard, typical of those built in the late nineteenth century as the city expanded. He wanted to decorate his house luxuriously and tastefully according to the latest fashions, so he scoured St Petersburg for furniture and, above all, paintings.

This brought him into contact with all kinds of dealers and artists. He bought works by established artists such as Kramskoy, Repin and Shishkin, and developed a taste for pieces by his friend Somov, from whom he also purchased some paintings. This new hobby taxed his income to breaking point. Little is known about his business activities at that time, other than

Somov, by Bakst

that he invested in the construction of an 'electric plant' in the vicinity.[17] He stated his intention of setting aside three to four thousand roubles a year to buy art.[18]

His new passion for the visual arts soon went beyond furnishing his apartment, and he conceived the idea of exhibiting his acquisitions. The person best placed to help him was, of course Benois, and Diaghilev began to see more of him around that time. The two youths, still students but already embarking on their social careers, and both on the verge of fame, grew closer to one another in those years. Though quite different in character, they were united by a shared passion. Diaghilev continually asked for advice, allowing Benois to indulge in his favourite role of mentor. His tuition soon made Diaghilev dissatisfied with his very first purchases, and he resolved to go abroad to buy Western art. An introduction from Benois led to a meeting with the Spanish artist Mariano Fortuny on his third visit to Venice. Though only a year older than Diaghilev, Fortuny had already made a name for himself as an artist and innovator in the fields of painting, photography, theatre, fabric design and stage lighting. Like Diaghilev, he had broad artistic interests and an entrepreneurial spirit. He was even a keen Wagnerian, and the two young men soon struck up a friendship.

But the main destination of this foreign trip was Germany. With the help of Hans Bartels, a contact of Benois, Diaghilev was introduced to Franz von Lenbach, the doyen of the Munich art scene, from whom he bought three paintings. In Berlin he also succeeded, unaided, in meeting the patriarch of the German art world, Adolf von Menzel, from whom he bought two works: watercolours this time. From Antwerp he wrote to Benois about his new experiences and purchases:

> I have been meaning to write you a couple of words for a long time, to remind you of me, but I just couldn't get myself to write anything sensible because I have too little time, for having looked at 24 museums (*sic!*) and visited the *ateliers* of 14 artists, it's not easy to convey the essence of the impressions I have assembled. And that's why until we meet and have a long conversation I am setting aside some possibly interesting artistic questions which I've come across during the marked practical experience I've had over the last month.
>
> I declare that this coming winter I am going to put myself in [your] hands and I hereby solemnly appoint [you] the custodian in charge of the Serge Diaguileff museum. I think the whole thing will really take off and perhaps in a few years together we'll achieve something worthwhile since the foundations are solid.[19]

By the time he returned to St Petersburg, in addition to the pieces by Lenbach and Menzel he had acquired works by Max Liebermann, Klinger, Jozef Israels, Puvis de Chavannes and Bartels. At the time these names reflected the most progressive taste in Russia, where the new French art movements were virtually unknown. Always a quick study, Diaghilev soon learned the ropes of this new world. Having reinvented himself as an art expert, he was keen to show off his trophies. The most cherished of these was a painting by Lenbach, signed by the artist with the dedication '*dem Mäzen*' – 'to [my] patron'.

Shortly afterwards, Diaghilev joined Benois, who was staying at his summer house in Martyshenko,

> elegantly dressed for travelling, wearing some special scent, all pink and drunk with excitement that he could have so much to boast of and to astonish with. He brought presents both for my wife and for myself. For her some fashionable trinkets, for me a good drawing by Max Liebermann ... I was deeply touched by the attentions of my friend, and this drawing in its original frame decorated my apartment to the very end of my time in Russia. Seryozha almost smothered us, Atya and myself, in his embraces.[20]

The two young men were, in fact, in the honeymoon of their friendship. When the initial ardour cooled, they would experience conflict, reconciliation and betrayal.

· 7 ·

Charlatan and Charmer

1895–1898

SOMETIME IN THE EARLY SPRING of 1895 Yury fell gravely ill. Sergey's house was converted into an infirmary; doctors were called in, and a diagnosis was quickly made: diphtheria, a respiratory infection that was not only potentially deadly, but also highly infectious. (It must have been around this time that Diaghilev developed his morbid fear of contagious diseases, which eventually progressed to the point where he would cover his mouth with a handkerchief whenever he ventured out in St Petersburg. He even insisted on riding in a closed carriage, no matter how hot the weather, because of an unshakeable belief that horses spread disease.)

Despite his burgeoning anxieties, he took good care of his beloved younger brother. He was afraid his parents would panic if he told them about Yury's condition by telegram, and so he sent Valentin to far-off Riga, where his father happened to be stationed, to break the news.[1] After a few months Yury's condition improved to the point that his life was no longer in danger. Even so, Yelena Diaghileva decided to move in with Sergey in order to care for her son. In the summer, after being laid up for four months, Yury had more or less recovered, and Sergey left on his grand tour of the artists' studios of Europe.

That summer Diaghilev wrote his stepmother a famous letter, the last few lines of which can be found in every single work on the great impresario.

The passage is a telling expression of his renewed self-confidence and self-knowledge. Yet his words are not merely the theatrical declaration of a great and ever-expanding ego that they are often taken for. The first few pages of the letter are devoted to his younger brothers; throughout the year he would send his stepmother updates on their comings and goings. Yury had been transferred to a less prestigious army unit, perhaps because of all the time he had missed on account of his illness, and Diaghilev tried his utmost to put a positive spin on this potentially humiliating news. He observed his younger half-brothers with the same unceremonious, cheerfully cynical gaze as he did himself, and, mannered though Diaghilev's self-analysis may appear, the letter as a whole contradicts the image of the super-narcissist held by many of his contemporaries.

> Yury's situation at the military school is not good, but there's still hope. It's likely we'll have to move him to the Nikolayevsky school, but it's only a matter of pride – if we're going to drink the cup of disgrace, then let's drain it. Joking aside – he'll probably have to finish there. At the end of the day does it really matter? I've arranged it so that on holidays they both go riding in the manège, that's very good for Yury. Isn't that so, Sir General? They're both wonderful boys. Linchik is better by nature and much more likeable when first met, but *au fond* he's much less likeable – he's coarse. Yury is much more corrupted, but his warmth and his tact are touching. He is going through a difficult period and of course he won't come out of it with as much brilliance as Linchik. I worry generally about Yury, but that's said in the abstract as it comes out of observation, not facts. As for myself, I have to say, again out of observation, that first of all I am a great charlatan, although one with flair; second I'm a great charmer; third I've great nerve; fourth I'm a man with a great deal of logic and few principles; and fifth, I think I lack talent; but if you like, I think I've found my real calling – patronage of the arts. Everything has been given me but money – *mais ça viendra*.[2]

Given his financial circumstances, he was in no position to act the patron, at least not in the traditional sense of the word. If he were to have any hope of attaining his ambition, he needed to establish a reputation as a connoisseur of the arts. In 1896 Diaghilev began writing art reviews for the newspaper *Novosti i birzhevaya gazeta*. One of his first pieces, a review of an exhibition of watercolours, was written under the pseudonym Lyubitel (amateur), probably because the show included works from his own collection. Subsequent articles were signed 'D' or 'SD'.

In those first few articles Diaghilev adopted a middle-of-the-road position. On the one hand he professed his respect for the Peredvizhniki, the society of itinerant artists who represented the prevailing school of 'critical realism' and nationalism and who were generally supported by *Novosti*. On the other hand, he championed a renewed orientation towards European art, which the Peredvizhniki had dismissed as irrelevant: 'It must come out both in active participation in the life of Europe and in bringing that European art to us; we cannot do without it – it is our one guarantee of success and our one weapon against the routinism that has kept our painting in fetters for too long.'[3] Yet Diaghilev also believed that European culture needed Russia, albeit for a very specific reason: 'But to be the victors in this glittering European tournament, we need thorough training and the courage of self-assurance.'[4]

As much as these words would seem to foreshadow the views of the future impresario, Diaghilev was then still quite conservative in many respects. The artists to whom he devoted the most ink were the ones he knew best: the German and Russian realists. Nevertheless, he did attempt to draw a distinction between the more progressive among them (like the landscape painter Levitan) and the more routine exponents of previous generations, such as Makovsky and Klever. In those first few years he scarcely dared cover artists from his own circle, confining himself, for instance, to noting that a particular exhibition failed to include Bakst. Indeed, his very first article even included a dig at Benois: 'I can add a couple of words about Alexandre Benois whose current exhibition hasn't been wholly successful. All the things he has shown are interesting in the studio but in the exhibition they fall short. They're just allusions, ideas, not even studies.'[5]

Undoubtedly this jibe was Diaghilev's way of signalling his independence to the editorial team of *Novosti*, who were, of course, aware of his friendship with Benois, but the effect must still have been hurtful. If nothing else, critical remarks like these would seem to undermine Benois's later claim that he had co-authored Diaghilev's first articles.[6]

At the same time that Diaghilev was finding his voice as an art critic, he was also taking his final exams. On 23 July 1896, he could finally wire his mother the good news: 'Done with university. Hugs and kisses. Sergey.'[7]

At the end of the summer Benois headed to Paris for an extended stay (he would remain there for two and a half years). There he worked as a buyer for Princess Tenisheva, who was assembling a vast collection of watercolours. It was a responsible and inspiring job, not only because the princess was willing to invest huge sums but also because the collection was meant to span the whole 'history of watercolours, starting with the European school and ending with the Russian',[8] a grand ambition that gave Benois the opportunity to broaden his knowledge of European art.

Maria Tenisheva, one of the most extraordinary women of fin-de-siècle Russia, committed the whole of her (or rather her husband's) fortune to promoting Russian art. She did this both by assembling a collection of her own and by sponsoring the establishment of the artists' colony Talashkino, which would become an important centre for the study and conservation of Russian folk art. Just after Benois left for Paris, Diaghilev also struck up an association with Tenisheva. He was a frequent guest at her mansion on the English Quay in St Petersburg, and together the two would attend public lectures by Adrian Prakhov, the grand old man of Russian art history.

In Paris, meanwhile, Benois was in the process of mounting an exhibition featuring pieces from the Tenisheva collection, to be held in St Petersburg in January 1897. At that same time Diaghilev was busy with plans of his own: a show of contemporary European watercolourists, largely featuring the work of the German artists he had encountered on his last trip. In need of a travel document, he asked his friend, Count Ivan Tolstoy, to approach the head of the Department of Foreign Relations, Baron Osten-Saksen, who personally issued 'a foreign passport ... to the nobleman S. P. Diaghilev' on 16 November 1896.[9] After having wangled a letter of recommendation from the Imperial Academy of Art (a process that also ran through the Department of Foreign Relations), Diaghilev left for Germany at the end of November to scout out pieces for his exhibition.

Of the two shows, Benois's was the first to open, in January. Diaghilev wrote a review for *Novosti*. It was a modest affair with a few pieces by Menzel, a Meissonier and many paintings by unknown French and German artists. Diaghilev tried to be diplomatic in his article, calling Princess Tenisheva 'virtually the only prominent and serious collector of Russian and international watercolours'. Intending to support Benois, he spoke favourably of works he had purchased by unknown Germans such as Hans Hermann and Ludwig

Dill, and went so far as to heap praise on one of Benois's own paintings, but by the end of the review he couldn't resist the temptation to vent his spleen about the quality of the Russian pieces in Tenisheva's collection. There you found naught but a 'deadly tedium'

> which reigns over this exhibition of watercolours ... All the rest are completely superfluous bits of coloured paper whose raison d'être no one could understand ... And we must give Princess M. K. Tenisheva some heartfelt advice: if she seriously wants her collection to become one of the foremost in Europe, then she must give up collecting Russian watercolour painting in its present manifestation until it is wholly revitalised from top to bottom and fill out her collection with examples of Western creative work in which art exists for art's sake and not just for the public and material gain.[10]

In a country where the art world felt comfortably superior to its Western counterparts and where utilitarian ideals enjoyed universal support, a review like this must have come as a shock. Tenisheva cannot have been pleased with the crack that a great deal of her hard-won collection consisted of 'bits of coloured paper'. Diaghilev's own exhibition opened in February. After various locales proved to be unavailable, Diaghilev settled for holding it at Tenisheva's mansion, which was not especially well suited to the purpose. Two weeks before the opening, however, Diaghilev managed to find a more appropriate venue: the main hall of Baron Stieglitz's new museum, a magnificent two-storey building with a colonnade and an enormous stained-glass dome. He immediately informed Tenisheva that he would have to 'abandon his plans to hold my exhibition in your most congenial residence'.[11]

The title that Diaghilev gave to his first major undertaking was 'An Exhibition of English and German Watercolourists', even though there was more on display than just watercolours and even though the 'English' artists were mainly Scots such as Paterson and Austen Brown, along with an American, Whistler. The core of the show consisted of German artists from Munich that Diaghilev and Benois now knew quite well: Bartels, Lenbach, Dill, etc. If the exhibition were to garner any interest today, it would be on account of the presence of twenty or so works by Menzel, a number of pieces by Böcklin and a handful of pastels and watercolours by Whistler. A week after the opening Diaghilev wrote a not uncritical review of his own show, signed 'S.D.'.

For the first time Diaghilev's contemporaries were given a glimpse of the energy and ambition of the young law graduate. In the span of just a few months, Diaghilev had organised an exhibition of 250 works, all of which were from outside Russia. He had presented them in a completely new, eye-catching setting and showed his finesse at using the media to advertise the project.[12] All of this was done entirely unaided. The correspondence and even the contracts with security personnel and coat-check girls were written in Diaghilev's hand.[13] Although it was clear to everyone that the show lacked a certain internal coherence – understandable, given the lack of preparation time – it was, in all its modesty, one of the greatest and most artistically rich presentations of non-Russian art yet seen in Russia. And it had all been initiated and organised by a twenty-four-year-old who had only recently stepped onto the public stage.

All the while Diaghilev's self-confidence grew. He perfected the public persona he had fashioned for himself the year before. From this point on he would be the theatrical agitator, the dandy, the fop: part over-sensitive aesthete, part coarse hussar – a combination that would remain his trademark for the rest of his life.

Benois was far from pleased with this new pose. After Diaghilev had visited him in Paris when he was preparing his own exhibition, he wrote to Kostya Somov:

> Seryozha was here for three days … He made an unpleasant impression on me although at first I was extremely glad to see him. His diabolical self-satisfaction, his grand ways which verge on rudeness, his foppish poses … and above all his offensive patronage of the arts, a stance so different from true patronage, one based on the most arrant and despicable ambition, the prostitution of art with a view to playing a glittering role – all of this angered me so much that we almost quarrelled … I don't like Seryozha, who I think is the only one of us capable of furthering his aims by making really wicked decisions.
>
> So, I've thrown mud at him, perhaps it's just one of those things, prompted by the anger which has been simmering in me these last three days during which I had to listen to all his theories and opinions and above all admire his grand ways – but perhaps it is right I should.[14]

Although Benois initially did not confront Diaghilev with his misgivings, outbursts like the above could not stay secret long in that tight-knit circle of friends. Soon afterwards Benois wrote a similar letter to Nouvel, which that eternal mischief-maker read out at a get-together in Diaghilev's presence, in a 'triumphant and caustic tone'. A hurt Diaghilev asked Benois for an explanation, making a half-hearted effort to defend himself: 'I know that my nature and my activities (if you can call them that) aren't very deep, God knows. My nature is not at all philosophical and not very in tune with this weighty atmosphere of scepticism. But the one thing I value and love in the people surrounding me, is when I am taken seriously, and it's just that which I don't find in those few with whom my spirit is comfortable.'[15]

In response Benois wrote what must have been a lengthy, humorous letter to his friend in which he spoke candidly about what irritated and repelled him about Diaghilev's behaviour and character. That letter did not survive, but Diaghilev's reply, the most beautiful letter he ever wrote, did. Above the salutation Benois made the note: 'Portrait of Seryozha'.

Shura, dear chap,
How could you get it into your head that I've become your enemy after your fine and sincere letter. Not everyone can write such letters just as not everyone can have a fine appreciation of them.

I still have an unbearable love for friendship, openness, sincerity, family feeling – in short for true *bourgeois* simplicity without any outside complications. When Dima and I read your letter, without any collusion we said that Valechka even if he gave his whole life to it wouldn't be able to find in our conversation *that tone* you accuse me of. Your letter gave me the feeling of something very pleasant, of closeness, of affection, and it's been a long time since anyone gave me that. Of course I don't altogether agree with you and find you are too keen on form and externals. Your whole letter comes down to the fact that you don't like my packaging, starting with my clothes and ending with the often insincere tone I use to speak of you in print. By the way your whole sermon about your relations with your well-wishers and your enemies, if a little cynical, is infinitely true and endearing in its sincerity ...

Of course I'm not going to become an eccentric, but to change my entire appearance would be petty and unworthy. I will be as I have been, and that's it. If needs must I'll go about in rags. As for the impression I make on those around me, that question is a bit more complicated and here I must ask you to believe every word of mine since I am offering you equal sincerity in return. All my life, starting from the age of 16, I have been in defiance of everyone. First my family raged at me – my family which was close to me yet has caused me many difficult and dramatic moments and one *tragic* one. Then began a war with a multitude of my more distant relatives. They condemned my every act, they offered me abuse and intolerance. Then I came to know all of you, who also started with countless mocking remarks and unpleasantnesses towards me.

Remember how for a long time you thought me a hussar *at heart*. Then began people's attacks on me for my frivolous appearance, pomposity, dandyism. It's now finally got to the point that everyone thinks me a rogue, a debauchee, a commercial vulgarian, in short God knows what, I'm all too well aware of it, yet I'll still enter the Nobles' Club with just the same look of *éclat*. You'll say this is just bravado. No. Here two feelings come together. First, a purely human feeling of hostility to that whole world of my ill-wishers mixed in with a big dose of scorn. And second a strong belief that this phase will pass if my life has success. Success, my friend, is the one thing that redeems everything and covers up everything. My family now dotes on me, my relatives are almost boasting about me, people have begun to say with a serious face, 'He's a really decent chap, very well dressed, just like a foreigner.' And these are the same people who were mocking my dandyism. I'll be successful as the promoter of great ideas, followers will gather round me, and success will be my lot – I'll be the best of all. *Tout est là, mon ami.* But if I should fail at all – O then all the wounds will reopen and everything will be set down against me.

I have a certain effrontery of spirit and a habit of spitting in people's faces, it's not always easy, but it almost always helps. It's got me where I am. There is a very, very small group of individuals in front of whom I lose all my boldness and whose judgement I await with bowed head. That's Dima, you, occasionally Valechka, and in certain questions of life Sasha Ratkov. Before you I become a man without any will and freedom of action.

I even think that everything I do I do just for you, or rather, because of you: you give your verdict and that's how it will be. And so you all are a second self for me. As for you personally I used to have a feeling of terribly wounded pride since you really often showed you didn't like me before. After your marriage you took a remarkable turn for the better, all your seriousness and simplicity date from then … In general I love

Somov, by Benois

you, I value you, I rely on you and I look on many things through your
spectacles ...[16]

We do not know how Benois responded. Of course, this letter, too, with
its provocative self-awareness and lack of modesty can only have fuelled his
irritation, but he must have also been impressed by the warmth, originality
and freshness of character revealed by this long epistle.

For the rest of his life Benois was alternately attracted to and repulsed (or
rejected) by Diaghilev. At times he seems to have been obsessed with him. In

March of that year he wrote to Nouvel, 'It is the Seryozhas in life that make the world go round; all glory and honour be unto him.' But in August he again questioned his friendship, writing to Somov from Paris: 'As for Seryozha he should be coming here tomorrow and he's planning to spend several days here. His visit is causing me a lot of anxiety: for me it will be the decisive and final test of the man – is he my friend or enemy? Now I don't know … I would like to love him as hating such a man would poison my existence.'[17]

The visit was a success, and the two were scarcely apart during those few days; their outings included a visit to the opera. And thus Diaghilev was able to coax Benois back into the fold. On 3 November Benois wrote to Nouvel, 'Seryozha is an extraordinary person, and I bow to him.'[18]

The only member of the circle who turned his back on Diaghilev completely, the only one who was incapable of tempering his repugnance, was Somov. Though he remained part of Diaghilev's entourage, he freely shared his true feelings about 'Mr High-and-Mighty' to anyone who cared to listen, describing his former friend as 'revoltingly bumptious' and 'sickening'.[19]

Oddly enough it was Nouvel, perhaps the member of the circle who was most fond of ridiculing Diaghilev, who grew closer to him and became a more loyal ally. The two knew each other very well, of course, because they played music together: either they would perform piano duets, or Nouvel would accompany Diaghilev while he sang. A better clue to their relationship might be the fact that it was the rather unsocial, down-to-earth Nouvel who first came out of the closet. He had at some stage tried to woo a woman, but he was as unsuccessful at attracting her interest as he was in stoking his own. 'That was', as Benois would later write, 'our friend's last attempt to enter the "cave of Venus". After that he made no further essays in that area, becoming the "confirmed" homosexual he would remain for the rest of his life.'[20] Around that same time Diaghilev wrote to his stepmother: 'I would like to see a bit of the *monde* and find myself a wife. That is harder than mounting an exhibition.'[21] If he did ever make a serious effort in that area, nothing ever came of it. Shortly thereafter, he informed his stepmother that for the time being he had 'no plans to get married'.[22] This was the last he would ever say on the subject. It is hard to say if Diaghilev ever seriously considered marriage. Nothing is known about possible candidates, aside from one stray remark by Benois, who wrote to Filosofov in 1898 that Sergey 'once dreamt, in jest, of marrying Sofia Panina. Apparently she even managed to attract pederasts.'[23]

It is the very casualness of Benois's remark that makes it so significant. As early as 1898 it was apparently perfectly acceptable to refer to Sergey as a pederast within the circle of friends. Indeed, this term described Diaghilev's sexual preference more accurately than the more general 'homosexual'; throughout his life it was generally boys, and not men, who excited his desire.

There is no way of knowing whether Diaghilev's plans to marry this Countess Sofia Panina were entirely 'in jest'. In many respects she was a logical choice. She was not unlike his beloved Aunt Anna. Besides being fabulously wealthy, she was politically active and progressive in her views (she financially supported political dissidents, for example) and a good friend of Leo Tolstoy to boot. She later became a member of the central committee of Kerensky's Kadet Party, playing an important role in the February Revolution in 1917. When the Bolsheviks took power, she fled the country.[24] She was the type of woman Diaghilev was drawn to: active, inspired and independent, just like his best friends later in life, Misia Sert and Coco Chanel.

In this context, the visit that Diaghilev paid to Oscar Wilde in May 1898 is significant. Diaghilev wanted to buy some pieces by the graphic artist Aubrey Beardsley, notorious for the decadent eroticism of his illustrations. Beardsley had only recently died, and Diaghilev was hoping that the illustrator's good friend Wilde would put him in touch with collectors who owned works by him. Shortly after Diaghilev's visit, Wilde wrote a note to his publisher Leo Smithers. It is clear from this little missive that, if nothing else, Diaghilev had succeeded in charming the Irish writer. Apparently Diaghilev left the highly questionable impression that he was both wealthy and 'a great collector': 'Have you a copy of Aubrey's drawing of Mlle de Maupin? There is a young Russian here, who is a great amateur of Aubrey's art, who would love to have one. He is a great collector, and rich. So you might send him a copy and name a price, and also deal with him for drawings by Aubrey. His name is Serge de Diaghilew.'[25]

Years later Diaghilev told Boris Kochno a story about his meeting with Wilde, which is undoubtedly apocryphal, but too good not to repeat. He claimed that when Oscar Wilde and he were walking along one of the Grands Boulevards, the streetwalkers stood on chairs to catch a glimpse of the notorious degenerate Wilde and the handsome young man with a lock of grey hair amid the black. It must have been an unforgettable scene, the Russian arm in arm with Wilde as they promenaded down the street, oblivious to the catcalls of the assembled strumpets.[26]

· 8 ·

'I'm full of big plans!'
1897–1898

THE OPENING of Diaghilev's first major exhibition at the Stieglitz Museum marked the beginning of a period of feverish activity. The whole thing started when a certain Balashov (a collector and vice president of St Petersburg's 'Association to Promote the Arts') commissioned him to mount an exhibition of works by contemporary Scandinavian artists, centring on such established figures as Anders Zorn and Fritz Thaulow. Petersburg society showed a lively interest in Scandinavian painters and writers, who as fellow 'Nordic' peoples were perceived to have an affinity with Russians. Diaghilev travelled to Kristiania (present-day Oslo), Stockholm and Helsinki in the summer of 1897, to select works for the exhibition. It opened on 11 October, and on the 26th Diaghilev gave a banquet for Zorn in Moscow, inviting all the leading lights of the Russian art world as well as the press, who reported on the event the next day. Diaghilev gave a long speech in French; Ilya Repin, the other guest of honour that evening, addressed Zorn in Russian. The exhibition established Diaghilev's position in the art world, and yet he was not happy. The art on show could hardly be described as progressive, and the venture incurred a loss of 285 roubles. Diaghilev ended up paying this sum out of his own pocket.[1]

By then his sights were firmly focused on another exhibition that he had begun to prepare, an ambitious project featuring works by progressive Finnish and Russian artists. Finland formed part of the Russian empire, yet it enjoyed a special status. The Finns had their own constitution and even a kind of parliament. Progressive Russians looked eagerly to Finland, hoping that they might one day enjoy similar political freedoms. Finnish artists were seen as progressive and less tradition-bound than Russians. Moreover, a sense of national awakening was taking hold in Finnish art, and this, too, appealed to Russians, who likewise saw art as a means of fostering national consciousness.

Diaghilev was attuned to the fashion for Finland. The main aim of the exhibition was to present new works by up-and-coming Russian artists, but by incorporating an overview of progressive Finnish culture, Diaghilev created an ideological framework that lent legitimacy to the venture. He had to tread carefully because at the time, Russian art was dominated by the Peredvizhniki, and new trends on the whole were met with suspicion, if not outright hostility.

The exhibition was also intended to launch a new, as yet nameless, artists' group that Diaghilev, eager to break the monopoly of the Peredvizhniki and other artists' associations, tried to set up in the spring of 1897. To this end he approached almost all young Russian artists of any standing, especially those attached to the Abramtsevo and Talashkino art colonies, the centres of neo-nationalist art in Russia.

But Diaghilev was not alone in his desire: Albert Benois, one of Alexandre's older brothers, wanted to found a society of Russian watercolourists. Diaghilev reacted furiously, as he always did to any form of competition – even if, as in this case, such competition posed no threat to his own activities. His response to Albert's plans reawakened the old tensions between him and Alexandre. The latter, of course, felt duty-bound to stick up for his brother and tried to pacify Diaghilev, but with little success. 'Albert's fickle,' Sergey wrote to Alexandre. 'He'll start something one day, and give it up the next.'[2] And later:

> I am writing you a couple of words to keep you abreast of what's going on. Nothing worthwhile will come out of Albert's society since its founding members are … abominations, and that's why *I am founding my own new avant-garde society*. The first year, as a group of young artists who met at my place decided, there will be an exhibition organised by me personally, and not

just every artist but every painting will be chosen by me. Then a society will be set up, which will see to that sort of thing from then on. The exhibition is planned at the Stieglitz from 15 January to 15 February 1898. You of course understand who will be joining the society: the young St Petersburgers, the Moscow lot who have really taken to my idea, the Finns (they're Russian too), and then some of the Paris Russians … And so I hope you'll join us rather than fall into Albert's swamp. What I am describing isn't just a project – it's a fait accompli. Let me know right away what you think of it.[3]

For Diaghilev it was indeed a fait accompli, because without waiting for Benois's answer he sent an open letter to all the young artists he wanted to involve in his plans by way of official invitation. He was clearly determined to assert himself as the leading exponent of modern art in Russia:

At the present moment Russian art is in the transitional situation into which history puts every burgeoning movement, when the principles of the old generation clash and struggle with the demands of the rising generation. This phenomenon, which has been repeated so often in the history of art, compels us every time to seek refuge in a rallied and concerted protest by the forces of youth against stale pressures and the opinions of old and moribund authorities. You can see this phenomenon everywhere and it manifests itself in such brilliant and powerful protest movements as the Secession in Munich, the Champs de Mars in Paris, the New Gallery in London etc. Everywhere talented young people have united and erected a new body of work on new foundations with new programmes and goals.[4]

Diaghilev also invited the artists to submit work for the planned exhibition of Finnish and Russian art at the Stieglitz Museum, promising that the exhibited works would then be shown in Moscow and at the prestigious annual salon of the Munich Secession.

In the same document, Diaghilev proposed that the members of the exhibition association refrain from drawing up official rules or creating an electoral body, and instead provisionally leave its organisation to his 'personal initiative' because 'it is easier for a single individual, exercising his personal choice and judgment, to give the new venture its own distinctive character and clear voice'.[5]

It looked, however, as if Diaghilev's plans might fall through when Benois wrote from Paris, expressing doubts about the new association and once more asking Diaghilev to join forces with the society his brother Albert was proposing to set up. Diaghilev was incensed and wrote back immediately. The letter ended on a prophetic note:

When I said a couple of years ago that I didn't want to have anything to do with Russian artists except to pay them back for their sheer vulgarity – I was right. I've had dealings with French, German, English, Scottish, Dutch and Scandinavian artists, and I've never had such difficulties as with our home-grown ones ... None of them has any sense of breadth or nobility. Every one of them confuses his pocket with his artistic principles. They're all cowards, all stuck in a rut. And now I've had a letter from you. All day I've been beside myself with disappointment. You have doubts, and then you suddenly advise me to make friends with Albert. Do you know something? Let's settle these questions once and for all. I think Albert is perhaps the most harmful of our artists ... Shura, come to your senses, don't mix up family feeling with your own artistic taste. You know all this, so why disguise it from yourself. You write – Albert is a fresh artist. My dear, that makes a mockery of both freshness and art. Don't be obstinate, admit you're wrong. It's time for us all to go about with our eyes open and to love the light. We've had enough of stifling fog and darkness ...

I want to bring up Russian painting properly, to clean it out and above all to show it to the West, to extol it in the West ...[6]

Diaghilev clearly could not do without Benois for a host of reasons: strategic, artistic and emotional. But Benois was in a bind. As he himself later wrote, in 1926:

My whole soul was with Diaghilev, who finally with the help of my closest friends was about to realise our long-held dream. But it was still painful for me to break with my brother ... However in two or three months my sufferings ended of their own accord. Albert felt that he shouldn't form a society and he returned to the bosom of the Imperial Society of Watercolourists; I felt completely free and could join my old group without any pangs of conscience.[7]

Whether Benois's soul was with Diaghilev, as he maintained in 1926, is debatable, because within the space of a year his loyalty to Diaghilev would take another knock. Meanwhile, Diaghilev left for Scandinavia to prepare his two exhibitions. First, though, he visited Benois in France – partly to rekindle the friendship and partly to discuss new plans.

When he returned to St Petersburg in early October 1897, he wrote to Benois to break the news of his plans to set up a journal as well as an association:

> You already know from Kostya [Somov] that I'm up to my neck in projects, each more grandiose than the next. I am now planning this journal in which I am thinking of bringing together the whole of our artistic life, i.e. to use its illustrations to show true painting, to use its articles to say openly what I think, and then to set up a series of annual exhibitions in the name of the journal, and finally to associate the journal with the new artistic movement that is developing in Moscow and Finland. In short, I am seeing the future through a magnifying glass. But for this I need help and of course to whom should I turn but to you? Besides, I believe in you as I do in myself, don't I? I expect from you five not especially long articles a year which are angry, good and interesting, it doesn't matter about what. Kostya has already helped out by promising to do a cover design and a poster. By the way, Kostya – what a wonderful talent. He is endlessly enjoyable and interesting. He says that in praising him I get carried away. My friends, it doesn't matter, it's so wonderful to get carried away![8]

Meanwhile, Diaghilev was busy laying the groundwork for his journal – crafting its programme and recruiting backers – while simultaneously finishing up preparations for the exhibition of Russian and Finnish artists. In the summer of 1898 a selection of the works shown at that exhibition were indeed on view at the summer salon of the Munich Secession. Diaghilev also organised the Russian contribution to the Munich exhibition. Almost all his correspondence during those months exudes urgency, tension and excitement.

The exhibition finally opened on 15 January 1898. In some ways it was the first major project to bear the unmistakable Diaghilev hallmark: subversive art in a lavish setting. There was a 'pompous opening'[9] with orchestral accompaniment, attended by invited guests and members of the press. Diaghilev distinguished himself from other exhibiting associations (which included the

Peredvizhniki) not only in content, but also in presentation, by seeking to make these exhibitions grand society events.

The exhibition was widely covered in the press and generally well received, though some bemusement could be detected: 'At this exhibition one finds not only contemporary art, but also the art of the future.'[10] But a polemical statement by the Young Turks of the art world had to provoke a conservative response. That response came, from no less a figure than Vladimir Stasov, the doyen of Russian critics.

Stasov was one of the most influential public intellectuals in Russia in the latter half of the nineteenth century and the most fanatical propagandist of the school of ideological realism. He started writing about the arts as early as 1847, and in the 1860s and 1870s his star ascended to great heights. He first made a name for himself as a music critic, being instrumental in the rise of the Five. He followed a similar path in the visual arts, where he was one of the driving forces behind the success of the Peredvizhniki. Mussorgsky and Repin, in particular, owed much to Stasov.

Stasov championed a utilitarian aesthetic: the sole aim of the arts should be to emancipate the people. To that end he prescribed a curious mix of strictly secular Enlightenment doctrines and Slavophile utopianism. According to Stasov, good art was 'healthy, true to nature and to life, authentic, profound and honest'.[11] Ever sure of himself, Stasov rabidly opposed any new movement in Russian art – especially if it had any links with western Europe – and he defended his opinions in the press with a self-righteous conviction and passion that was unmatched, even in the hot-tempered world of the Russian arts.

In private he was friendly, open-hearted and generous. His enthusiasm was infectious, and he succeeded in winning many to his causes. He had a huge social network, corresponded with all and sundry and was received everywhere. His passion, combined with his aura of integrity and intellectual purity, made him unassailable. Even those who loathed him, such as Turgenev, did not sever contact with him, and were still willing to assist him if called upon. Igor Stravinsky met him as a small boy, because Stasov regularly visited his father, the leading bass at the Imperial Opera. When Stasov died, Stravinsky remembered how odd it was to see him lying in his coffin with his arms crossed, because 'he was the most open-armed man in the world'.[12]

Diaghilev and Stasov must have met fairly regularly at Bogdanovskoye.

Anna Filosofova was one of Stasov's dearest women friends, and the writer was a frequent guest. In the 1860s and 1870s Bogdanovskoye was a centre for critical, left-wing intellectuals. Diaghilev and Filosofov, for their part, used the estate as a retreat where they could continue to work on their plans. Aunt Nona was torn, forced to choose between her closest relatives and her Stasovian convictions. As she herself wrote: 'For me, a woman of the 1860s, all this was so outrageous that I could barely contain my indignation. Everyone can understand what I was going through while 'the Decadence' was coming into being in my house!'[13]

Stasov, too, later wrote in a letter that for Anna's sake he had initially made an effort to restrain himself and spare Diaghilev:

> During 1896 and 1897 Diaghilev caused me frequent and great embarrassment with his articles in various journals. I found nothing there but coarse ignorance, arrogance, self-importance, and above all intolerable *shallowness* and endless *superficiality*. Most intolerable of all was Diaghilev's sermon that art needs no 'subject' or 'content', but that 'artistic execution' is enough. For a long time I restrained myself, I didn't *want* to touch Diaghilev because he is the nephew of a lady I love and respect … But eventually my patience snapped, especially when I began to see that those of our young artists who are weaker in intellect or character, and sometimes both at once, listen to Diaghilev's follies with a kind of 'respect', and add them to the follies they themselves have got direct from Paris …
>
> As I got angry with the lack of seriousness and taste, the lack of reason and discrimination among our little artistic *monkeys* who are just *yes-men* to the whims of others, one fine day I stopped holding myself back and wrote a major critique of 'Diaghilev's exhibition'.[14]

Stasov's article was nothing less than a frontal assault on Diaghilev's aesthetic agenda, clearly with no other intention than to compromise Diaghilev to such a degree that he would cease his activities. The article was published on 27 January 1898 in *Novosti i birzhevaya gazeta*, a newspaper to which Diaghilev himself was a fairly regular contributor. At Diaghilev's exhibition Stasov saw 'much that was off-putting, and much that was simply pointless'. He regarded the work of such artists as Mikhail Vrubel and Konstantin Somov as 'decadent absurdity and ugliness' and 'an orgy of debauchery and madness'. At the exhibition 'chaos reigned supreme […] while Mr Diaghilev sat enthroned above this decadent rubbish like a decadent village elder'.[15] The conservative camp gratefully seized on that final crack, and 'decadent village elder' became a popular slur. Diaghilev had to defend himself, of course, and two days later wrote a fierce polemic which mocked Stasov's age and musty ideas:

A letter to the Editor.

… Between you and me there is a 50-year difference in age. So, as I take up my pen to reply to your lengthy and substantial comments (*Novosti*, no. 27) in which you mention my name a dozen times, I feel a certain involuntary sensation of embarrassment; I feel strangely like a grandson answering the stern voice of his old grandfather …
    … Take a look at yourself, at your head covered with grey hairs … perhaps there will stir, involuntarily and for the first time, the recognition that you have said all that you had to say, that your theories have been acknowledged and accepted, that you are no longer a fighter gradually getting stronger in the thick of battle, that, let me say it directly, you are just repeating yourself, that you are finished, that you have left the stage and that your mighty voice will never again arouse that passion that you could previously evoke.[16]

Diaghilev continues in this vein for some time, although he does occasionally try to insert a more serious comment between insults. To no avail, however: not a single newspaper dared to print the article, so great was Stasov's status. Diaghilev then took an unusual step. He wrote a letter to Stasov, containing his own article and the following request: 'I am asking you whether you could help and state in print a few words in my support, since the enforced silence of your opponents can hardly correspond to your wishes'.[17]

Stasov was predictably irked ('the insolence, the preposterousness, the effrontery of it all!'),[18] but nevertheless attempted to foist the article on various editorial boards, or so he claimed. However, his efforts were fruitless, and he returned the piece to its author.

Nothing daunted, Diaghilev tried a different tack. He went to the national library, where Stasov worked as head librarian and, bearding him in his den, asked him whether he would be prepared to submit articles on art

PEPIN, RUTH ELISE

Until:	Thu 08 Mar 2018
Patron barcode:	20027000629310
Pickup location:	Limerick Granary
Notice type:	---
Item barcode:	30012006338726
Mobile:	0892489916

Author: Scheijen, Sjeng.

Title: **Diaghilev / Sjeng Scheijen**

Hold Note:

history to the periodical that Diaghilev was setting up. Diaghilev was such an admirer of Stasov and had such 'faith in his expertise', and always read his 'highly talented pieces' with 'considerable pleasure'. Diaghilev then shook the dumbstruck Stasov warmly by the hand.[19] Such heavy sarcasm was not lost on the critic. Once again he described Diaghilev's behaviour as the height of 'impertinence and effrontery'.[20]

The extent to which Russia's art world was rent by conflict at the turn of the century is astonishing. These feuds were nominally about ideas, but the combatants' vehemence and intractability suggest a Darwinian struggle for survival in a limited economic niche. The market for art was still very small, and private patrons, though growing in number, were thin on the ground. Diaghilev's ability to find funding for his activities and attract public interest while others were doomed to obscurity must have fuelled the fierce opposition shown by some of his contemporaries. Tellingly, Stasov's main grudge against Diaghilev was that he had managed to obtain funds from businessmen and the nouveaux riches. 'That shameless and brazen piglet is trying to get all kinds of merchants, traders, industrialists and so on to subscribe to his publication.'[21]

The conflict with Stasov polarised the Russian art world. It had become abundantly clear that Diaghilev and his friends needed their own platform to showcase their ideas. In March Diaghilev was given the green light by his sponsors, and could move on to the next step. He tried to engage as many contributors as possible, looking beyond his own group to artists who showed progressive leanings but were not considered decadent.

The authority and status of the new group was greatly enhanced when Valentin Serov joined its ranks. Despite being fairly young – he was only seven years older than Diaghilev – Serov had established himself as Russia's most sought-after portraitist. He had been a child prodigy, receiving lessons from Repin at the tender age of nine, and since the mid-1880s he had made a name for himself with his brilliant and (by Russian standards) groundbreaking paintings. Although Serov exhibited with the Peredvizhniki and his paintings were bought by Pavel Tretyakov, a wealthy collector and patron of that group, he was viewed as worryingly unorthodox by the art establishment. Serov's father, Aleksandr, was a composer and Russia's most high-profile Wagnerian. He and Stasov had clashed furiously on the issue of Wagner many years earlier, so Valentin was familiar with the more intolerant and aggressive aspects of the 'liberal' camp. He was an outspoken critic of the tsarist regime, with a strong sense of social justice. Many were surprised that the reserved Serov had joined Diaghilev and his circle.[22] But Serov felt isolated in Russia's suffocating cultural climate, and Diaghilev's pluralist, chaotic entourage seemed like a breath of fresh air. Diaghilev and Filosofov had got to know him shortly after the exhibition of Russian and Finnish artists, and he was quickly taken to the group's bosom. 'Serov is undoubtedly one of the most sympathetic of our new friends,' Filosofov wrote to Benois on 30 March. 'We even "drank brotherhood" with him. I think he's one of us.'[23] Being older than the rest, and having secured his position as one of Russia's greatest living artists (along with Repin and Vrubel), Serov became a kind of guide and moral authority. Both Benois and Dobuzhinsky referred to him as the group's 'collective soul'.[24] As Stravinsky commented, observing Serov's friendship with Diaghilev in 1910 and 1911, 'Serov was the conscience of the *Mir isskustva* circle, but when Diaghilev referred to him as "*la justice elle même*", he did so with regret, for Diaghilev wanted to sin.'[25]

Diaghilev pulled off another great coup when he succeeded in recruiting Yelena Polenova as a staff member of his new periodical. Not only was she the sister of the landscape painter and Peredvizhnik Vasily Polenov and a highly regarded artist and designer in her own right, she was also one of Stasov's closest friends. Diaghilev staged an even greater coup on 13 September 1898 when he informed his friends that the journal had managed to bag the biggest prize of all: Ilya Repin, Stasov's most important protégé and Russia's most revered artist.[26]

But while Diaghilev was winning victory after victory at the front, dissatisfaction was simmering among his foot soldiers, stirred up by Alexandre Benois. In previous months he had repeatedly expressed open hostility to Diaghilev's plans in letters to Filosofov and Nouvel,[27] and his involvement remained in doubt. Benois, who still enjoyed a great deal of influence within the group, was the only one still capable of undermining Diaghilev's authority. When he wrote to Diaghilev from Paris (in a letter that has now been lost) to announce that he was withdrawing from the project, Diaghilev once again had to dash off a reply in an effort to keep him on board:

When you're building a house, God knows how many masons, plasterers, carpenters, joiners, painters surround you, God knows how much trouble you have to have with the building committee or some other committee. It's bricks or beams or wallpaper or all manner of other trivial stuff. You're sure about just one thing – that the façade of the house will be successful since you believe in the friendship and talent of the architect. And now it's the reverse: you've come out from under the wood and beams all covered in dust and sweat and your architect says to you that he can't finish the building, and what's the point of building the house anyway, is it really necessary etc. And it's only now that you're struck by the sheer horror of bricks and the sheer stench of wallpaper and glue and the sheer stupidity of workmen etc... .

I cannot and would not ask my parents to love me; in the same way I can't ask you to feel for me and help me – not just with your support and blessing, but directly, firmly and effectively through your work. In short I can't prove to you or ask you anything, and there just isn't time to give you a good shake, now when they might wring my neck any minute. That's it; I hope that the sincere and friendly tone of my abuse will have some effect on you and that you'll stop acting like a stranger and will throw on a dirty apron like all of us to mix this steaming lime.[28]

The letter had the desired effect. Benois returned to the fold and promised to write an article for the first issue. His shilly-shallying and moaning must have been infuriating, but his behaviour was understandable. Though intellectually superior to Diaghilev, he was forced to look on helplessly as the latter hijacked his ideals and realised all his dreams in a way he never could have. As Filosofov later wrote, 'Benois found it hard to switch from a purely friendly relationship to a more businesslike partnership. Diaghilev's power seemed to smack of despotism to him.'[29] Benois found it galling to defer to him. But a ship can only have one captain and, as Filosofov put it, 'Diaghilev's relentless energy and organisational zeal meant he could never play second fiddle.'[30]

With harmony having been restored for the time, the band of friends spent the remaining months working round the clock to publish the first issue on time. 'I spend all my evenings with Seryozha,' Nouvel wrote to Benois. 'The journal thrills us; we are consumed with excitement and tackle everything with a fiery passion. There are heated debates every single day.'[31]

On 7 November the board of censors gave Diaghilev permission to publish. Two weeks later, over a month before the official launch had been planned, *Mir iskusstva* – 'The World of Art' – rolled off the presses and sent shock waves through Russia's artistic community.

· 9 ·

The World of Art
1898–1900

BY MARCH 1898 DIAGHILEV had received a firm commitment from his backers to put his plans for the journal into action. The backers in question were Princess Tenisheva and the railroad magnate Savva Mamontov. The two signed a contract stipulating that they would each donate 15,000 roubles to cover the costs of the first year.

For the Russian fin-de-siècle art world, Savva Mamontov was just as important as Princess Tenisheva. The two espoused much the same artistic ideals, though they differed in terms of their backgrounds, temperaments and the source of their wealth. Tenisheva was a high-born woman who lived off her husband's fortune. Mamontov, by contrast, was from the merchant class and a self-made entrepreneur.

Like Tenisheva, Mamontov founded an artists' colony, Abramtsevo. He invited artists there, to work amid a natural setting as members of a community. In the 1890s Mamontov's Abramtsevo and Tenisheva's Talashkino became centres of a Russian Arts and Crafts movement now commonly referred to as the neo-nationalist school of Russian art. The international revival of applied art, of which the Arts and Crafts movement was one facet, came to Russia relatively late, but it emanated a vitality that exceeded that of similar movements in western Europe. Broadly speaking, there are two reasons for this. First, the values of the movement appealed to the quest for a native Russian identity, a cause that seemed all the more urgent at the end of the century, as the pace of internationalisation quickened. Second, the movement's focus on the languishing status of trades and applied arts in the life and development of the peasantry dovetailed neatly with the social ideas that dominated the art of the 1870s and 1880s.[1]

Russian neo-nationalism was widely embraced and imitated, not only within the world of the applied arts, but also in painting, theatre and, to a large extent, music. In fact, all progressive visual artists of any stature were affiliated with Abramtsevo or Talashkino.

Diaghilev made his first public statement about the new magazine in a joint interview with Mamontov for the *Peterburgskaya gazeta*. 'The journal must bring about a revolution in our art world, as among the public, who have hitherto fed on the scraps of movements which have already begun to pall in Europe.'[2]

In the first few issues of *Mir iskusstva* the section on art criticism consisted almost entirely of a long article by Diaghilev which set out his theoretical manifesto. Entitled 'Difficult Questions', it was published in parts and consisted of four chapters: 'Our supposed decline', 'Eternal conflict', 'The search for beauty' and 'The principles of artistic evaluation'. At over 12,000 words, it is by far the longest and certainly the most ambitious essay Diaghilev ever wrote. It was written in close collaboration with Filosofov during Diaghilev's stay at Bogdanovskoye in June and August. Nouvel claimed that the 'historical and theoretical portion of "Difficult Questions" was entirely Filosofov's work', seeing Diaghilev's hand only in the polemical digs and certain 'succinct phrasings' in which he proclaimed 'our creed': 'the exaltation and glorification of individualism in art'.[3] Yet there is no reason to doubt that Diaghilev was ultimately responsible for the piece as a whole. The choice and arrangement of the subject matter was his, and all his contemporaries (and not just his friends) regarded him as the sole author of the text. Besides, the whole essay – composed in a tone that varied from polemical to supercilious to fashionably blasé – bears the unmistakable Diaghilev touch.[4]

In its weakest passages 'Difficult Questions' is unbalanced, pretentious and unduly arrogant, while in its best it is flamboyant, compelling and thrilling. Diaghilev attempted to rise above the prevailing debate between utilitarianism and aestheticism. He had no desire to get bogged down in another shouting match with Stasov and decided against including his 'Reply to Stasov' in the first issue. He sought to establish the journal as the voice of a new generation, who aspired to operate at an entirely different level from their petty-minded forebears. Above all he attempted to present *Mir iskusstva* as a journal that would transcend national and historical boundaries. To emphasise the international and timeless nature of the magazine, Diaghilev dropped names with abandon – from Raphael and Leonardo to Alma-Tadema and Van Gogh, and from Sophocles and Shakespeare to Tolstoy, Huysmans and Zola. The idea was to impress a public for whom the vast majority of the artists, composers and writers mentioned were, at most, famous names they had heard somewhere.

It is in 'Difficult Questions' that Diaghilev first disassociates himself from the label 'decadent', which was then applied willy-nilly to anyone who happened to stray from the mainstream:

> We have been called the children of decadence, and with bowed heads we coolly accept the meaningless and insulting name of 'decadents' … But I would like to ask: where is that flowering, that 'high point' of our art from which we are rushing towards the chasm of decay?[5]

Then he tries to reconsider the conflict between utilitarianism and aestheticism, in an attempt to move beyond what he viewed as an obsolete dichotomy and create the freedom for individual expression and a diverse artistic output:

> The war between the utilitarians and the adherents of art for art's sake – that old squabble – should have died down long ago, yet it is still smouldering today. Although the fundamental question of the relationship of ethics to aesthetics has always existed, narrowly utilitarian tendentiousness in art is a creation of the nineteenth century, and it is difficult to get rid of one's bad habits … The theory of art for art's sake never enjoyed a clear victory in Russia … Chernyshevsky has not yet been digested, and deep down our artistic judges still cherish the barbaric image of him touching art with his dirty fingers … In my view, the demand that art should serve society on the basis of set rules is completely incomprehensible.

By way of a critical explication of the aesthetic theories of Ruskin and Tolstoy, Diaghilev teases out a theory of his own:

> I see the forward movement of the entire history of the arts in the development of the artistic personality alone, independent of any objective conditions, and from this point of view all eras in the history of art are of equal significance and worth ...
>
> ... We were brought up on Giotto, on Shakespeare, on Bach. They were the first and greatest gods of our artistic pantheon. But it is true that we were not afraid to rank alongside them Puvis de Chavannes, Dostoyevsky, and Wagner ... Our whole attitude to art was based on the premise of independence and freedom ... We rejected any notion of art as dependent; our point of departure was man himself, as a uniquely free creature.

As mentioned above, the other great question to dominate Russia in the closing decades of the nineteenth century was the role of nationalism. A sense of national consciousness had been growing across Europe throughout the 1800s, but in Russia the issue was so pervasive that it coloured all other debates. There were a number of reasons for this. Nationalism was, as always, a by-product of internationalisation, which in Russia unleashed social upheaval owing to the rapid modernisation of the economy. Moreover, the radicalisation of the progressive movement tainted almost every form of emancipatory engagement. Only the campaign for national consciousness escaped this erosion of ideals; indeed, in some ways it emerged even stronger than before. Diaghilev, too, had to take a stance in this debate:

> Nationalism is still a sore issue in modern art, especially Russian art. Many people see in it our entire salvation, and they attempt to preserve it in us artificially. But what could be more destructive than the wish to become a national artist? The only possible nationalism is the unconscious nationalism that is in the blood ... until we see in Russian art an elegant, grandiose harmony, a majestic simplicity and rare beauty of colour, we will have no real art. Take a look at our real pride: the icons of ancient Novgorod and Rostov – what could be nobler and more harmonious? ... We must be as free as gods ... We must seek in beauty the great justification of humanity and in the individual its highest manifestation.

The journal contained articles on ancient and modern art, arts and crafts, art criticism and literature as well as a 'chronicle' with announcements and previews. The reproductions, some better than others, were printed on different paper; Diaghilev and his team had had huge difficulty ensuring their quality. At that time in Russia no periodical came close to meeting the high technical standards Diaghilev and his friends had set for themselves. Russian printers and lithographers lacked the necessary skills and technology. Paper was imported from Finland, and the stereotypes were made mostly by printers in Berlin, Meisenbach and Frisch.[6] After searching long and hard for a suitable typeface, they opted for a font from the period of the Empress Elizabeth, the moulds of which had to be carted in from the archives of the Academy of Science. Bakst designed a logo – a spread eagle – which adorned all their correspondence and publicity material. A system of accounts had to be set up to handle subscriptions, and someone needed to oversee the distribution network, which consisted of a few select bookshops. The journal was also sold abroad in a handful of cities including Kristiania and Milan – hardly the most obvious choices.[7]

Diaghilev's apartment on the Liteyny Prospekt served as the editorial office, and it was also there that the lithographs were designed and, if necessary, retouched. The editorial team met on Mondays (as of 1903, Tuesdays). Diaghilev's apartment was a hive of activity, and the whole clique pitched in to help, usually for free. It was Diaghilev's boundless energy which, Benois wrote,

> made us forget the risks and our exhaustion, made us look at this 'first worker among us' as a true leader whom you would follow through thick and thin – although there was no real need for that. Diaghilev – this operator, this man of business – had an individual gift of creating a romantic working climate, and with him all work had the charm of a risky escapade … Periods of idleness and apathy alternated with sudden bursts of extreme activity and it was only then that Diaghilev felt himself in his element. It wasn't enough for him to overcome the difficulties that naturally arose to block his path; he liked to create new ones for himself and to overcome them with redoubled fervour.[8]

The core group consisted of Bakst, Benois, Diaghilev, Filosofov and

Serov's vision of Diaghilev and Nouvel fifteen years on

Nouvel. Filosofov was in charge of the literary section and treated it as his own personal fiefdom. Bakst, a mere shadow of the celebrated Parisian artist he would later become, oversaw the quality of all the printed matter. Nouvel, who acted as the journal's secretary alongside his job at the court chancery, could always be found at the 'office':

> One can't even imagine *Mir iskusstva* without seeing his small, restless figure, always elegantly dressed, darting about the room with a cigar between his teeth, or perched on the very edge of the sofa, one leg over the other ...
>
> Nouvel had absolutely no interest in his official job. For him it was just a way of earning a living and we only knew about it because he sometimes appeared at the editorial office in his service uniform.[9]

When Benois returned to St Petersburg from Paris in the middle of 1899, he gradually took up his old role as the group's intellectual conscience. There were also many new faces who drifted into Diaghilev's entourage because of their association with the journal. First of all, there was Alfred Pavlovich

Nurok, another dilettante, who, like Nouvel, was a ministry official. Apart from his many satirical contributions (which sparked more than their share of scandals), this 'witty cynic, with his imperturbable Mephisthophelean face'[10] was mainly active as the *Mir iskusstva*'s music critic. He was an ardent admirer of the European decadents, a lover of erotica and a connoisseur of French and German poetry. Of the group, Nurok was fondest of shocking the bourgeoisie. This was doubtless why he always kept a volume of the Marquis de Sade, who was banned in Russia, in his jacket pocket.

Another important addition to the *Mir iskusstva* stable was the young artist and art historian Igor Grabar. Grabar lived and worked in Munich, where he wrote a column about artistic trends in Germany. He was far more progressive than either Diaghilev or Benois, being open to post-Impressionism, for example. Grabar would later become the most prominent art historian of the Soviet Union, and it is undoubtedly his association with the Soviet regime that is responsible for his lack of renown in the West.

Vasily Zuikov, Diaghilev's valet, was another 'regular' at these editorial meetings. The editorial disorder was notorious, but Vasily always seemed to know where everything was, and not only Diaghilev, but the entire staff, addressed themselves to him when a book, an article or a drawing was missing.[11]

Diaghilev's nanny Dunya (Avdotvya Aleksandrovna Zuyeva)[12] was another fixture:

> [W]ith her brown clothes and unhurried movements she brought to Diaghilev's metropolitan and 'decadent' apartment the style and cosiness of an old world country landowner's estate. This feeling was enhanced when the master of the house himself sometimes dropped his 'Napoleonic' persona and appeared at the tea table in just a dressing gown like Oblomov's – an elegant flowered one, to be sure.[13]

Bakst's decision to include the nanny in the background of his famous portrait of Diaghilev, gazing solemnly at the man she had served since his birth, is a visual reminder of the patriarchal traditions that were part and parcel of Diaghilev's personality.

Diaghilev was never one to pay much attention to the bourgeois distinction

Diaghilev's nanny Dunya, by Serov

between the personal and the professional. Both now, at the start of his career as a 'cultural entrepreneur', and afterwards, when he led an organisation that employed hundreds of people, his friendships, familial relationships and romantic entanglements overlapped almost completely with his business relations and connections. His two half-brothers, Valentin and Yury, could often be found at the editorial office, along with the inevitable Pavka, and they were all put to work on various tasks. Within his group of close associates, Diaghilev always tried to maintain a homely atmosphere, in which intimacy intermingled with professionalism. The advantages were obvious: it fostered a mood of shared responsibility, where there was no place for self-interest and where personal considerations always had to yield to the needs of the collective. Many outsiders were struck by the cohesiveness of the group, as if they were inseparable and always acted as a single entity.[14] The drawbacks of this approach were also readily apparent: workplace conflicts had a direct, enervating effect on Diaghilev and the people around him. This was evident in his recurring rows with Benois and especially Somov (at one point, feelings ran so high that Diaghilev actually challenged Somov to a duel – though fortunately nothing came of it). Another casualty was his relationship with Filosofov.

During the early years of *Mir iskusstva* he maintained an intense working relationship with Dima. The enormous pressure of the job brought the cousins and lovers even closer together and revealed Diaghilev's dominance all the more plainly. Or, as Somov put it: Dima was 'Diaghilev's slave'.[15] He was not the only one who felt that way; others too remarked on how Dima 'was completely under Diaghilev's control'.[16]

It should be noted that Filosofov did have a personal life outside of Diaghilev, though the latter scarcely took any notice of it. Dima's literary pursuits had, in recent years, been overtaken by his growing preoccupation with religious philosophy. This new interest was strongly encouraged by his friends Dmitry Merezhkovsky and Zinaida Gippius, a married couple, both writers, who became closely involved with the magazine at his instigation. Merezhkovsky and Gippius were among the most important theoreticians of what is commonly called the first generation of Russian symbolism. They had already made a name for themselves, and they were now interested in Filosofov – and not only for his intellectual gifts. Filosofov drew them into the sphere of *Mir iskusstva* and saw to it that they were accorded a special status. Lambasted by the other contributors but staunchly defended by Filosofov, they both published long articles in the journal on a regular basis. In 1900 the relationship between Filosofov and the couple was still primarily an intellectual one; at that time, for example, they still addressed each other by the formal 'you'.

Gippius was a keen observer. Her clear distaste for Diaghilev did not prevent her from offering a balanced portrayal of him in her memoirs:

> He was all too perfect. All dictators are more or less perfect, they're *prédestinés*. And Diaghilev, I repeat, was a born dictator, Führer, leader ...
> Many were repelled by Diaghilev, the born dictator, and we were too. Without any sense of hostility (we were, after all, merely outside observers), recognising all his talents and merits, believing in his future success but always feeling there was something unacceptable about him – about his aristocratic ways, the intonations of his voice, his thickset figure, his full, pink, then really rather handsome face with its low forehead and the white streak of hair above it on his round black-haired head. People said he was capricious and obstinate. But I don't see him like that. He was a man who was strong in his own way, bent on achieving his will and therefore

necessarily completely confident in himself. If that self-confidence was
offensive, it was a failure of his clever mind ... which his broad knowledge
made redundant; it was overshadowed by his versatile talent and deep
intuition.[17]

In Merezhkovsky and Gippius, *Mir iskusstva* had managed to enlist two
talented writers who were held in high regard in progressive literary circles.
Through them, other writers, including Vasily Rozanov and Valery Bryusov
and later Andrey Bely, would join its ranks. Yet the literary section would
never quite mesh with what was generally regarded as the journal's mission:
propagating a renewal of the visual arts.

From the beginning, the editorial staff had their hands full parrying the
many attacks directed at their publication. Several polemical asides in the
'chronicle' managed to stir up even more antagonism. In the events section of
the very first issue Nurok wrote sarcastically about an exhibition in England
of the painters Yuly Klever and Vasily Vereshchagin: two older, respected,
serious Peredvizhniki: 'Poor England is being threatened with an exhibition
of work by the painters J. Y. Klever and V. Vereshchagin. How can we prevent
Russian art and the English public from being subjected to such an unpleasant surprise?'[18]

Snide cracks like this raised the hackles of more moderate forces (like the
powerful collector Pavel Tretyakov) and strengthened the case of the most
reactionary critics. Stasov was characteristically blunt in his verdict on the first
few issues of *Mir iskusstva*: 'Silliness, depravity and filth again set the tone.
What clumsiness, dull-wittedness and tastelessness the editor shows in all
his choices!' But the journal had more trouble dealing with the verbal salvos
of Viktor Burenin, a young polemicist with a conservative agenda and a chip
on his shoulder, who wrote for the popular *Novoye vremya* (New Age). On 16
April, Good Friday of that year, Burenin launched a personal attack on Diaghilev: 'I don't know whether Mr Diaghilev is the type of clown who follows every
recent European fashion or whether he belongs to the ranks of charlatan dilet-
tantes ... But without any doubt this upstart dilettante is the most ludicrous
as well as the most unabashed of the self-appointed modern judges of art.'[19]

Stasov's broadsides were one thing: at least he was a worthy opponent
with an established reputation. Burenin was nothing more than an agitator
('an unscrupulous obscurantist' in Benois's estimation).[20] To waste column

Cover for Mir iskusstva, *1902, no. 8, by Bakst*

space responding to his attack would only legitimise his position. With this
in mind Diaghilev and Filosofov hatched another plan for dealing with this
troublemaker:

On Easter night just before the early morning service Diaghilev and Filosofov went to Burenin's flat – but not to give him Easter greetings ... Having briefly explained to him the purpose of their visit, Diaghilev struck him on the face with his top hat to teach him a lesson, and then both visitors quietly departed, as the furious Burenin yelled and cursed at them down the stairwell.[21]

Diaghilev's run-in with Burenin was soon the talk of the town.

Despite, or more likely because of all the scandals, *Mir iskusstva* was a great success in its first year. The men behind it had planted their standard on the summit of the Russian Parnassus, and with both the journal and the exhibitions they became the undisputed arbiters of all things progressive and fashionable in St Petersburg. But that success did not translate into financial security. Indeed, at the close of the year the journal was down 5,686.24 roubles. They took in less than 20,000 roubles from subscriptions, single-issue sales and advertising. That meant that none of the 30,000 roubles pledged by Tenisheva and Mamontov could be paid back. This situation was exacerbated by the fact that Mamontov was embroiled in financial difficulties of his own. He even served a short prison term for defaulting on his financial obligations. As a result, he was only able to pay 9,500 of the 15,000 roubles he had promised, forcing Tenisheva to cough up 20,500 roubles to make up the deficit. Nevertheless a large shortfall remained, which fell 'entirely to the editor's account', according to the official report Diaghilev sent to Tenisheva.[22] Diaghilev had allotted himself a salary of just a few thousand roubles, but even that was insufficient to keep the journal in the black.

What did Diaghilev live on? Perhaps he was still collecting income on property he had bought with the inheritance from his mother, but this couldn't have been much. It is more likely that, even then, he was living off the money generated by his various business ventures – not only the journal, but also the exhibitions. Moreover, *Mir iskusstva* had other sponsors, whom Diaghilev kept off the official books. Even then, he understood that it was better to operate in the red if you were dependent on external backers. The painter Korovin claims to have contributed 5,000 roubles during that first year, but that amount does not appear in the annual accounts.[23] Grabar maintains that Serov also put in some money, another contribution that never found its way into the books.[24] While all this was going on, Diaghilev was still supporting his parents and at least partially funding his brothers' education.

Not only did the journal close that year at a loss, its two principal backers pulled out. Mamontov was ruined and in no position to act as patron of the arts. Tenisheva, too, refused to continue funding *Mir iskusstva* for a second year. To begin with, her association with Mamontov made things awkward, but more importantly, she deeply resented the vitriolic attacks on the journal by the Russian press. A cartoon by the popular caricaturist Shcherbov, depicting her as a cow being milked by Diaghilev, couldn't have helped matters.

Diaghilev now had to find new sponsors, and fast, if his periodical was to have any hope of surviving. Just then, an offer of help came from an unexpected source. At the time Serov was working on his famous portrait of Tsar Nicholas II. During the long sittings, Serov could speak freely with the tsar, and on 24 May 1900 he told him about the problems facing the journal. 'But I have no head for finance,' said Serov. 'Nor do I,' replied the tsar.[25] But Nicholas was for some reason well disposed to the magazine, and prepared to offer his support. Diaghilev only had to submit an official request. On 31 May he had an official meeting at the palace with the head of the chancery, where he was promised 15,000 roubles a year for a period of three years.[26] By 4 June the money had already been transferred to the editorial staff.[27]

'I couldn't venture to say what would have happened if we hadn't got that grant,' wrote Filosofov. 'We probably would have had to close up shop.'[28] The tsar's support also helped restore the journal's stature, which had suffered a blow when Tenisheva bowed out. Now that *Mir iskusstva* had the imperial seal of approval, attracting other sponsors would be much easier.

The St Petersburg art world was abuzz with the news of Diaghilev's triumph.[29] But during *Mir iskusstva*'s first year something even more important happened in Diaghilev's life, following the appointment of a new managing director of the Imperial Theatres, Prince Sergey Volkonsky. Diaghilev was well acquainted with Volkonsky, who was twelve years his senior and also gay; they had met at one of his Aunt Tatusha's musical soirées. Volkonsky later said that he had immediately felt a warm sympathy for his hostess's musical nephew.[30] Volkonsky, whose family belonged to the very highest stratum of the Russian nobility, was a great connoisseur of the theatre, a brilliant man and keen traveller who had visited many countries, including the United States. He was a trained historian with a special interest in the

Decembrists, an early-nineteenth-century revolutionary group of whom one of his ancestors had been a significant member. His critical essays, which displayed his erudition in the fields of history, literature and theatre, appeared in leading newspapers and magazines. In addition, Volkonsky was a passionate amateur musician and composer. At an intimate concert at Bogdanovskoye in 1893 Diaghilev once sang Volkonsky's romance, 'Es hat die Rose sich beklaget' (The rose's lament).[31] The two men had stayed in touch, and Diaghilev asked Volkonsky if he would be interested in becoming a contributor to *Mir iskusstva*.[32] Volkonsky saw a great future in Diaghilev: even before his appointment as director, he had approached the younger man about taking on a managerial position in the Imperial Theatres.

And this is exactly what happened, though it took some effort on Volkonsky's part: on 22 September 1900 Diaghilev was hired as 'a functionary for special assignments for the management of the Imperial Theatres'. His bland official title was, oddly enough, 'government secretary'. Diaghilev's appointment met with a storm of protest (a certain Molchanov promptly resigned rather than work under him).[33] These protests only intensified when, two weeks later, strenuous lobbying by Diaghilev resulted in the appointment of Filosofov to the repertoire committee of the Alexandrinsky Theatre, the most important stage in the country, which also fell under Volkonsky's purview. The cousins had hit the big time. They not only ran the most progressive art magazine and the most important exhibiting association in the country, they now also occupied key positions in the world of theatre. Diaghilev was twenty-eight years old and at the top of his game. Who could suppose that his new job would lead to the first and perhaps most dramatic setback of his professional life?

· 10 ·

The *Sylvia* Debacle
1900–1902

DIAGHILEV'S FIRST MAJOR ASSIGNMENT was to edit the annual of the Imperial Theatres. These annuals were impressive, costly publications in which the management presented its artistic vision for the coming year and introduced musicians, actors and dancers to the public. The Imperial Theatres comprised two large opera houses in St Petersburg and Moscow (the Mariinsky and the Bolshoy), the main theatres in both capitals, and all the companies performing at these venues. A bureaucratic behemoth, in other words, ill-suited to nourishing creativity. Diaghilev was to be paid an annual fee of 2,400 roubles for the job.

Prince Volkonsky had approached Diaghilev not just because of his creative powers and organisational skills, but also because he would bring in young artists who could breathe some much-needed life into the organisation.

Virtually from the moment he was hired, Diaghilev bombarded Volkonsky with a volley of ideas, only a few of which were destined to see the light of day. On 17 November 1900 he proposed abandoning the annual format and instead publishing a bimonthly glossy magazine that would allow for a much more topical approach. He had already thought of a name: *Panteon*. The editor-in-chief would be none other than Sergey Pavlovich Diaghilev. He immediately tried to rope in Somov and others, but was brought to heel by Volkonsky.[1] A similar fate awaited an ambitious plan for a series of guest concerts by the German conductor and Wagner specialist Felix Mottl, to be organised by Valechka Nouvel. Diaghilev advised Nouvel: 'Go for the Bach Passion, Berlioz and *Parsifal* … In a programme of individual works I'd like to see a Brahms symphony, something major by Richard Strauss and something new, but no rubbish.'[2]

The most striking item on the proposed programme is not so much the 'major' work by Richard Strauss as the Bach *Passion* (it seems safe to assume he meant the *St Matthew Passion*). However, this plan, too, came to naught. Diaghilev soon found himself at the mercy of an intractable and capricious bureaucratic apparatus. It was a very different world from *Mir iskusstva*, where he was the sole decision maker and could overcome obstacles by sheer force of will.

These first two stillborn projects reminded Diaghilev that he was no longer at the top of the pecking order. Nevertheless, the March 1900 edition of the annual bore his unmistakable stamp. It was glossier than any previous publication, full of high-quality reproductions of works by Repin, portrait drawings by Serov, Bakst and Braz, and vignettes by Somov and Bakst. Benois contributed an article and, as with *Mir iskusstva*, Bakst was in charge of the book's design, including the cover and typography. The quality of the paper and binding and the technical standard of the printing left previous annuals in the shade. The edition, which consisted of two separate volumes, is still seen as a landmark in Russian publishing. Volkonsky went so far as to claim that the entire resurgence of graphic design in the twenty years preceding the Revolution 'sprang from the wellspring tapped by Diaghilev with his annual'.[3] According to Benois:

> The annual was extraordinarily successful, and – crucially for its editor –
> not only confirmed his position among the management and his colleagues
> but also received the approval of the tsar himself … A copy of the book in
> a particularly luxurious binding caused a real sensation among those who
> sat in the imperial box. Nicholas II went through the whole volume page
> by page, now and then expressing his pleasure.[4]

While Diaghilev enjoyed ego-boosting success in the beau monde, an entirely new passion led him to the less glamorous setting of Petersburg's archives and palace depots. He would spend days ferreting through these dusty locations, in search of works by and information about largely obscure eighteenth-century Russian artists such as Dmitry Levitsky, Vladimir Borovikovsky and Mikhail Shibanov. An interest in the eighteenth century (or more specifically the period from the reforms of Peter the Great to the invasion of Napoleon in 1812) was common among the Miriskusniki (as the *Mir iskusstva* group were called), though the fact is often overlooked. It is, of course, easy to see why such an outward-looking era, with its emphasis on formal mastery, inspired rebellion against the Peredvizhniki, whose focus was on content, morality and isolationism. But the interest in eighteenth-century artists was also prompted by nostalgia for an age when art was still firmly embedded in elite culture, and when Russian culture was a peripheral yet undeniable part of a pan-European whole. Diaghilev's idealisation of the eighteenth century is illustrative of two seemingly contradictory ambitions: promoting national consciousness and repositioning Russia within the constellation of Europe's diverse cultural elites.

This passion for the eighteenth century was sparked mainly by Somov and Benois, and it was initially they who drew Diaghilev's attention to its forgotten masters. But by 1900 Diaghilev knew more even than Benois about the painting of that era, and he planned a series of monographs on its greatest portraitists, starting with Catherine's court painter Dmitry Levitsky. While working on the annual he began to research Levitsky, delving into the Petersburg archives and visiting the estates of old noble families in search of undiscovered works.

Given the diversity and depth of Diaghilev's activities during those years, it is not hard to see why he was so headstrong and dictatorial. How else could he manage various organisations devoted to groundbreaking projects, while constantly setting himself new challenges in areas requiring financial acumen as well as intellectual discernment? But his ambition was making him more and more enemies. He was a raging bull in the china shop of Petersburg society, blithely unaware of the trail of trampled egos and hurt feelings he left in his path.

Diaghilev had a few important allies: Grand Duke Sergey Mikhailovich, a cousin of the tsar, who was actively involved in the theatrical world, and the ballerina Matilda Kshesinskaya who, as Nicholas's former mistress, had a great deal of influence. Diaghilev believed that with their support he could win any battle, however many enemies he made. An initially neutral observer was the deputy director of the Moscow theatres, Vladimir Telyakovsky, whose plodding diary entries provide posterity with the fullest account of events.

Around the end of 1899 Diaghilev hatched a new, highly ambitious plan: to perform Léo Delibes's mammoth ballet *Sylvia* with the help of Bakst, Benois, Serov and Nouvel. Benois cultivated a boyish enthusiasm for the music of the French composer, whom he referred to as 'one of my two gods'[5] (the other being E. T. A. Hoffmann). Perhaps more tellingly, their hero Tchaikovsky took Delibes as his inspiration when composing his own ballets and regarded *Sylvia* (never performed in Russia) as Delibes's masterpiece, a fact of which Diaghilev was probably aware.[6]

He put his plan to Volkonsky, who in early January gave him the go-ahead, together with full authorisation to direct the production as he saw fit. A day later the entire group of friends gathered in Diaghilev's apartment to discuss the project with the choreographers Nikolay and Sergey Legat. Diaghilev and Nouvel sat at the piano, playing the score for the Legat brothers, while Benois commented on each scene in turn.[7]

With hindsight it seems logical that Diaghilev chose a ballet rather than an opera for his first theatrical production, but the choice was by no means an obvious one at the time. Prior to 1900 he had seen very few ballets and shown little interest in what many Russians (and Europeans in general) regarded as a frivolous art form unsuited to serious artistic expression. But in Nouvel the group possessed a fervent and tireless champion of ballet. His conviction that an innovative form of ballet could convey the most elevated and contemporary artistic ideals informed the group's collective thinking on dance. As early as 1897 Nouvel had written:

> I think ballet has a great future ahead of it, but of course not in the form
> in which it exists at present. Our decadent aesthetic and sensual demands
> can't be satisfied by the ideals of plasticity and beauty of movement that
> existed thirty years ago. We must make it the exponent of our tender,
> refined, morbid feelings, sensations and aspirations. We must make it
> sensual *par excellence*, but sensual aesthetically and if you like symbolically.
> That vague, inexpressible, elusive feeling, to which modern literature is

trying to give voice, obeying the clamorous demands of the modern spirit, must find, and in all likelihood will find, its realisation in ballet.[8]

Whatever the personal merits of 'the little, untalented Nouvel', as Princess Tenisheva called him,[9] he played a crucial role in the genesis of a ballet cult within the group, and thus in the revival of dance throughout the world – not as the fuel or the fire, but as the igniting spark.

Prior to the turn of the century, Diaghilev had nothing but scorn for Nouvel's enthusiasm. 'Valechka will go on about ballet!' he wrote to Benois.[10] Why, in 1900, he should suddenly focus his energies on staging a ballet is not entirely clear. Perhaps because it was cheap and relatively simple to produce. Perhaps because he saw ballet as an art form in decline, in contrast to opera, which was undergoing a revival thanks to the artistically progressive productions at Mamontov's theatre. Moreover, organising an opera was a complex undertaking. It would be difficult to impose his own will, and Diaghilev always needed to be in complete control of any venture he was involved in, as the subsequent turn of events would show. Ever attuned to anything that might win the tsar's favour, he may also have been thinking that the imperial court, and especially Nicholas himself, were great ballet aficionados.

By January 1901 the group of friends had been occupied for many months with preparations for their production of *Sylvia*, which was programmed for the coming season. Volkonsky had promised to give Diaghilev full control over the project. The latter's rise within the Imperial Theatres had already caused unruly mutterings, as Telyakovsky's journal relates, and this decision provoked further protest. As Volkonsky prepared to announce it officially in the internal bulletin, the rumour went round 'that various civil servants had sworn never to take orders from Diaghilev'.[11] His main opponent was the painter and theatrical designer Vladimir Polenov, a conservative Peredvizhnik. Telyakovsky proposed that Volkonsky talk to Polenov and the other mutineers before making Diaghilev's appointment official – a piece of advice he took to heart.

Those talks caused Volkonsky to change his mind. Realising that Diaghilev lacked the backing of the organisation, he decided not to publish his appointment in the bulletin. Thus Diaghilev would be allowed to produce *Sylvia*, but under Volkonsky's authority. Volkonsky hoped, by means of this compromise, to pacify the dissenters in the ranks and at the same time to retain Diaghilev's services. Volkonsky informed him of the situation on or around 27 February 1901. Diaghilev was furious, fearing that if he were not officially in charge, he and his friends would forfeit artistic control. Confident that his powerful allies would help him, Diaghilev complained directly to Grand Duke Sergey Mikhailovich, who in turn informed the tsar. Diaghilev told Volkonsky that if no official announcement were published in the bulletin, he would refuse to edit the next annual, which was already in production. That same day Filosofov, Benois and Bakst each wrote to Volkonsky, expressing support for Diaghilev and terminating their professional association with the Imperial Theatres. The director now had another revolt on his hands, this time by the artists who were not only collectively responsible for the huge success of the latest annual, but who also figured prominently in his new artistic vision for the Imperial Theatres. Diaghilev speculated openly that the leading modern artists would side with him, thus forcing Volkonsky's hand.

On 28 February, Volkonsky showed the letters to Telyakovsky, who suggested talking to Diaghilev. Telyakovsky described the subsequent, hastily arranged meeting with Diaghilev in his journal:

> I got to Diaghilev's at 4.30 and found there the entire company; they told me their decision was firm – they had lost faith in the prince's promises and now weren't prepared to work unless he gave them promissory notes ... Having talked away for a couple of hours and exhausted all my oratory, I failed to convince them and we decided to send for the prince. At first he said on the phone that he couldn't come, but when Diaghilev refused to go to him, Volkonsky relented. He was criticised for repeatedly letting everyone down, and they began to list all his mistakes, criticising the Director for weakness and lack of character – they even told him to his face that he couldn't be Director with such an attitude to the job. He shrugged his shoulders and insisted that he couldn't give way on the bulletin, and all the talks came to nought ...

By seven-thirty, after a fruitless, four-hour discussion, Telyakovsky and Volkonsky withdrew.

> When I was going downstairs with the Director, he said to me, 'But they're still such nice people, and it's a pity to lose them.' I replied that he must

first think things over a hundred times. It's easy to find administrators, but we have no more artists.

The following day Telyakovsky wrote to Volkonsky, once again urging him to come to some sort of agreement with Diaghilev and not to fire him whatever he did, because 'there are no more artists in Russia'.

The issue had by now reached the ears of the tsar, who had already confided to Telyakovsky a few days earlier that 'Volkonsky had allowed [the Polenov group] to walk all over him'. However, Volkonsky found Diaghilev's outburst in his apartment 'so vicious that he considered further cooperation to be impossible'.[12]

On 1 or 2 March, Volkonsky gave Diaghilev five days to tender his resignation. The latter did not react. On 5 March, Polenov and his cronies reiterated their intention to resign if Diaghilev were given official responsibility for *Sylvia*. On 6 March, Volkonsky made an official application to the court to dismiss Diaghilev.[13] That same day Volkonsky received a message from Diaghilev that he had once again put the case to the tsar. Nicholas had allegedly said that 'under no circumstances was Diaghilev to be dismissed'.[14] Diaghilev was now even less inclined to resign than before. But by the time Volkonsky received this letter, the announcement of the dismissal had already been published in the government gazette.

Up until that moment, Diaghilev may have reckoned with the possibility of defeat, but he could never have imagined he would fall so far. Even at that stage he believed that with the tsar's backing he would come out on top, Volkonsky would clear the field, Grand Duke Sergey would run the theatres and he would be made artistic director. But when, on 7 March, Diaghilev 'had a look at the paper before getting out of bed', he read the following cruel lines in the government announcements section: 'S. P. Diaghilev, functionary for special assignments, has been given a category-three dismissal, without right of appeal or pension.'[15]

That last designation, 'category-three dismissal', was rarely seen, except in cases of improper conduct, corruption or embezzlement, and implied that the individual in question could never return to government service.[16] According to Benois it meant that Diaghilev 'had been publicly shamed', and that he had been 'damaged and trampled upon, and dragged through the mud'.[17]

Exactly why Diaghilev was dismissed in this way remains unclear. Accord-ing to Telyakovsky, it was on Volkonsky's insistence, but that is not evident from the official application for dismissal.[18] Benois believed that it was because the dismissal was not dealt with by Baron Frederiks, the responsible minister, but by his deputy, General Rydzevsky, who apparently held a grudge against Diaghilev and saw this as an opportunity to take revenge. Benois does not provide any details, and Rydzevsky is not mentioned in other sources.

Diaghilev believed himself to be the victim of a plot by higher-ups, as is evident from a letter he wrote to Telyakovsky on 10 March. Though he clearly thought that Telyakovsky could still salvage the situation, he was by no means sanguine about the outcome:

> I am writing you these lines in the midst of tumultuous chaos and frightful, inexpressible confusion ... After our four-hour conversation no attempt was made to clarify this business and it became crystal clear to me that this whole 'feud' was far from accidental but was rather the result of a long-standing, wholly conscious plan of action by a certain 'invisible hand'. You know that a wide variety of influences play a part in the current state of affairs, and at the present moment these influences are against me. This is clearly borne out by the fact that a couple of days after our conversation I received a categorical demand for my resignation, and a day later a confirmation of that, but this time through official channels, specifying I have no right to apply for State service and giving me one week to put in my resignation. You as an official yourself will understand what it means for an official attached to the director of the Imperial Theatres – and one so 'well known' as a decadent – to get an order to resign immediately in St Petersburg in the middle of winter, and with no rights to boot!! All this of course is causing an extraordinary scandal and I don't know to whose advantage! ...
>
> I know you'll accuse me of a certain impulsiveness, of an excess of youth, and that you generally think of me as a young *Bashibazouk* ... I sympathise with all arguments for caution and tact, which are necessary in politics, but sometimes these praiseworthy qualities aren't enough, one has to be a human being, a man of action!![19]

All things considered, it would seem that the tsar was indeed on Diaghi-lev's side, but simply had no control over his own officials. The affair showed that the apparatus of power was essentially a rudderless ship, at the mercy of powerful cliques. Any attempt at enterprise or innovation was doomed from the outset.

Diaghilev's reaction to the events was typically stoical. But in his memoirs, Benois reveals that Diaghilev was deeply hurt, to an extent he could not hide from his friends.

> He didn't curse fate, he didn't abuse the authors of his misfortune, he didn't require any kind of sympathy from us, he only asked us not to talk to him about what had happened. Everything had to go on in its usual way 'as if nothing were the matter'! When visitors came to the office of *Mir iskusstva*, he went out to meet them in the reception with that 'radiant' look of a Russian grandee which was his stock in trade, but as soon as he was alone with his intimates, he immediately subsided, he sat down in a corner of the sofa and stayed motionless for hours, answering questions with an air of desperate distraction and hardly taking part in the conversation going on around him. Alone with Dima he showed more of himself, sometimes he even wept or gave in to stormy outbursts of rage, but that took place in the quiet of his bedroom at the end of the corridor, where apart from Dima, his manservant Vasily and his Nyanya no one was allowed.[20]

During the next few months of 1901, Diaghilev immersed himself in his archival work and his research on Levitsky, publishing a monograph on the artist that autumn. As was to be expected, it was a lavish, beautifully designed publication, but its real value lay in the extensive and carefully annotated list of works compiled by the author. He succeeded not only in tracing and identifying paintings that had been thought lost, but also in recognising works by Levitsky that had been attributed to other artists. The book heralded a period of renewed interest in the forgotten art of the eighteenth century which, as Diaghilev put it, 'had been crowded out at the beginning of the nineteenth century by raucous pseudo-Classicism'.[21]

Diaghilev's monograph was very well received, by academics as well as the general public. On 23 October he telegraphed his stepmother that it had won the prestigious Uvarovsky Prize, the highest award of the Imperial Academy of Sciences.[22] It had not been bestowed in the previous six years. After all the setbacks of that year, the prize came at just the right moment for Diaghilev, who had repeatedly expressed frustration that he was not taken seriously by the intelligentsia.

This frustration had recently been exacerbated by his not being invited to join Novy Put' (The New Path), a new religious and philosophical association that had been set up in November 1901 by a group that included Dmitry Merezhkovsky, Zinaida Gippius and Dima Filosofov.[23] Diaghilev was certainly not unreceptive to the religious and spiritual craze sweeping Russia at the turn of the century, and might well have wished to join this relatively moderate association, with its civilised aspirations. He felt painfully snubbed.[24]

Perhaps the group did not want Diaghilev as a member because of his domineering character, but it is more likely that Merezhkovsky and Gippius wanted to separate Diaghilev and Filosofov. As Nouvel (who did go to the meetings) waspishly remarked to Gippius, it was 'not God that she was looking for, but Filosofov, because she was attracted to him'. Nouvel also commented that 'if Gippius were not in love with Filosofov, he would lose all interest in her and in the cause'.[25] The last assertion was certainly untrue because he had for many years showed a serious interest in all kinds of religious matters, but it did suggest the nakedness of Gippius's desire for Filosofov. Filosofov, for his part, seemed more interested in Merezhkovsky. Diaghilev, however, appeared to close his eyes to all this. In a letter to Vasily Rozanov (another important member of the group) on the subject of his 'rejection', he seems mainly to be upset about not being taken seriously as an intellectual:

> I have joined the ranks of men of 'action', whereas you all are men of 'contemplation'. This sobriquet, given to me with a slightly patronising air, I bear without shame; people like that are needed too, maybe. But in view of my famous 'energy' and 'muscle' – qualities associated with athletic rather than intellectual activities – I was understandably afraid and still am afraid to join the men of 'contemplation' and I only regard them from a distance, though I feel a certain kinship with them which no sobriquets will ever destroy.[26]

Diaghilev went on to remind Rozanov that all kinds of people who were much less qualified to be referred to as 'men of contemplation' were being admitted to the group. It was particularly painful to him that his aunt Anna

Filosofova, and even his beloved stepmother, faithfully attended the group's meetings.

Filosofov spent more and more time with Merezhkovsky and Gippius, but Diaghilev still had a hold on his cousin, and this would ward off a split for a while. In the spring of 1902 Filosofov had a tiff with Gippius and ran back to Diaghilev. Merezhkovsky tried to patch things up, even turning up at Diaghilev's apartment to talk to Filosofov, but he was politely asked to leave.[27]

Around this time Diaghilev's fortunes took a turn for the better. Friends had been hard at work behind the scenes to limit the damage caused by his dismissal from the Imperial Theatres. This resulted on 31 January 1902 in an imperial decree quashing the 'category-three' designation,[28] which cleared the way for Diaghilev's re-entry into government service. Another conflict had claimed Volkonsky himself as a victim, shortly after Diaghilev's departure, and Telyakovsky was now managing director. Diaghilev flattered himself that Telyakovsky would reinstate him, but this proved a vain hope. He was given a post in the tsar's personal chancery, presumably by way of compensation, though this notional, unsalaried job was hardly a sinecure. What it precisely entailed is unclear. Diaghilev spoke of it in a letter dating from 1926,[29] and Benois, too, remembered it. According to Benois, the position was honourable but purely bureaucratic, and Diaghilev hardly ever bothered to turn up at the office.[30] No one else in his circle recalled that he had officially been in the tsar's service, and it is not known how long he held this post.

In any case, he again went on a journey with Filosofov in the summer of 1902. During a long stay in Venice, he wrote the two letters quoted in the introduction. He continued to edit *Mir iskusstva* by post from his various European ports of call. On 9 September he wrote to Benois from Graz:

> We spent one and a half months in Venice and now we're in Graz, in the
> sanatorium of the famous Krafft-Ebing. Don't think we've gone mad,
> but my accursed nerves need some looking after. But we can talk about
> ourselves when we meet – I don't yet know how soon that will be. Dima
> will return in three weeks but perhaps I'll hang around here a bit longer, for
> they think I'm ill.[31]

Baron Richard von Krafft-Ebing was a celebrated Austro-German psychiatrist and sexologist, best known for his studies of sexual aberrations: sadism, masochism (both of which terms he coined) and homosexuality. His conclusion that homosexuality was not a psychological or moral problem but an incurable pathological deviation – strange though it might sound to modern ears – did much to further acceptance of homosexuality, and became an important weapon in the battle to decriminalise it. It would seem that it was during his stay in Graz that Diaghilev first fully acknowledged his sexuality.

That Diaghilev's nerves were indeed on edge is painfully clear from a letter he wrote to his stepmother from Warsaw, on his way to southern Europe:

> You're my chubby darling, you're a sweetie, I love you, I'm still not happy but frightened, so frightened that I think I'll die any minute and that it would be less frightening than now. I feel it will pass and I'll be happy. Dear Lepus, will I never be cured of this fear of I know not what? I am frightened of everything: frightened of life, frightened of death, frightened of fame, frightened of scorn, frightened of faith, frightened of the lack of faith. Such decadence. My darling, you're cross with me and you're right. I have stopped being interesting, I'm no longer young at heart, but there can be beauty in old age too. But I'm frightened of old age.[32]

In the autumn of 1901 Diaghilev returned from Europe a sadder but a wiser man. The previous year had been the most demanding of his professional career, and he had not escaped entirely unscathed. And his problems were not over yet. His relationship with Dima was still strained and new crises seemed inevitable.

At the end of that year, on 20 December, a cultural event took place in Petersburg that would have great significance for Diaghilev, even though he had nothing to do with its organisation. On that day a group including Nouvel and Alfred Nurok held the first Contemporary Music Evening, a concert series which showcased works by Russia's most progressive musicians. One of the pianists who took part in that first concert was the young law student Igor Stravinsky.[33] History does not relate what he played, but it certainly wasn't his own music. Neither Diaghilev nor Stravinsky ever recorded their impressions of this evening; they probably did not even notice one another. They had, however, already met. Diaghilev knew Igor as the son of the Imperial Opera bass Fyodor Stravinsky.[34] For his part, Stravinsky must have known of Diaghilev simply because no one with the remotest interest in the fine arts could have been unaware of his existence.

In the course of their ten-year existence, these Contemporary Music Evenings would confront the Russian public with the music of Reger, Debussy, Ravel, Strauss, Mahler and Schoenberg and the debuts of Stravinsky, Prokofiev and Nikolay Myaskovsky.[35] At that first concert, Diaghilev and Stravinsky passed one another like the ghosts of things to come. It would be eight years before the young Igor made his debut as a composer on just such an Evening, providing the first impetus for a partnership that was to make a lasting mark on the sound and rhythm of the twentieth century.

· 11 ·

The Hour of Reckoning
1902–1905

UPON RETURNING TO ST PETERSBURG, Diaghilev resumed his daily routine: editing *Mir iskusstva* and organising exhibitions. His parents moved to Peterhof, where Pavel Pavlovich had been charged with overseeing construction work in the village near the palace complex. It seemed as if the family had finally weathered its financial storm.

The political situation in the country, however, was turning grim. A new terrorist organisation, the Socialist Revolutionaries, was making its presence felt. Its members were not only more numerous, but also better organised than their precursors from the 1870s and 1880s. The government's response was typical: more spies, tighter controls, increased restrictions on civil rights. Prospective spies had to meet strict criteria. At the bare minimum, they had to be debt-free members of the hereditary nobility who had served in the army for at least six years. Needless to say, Catholics and Jews were out of the running.[1] It didn't take a Socialist Revolutionary to perceive a deeply discriminatory system.

The government's tentacles reached into every aspect of daily life: the busiest department at the main post office in St Petersburg was the 'black cabinet', where 500 letters an hour were steamed open, copied and then resealed. When letters bore a wax seal, the seal was first copied by specialists and then broken. After the contents had been read, a fresh seal would be affixed to the envelope.[2] From this one example alone it should be clear that the machinery of control placed an immense burden on the state. But even this bizarre secret bureaucracy could not prevent the assassination of foreign minister Dmitry Sergeyevich Sipyagin by a student on 21 April 1902. Attacks were a monthly occurrence. Targets included the governor of Kiev, the governor of Ufa and the ultra-conservative ideologue of tsarist autocracy, Konstantin Pobedonostsev (twice). Life was cheap in Russia, especially the lives of politicians, and in a climate like this it was hardly surprising that the moderates in the government began to feel the squeeze.

Diaghilev did his best to avoid politics – an understandable decision, given that his journal was sponsored by the tsar and that he himself was an employee of the imperial court. Nevertheless, within his circle there was a growing antipathy to the regime, which was unable to quell the terrorist threat and yet resolutely refused to introduce any reforms that would stabilise the economy, protect small businesses from corruption and redress the appalling social injustice. The most critical of his associates was Valentin Serov, who in 1901 refused to work for the Romanovs any longer. An attempt by Diaghilev to change his mind (prompted, in all likelihood, by his contacts at the court) was rebuffed by Serov with a one-line telegram: 'I don't work in that house any more.'[3]

Diaghilev was now facing dissent within his own ranks. As early as 1900 a large group of artists who regularly showed their work at his exhibitions demanded a greater say in the content of these events. In response an editorial board was set up, which included Diaghilev, Benois and Serov. New artists seeking to exhibit their work needed the written permission of at least seven members of the core group of twenty *Mir iskusstva* artists.[4] This new vetting policy seriously curtailed Diaghilev's power. But in practice it was often ignored, and he went on calling the shots.

In 1902, however, Diaghilev was confronted with a rival: a new collective of Moscow-based artists that would later merge into the Union of Russian Artists. The group was a mixture of the more progressive *Mir iskusstva* artists and some neophytes who felt little affinity for the 'decadent' aesthetics of *Mir iskusstva*. There was a general feeling that Diaghilev was becoming passé and that his journal no longer represented the progressive face of Russian art. Looking back, we can see that the two groups overlapped to a significant degree, but in 1902 the creation of this new association was seen as a minor coup, and people began speculating openly that, as Bakst put it, 'Diaghilev had had his day.'[5]

The fact that *Mir iskusstva* was partly funded by the tsar was, for many, evidence enough that it was the mouthpiece of the establishment. The court was plainly of the same opinion: in July 1902 the tsar decreed that *Mir iskusstva* would continue to be subsidised in the years ahead (the first grant was set to expire at the end of 1902), though at the lower rate of 10,000 roubles a year.[6] This time Diaghilev had discussed the matter with Sergey Witte, the liberal finance minister. From the correspondence between Witte and Tsar Nicholas we also know how many subscribers the magazine had: 1,309. A paltry number – *Mir iskusstva* was and would remain a niche publication and thus highly dependent on external backers.

Yet the greatest threat to the journal was not posed by its tenuous political position or rival groups of artists, but rather by a figure at the very heart of the organisation: Dima Filosofov. Diaghilev's relationship with his cousin remained tense, and that tension increasingly showed in the disjunction between the magazine's two 'departments': literature and the visual arts.

On 16 February 1903 the participants in the latest *Mir iskusstva* exhibition held a meeting to address, among other things, the antagonism between the Moscow and the Petersburg groups. Grabar reported:

> Never had so many artists assembled in one place before. Apart from the Petersburg group all Moscow was there. Diaghilev, opening the meeting which took place in the editorial offices, made a speech in which he said he had been told there was some dissatisfaction among the participants with the jury's actions, and so he felt it his duty to ask if it wasn't now time to think of alternative forms of organising exhibitions. He also alluded to the dissatisfaction with his own dictatorial powers which had been openly manifested in Moscow. Unwillingly at first, but then ever more boldly and resolutely, one after another began to speak. All that was said clearly led to the conclusion that it would be better to have a somewhat broader jury, and of course no 'dictatorial tendencies'.
>
> I said nothing, beginning to understand that there was open war between Moscow and St Petersburg ... But the most surprising thing was that a number of the Petersburg artists ... sided with Moscow. Even more unexpected was a speech from Benois who also spoke in favour of

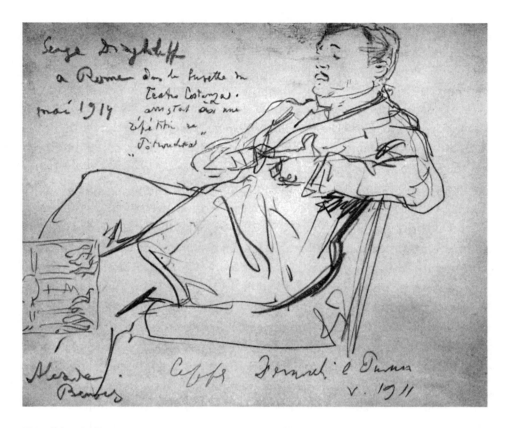

Diaghilev, by Benois

the organisation of a new society. Diaghilev and Filosofov looked at one another. The first was very agitated, the latter sat quietly with a sarcastic smile on his face. So a resolution was reached and everyone got up. Filosofov said loudly, 'Thank God, that means it's over.'[7]

According to Grabar the downfall of *Mir iskusstva* as an exhibition association was primarily due to discontent over the perceived excess of literary and philosophical content at the expense of the arts, or, as he termed it, 'Filosofov's power grab'.[8]

Of all the participants Grabar offers the most convincing account of events, being one of the few who was not a follower of either party. In his efforts to keep Filosofov to himself, Diaghilev would seem to have been too accommodating toward Merezhkovsky and his camp. The latter had done well not to invite Diaghilev to their religious meetings; clearly, the man's judgement was clouded by his pique at being excluded.

Around 1903 Diaghilev began a campaign to bring in Anton Chekhov as *Mir iskusstva*'s literary editor. 'I would do almost anything within my power to work with you,' he wrote to Chekhov on 22 November 1903.[9] At that time Chekhov was arguably Russia's most admired playwright, still riding high on the success of *The Seagull*, *Uncle Vanya* and *Three Sisters*, and even better known for his fiction. The decision to approach him sprang from a desire to change course artistically and abandon the religiously charged symbolism of Merezhkovsky and his ilk. With Chekhov on board, Diaghilev could give the journal a fresh impetus and break Merezhkovsky's hold. Diaghilev also felt an intimate connection with Chekhov's work, which deals with the decline of nineteenth-century rural life – a subject Diaghilev knew all too well. *Three Sisters* was even set in Perm, and the playwright's description of the milieu of cultivated provincial officers and their inability to respond to the modern age must have resonated deeply with Diaghilev. Around this time his favourite half-brother Yury began writing stories in the style of Chekhov, which were published in *Mir iskusstva* under the pseudonym Yury Chereda. Diaghilev's conviction that Chekhov would be his magazine's salvation shines through the tremendous effort he made to win over the great writer. In the autumn of 1903 Diaghilev wrote him five long letters,[10] one after the other, an honour he had never bestowed on anyone before.

But Chekhov wasn't to be won over. His fragile health ruled out a move to St Petersburg. What's more, he clearly had no desire to work with Merezhkovsky.

> I can't be editor of *Mir iskusstva* as I cannot live in St Petersburg, and the journal won't move to Moscow for me; editing by post and by telegraph is impossible and there is no point in having me as editor in name. That's the first thing. Secondly, just as only an artist paints a picture and only an orator makes a speech, so too a journal is edited just by one individual. Of course I am not a critic and would probably edit the critical side none too well, and moreover how would I accommodate myself under one roof with D. S. Merezhkovsky who is a firm believer, and a believer who teaches, whereas I have long since lost my faith and can only regard religious

intellectuals with incomprehension … All the same – whether my attitude to the matter is wrong or not, I have always thought and am just as certain today that there has to be one editor, only one, and that *Mir iskusstva* in particular can only be edited by you. That's my opinion and I don't think I shall change it.[11]

Diaghilev sent several more letters to Chekhov, but in vain. He even managed to finagle a meeting with Chekhov's wife, Olga Knipper, in Moscow, but she was less than charmed ('He is refined and repulsive,' she wrote to her husband)[12] and refused to be talked into using her influence on the writer. But in the end none of this made any difference. Chekhov had just a few months to live (he died on 15 July 1904 in Badenweiler, Germany), and so did *Mir iskusstva*.

In February 1904 Russia became embroiled in a war with Japan. Both countries had expansionist ambitions in the Far East, with Port Arthur as the main bone of contention. Now known as Lüshunkou, this Chinese city was the northernmost ice-free port on the Asian continent. In an uncharacteristically aggressive move, Russia demanded (and obtained) exclusive use of the port from the Chinese. The Japanese, however, saw Russian expansionism as an infringement of their 'natural' sphere of influence and a challenge to their own imperialist policy in China. Amid rising diplomatic tensions, Japan attacked Port Arthur on 8 February, leaving Russia little choice but to declare war, which it did two days later. One of the casualties of the attack was Ivan Diaghilev, an older cousin of Sergey's, the brother of Kolya, for whom he had once written a cello sonata.[13] Diaghilev's father was forced to move to Odessa in early 1904, probably as a result of the war.

Officially *Mir iskusstva* was still entitled to an annual subsidy of 10,000 roubles from the tsar, but it is quite conceivable that payments were delayed or suspended entirely during the war. In any case Diaghilev had no reason to hope for an increase, partly because he was now preoccupied with raising money for his next big project: an exhibition of historical portraits. This show was a long-cherished dream of his. After the Levitsky book he hadn't been able to add a new volume to his planned series of monographs on forgotten eighteenth-century painters, though he remained active on that front. He was harsh in his judgement of art historians and exhibitors who, in his view, failed to appreciate older Russian art, and he continued to comb through archives and old collections. Sometime in 1903 he hit upon the idea of mounting a comprehensive exhibition of Russian portraiture since 1705, and by 1904 all his energy went into this new venture.

This put pressure on *Mir iskusstva* for a number of reasons. Not only did the journal suffer for want of Diaghilev's strong leadership, but in the never-ending struggle for funding it now had to take a back seat to a large-scale, costly exhibition. The financial difficulties were compounded by ongoing disagreements about the journal's artistic programme and personal conflicts between Diaghilev and Filosofov. In his spare moments Diaghilev continued to trawl for backers for *Mir iskusstva*.[14] In a last-ditch effort to save the magazine, overtures were made to Princess Tenisheva, but in exchange for her support she demanded a large measure of editorial control as well as personnel changes. In 1904 Benois had become co-editor with Diaghilev, with editorial responsibility alternating from issue to issue: Benois's issues were dedicated exclusively to 'older' art, antiques and architecture, while Diaghilev's focused on contemporary and European art. Tenisheva objected to both the historical and the internationalist tendencies. In her view the journal should return to the purely neo-nationalist course it had pursued in its first two years. It might have been possible to accommodate her on this point, but Tenisheva also demanded that Benois be fired and replaced by her idol, the artist Nikolay Rerikh, or as he is more commonly known outside Russia, Nicholas Roerich. Roerich played a significant though somewhat obscure role in Diaghilev's activities. He is mainly known in the West for writing the libretto and designing the costumes and sets for *Le Sacre du printemps*. Yet there was a great deal more to the man than that. His often unorthodox spiritual and political ideas won him legions of followers, and even today his work continues to attract interest around the world, especially in more 'alternative' artistic circles. He was a serious amateur archaeologist, making an important contribution to the study of pre-Christian Russia. In the early twentieth century he shot to fame in St Petersburg with his original, colourful canvases, which featured elements of his historical research. His style is instantly recognisable, with its idiosyncratic subject matter, original textures and use of colour, though as time wore on his art became increasingly schematic and banal.[15]

Diaghilev realised that bringing in Roerich would only complicate matters

Diaghilev and Ostroukhov, by Serov

further. Was Tenisheva's support worth the loss of Benois? Diaghilev had few qualms about ditching even his closest friends if he thought that that would improve the quality of his productions. Yet it would be unfair to dismiss him as an unscrupulous opportunist. And thus, after an abortive attempt at compromise, Tenisheva's proposal was rejected.[16] The princess withdrew her support and Diaghilev found himself back at square one. Without external funding the journal could not continue, and the eleventh issue of that year would be *Mir iskusstva*'s last.[17]

The journal's downfall can thus be ascribed to a complex of factors, chief among them Diaghilev's own waning interest. If he had devoted all his energies to resolving the financial, artistic and interpersonal problems plaguing the magazine, he might well have turned things round, but by 1904 his heart was simply no longer in it.[18]

The financial consequences of the journal's demise were not inconsiderable. Diaghilev was forced to sell (in secret) a number of his best paintings (a Bartels, a Kramskoy and a Repin, and perhaps others) to the wealthy collector Ilya Ostroukhov. 'If you only knew how fed up I am with the financial headache this journal has landed me with,' he wrote to Ostroukhov on the occasion.[19]

Diaghilev had little time to mourn the loss of his magazine and his art collection. In February 1905 his Exhibition of Artistic and Historical Portraits opened its doors at the Tauride Palace in St Petersburg. With more than 4,000 portraits painted between 1705 and 1905 on display, it was a monumental overview of two centuries of imperial Russian history.[20] The show, which was opened in grand style by the tsar, also became a celebration of Russian self-confidence and provided a much-needed dose of national pride at a difficult time. The war with Japan was going badly; in early January Port Arthur had fallen to the 'yellow monkeys' (as the Japanese were called in the official propaganda), but the Russians still cherished the hope that the arrival of the Baltic fleet would turn the tide.

The exhibition would be Diaghilev's greatest triumph in his homeland. In terms of both money and logistics, it remains a mystery how he managed to organise such a vast undertaking in just a year. Diaghilev's contemporaries were equally surprised by his punishing work ethic. Once the great thaw set in after the long Russian winter and the roads were again more or less passable, he travelled to remote country estates (more than a hundred of them in total) in search of portraits by forgotten masters.

The young artist Mstislav Dobuzhinsky, who had grown close with the Miriskusniki and lent a helping hand getting the Tauride Palace ready for the exhibition, described the arrival of the paintings:

> I remember how, an overcoat over his shoulders, [Diaghilev] used to sort the paintings as they were taken out of the crates (whole 'galleries of ancestors' were indiscriminately brought in from those country estates) and his shrill and abrupt voice – 'rejected!' or 'accepted!' – rang out in one or other apartment of the palace; he flew about everywhere, giving directions and orders, like a true commander on the field of battle – he was omnipresent. What was remarkable in him – for all his 'commander's' ways, Diaghilev had an eye for detail; nothing was trivial for him, everything was important, and he wanted to do everything himself.[21]

Diaghilev's strength lay not only in his superior organisational skills but also in the breadth of his knowledge. Since his book on Levitsky, Diaghilev remained immersed in the world of eighteenth-century and early nine-teenth-century Russian painting, acquiring an unparalleled level of expertise. Igor Grabar, who was no autodidact like Diaghilev but a trained art histo-rian, expressed surprise at the latter's discerning judgement: 'He possessed a unique visual memory and an iconographic nose, and as we were assembling the exhibition, he put the rest of us to shame. On occasion we would come across a particularly obscure work that had been sent in from some forgotten country estate. No one would know who had painted it or what it depicted. After a half hour, Diaghilev would tear himself away from some other urgent matter. With his charming smile he would say in a friendly tone: "Funny people, can't you see: it's a Lüders of course [David Lüders, a German painter who worked in Russia in 1759], of Prince Alexander Mikhailovich Golitsyn as a young man." ... He was quick in his judgements and there was no appeal; he also made mistakes of course, but he made mistakes much less than others and not so hopelessly.'[22]

Every time Diaghilev modified his list of proposed works, he needed the approval of the tsar, who stood surety for all the loans. The third list he submitted contained more than 550 lenders, 149 of whom lived in distant provinces and sixteen in foreign countries.[23] The catalogue for the exhibi-tion, which was published shortly after the opening and which was edited and largely written by Diaghilev, contains 2,228 entries describing an even greater number of artworks. Besides giving signatures and dates and specify-ing media, it provided a great deal of historical and genealogical information about the subjects. Today, the catalogue is a valuable historical document and a milestone in the history of Russian art. As a testament to Diaghilev's extraordinary creative and organisational talents, this exhibition ranks with the greatest achievements of the Ballets Russes.

At the opening Diaghilev kept something of a low profile: he gave no speeches, and no official thanks were offered. He knew that he had stepped on too many toes on his way to the top to be constantly fêted by the estab-lishment. But after the opening a group of artists and art lovers invited him to a gala banquet at the Metropole, Moscow's classiest hotel. Diaghilev was honoured, and in the space of a day he cobbled together an impressive speech which he delivered at the banquet. It was published the very next day under the title 'The Hour of Reckoning' in the magazine *Vesy*, the new domain of many of the symbolist writers of *Mir iskusstva*:

I think many of you will agree that the idea of a reckoning, of things coming to an end, is one that increasingly comes to mind in these times. And it's one that kept on coming to me the whole time I was recently going about my work. Don't you feel that the long gallery of portraits of people great and small with whom I have tried to fill the magnificent halls of the Tauride Palace is nothing more than a grandiose and overwhelming inventory of a brilliant but regrettably dead period in our history? …

I have earned the right to say this loud and clear, for as summer was breathing its last I ended my long journey across the length and breadth of infinite Russia. And it was indeed after those acquisitive trips that I became especially sure the time of reckoning had come. I saw that not only in those brilliant portraits of our ancestors, so obviously distant from us, but especially in the eyes of their descendants, who were approaching the end of their time. The end was here in front of me. Remote, boarded-up family estates, palaces frightening in their dead grandeur, weirdly inhabited by dear, mediocre people no longer able to bear the weight of past splendours. It wasn't just men and women ending their lives here but a whole way of life. And that was when I became quite sure that we are living in a terrifying era of upheaval; we must give up our lives for the resurgence of a new culture, which will take away from us the remnants of our tired wisdom. This is what history teaches us, and aesthetics confirms. And now, immersed in the history of painted effigies, and thus made immune to accusations of extreme artistic radicalism, I can state frankly and firmly that such conviction as I have cannot be wrong: we are witnessing the greatest historic hour of reckoning, where things are coming to an end in the name of a new, unknown culture, one which we will create but which will in time also sweep us away. And therefore, without fear or doubt, I raise my glass to the ruined walls of those beautiful palaces, and in equal measure to the new commandments of the new aesthetic. And the only wish that I as an irredeemable sensualist can make is that the coming struggle will not insult the aesthetics of life, and that death may be as beautiful and as radiant as the Resurrection![24]

One is almost forced to conclude that Diaghilev wanted to hold up his own family's ruin as an example for his tablemates, as if he suddenly realised that his ambition never would have taken him so far if he hadn't had to fight for his social position, his opportunities and his money.

But of course, most of his audience would have seen his speech through

Diaghilev, by Dobuzhinsky

a political prism. The war with the Japanese demonstrated once more that despite spectacular economic growth, scientific progress and artistic achievements, Russia remained a backward country with respect to its social structure and its institutions. A few months after Diaghilev's speech, on 27 and 28 May 1905, two-thirds of the Russian fleet was destroyed by the Japanese navy (which suffered minimal losses) at the battle of Tsushima Strait. Any hope of a Russian victory vanished. Less than a month later there was another high-profile assassination: on 23 June Count Shuvalov, the governor-general of Moscow, was killed by a terrorist. People braced themselves for the trying times ahead.

For his part Diaghilev had his own war to wage – with Dima. In April they travelled to Odessa to visit Diaghilev's parents and to relax in the sun. But while Sergey returned to Petersburg at the end of the month, Dima left Odessa for Yalta, where Merezhkovsky and Gippius were staying. During his time in Yalta, Filosofov was persuaded to go to Paris with the couple, for a few years at least. A split with Sergey was now inevitable. Filosofov did not go back to Petersburg from Yalta, instead spending a few weeks with his mother at Bogdanovskoye. Yet he was afraid to tell his mother about his plans and eventually left for Petersburg without saying a word about Paris. For the next few months Filosofov, still unsure about what to do, kept his friends and family in the dark, evidently still considering his options. But on 2 August 1905 he wrote to his mother:

You've known for a long time that I am extremely dissatisfied with myself, and that because of the way my life has turned out, what I say and what I do aren't in line with each other. And so finally I've decided to make a clean break ... It's difficult for me to acquaint you with all the details and it's not necessary. I'll only say that my path and Seryozha's have parted; and because of our close personal relationship, I want to ensure that this intellectual opposition doesn't turn into enmity. Therefore, I've decided to get away for a while from him and from *Mir iskusstva*.[25]

It is unclear if Diaghilev was starting to become suspicious at that point; Filosofov certainly hadn't told him anything.

In itself, Dima's and the Merezhkovskys' flight to Paris was hardly exceptional. Many Russians were emigrating at that time, to escape the unrest in their homeland. Benois and his family had already left for France in January, after peaceful demonstrators in St Petersburg had been gunned down by government forces on Bloody Sunday (22 January). But everyone knew that Dima was not fleeing political violence but Sergey, and perhaps the *Mir iskusstva* group as a whole. After all, Merezhkovsky and Gippius were hate figures among that circle of friends, who blamed them for the downfall of their journal.

Shortly after sending the above letter to his mother, Filosofov broke the news to Diaghilev, whose initial reaction was cool. He knew, of course, that any 'decision' made by the doubt-ridden Dima was of little value. Oddly enough it was Benois, from his new home in Brittany, who was most incensed by Dima's defection to the 'camp' of Merezhkovsky and Gippius: 'I cannot come to terms with our separation, in the knowledge that he is leaving us for that jungle of mystical affectation, with which he desires to amuse Merezhkovsky.'[26]

In faraway France, Benois was already feeling left out and lonely. He tried to distract himself with a steady stream of letters to his friends in Petersburg. Yet Sergey's failure to reply only compounded Benois's despair.

From his vantage point in France, Benois had a much more balanced view of the political situation in Russia than did most of his friends:

That whole affair in Odessa [the *Potemkin* mutiny], the assassination of

Shuvalov etc., are incredibly unfortunate and wrong-headed. All these things do is make people resigned to the notion of a dictatorship as the only means of saving the country from perdition. In fact I bet that certain hard-line reactionaries are even now rubbing their hands with glee ... Or would you advise me to wait for the rule of the Social Democrats? By that time all those palaces I love would be mere piles of rubble, don't you think?[27]

Diaghilev finally replied to Benois on 16 October, at the height of what had become a popular revolution. In September the government had signed a peace treaty, ceding large chunks of Russian territory to the Japanese. Yet even with the war at an end the authorities were unable to curb the unrest. Strikes broke out across the country; demonstrators took to the streets, and the army and navy were plagued by mutinies. Liberal factions had signed a manifesto in August outlining a parliamentary democracy. The tsar even had to deploy his Cossack regiments to keep order. Against this background, Diaghilev wrote to Benois:

Don't be angry at my silence. It's impossible to describe what's going on here: we're shut in on all sides, in complete darkness, no chemists, trams, newspapers, telephones or telegraphs and nothing to do but wait for the machine guns!

Yesterday evening I walked along the Nevsky amidst a huge black mass of a most diverse crowd. There was complete darkness, save for a beam of electric light directed from the top of the Admiralty along the whole Nevsky from a huge naval searchlight. The impression and the effect were amazing. Black pavements, the middle of the street brilliant white, people like shadows, houses like a cardboard set.

You'll understand that one doesn't want to think or talk about anything.

I closed the exhibition almost without any scenes, and thank God for that. But I am not sure that the pictures will get back to their rightful owners! I am dreaming of getting down to the publication of my *Dictionary of Russian Portraits*, but at present I am just tediously and mindlessly waiting for events without knowing where they will take one.

Dima wants to go and do a Herzen abroad in the train of the Merezhkovskys. Whether this is necessary and opportune – I leave it to everyone to judge for himself. At all events one can now do one of two things – either go out into the town square and give oneself up to every momentary madness (which is only natural) or wait in one's study, cut off from life. I can't choose the first solution, for I like town squares only in opera or a small Italian town, but for the study option, one needs to be a 'study man', and that's just not me. So things are turning out badly – it can't be helped, all one can do is sit around and kill time, but when will there be an end to this wild bacchanal time, which is not without a certain elemental beauty but which like every tempest brings so much hideous misery? That's the question which everyone is now asking themselves and with which one is eternally preoccupied.

Until it's settled, I envy you and I would give untold riches to get out of here. And so don't complain about me. I believe that our time too will come. I embrace you.[28]

The day after, Tsar Nicholas signed a liberal manifesto authorising the creation of a legislative body, the Duma. Even for Diaghilev, who told Benois that he held himself aloof from all the political wrangling, that moment was too beautiful not to celebrate. He bought a bottle of champagne and rushed over to the Filosofovs. Aunt Anna wrote to her daughter the next day to congratulate her on the manifesto. 'What joy! Yesterday there was even champagne. Brought by ... Seryozha! What a miracle!'[29]

Yet amid the mood of optimism Benois remained sceptical. In one of his letters Nouvel attempted to explain why he and Diaghilev felt as they did.

You fear it [the revolution] and, alas, you curse it, but we welcome it. We welcome it not as an 'eternal dream or final objective', but as a gigantic global upheaval, a spontaneous influence that can bring forth new fruit, as unknown as it is unexpected ... I relish the revolution, not only in an aesthetic sense, but as a means of gaining historical and philosophical insights. Each day nourishes my intellect, imagination and consciousness. How could this fail to make me happy?[30]

It remains unclear if this accurately reflected Diaghilev's state of mind, but there is no question that in the autumn of 1905 he was caught up in the dramatic political events, if only momentarily.

But the hope of a better future cherished by him and Nouvel was a vain one. It soon became clear that the Duma had no real power. Everyone realised that the yawning divide between the Russian political system and that of western Europe would not be bridged any time soon.

And in all the commotion Dima, after months of hemming and hawing, ultimately decided *not* to go to Paris. As he put it, he felt 'a kind of violation of the balance of our trinity'[31] (as Filosofov called his relationship with the couple). It was now Diaghilev who turned his gaze to the West.

· 12 ·

The 'Homosexual Clique'
1906–1907

DIAGHILEV'S RELATIONSHIP with his cousin was more than a mere romance or fling. The two enjoyed an intimacy and affinity that permeated their professional lives and nourished their aesthetic ideals. They were twin souls united by a single philosophy and a single ambition, and although Sergey was quite aware that Dima had other interests (philosophical as well as romantic), he was convinced that nothing could ever come between them. Zinaida Gippius, that hostile but sharp observer of Diaghilev's psyche, perfectly understood that he 'certainly didn't expect to lose someone who had been his trusty helper for so many years, and he had no doubt that they would go on together down the future path they had planned'.[1] Even Dima's intention to leave St Petersburg did not upset Diaghilev, as if he knew his cousin could be relied upon to change his mind.

By now the relationship may have become entirely platonic; it was certainly less exclusive. Diaghilev had the occasional affair on the side, as did Dima. And it was a sordid little incident arising from one of these affairs that finally drove them apart. Trivial enough in itself, it was the spark that set off the powder keg. Tensions that had been smouldering under the surface now flared into an ugly conflict.

Just before Christmas 1905, Nouvel had apparently told Sergey that Dima

Filosofov, by Bakst

was trying to steal his current lover, a Polish student called Vika. When Diaghilev heard this he flew into a rage and ran to Donon's, a smart restaurant on the Moyka Canal, where he knew that Filosofov was dining (with Zinaida Gippius as it happened). There he created such a scene as to attract a crowd of goggling waiters, and a terrible scandal ensued.[2] Shortly afterwards, Diaghilev wrote to his aunt Nona, asking her forgiveness for the fact that 'he could no longer visit her house for personal reasons'.[3]

Diaghilev was also the driving force behind the very last act of the drama – their separation. Dima suddenly found it easy to leave St Petersburg: 'While I did everything to make our parting a matter of principle – that didn't work out in the end. At the first grubby little incident – something that made me feel personally dirty – Seryozha had no trouble making a complete break …'[4]

On 10 February 1906, Dima decided to leave the city ahead of Gippius and Merezhkovsky. Diaghilev was not informed of his plans. Dima's train left at noon from Warsaw station, the point of departure for all of his and Diaghilev's trips abroad. Diaghilev arrived at Moscow on the night train at eleven o'clock that same morning. There he learned that Dima would be leaving within the hour from a different station. As soon as he heard this, he made a headlong dash across the snow-covered city centre: 'Five minutes before the train's departure Seryozha arrived. We kissed one another fervently. It was so terribly hard. My spirit was flooded with regret. I was scared. It was a dreadful scene. O Lord, somehow everything will be all right.'[5]

This was the formal end of their relationship.

Throughout 1905 and 1906, the political situation remained tense, and this tension would have an effect on the world of the arts. None of Russia's main cultural institutions – theatres, museums, conservatories and art colleges – enjoyed any administrative autonomy; they were part of an immense bureaucratic apparatus, headed in almost every case by a grand duke (a brother or cousin of the tsar). The possibility of allowing cultural organisations more independence had been cautiously mooted prior to 1905, but nothing had come of it. Riots and protests broke out among the students of the Petersburg conservatory, which was headed by the composer Rimsky-Korsakov. Their demands included a greater say in decision-making and the abolition of corporal punishment (one professor, the celebrated violinist Leopold Auer, used to strike students over the head with his bow).[6] When Rimsky-Korsakov sided with the students in a reasonable and restrained open letter to the newspaper, he was promptly fired. His sacking led to new protests and the resignation of a number of teachers. Rebellious students were expelled, and the government forbade the performance of Rimsky-Korsakov's 'revolutionary' operas.

Storm clouds were also gathering over the Imperial Theatres. Although Diaghilev had steered clear of the discussion surrounding Rimsky-Korsakov and the conservatory, he threw himself into the theatrical revolt with angry zeal, impelled by the tragic event that had sparked the unrest in the first place: the suicide of the choreographer Sergey Legat.

That autumn a strike had broken out among the ballet dancers, who demanded greater artistic autonomy. A committee was formed, three of whose members would later become leading lights of the Ballets Russes: Anna Pavlova, Tamara Karsavina and Mikhail Fokine. The director (still Vladimir Telyakovsky) threatened to punish the agitators and demanded that all dancers and choreographers sign an oath of loyalty. The rebellion brought Fokine and Diaghilev into close contact. Nouvel remembered that 'Fokine often visited Diaghilev to consult him and ask for advice'. Diaghilev encouraged Fokine to continue his protest 'in the hope of provoking further commotion'.[7] He himself stayed on the sidelines for the time being, but this was to change when events took a dramatic turn.

One of those who had signed the oath of loyalty was Sergey Legat, with whom Diaghilev had worked on his doomed *Sylvia* project. It was claimed that Legat had only signed under duress and was ashamed of having betrayed the other dancers. Overcome by remorse, he slit his throat with a razor on 17 October.[8]

Nouvel later wrote that Diaghilev was deeply affected by Legat's suicide, which he blamed on the culture of the Imperial Theatres, where careers were not determined 'by talent, but by toadying, tattling and malicious gossip'.[9] Eleven days after Legat's death, Diaghilev published an agitated, rather incoherent piece entitled 'Plyaska smerti' (The dance of death), in which he blamed Legat's death on Telyakovsky. He concluded, 'At the present moment Russia is donning new dress. In the field of art, that essential motor of all culture, hasn't the time come for renewal and new people?'[10]

It is hard not to suspect Diaghilev of opportunism, for he still had a bone to pick with Telyakovsky, but judging by the reactions of his friends, his outburst was generally held to be sincere.[11] He was the only major public figure to take up the dancers' cause directly, which must have added to the awe with which they already regarded him.

Many former *Mir iskusstva* artists, including Grabar, Dobuzhinsky and Serov, came together in mid-1905 to launch a satirical magazine called *Zhupel*

(Bugbear), in which they gave vent to their political dissatisfaction by lampooning various figures. Diaghilev was only tangentially involved, probably because he realised that the censors would never permit publication. The magazine was indeed banned by the government after only three issues, and the editor-in-chief, Zinovy Grzhebin, was imprisoned. Diaghilev subsequently used his influence to obtain Grzhebin's release.[12]

Diaghilev tried to tread carefully in this political minefield. He did not want to offend his government contacts, but neither did he wish to alienate left-wing, progressive forces in the artistic community. He made no open criticism of the government, but he did support radical change and critics of the regime in his articles. He even briefly allied himself with Maxim Gorky, one of Russia's best-known radical left-wing intellectuals. Gorky and Grabar wanted to launch a magazine about the arts, and they asked Diaghilev for assistance. Though he showed enthusiasm initially, he probably wasn't heartbroken when the venture failed. Up to now, none of his artistic enterprises had succeeded without the help of the authorities. He was fully aware that if he wished to continue working in Russia, he needed the help of both the government and the court.

There was another reason Diaghilev had to be careful: his ever more open homosexuality. Although the higher echelons of tsarist society were remarkably tolerant of 'deviant' sexual behaviour, homosexuality (always referred to as 'sodomy') was officially a crime under the penal code. As so often in Russia, the law was not always consistently enforced, but convictions did occur – even among the upper crust. Offenders could be banished to Siberia; they were also sentenced to hard labour if minors were involved.[13]

In principle, Diaghilev had little to fear. He was well respected and the authorities did not actively look for offenders. The public prosecutor's office took action only if an offence was reported, and convictions tended to be confined to cases of assault or rape.[14] Nevertheless, this meant that every time Diaghilev picked someone up, he was committing a serious offence. It was not unthinkable that the authorities might suddenly decide to tackle the decline of public morals. They would have no difficulty finding a prominent homosexual to make an example of, and Diaghilev knew all too well what had happened to Oscar Wilde in England. In other words, he had every reason to keep up his connections with court and high government officials.

Illegal or not, a fairly open homosexual subculture had emerged over the last decade, mainly in St Petersburg, and Diaghilev was a prominent

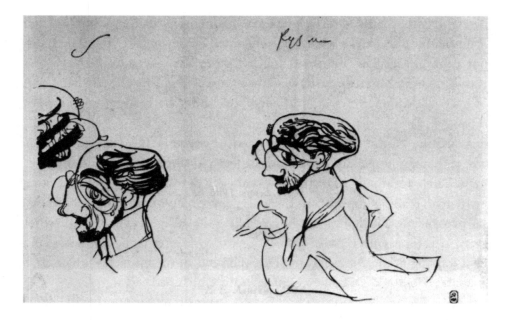

Kuzmin, by Dobuzhinsky

figure in these circles. Many would have been aware that, in Europe, views on homosexuality were becoming more progressive. *Psychopathia Sexualis*, an authoritative work on 'sexual deviance' by Krafft-Ebing, had already been translated into Russian by 1887.[15]

Yet this growth in tolerance and openly homosexual behaviour was sparking a backlash of criticism and repugnance. From 1905, satirical pieces appeared fairly regularly in the papers, attacking the 'homosexual clique' and painting it as debauched and dangerous. In his diary, the poet Alexander Blok described his own revulsion at Diaghilev's lifestyle: 'There is something frightening about him, and he is not the only one: art, he says, is a stimulus to sensuality … A very black impression, a terrible epoch, reality has far out-stripped imagination. Everything about Diaghilev is terrible and significant, including his "active homosexuality".'[16]

One of the central figures of the homosexual community was the poet and composer Mikhail Kuzmin. Diaghilev had met him through Nouvel, who was Kuzmin's close friend and perhaps lover.[17] In 1905 Kuzmin pub-lished *Krylya* (Wings), an explicit coming-of-age novel. He was a great music lover, sharing with Nouvel and Diaghilev an unfashionable passion for music by eighteenth-century Italian and French composers such as Cimarosa and Rameau. He also liked a wide range of contemporary music – though he was not a fan of German composers – being particularly keen on Debussy and Ravel. Kuzmin kept a diary in which he chronicled his own love life and that of his friends, sometimes in lurid detail. Diaghilev starts to figure in it as of 1905.

Kuzmin, Nouvel and Diaghilev liked to cruise in the Tauride Garden, where they could pick up schoolboys, cadets and students for sex, sometimes in exchange for money: 'Diaghilev was already in the Tauride Garden with a gentleman (calling himself Stasa) and a cadet, Chichinadze. Not far from me sat two queens, a little Jew in a bowler hat and black gloves and a bit farther away, in a straw hat, a Finnish type with narrow, shining, languorous eyes who kept looking at me. Nouvel turned up, then Bakst; there was no "khaki" [i.e. soldiers] about and Diaghilev went off with Chichinadze.'[18]

They boasted of conquests and passed lovers on to one another: 'Diaghilev told me of Ruslov, a Moscow grammar-school boy ... who thinks himself a Dorian Gray. He always has 30 boyfriends available *par amour*, and sought out Diaghilev himself etc. Maybe we'll go to Moscow together.'[19]

One of the youths that Diaghilev had been pursuing for some time was a student by the name of Poklovsky-Kozell – a grandson of Alfons Poklovsky-Kozell, the businessman from Ekaterinburg who had driven the family into bankruptcy in Perm. By a wry coincidence, Alfons had given Bikbarda to his son Vikenty, making the latter Sergey's successor as 'son of the house'.[20] An habitué of various gay haunts (always with a different companion), he appears to have been a sought-after item. Kuzmin's diary relates a number of failed attempts to get into contact with this youth, usually simply referred to as 'the student'. Ultimately, however, his hopes were dashed by Diaghilev: 'Diaghilev is awfully nice, although he told me that my student he's been pursuing for two years is Poklovsky-Kozell, who has four million and so is indifferent to the question [of money].'[21]

In the course of 1907 the two men grew closer, and Diaghilev wrote several (alas unpreserved) letters to Kuzmin from Europe. This was a great honour, because Diaghilev had by then developed an aversion to letter writing. Instead he sent cables or used the telephone. Typically, he would wire his business contacts but ring his friends and family (by that time around 40,000 Petersburg households had telephones). The affection between Kuzmin and

Diaghilev did not go unnoticed. Kuzmin wrote in his diary, 'It would seem that Nouvel suspects I have feelings for Diaghilev.'[22] Nearly two months later he writes, 'There are all sorts of rumours making the rounds about Diaghilev and me. "*Quelle farce*".'[23]

To his many one-night stands and brief affairs Diaghilev added a new and more enduring friendship with the young graphic designer Aleksey Mavrin. The latter was soon employed as his secretary, living with him on and off and accompanying him on his trips abroad. The relationship with Mavrin was only to last a few years, but it continued a pattern that started with Dima, whereby Diaghilev involved his lovers in his professional life.

In early 1906, Diaghilev was still trying to drum up funding for his planned monographs on eighteenth-century masters, without much success. In May 1905 he had managed to extract a subsidy of 6,000 roubles from the Academy of Arts and a 3,000-rouble advance on the purchase of 200 copies of the edition. But the actual costs would far exceed these sums, and Diaghilev was unable to raise the money. His failure may reflect his waning interest in the project. The 9,000 roubles were not paid back. Diaghilev, ever the optimist, hoped that this very large debt would eventually be forgotten – but this was not to be.

New projects jostled for attention. Diaghilev wanted to hold a final *Mir iskusstva* exhibition (almost three years after the previous one), to be mounted completely independently. The exhibition, which opened in the Catherine Room at 3 Malaya Konyushennaya Street in February, was his most progressive ever. Even as he devoted his energies to fostering a renaissance of eighteenth-century art, his interest in the latest French art movements had been growing. The last issues of the magazine he edited also reflect his interest in neo-Impressionism. It was the first Russian publication to reproduce works by Gauguin, Sérusier, Toulouse-Lautrec, Cézanne (misspelled 'Sezanne'), Matisse and Van Gogh. It also contained an article on a young Russian painter working in Munich: Vasily Kandinsky. *Mir iskusstva*'s reputation for following the latest trends in Europe is almost entirely based on those last issues.

Diaghilev kept to the cutting edge in his last exhibition. Besides the Miriskusniki, the show spotlighted works by young artists such as Mikhail Larionov, Aleksey von Jawlensky and Pavel Kuznetsov, revealing a growing divide between Russia's progressive art movements. Whereas the Miriskus-niki were preoccupied with line and with flat, almost graphic planes, Larionov and Jawlensky (in their own very different ways) focused on colour and mass, using an impasto, painterly technique. The Miriskusniki favoured an intellectual, cool, almost emotionless form of expression, whereas Larionov, Kuznetsov and Jawlensky opted for an expressive, primitive and spontaneous approach. Finally, while the Miriskusniki used their extensive knowledge of European cultural history to create a highly original pictorial language, Larionov and Jawlensky were attuned to the latest European trends and sought to position themselves within these international movements.

Perhaps Diaghilev already felt that his friends' art would ultimately lose ground to the new schools developing in Moscow, Paris, Munich and the artists' colony of Worpswede near Bremen. In any event, he began to adopt a more independent stance, distancing himself from Benois, who despised the neo-Impressionists. Instead, he took his lead from what he observed happening in Europe and from Grabar, a staunch defender of Van Gogh and Gauguin.

This exhibition was the real swansong of *Mir iskusstva* and Diaghilev's last public venture in his native country. He was only thirty-four years old, but his professional life in Russia had come to an end. Shortly after the exhibition opened he and Mavrin left on a long trip to Athens (where he saw the Olympic Games), Istanbul and Italy. During that journey he began to hatch a new plan.

The idea that Russian art should present itself abroad had been in the air for some time. Although works by Russian artists had found their way into various international exhibitions, a major overview of Russian art had never been held outside the country. Even Benois believed that Russian artistic culture could now compete on an equal footing with the great cultures of Europe. At the beginning of 1906 he tried, without success, to find French backing for an exhibition of Russian art in Paris. Around that time he must have spoken to Diaghilev about his plans. He received the following letter from Sergey, who was then in Constantinople:

Don't be surprised by this address. You probably know that tomorrow I am sailing for Athens, and I am thinking of passing by Paris in a month's time

Diaghilev, by Benois

(approximately). What do you think of raising the question of a Russian section in the present Salon d'automne? Petersburg approves of the idea; I too am ready to take the thing on. Could you put out a feeler? The French would be fools not to agree. I'll show them the real Russia.[24]

Exactly what that 'real Russia' entailed was probably already clear in Diaghilev's mind: an exhibition of Russia's most progressive schools, with emphasis on the youngest generation of Moscow painters like Larionov, a large selection of eighteenth-century and academy art, and numerous old Russian icons from the collection of the historian Nikolay Likachov. That latter component would be unique, because even in St Petersburg, serious interest in icons was a daringly modern fashion.

Within a month of writing to Benois, Diaghilev was already in Paris, busy arranging his exhibition. 'Diaghilev is here,' wrote Benois, 'he is cheerful, lively and full of grand plans. I'm steering him round the local authorities.' In the last week of May, Benois introduced Diaghilev to Léon Benedict, a curator at the Musée de Luxembourg, who was soon won over by the Russian's charm.[25] He put the two men in touch with the organisers of the Salon d'automne, which had been set up in 1903 as a modernist alternative to the more conservative Paris salons. It had become known as the main venue for post-Impressionists and Fauves, and its organisers included future Diaghilev designers André Derain, Henri Matisse and Georges Rouault.

Though the Russian exhibition was mounted separately, visitors to the Salon d'automne in the Grand Palais could view it free of charge. Diaghilev was at first allocated ten rooms; this was later increased to twelve.[26] He chose Bakst as designer, and on 2 June a list of artists was drawn up over a pot of tea in a patisserie on Rue Royale.

Once Diaghilev got to work with his 'two satellites'[27] Bakst and Benois, it was just like the old days of *Mir iskusstva*, with Diaghilev and Bakst at loggerheads, and Benois agonising over 'the cheap and trivial impression' made by Bakst's decorations. In fact Benois disapproved of just about everything – the choice of artists (too few Petersburgers, too many Muscovites – 'Seryozha was cruelly unjust!'), the background colours, the greenery and the silk drapery in different colours: 'Setting up the exhibition went as usual. Seryozha paid no attention to anyone, didn't pay calls where he should have done, but spent whole days hanging and rehanging the pictures, driving the decorators crazy. As always, everything seemed chaotic till the last moment and then suddenly everything fell into place.'[28]

The final month saw an invasion of Petersburgers: Nouvel (who was increasingly settling into his role as Seryozha's secretary) came to lend a hand, along with the 'indefatigable' Grabar, and Prince Vladimir Argutinsky-Dolgorukov, an immensely rich collector and art lover who in recent years had become a important presence among the Miriskusniki.

Dima's absence cast a strange shadow over the proceedings. He was in Paris but did not show himself. In fact, so keen was he to avoid bumping into his former lover and the rest of his friends that he kept to the left bank throughout September and October.[29] His non-attendance did not go unnoticed. 'They [Filosofov and the Merezhkovskys] didn't come to the exhibition at all. That was quite a blow; I never saw them once,' Diaghilev wrote to his stepmother.[30]

The exhibition was opened by President Fallières of France on 6 October. Diaghilev's twelve rooms in the Grand Palais contained almost 750 works, from many different collectors. Bringing them together had not been easy. Celebrated collectors like the merchant Pavel Tretyakov and Princess Maria Tenisheva had refused, for various reasons, to loan works, as had the Russian

Museum in St Petersburg. As a result, the Peredvizhniki were scarcely represented, and that was perhaps for the best. After all, the ordinary (French) rooms of the Salon d'automne were full of works by Cézanne, Gauguin, Matisse and even Picasso. If pieces by contemporary painters like Vasily Surikov or Ivan Kramskoy had been hung next to them, it would undoubtedly have been harder for Russian art to shake off its provincial reputation. Diaghilev knew this very well, which is why he gave so much prominence to Mikhail Vrubel (who had just died and had a whole room to himself) and to young artists like Larionov, Goncharova, Sudeykin and Sapunov. He even had Larionov, whom he and Bakst regarded as the most talented of the young artists,[31] travel from distant Tiraspol to be present at the opening.[32]

The exhibition was very well received. *Le Figaro* devoted a long article to it, singling out Vrubel for special praise. Diaghilev was made an honorary member of the Salon, along with Bakst, Benois, Roerich and Vrubel (posthumously), while Larionov and others were made ordinary members.[33] Yet it was by no means a triumph or a sensation. Russian art had made an impressive entrance in France, profiting from the charm of novelty. But was it really equal to the explosion of inventiveness in French art of the same period? What's more, the exhibitors had, as it were, shot their bolt. The best Russian art had already been shown, and a subsequent exhibition could only promise more of the same. If Diaghilev wished to trump his latest achievement, he would have to look further than the visual arts.

After the Salon closed, the Russian exhibition travelled on to Berlin and later, in a radically slimmed-down version, to the Biennale in Venice. It was a success in Berlin, too: 'The Germans like it. There have been hordes of visitors. We've done it again!' Diaghilev wrote to Nouvel. He was still not a great fan of Berlin, though: 'On Monday I'm leaving this boring and tedious Berlin ... The only interesting thing was chatting to Wilhelm [II], but he talks such nonsense one wants to block one's ears. He has more aplomb than I do ...'[34]

He returned to St Petersburg for a few weeks at the beginning of December, but by the 23rd he was back in Paris for the Christmas holidays. By now he had amassed a circle of acquaintances from the highest echelons of the Parisian beau monde. His main new allies were Elisabeth, Comtesse Greffulhe, a wealthy art patron, and her cousin, the poet Robert de Montesquiou. Diaghilev had probably met the Countess through Montesquiou, the two men's paths having crossed briefly in 1898.[35] Montesquiou, a well-known gay dandy and aesthete, was just the man to introduce Diaghilev to the Parisian homosexual subculture. They hit it off so well that Montesquiou accompanied Diaghilev to St Petersburg after Christmas.

Both the Countess and Montesquiou were the kind of people with whom Diaghilev had an immediate affinity. They were wealthy, art-loving aristocrats: refined, yet open to new fashions and not averse to crossing boundaries. Like Diaghilev, their identities were constructed around their artistic preferences and activities. That they saw no difference between life and art is nowhere better exemplified than by the fact that they served as models for Baron de Charlus and the Duchesse de Guermantes in Proust's *À la recherche du temps perdu*.

Diaghilev needed them for their money and their contacts, but at the same time they confirmed his own identity and undoubtedly provided scintillating conversation. To them, Diaghilev had the charm of the ambiguous. An aesthete with a remarkable knowledge of the arts, but at the same time a man of action: businesslike, expansive and cosmopolitan. Perhaps they were amused by the notion that a passionate Tartar lurked behind that well-trimmed little moustache, those pince-nez and that pomaded hair, but they were quick enough to grasp that this quaint figure was not primitive, but rather exceptionally modern.

· 13 ·

Tsar Boris and Tsar Sergey
1907–1908

UPON RETURNING TO PARIS, Diaghilev hurriedly attempted to throw together a coalition which would help realise his latest plan: a series of five 'historic' Russian concerts at the Grand Opéra in Paris. This idea had been brewing since at least September 1906, before the opening of the Salon d'automne exhibition.[1] Diaghilev's first ally in Paris was the Comtesse Greffulhe, whom he won over with an impromptu concert of Russian music on her grand piano.[2] In Russia he found support from Alexander Taneyev (not to be confused with Sergey Taneyev), a mediocre composer with friends in high places, and Grand Duke Vladimir, the tsar's senior uncle, who had chaired the committee of recommendation for the exhibition at the Salon d'automne. His admiration for Diaghilev proved to be valuable, a fact the latter may not have fully appreciated until Vladimir's sudden death in early 1909.

The biggest individual donor was Hendrik van Gilse van der Pals, a Dutch rubber merchant from Rotterdam who had been living in St Petersburg since 1863. Van der Pals, whose son Nikolaas became a leading musicologist and Rimsky-Korsakov's first biographer, was a well-known patron of the city's musical arts.[3] He became acquainted with Walter Nouvel, and it was through him that he met Diaghilev. Van der Pals was not indifferent to marks of distinction (in 1914 he became the Dutch consul in St Petersburg),

and Diaghilev rewarded him with a place on his committee of recommendation, where he sat among such eminent figures as Glazunov, Rachmaninov
and Rimsky-Korsakov.[4]

As the year drew to a close, Diaghilev had evidently accumulated substantial financial pledges, though his personal finances were in such a deplorable state that he had to borrow 500 francs from Benois to make it through
the next few months.[5] Despite these difficulties, by January Diaghilev was
hard at work on the concert series.

Diaghilev resolved to spend most of his time abroad for the foreseeable
future. Sometime in 1907 he cleared out of his apartment on the Fontanka,
from then on staying at the Hotel Europe during his increasingly infrequent
trips to St Petersburg. His old nanny moved into his parents' little apartment
in Peterhof.[6]

There has been much speculation about why Diaghilev was so keen to
move his base of operations abroad. As so often, the decision was prompted
partly by the exigencies of the moment and partly by a strategy that had
been mapped out long before. To start with, there were personal reasons: his
break-up with Dima had put his relationship with his family under strain.
His decision not to see the Filosofovs affected his usual closeness with his
stepmother. The few letters he sent her around this time betray none of
the affection and intimacy so characteristic of their earlier correspondence.
Undoubtedly, the Merezhkovskys also played a part in all this. Diaghilev's
father and stepmother continued to associate with them, and Sergey regarded
this as a painful betrayal. It certainly couldn't have helped matters that in the
summer of 1905, as the last threads of his romance with Dima were unravel-
ling, Merezhkovsky and Gippius went off to stay with Diaghilev's father in
Odessa for a few days.[7]

He also had professional reasons for setting his sights on more distant
horizons. Simply put, Diaghilev felt he had exhausted his career opportunities in St Petersburg. As early as 1901 rumours were circulating that he
was making 'frantic efforts to become Minister of Culture'.[8] His dismissal
from the theatre had seemingly ruled out that option, but the Revolution of
1905 opened up the prospect of a senior post in the cultural bureaucracy. In
the wake of the protests by the ballet company, Telyakovsky's position had
become tenuous, and Diaghilev hoped that Prime Minister Sergey Witte,

whom he knew and respected, would intercede on his behalf.[9] Yet by the end of 1905 Witte's star began to fade and with it, Diaghilev's hopes. A final opportunity to obtain a high-ranking official position in Russia presented itself in 1907. The elderly Count Ivan Tolstoy had been vice president of the Academy of Arts for years, and he was nearing retirement. (The Academy's president, invariably a grand duke, was a mere figurehead, while the vice president held the real power.) Speculation was rife that Diaghilev was the only serious candidate to succeed him, but the thought of allowing him to wield the sceptre over such an august institution was anathema to many. Even moderate critics reached for their pens to warn of the disaster that would ensue if the post were given to Diaghilev. The esteemed art historian Ivan Lazarevsky wrote on the subject in a leader in *Slovo* (The Word):

> In Mr Diaghilev's career, apart from an exhibition of portraits and an exhibition abroad of the work of Russian painters, it is difficult to point to anything worthy of remark which could have a serious impact on the development of Russian art … One can imagine what our Academy would turn into if the reins of government went to Mr Diaghilev, a man of party and in his artistic beliefs an extremist![10]

Despite his many successes, Diaghilev remained a controversial figure – even a hate object – in his homeland, and the last thing the authorities needed was a new cause for unrest in the art world. The effect of this state of affairs was twofold: to begin with, Diaghilev was driven abroad by the impossibility of furthering his career in Russia; yet at the same time, the government was all too happy to fund his activities in France, provided this would keep the troublemaker out of their hair. Working abroad, he could boost Russia's international image, which had suffered on account of the war. More importantly, in far-off France he could do less damage. The powers that be had the 'Hottentot' and '*Bashibazouk*' Diaghilev right where they wanted him: far away and tied to their purse strings.

But of course, Diaghilev's conquest of Paris was not down to negative factors alone. His patriotic pathos should not be underestimated. So often did he express his desire to propagate Russian culture in the West to his friends and associates that it cannot be seen as an empty slogan to curry favour with his official backers. For him, the triumph of Russian culture was vitally important. Equally important was his growing interest in the French artistic avant-garde, which was evident from the last issues of *Mir iskusstva*. His passion for modern French music, stoked by Nouvel and Kuzmin, also fuelled his interest in artistic goings-on in Paris. Back in his student days Diaghilev's musical universe had been defined by the contrast between Tchaikovsky's romantic classicism and Wagner's harmonic experimentation. The new music of Debussy and Ravel, in which harmonic innovation went hand in hand with a classical sense of proportion and precision, offered a way out of this dichotomy.

Nouvel arrived in Paris in early April, and he was often in Diaghilev's company. Benois was still in town as well but had only a peripheral involvement with the organisation. He described Nouvel and Diaghilev's Parisian lifestyle to Serov thus:

> Generalissimo Diaghilev's staff are beginning to gather here. Yesterday I found him in real Potemkin style (and that's how you should paint him) – in a loose golden silk dressing-gown and horizontally striped pants. It was already about one p.m. but his serene highness had only just deigned to roll out of bed. Here too is Valechka Nouvel, a dark little chap with a touch of yellow. He ties his tie with amazing skill.[11]

Diaghilev stayed at the Hotel Mirabeau on rue de la Paix, where he rented two rooms for himself (and probably Mavrin) and a third for his manservant Vasily. In one of the rooms there was a grand piano where groups of Russian expatriates would hold intimate musical *séances*, with Scriabin at the keyboard and Chaliapin singing.[12]

In retrospect it is not entirely clear on what basis Diaghilev devised the programme for his concert series. Russian music was hardly unknown abroad; both Tchaikovsky and Rubinstein had performed extensively in the West, though they attracted few followers. Little interest was shown in the neo-nationalist Five, with the exception of Mussorgsky, who had achieved a certain cult status in France. In Russia itself, opera was regarded as the country's greatest musical asset, though the opportunities for staging Russian opera abroad were few and far between. This proved to be Diaghilev's biggest obstacle. The time was not yet ripe for opera, and Russia's

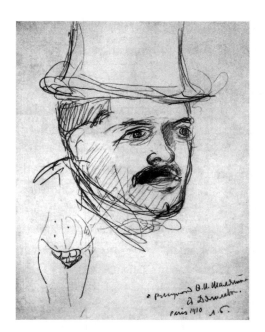

Diaghilev, by Chaliapin

most renowned symphonist, Tchaikovsky, was dismissed by the French as inauthentic. Tchaikovsky did find his way onto Diaghilev's programme, in the form of the ill-chosen Second Symphony (perhaps selected for its supposed nationalist character) and the symphonic poem *Francesca da Rimini*. Diaghilev also tried to squeeze in as many opera arias as he could, including selections from Mussorgsky's *Boris Godunov*, Borodin's *Prince Igor*, Balakirev's *Thamar*, Glinka's *Ruslan and Lyudmila* and several works by Rimsky-Korsakov (*Christmas Eve*, *The Tale of Tsar Saltan*, *The Snow Maiden*, *Mlada* and *Sadko*). The younger generation was represented by Sergey Rachmaninov, who performed his own Piano Concerto No. 1. The only truly daring choice was the planned world premiere of Alexander Scriabin's *Poème de l'extase*. But even though Scriabin worked 'day and night' to have the piece ready by the third week in May, he did not manage to finish in time.[13] It was replaced by two of his more conservative works, the Second Symphony and Piano Concerto.

This eclectic and somewhat imbalanced programme contained a great deal of rarely heard music, but there was little that could be called groundbreaking or adventurous. A number of pieces, including music by Lyapunov and the inevitable Alexander Taneyev, were downright weak. To transform this programme into the brilliant success he envisioned, Diaghilev had to engage the best and most spectacular instrumental soloists, vocalists and conductors.

The star was indisputably the bass Fyodor Chaliapin, who was already an established artist in the West, thanks to performances at major venues like La Scala. He was brought in for the quite reasonable sum of 1,200 roubles.[14] Other major soloists were the soprano Felia Litvin and the tenor Dmitry Smirnov. Diaghilev's greatest challenge, however, was recruiting the elderly Rimsky-Korsakov to conduct his own pieces. Widely regarded as the most important composer in Russia, Rimsky-Korsakov was the last living link to the music of Mussorgsky and Borodin. His presence was crucial to the artistic prestige of the series and to Diaghilev's faith in his own enterprise. But in principle the composer was still a member of Stasov's camp – albeit a fairly independent one – and his relationship with Diaghilev had not improved since the latter's abortive attempt to become his pupil years before. Diaghilev's tireless efforts to win over Rimsky-Korsakov sprang solely from his boundless admiration for the composer's talent.

At first Diaghilev's pleas fell on deaf ears. Rimsky-Korsakov had shown himself to be an obstinate man on other occasions, for instance during the student revolts, and he was unmoved by appeals to his vanity. Promises of fame and fortune were similarly ineffectual. His initial response gave little cause for hope: 'Paris? No! I'm not going to stand before an audience that didn't appreciate our Tchaikovsky.'[15]

Diaghilev wrote to him several times in the spring to consult with him and keep him apprised of the situation, all the while continuing to plead for his personal participation:

> I am not giving up hope of your taking part in Paris. For all the endless difficulties which this business presents, I can't work without the thought of support from a loved and dear teacher. Just think how sad you will make us with your refusal, and worse still – of the harm you will do to a cause for which you have expressed your sympathy. For God's sake, agree to our request, the journey won't be exhausting, we will take care of you in every way, we'll be at your complete disposal, and you will do us the greatest of favours and help us as no one else can.[16]

Sergey Diaghilev

Not long after, Rimsky-Korsakov paid several visits to Diaghilev in St Petersburg to discuss the matter further. Diaghilev wrote that the composer

> appeared in a huge fur coat and misted-over glasses, he was in a state, he wagged a long finger threateningly, he condemned the whole of French music, and then upon coming back home I suddenly found his little visiting card on which was written, "If one has to go, one has to go!" cried the sparrow as the cat dragged him downstairs.' And he went.[17]

That spring Diaghilev was also preoccupied with expanding his list of contacts in Paris and strengthening existing connections. The musicologist Michel Calvocoressi was an important collaborator, being not only an authority on Russian music (a rarity in France), but also conversant with the tastes of the French public. While continuing to work with the Comtesse Greffulhe (who arranged contacts with the beau monde) and Robert Brussel, the powerful music critic of *Le Figaro* (from whom the rest of the press took their lead), Diaghilev also became acquainted with Gabriel Astruc around this period. Astruc proved to be the right man at the right time. On the one hand, he was a serious businessman, who was active in the field of high culture. As a publisher he put out the music of Glinka, Rimsky-Korsakov and

Aleksandr Dargomizhsky, and as a concert promoter he had attempted to organise a European tour for Scriabin in 1904. But Astruc also had a good feel for the lowbrow end of the cultural market. In 1905, for example, he rushed to become the manager of Mata Hari, whose 'exotic' dancing was the talk of Paris. He was also at home with French bureaucratic codes, infrastructural issues and the workings of financial institutions – none of which Diaghilev knew anything about. This inevitably affected the power dynamic between the two men. It was not for nothing that Diaghilev was said to be 'completely under [Astruc's] thumb' and uncharacteristically 'quiet and modest' in Astruc's presence.[18]

The first concert was given on 16 May, in the presence of four grand dukes, the Russian ambassador, Richard Strauss (who sat in Diaghilev's box) and the cream of Parisian society.[19] The ovation that followed Chaliapin's performance of an aria from *Prince Igor* refused to die down, even after conductor Arthur Nikisch stepped up to the podium to begin the next piece (*Kamarinskaya* by Glinka). Nikisch attempted to calm the audience, but to no avail: again and again they called out for Chaliapin. Enraged, Nikisch threw down his baton and stormed off. Diaghilev recorded the scene:

> The audience didn't know what to do, many began to leave; in the gods they started to make a noise; in a moment of silence a booming Russian bass rang out from the top of the theatre through the whole auditorium, 'F*** your *Kamarinskaya*!' Grand Duke Vladimir Alexandrovich, who was sitting next to me in the box, got up and said to his wife, 'Well, Princess, I think it's time for us to be going home.' That was the end of my Parisian debut![20]

The following concerts, on 19, 23, 26 and 30 May, proceeded without incident, though the reception was no less enthusiastic. It seems, though, that this artistic triumph did not translate into financial success. According to Scriabin, 'some people lost out. One of them was Nicholas II … Yes, they say the loss from these concerts was 100,000 francs even though the theatre was packed.'[21]

If this is true, the parties in question evidently saw no reason to withdraw their support, for preparations for the next season of Russian music, which had started before the concerts even began, now shifted into top gear.

A highly unexpected visitor appeared in the person of Dima Filosofov, who had finally screwed up his courage and crossed the Seine. Diaghilev and Nouvel were happy to see him. Filosofov also attended the concerts and even spent the night in Diaghilev's hotel room.[22] When he confessed this to Gippius, she flew into a rage, calling Diaghilev 'that devil' and 'that stuffed shirt'.[23] But she had no cause to worry: this was nothing more than the dying gasp of their friendship and love.

In Paris, Diaghilev was far too busy to waste time thinking about this last encounter with Dima. Yet that summer, despite his many professional commitments, he would embark on a new relationship that was to have a profound influence on the rest of his life.

The seventeen-year-old dancer Vaslav Nijinsky was already a minor celebrity in the ballet world. The first reviews he received (one just before his sixteenth birthday, the other a year later) express wonderment at this manifestation of 'a rare natural gift' in a dancer with a 'phenomenal *ballon*'.[24] One critic wrote, 'His leaps are high, his elevation is such that he appears to fly through the air like a bird; his entrechat and pirouettes are daring and pure: he makes it look easy.'[25] Early on, critics realised that Nijinsky's talents went beyond his exceptional athletic abilities. 'The artistic quality of his dancing is extraordinary,' wrote the famous critic Valerian Svetlov, who later became one of Diaghilev's closest advisers, 'but he has also shown himself to be a gifted mime.'[26]

The relationship that would develop between the young dancer and the eighteen-year-older Diaghilev, which Richard Buckle describes as 'the most notorious since that of Oscar Wilde and Alfred Douglas',[27] has become the stuff of legend and controversy, and the accounts that have come down to us are often vague, contradictory and biased. In relating the story of their meeting I have relied heavily on Walter Nouvel, for two reasons. First of all, Nouvel was one of the few steadfast members of Diaghilev's inner circle throughout that period; indeed, the two were virtually inseparable. Secondly, since Nouvel's writings on the subject were never intended for publication, they are less likely to be tainted by the personal agendas, hidden and overt, that mar other accounts.[28]

In 1907 Nijinsky was under the protection of Prince Pavel Lvov. At that time it was customary for ballet dancers, male and female alike, to be 'looked after' by a patron who would finance them and introduce them to high society, typically in exchange for sexual favours. There was an implicit hierarchy whereby the best or most beautiful dancers paired off with the richest patrons, often through the intervention of a middleman.[29] This was exactly how Nijinsky came to the attention of the fabulously wealthy Pavel Lvov, a distinguished gentleman from a prominent family, who 'led an independent existence dedicated solely to the pursuit of pleasure'.[30] He had courted other dancers in the past, but 'Lvov's tastes were highly varied though he leaned more toward the stronger sex … He was a man of average intelligence, but of exceptional charm.'

Lvov was generous, showering Nijinsky with gifts and supporting his family, 'to the neglect of his own financial affairs, which were always a complete shambles'. Lvov admired Nijinsky as a dancer, but he was no ballet fanatic; if anything he was a sports aficionado. Even though he did not know Diaghilev well, Lvov encouraged the impresario 'to work with the young dancer to help cultivate his culture and talent'. According to Nouvel, Lvov became obsessed with 'the idea of coupling Nijinsky with Diaghilev'. Nijinsky was equally taken by this idea and, as Nouvel wrote, did everything 'to please Diaghilev and attract his attention'.

At first Diaghilev was less than charmed by Nijinsky, whose looks were not to his liking and whose conversational skills were rudimentary at best (hardly surprising, given his age). 'Despite Lvov's urgings and Nijinsky's unmistakable advances, Diaghilev maintained a cool reserve in his dealings with the young dancer.'

There has been a certain amount of speculation about why Lvov was so keen to bring Nijinsky into Diaghilev's fold. Surely, the prince knew of the older man's homosexual reputation. It seems unlikely that money had anything to do with it: Lvov was rich and Diaghilev poor. Some have suggested that, while Lvov admired Nijinsky's talent as a dancer, he was less enthusiastic about his amatory skills and was eager to get rid of him.[31] Nouvel, however, makes it clear that Nijinsky was at least as fervent in his pursuit of Diaghilev as Lvov. Nijinsky's biographers have always cast the dancer in the role of the victim, stressing his timid and helpless character[32] and portraying Lvov as a wicked sybarite who handed over a passive Nijinsky to Diaghilev on a whim. In reality, it would seem that Nijinsky was not the passive victim later observers claimed him to be. In the light of Nouvel's comments, Nijinsky's interest in Diaghilev seems to be a classic case of a young person taking an older lover to further his career, intellectual growth and social development. That would explain Diaghilev's initial reluctance to respond to Nijinsky's advances. Maybe Lvov was eager to unload Nijinsky on someone else, or maybe he was genuinely interested in the artistic growth of his protégé and knew that Diaghilev would have much to offer in this respect.

During the winter of 1907–8 Diaghilev and Nijinsky dined in the company of Lvov and Nouvel on three occasions. In late December, Diaghilev 'spoke highly of Nijinsky'[33] to Kuzmin, whom he asked for advice about the situation, though according to Nouvel made no decision. In the early spring of the following year Diaghilev returned to Paris to continue working on his new programme for the Grand Opéra, and for the next few months, Nijinsky was out of sight.

This new programme sought to redress the one major shortcoming of its predecessor – the absence of staged opera. The new season at the Paris Opéra would be the first to showcase *Boris Godunov*, considered by many to be Russia's greatest opera, and possibly *Sadko* by Rimsky-Korsakov. Both productions would again require the collaboration of Rimsky-Korsakov, in the case of *Boris* because Diaghilev preferred to work with Rimsky-Korsakov's reorchestration, rather than Mussorgsky's original version.

The plan was to stage *Boris* in Russian and *Sadko* in French. Before the Second World War it was common practice to present operas in the language of the country where they were performed. In Amsterdam, for instance, Tchaikovsky was sung in Dutch. All the costumes and sets were specially made for the production, so they could be left in Paris for possible revivals. Diaghilev had other plans, for which he would need Rimsky's help. In early June lengthy negotiations got under way, straining Diaghilev's charm to the utmost. 'I very much hope you will help us in this respect and will believe that I am wholly enthusiastic about this idea, which seems brilliant.'[34]

Shortly after his first letter of 5 June, Rimsky-Korsakov invited the impresario to visit him at his country estate, but Diaghilev declined, for practical reasons. Diaghilev had to reassure the chauvinistic Rimsky-Korsakov that they would not go out of their way to conform to the tastes of the French. That was no easy task, as Diaghilev already planned on making a number of significant cuts to both operas. Since his first encounter with the work of

Rimsky-Korsakov, by Serov

Wagner in Bayreuth, he felt that most operas should be abridged, especially new or unfamiliar works: '... one mustn't forget that even someone as impatient as Wagner hesitated before putting *Tannhäuser* on in Paris and even ... rewrote it for Paris ... the only good lecturer is one who knows his audience and does not despise those he is addressing'.[35]

Diaghilev gradually tried to prepare Rimsky-Korsakov for the shock of losing a number of crucial scenes in both operas. The following excerpt of a letter of 11 August is a witty highlight of Diaghilev's campaign of persuasion. By mocking a Petersburg performance of *Boris Godunov* at the Olympia summer theatre, he hints at his own plans for Paris.

Yesterday I went off and saw the first performance of *Boris* on the stage of the wooden Olympia theatre. In general it was done decently and the music was superb but … I cannot remember a more tiring evening. They put us in reasonably comfortable seats at 8.30, when it was already completely dark, and let us go at 12.30, when everything was shrouded in stinking fog and the sewage-disposal carts trundled to meet us along Basseynaya with the drivers dozing on the box.

During this endless period we were treated to numerous musical tableaux, a few *absolutely perfect* musical sensations and no fewer than seven identical, intolerably offensive intervals: seven times they lowered the curtain in front of our noses with its advertisement for Omega watches and Pink laxative pills; seven times my neighbour, a civil servant in the Excise, took his fat spouse out for an airing; seven times the same young man appeared in the next box and seven times said the same banalities to the same young ladies. It was intolerable, there was something wrong with it, it lacked any kind of architecture.

When I got home about one in the morning … I opened a score of *Boris* published in Mussorgsky's lifetime and with some amazement read on its first page the following informative words: '*A complete arrangement* for piano and singers, *including the scenes which are not intended for stage performance.*'

The hour was late and I thought I was beginning to hallucinate through exhaustion. Next to it lay the piano score of *Sadko* but I couldn't now bring myself to look in it. What if, I thought, it too included something equally unexpected![36]

Unfortunately for Diaghilev, Rimsky struck back with iron logic:

If *Sadko* in its present form is too difficult for the imbecile French audience in its tails, which drops into the theatre for a little while and pays heed to the venal press and its hired claques, then it shouldn't be put on.

If my opera is fated to enjoy a long life on this earth and not languish or fade away, then its time will come and the French will hear it out, but if it isn't, then its life won't be prolonged by a giddy French success. An author doesn't agree to the mutilation of his work, especially since by doing so, he sanctions such mutilations for ever and the opera will go on everywhere with ugly cuts.[37]

The remarks about claques and the 'venal press' may have cut a little too close to the bone for Diaghilev. 'Your last letter hurt me deeply,' he wrote to

Rimsky. 'I will refrain from going into the painful details and confine myself to the most essential points.'[38] As an alternative form of truncation, Diaghilev then suggested performing selected acts, unabridged, from *Sadko*, rather than the whole opera. Rimsky agreed,[39] and Diaghilev presented this compromise to the management of the Opéra. On 17 November, Diaghilev wired Rimsky from Paris that an agreement had been reached and that *Sadko* would be performed in October 1908.[40] And this was the very last that was ever heard about this planned collaboration: *Sadko* would never be produced by Diaghilev.[41] The exact reason is unclear, but in all likelihood Diaghilev began to realise that the high cost of an opera like *Boris* would preclude a second production.

In early 1908 Diaghilev signed a contract in Paris for *Boris Godunov*, stipulating that the performances take place on 19, 21, 24, 26 and 31 May. The director of the Opéra, Leimistin Broussan, was brought to St Petersburg and received in audience by Nicholas II. Chaliapin and Smirnov were again hired to sing the leads, the former for the princely sum of 55,000 francs.[42] The production would be directed by Alexander Sanin, a veteran of Stanislavsky's Moscow Art Theatre and an old hand at managing large crowd scenes.[43] The chorus was from the Bolshoy Theatre in Moscow, as were a group of Russian stage managers headed by theatre technician Karl Valts. According to Valts, they were there because 'foreign manual labour was extremely expensive',[44] but Diaghilev also wanted to forestall any potential problems with the Opéra's technical staff. By that winter, preparations were in full swing, and Paris was awash with Russians.

Diaghilev had invited a group of artists – Konstantin Korovin, Ivan Bilibin, Aleksander Golovin and Benois – to design the sets and costumes.[45] Conceptually speaking, the production was rooted in neo-nationalism, an artistic movement long past its early-nineteenth-century heyday. 'Early' Mir-iskusniki determined the overall look of the production, and the direction emphasised illusionistic and naturalistic elements. For this first production Diaghilev fell back on trusted methods, eschewing wild conceptual experimentation. Yet it was the unique costume and sets that distinguished this *Boris* from previous productions.

Diaghilev sent Bilibin, who had published a monograph on arts and crafts in northern Russia, to villages and settlements in Archangelsk and Vologodskaya to buy old *sarafans* (traditional dresses), embroidered fabric and head coverings. According to Diaghilev, the garments and material were 'so valuable and beautiful that I organised an exhibition of them at the Imperial Hermitage, at the request of Grand Duke Vladimir'.[46] Diaghilev and Benois themselves browsed the Jewish and Tatar booths at the Alexander market in St Petersburg. 'Sergey was particularly smitten by the headscarves embroidered with gold and sequins. It was his idea to use them to make turn-down collars for the boyars' kaftans and coats.'[47]

Thus the costumes for *Boris Godunov* were assembled from a wide variety of traditional fabrics, representing different regions and frequently divorced from their traditional context. The end result was far from the authentic presentation of medieval Russia the makers promised. Rather, it was one big multiethnic, ahistorical hotchpotch of the most eye-catching exotica the Russian empire could offer. It was this very quality, this hyperbolic visual free-for-all, that would be Diaghilev's recipe for success during his first five years at the theatre.

The technical preparations at the Opéra proceeded in frenzied chaos, as the aristocratic management and the labourers of this venerable French institution locked horns with the hundreds of imported Russians – '*une horde des barbares*' – only three of whom spoke good French.[48] There were constant conflicts between the Parisian technicians and the Russians, which Diaghilev managed to smooth over thanks to his authority and strategic acumen. At least, that's how Benois tells it. Diaghilev himself attributes his success as a mediator to the substantial bribes he regularly slipped to the technicians.[49]

Three days before the premiere the whole production was still in a state of utter disarray. The technical installations had not yet been tested, and the backdrops had still not been hung.[50] Diaghilev remembered being told that they would not be able to erect the sets in their entirety until the day of the premiere. He decided to call a meeting of the whole team – carpenters, technicians and make-up artists – and ask the assembled crew what they wanted to do: postpone the premiere or let the show go on as scheduled? 'Plainly Sergey was seriously concerned,' wrote Benois, 'considering that he resorted to such "democratic" methods, which was certainly not his typical way of working.'[51] Amid cries of 'We mustn't disgrace Russia' and 'We won't go down without a fight', the carpenters and make-up artists insisted that the opera would go on as planned.[52]

A dress rehearsal was out of the question. On the night before the premiere, Chaliapin was so nervous that he ended up spending the night on Diaghilev's sofa. As Diaghilev wrote, 'The sets had to be hung without any mistakes in a theatre which none of us knew, sets which no one [in the company] had yet seen in their entirety … The sets were hung a few minutes before the beginning of the performance. I barely had the strength to stand when the curtain went up.'[53] Dressed in a tailcoat and white gloves, he helped the stage managers set out the props during the intermission.

Boris Godunov met with a rapturous reception. There was already a warm ovation before the first intermission, and by the end the audience could no longer contain its enthusiasm. The imperial court was not represented at the first performance, fearing a scandal, but after the initial notices began trickling in, Grand Duke Vladimir went to Paris to congratulate Diaghilev and the rest of the company.

One member of the audience that night was a Franco-Polish pianist and socialite, with Russian and Belgian roots. Married no fewer than three times, she had several surnames in her lifetime, but she is best known today as Misia Sert (the Spanish painter José-Maria Sert was her first lover and her third husband). A patroness of the arts, she had a famous salon in Paris and sat for such renowned painters as Renoir, Félix Vallotton, Vuillard, Toulouse-Lautrec and Bonnard. Misia was almost the same age as Sergey (she was born on 30 March 1872), and she never knew her mother, who died in childbirth. Such coincidences were of great significance to Diaghilev, who believed deeply in omens and mystic links.

Misia was so impressed by *Boris Godunov* that she not only attended every performance but also bought up all the unsold tickets and distributed them among her friends. Although Misia and Sergey had already met in 1899, it wasn't until May 1908 that their acquaintance blossomed into friendship. They saw each other at Pruniers and struck up a conversation: 'We remained [at the restaurant] until five in the morning,' wrote Misia, 'and found it intolerable to have to part. The next day he came to see me, and our friendship ended only with his death.'[54]

The friendship between the two was indeed close and would profoundly influence Diaghilev's work in the theatre. It could be argued that Misia Sert was the most important woman in Diaghilev's life after his stepmother, whose place she came to occupy.

Drunk on champagne, Diaghilev's entourage staggered home, arm in arm, after the premiere. Benois's hotel was separated from Diaghilev's by a small courtyard, and the two friends continued to converse through their windows for the rest of the night. At daybreak the 'esteemed gentleman' Pavka Koribut tumbled into Benois's room in a state of prodigious intoxication. 'After all the tensions of the past few weeks, he couldn't sleep and moaned that he needed to pour out his heart to a friendly soul.'[55] When he realised he could talk to dear old Seryozha through the window, he began to shout so loudly to his cousin that the other guests opened their windows to vent their feelings. Benois finally managed to yank Pavka away from the window and steer him to the sofa.

Upon returning to St Petersburg, Sergey was met by an admirer. Stories about Diaghilev's Parisian triumph had spread far and wide, nowhere more so than in the grand corridors of the Imperial Theatres, where Nijinsky was taking daily lessons and rehearsing. Now as never before, Nijinsky realised that Diaghilev had more to offer than Lvov.

Nouvel spent two days at Lvov's estate, where Nijinsky also lived. According to Nouvel, Nijinsky was in a foul mood the whole time, prompting Lvov to complain about his young friend's difficult and capricious character and penchant for making scenes. 'He also spoke to me of Nijinsky's admiration for D.[iaghilev] and returned again and again to his aim of bringing D. and the young man closer together, claiming that this was his most fervent wish.'[56]

Sometime around the early autumn of 1908 Nijinsky started to become intimate with Diaghilev, and Lvov gradually faded from the scene. This was the start of a passionate, five-year love affair, which would cast its light (and shadow) on far more than the lives of these two men alone.

· 14 ·

The Rise of the Ballets Russes
1908–1909

EARLY THAT SUMMER, shortly after the last performance of *Boris Godunov*, Diaghilev was back in St Petersburg, busy forming a committee to organise a new season in Paris, this time to include ballet. Since the Opéra was not available, Diaghilev had to shift operations to the Théâtre du Châtelet, normally a venue for operetta and variety shows. The first committee meeting, which was attended by Bakst, Nouvel and Prince Argutinsky among others, took place on 29 June.

The plan to feature ballet as well as opera in the 1909 programme had been in the works for some time, as dance became more and more important to the Miriskusniki. As an anti-naturalistic art form that married the sensual to the formal, ballet was the ideal vehicle for the group's aesthetic programme. Benois summed up their position thus in 1908:

> Ballet is perhaps the most eloquent of all spectacles inasmuch as it allows two of the supreme conductors of thought – music and gesture – to display all their fullness and depth, without imposing words on them; words which always put fetters on thought, bringing it down from heaven to earth. Ballet possesses that sense of liturgical ritual of which we have lately dreamt so intensely.[1]

It was precisely this 'liturgical' aspect of ballet that promised to bring together the full range of sensual experience in the way envisaged by the Miriskusniki. Though Diaghilev's *Sylvia* project had fallen through, they still hoped to propagate their ideas through ballet. In the early years of the new century, both Bakst and Benois had made a name for themselves as theatrical designers. It was Bakst who was the first to take on a ballet. In 1903 the Imperial Theatres asked him to design *Feya Kukol* (the Russian version of *Die Puppenfee*, the classic Austrian ballet that Diaghilev had seen in Vienna in 1890). In 1905 Diaghilev and the ballet critic Valerian Svetlov tried to set up a society to promote ballet. They apparently got as far as renting an apartment for meetings, but the initiative died a quick death.[2]

Within a year, though, Diaghilev's plans to stage ballets in Paris were well on their way to fruition. Back in the days when he was preparing for the exhibition at the Salon d'automne, he had talked to the tsar's uncle the Grand Duke Vladimir about his wish to bring Russian opera and ballet to Paris, the ballets being *Raymonda* (Glazunov) and *Pavillon d'Armide* (Nikolay Tcherepnin), together with a new commission.[3] When Robert Brussel visited Diaghilev in Russia in the winter of 1906–7, he too was told about the latter's plans to bring the imperial ballet to Paris.[4]

Of all the items on this wish list, *Pavillon d'Armide* is the most striking. It was far from finished in 1906: only Tcherepnin's score and Benois's libretto had been completed. Why should Diaghilev have included a work whose performance was such a distant reality?

The germ of the idea of *Pavillon d'Armide* dated back to 1902, shortly after Diaghilev's dismissal from the Imperial Theatres. Benois was looking for a theme for a ballet to be written by the young composer Nikolay Tcherepnin and found it in the form of a story by one of his heroes, Théophile Gautier. Gautier was a nineteenth-century French writer, poet and critic, whose works included ballet librettos and plays. In the diversity of his output and his productivity Benois even resembled his hero somewhat – perhaps through conscious imitation. But Benois was not alone in his admiration. The Miriskusniki as a whole were greatly influenced by Gautier, and his reverence for ballet as an art form (he was the librettist of *Giselle*) undoubtedly strengthened their conviction that ballet could be the medium for great art. Tcherepnin was soon won over to the idea and wrote the music in 1901. However, the project stalled as relations between the Miriskusniki and the management of the Imperial Theatres deteriorated.

Tcherepnin, by Benois

In 1907 Benois was approached by the innovative young choreographer Mikhail (or Michel) Fokine, who volunteered to choreograph *Pavillon d'Armide*. Progress was rapid, and the ballet premiered on 25 November of that year at the Mariinsky Theatre, with Anna Pavlova, Pavel Gerdt and Vaslav Nijinsky – whom Diaghilev had just met for the first time – in the leading roles.[5] At Fokine's request, Benois had gone so far as to insert a new role in the libretto, so as to exhibit Nijinsky's talents to the full. And it was, incidentally, Nijinsky's unparalleled talent as a dancer, far more than his personal charms, that opened Diaghilev's eyes to the seventeen-year-old.

The premiere of *Pavillon d'Armide* marked a new era in the ballet culture of St Petersburg, the first collaboration between the most progressive dancers and choreographers of the Imperial Theatres and the Miriskusniki: a collective that would ultimately be responsible for all the new productions of the Ballets Russes in the first three years of its existence. Fokine was a pivotal figure in this professional union. No mean dancer himself, since 1905 he had been cementing his reputation as one of the most notable young choreographers of the capital. A man of formidable drive, he produced no fewer than two dozen choreographies between February 1906 and March 1909.[6] Russian dance had become dusty and antiquated, and Fokine tried to invigorate it with ideas from the world of theatre. In doing so he took his inspiration from a variety of sources: from the naturalist theories of Konstantin Stanislavsky to the symbolism of Vsevolod Meyerhold. And though Fokine's innovations were by no means radical – he never departed from classic ballet techniques – official circles looked on him with extreme disfavour. The vast majority of his choreographies had to be produced outside the official circuit, to his great displeasure, for his ambition seemed suited only to the largest houses. His association with the Miriskusniki was born more of shared frustration at the intractability of the artistic establishment than of a common aesthetic programme.

Ballet occupied a much more prominent place in Russia's performing arts culture than in that of any other European country, even France or Italy, the birthplace of classical ballet at the beginning of the nineteenth century. It enjoyed considerable standing in court circles, as well as generous funding. The Russians had the best ballet schools in the world and recruited Europe's top instructors and choreographers. From 1870, Russian ballet underwent a renaissance under the inspired direction of the Petersburg ballet master Marius Petipa. After 1890, however, it seemed as if Petipa had run out of ideas, and the new generation of ballet aficionados, headed by Diaghilev and his group, became bored with the imperial ballet productions.

The debut of the American dancer Isadora Duncan in Petersburg on 13 December 1904 was to have a defining effect on the capital's dance culture. Duncan categorically rejected classical ballet, which was by now more or less standardised throughout Europe (with slight national variations). To her, expression and improvisation were more important than technique and fixed choreographies. She danced barefoot, in a revealing Greek tunic, to music that had not been written especially for the ballet (by composers such as Wagner, Beethoven and Chopin). Fokine, Diaghilev, Bakst and Benois saw her dance in 1904 and were deeply impressed. They joined her at a dinner at Anna Pavlova's house after her performance.[7]

'Duncanism', which Nouvel described as a 'violent revolt against Petipa's routine',[8] became the subject of heated debate. Some years later, Diaghilev was very definite about Duncan's influence on the genesis of the Ballets Russes. 'We do not deny that Duncan is a kindred spirit. Indeed, we carry the torch that she lit.'[9]

In *Mir iskusstva*'s later years, Diaghilev had been highly critical of the premieres of imperial ballet performances under Telyakovsky, and his biting attack after Legat's suicide had not gone unnoticed by progressive dancers and choreographers. It seemed only a matter of time before the Miriskusniki extended their activities to the world of ballet.

The production of *Pavillon d'Armide* in 1907 proved to be a tremendous headache. Benois was initially given considerable artistic and financial leeway, but his overspending and headstrong manner soon led to clashes with the management. When Diaghilev arrived to view a rehearsal, he found his way barred by a police officer who 'requested [him] politely but firmly to leave the theatre', which made Diaghilev 'feel as bitter as when he'd been fired'.[10] Upset by all the commotion, Matilda Kshesinskaya, the prima ballerina who was to dance the leading role, walked out shortly before the premiere. Anna Pavlova, a brilliant young dancer who had been one of the leaders of the student rebellion of 1905, volunteered to stand in for Kshesinskaya. *Pavillon d'Armide* thus became the exclusive product and artistic manifesto of a new generation.

When Diaghilev decided to bring Russian ballet to France in 1909, *Pavillon d'Armide* was his first choice. He was also set on staging Rimsky-Korsakov's *Maid of Pskov*. That opera had been on his list right from the start, but by 1908 it had become an absolute necessity, being an ideal vehicle for the great bass Fyodor Chaliapin, whose superstar status dictated that he feature prominently on the bill. Other productions initially considered by Diaghilev included the ballet *Giselle*, Borodin's opera *Prince Igor* and a reprise of *Boris Godunov*.

Such a wide-ranging programme required far greater organisational capacity than had been needed for *Boris Godunov*. So the role of the 'committee', as Diaghilev called the band of aficionados and professionals that he had grouped around himself, became ever more important. During the winter of 1908, besides Bakst, Benois, Nouvel and Fokine, the group included Prince Argutinsky, Valerian Svetlov, the balletomane General Bezobrazov and Sergey Grigoriev. The last of these, a former dancer, had been sent to Diaghilev by Fokine on account of his organisational talents. Svetlov gave a detailed description of the committee's working methods and atmosphere:

> The new Diaghilev ballet does things quite differently. It brings together artists, composers, ballet masters, writers and in general people who are close to art, and together they discuss the plan of the coming work. A

subject is put forward and then worked out in detail. One person makes
a suggestion as it comes into his head, the others either accept or reject it,
making it difficult to establish who is the true author of a libretto in this
collective creative enterprise. Of course, it's the one who puts forward the
idea for a work; but the corrections, the elaboration, the details belong
to everyone. After that the character of the music and the dances is
collectively discussed ... That's why there is a unity of artistic intent and
execution.[11]

One of the advantages of this method was that all those involved felt
collectively responsible for the success of the venture. Of the committee
members, only Diaghilev, Benois and Nouvel had any experience with organising this kind of international event. Neither Fokine nor Grigoriev spoke a
word of French. The project was far more ambitious than that of the preceding season. There were now eight productions for which sets and costumes
had to be designed and made. An army of dancers somehow had to be transported to France, to say nothing of an entire opera company, complete with
orchestra and choir. All the opera and ballet soloists, and the conductors of
the choir and orchestra had to be contracted separately. There was no handy
infrastructure; rehearsal rooms, costume studios and set-building workshops
all had to be found and rented. Diaghilev ordered much of the music to be
reorchestrated, or replaced entirely. As a result, many of the productions could
not use existing scores, and all the parts had to be copied out by hand, which
in turn necessitated extra rehearsals.

In this way, eight premieres – enough to fill three evening programmes
– were produced in the space of a few months. An incredible feat, when one
considers that the largest modern opera and ballet companies (with elaborate
professional machinery in place and the latest technology and means of production) would devote years of preparation to such an undertaking.

In his search for funding Diaghilev turned, as he had before, to wealthy individuals and to the tsar. He managed, once again, to extract a huge contribution from Hendrik van Gilse van der Pals and other rubber barons. Sergey
and his friends sniggeringly referred to the manufacturers as the *galoshisty*, or
'the rubber gang', a nickname that has the same prophylactic connotations in
Russian as it does in English.[12] To cut costs Diaghilev decided not to make

costumes and sets as they had done in 1908, but to borrow them from the Imperial Theatres. In October 1908 he tried to persuade Telyakovsky to lend him what they needed, but could only get his hands on costumes for *The Maid of Pskov*.[13] Diaghilev then appealed to his old patron, Grand Duke Vladimir, who put the case to Tsar Nicolas. By January 1909, 'the matter of propagating Russian art in the West had fallen under the personal patronage of His Imperial Highness'.[14] The Tsar gave Diaghilev 25,000 roubles (out of a total budget of 120,000) and access to rehearsal rooms and workshops, though the impresario was once again refused the use of existing costumes.[15] All this support had been promised on an informal basis; Diaghilev had yet to receive official written confirmation of Nicholas' patronage. The tsar was legendary for his indecisiveness, and this should have given Diaghilev pause.

Little by little the programme began to take shape. Besides *Giselle*, a showcase for Pavlova in her best role, it included a series of ballets by Fokine. His choreographic suite *Chopiniana* had been a hit at the premiere of 1908, and Diaghilev wanted to put it on in Paris too, though under the name *Les Sylphides*. Duncan's influence was much more evident in this ballet, which was plotless and danced to pre-existing music (orchestrated piano pieces by Chopin). *Les Sylphides* entered history as the first 'abstract' ballet, and it prefigured the future of dance more than any other Diaghilev production in the early years of the Ballets Russes.

The two other ballets to be presented that season were *Cléopâtre* and *Le Festin*. The first was a reworking of Fokine's 1908 ballet *Egyptian Nights*, which had originally been danced to music by Anton Arensky. Diaghilev, however, found the score too monotonous; his plan was to create variety by adding a dash of Glazunov, Rimsky-Korsakov, Mussorgsky, Sergey Taneyev and Tcherepnin. In an effort to convince Fokine and Nouvel, Diaghilev demonstrated the pieces he had chosen on the piano. 'He played very well,' wrote Grigoriev, 'biting his tongue throughout, especially during the tricky passages.'[16] Nouvel saw straightaway that the work would suffer from such a jumble of musical styles, dismissing the final product as a 'mediocre "salade russe"'.[17] Musically speaking, he was right, but the ballet's historical importance lay not in its musical concept or choreography, but in its launch of two of Diaghilev's new stars: Lev Bakst and Ida Rubinstein. At the age of forty-two, the former suddenly found a new calling, creating exotic sets and costumes that conjured up the Mysterious East. His costumes were graceful, outlandish and unabashedly erotic. Combining a Beardsleyesque line with daring colour schemes, he never missed a chance to dazzle his audience with the glitter of bejewelled fabrics or tantalise them with flashes of painted skin.

Ida Rubinstein, who danced the lead role, was a recent discovery of Bakst's. An orphan from a fabulously wealthy family of Jewish industrialists, she had decided some years earlier to devote her personal fortune to the pursuit of an artistic career. She asked Fokine to teach her to dance and Bakst to design costumes for the performances she staged. As a dancer she lacked classical skills, but her body language was unusually expressive. On 20 December 1908, in the main auditorium of the conservatory, she performed the Dance of the Seven Veils from Wilde's play *Salomé* to music by Glazunov, casting aside the last veil to appear completely naked before the audience. Benois was most impressed: 'To achieve her artistic aims she was prepared to test the limits of social tolerance and even decency – indeed, to go so far as to bare herself in public.'[18]

The performance provoked a scandal, less so because of the nudity than the subject matter itself. The Russian Orthodox Church strictly forbade any depiction of sacred characters on stage, and the Holy Synod had accordingly banned *Salomé*. But the ban applied specifically to the text of Wilde's play, and the resourceful Rubinstein decided there was nothing to prevent a mimed version of the work. The authorities were not amused. On the day of the performance, the police arrived to impound the papier-mâché head of John the Baptist that Rubinstein had used as a prop in the Dance of the Seven Veils. But the show went ahead – albeit headless.

The last Fokine ballet, *Le Festin*, was even more of a 'salade russe' than *Cléopâtre*, being little more than an excuse to show off Nijinsky's talents. Besides the *Maid of Pskov* (renamed *Ivan le Terrible* for the Paris performance) the programme featured isolated acts from a number of other operas: the second act of Borodin's *Prince Igor* (which also included spectacular dances choreographed by Fokine) and the first act of Glinka's *Ruslan and Lyudmila*. At that stage (early 1909), a reprise of *Boris Godunov* was still being planned.

Allocating dance roles proved problematic. St Petersburg had two big female stars, Anna Pavlova and *prima ballerina assoluta* Matilda Kshesinskaya. The latter was thirty-six (almost as old as Diaghilev) and clearly past her prime. But she had been the mistress of Nicholas II when as tsarevich he had sowed his wild oats, and enjoyed the protection of the court. She had to be involved, if only because of her closeness to the Romanovs. She did not get on well with Fokine, though, and he was violently opposed to her dancing either in *Giselle* or *Les Sylphides*. Under pressure from Diaghilev, he reluctantly assigned her the leading role in *Pavillon d'Armide*, which she had earlier refused in 1907. This did not mollify her, however. She loathed the notion of playing second fiddle to Pavlova, who was clearly intended to be the star of the Paris programme. Kshesinskaya plotted revenge, but could do little while Diaghilev still enjoyed the protection of the tsar's uncle, Grand Duke Vladimir.

But everything changed abruptly when the latter suddenly died on 4 February 1909. A shocked Diaghilev hastened to his palace on the bank of the Neva, where the body lay in state. Vladimir Alexandrovich had only recently come to his aid when he was accused of having lost considerable sums of money, and the memory of their last conversation, in which the grand duke had kissed him and made the sign of the cross over him 'to protect him against intrigues', was still a vivid memory. Diaghilev wrote in his memoirs: 'I got to the palace before everyone else and went into the room where Vladimir Alexandrovich lay on a bier. I wept and suddenly I saw beside me the figure of a man. It was the tsar. He came in, crossed himself, looked at me and said to me as if replying to something, "Yes, he was very fond of you."'[19]

This anecdote is reminiscent of the account of Tchaikovsky's death, in which Diaghilev also constructed a special, personal relationship around the passing of a revered figure. Whatever the truth of the matter, the story shows how much Diaghilev was affected by the death of his patron, and how the subject of death continued to fascinate him.

Whether or not the tsar materialised like a benign ghost in the chamber where the body lay, scarcely a month later he was to prove much less well disposed towards Diaghilev. On 3 March Diaghilev asked Alexander Mossolov, the head of the chancery, for permission to rehearse in the tsar's personal theatre at the Hermitage. On 11 March Mossolov informed him that the tsar had no objection, and that same day Diaghilev moved in with his entire entourage, sets and costumes. Rehearsals started immediately. 'During the breaks, the tsar's footmen brought us tea and hot chocolate,' Chaliapin recalled.[20] On 14 March Nicholas even went so far as to officially place the entire enterprise under the protection of the court, naming the rakish Grand Duke Boris (one of the sons of the lately deceased Vladimir Alexandrovich) as official patron. But, as the Psalmist so wisely enjoined, 'Put not your trust in princes'. On 17 March a telegram arrived ordering the immediate cessation of rehearsals and the seizure of sets and costumes. It was signed 'Nicholas'.[21]

The news came like a thunderclap. Why had the tsar suddenly gone back on his offer? Why was he now so set against the venture? Word had it that it was Kshesinskaya's doing. Insulted at being given an insignificant role, she was said to have used her influence with Grand Duke Andrey Vladimirovich (another son of Diaghilev's late patron, whose mistress she was and whom she later married) to get her own back. Diaghilev, meanwhile, invoked the aid of the duke's brother Boris, in an attempt to change the tsar's mind. A day later, Andrey Vladimirovich wrote the following letter to Nicholas:

> Your telegram wrought terrible havoc in the Diaghilev camp and to save his dirty little enterprise, Diaghilev used every trick in the book, from flattery right through to lies.
>
> Tomorrow Boris is in attendance on you. According to all the information we have, he has been moved by Diaghilev's lies and is going to ask you ... to return the costumes and sets for Paris. We very much hope you won't swallow this bait ... it would be just pandering to a dirty business that is a blot on the good name of our late father.[22]

On 20 March Diaghilev wrote to Baron Frederiks asking him to 'help win back the tsar's favour' but Frederiks refused to assist him.[23]

What Kshesinskaya told the tsar to make him change his mind remains a matter for conjecture. There was certainly enough damning material to choose from. First, there was the growing talk about Diaghilev's intimate relationship with the young star of the Imperial Theatres' dance troupe. The scandal surrounding Ida Rubinstein must also have come to Nicholas' ears. Her performance had, after all, been banned by the Holy Synod. And, finally, Diaghilev's open support for the striking dancers in 1905 had also caused irritation. Homosexual entrepreneurs, blasphemous Jews, mutinous dancers – grounds enough, possibly, to make Nicholas withdraw his support.

With only two months to go before the premiere in Paris, Diaghilev had lost all his sets and had nowhere to rehearse. He telegraphed Astruc, who was still managing his affairs in Paris, telling him that the Russian programme could not go ahead unless he drummed up extra local sponsorship.[24] Astruc managed to raise the money within a few weeks, with the help of the Comtesse Greffulhe and Misia Sert (at the time married to the newspaper magnate Alfred Edwards). Though by no means sufficient, it at least covered the initial costs and gave backers confidence that the show would go on. Diaghilev used subscribers' financial pledges and advances on ticket sales to cover running costs, pushing poor Astruc to the brink of bankruptcy.[25]

Within a day of leaving the Hermitage, Diaghilev had found somewhere else to rehearse: the Catherine Hall on the eponymous canal (now Griboyedov Canal). Benois recalled the motley caravan that wound from the Hermitage to the new premises: 'M[avrin] and I headed the procession in one cab, all our artists, dressers with their baskets and stage hands followed behind in others. The long procession stretched across the whole town ... The atmosphere of adventure – almost of a picnic – seemed to soften our slight feeling of shame at having been "turned out".'[26]

Diaghilev's opponents were shocked by his refusal to even think of abandoning the project; his dogged persistence was a continuing source of amazement to the court. On 19 March the Grand Duke Andrey wrote to his brother: 'He is continuing the work on a wholly private basis and thinks the enterprise completely sure of success both without patronage and without sets.'[27]

As Diaghilev himself wrote a year later, 'There was nothing for it but to have all the sets, costumes and props made again ... at superhuman effort and cost'.[28] A few changes did have to be made to the programme. *Boris Godunov* had to be scrapped, as did *Giselle*. *Judith* replaced *Boris*, but no real alternative could be found for *Giselle*.

Diaghilev now met with another major setback. Anna Pavlova, the intended star of the programme, turned out to have organised her own tour of European cities (including Berlin, Vienna and Prague), fearing that Diaghilev's venture might fall through. The cancellation of *Giselle* must have only strengthened her resolve. Pavlova was the only one of the dancers whose fame had spread to Europe. She was regarded as the greatest ballerina in Russia, and therefore the world. Diaghilev had ordered giant posters to be made of her (based on a chalk portrait by Serov), to be displayed all over Paris. He tried desperately to persuade her to cancel her tour, but she remained adamant. In the end, she did come to Paris after completing her own performances, two weeks after Diaghilev's season opened.

Pavlova, by Bakst

Pavlova's initial absence had two consequences. The first was to greatly increase the publicity surrounding Nijinsky, invariably billed as 'the new Vestris' – a reference to Auguste Vestris, a legendary French dancer of the late eighteenth century. The second was to launch the career of Tamara Karsavina, the dancer who would take over most of Pavlova's roles in the first two weeks. Karsavina lacked Pavlova's technical perfection, but she was highly intelligent (her book *Theatre Street* stands out among the memoirs about the Ballets Russes), much less conservative than Pavlova and considerably more interested in the artistic development of dance. In her memoirs, Karsavina comes across as a warm, creative person with the spirit of a peacemaker. A faithful and affectionate friend to Diaghilev, she helped to bind the new company together.

Rehearsals at the Catherine Hall began at four o'clock on 2 April 1909. The only prior rehearsal (at the Hermitage) had been for an opera, so the ballet company was now assembled for the first time. Diaghilev had not yet met many of the dancers. Grigoriev introduced them to him and, in seigneurial manner, Diaghilev gave a brief speech expressing the hope that they would all be able to work harmoniously together. He added that he was 'very happy to give Paris its first taste of Russian ballet – as I believe ballet to be the most charming of the arts, and our ballet to be unique in Europe'.[29]

Despite the great tension they must have been under, the mood (according to all who recalled the preparations in St Petersburg) was exceptionally amicable, cheerful and inspired. The dancers of the Imperial Theatres were used to a strict, official regime, and Benois reports that they relished the easy, informal atmosphere.[30] They were apparently indifferent to the malicious rumours being spread by the court, for instance, that they were dancing in the nude, and that Diaghilev's enterprise was an anti-government cabal.[31]

After a month of rehearsals, the dancers left for Paris on 2 May. Diaghilev arrived a day later. Shortly before his departure he arranged a last meeting with Prince Lvov, who had hinted that he wanted to follow Nijinsky to Paris. According to Nijinsky's mother, Diaghilev demanded that Nijinsky break off the relationship, telling the prince that if he genuinely wished Nijinsky well, he would remain in Russia. Lvov not only agreed; he went so far as to give Diaghilev money to fund his Paris programme. On the day of their departure, the prince visited Nijinsky's mother and sister Bronya, and took tearful leave of them.[32]

On arrival in Paris the 250 dancers, singers and technicians, plus an eighty-piece orchestra, took over the Théâtre du Châtelet.[33] The dancers stayed in little hotels on Boulevard Saint-Michel. Nijinsky, his mother and sister (who was also in the dance troupe) boarded in a hotel on rue Danou, not far from the Hôtel de Hollande, where Diaghilev and Mavrin were staying. The latter had made himself very useful in the previous hectic months – indeed, he had become indispensable – but his presence was becoming awkward as Diaghilev and Nijinsky grew increasingly open about their affair. For the time being, though, tensions had to be kept bottled up, because there simply wasn't time for romantic drama.

The publicity had been very well managed. Serov's posters could be seen all around the city, and the papers regularly reported on the Russian company in the days before the premiere. *Figaro* reporter Robert Brussel wrote a daily column on the rehearsals and preparations. Meanwhile, Diaghilev had ordered the complete refurbishment of the theatre. A new stage was constructed, and the floors were recarpeted. Under the guidance of the designer Karl Valts, technical improvements were made, enabling a lightning-fast change of scene in *Pavillon d'Armide*. Pipes were even installed under the stage so that water from the Seine could spout from the fountains in the final act of that ballet.[34] Astruc sent invitations to the premiere to attractive young actresses, placing them all in the front row of the balcony. 'I took great care to alternate blondes with brunettes,' he wrote. He felt that it was only by stooping to these kinds of tactics that he could win over the artistic avant-garde, or, as he called them, '*mes chers snobs*'.[35]

The premiere on 19 May, featuring *Pavillon d'Armide*, *Prince Igor* and *Le Festin*, has gone down as a legendary event in twentieth-century theatrical history.[36] All contemporary sources speak of a shocking, entirely novel, even life-changing experience. 'Invasion', 'explosion', 'outburst' – no hyperbole was left unused. The poet Anna de Noailles, who attended the first performance, described it as follows: 'It was as if Creation, having stopped on the seventh day, now all of a sudden resumed ... Something completely new in the world of the arts ... a sudden glory: the phenomenon of the Ballets Russes.'[37]

The public response to this and subsequent Diaghilev productions will forever remain something of a mystery. Almost all famous eyewitness accounts of those first evenings were written years, sometimes decades later – a fact that undermines their reliability and makes the emotions they describe difficult to comprehend. But contemporary descriptions of Diaghilev's first season do show that the legend is not a historical construct. Sitting in the audience that night was the young German diplomat Count Harry Kessler. Kessler was a cosmopolitan aesthete, very much au fait with the latest trends in the visual arts, dance, literature and music. He was a close friend of Hugo von Hofmannsthal and knew Richard Strauss well. Other friends included the sculptors Maillol and Rodin, and Edvard Munch, who painted a striking full-length portrait of him. He had a huge, highly progressive art collection: even before 1900 he owned works by Van Gogh, Cézanne, Signac and Seurat. Kessler was passionate about modern dance. He had seen Isadora Duncan perform, but was chiefly under the spell of another American dancer, Ruth St Denis. In short, Kessler was not one of Astruc's '*chers snobs*', but a sophisticated intellectual, conversant with all that was happening in the world of art. From 1911 he became a fixture in Diaghilev's circle. But in 1909 he knew none of the Russians, nor any of their French entourage, a fact that gives his account extra weight.[38] Kessler's description of events, recorded in his diary and in his correspondence with Hugo von Hofmannsthal, provides us with a direct reaction to those evenings in May and June in the Châtelet.

He described his first impression of Nijinsky in a letter to Hofmannsthal: '[Nijinsky is like] a butterfly, but at the same time he is the epitome of manliness and youthful beauty. The ballerinas, who are just as beautiful, are completely eclipsed by him. The audience went mad. If you ever write a ballet (with Strauss) we must get hold of this young Nijinsky.'[39]

The female dancers soon rose in his estimation. After seeing *Cléopâtre* and *Les Sylphides* on 4 June, he wrote in his diary:

> Nijinsky and Pavlova together in 'Sylphides', the embodiment of Amor and Psyche; both extraordinarily young and beautiful, light and graceful; not the slightest trace of sentiment. Both beguilingly elegant. Nijinsky virile, but as beautiful as a Greek god. Cléopâtre, a Jewess, Ida Rubinstein, in a blue Egyptian wig; a slender boyish body; her movements displaying a refinement that could hitherto only be observed in ancient Egyptian or ancient Chinese pictures. All in all, this Russian ballet [is] one of the most remarkable and significant artistic manifestations of our time ...[40]

The next day he once again wrote to Hofmannsthal to recount his impressions of the previous day:

> I could never have dreamt of a *mimetic art* that was so beautiful, so refined, so far beyond any theatrics ... Strange but true: since seeing 'Tristan' for the first time, I don't think I've ever been so deeply impressed by a theatrical production ... These women (Pavlova, Karsavina, Rubinstein), and these men, or rather, boys, Nijinsky and a few others, seem to have descended from another, higher, more beautiful world, like young living gods and goddesses ... We are truly witnessing the birth of a new art ... To achieve such effects is a measure of our modern refinement; it testifies to an aesthetic appreciation that verges on the perverse.[41]

Is it still possible to form an objective judgement of the novelty and quality of Russian ballet as presented in Paris in those heady days in May? Our modern view is clouded by the more vulgar aspects of the whole enterprise – the manufacture of celebrity and the hype ('Nijinsky, the new Vestris') – because we associate them with the economics of pop culture. The marketing of the venture has obscured its artistic achievements, which are also difficult to convey historiographically. *Les Sylphides* and the dances from *Prince*

Igor are still performed today, but very few will be able to see in these ballets 'the birth of a new art'.

But if we are to understand what happened, we must take the rapture shown by Kessler and others at face value. The surprise and excitement sprang from a combination of factors. The sets were not in themselves innovative. They were elaborate and ornate, the handiwork of celebrated artists rather than stage painters, but technically they were no different from the illusionist decors that were the norm in theatres all over the world. What made the production unique was the care with which sets and costumes had been coordinated and integrated into the visual spectacle. 'The decors,' Diaghilev said in an interview, '… must provide a symbolic, or rather artistic cum symbolic framework that enhances the meaning of the performance.'[42] The music was probably the ballet's weakest point. Tcherepnin's score had a kind of Hollywood appeal, but the Arensky hotchpotch for *Cléopâtre* was nothing special, and the less said about the orchestrated Chopin the better. The only outstanding music was by Borodin; it could pass as new in France, even though the composer had been dead for nearly a quarter of a century. Even the dance was not essentially new. It was ballet in the classical sense, albeit of a higher technical standard and invested by Fokine with a more dramatic and 'mimetic' vocabulary.

Diaghilev and his team made every effort to integrate the various components of their performances. 'Our ballet is the synthesis of all existing art forms,' commented Bakst in 1910.[43] But synthetic theories had dominated the performing arts since 1850,[44] so, in a conceptual sense, Diaghilev's ballet was by no means new. It was the level of performance, and the care, seriousness and dedication which Diaghilev, Fokine, Bakst and Benois brought to every detail that raised the ballet to a new level of dramatic expression – ballet as 'total theatre'. The shock that Kessler experienced lay not in discovering something entirely new, but in recognising the potential of something that already existed.

In those days, Diaghilev lived in an intoxicated, enchanted world.[45] He sat in Misia Sert's box every evening, gazing at his dancers 'through a diminutive pair of mother-of-pearl opera glasses'.[46] Despite all the tension of the past weeks, and the looming spectre of financial difficulties, he was happy. His protégé Nijinsky had exceeded expectations, and Diaghilev had become more

Nijinsky, by Serov

confident of his ability to recognise and launch talent. Mavrin, his former favourite, was meanwhile forced to witness the painful sight of Diaghilev and Nijinsky becoming more and more intimate. He decided to get back at Diaghilev in a way that was to set a pattern for subsequent lovers: he had an affair with a woman.

The woman in question was the dancer Olga Fyodorova. Mavrin had selected her very deliberately; even Diaghilev was forced to acknowledge her beauty. He allegedly told Benois that she 'was the only woman with whom he could fall in love'.[47] Diaghilev responded predictably enough to provocation by sacking Mavrin.[48]

Nijinsky and Diaghilev were by now very much an item. As a sign of their bond, Diaghilev gave the dancer a platinum Cartier ring, adorned with a huge sapphire. According to Lifar, 'Nijinsky was Diaghilev's pride and joy.'[49] Nevertheless, when Nijinsky was diagnosed with typhoid fever shortly after the last performance, Diaghilev was so terrified of getting infected that he didn't dare enter his lover's hotel room, but communicated with him through a crack in the door.[50]

Diaghilev, Bakst, Misia and Nijinsky spent the summer in Venice, and there Nijinsky corresponded with his mother and sister. Bronya recalled:

Vaslav wrote that he had met Isadora Duncan at one of Diaghilev's parties, where he was seated next to her at dinner. She made the following proposal to him: 'Nijinsky, we should get married – think what wonderful children we would have ... they would be prodigies ... our children would dance like Duncan and Nijinsky.' In the letter, Vaslav told us what he had said in reply. He said that he didn't want his children to dance like Duncan – and that, besides, he was too young to get married.[51]

In Venice, plans were made for the seasons ahead and Diaghilev was once again on the hunt for patrons. He wrote to Benois that he had been in touch with the Grand Duchess Maria Pavlovna, the formidable widow of Vladimir Alexandrovich and the unquestioned doyenne of Petersburg high society. She allegedly promised that Diaghilev would be placed under 'the exalted protection of Her Highness'.[52] He was also preparing to approach the tsar with a request for money.

Looking back, Diaghilev's naivety seems almost comical. Did he really believe he could regain the court's favour? Did he really not see what was happening around him?

· 15 ·

Bakst and the Art of Seduction
1909–1910

A FLOCK OF LETTERS flew from Venice to Paris and St Petersburg, detailing plans for a new programme of opera and ballet in various European cities. At this point Diaghilev took two major decisions. The first was to mount a number of world premieres every year: he had no desire for the Ballets Russes to become a mere repertory company. The second was to employ the talents of non-Russian (primarily French) artists and composers.

The first two composers Diaghilev approached were Maurice Ravel and Claude Debussy. The latter was generally regarded, particularly after the 1902 premiere of his opera *Pelléas et Mélisande*, as the leading French composer of the day and France's answer to Wagner. His harmonic innovations were a source of inspiration to young composers, and his influence extended far beyond France. Debussy knew Russia well: as a young musician he had worked there as a private tutor, though his experience had done little to foster an appreciation for Russian culture. At first Debussy was sceptical about Diaghilev and his Ballets Russes, though he was sufficiently intrigued not to dismiss the idea out of hand.

In September, Diaghilev wrote to Benois to describe his ideas about the Debussy ballet:

Debussy expressed great readiness to write a ballet and he's already begun the music. He's writing the libretto himself and by a fairytale coincidence it's set in eighteenth-century Venice. Of course you'll understand that it's your sacred duty to do this ballet, and although you have masses of material from the period, still, taking advantage of my stay here, I have bought some photographs which will send you into ecstasy ... The setting is a Venice square with a canal with gondolas floating down it.[1]

Diaghilev had gone to great lengths to persuade Debussy. As late as 18 July Debussy was writing to his publisher Jacques Durand that he could not 'produce ballet subjects on demand. And certainly not one set in eighteenth-century Italy! ... For Russian dancers that strikes me as rather contradictory.' The composer was moreover decidedly unimpressed by Diaghilev himself. 'I ran into Monsieur S. de Diaghilev ... [His] lack of French skills impeded the conversation somewhat.'[2] But a few weeks later Debussy was more optimistic and suddenly much more complimentary about Diaghilev's French skills. '[W]e are dealing with a Russian who understands French very well ...' He wrote to Louis Laloy a musicologist, who would flesh out the libretto, that he had sketched out the synopsis of the ballet and that Nijinsky and Karsavina would be the two protagonists. He chuckled at the many far-fetched interpretations imposed on the work of the Russian ballet: 'I do not require Nijinsky's legs to describe symbols or Karsavina's smile to explicate the doctrine of Kant. I intend to amuse myself writing this ballet, an excellent state of mind for a divertissement. I hope you will enjoy it nonetheless.'[3]

Ravel – a mere thirty-four to Debussy's forty-eight – was regarded as the most modern composer in France. His music was performed within Kuzmin's circle and at Nouvel's Contemporary Music Evenings, and in that sense he was an obvious choice, though Diaghilev could just as easily have gone to more established figures like Dukas, d'Indy or Saint-Saëns, whose names also cropped up on lists he was making at that time. But in the end, it was Ravel's ballet that was the first to be produced by the company, testifying to the esteem in which Diaghilev held the young composer.

Despite Diaghilev's own enthusiasm for Ravel, the conservative wing of his entourage, led by Bezobrazov, was clearly appalled: 'One [ballet] has already been commissioned, *Daphnis et Chloé*. By the combined efforts of Bakst, Fokine and Ravel we've worked out a detailed programme ... Ravel

Ravel, by Benois

is blazing away like a candle. I think he'll make an absolute masterpiece, an *absolu chef d'oeuvre*, as he himself told Fokine, but … can you picture the faces of Bezobrazov and Co? It's hilarious!'[4]

The idea for *Daphnis et Chloé* came from Fokine, who had been trying to produce a ballet based on this story since 1904. By letting Fokine have his way, Diaghilev managed to assure himself of the choreographer's loyalty, which could be fickle at times. In a letter to a friend, Ravel discusses the difficulty of conveying his ideas to Fokine:

> I must tell you that I've just had an insane week: preparation of a ballet libretto for the next Russian season. Almost every night, work until 3 a.m. What complicates things is that Fokine doesn't know a word of French, and I only know how to swear in Russian. In spite of the interpreters, you can imagine the savour of these meetings.[5]

Diaghilev's greatest challenge was finding a new Russian (i.e. neo-nationalist) ballet, a story that would not only lend itself to the treatment that had made *Boris Godunov* so successful – the depiction of historical Russia,

rich in quasi-anthropological detail – but which could also be turned into a
Fokine production à la *Pavillon d'Armide*. The first composer he approached
was Fyodor Akimenko, and there was talk of a ballet to be entitled *The
Icehouse*.[6]

Akimenko may have been suggested by Nouvel, since his music was
played at the latter's Evenings, or by Kuzmin, who played it at home.[7] Many
have wondered what Diaghilev ever saw in him, Diaghilev not least among
them: 'The more we got to know Akimenko, the less we liked him,' he wrote
to Benois on 12 September. '[He is] a slow-witted bumpkin.'[8]

According to Benois, Tcherepnin had long been in the running to
compose a new ballet, and he was also a member of the organising committee, but for some reason he did not make the final cut.[9] The next candidate
was Anatoly Lyadov, a leading pedagogue and a well-established composer
who was known for his painstaking working habits and technical mastery.
In short, a typical representative of the Petersburg school. Diaghilev knew
Lyadov, of course, and did not hesitate to approach him.

> You told me, and I'd like to believe you, that you aren't against what I'm
> doing and that you like some things about it. You told me that 'your music
> needs to be commissioned a year in advance'.
>
> Taking all this into consideration, I am making you a proposal or, to
> put it more modestly, requesting you to work with us. I need a ballet, and a
> Russian one – the first Russian ballet, for there aren't any – there's Russian
> opera, Russian symphonies, Russian song, Russian dance, Russian rhythm
> – but no Russian ballet … I don't need a three-act ballet – and the libretto
> is ready – Fokine has it and it's been composed by the collective efforts of
> all of us. It – *Firebird* – is a ballet in one act and maybe two scenes.[10]

The libretto drew on a number of fairytales involving the figure of the
firebird, all taken from a well-known anthology assembled by Aleksandr
Afanasyev. In all likelihood Diaghilev and Fokine, who had followed Diaghilev to Venice, had sketched out the scenario during their time in Italy. Lyadov
expressed interest in the project, and he and Fokine were soon put in touch.
Aleksandr Golovin, who had designed *Boris Godunov* in 1908, was hired to
make the sets and costumes.

It was around this time that Diaghilev decided to drop Debussy, perhaps because of the rapid progress being made on *Firebird*. The composer was not accustomed to this kind of treatment, and he was understandably incensed, writing to Laloy: 'Our Russian friend acts as if the best way to treat people is to start off by deceiving them … Be that as it may, none of this will affect our relationship. The main thing is to rise above Diaghilev and his duplicitous band of Cossacks.'[11]

It would be some time before Diaghilev and Debussy patched things up, though the Frenchman would never quite lose his distrust of the Russian. Plainly, Diaghilev wasn't concerned about the lack of new works for the upcoming season, because in Venice he had already hatched plans for another new ballet, with the help of Bakst and Nijinsky. In a letter to his sister, Nijinsky urgently requested a Russian edition of *One Thousand and One Nights*.[12] This was the genesis of the ballet that would become *Schéhérazade*.

Although Lyadov had agreed to write the music for *Firebird*, Diaghilev was uneasy. The composer was ruthlessly self-critical, a quality that made him an exceptionally slow worker. Diaghilev suspected problems were brewing, and he asked Benois in St Petersburg to 'lean on' Lyadov. 'If worse comes to worse, and Lyadov cancels on us, we'll have to ask Glazunov, but I would much rather have the former!'[13] What could Diaghilev do? Glazunov was not an attractive option, but there were so few good young composers. Nouvel had long complained about the lack of new pieces for his Contemporary Music Evenings.

Fokine gave his scenario to Lyadov, who promised to get to work on it. Many weeks later, the story goes, Golovin ran into Lyadov on the street and asked him how things were coming along. 'Oh excellently. I've already bought the music paper,' Lyadov is said to have replied.[14]

Diaghilev promptly wrote off Lyadov and, undoubtedly exasperated by the difficulty of finding a Russian composer for his ballet, took a daring decision. He sent a telegram to Ustilug, a village in Ukraine, where a young composer, a former pupil of the recently deceased Rimsky-Korsakov, was staying at his family's country house. That composer was Igor Stravinsky.

By then Diaghilev had known Stravinsky for several years. He undoubtedly knew Igor's father, Fyodor, whose twenty-fifth anniversary gala as bass at the Mariinsky he had almost certainly attended, as he was then still in the employ of the Imperial Theatres. He may also have met the composer at

Stravinsky, by Fokine

Nouvel's, at the latter's first Contemporary Music Evening, where Stravinsky was one of the accompanists.[15] Diaghilev was in St Petersburg when Stravinsky played his *Pastorale* and the first of his *Deux melodies* op. 6, at Nouvel's thirty-ninth Evening on 27 December 1907, and it is quite possible that he was in the audience.

We know for certain that Diaghilev was present at a conservatory concert when Stravinsky's orchestral showpiece *Fireworks* was played, sometime in the spring of 1909. Diaghilev had taken Fokine along, and he subsequently told Grigoriev that the composition had made a deep impression on him: 'It is new and original, with a tonal quality that should surprise the public.'[16] Stravinsky later recalled that

> [Diaghilev] sent round his card with a note, asking me to call the following day at 3.00 p.m. Of course, I knew who he was, everyone did, so I went. The door was opened by a servant whose attitude was very [haughty]. He said, 'Sit down and wait.' There was a small entrance hall, I sat and waited. Laughter could be heard from an inner room. Time passed. You know, I was young, but already impatient. I grew restless. After twenty minutes I got up and moved to the street door. As I grasped the handle, a voice behind me said, 'Stravinsky, *pridite, pridite*,' come in.[17]

Diaghilev's first commission for Stravinsky was decidedly mundane: an orchestration of Chopin's *Nocturne* op. 32 and the *Valse brillante* op. 18, to be used in *Les Sylphides*. Diaghilev wired Ustilug to sound out Stravinsky about writing the music for his planned fairytale ballet, though he stopped short of actually offering the young composer the commission outright, on the off-chance that Lyadov would come through for them after all. In December Diaghilev rang Stravinsky with the news. 'I remember the day Diaghilev telephoned me to say go ahead, and I recall his surprise when I said that I had already started.'[18] What Stravinsky did not know, however, was that the chances of a new season in Paris were dwindling with each passing day.

The 1909 season had closed at an enormous loss of 85,000 francs, an amount that Diaghilev now owed to Astruc. Rather than devote his energies to paying off this debt, Diaghilev entered into secret negotiations with the Grand Opéra about the possibility of a new Russian season. Astruc felt cheated and feared that he would be saddled with the debt. To make matters worse, he had already booked the New York Metropolitan Opera for the Châtelet for the same period, which Diaghilev knew perfectly well. Diaghilev's new venture would thus be in direct competition with Astruc's own concert series. This was the last straw for Astruc, and he embarked on a campaign 'to eliminate Diaghilev as an artistic rival', as Lynn Garafola put it.[19] Anyone willing to listen was told of the Russian impresario's 'fraudulent' business practices. The effectiveness of Astruc's smear campaign is apparent from a letter from Pierre Gheusi, a senior manager at the Opéra, to Misia Sert. Misia had asked Gheusi for help, just before she and her lover, José Maria Sert, were to leave for Venice with Diaghilev. She received the following letter in Italy, and we can only assume that she shared its contents with Diaghilev.

> We received your card, dear friend, a few hours after having learned of your departure. I see that your friendly concern is following you to Venice, you and Sert. But I must tell you this: I dined by chance with Serge the Muscovite and Astruc … the other evening … I then took the precaution of getting the opinion of Astruc himself about his Slavic associate.
>
> Oh … My dear friend! … What I learned then, with no room for doubt, makes it *absolutely* impossible for me to join forces with this ostentatious, conscienceless man … Benois is a perfect gentleman as well as

a great artist. But the other!!! ... In short, *I must not, I cannot* be associated in any way with Monsieur S de D. I'll give you more details when you return.

There will be no *official* Russian season in Paris next year. That is the *formal* wish of the Russian court and the grand dukes ... I myself am *with* Sert, with all my heart – with you. But my strict duty is to advise you, both of you, not to get mixed up with certain others. Is that clear?[20]

Astruc also began to seek out Diaghilev's enemies in St Petersburg. He wrote to Kshesinskaya on 2 August to ask if she was aware of Diaghilev's plans at the Opéra. In mid-November he contacted Grand Duke Andrey, the same man who had helped sabotage Diaghilev's agreement with the tsar the year before. At the latter's suggestion, Astruc turned his attention to Baron Frederiks, the Minister of the Court,[21] who in turn advised him to write a report to the Russian government on Diaghilev's activities in Paris. 'The Russian I did business with last year has the audacity to return to Paris and go into competition with me,' Astruc wrote at that time to one of his business partners.[22]

In the eleven-page 'report' Astruc sent to Baron Frederiks, it is actually Astruc himself who comes across as an unscrupulous schemer, though the document also contains prime examples of Diaghilev's rather cavalier attitude toward the truth. Astruc complained, for example, that Diaghilev had deceived him by repeatedly introducing himself in correspondence as '*attaché à la Chancellerie Personelle de Sa Majesté l'Empereur de Russie*'. And sure enough, Astruc's estate contains a number of documents in which Diaghilev uses that title. That may not have been actually fraudulent, strictly speaking, because Diaghilev had been in the employ of the imperial chancery since 1902 or 1903,[23] though his was the kind of position unique to the Russian imperial bureaucracy: a purely ceremonial function, with no status, no salary and no pressure to show up at the office. But of course to any outsider, such a lofty title would suggest that Diaghilev was an official representative of the government – which was plainly not the case. Astruc clearly had a point there. The rest of the report, however, is a vicious, unrelenting attack on the man, with sentences like 'In the interest of protecting the reputation of the Russian performers and the dignity of the Imperial Theatres of Russia, it might be best to refrain from conferring official protection on the activities of an amateur impresario whose credibility has been seriously undermined in Parisian commercial circles.'[24]

This report was dispatched to St Petersburg under the strictest secrecy, where it undoubtedly delighted Diaghilev's enemies. In the meantime Astruc had found his own way of dealing with Diaghilev's debt: selling off Diaghilev's inventory – all the costumes and sets for the 1909 season – to the management of the Monte Carlo opera for 20,000 francs.[25] This was a double coup for Astruc, as it not only offset some of his losses, but also prevented Diaghilev from restaging the 1909 repertoire in Paris. Meanwhile, Diaghilev was raising money wherever he could, and this restored the Grand Opéra's faith enough to enter into a 100,000-franc contract with him on 24 December for the following summer.

The St Petersburg press was abuzz with all sorts of juicy gossip. Benois wrote to Argutinsky that the papers 'said God knows what about Seryozha and Nijinsky and the distortions of opera etc.'. It was said that 'Ida Rubinstein paid Seryozha 30,000 francs for every appearance and that sort of thing. Rubbish! You can't imagine what heaps of sarcasm (jealousy?) and scepticism and general nastiness have greeted the victors in their own country. Seryozha's share price hasn't exactly gone up, I fear.'[26]

Even without Astruc's report, the title-tattle of the press would probably have been reason enough for the court to sever its ties with Diaghilev once and for all. Yet in February 1910, Diaghilev once again asked the tsar for money. 'Last year's success', Diaghilev wrote to Nicholas, 'not only guarantees a new triumph of Russian art, it will also be sufficient to cover earlier losses.'[27] Astonishingly, on 9 April, Nicholas decreed that Diaghilev be given 25,000 roubles, with the comment that 'His Majesty regards it as undesirable that resources from the exchequer should continue to be furnished for this purpose, and therefore no further funds will be forthcoming.'[28]

But this time, the ever-vacillating Nicholas changed his mind more rapidly than usual. Six days later he gave the order to rescind the subsidy issued to Diaghilev.[29] We can only guess at his motives, but it seems likely that sometime between 9 and 15 April Baron Frederiks drew the tsar's attention to Astruc's report.

The air of scandal that clung to Diaghilev caused even his most loyal supporters to doubt him. It can be inferred, for example, from a letter sent by Benois to Sert that even the latter had qualms about the way Diaghilev operated. The same letter also reveals how Diaghilev's friends dealt with his 'unorthodox' working methods:

> [His conduct] is more or less phantasmagoric and will not cease to be so till the moment the curtain goes up at the first *répétition générale*. But that has always, always been the way he conducts his affairs, and I begin to believe he is right, seeing that, in spite of his numerous gaffes, his negligence, and the tricks he has the habit of playing, he also has the habit of success.
>
> I am so accustomed to this somewhat bizarre 'system' that I no longer protest but just wait patiently and with confidence. Besides, I am quite convinced that the great bullfighter will quickly dispel all your fears; at least, that's the way he operates with his close apostles.[30]

Indeed, in spite of everything, Diaghilev had garnered so much admiration and trust that he found enough people who believed in him and were willing to offer their support. The only real consequence of Astruc's campaign was that it effectively prevented Diaghilev from returning to Russia. Diaghilev's hope that his success abroad would secure him a senior position in the cultural world of St Petersburg had been shattered. In a sense, Astruc had accomplished exactly the opposite of what he had meant to do: hound Diaghilev out of France. Now that his former partner had burnt all his bridges in his homeland for him, Diaghilev redoubled his efforts to conquer the rest of Europe – for he had no other option.

By mid-February Diaghilev had repaid the remainder of his debt to Astruc and bought back some of his sets and costumes from the Opéra de Monte Carlo. At that point Astruc tried to make the best of a bad situation by reaching a compromise with Diaghilev. Diaghilev agreed not to schedule any performances on those dates that the Metropolitan Opera was playing the Châtelet and arranged for Astruc's agency to oversee the whole publicity campaign.[31]

But as usual, Diaghilev was getting ahead of himself. There was still the small matter of securing funding for the upcoming season. New sponsors were approached, chief among them the banker Dmitry Gintsburg, who went by the name Gunzburg in France. In return for a substantial sum of money, he would become 'co-director' of Diaghilev's dance company and his name would appear on all Ballets Russes posters.

At the same time the impresario had to streamline his budget. When the tsar's funding fell through, Diaghilev abandoned plans to stage any operas in Paris during the coming season. Pre-existing agreements were terminated. 'All my manoeuvring has come to naught,' he wrote to the singer Petrenko, one of his stars, 'and it is with a heavy heart that I must inform you that we will not be presenting any opera abroad this year.'[32]

Meanwhile Ravel was way behind schedule on *Daphnis et Chloé*. This was actually a blessing in disguise for Diaghilev, since it spared him from having to mount such an expensive production that season. London performances could not go ahead, but in their place Diaghilev had managed to book the Theater des Westens in Berlin and the Théâtre Royal de la Monnaie in Brussels. Bit by bit his programme for the summer began to shape up. At the very least the company would be putting on *Firebird*, *Schéhérazade* and *Carnaval*, a ballet by Fokine to music by Schumann, with sets and costumes by Bakst.[33] Not for the first time, Benois pushed for *Giselle*, but Diaghilev had his doubts, preferring to concentrate on new, modern productions rather than the standard repertoire. Though he had programmed *Giselle* the year before as a showpiece for Pavlova, the prima ballerina would not be dancing for him in the new season. In the end Benois got his way, on the argument that a performance of *Giselle* – the most important French ballet of the Romantic period, but now all but forgotten in France – would serve as a tribute from the Russian ballet to the French.[34] Yet *Giselle* would form a sharp contrast with the modern style Fokine had been cultivating these past few years. It would seem that Diaghilev's chief motive in including the ballet was to placate Benois by allowing him to design the sets and costumes. The last addition was a new *divertissement*, a Russian medley with various showpieces, danced to the music of Glazunov.

Rehearsals began in the spring, again at the Catherine Hall, with *The Firebird* as the main focus. Today, it is hard to imagine that the score to this ballet, so redolent of Stravinsky's master Rimsky-Korsakov, was criticised for its lack of melody, with some critics sneering 'that it did not sound like music at all'.[35]

Stravinsky regularly attended the rehearsals to indicate the exact tempos and rhythms from the keyboard. To the dancers it sounded like he was demolishing the instrument, rather than playing it: 'He ... used to hammer out [the rhythms] with considerable violence, humming loudly and scarcely caring whether he struck the right notes.'[36]

Karsavina as the Firebird

The title role was given to Tamara Karsavina, with Fokine as Prince Ivan. Karsavina and Nijinsky would dance *Giselle*, while Ida Rubinstein would play the role of Zobeïde, the favoured harem girl in *Schéhérazade*, with Nijinsky as the 'golden slave'. Nouvel couldn't help but remark to Diaghilev how odd it was 'that Nijinsky should always be the *slave* in your ballets – in *Pavillon d'Armide*, in *Cléopâtre* and now again in *Schéhérazade*! I hope, Seryozha, that one of these days you'll emancipate him!'[37]

In mid-May 1910 the dancers left for Berlin, where they had their first performance on 20 May. Nijinsky had turned twenty in March, and he continued to grow as a dancer. His sister Bronislava, who was a year younger and a talented ballerina in her own right, joined them for this tour, and in her memoirs she described her brother's progress, with an eye for detail that one would find only in a fellow dancer:

> While Vaslav, apart from the others, practised his dance exercises alone, I observed him from a distance. He executed all his exercises at an accelerated tempo, and for never more than forty-five to fifty minutes; that would be his total practice time. But during that time he expended the strength and energy equivalent in other dancers to three hours of assiduous exercises … Vaslav seemed more intent on improving the energy of the muscular drive, strength, and speed than on observing the five positions … He worked on the elasticity of the whole body in the execution of his own movements. Even when holding a pose, Vaslav's body never stopped dancing. In his *adagio* exercises, in the *développé* front, he could not raise his leg higher than ninety degrees; the build of his leg, his overdeveloped thigh muscles, as solid as a rock, did not permit him to attain the angle possible for an average dancer.
>
> In the *allegro pas* he did not come down completely on the balls of his feet, but barely touched the floor with the tips of his toes and not the customary preparation with both feet firmly on the floor, taking the force from a deep *plié*. Nijinsky's toes were unusually strong and enabled him to take this short preparation so quickly as to be imperceptible, creating the impression that he remained at all times suspended in the air.[38]

There were no premieres in Berlin, with the exception of *Carnaval* and *Cléopâtre*. The latter was a hit with the audience, including Kaiser Wilhelm, who was present for the opening night. Afterwards Wilhelm had 'called together the members of a society of Egyptologists of which he was president to talk to them about the cultural significance of the ballet and to urge them to study Diaghilev's mise-en-scène'.[39] Both *Les Sylphides* and *Le Festin* were presented to full houses in Berlin. 'This fortnight in Berlin,' wrote Grigoriev, 'also served, from our point of view, as a prolonged dress rehearsal for Paris.'[40]

When the company returned to Paris at the end of May, there was much to be done. The stage of the Opéra had to be modified, the dancers housed, and the new season publicised. Diaghilev wanted to spotlight Stravinsky, the boy genius of Russian music. With this in mind, earlier that spring he had invited Robert Brussel to St Petersburg, where the reporter was treated to a private performance of the new ballet in the flat Diaghilev had just rented a short time earlier in Zamyatin Lane.[41] In this way Diaghilev hoped to create a buzz around the young composer. The impresario was confident of his discovery's future success. During rehearsals he said to the musicians, pointing to Stravinsky, 'Mark him well ... He is a man on the eve of celebrity.'[42]

Golovin's sets for *The Firebird* are as breathtaking today as they were a century ago, ranking among the best work the Ballets Russes produced in the pre-war years. The scenery for the second act, 'The Realm of Kashchey', in particular, is a high point of Russian stage design. Yet this would be Golovin's last production for Diaghilev. The reason for his departure was most likely political, rather than artistic: Golovin was a close friend of the despised Telyakovsky, director of the Imperial Theatres.

Stravinsky's music met with an enthusiastic response, achieving exactly what Diaghilev had hoped for: the recognition that his company belonged to the world of the avant-garde, in music as well as dance. Even Debussy was won over, writing to Jacques Durand: '[*The Firebird*] is not perfect, but in certain respects it's quite good, since the music is not the docile slave of the dance ... And now and again you hear completely unfamiliar rhythmic combinations! French dancers would never have agreed to dance to such music ... Ergo Diaghilev is a great man, and Nijinsky is his prophet ...'[43]

Yet it was *Schéhérazade* that created the greatest stir that evening. With its daring depiction of violence and Eastern sensuality (or at least what passed for Eastern sensuality in pre-war France), it tapped into the longstanding vogue for orientalism in French art and literature, while its erotic and violent imagery tied in with the emerging cult of primitivism. The plot of *Schéhérazade*, which has been summarised as the 'tale of a harem of beautiful women using the absence of their lord and master to indulge in an orgy of group sex with a band of muscular Negroes, ending in a bloodbath of vengeance',[44] created a sensation. The highlight was an erotic dance between Zobeïde and her favourite African slave. In reality the ballet just did what orientalist art had been doing since Delacroix and Ingres: rendering erotic tableaux socially acceptable by placing them in an Eastern context. The exotic, semi-barbaric surroundings of the Orient validated a dark sexuality that would have been impossible even in a classical setting. The Russians, for their part, used the ballet to exploit stereotypes about their own supposedly savage nature, much though Diaghilev would later decry the Western penchant for portraying Russians as uncivilised.[45]

Rubinstein and Nijinsky were lauded for their work, but the real star of the show was Leon Bakst. It was his spectacular sets, with their vibrant colours and lavish use of costly materials, that gave the work artistic unity. Diaghilev called him 'the hero of our ballet' shortly after the performances in Paris.[46] Bakst was more surprised than anyone at the success of his ballet. Diaghilev had invited a number of prominent artists to one of the last rehearsals, and their response was nothing short of ecstatic. As Bakst wrote to his wife: 'What a success I had among the artists (Vuillard, Bonnard, Seurat, [Jacques-Emile] Blanche and others)! Seryozha embraced and kissed me in front of everyone and the whole ballet exploded into applause and then set about chairing me on their shoulders on the stage. I barely managed to escape but they are threatening to chair me "formally" after the dress rehearsal.'[47]

With Bakst having largely faded into obscurity, it is hard to imagine the magnitude of his celebrity in 1910 and the years that followed. In 1892, when still a young man, Bakst had told his friends that his greatest wish was to become the most famous artist in the world,[48] and with the premiere of *Schéhérazade* it seemed that his dream had come true. The rising star was interviewed in fashionable magazines, his art was exhibited in galleries, and his designs for the ballet were purchased by the Musée des Arts décoratifs in Paris. American and French actresses approached him to design dresses for them, and chic Parisian boutiques sold '*étoffes Scheherasades*'.[49]

The most famous artists and fashion designers of the capital all wanted to rub shoulders with the Russian. On 25 June, even before the season had come to a close, he wrote: 'I'm still surrounded by a lot of noise and success … In four days I'll put down the deposit on a studio which I am taking for six months. It's Matisse's studio. He's very nice, uncomplicated, and I feel we'll be friends. In spite of everything he's a shy and serious man of a simple sort … Have you heard of Poiret, the dressmaker? He's the *dernier cri*. The other day he offered me 12,000 francs for twelve drawings of fashionable outfits.'[50]

Bakst was no overnight sensation – he was forty-four in 1910 – but for those who had been following his work, this sudden acclaim did not come out of the blue. His contribution to *Mir iskusstva*, mainly as a graphic designer, had been relatively modest. Yet as of 1905 his reputation as an artist in his own right took off as he won admiration for his dark, idiosyncratic vision. Paintings like *Vase: Self-portrait* (1906), *Elysium* (1906) and *Terror Antiquus* (1908), which were defining works of Russian symbolism, confirmed his status as a major artist. In 1904, Bakst married Lyubov Gritsenko-Tretyakova, a daughter of Russia's greatest art collector, Pavel Tretyakov – a liaison that marked the summit of Bakst's climb up the social ladder. Before he could take Tretyakov's daughter as his wife, however, he had to renounce his Jewish faith and enter the Russian Orthodox church. According to some, this plunged him into a spiritual crisis. His letters to his wife suggest that theirs was a friendly and intimate relationship rather than a passionate one.

His earlier success in Russia was soon outstripped by the celebrity status he acquired in France, where Bakst was a favourite topic of the gossip columnists and famous enough to figure in Cole Porter's 'Since Ma Got the Craze Espagnole':

> To show to what limits our nerves have been taxed:
> Why, she just had the bathroom done over by Bakst.[51]

If Bakst was the big winner to emerge in the wake of *Schéhérezade*, the loser was unquestionably Alexandre Benois. Not only had he had a close hand in writing the libretto of the ballet, he had also invested a great deal of time and energy in its dramatic composition. Benois was not present for the start of the Russian programme in Paris because he had been held up in St Petersburg. When he arrived in Paris in mid-June he was dismayed to see that the programme credited only the '*célèbre peintre*' Bakst as author of the ballet.

This was more than Benois could stomach, and he demanded an explanation from Diaghilev: 'I asked Seryozha what this meant and how it could have happened, and quick as a wink he retorted: "*Que veux tu?* I had to give something to Bakst. You have *Pavillon d'Armide*, so let him have *Schéhérazade*."'[52]

Benois was so incensed by this slight that he left Paris and refused to attend a single performance the whole season. This prickly situation was exacerbated by the cavalier treatment of his sets for *Giselle*. When it came time for the backdrops to be painted, there was general dissatisfaction with Benois's design, and Bakst was brought in, perhaps at Diaghilev's behest, to make some changes. Such last-minute changes were not unusual, but in this case the decors were altered without the consent of the designer. An angry Benois wrote to ask that his name be removed from the ballet pro-gramme. Bakst and Diaghilev took no notice of his wishes and credited him as the production designer in all the promotional material for *Giselle*. This just added fuel to the fire.[53]

The issue of the authorship of the two ballets refused to die, partly because of the difficulty of assigning responsibility for a collaborative work by such a close-knit group of artists, and partly because of Diaghilev's chaotic and dictatorial methods. For once, Diaghilev had done little that could be called blameworthy. The idea for *Schéhérezade* had been conceived in Venice, by Diaghilev and Bakst, a fact that Benois did not dispute. Indeed, no one could deny that the artistic and popular success of the ballet was first and foremost down to Bakst. Yet Benois had left his own mark on the libretti of both *Schéhérezade* and *Firebird*, while receiving no credit for either. In retrospect Benois's claim that he pored over Rimsky's score night after night to tailor the action to the music seems far-fetched: if any aspect of the work could be called vulgar or trite, it is the plot. Benois's frustration, however, had deeper origins. Of all the Miriskusniki, he had been most committed to the idea of transforming ballet into an art form with a whole new range of artistic pos-sibilities. Now that they were finally in a position to realise that old dream, his own contribution was far less significant than he had hoped. The year before, *Pavillon d'Armide* had been a great success, but its producers must already have known that it had little chance of becoming part of the repertory. This year he had only *Giselle*, tossed his way more or less as a consolation prize – and even then Diaghilev was not above meddling with his designs. When *Giselle* failed to generate the excitement of the Bakst productions, Benois's disappointment was complete. Bakst's unexpected fame, and the money, attention and women that followed in its wake, made him feel all the more slighted. It was particularly galling that Bakst, of all people, should suddenly be the toast of Paris, for Benois had always seen him as a minor figure, the least likely of his friends to threaten his feelings of superiority.

There may be some truth to the claim that Benois's downfall was the result of an active campaign by Diaghilev to push his old friend to the sidelines because he had grown tired of his conservative ideas and found him harder to dominate than the others. At the same time Diaghilev believed that Benois would eventually come to his senses, confident that his desire to be a part of future projects would outweigh any differences of opinion they might have. But Benois had dug in his heels more deeply than Diaghilev realised.

· 16 ·

Emergence of a Genius
1910–1911

THE FINAL YEAR of the decade proved to be a significant one for Diaghilev. He had demonstrated, first of all, that he did not need an opera to have a successful season. His premieres had been a hit with the Parisian public. What was more, the performances in Berlin and Brussels had shown that Russian ballet was popular elsewhere – a good thing too, since Diaghilev needed to branch out to secure the company's future. Yet his main accomplishment had been to establish himself firmly as an artistic trailblazer among the Parisian avant-garde. Marcel Proust, who attended two of the Russian performances in 1910, compared the excitement around Diaghilev and his group with the brouhaha sparked by a contemporary cause célèbre, describing the season as a 'charming invasion, against whose seductions only the critics who were devoid of taste protested, [and which] aroused Paris … with a fever of curiosity that was less bitter, more purely aesthetic, but perhaps quite as intense as the Dreyfus Affair'.[1] When Bonnard, one of France's most prominent painters, was asked whether the Russians influenced his work, he answered, 'But they influence everyone!'[2]

The 1910 season also cemented friendships with notable Parisians who had been following Diaghilev since 1906. Among the members of Diaghilev's 'honorary consulate', presided over by Misia Sert, was the young poet

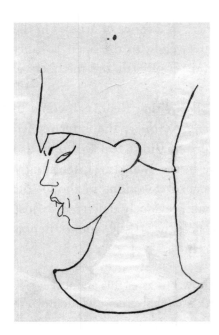

Nijinsky, by Cocteau

Jean Cocteau, who soon made himself a permanent attaché. Never missing a performance, he attended rehearsals, wandered about behind the scenes and tagged along to the post-performance suppers at Restaurant Larue. 'God knows, Jean was irresistible at twenty,' Misia said, remembering him dancing on the benches at Larue's.[3] By then Cocteau had already made a name for himself as poet and socialite, a striking presence in lipstick and rouge.

But things never went smoothly for long, and Diaghilev meanwhile had to deal with another mutiny in the ranks. Benois had spent the whole of the season sulking in the little Swiss village of Montagnola on Lake Lugano, where he had rented the imposing Casa Camuzzi, a palazzo that was later to be Herman Hesse's home for over a decade.[4] Benois had to be coaxed back into the coterie at all costs. In some ways the relentless sparring between the two friends was a source of creative energy, but it also caused rifts, and this latest row would be difficult to patch up. Conflicts like this were meat and drink to Diaghilev but they exhausted Benois.

Diaghilev needed Benois. He was the group's moral conscience – even though his self-styled intellectualism sometimes lacked substance – and his dedication to the common cause was beyond question. Furthermore, his standing in Russian artistic circles was still high. In previous years, he had reported on Diaghilev's foreign enterprises in a series of articles in the Russian press, providing an important counterweight to the open hostility evinced by segments of the art world, government officials and members of the court.

Diaghilev sent a telegram to Montagnola inviting Benois to come to Paris to settle their problems and discuss '*projets futurs*'. The latter replied promptly that he wouldn't be coming because he didn't feel well, but also because he had doubts about his future role in the company. Interestingly, he quoted Diaghilev's own description of his chaotic working method – 'the psychology of the hectic' – which Benois had previously defended to José Maria Sert, but which he now saw as responsible for artistic failures. Benois was unusually candid and did not spare himself:

> Am I so needed for *projets futurs*? I don't know, but after this awful year I'm so low, in such a *purée mode*, that I think my involvement would be completely superfluous. To a significant degree my nervous tension was caused by the lack of clarity about my position in the organisation. To be just a 'consultant' bores me, to be 'the heart and soul of the company' isn't on the cards, mostly because even without me there are enough 'hearts and souls'. And then this continual wavering, rolling this way and that. I've developed a kind of spiritual sea-sickness and when I started smashing glass, it was from a desire to jump out into the fresh air, to get away from that heaving sensation. The results were unexpected and perhaps fateful for my future involvement. The first days I felt terribly upset I wasn't with you, I thought my presence was essential, that without me you'd be lost and I begged the doctor to release me, but when it emerged that everything had worked out excellently *without me*, I felt a kind of relief and at the same time something snapped in me. It emerged I wasn't needed even though I was ready to make the craziest sacrifices (and I had already made many) if I knew I was essential …
>
> Generally speaking I like clarity, and in my relationship to the organisation and in the whole organisation itself there is too little clarity. I know: you think this makes a 'valuable' environment, the psychology of the hectic, everything on the boil. However it isn't like that. For true creativity, one that is good and great, not stormy but sunny – one needs more of a system. Disgraces like the present *Giselle* or last year's *Armide* sap creativity. You've got to understand that! …

I can't stand being the fifth wheel. If you were to ask me what I *really* want, then I'd say you should know that better than me and if you don't, it's pointless for me to want anything. Furthermore I am stupidly proud to the point of never wanting anything definite, so as to spare myself the insult of a refusal. It's difficult with me there, and for that reason it's probably better to be without me.[5]

After this letter arrived Bakst, too, was urged to write to Benois, to explain what had happened with *Giselle* and to convince him that 'everyone here, both Russian and French, sorely misses you'.[6]

After the performances in Paris, Diaghilev and Bakst travelled to Montagnola in the hope of burying the hatchet.[7] Whether this meeting led to a direct reconciliation is unclear. According to Nijinsky's sister Bronislava and Grigoriev it did; Benois, however, claimed that he initially stuck to his guns, refusing to work with Diaghilev ever again.[8] Bronislava relates that Diaghilev then headed for Venice. Bakst travelled to Carlsbad to pick up Nijinsky, who was staying there with his family, and the two then joined Diaghilev in Italy.[9]

The three had a relaxing time in Venice. Bakst painted Nijinsky in his swimming trunks on the Lido, while curious onlookers jostled to get a sight of him. Diaghilev never ventured into the sea himself, but loved watching Nijinsky as he sported about in the water. Bronislava recalled her brother's prowess as a swimmer. She remembered strolling along the bank of the river near their home while Vaslav swam, keeping pace with them: 'So I knew that many of those watching Vaslav in Venice, on the Lido, would also be admiring the extraordinary, beautiful style of his swimming, his strength and endurance in the water, for, whether on the surface of the water or underneath, he was like a fish.'[10]

By early October Diaghilev was back in Paris. The success of the new season had naturally not gone unnoticed in Russia, but instead of being proud of the fame he had garnered abroad, his compatriots were quick to berate him. Diaghilev was attacked in turn by Pavlova, Telyakovsky and Rimsky-Korsakov's widow. He wrote a number of articles in his defence, giving as good as he got. Pavlova's comments on Diaghilev were fairly innocent, her worst accusation apparently being that she had not taken part in his programme because 'she wanted to punish him for his disrespectful attitude toward the ballet dancers'.[11] Diaghilev hit back, accusing Pavlova of having sold out artistically by dancing in variety theatres like the London Palace and the Paris Olympia, where she performed between dog acts. He expressed outrage that a dancer of the Imperial Theatres would stoop so low, predicting that 'at this rate our choreographic arts will soon end up being performed in pubs thanks to the example set by Miss Pavlova and her lackeys'.[12] Of course, the real target of Diaghilev's ire was Telyakovsky, who had supplied Pavlova with dancers and sets for her tour of the variety theatres, in open opposition to Diaghilev.

Telyakovsky could not let this slight go unanswered. He retorted angrily in an interview with a journalist, accusing Diaghilev of being motivated by personal gain rather than a genuine desire to propagate Russian art. Telyakovsky added that he 'did not regard Diaghilev's performances as art at all'.[13] He then went on to beat the nationalist drum: 'If resources allowed, the management [of the Imperial Theatres] would organise a tour of the opera company to the big towns of the provinces. It's in our interests to promote Russian art among the Russian people: "We must work for Russians, not for foreigners."'[14]

Diaghilev hit back, claiming that Telyakovsky had never done anything for Russian art because he simply couldn't understand that Russian art 'can have a serious and lasting significance in the history of European art! One must have a fanatical belief in the strength and individuality of Russian art, in the essential importance of Russian talent for the life of modern Western culture.'[15]

Aid came to Diaghilev in the person of Valentin Serov, who had been closely involved in the last season in Paris. Serov brought his considerable reputation to bear on defending his associate. In an article published in the influential journal *Rech*, Serov mainly attacked the brash assertion that Diaghilev saw the company primarily as a money-making venture. In fact, Diaghilev was so hard up that he was temporarily unable to pay many of his artists (as of August, thirty-one people were still waiting for their salaries, including his manservant Vasily).[16] Against this background, even the slightest accusation that he had grown fat on his box-office takings was potentially very damaging.

But the most serious complaint came from Rimsky-Korsakov's widow, who was greatly upset that Diaghilev had excised parts of her late husband's *Schéhérazade* suite without permission. All Diaghilev could say in his defence was that the cuts had been necessary because theatres imposed different demands than concert halls. He pointed out that Rimsky-Korsakov had himself altered and abridged scores by the late Mussorgsky. And he added, somewhat lamely, that he had 'respected and loved Rimsky-Korsakov from the bottom of his heart and that his memory was exceptionally dear to him'.[17]

It took more than a gaggle of bureaucrats, ballerinas and widows to get the better of a master polemicist like Diaghilev. But the press persisted in painting the Russian ballet in Paris as a murky, contentious affair. After all the adulation that had come his way in France, Diaghilev must have found it most unpleasant to encounter so much suspicion and hostility in St Petersburg.

His success had yet another drawback: the profitability of the Russian ballet lured all kinds of impresarios out of the woodwork. Diaghilev's ballerinas were enticed into performing in music halls and variety theatres, especially in England and the US, where such establishments were thick on the ground. Karsavina had long annual guest appearances in England, reducing her availability for Diaghilev. The young Lydia Lopokova (she was only seventeen when she began to work for Diaghilev) who had been Karsavina's understudy in *Firebird*, was brought to America, where she stayed until 1916. There was a constant danger that members of Diaghilev's team would opt for artistically less elevated but more lucrative contracts. Pavlova had since formed her own touring company, which performed mainly in the US and Britain. Russian ballet dancers were taking the world by storm, and although they mostly confined themselves to old-fashioned, nineteenth-century ballets, they were serious competition for Diaghilev's productions.

With her immense private fortune, Ida Rubinstein had no need of Diaghilev. She settled in Paris and began to plan her own productions. Most alarming of all, Fokine seemed poised to jump ship. He tried to set up his own ballet company, entering into negotiations with the Alhambra Theatre in London for a Russian season in 1910.[18] Fortunately for Diaghilev, Fokine's demands were so absurd that the Alhambra lost interest. But in the autumn of 1910 it was unclear whether Diaghilev still had a choreographer.

That didn't prevent him from devising all kinds of new ballet projects, with a key role for Igor Stravinsky. Diaghilev proposed that Stravinsky write music for a ballet based on the Edgar Allan Poe story 'The Masque of the Red Death'. But Stravinsky had other ideas. Before leaving for Paris he had got together with Nikolay Roerich to devise a new ballet. Subsequently, each man would claim to be the sole originator of *Le Sacre du printemps* – for this was the work in question. In the words of his biographer Stephen Walsh, 'Stravinsky's own account ... has entered the folklore of twentieth-century music:'[19]

> One day, when I was finishing the last pages of *L'Oiseau de feu* in St Petersburg, I had a fleeting vision which came to me as a complete surprise, my mind at the moment being full of other things. I saw in my imagination a solemn pagan rite: sage elders, seated in a circle, watched a young girl dance herself to death. They were sacrificing her to propitiate the god of spring.[20]

According to Roerich, it was he who had proposed the notion of a prehistoric ballet to Stravinsky, a claim he repeated twice in 1910 in interviews with Petersburg newspapers.[21] Both Viktor Varunts, the exceptionally well-informed editor of Stravinsky's correspondence, and Stephen Walsh ultimately give Stravinsky the benefit of the doubt, but the matter remains a mystery.[22] There is in any case no doubt that before the premiere of *The Firebird* Roerich and Stravinsky had collaborated closely on the first sketches for *Le Sacre*, then still called *The Great Sacrifice*. When, in Paris, shortly before *Firebird*'s premiere, Diaghilev proposed the Poe ballet to Stravinsky, the latter was forced to refuse because he was already working on another. Stravinsky described the situation to Roerich:

> The success of *Firebird* understandably fuelled Diaghilev's interest in future colloboration and that sooner or later ... I would have to tell him of our agreement. Circumstances did not make us wait long for this. Diaghilev proposed I should write a new ballet, to which I replied that I was already engaged on the composition of a new ballet, the subject of which I didn't want to talk about for the time being. That maddened Diaghilev! How can you keep things from me, he says? Everyone is keeping secrets from me – first Fokine, now you (that's me) – I'm working myself silly etc., etc.[23]

Although Diaghilev expressed enthusiasm for the *Great Sacrifice* project fairly early on, he was not without his qualms. Since the idea had not been conceived within his committee, Roerich and Stravinsky were under no obligation, moral or otherwise, to allow him to produce the ballet. What's more, the two had already discussed the project with Fokine. As Diaghilev had not yet reached any agreement with the latter, there was a very real chance he would miss out.

With this in mind, Diaghilev sought a way to involve Stravinsky more closely in the organisation, and in the autumn of 1910 an opportunity presented itself to do just that. When he looked the composer up in Clarens, Stravinsky played two new pieces – 'Russian Dance' and 'Petrushka's Cry' – that he intended to incorporate into a concert piece about a doll that comes to life. Diaghilev was quick to suggest that this music would be perfect for a new ballet about Petrushka, the Russian version of Punch (from Punch & Judy). Stravinsky was immediately taken by the idea. Indeed, he was even prepared to give priority to the Petrushka ballet, since he had already written some of the music. Diaghilev, the master tactician, was quick to spot another advantage. Benois had always adored Russian puppet shows; surely he could not resist the lure of designing a ballet on that theme?

Diaghilev immediately wrote to him in Montagnola: 'Enough sulking. Put aside old grievances. You must make the ballet which Igor Stravinsky and I have in mind. Yesterday I heard the music of the Russian Dance and Petrushka's shrieks which he has just composed. It is such a work of genius that one cannot contemplate anything beyond it. You alone can do it …'[24]

Roerich was naturally disappointed that his ballet had been put on the back burner. In an attempt to appease him, Diaghilev proposed that he design a ballet to an excerpt from Rimsky-Korsakov's opera *Sadko*. Diaghilev ended his letter with the remark: 'What a shame that Stravinsky won't get his ballet [*The Great Sacrifice*] finished by spring, but what's delayed isn't lost.'[25] But Roerich was in no mood to be conciliated, and Diaghilev passed on the assignment to Boris Anisfeld, who until then had worked for him mainly as a set painter.

Twenty years later, Benois wrote that he 'set straight to work' on hearing Diaghilev's proposal, but nothing could be further from the truth.[26] In early November Stravinsky was still trying to find out whether Benois would accept the assignment, and it wasn't until 22 December that the latter finally committed himself.[27] Six weeks later, when he and Stravinsky had made considerable progress on the libretto and the piano score of the new ballet was almost finished, Benois wrote to Diaghilev to say that he was opting out of the project after all, this time for financial reasons (he still hadn't been paid for his previous season's work).[28] Diaghilev stumped up and Benois resumed work. His ultimate involvement in *Petrushka* – the production that is most associated with Benois and did the most to make his name – is much less self-evident than he would later claim.

Diaghilev's main problem for the coming season was the status of his enterprise. He could no longer present himself as the official representative of the Imperial Theatres as he had the year before. Indeed, the entire state apparatus, including the embassies in Europe, had been explicitly forbidden to assist him in any way.[29] And then there was the problem of competition. Russian dancers were by now thick on the ground in music halls and variety theatres. Although the shows in which they appeared did not present an artistic threat, they were much cheaper to produce. Diaghilev responded in the same way he always did when danger threatened: by expanding. He wanted to set up a permanent company for touring Europe – not just in the summer months, but all year round. Only by bumping up the number of performances could he go on producing the cripplingly expensive shows that had made him famous. In the last two years he had built up enough of a repertoire to tour the cultural centres of Europe.

Up to then, dancers of the Imperial Theatres had worked for him during the summer months, when they had no other commitments. Clearly, though, they could not form part of a permanent company. Finding dancers for the corps de ballet was not such a problem; the main difficulty was securing the services of his stars. Karsavina had become a prima ballerina, which meant that her time was more her own, and that she could take extended leaves of absence, sometimes for months at a time. It was questionable, though, whether she would trade in her reasonably carefree existence as a prima ballerina in St Petersburg for a stressful stint with the Diaghilev circus. Persuasion seemed necessary.

In her memoirs, Karsavina wrote that Diaghilev had an 'almost hypnotic power' over her:[30] 'I dreaded the telephone, as it was not easy to resist Diaghilev's pressure. He would wear out his opponent, not by the logic of his arguments, but by sheer stress of his own will ...'[31] When she once dared to remark that she, too, might care for some rest every now and then, Diaghilev answered, 'What an odd creature you are! Can't you realise that the present moment is the hey-day of ballet, and incidentally yours? Of all the arts it has the greatest success, and you the one who has the greatest success in it ... A rest, what for? Have you not all eternity to rest in?'[32]

Karsavina, by Serov

Karsavina ultimately signed up for another two years, though she was not permanently available.

Diaghilev's biggest star was of course Nijinsky, and there was no question of taking him away from the Imperial Theatres for extended periods. 'Le Dieu de la dance' was, in the strict hierarchy of St Petersburg, a mere neophyte. Like all dancers who had completed their training at the Imperial Ballet Academy he was obliged to work for the Imperial Ballet for five years before being entitled to a greater say in his engagements, and this term of service was far from over. And yet without Nijinsky, Diaghilev had little prospect of realising the great successes he envisioned. To make matters worse, he was already besotted with the boy. The situation seemed hopeless, but an unexpected chain of events suddenly turned things round.

On 23 January 1911 the audience at the Mariinsky Theatre would see Nijinsky dance the male lead in *Giselle* for the first time in Russia. Expectations were high. Nijinsky was better known in Paris but his reputation had preceded him, and the Russian public wanted to see how their star would interpret the role of Prince Albrecht, possibly the most prestigious male role in the classical dance repertoire. It was an illustrious audience. The mother of

Nicholas II, Maria Fyodorovna, was there with her daughter Grand Duchess Xenia and Grand Dukes Sergey Mikhailovich and Andrey Vladimirovich, who had perhaps done more than anyone to thwart Diaghilev. Baron Frederiks (no great fan of Diaghilev either) was in the audience as well.

Nijinsky had decided to dance in the same Benois-designed costume he had worn in the Paris performance – a departure from Petersburg conventions. The traditional costume featured a jacket that covered the torso and extended down the thighs. The revealing nature of Nijinsky's outfit, which consisted of extremely tight tights and a short, belted tunic, caused offence in the imperial box. In the interval, Maria Fyodorovna sent Grand Duke Sergey to Nijinsky 'to find out what costume Nijinsky would wear in the next act, because if it were the same one, she and the grand dukes would have to leave the theatre'.[33] The grand duke then demanded that Nijinsky first show him his costume before going on stage, which Nijinsky initially refused to do.

After exceeding the time allotted for the interval, the dancer showed himself to the grand duke, dressed in a long black coat, which covered the offending garment: 'Making no attempts to approach him, he bowed to no one in particular and again stood motionless. Suddenly he threw open his cloak to reveal the costume for the second act. He turned around with a sweeping gesture, wrapped the cloak back around himself, and threw one end over his shoulder. Then, with no attempt to hide his anger, he strode off the stage.'[34] The grand duke left the wings and a few minutes later Nijinsky went on for the second act.

Nijinsky's refusal to change his costume and his arrogance towards the grand duke were taken as a grave insult. The very next day he was rung by the deputy director A. D. Krupensky and summoned to the offices of the Imperial Theatres. There he learned that an order had been received from Baron Frederiks to dismiss him within twenty-four hours for wearing an indecent costume in the presence of the mother of the tsar. Telyakovsky wrote in his diary that Nijinsky responded that he was astonished by the St Petersburg public, 'which goes to the ballet as if they were going to a bar, and has no appreciation of proper costumes'.[35] Since the management did not want the affair to escalate any more than they wanted to lose Nijinsky, he was told that if he immediately proffered a written apology, he would most likely be reinstated. When Nijinsky failed to respond, he was offered the prospect of a better contract on submission of an apology. This, too, he refused, with the parting shot:

> I, Nijinsky, do not wish to return to the Imperial Ballet from which I was thrown out as if useless. I now consider myself to be an outsider, and if you want me to return to the Imperial Theatres, then I suggest to you, to the directorate of the Imperial Theatres, that I should be sent an apology for the wrong done me, no matter whether it was due to a mistake or a misunderstanding, and also that I be sent a petition requesting my return. I will consider such a petition and, in due course, will inform you of my decision.[36]

Nijinsky then returned home and told his sister: 'That is all, I am no longer an Artist of the Imperial Theatres. I am now only an artist of the Diaghilev Ballet. I will telephone Seryozhka and tell him. I can imagine how happy he will be.'[37]

Diaghilev saw the scandal mainly in terms of its publicity value. Immediately after the performance he telegraphed Astruc in Paris:

> After triumphant début presence [sic] all Petersburg Vestris [i.e. Nijinsky] was dismissed within twenty-four hours ... Monstrous intrigue. Press indignant this morning. Interview director announcing willing take back Vestris who refused. Appalling scandal. Use publicity.[38]

The French papers were full of articles condemning the shabby way in which Russia treated its artists. Igor Stravinsky wrote to Benois from Switzerland: 'I read the news about Nijinsky in just about every Parisian paper. Marvellous stuff!'[39] The Petersburg newspapers bristled with reports of Parisian reactions to Nijinsky's sacking. This was a victory for Diaghilev, because Russians in general – and government officials in particular – were extremely sensitive about their reputation in western Europe. Not only did Diaghilev now have permanent access to Nijinsky, but he could also use the winter months to drum up publicity for his company in Paris, thanks to this heaven-sent scandal.

The exact circumstances of the scandal have never been fully clear. Nijinsky's sister laid the blame at Kshesinskaya's door. She had allegedly set the grand dukes and the tsar's mother against Nijinsky; the uproar over the costume was just a flimsy excuse to get at him. Kshesinskaya's loathing of Diaghilev and Nijinsky was fuelled by their continuing success in Europe, despite all her machinations. When Nijinsky refused to dance with her in the winter of 1910–11 in a benefit performance celebrating her twentieth anniversary, her anger, according to Nijinsky's sister, knew no bounds. Kshesinskaya then threatened Nijinsky that she would find a way to get some of the group fired.[40] Telyakovsky too wrote in his diary that Kshesinskaya regarded it as 'her mission to break Diaghilev in any way possible'.[41] The least likely explanation is the one most often given: Diaghilev had himself orchestrated the whole affair by pressuring Nijinsky to wear Benois's costume.[42] But there is no evidence whatsoever for this, and the idea that Diaghilev could have predicted the chaotic chain of events that ensued is absurd. The various sources – Telyakovsky's diary, Nouvel's eyewitness account and Bronislava Nijinska's memoirs – all suggest that it was Nijinsky himself who escalated matters through his stubborn pride and social ineptitude. None of the eyewitnesses even mention Diaghilev's presence that evening.

As far as the costume itself is concerned, everyone agrees that it left little to the imagination, but the extent of its indecency is moot. Benois writes that Nijinsky's tunic was made five centimetres shorter at Diaghilev's behest in order to accentuate the shape of his buttocks.[43] This is not entirely implausible, but no one close to Nijinsky, and none of the eyewitnesses or memoirists, mentions a shortened tunic and no contemporary reviewer made any mention of any uproar in the audience. Two critics did, however, refer to Nijinsky's costume. One concluded that the tights 'emphasised the lines of his body in an ugly way'. The other wrote that 'the impudence of Nijinsky's costume attracted attention'.[44] The majority of the reviewers were struck only by Nijinsky's peerless performance. In his diary, Telyakovsky remarked dryly that 'Paris is tolerant of things that would be out of the question in St Petersburg, especially on the imperial stage',[45] and that is probably the only sensible thing that could be said about the matter.

Long before Nijinsky's dismissal, Diaghilev had started to conclude contracts that would form the foundation of his new company, but now, with his star dancer entirely at his disposal, his plans went into high gear. On 15 February Bronislava Nijinska also tendered her resignation from the Imperial Theatres, unhappy with the way her brother had been treated. She was an exceptional dancer, almost as talented as he. In recent years she had made rapid progress and was now ready to take on leading roles. Her resignation was a great blow to Telyakovsky; he invited her to come and talk things over, but she refused. Now that Nijinsky and his sister were on board, Adolph Bolm, the star of *Prince Igor*, felt confident enough to cancel his contract with the Imperial Theatres and sign up with Diaghilev.

A fresh crisis arose, in the shape of an under-strength corps de ballet. General Bezobrazov was dispatched to Poland in search of dancers, and Enrico Cecchetti, a famous Italian dancing master who had worked in St Petersburg for many years, was given the job of moulding the new company into a cohesive unit. In the spring of 1911 things began to take shape, and Diaghilev started using a new letterhead for his correspondence: 'Les Ballets Russes de Serge de Diaghilew'.

An effort was made to placate the two most difficult members of his company, Fokine and Benois, by making them directors – though their appointments were strictly ceremonial in nature. Fokine was made *directeur choréographique* and Benois *directeur artistique*. The latter function was particularly meaningless, because Benois had refused any kind of involvement up to the end of 1910, contributing almost nothing to the programme. It should have been clear to Diaghilev that an empty title of this kind could not assuage Benois's gnawing dissatisfaction or his sense of exclusion.

· 17 ·

Petrushka
1911–1912

DIAGHILEV HAD BEEN ABLE to book a long series of performances for 1911. That year, the focus was to be London, where the company was scheduled to play Covent Garden from 21 June to 31 July and from 16 October to 9 December. Their time in Paris would be considerably shorter: just ten days in June at the Châtelet and a mere week in December at the Grand Opéra, following a series of engagements in Rome at the Teatro Costanzi. Since the Ballets Russes were an as yet unknown quantity for British audiences, the stint in London would be a risky undertaking that would make or break the company.

Diaghilev needed a base of operations, a place to rehearse and prepare new productions, to store costumes, sets and props. If the company was to perform in Europe the whole year round, Diaghilev could no longer run things from St Petersburg. Monte Carlo became his new headquarters and would remain so until the First World War. On 6 April the Ballets Russes would have their premiere at the Salle Garnier, the principality's small, ornate opera house.

Before all the Russian dancers left for Monte Carlo, Diaghilev went to Paris with Nijinsky and Bakst to see some friends and to talk business with Astruc. One of the matters to be discussed was the participation of Ida Rubinstein. The twenty-five-year-old actress had inherited a vast fortune, and over the past few years she had acquired a reputation as an actress, society figure and extravagant patroness of the arts. She cultivated eccentricities that were typical of pre-war Parisian cultural life and reminiscent of Sarah Bernhardt at her most outlandish. This was hardly surprising, as Rubinstein viewed the actress as a role model. Her romantic conquests included both Gabriele d'Annunzio and his wife Natalia de Goloubeff, as well as the American artist Romaine Brooks. She rented an enormous apartment in Paris, where she kept all manner of wild animals, including a panther and a tiger. She commissioned the play *Le Martyre de Saint Sébastian* – d'Annunzio signed the contract in his own blood, Diaghilev later told Kessler[1] – and asked Bakst to design the costumes and Debussy to compose a fitting score. This infuriated Diaghilev, who wanted to keep his star designer for himself and wasn't keen on having Debussy work with other Russians. Nonetheless Diaghilev needed Rubinstein: unbeknown to her, he had entered into a contract with third parties that stipulated a certain number of performances from her.

The visit Diaghilev paid to her apartment to discuss the details of a new contract took a bizarre turn courtesy of Rubinstein's panther. The big cat's reputation preceded it. A few months before, Bakst and Debussy had been invited to Rubinstein's. When they arrived, they found their hostess stark naked, being dragged across the floor on a chain by the panther. Rubinstein and Bakst later described Diaghilev's visit to an interviewer:

> [Diaghilev] was wearing a large frock-coat, to which the panther, waking up from a nap, took an instant dislike. It bounded in Diaghilev's direction and he promptly leapt up on to a table with a cry of terror. This, in turn, frightened the young animal. It took refuge in a corner where it crouched, howling and snorting, its whiskers bristling. Ida thought that she would die of laughter as she picked the panther up by the scruff of the neck and threw it into the next room. Diaghilev was saved.[2]

According to Rubinstein's biographer, Diaghilev never forgave her for the incident. That may be, but the real reason for their estrangement was Rubinstein's independence, a quality Diaghilev had difficulty appreciating in anyone but himself. In the end she performed *Schéhérazade* again at the Châtelet starting on 24 April, but after that, Diaghilev made no further effort to engage her services.

In Monte Carlo the group set to work, planning out the new season. The many new dancers were unfamiliar with the previous season's ballets, and they had their work cut out for them learning the company's existing repertoire. On top of that, the premieres had to be staged and rehearsed. Besides *Petrushka*, the most important new works of 1911 were *Narcisse*, by Tcherepnin and Bakst, and *Le Spectre de la rose*, a short ballet based on a scenario idea by the French poet Jean-Louis Vaudoyer and danced to the music of Weber. *Spectre* was conceived as a showpiece for Nijinsky, a chance to 'give him ample opportunity of exhibiting his extraordinary *élévation*', in the words of Grigoriev.[3] As such, it was a resounding success, and would become one of the mainstays of the Ballets Russes. *Narcisse*, which was a more ambitious project, attracted far less praise from the critics. Fokine and Bakst certainly shared a passion for ballets on Greek themes, but the main reason *Narcisse* found its way onto the programme was that Ravel still had not finished *Daphnis et Chloé*. If *Narcisse* is remembered at all today, it is thanks to Bakst's costumes, which were some of the most eye-catching designs he ever committed to paper. His conceptions for this ballet are artistic miniatures that transcend the theatrical world in their ambition; indeed, in many cases the drawings are scarcely recognisable as costumes at all. Almost never exhibited, their rare showings always elicit astonishment and awe. The vitality of Bakst's dancing figures, the simplicity and elegance of line, the uncharacteristically conservative use of colour, and the contrast between static decorative elements and the moving figures of the dancers make these designs exceptional. Unfortunately, however, their undeniable eccentricity resists easy classification, making it unlikely that Bakst will ever find his way into the canon of great Western art.

The company's considerable success in Monte Carlo obscured the fact that they were well behind schedule for the Paris premieres. That became clear in Rome, where they set up shop in May. In a letter from Paris, Bakst claimed that he was wasting away, working till ten every night and only putting down his brush when he was overcome by exhaustion. Even though Astruc had given him five assistants, he worried he would not be finished in time.[4]

Fokine had his share of problems too. Rehearsals for *Petrushka* did not begin until after the move to Rome, and now that they were under way, the rhythmically complex score was proving more difficult to choreograph than anticipated. Diaghilev was irritated: 'Fokine shouldn't have wasted his

Fokine, by Serov

time rehearsing the old stuff. He should have worked at Monte Carlo on *Petrushka*; and he must find time now, even if he has to keep at it morning, noon and night!'[5]

With Stravinsky at the piano, he did just that. The tremendous pressure strained tensions to breaking point. Stravinsky, in particular, found himself constantly at loggerheads with 'the wilful and autocratic and at the same time insufficiently sensitive Fokine'.[6]

In the evening Stravinsky continued to work on his music: just a month before the premiere, it was still not done. Benois wrote that

[we] decided to begin the production before the music was quite finished. As the management of the theatre could not find a more suitable building, the rehearsals had to take place in the restaurant of the theatre …
The weather was terribly hot and everybody suffered from it, most of all Fokine, who was always moving, and Stravinsky, who for hours performed the duties of a pianist – for who but the composer himself

could read the complicated manuscript or simplify the music to make it comprehensible to the dancers? Even Fokine used at moments to have difficulty in mastering some of the rhythms (which were indeed unusual) and memorising the themes ... Seryozha, immaculately dressed from early morning, appeared almost daily at these rehearsals. He looked extremely tired, for the burden he had taken on himself was weighing heavily on him and the coming season in Paris would demand a still greater expenditure of energy and strength.[7]

The initial reaction to Diaghilev's company in Rome was tepid. Chauvinistic Italians felt that no one could teach them anything when it came to dance and ascribed the Russians' success in Paris to sheer snobbishness. They were especially irked that a number of operas had to be cut from the programme of the Teatro Costanzi to make room for the Russian ballet. Diaghilev felt compelled to write a diplomatic open letter to the Roman newspaper *La Tribuna* to reassure the public.[8] Before the first performance he told his dancers not to be rattled by hissing or whistling. He had been warned that the Italians planned on staging a protest and that a claque had been hired and positioned at strategic points around the theatre.[9] Russian journalists in Rome also mentioned 'the rumours that the premiere of the ballet may be disrupted by fights organised by a claque'.[10]

According to Benois, the technical crew did not bother to turn up on the night of the premiere, so that he and Diaghilev were forced to operate the technical machinery themselves: 'During the performance of *Le Pavillon d'Armide* I had to stand at the switch board myself and give the signals for the different changes. I had to press different buttons every minute and heaven knows what would have happened had I made a mistake. At the same time Seryozha, sitting under the stage, was directing the lighting effects ...'[11]

The dancers were even advised by the Russian ambassador to be on the lookout for nails and shards of glass on the stage and in the wings, scattered there by a decidedly unreceptive public.[12] The evening was saved by the king of Italy, who burst into applause after Nijinsky's first solo variation. 'Now we have nothing to worry about,' Diaghilev supposedly exclaimed. 'The King is in the Theatre and he has applauded us. For the Italians this means everything – the King's approval.'[13] Of course, the Russians were not without national pathos themselves. According to Grigoriev, 'venerable Rome, no less than Paris, seemed to have submitted to a Russian conquest',[14] while Serov claimed that the company's catchphrase now was 'Rossia über alles'.[15]

After their stint in Italy, the group decamped to Paris, which was full of posters designed by Jean Cocteau announcing the new season. Diaghilev's first order of business was to pacify Fokine, who was ready to 'throw in the towel because Rimsky-Korsakov had received more prominent billing on the poster for *Schéhérazade*!'[16] Diaghilev was nervous; he needed a success in Paris to hold his company together. 'It is not enough to take the Tuileries. The problem is to stay there,' said Diaghilev, echoing Napoleon.[17] As Grigoriev tells it, though, Diaghilev had no cause for worry: people were fighting to get into the Châtelet. The opening-night programme consisted of *Narcisse*, *Le Spectre de la rose* and *Sadko*, along with some older pieces. *Spectre* proved to be an audience favourite; *Narcisse* was notably less popular, however. The young conductor Pierre Monteux was asked to lead the rehearsals for *Petrushka* because the other regular conductors, Tcherepnin and Pierné, were both unavailable. Monteux was less than thrilled with the assignment. He knew little of Russian music or modernism, but there was simply no one else to do the job.

For all that, he was deeply impressed by the young Stravinsky: 'This very slight, dynamic man, twenty-nine years of age, darting like a dragonfly from one end of the foyer to the other, never still, listening, moving to every part of the orchestra, landing at intervals behind my back, and hissing semi-voce instruction in my ears, intrigued me. I should add that he in no way annoyed me, as I was by that time completely subjugated by the music and the composer.'[18]

The dress rehearsal on 13 June, which all Paris had turned out to see, did not go as smoothly as they would have liked. Twenty minutes after the scheduled start, the curtain had still not gone up, and the audience began to get restless. Misia Sert wrote:

> Opera-glasses fell from impatient hands, fans were being fluttered, programmes rustled. Suddenly the door of my box flew open. Pale, dripping with perspiration, Diaghilev rushed up to me: 'Quick – have you got 4,000 francs?'
>
> 'Not here, but at home. Why? What's happened?'
>
> 'The costumier refuses to leave the clothes without being paid. It's

ghastly. He says he won't be duped again and he'll take all the stuff away if he isn't paid at once!'

Before he had finished speaking I was gone. Those were the happy days when there was no doubt that your chauffeur would remain at the spot where he had left you. Ten minutes later the curtain rose.[19]

The cultural background to *Petrushka* is complex. In fin-de-siècle art, the stock figures of the commedia dell'arte and puppet theatre (Harlequin, Punch/ Pulcinella, Columbine, Pierrot, etc.) reappeared again and again in various guises, serving as inspiration for a wide range of composers and dramatists, from Leoncavallo (*I Pagliacci*) to Schoenberg (*Pierrot Lunaire*). In Russia these characters were frequently used by symbolist playwrights and directors. Blok's drama *Balaganchik*, as staged by Meyerhold, is the most famous example, but these figures were ubiquitous in Russian art of the period: in poetry, and in paintings by Somov and Benois and by artists such as Boris Grigoriev, Nikolay Sapunov, Alexandre Jacovleff and Serge Sudeykin, who in some sense kept the spirit of *Mir iskusstva* alive in St Petersburg. This was the climate in which *Petrushka* emerged, though the ballet is also indebted to an entirely different source: the mimetic dramatic techniques of Konstantin Stanislavsky, which trace their origins back to the Russian realism of 1850–70. To a greater degree than in *Schéhérazade* Fokine experimented in *Petrushka* with a new role for the corps de ballet, which was given a more dramatic presence and greater freedom of movement. The strict division between soloists and the corps was abolished, and all the dancers in the company were allocated individual roles. Fokine went so far as to sketch out mini-biographies for each of these supporting roles, ordering the dancers to immerse themselves in their characters and to bring them to life with the help of his notes. With its mimetic nature *Petrushka* also struck a subtle blow against the empty acrobatics of the academic style, which was becoming passé. This underlying programme was made explicit by having one of the supporting characters (the street dancer, as portrayed by Bronislava Nijinska) perform a parody of Kshesinskaya's cabrioles and relevés en pointe from the ballet *Le Talisman*, which had been so ridiculed by the '*diaghilevtsy*'.[20]

Petrushka's sinister libretto deserves special mention. The action takes place at the time of *maslenitsa*, a pre-Lenten Russian festival not unlike carnival. At the annual fair at the St Petersburg parade grounds, an 'old wizard', the proprietor of a puppet theatre, brings three of his puppets to life: Petrushka, the Ballerina and the Moor. Petrushka is in love with Ballerina, but he is no match for the virile Moor. After the day's show, the wizard puts the puppets away together, hoping to amuse himself with the conflict that is sure to arise. The Moor plays with a coconut (this was one of Fokine's additions to the scenario[21]), trying to crack it open with a knife. When this fails, the Moor gets it into his head that the coconut is a god and begins to worship it. According to Benois, the Moor symbolises an 'almost bestial senselessness'.[22] (It is remarkable how few commentators over the years have mentioned the explicitly racist character of the ballet.) At the climax of the Moor's religious ecstasy, the Ballerina enters, unable to resist his raw masculinity. Petrushka is mad with jealousy, but the Moor chases him away so he can have his way with the Ballerina. Once he is through with her, he dispatches Petrushka with his scimitar. The wizard, who has been observing the whole spectacle, takes the lifeless puppet away to repair him, but then suddenly the ghost of Petrushka appears above the theatre, shaking his fist at his creator, who quickly takes to his heels.

Like the storyline, the music drew on a wide variety of sources. In his score Stravinsky incorporated folksongs and popular tunes, some of which he knew from memory, others he discovered in recent compilations of folk music. They were then fleshed out, telescoped or otherwise recast and embedded in an orchestral setting that was still imbued with the harmonic principles of Rimsky-Korsakov, though in a way that none of his peers seemed to recognise. The bag of musical tricks so favoured by the Five, with their ornamental orchestral glissandi and habitual alternation between chromatic and diatonic motives, had been abandoned, at least in its most clichéd, recognisable form.

Contemporaries like Serov saw Stravinsky as a new kind of composer who owed no debt to his predecessors: 'This time the best thing is *Petrushka*, a ballet of Stravinsky's. It's a real contribution to modern Russian music. It's very fresh and sharp – there's nothing of Rimsky-Korsakov, Debussy etc., it's a completely independent piece, witty, comically touching.'[23]

Perhaps Stravinsky's greatest achievement was to fashion a unified work of art out of the many heterogeneous elements of his score and the various mood changes dictated by the libretto, and to give his listeners the sense that every note and every shift in metre was absolutely necessary. 'In essence my scores are like bank cheques,' Stravinsky said to Tcherepnin at the time. 'Remove one minor detail, and they cease to be authentic.'[24]

Not surprisingly, the ballet fired the passions of the critics. Stravinsky wrote to one of Rimsky-Korsakov's sons, a friend: 'On the subject of *Petrushka* I'll say that its success was many times greater than that of *Firebird*, its success was colossal – and it continues to grow. You're wrong in thinking that the press was bought by Diaghilev. I see from that you're out of touch.'[25]

That was definitely not the case, as an increasingly clear division was starting to appear among the French critics, between the conservatives, who were becoming more and more hostile toward Diaghilev's newfangled experiments, and progressive journalists, who fell over themselves hailing the ballet's innovations.[26]

Stravinsky and Diaghilev were thrilled by and relieved at the enthusiasm displayed by the normally sceptical Debussy, who expressed his feelings about *Petrushka* in a letter to the Swiss musicologist Robert Godet a few months after the premiere, when Stravinsky himself was already back in Switzerland: 'Are you aware that not far from you in Clarens there is a young Russian musician, Igor Stravinsky, who has an instinctive genius for colour and rhythm? I feel certain that he and his music would please you to no end ... It is at once child-like and savage. Yet the overall construction is extremely delicate.'[27]

Six months later, after having received a score of *Petrushka*, Debussy wrote to Stravinsky:

> Thanks to you I spent a wonderful Easter holiday in the company of Petrushka, the terrible Moor and the delightful Ballerina. I can imagine you must have spent many an unforgettable moment with those three puppets ... It is full of a kind of sonic magic, a mysterious transformation of the mechanical souls that become human through a magic spell, which so far only you seem to know. At any rate there is an orchestral *assurance* I have only ever encountered in *Parsifal*. You know what I mean, I'm sure. You will produce greater works than *Petrushka*, I've no doubt of it, but this is already a feather in your cap.[28]

The success of *Petrushka* was crucial for the Ballets Russes because it demonstrated that the company was capable of more than mere showmanship or Russian-cum-oriental exoticism. In *Petrushka* the flashiness was kept to a minimum: Nijinsky had almost no leaps, and he had to rely fully on his

Benois, by Dobuzhinsky

gifts as a mime. Stravinsky later wrote that the success of *Petrushka* had been significant because it gave him 'the absolute conviction of my ear just as I was about to begin *Le Sacre du printemps*'.[29] Before the premiere Diaghilev had urged Stravinsky to alter the last few bars, which were among the most harmonically daring of the whole piece, so as to ensure 'a tonal ending', but Stravinsky refused.[30] After the triumph of *Petrushka* the ballet's creators grew more confident and began to explore more experimental avenues.

The only one who took no pleasure in the ballet's success was Alexandre Benois. Shortly before the premiere a new conflict had erupted between him and Bakst, one that was even more trivial than their spat of a year before. One of the decors for the second act – the painted head of the wizard, which was supposed to look down on the title character – had been damaged in transit and had to be repaired. Benois was at home sick at the time, and so Bakst took it upon himself to repaint the head, altering the composition in the process. When Benois came to watch the dress rehearsal and saw what had been done to his design he accosted Bakst, berating him even as the rehearsal was still going on: 'I shall not allow it! Take it down immediately! I can't bear it!'[31] The hysterical Benois launched into an anti-Semitic tirade against Bakst

– 'with his Yiddish mug'[32] – and stormed out of the theatre, never to return, not after apologies from Diaghilev and Bakst, not after an attempted mediation by Nouvel and not even after Serov repainted the portrait according to Benois's original specifications.

In his anger, Benois even lashed out at poor Serov, who was the most mild-mannered of men and always the soul of reason: 'Poor Benois acts like a completely hysterical woman – I don't like it. It's very painful to witness such frightening and alienating scenes. He absolutely can't stand Bakst. I don't know what this is about, maybe jealousy of his (deserved) triumph in Paris.'[33] Benois sent Diaghilev a note to straighten out a few last technical details related to the production. It ended as follows: 'Of course my name must not appear any more on the poster as *directeur artistique* since I'm having to give up my responsibilities.'[34]

The previous year's row about the authorship of *Schéhérazade* was still evidently fresh in his mind. Serov wrote to Benois expressing the hope that, once tempers had cooled, everyone would be able to come together again and talk things out. He did however add: 'In any case your abuse of him and his "Yiddish mug" is pre-eminently unworthy of you and by the way hardly appropriate in someone who looks so Jewish himself. But Jewishness isn't the point …'[35]

Benois gives a detailed, unsparing account of this incident in his memoirs, though he carefully glosses over his anti-Semitic outburst. He even mentions Serov's letter: 'The kind Antosha [Serov] wrote me a letter which showed that some words of mine had hurt him personally. I did not reply …'[36] This was not true, however. He did write back to Serov, but it was the sort of letter one prefers to forget. This is what he wrote to 'kind Antosha':

I find the whole of your letter offensive. I pass over the tasteless passage, one unworthy of you, in which you comment on my Jewish appearance (a phrase repellent in its cold and wounding deliberateness. At an intellectual level it doesn't affect me because I long ago became reconciled to what I look like, but I'm talking about your attitude.) This deliberateness is much worse than that clichéd phrase of abuse which I let fly at Bakst and which so often came from our lips and especially from those of your adored Diaghilev – Seryozha really made it a cliché.

I have absolutely never despised Jews, in fact I rather have a weakness for them, but I know their peculiar faults and hate them as I hate all peculiar faults.

Bakst is peculiarly Jewish in that he is soft and greedy, *coulant* [compliant] – the combination gives him something slimily predatory, snakelike, i.e. repellent …

At that point Benois returned to the subject of *Schéhérazade*, restating his position on that vexed question at some length. He ended the letter brusquely:

So many grievances have built up over my fifteen years of 'collaboration' with Seryozha, or rather of his shameless exploitation, which has brought me at the age of forty to a state of complete disintegration, complete demoralisation.[37]

Anti-Semitism was a fact of life in tsarist Russia, and Diaghilev's circle was no exception in this regard, but the rabid tone of this letter is unique in the group's correspondence and memoirs. It is unclear how Serov responded. He did not write back, apparently waiting for a letter of apology for some time.[38] Given that no one else mentioned Benois's letter, it seems unlikely that Serov showed it to anyone. On 22 July Benois wrote a review of *Narcisse* in *Rech*, in which he vilified Bakst's sets and costumes. Up to that point Benois had always risen above internal conflicts in his articles for *Rech*, which he often used to promote the company. Now, though, the press became an outlet for his anger. This did not go unnoticed, of course, and it only served to further undermine his position with the Ballets Russes.[39] Although Diaghilev and Benois eventually patched things up, things would never be the same again, and the central role Benois had previously played was history. For the whole of the next season Benois would be almost completely absent from Diaghilev's life.

Diaghilev, not surprisingly, was too busy to waste any time thinking about the loss of Benois. He had to shepherd his company to London, where they were set to perform in the festivities surrounding the coronation of George V, cousin to Nicholas II, to whom the British monarch bore a striking resemblance. There, they danced a more conservative programme than in Paris. Diaghilev set aside the two Stravinsky works, which he deemed too progressive for London.[40] In their stead they performed *Pavillon d'Armide*, *Spectre de la rose*, *Schéhérazade* and *Cléopâtre*, supplemented by *Carnaval*, *Les Sylphides* and *Prince Igor*.

The London premiere, on 21 June 1911, was a huge success, maybe the company's greatest triumph up to that point. Covent Garden was sold out for days on end and the press devoted long, adulatory articles to the Russian dancers. At the coronation gala on 26 June Covent Garden was awash in a sea of roses and orchids; on the balcony, 'India' had been spelled out in garlands (George V was, of course, also the emperor of India): 'The stalls and the tiers were glittering with diamond tiaras and a myriad of jewels worn with beautiful décolleté gowns. The men wore their sparkling decorations and medals on splendid dress uniforms. In the Grand Tier sat the oriental potentates and maharajas with precious stones in their bejewelled turbans.'[41] According to Diaghilev, there were 'almost as many maharajahs as roses'.[42]

This was an occasion for the British empire to display its wealth and power, and it was a great honour for the Russian dancers to be invited to perform at such a prestigious event. They danced a section of *Pavillon d'Armide*, their most 'courtly' ballet. Two days later Diaghilev cabled Astruc: 'Announce unparalleled triumph … audience indescribably smart. London has discovered Nijinsky and given warm welcome Karsavina, … Fokine, Tcherepnin.'[43]

In London, Diaghilev would always present a more conservative programme than in Paris. Almost all their major new productions had their premiere in Paris. Only after withstanding the discriminating audiences of the French capital was a production moved to London. Even so, Diaghilev had a much larger and more loyal public in London, and it was that city that would come to provide the company's financial foundation. The triumph in London had another effect: the St Petersburg establishment, which had shown little interest in Diaghilev's 'avant-garde' success in Paris, pricked up its ears at the news that the company had won over the upper crust of London society. Doors that had long been closed to Diaghilev suddenly flew open.

When the engagement in London was over, the future looked bright for the Ballets Russes. In October there would be another lengthy residence in London, and in the winter they would perform at the Grand Opéra in Paris. At the very least, such a full calendar meant a modicum of financial security and thus the freedom to try new things. Diaghilev had two great ambitions for the near future. The first was to undertake a major overhaul of the repertoire, in the form of more innovative music (especially by the French modernists) and a new type of choreography. Diaghilev had already hinted to his closest associates that he had had enough of Fokine. Karsavina was shocked when he told her that the repertoire they had assembled such a short time before was already starting to pall on him. 'What are you going to do with Fokine's ballets, Sergey Pavlovich?' she asked him. 'Oh, I don't know. I may sell it all, lock, stock and barrel.'[44] We find similar sentiments in Benois's memoirs. When he once claimed that they ran the risk of losing Fokine if Diaghilev tried to pursue more avant-garde projects, Sergey replied: 'That wouldn't be so terrible. What's a choreographer, after all? I could make a choreographer out of this inkwell if I wanted to.' 'And the awful thing,' Benois added, 'is that it wasn't just bravado on Seryozha's part; he really meant it!'[45]

For Benois, who wrote at the time that he was 'completely satisfied' with Fokine's work, such overconfidence could only spell disaster. But this was no impulsive decision on Diaghilev's part. He had already persuaded his most progressive associate, Stravinsky, that Fokine would have to be replaced over the long term. Stravinsky told his wife: 'As I got to know him [Fokine] (and his work) really closely, I saw (and I wasn't alone in this, Diaghilev and Benois and others did too) that he isn't *modern at all* and isn't even trying to be.'[46]

It is surprising to find Benois's name in this list. Perhaps Stravinsky wrongly anticipated that Benois would take his side. At this point, however, neither Stravinsky nor Benois knew whom Diaghilev had in mind as Fokine's successor: Nijinsky, who had been working in secret for over a year with his sister, to develop a revolutionary new expressive language.

Diaghilev's second great ambition was to take his new company to Russia and show off the groundbreaking work they had been doing in the West. It was time for a homecoming for Diaghilev and his ballet. To achieve this, the great impresario was prepared to enter into a very unexpected alliance indeed.

· 18 ·

Prelude to a Scandal
1911–1912

WITH THE PERFORMANCES IN LONDON finished, the company had two months off, giving Diaghilev a little time to sort out his affairs. On 8 August 1911 he and Nijinsky returned to Paris, where he arranged to meet Harry Kessler the next day.[1] A devotee of the company since 1909, Kessler had made several attempts to get on a closer footing with the Russians. It was probably Misia Sert who eventually introduced him to Diaghilev. Kessler was keen to team the impresario up with the poet Rainer Maria Rilke, whom he had dragged along to the ballet, but his efforts proved fruitless.[2] In 1900, Rilke had invited Diaghilev to take part in an exhibition in Vienna, and a correspondence had resulted. Nothing came of the plan, however, probably because of a lack of personal affinity between the two men.[3] Undaunted, Kessler tried another tack. For some time he had been preoccupied with a project to erect a gigantic monument to Nietzsche in Weimar, consisting of a stadium and a temple, the central feature of which was to be a statue of Apollo sculpted by Aristide Maillol. Kessler wanted Nijinsky to model for the Nietzschean Apollo – an idea that charmed Diaghilev.

Kessler was fascinated by Nijinsky. Sitting opposite the dancer at breakfast, before setting off to meet Maillol, he could scarcely contain his amazement: 'Nijinsky first had to eat his breakfast, which he did very slowly and deliberately. He paused at every little dish on the buffet to ask Diaghilev if he thought that he, Nijinsky, would like this salad or this fish, which in each case led to lengthy deliberations and protestations of doubt. The more you get to know him, the more he seems like a spoilt, pampered child.'[4]

Maillol made some nude sketches of Nijinsky, but he stressed that he would not be able to start sculpting until 1913 – far later than Kessler had hoped. Maillol described Nijinsky's body as follows: 'He has no chest muscles, enormous thighs, a wasp waist: most attractive, but it will have to be altered to convey my idea.'[5] With the Apollo project left up in the air, Diaghilev proposed that Kessler write a ballet with Hugo von Hofmannsthal, to music by Richard Strauss. Kessler agreed to mull over the idea. In October he went to London to see Diaghilev's performances there.

In mid-August, Diaghilev travelled to Carlsbad, dispatching Nijinsky to Venice with his mother and sister.[6] He stayed with Ostroukhov who, like so many other Russians, was holidaying in the Bohemian spa town. Stravinsky was instructed to join him, to discuss new projects. By the time Stravinsky arrived in Carlsbad, Diaghilev had returned from two excursions, this time to Munich and Bayreuth. He told Ostroukhov that the latter visit was because he wanted to produce 'Parsifal [!], which is under a ban until 1913'.[7] (Wagner had prohibited the performance of his opera outside Bayreuth, and his second wife, Cosima, fiercely maintained this tradition long after his death.) The idea of being the first to break the Bayreuth monopoly undoubtedly appealed to Diaghilev, but nothing more was ever heard of the plan. Clearly, his love of Wagner and of opera in general had by no means cooled.

When Stravinsky arrived in Carlsbad, Diaghilev tried to rekindle his enthusiasm for the Poe ballet, but the composer was unmoved by his blandishments. He wanted to finish his sacrificial ballet with Roerich first, and Diaghilev capitulated. While he surely appreciated the possibilities of such a work, the fact that it would be outside his artistic control was hard to swallow.[8] Diaghilev suggested a few minor changes to the libretto and urged Stravinsky to visit Montagnol, to ask Benois's advice. Stravinsky was almost the only one of Diaghilev's band of collaborators still on speaking terms with Benois – in fact the two got on excellently – so in sending him to Switzerland, Diaghilev was also hoping to lure Benois back.

After Stravinsky's departure, Diaghilev paid a short visit to Baden-Baden, where Bezobrazov was spending his holidays. The old general was once again ordered to Poland to scout out new dancers: the corps de ballet had not been up to scratch that year, and the company was in constant need of fresh talent. Back in Carlsbad, Diaghilev took leave of Ostroukhov and left for St Petersburg in the first week of September.

Diaghilev's burning ambition was to bring the Ballets Russes to St Petersburg, and now that he had his own company, all he needed was a suitable location. But the management of the Imperial Theatres controlled almost all the venues in St Petersburg, and Diaghilev was of course on bad terms with Telyakovsky. Indeed, he was persona non grata with many people in high places. With that in mind he decided to take drastic action and make peace with one of his arch enemies, Matilda Kshesinskaya.[9] Diaghilev's trump card was his planned season in Covent Garden, due to start in mid-October. Accounts of the Ballets Russes' London triumphs had not gone unnoticed in St Petersburg. Paris, with its Bohemian public and fondness for newfangled ballets, may not have held great appeal for Kshesinskaya, but London, with its aristocrats and old-world glamour, was an altogether more attractive prospect. By early September she and Diaghilev had reached an understanding.

Diaghilev also needed Kshesinskaya for another reason. Nijinsky was liable for military service. Dancers affiliated with the Imperial Theatres could request an exemption, but independent artists enjoyed no such protection. A stint in the army would spell the end of Nijinsky's career – no dancer could go for months without practising or performing – and that in turn would mean curtains for the Ballets Russes. Nijinsky could, of course, evade military service by staying away from Russia for a few years, but this would torpedo Diaghilev's dream of bringing the Ballets Russes to his homeland. He hired a lawyer to apply for a dispensation, but the chances of success were slim, given his lack of influence in high circles. Kshesinskaya promised to try and intercede, and according to Bronislava, Diaghilev depended 'entirely on Kshesinskaya's influence to settle Nijinsky's military service status'.[10]

Diaghilev clearly stood to gain from a truce with the ballerina, but it was uncanny how easily the two foes managed to bury the hatchet, having only recently been quite literally mortal enemies.[11] Kshesinskaya, for her part, had seen how other Russian ballerinas conquered foreign audiences. A few years earlier she had tried to mount her own tour of London, but that had fizzled out. She had turned forty in August and was past her prime. If she wanted to perform at the highest level for a few more years, she had to act quickly. Diaghilev had agreed with Kessler that in London she would dance *Swan Lake* (in the old Petipa–Ivanov version, albeit with sizeable cuts by Diaghilev) and in 'Aurora and the Prince', a *grand pas de deux* from the final act of Tchaikovsky's *Sleeping Beauty*. Diaghilev had also managed to contract Anna Pavlova to dance *Giselle* and to induce Karsavina to perform in some Fokine ballets in the first half of October. It was a legendary season, with the three great dancers of their day performing in a single Diaghilev programme: a unique event. At the same time it was the most conservative of all his programmes, and definitely not something he would want to repeat.

Not all Diaghilev's friends could stomach his opportunism. Serov was especially disappointed. On 11 September he wrote to Nouvel in his typically dry style:

> First, for all her gymnastic virtues she isn't an artist.
>   Second, she is Kshesinskaya – that's nothing to sneeze at …
>   I don't see any real need to put on *Swan Lake*.
>   Isn't there any desire to get close to and have dealings with the so-called 'highest circles', i.e. the grand dukes etc. etc.?
>   All this is very sad and takes away, for me at least, the wish to have any connection with the ballet, for which I do have a certain attachment.
>   In London I thought this business wouldn't come off but since Kshesinskaya herself is announcing it – it must be so …[12]

Telyakovsky, too, was surprised by the alliance between the impresario and the dancer, and an uncharacteristic note of despondency crept into his otherwise stolid diary: 'Life becomes harder by the hour. Kshesinskaya and Diaghilev are now hand in glove.'[13]

At the end of September, Nijinsky's application for exemption from military service was denied. Diaghilev's lawyer had botched the matter by sending his assistant to the court hearing, and Nijinsky was now officially a draft dodger. His mother was prostrated by this unexpected setback, but Diaghilev reassured her that things would turn out all right in the end.[14]

In mid-October, Diaghilev wrote to Kshesinskaya from London, asking her to parley with Telyakovsky in the matter of renting the Mikhailovsky

Theatre (now the Mussorgsky Opera and Ballet Theatre). Diaghilev hoped to rent it 'three days a week for five consecutive weeks in the period after 15 December'.[15] But Telyakovsky was not to be cowed by Diaghilev's powerful ally and flatly refused to cooperate. Shortly afterwards, Diaghilev announced that he had rented Narodny Dom (the People's Palace) in Aleksandrovsky Park for a number of performances in February. The building belonged to the tsar and had presumably been secured with Kshesinskaya's aid. A large theatre had been added to it not long before, but the venue was by no means ideal. It lacked cachet and was poorly equipped; Diaghilev had little choice, however.[16]

The London season was yet again a success. Kshesinskaya and her coterie of grand dukes and Russian aristocrats were themselves enough of a spectacle to make the press come running. As befitted a prima donna, she made a great public display of her jewellery, which had travelled to London separately. She told a *Daily Telegraph* journalist, '"One million roubles, my jewels?" Yes, I suppose so. I have two sapphires on a chain that alone are worth 45,000 roubles. This is the bandeau I will wear on Tuesday night. See how big the sapphires are!'[17]

By way of relaxation, Diaghilev went to see *The Mousmé*, a now long-forgotten operetta by Lionel Monckton. (He was also a fan of Gilbert and Sullivan; he and Stravinsky had gone to see several of their shows.)[18] He was accompanied by Kessler and 'a young Cambridge student – a mere boy – whom Diaghilev addressed ... as "mon petit"'.[19] The youth accompanied Diaghilev back to the Savoy, where he was staying. By then, he and Nijinsky were sleeping in separate rooms. A month earlier, in St Petersburg, Diaghilev had been chasing after students as usual, making the rounds of the city's bathhouses with Nouvel and Kuzmin.[20] But the St Petersburg nightlife was dull, and Diaghilev made a 'restless impression' on Kuzmin.[21]

Diaghilev must have spent some happy weeks basking in his London triumphs and revelling in the prospect of performing in St Petersburg in February, but his joy was cut short by the news of Valentin Serov's unexpected death on 5 December. Diaghilev was 'prostrated by grief',[22] but could not attend the funeral.

These were hectic times. Every day that the company did not perform cost money Diaghilev did not have, so new contracts had to be arranged all the time. Performances were sometimes scheduled with only a few weeks' notice; the dancers and production staff lived out of suitcases. Their next destination was Paris, after which the company was due to appear in Berlin's Theater des Westens in January, shortly before the St Petersburg season.

On 20 January, Diaghilev received yet another blow when he heard that the Narodny Dom had burnt to the ground. He made desperate efforts to find an alternative venue, fixing his hopes on the theatre of the Literary and Artistic Association (now the Bolshoy Drama Theatre) on Fontanka Embankment, which was run by Alexey Suvorin, a highly reactionary newspaper magnate and writer. In many respects he was an even less suitable partner than Kshesinskaya – Serov would have given Diaghilev a flea in his ear, had he still been alive – but Diaghilev was prepared to go to any lengths to secure a venue. Suvorin, however, was not interested, and, being immensely wealthy, did not have to play ball. He named a sum that Diaghilev could not possibly afford, and with that, the matter was closed. Diaghilev was shattered, as was the rest of the company. Stravinsky wrote a furious letter to Benois:

> I've just heard from Mama that Diaghilev won't be performing in Petersburg. That's how our country welcomes us. It's clear how much she needs us – the Theatre of the Literary and Artistic Association … set such an unbelievable price that Diaghilev for all his brilliant resourcefulness couldn't do anything! The truth is that in Russia the word 'Art' must be taken in an ironic sense. Horrible little tradesmen and crooks – they only serve what is filthy, vulgar, debased, the Burenins, Suvorins and other scum who bring no good to Russia – it makes you choke.[23]

Although Diaghilev had by no means given up his dream of taking his company to Russia, he now had little choice but to find an alternative booking for February – Dresden, as it happened.

Meanwhile, the impresario had reason to feel more cheerful: a secret project of Nijinsky's was beginning to take shape. Unbeknown to everyone except Diaghilev, he had been working for over a year on a choreography of his own. Diaghilev encouraged his protégé's efforts, but he was also wary. For one thing, Fokine would not tolerate competition from within the company. For another, there was the danger that Nijinsky would go public too early with an immature choreography that could harm his career.

Fokine did not go to Berlin with the company in January, so the coast was clear to start rehearsing the work: *L'Après-midi d'un faune*. The idea of using Debussy's symphonic poem for Nijinsky's choreographic debut was Diaghilev's.[24] People were familiar with the music; it was cheaper to use a pre-existing piece than commission a new one; the idealised Greek setting lent itself to a Bakst design and, most important of all, the work was only ten minutes long.[25] If it flopped, the embarrassment would at least be short-lived, and the dance could be scrapped from the programme without having to be replaced. By 26 October Diaghilev had already received permission from Claude Debussy to use his 1894 piece, which had been inspired by a Mallarmé poem. Production could now go ahead.

The ideas and artistic sources that inspired *L'Après-midi* are too many and varied to be fully reconstructed, partly because the ballet's authorship is unclear and partly because so many different ingredients went into its creation. The visual arts were an important influence, from the Greek reliefs that Bakst and Nijinsky so admired to Gauguin's Polynesian paintings.

Diaghilev had also recently immersed himself in new theories about theatre and dance. He was by no means alone in this; the whole of theatrical Europe was abuzz with them. The proponents of the various schools locked horns, but also freely borrowed one another's ideas. Almost all wanted to do away with illusionism and realism – to dispense with wings, floodlights, tricks of perspective and the division between stage and auditorium. Theatre should be accorded the status of a fully independent art form, and not treated as a poor cousin of literature. Fixed scripts and method acting were out – improvisation, mime, garish make-up, marionettes and artificial lighting effects were in. No wonder these pioneers were attracted by dance, with its direct, 'primitive', anti-mimetic power of expression and its perceived independence from other art forms.

Diaghilev followed and took part in these discussions, and the various theorists welcomed his practical input. He had lengthy talks with Edward Gordon Craig, the British director and theatrical designer, a close friend of Kessler's. The latter once remarked that Craig 'firmly denied that [the Ballets Russes'] performances were Art and dismissed its incontrovertible achievements as tricks or plagiarism'.[26] Diaghilev, for his part, was not particularly charmed by Craig, and their various attempts to collaborate ultimately petered out. Diaghilev was also in communication with his fellow countryman Vsevolod Meyerhold, possibly Europe's foremost director and theatrical innovator of the pre-war period, having got to know him quite well previously. They had even been to committee meetings together in St Petersburg. Then there was George Fuchs, whose treatise on dance had been translated into Russian in 1910, and the Swiss music pedagogue Emile Jaques-Dalcroze, who was first introduced to a Russian public by Prince Sergey Volkonsky, the man who had Diaghilev dismissed from the Imperial Theatres in 1901. Shortly after visiting Diaghilev in Carlsbad, Stravinsky wrote to him enthusiastically about Fuchs's book and Volkonsky's first article about Dalcroze.[27] The reason behind Diaghilev's trip to Munich may well have been to talk to Fuchs, who worked in the Künstler-theater there.

Diaghilev was particularly enthralled by Dalcroze's theory that in dance, music was subordinate to, and should be comprehended through, movement, rather than the other way round. Perhaps he hoped that Dalcroze's exercises might compensate for Nijinsky's lack of musical knowledge – a shortcoming of which Diaghilev was all too aware. As luck would have it, Dalcroze had just opened a school in Hellerau, a suburb of Dresden, the very spot where the Ballets Russes found themselves in February after the cancellation of their performances in St Petersburg. Whenever an opportunity arose, Diaghilev would travel to Hellerau with Nijinsky, to take lessons from Dalcroze. Reams have been written in histories of dance about the collaboration between the three men, but it might well never have come to pass if the Ballets Russes hadn't landed on Dalcroze's doorstep.

The direct influence of Dalcroze's theories on the choreography of *L'Après-midi* cannot have been very great, because the work had already been sketched out before the first visit to Hellerau. Nijinsky's subsequent choreographies clearly owed something to Dalcroze, however, largely thanks to one of his pupils, the Polish dancer Marie Rambert, whom Diaghilev employed to work with Nijinsky on his technique.

After Dresden the company made its debut at the Hofoper in Vienna with a conservative programme, travelling on to Budapest in March. Diaghilev remained behind for a while in Vienna to discuss a possible tour of South America. The company then returned to their base in Monte Carlo, to rehearse the new premieres for the next Paris season. At the end of the month Diaghilev heard that his aunt, Anna Filosofova, had died on 17 March. He sent a large wreath, which was laid on the grave together with seventy-five other floral tributes, mostly from feminist groups.[28] He wired the family: 'I share this loss with you, dear friends. Our most joyous moments are linked inextricably with her memory. Seryozha.'[29] If he wrote a personal letter to Dima, it has not been preserved.

The mood of the rehearsals in Monte Carlo was much less ebullient than it had been the previous year. The honeymoon period was over; people quarrelled and sulked, mainly about *L'Après-midi*. Fokine and Nijinsky argued about rehearsal times and dancers' availability, and the former chafed at not getting enough attention from Diaghilev. According to Nijinska, *L'Après-midi* required ninety rehearsals. Rambert put the figure at a hundred and twenty.[30] Whichever was correct, it was clearly a huge burden for a ten-minute ballet. The dancers complained at the tedium of the rehearsals and protested at having to learn a new theory of dance from Nijinsky. There were also rumblings among the more conservative members of Diaghilev's team of advisers. Bezobrazov was the most fervent opponent of the new ballet, and squabbled with Nijinsky on the subject.

Diaghilev's ability to spot the potential of an idea or the talent of an up-and-coming artist was offset by a tendency to panic, lose all self-confidence, and suddenly slam on the brakes. According to Nijinska, this is exactly what happened in Monte Carlo, when he became so riled by Bezobrazov and his sympathisers that he refused to sanction the ballet premiere and even threatened to disband the company. While Diaghilev's threats were to some extent a conscious part of his 'psychology of the hectic', it does seem as if there was an element of real doubt this time.

Bronislava increasingly mediated between Diaghilev and her brother. Diaghilev told her: 'You should have heard what scandal Vaslav caused today … in the presence of Bezobrazov. This is a debut for Vaslav as a choreographer. He must understand that he might be wrong. Vatsa is still a boy. He is only twenty-one [he was in fact twenty-three, as Nijinska noted] but he refuses to listen to a single word about his ballet.'[31]

The crisis was resolved by Bakst, who arrived in Monte Carlo a few days later. He was captivated after seeing a rehearsal, claiming 'You will see … how wild Paris will be for this'.[32] Diaghilev was reassured, and uncharacteristically ready to admit that he had been in the wrong. 'You know Bronya,' Diaghilev said a few days later, 'I have never seen Bakst so enthusiastic. Levushka said

Nijinsky as Le Dieu Bleu

that *L'Après-midi d'un faune* is a "super-genius" creation and that we are all fools not to have understood it ... But you can imagine how triumphant Vaslav is. Now it is all over and he will never listen to me again.'[33]

Three major premieres for the next Paris season, all of them choreographed by Fokine, also had to be rehearsed. *Le Dieu bleu*, with a libretto by Jean Cocteau, was the kind of oriental ballet that had become a company trademark. The music had been written by Reynaldo Hahn – not exactly a giant of the concert hall, more the darling of salons and cafés. It was sheer luck that he became the first French composer to have a commissioned piece premiere with the Ballets Russes: Debussy and Ravel had still to finish their own works. One of the other new ballets was *Thamar*, an exotic Caucasian tale, with bombastic music by Balakirev.

Musically speaking, the final premiere of 1912 – Ravel's oft-postponed *Daphnis et Chloé* – was by far the most significant event of the year. *Daphnis* was one of Diaghilev's most ambitious pieces, taking almost an hour to perform and requiring a large orchestra and choir. Fokine had put his all into the ballet, but Diaghilev was so preoccupied with *L'Après-midi* that *Daphnis* suffered. The scheduling of the premiere, at the tail-end of the Paris season, also betrayed his indifference to the work. As a rule, if a production dragged on too long, Diaghilev began to lose interest, but on this occasion his waning enthusiasm was particularly unfortunate, as Ravel's score is one of the best the Ballets Russes ever brought forth.

Friends and guests were always coming or going in Monte Carlo. Somov dropped by, as did Chaliapin. Stravinsky stayed on a couple of occasions and played the first half of the still untitled sacrificial ballet. He told Benois, 'Seryozha seemed to be dumbfounded by my sacred "inspirations".'[34] Diaghilev did have to break it to Stravinsky that the premiere of his new ballet had been put off for a year, because Fokine simply couldn't have coped with yet another work. In fact, neither of them wanted Fokine to choreograph the ballet, so the delay gave them an opportunity to look for someone else.

Around this time Diaghilev received an odd visitor from a small town in the Dutch provinces: Grietje Zelle, alias Mata Hari. Now that Ida Rubinstein had left the company, Diaghilev needed exotic dancers for the mimed roles in his oriental ballets. There was a plum role for such a dancer in the new *Dieu bleu*, whose choreography was inspired by Siamese temple dances.

Dancers who performed nude or semi-nude had been all the rage in Paris for a decade. Diaghilev's passion for avant-garde trends in drama and music had not affected his grasp of lowbrow theatre, and he knew that stars of this kind could pull in the crowds. He had asked Astruc to look out for suitable performers for St Petersburg, and the latter had come across Mata Hari in his portfolio. Diaghilev approved, offering her 3,000 francs, but when the performances in St Petersburg were cancelled, that contract fell through.[35] He obviously hadn't entirely abandoned the idea of presenting Mata Hari with the Ballets Russes, though, because he summoned her to Monte Carlo to see her dance.

But according to her biographer Sam Waagenaar, Mata Hari didn't want to audition; she regarded it as beneath an artist of her calibre.[36] Diaghilev was not to be denied, however; in the end she did perform for him, Fokine and Nijinsky – with predictable consequences, as she had no proper training as a dancer. 'Diaghilev made me come all the way to Monte Carlo for nothing,' she wrote to Astruc.[37] Apparently Diaghilev didn't reject her out of hand, because shortly afterwards she met Bakst to talk about the costume – though it seems Bakst might have had other things on his mind. 'I stripped off entirely for Bakst in my room,' she wrote on 2 April, 'and that's quite enough. I don't see any reason to do so again on the Beausoleil stage, with all the stage hands wandering in and out.'[38] At any rate, Diaghilev abandoned the idea of hiring Mata Hari for the time being.

On 5 May 1912 the company left Monte Carlo for Paris. The season opened on 13 May, with *Le Dieu bleu* and *Thamar*. Both got a rather lukewarm reception – a particular disappointment in the case of *Thamar*, which the team had hoped might be a second *Schéhérazade*. *Dieu bleu*, on the other hand, had never enjoyed much confidence. According to Grigoriev, '[Diaghilev] was doubtful in particular about Reynaldo Hahn's music, which he had been obliged to accept for reasons of policy.'[39] Quite what he meant by this has never been exactly established, but Hahn was a French celebrity, a former lover of Marcel Proust, and popular in moneyed circles – in other words, among potential backers. Disaster loomed for the Paris premieres. All efforts now focused on *L'Après-midi*. It simply had to succeed.

Diaghilev increasingly relied on the judgement of his friend Misia Sert, who had a huge network of aristocratic, artistic and business connections, and a gift for manipulating the press and the public that rivalled Diaghilev's. She was also a reasonably accomplished pianist, with an insider's knowledge of the Parisian musical scene. Although she had probably lobbied to get Hahn the commission for *Dieu bleu*, its failure hadn't dented Diaghilev's confidence in her. On the contrary, their dramatic spats, followed by tearful reconciliations, were an expression of their intimacy. In a sense Misia took over from Diaghilev's stepmother the role of confidante; the tone of his correspondence with the two women, to judge by the few letters to Misia that have survived, is very similar. Misia's love and admiration for Diaghilev were unbounded. He was 'a permanent miracle' and 'diabolically gifted',[40] a man who 'saw, heard, criticised and improved everything at once, fervently moulding the chain of miracles which so startled the world every time the curtain went up on one of his new productions'.[41] She also strongly resembled his stepmother in her unqualified affection.

Diaghilev, for his part, accepted this love as his due, and not infrequently accused her of failing to pay him enough attention: 'I know nothing more absurd [he wrote] than this fatality that brings you to a town at the precise moment when I have to leave it, or forces you away from another when I land in it and have an urgent need to be with you, if only for a few hours ... Really, these last few weeks you have shown such indifference to all that touches me, all that I hold dear, that it would be better to have a frank explanation.'[42]

Such rows were commonplace. According to Misia, the aim was always to make her feel guilty, and she invariably caved in to his demands. Sometimes she felt used: '[H]e only bombarded me with telegrams, but never took the trouble to write.'[43] They once discussed this at length, on a train journey, and afterwards Diaghilev wrote her the following letter:

> You maintain that it isn't I that you like, only my work. Well, I can say the opposite about you, for I love you with all your numerous faults, and feel towards you as I would feel towards a sister, if I had one. Unhappily, I haven't got one, so all this love has been concentrated on you. Please remember that not very long ago we came to a *very serious* agreement on the question that you are the only woman on this earth that I could ever love. Therefore I find it infamous on the part of a 'sister' to kick up such a fuss just because I don't write to you ...[44]

Misia's connections were sorely needed for *L'Après-midi*. As soon as he arrived in Paris, Diaghilev busied himself to ensure that the ballet was well received, mainly by inviting potentially useful individuals to attend rehearsals. But he remained deeply concerned about its reception. The originality of Nijinsky's choreography was a problem in itself, but its eroticism had real potential to cause a scandal. At the end of the short ballet, the faun lies down on a veil he has captured from a nymph and mimes copulation. According to Stravinsky, this 'representation of the act of love [was] entirely Diaghilev's idea'.[45] Diaghilev may have been capable of arranging some favourable reviews, but he certainly did not have the entire press in his pocket. His fears would lead him and Astruc to undertake a remarkable piece of deception that has only recently come to light.

Diaghilev needed someone of great standing in the French art world who was well disposed towards the Ballets Russes and would, if necessary, defend Nijinsky and his choreography publicly. Someone came up with the idea of approaching Auguste Rodin. He certainly had sufficient standing – he was an international superstar, the grand old man of French art, who lived in a grace-and-favour apartment in the magnificent Hôtel Biron – but he could hardly be called a balletomane. In fact he had never been to a ballet in his life. In recent years, however, he had expressed an interest in dance and, what was more, he was known to have a high tolerance for explicit eroticism. Six days before the premiere Diaghilev asked Harry Kessler, who knew Rodin well, to invite the sculptor to a rehearsal on 27 May. Diaghilev made his intentions quite clear, telling Kessler that the idea was for Rodin to give them a useable quote on the performance 'because Nijinsky and Diaghilev were afraid it might put the public off'.[46] Rodin agreed to come along.

He did indeed turn up on the 27th and was impressed by Nijinsky and the choreography. But there was no question of him writing an article; the seventy-one-year-old sculptor appeared to be losing his mind. The next day Roger Marx, a journalist who worked for *Le Matin* and who was well disposed to Diaghilev, was dispatched to Rodin to collect some statements about *L'Après-midi*. But his mission was a failure. Jean Cocteau told Kessler that he 'could get nothing out of Rodin other than "C'est de l'antique, c'est de l'antique," which he repeated over and over. I [Kessler] said that this seemed rather a slim basis for an article. Cocteau reassured me: "Marx will manage something."'[47]

Around a hundred and fifty guests had been invited to the dress rehearsal. Besides Jean Cocteau and Misia Sert they included the writer André Gide, the painters Jacques-Emile Blanche, Pierre Bonnard and Edouard Vuillard, the German theatre director Max Reinhardt, the poet Hugo von Hofmannsthal and the sculptor Aristide Maillol. Not everyone was enthusiastic – Misia and Vuillard even got into a post-rehearsal row.[48]

L'Après-midi premiered on 29 May 1912, and according to Kessler, the Châtelet audience was the most brilliant he had ever seen.[49] The atmosphere was hushed during the performance, but as soon as it ended, enthusiastic applause broke out, mixed with boos, catcalls and hisses. Grigoriev recalled that 'Diaghilev appeared on the stage flushed and agitated – when suddenly we heard shouts of "Bis, bis!" from the auditorium, which quite drowned the hissing of the objectors. Diaghilev seized on this demonstration to order a repetition of the performance. This took place in a somewhat calmer atmosphere; and though by the end opinion was still of course divided, the excitement had noticeably abated.'[50]

The next day the papers were split into two camps. *Le Figaro* had previously been a faithful ally of Diaghilev's, but Gaston Calmette, the paper's reactionary editor-in-chief, had had enough. He replaced the puff piece written by his reporter Robert Brussel with a front-page article of his own, in which he heaped scorn on the ballet, dismissing it as 'neither a pretty pastoral nor a work of profound meaning. We are shown a lecherous faun, whose movements are filthy and bestial in their eroticism, and whose gestures are as crude as they are indecent.' Calmette ended his tirade with a dig at the Russians: 'This is the sort of show to give the public, with its charm, good taste, *esprit français* ...'[51]

That same morning an article appeared in *Le Matin* entitled 'The Renewal of Dance' and signed by Auguste Rodin. It contained the following remarks:

Nijinsky has never been so remarkable as in his latest role. No more jumps – nothing but half-conscious animal gestures and poses ... Form and meaning are indissolubly wedded in his body, which is totally expressive of the mind within ... His beauty is that of antique frescoes and sculpture: he is the ideal model, whom one longs to draw and sculpt. When the curtain rises to reveal him reclining on the ground, one knee raised, the pipe at his lips, you would think him a statue; and nothing could be more striking than the impulse with which, at the climax, he lies face down on the secreted veil, kissing it and hugging it to him with passionate abandon.[52]

Diaghilev wrote to *Le Figaro*, defending Nijinsky and enclosing a letter from the symbolist painter Odilon Redon, who took up cudgels on the dancer's behalf. He also quoted extensively from Rodin's piece in *Le Matin*. The fact that Diaghilev associated himself so openly with that article suggests that he may not have been entirely au fait with its origin.

The unwitting Rodin – who of course hadn't written a word of the article – suddenly found himself in the middle of a hornets' nest. The day after its publication Calmette resumed his attack on Nijinsky in *Le Figaro*, but this time he also tore into Rodin, accusing him of living at the taxpayers' expense at the Hôtel Biron and of bringing shame on France with his indecent drawings. Kessler felt responsible for Rodin's involvement in the case, and took Diaghilev along to the sculptor's to discuss how to proceed further. Rodin looked crestfallen, according to Kessler, 'as if someone had wilfully destroyed one of his finest marble statues'.[53] He nevertheless said that he did not wish to retract 'a single word of the article' under which his name appeared. He went on to add, 'I would of course have preferred it if Marx had listened to me and co-signed the article. But since the article reflects my views, I have no objections to it.'[54] Diaghilev was somewhat reassured, but four days later the whole house of cards was again teetering on the brink of collapse. *Le Matin*'s editors had found out not only that Rodin was not the author of the article, but also that Marx had gone so far as to forge his signature – a fact admitted by the sculptor, whom they had visited in the meantime. This sensational scoop was to be front-page news the following day. Misia Sert asked Kessler to go once again to Rodin, to persuade him to retract this admission, and Kessler complied. He told the poor old man – who once again seemed befuddled by the whole situation – that it would greatly harm his reputation if it were to emerge that he had sanctioned the publication of ghost-written articles. Rodin caved in, and Kessler dictated a letter to him, requesting another meeting with the editor-in-chief of *Le Matin*. Thus the affair was eventually hushed up.[55] Kessler later told Diaghilev all about it:

I first informed Diaghilev in Nijinsky's hotel room as to my dealings with Rodin, whereupon Diaghilev rang Astruc to let him know how things stood. He took the opportunity to ask him why in the world Marx, whom he scarcely knew and who was under absolutely no obligation to him, had been prepared to go to such lengths to commit this forgery. Astruc mumbled something about an 'ami de trente ans'. But the true motive never came out.[56]

This last revelation appears to show beyond doubt that Astruc was behind the whole affair, though it is scarcely credible that Diaghilev knew nothing about Marx's shady tricks. All in all, Rodin had been grossly manipulated, and the matter – which was not fully revealed until the publication of Kessler's diaries in 2005 – reflects very badly on those involved.

In the midst of all these shenanigans, *L'Après-midi* had had a second performance on 31 May, with a slightly altered ending. Now the faun did not grind his crotch into the shawl, but knelt on it instead. The revised version was received with cheers and cries of 'Encore!'

The post-performance party at Larue went on into the small hours. Nijinsky had earned his spurs as a choreographer, and Diaghilev had been rewarded for taking a gamble on the twenty-three-year-old. The result was the most radical break with the language of formal ballet ever initiated by a classically trained dancer. It heralded a new phase for Diaghilev's ballet company, which had taken its reputation for artistic innovation to unprecedented heights. Though at this point, of course, no one could foresee that Nijinsky's experiment would be a mere flash in the pan.

· 19 ·

A Year of Risky Experiments
1912–1913

TWO WEEKS AFTER THE PREMIERE of *L'Après-midi d'un faune*, house choreographer Mikhail Fokine left the Ballets Russes. The break between Fokine and Diaghilev, which may have been inevitable, was hastened by the squabbling that surrounded the premiere of *Daphnis et Chloé* on 8 June 1912. The many rehearsals that were necessary for *L'Après-midi* threatened to jeopardise Fokine's work, and shortly after the premiere the choreographer accused Diaghilev of being 'utterly indifferent to ballet'.[1] This is confirmed by Grigoriev, who asserts that the only reason Diaghilev let the work go ahead was to spare Ravel's feelings.[2] During rehearsals, Fokine mischievously exacerbated the conflict with Nijinsky by incorporating parodies of the latter's *L'Après-midi* in *Daphnis*. Though these touches might not have registered with the general public, the dancers – some of whom were just as hostile to Nijinsky's experimentation as Fokine – recognised them for what they were: a clear swipe at the younger choreographer.[3] For Nijinsky, this was just another reason to ratchet his feud with Fokine up a notch. The latter, for his part, was irritated at Diaghilev for postponing the ballet's premiere by three days, meaning that it would be performed only twice in Paris. The exact course of events leading up to Fokine's departure is difficult to reconstruct, but plainly, he was not the only one who had had enough. Nijinsky, whose self-confidence was growing by the day, had said that 'either he or Fokine had to go'.[4]

Although Diaghilev's loyal associates (including Stravinsky) shared the latter view, others were shocked by this apparently rash decision. Fokine *had* choreographed *Schéhérazade*, *Spectre de la rose* and the *Dances polovtsiennes*, three regularly performed ballets that formed the commercial bedrock of the Ballets Russes. Furthermore, while Nijinsky may have been an inspired innovator, he was not a professional choreographer like Fokine, who could turn out successful productions on a variety of themes at short notice with a limited number of rehearsals. Did Diaghilev really think that Nijinsky's new language of movement could charm provincial audiences in Germany, France and Austria-Hungary? A month later Harry Kessler stayed up with Diaghilev till deep in the night, urging him to bury the hatchet with Fokine, but to no avail.[5]

A few days later Lady Ripon, Diaghilev's biggest sponsor in London, made a similar appeal, recorded in his diary by Kessler:

> She wanted him to keep Fokine and make certain concessions to the public and suchlike. Diaghilev's almost impudent reply was that the public was there to be ravished: '*Si nous ne donnons pas les lois, qui les donnera?*' [If we don't lay down the law for them, who will?] Here we were given a taste of the Tartar, an insolent but impressive temperament. She wilted completely and her tone verged on begging, though she repeated her position and chastised Diaghilev for his rudeness, saying, 'It doesnot [sic] matter; I donot [sic] mind, how you speak to me, for I am a man; but …' [English in original] They parted in anger. On the way back I tried to make Diaghilev understand how foolishly he had behaved, insulting a woman like Lady Ripon with unnecessary insolence. He maintained that that was the right treatment for that kind of woman.[6]

The next day things went from bad to worse. Diaghilev had been invited back to Lady Ripon's, this time in the presence of the Queen Mother Alexandra, an aunt of Nicholas II, and other high-society figures including the American novelist Edith Wharton, the art historian Bernard Berenson, the composer Percy Grainger and Princesse de Polignac.[7] Nijinsky danced for them, but there was 'awkwardness', and Diaghilev ended up leaving the party without saying goodbye. Kessler was called in to patch up the situation, 'but Diaghilev was completely beside himself with anger. He just kept talking about "*cette cochonne*" [that sow], about how he was going to sue her. He swore he would never speak to her again.'[8] Fortunately Kessler knew Diaghilev and his moods, and he had an idea of how to bring him to his senses. Two days later there was a matinee performance of the ballet, which the Queen Mother attended with Princess Victoria. Kessler had prevailed upon Lady Ripon to ask the Queen Mother to invite Diaghilev to stop by her box and to 'say a few friendly words'. This is exactly what happened. 'After a short time Diaghilev came out of her box beaming, walked up to us [Kessler and Ripon] and kissed the lady's hand, coldly but politely. She got up, walked a few steps and then fell to the floor in a half-swoon of excitement.'[9]

Stravinsky remembered another incident that took place at Lady Ripon's, this one involving Nijinsky. In all likelihood it was the very same party described above, and the anecdote gives a sense of what Kessler meant by 'awkwardness':

> Lady Ripon proposed a parlour game in which we were all to decide what sort of animal each of us most resembled – a dangerous game. Lady Ripon initiated it herself by saying that 'Diaghilev looks like a bull-dog and Stravinsky like a *renard* [fox]. Now, M. Nijinsky, what do you think I look like?' Nijinsky thought a moment, then spoke the awful, exact truth: '*Vous, Madame – chameau*' – just the three words; Nijinsky did not speak much French. Lady Ripon did not expect that, of course, and in spite of her repeating: 'A camel? How amusing! I declare. Really? A camel?' – she was flustered all evening.[10]

Diaghilev's desire to 'lay down the law' for the public and continually rejuvenate the company's artistic basis clashed with an unfulfilled ambition: taking the Ballets Russes on a tour of Russia. With Nijinsky as a choreographer, the company's artistic course was drifting ever further from the culture of St Petersburg. As Diaghilev said himself, '*L'Après-midi* is not like the innocent tights of *Giselle*. If we were to present it in Petersburg, we'd be hauled off at once to the St Nicholas the Thaumaturge Lunatic Asylum, or sent to Siberia for hooliganism.'[11]

There were also certain practical obstacles that made a trip to Russia seem less likely than ever. Diaghilev's inner circle was becoming increasingly negative about the state of Russia's artistic life. Stravinsky frequently disparaged St Petersburg, contending that 'true artistic taste' existed only in France and that he was 'considering emigrating'.[12] The deteriorating political situation did not help matters. On 12 September 1911 the Russian prime minister Pyotr Stolypin was murdered by a Jewish terrorist, who happened to be on the payroll of the secret service. Anti-Semitic laws were quickly adopted (the tsar believed that 'nine-tenths of the troublemakers [were] Jews'[13]). Within the Ballets Russes this backlash had immediate repercussions for Bakst. In early October he was notified that, as a Jew, he could no longer remain in St Petersburg. Absurdly, one of the most famous Russian artists in the world was no longer welcome in his homeland's capital, where he had spent most of his life.[14] There was still also the problem of Nijinsky and the draft, which was no closer to being resolved. Yet despite all this, Diaghilev had not given up on his dream of a homecoming tour. He spoke to a journalist on the subject in October 1912, during a short visit to St Petersburg, apparently to publicise Telyakovsky's refusal to cooperate. He told the reporter that he still

> dreamed of bringing his company to Petersburg and showing its inhabitants a whole range of his ballets … The whole problem is the location [the journalist continued]. The only suitable one is the Mikhaylovsky Theatre which is free till the end of September. But it's doubtful that the management of the imperial theatres would agree to put this theatre at Mr Diaghilev's disposal. V. A. Telyakovsky isn't too well disposed to Diaghilev, especially after last year's controversy over the ballet [the row about Nijinsky].[15]

Even if Diaghilev did succeed in surmounting all these obstacles, trying to shoehorn a Russian tour into the company's already full calendar was a near impossibility. After Paris the company would go to London (until the end of August) and from there to Deauville, Cologne, Frankfurt, Munich and finally Berlin, where they would play the Kroll Opera House for a month.

On 20 September, a few weeks before his visit to St Petersburg, Diaghilev's grandmother died. He did not learn of her death until six days later and responded with a telegram: 'I only just heard about Grandma's death. It pains me that I cannot be with Mama right now. I will be there on Saturday.

My warmest embrace. Seryozha.'[16] But that Saturday he was in Paris, and it would be some time before he would find his way back to St Petersburg. He called Peterhof to offer his apologies. The conversation was awkward, and he wrote the following letter right afterwards:

> My darling, my little old woman,
>
> I said goodbye to you on the telephone and then I cried; from being calm, Western, official, business-like I became for a minute completely feeble and unhappy, terrified of life, loving you not as I would like to; but still you must <u>believe</u> me – you are very close to my heart, in my small heart you have your own corner, the innermost and warmest corner.[17]

Diaghilev's biggest worry in the autumn of 1912, however, was programming the upcoming season in Paris and London. The last season had been a lean year: there were only two premieres, one of which was the very brief *L'Après-midi*. This year there would have to be more, and the company would have to get by without the services of Fokine. In the meantime Nijinsky had begun working on two new choreographies, but neither contained any roles that would showcase Diaghilev's leading lights. Karsavina, in particular, mourned Fokine's departure because she realised that Nijinsky would never make the kinds of dances in which she could shine. To pacify her, Diaghilev commissioned an exotic ballet from the young Muscovite choreographer Boris Romanov, to be based on the seemingly inexhaustible Salome theme. No new music was composed for the piece. Instead they made use of a 1907 score by the French composer Florent Schmitt. The result, *Le Tragédie de Salomé*, was one of the company's least ambitious pre-war ventures, though at least it satisfied Karsavina.[18]

Opera would be unexpectedly prominent in the planned season. After two years without any operas, Diaghilev programmed three major productions in 1913, including one premiere. Diaghilev was certainly not the only driving force behind these works. The conductor Thomas Beecham, heir to an immense pharmaceutical fortune from his grandfather, had become a leading figure in the musical life of the British capital. In 1913 Beecham planned an ambitious programme of Russian opera and ballet, and to that end he approached Diaghilev. Beecham desired to mount groundbreaking new productions, and money was no object. In his memoirs he describes his search for 'some new and vitalising force [that] could lift opera out of the deplorable stagnation in which it was languishing[,] ... and it was at least imaginable that another one hundred per cent Russian institution might be the key to the enigma.'[19]

Although Diaghilev had recently been concentrating more on ballet, his spectacular opera productions of a few years before had not been forgotten. Despite the success of the Ballets Russes, opera remained the preeminent form of musical theatre, and Beecham was determined to programme it. For his mixed bill of opera and ballet he rented Drury Lane Theatre, and it was there that Diaghilev would produce his new programme of opera and ballet in 1913.

For years, Gabriel Astruc had been overseeing the construction of his own theatre complex in Paris; it was due to open in 1913. This theatre, now known as the Théâtre des Champs-Élysées, was the work of Auguste Perret, the future teacher of Le Corbusier, who envisioned it as an example of ultra-modern design. To secure his position in the Parisian theatrical world, Astruc wanted his first season to be an event. Like Beecham, Astruc was interested in a marriage of opera and ballet and he approached Diaghilev to assemble a programme. Diaghilev suggested restaging *Boris Godunov* together with a revised version of *The Maid of Pskov* (which would have its London premiere under the title *Ivan the Terrible*) and a new production of Mussorgsky's *Khovanshchina*. This meant that there would be three complete operas for the 1913 season, even more than in 1909.[20] Unlike then, however, ballets were not being produced to plug gaps in an opera series that would have otherwise been too expensive; rather, operas were now being staged to finance experimental dances. Diaghilev was a tough negotiator when it came to the fee for the operas, which would pay for the extra rehearsal time needed for Nijinsky's new choreographies. The contract between Diaghilev and Astruc would, in fact, plunge the latter into bankruptcy before the year was out. Many years later Astruc described the negotiations to Arnold Haskell:

'I had said to Diaghilev,' says Astruc, 'This year no more Opéra, no more Châtelet! You are coming to me.'

'But my dear friend, the directors of the Opéra want me.'

'So. And how much are they offering you? Doubtless twelve hundred francs, your usual price.'

'Yes, but you must understand that for six years now people say that Astruc invented the Russian Ballet. That, my dear friend, must be paid for.'

'How much?'

'At least 25,000 francs a performance.'

'Even for twenty performances?'

'Even for twenty performances.'

The signing of this contract, Astruc goes on to say, meant his death warrant … Gallantly he says, 'That mad act, that I had not the right not to commit, allowed the creation of *Sacre*, and cost me the life of my management.'[21]

Of the three operas, only *Khovanshchina* was an entirely new production, and Diaghilev asked Stravinsky and Ravel to make a new orchestration, since the work had been left incomplete at the time of Mussorgsky's death. There was already an orchestration by Rimsky-Korsakov in circulation, but Diaghilev had his reasons for bypassing that version. In the first place, Stravinsky and Ravel would do more or less what he wanted, enabling him to indulge his passion for cuts. Diaghilev had been interested in staging *Khovanshchina* since 1910, when he had hoped to present the opera as part of an all-Mussorgsky programme. The 1913 production, however, had a special significance and certainly aspired to be much more than 'a starring role for Chaliapin'.[22] Diaghilev intended to use his Parisian production of *Khovanshchina* to reaffirm his status as guardian of Russia's cultural heritage to the naysayers in St Petersburg. In an interview with the *Peterburgskaya gazeta* he pointedly remarked that 'that magnificent opera [had] never been performed on an Imperial stage'.[23] This was an open swipe at Telyakovsky. In that same article he made much of his intention to 'reconstruct a number of scenes in the opera that did not find their way into Rimsky-Korsakov's version and can only be found in Mussorgsky's original manuscript from the public library'.[24]

Diaghilev's claims to authenticity seem laughable, considering the radical cuts he made to Mussorgsky's 'original manuscript', but it is clear that he was concerned about the production's reception in Russia.

In Europe, Diaghilev attempted to coax the public in the direction of his own (modernist) artistic sensibilities. It was time that the audiences of Berlin and Vienna, who had thus far only been exposed to conservative fare, were given a taste of the Stravinsky ballets and *L'Après-midi*. The tour of Germany would have major artistic ramifications for the years ahead. First of all, there was a meeting on 8 August with Richard Strauss in Garmisch-Partenkirchen to discuss the production of a ballet to a libretto by Harry Kessler and Hugo von Hofmannsthal (Mrs Strauss had put on a 'traditional grass-green Alpine dress' especially for the occasion).[25] The ballet, which Kessler had been in talks with Diaghilev about for some time, would become *La Légende de Joseph*. Strauss may have been an unusual choice for a Francophile like Diaghilev, but at the time he was probably the most famous composer in the world, and now that Kessler's friendship with the impresario had brought Strauss into the orbit of the Ballets Russes, it seemed a pity not to enlist his talents. Kessler's diary entry for that day also mentions Strauss's proposed fee for the commission: the astronomical sum of 100,000 marks.[26]

Scarcely two weeks later Diaghilev went to Bayreuth, accompanied by Stravinsky, whom he had taken to see *Die Meistersinger* and *Parsifal*. Stravinsky's witty account of the *Parsifal* performance in his 'autobiography'* – with its numerous digressions on the constrained, quasi-religious atmosphere, the architecture of the Festspielhaus ('like a crematorium'), the sausage and beer fests that constituted the intermissions – should be seen in the light of the anti-German mood of the twenties and thirties, when the book was written.[27]

In Berlin on 21 November *The Firebird* had its first performance in Germany. Strauss had travelled up to the capital for the occasion, and when asked by journalists what he thought of the piece, replied that it was 'always interesting to hear your imitators'.[28] Another major composer was also in the audience for the Stravinsky ballets (on 4 December *Petrushka* was danced as well): Arnold Schoenberg. He had been invited by Diaghilev, who, according to Stravinsky, had wanted to give him a commission.[29] 'Diaghilev and I spoke German with Schoenberg,' wrote Stravinsky, 'and he was friendly and warm and I had the feeling that he was interested in my music, especially in *Petrushka*.'[30] Not long afterwards Schoenberg invited Diaghilev and Stravinsky to attend the last matinee performance of *Pierrot Lunaire*, his cycle for narrator and small ensemble, which had had its world premiere

---

*Actually written by Nouvel.

shortly before.[31] 'Diaghilev and I were equally impressed with Pierrot, though he dubbed it a product of the Jugendstil movement, aesthetically.'[32] Months later Diaghilev and Stravinsky were still talking about the impression that Schoenberg's music had made on them: 'Stravinsky and Diaghilev are still going on about the Austrian Schoenberg,' wrote Bakst in March 1913. 'Really, I can't make head or tail of [his music] – without tonality – and even if he is a genius: who's ever heard of the man?'[33]

Stravinsky wrote to Florent Schmitt, 'Schoenberg is a remarkable artist – I feel it!'[34] And three weeks later he told a *Daily Mail* reporter that 'Schoenberg is one of the greatest creative spirits of our era'.[35] It is not entirely clear how the composer came to Diaghilev's attention in the first place. Unquestionably his radical music was being talked about in artistic circles, but Kessler was not familiar with him, and apparently neither was Stravinsky. The initiative to meet Schoenberg was plainly Diaghilev's, as we can read in Stravinsky's memoirs. The most likely scenario is that Diaghilev was informed by Nouvel or Nurok, who had caused a scandal in June 1911 by programming Schoenberg's *Drei Klavierstücke*, op. 11, with a twenty-year-old Sergey Prokofiev at the keyboard.

Even then Prokofiev had acquired a reputation as a composer with a highly original, albeit unpolished talent. By the time of the June concert he had already appeared at the Contemporary Music Evening a few times before, performing his own works. His interpretation of the Schoenberg pieces, which was greeted with loud jeers and derisive laughter, provoked an ecstatic response from the organisers. On stepping down from the podium Prokofiev was 'surrounded by a noisy and ecstatic crowd of the main organisers of the Evening. My performance caused a sensation; they didn't expect that one could make something which sounded like "real" music from these pieces, of which none of them had the patience to understand three bars.'[36]

A 'sensation' of this magnitude must have attracted Diaghilev's attention, and from then on the names of both the Viennese composer and the Petersburg pianist were etched in his memory.

In February 1913 Diaghilev began planning a ballet for which Schoenberg would write the music. He also had a candidate in mind for the set design: the experimental theatre practitioner Edward Gordon Craig. Diaghilev had had his eye on Craig for some time, but in earlier conversations the

Englishman had proven to be difficult and inflexible. To complicate matters further, he was no fan of the aesthetics of the Ballets Russes. Nevertheless the opportunity to design a production for such a prestigious company was too good for Craig to resist. For the subject of the new ballet, Diaghilev returned to ancient Greece, this time the story of Cupid and Psyche. When Diaghilev suggested Schoenberg as the composer of the ballet, Craig balked. According to Kessler, 'He wanted nothing to do with Schoenberg, whom he incidentally didn't even know, but instead insisted on Vaughan Williams.'[37] Kessler, ever the diplomat, wrote to Craig that 'there is a grave danger of the whole plan of a ballet by you for the Russians coming to nought, if you are uncompromising on the question of the musician [i.e. composer]'. Kessler then suggested that Craig might do well to leave the choice of composer up to Diaghilev: 'This course I should think pretty safe, as Diaghilev has a very sound and fine taste in music, and I do not think him capable of suggesting anything incongruous.'[38] Diaghilev was optimistic enough to release reports to the press about Craig's ballet.[39] 'Diaghilev wanted Schoenberg to do the music,' wrote Kessler. 'Nijinsky and he felt that Schoenberg's weird, ultramodern music was well-suited to the fantastic, poetic theme.'[40] But Craig, who was irked by the idea that his prospective employers apparently also regarded his own work as 'weird' and 'ultramodern', insisted on the treacly strings of Vaughan Williams, and *Cupid and Psyche* sank into oblivion.

Diaghilev, however, was still at the height of his 'ultramodern' phase. Along with the Schoenberg project, two of Nijinsky's dances were well on their way to completion, and it was Diaghilev's hope that they could be programmed for the summer of 1913. The works in question were the sacrificial ballet by Stravinsky and Roerich, and *Jeux*, set to music by Debussy.

A contract had been signed with the latter in June 1912, and there had already been some discussion of the dance's subject matter.[41] Diaghilev and Nijinsky had come up with a modern theme. The ballet, as the title suggests, would be about sport and there would be just three dancers on stage, in tennis attire (or at any rate, costumes that were meant to suggest tennis attire). In the background an aeroplane would fly by. According to Diaghilev's sometimes cryptic description of the libretto, which he sent to Debussy in 1912, a Zeppelin would hover over the stage at the end of the piece, startling the dancers and bringing the plot to a close. Diaghilev explicitly notes that, in contrast to the Zeppelin, the aeroplane would not frighten them, or even attract their interest. This may be because even before the war dirigibles were being fitted out as bombers, and the general public was apparently convinced they posed a greater threat than planes. In addition, the Zeppelin was primarily a German weapon, and its appearance may well have had certain national connotations. Whatever the case, Debussy saw little point in such a prop. Instead, he wanted to end the action with a more prosaic rainstorm.[42] Diaghilev tried to wrap up the matter in a letter to Debussy in which he again ran through the various options. In it he also proposed a choreographic first:

My dear Maestro,

If you do not care for the airship, we will get rid of it. Obviously, I envisioned the aeroplane as a decorative panel, to be painted by Bakst, which would move along the backdrop and give a new effect with its black wings. Given that the ballet is set in 1920, the appearance of such a machine is of no interest to the characters on stage. They are only afraid of being sighted by the airship. But no matter, I won't insist on it. I'm just not entirely happy with the 'downpour'. I think we can end everything nicely with the kiss and the exit of all three in a final leap.

As regards the style – of the ballet – Nijinsky says that he mainly envisions 'the dance' – scherzo, waltz – as lots of *pointe* work for all <u>three</u>. This is top secret because until now, no man has ever danced *en pointe* before. He would be the first, and I think it will be very elegant. He sees the dance as a whole, from beginning to end, as with *Spectre de la rose*. He says he is trying to preserve a uniform style for all three dancers, in order to make them as nearly identical as possible. This is the general style, and as you can see, it has nothing in common with the ideas he expressed in *Faune*.

I think this information should suffice. We are looking forward to a new masterpiece from you. I hope you have already started on it. Time is of the essence.[43]

Shortly after this letter was written, Diaghilev and Nijinsky called on Debussy in the hope of hearing something about the new piece, but Debussy was less than forthcoming with details, as he wrote to his publisher Durand: 'I was paid a visit by Nijinsky and his *nyanya* (S. de D.). I refused to play them what I'd written, as I don't like to have barbarians sticking their noses into my personal chemistry.'[44]

But the score was due on 1 September, and on that very day Diaghilev again came to call, this time in the company of Marie Rambert ('a woman, as dry as a mosquito', in Debussy's words[45]), who would lead the rehearsals. 'Diaghilev seemed satisfied; he only asked me to stretch out the ending slightly.'[46] Five days later Debussy had to admit that the barbarian's advice had done his music no harm. 'The few measures that D. requested obliged me to rewrite the ending of *Jeux* – fortunately. It now works much better and positively oozes sumptuousness.'[47]

Debussy's score for *Jeux* is some of the best music he ever wrote, a fact Diaghilev was quick to acknowledge. In an interview he gave shortly after hearing the work, he presented the new ballet as the cornerstone of the new season, surpassing even *Sacre*: 'The performance [of *Jeux*] will be a major event in Europe's artistic and musical life.'[48] Stravinsky shared the impresario's enthusiasm, calling it 'the freshest and most youthful work by Debussy in recent years'[49] and admitting that he 'never would have expected such youthful élan from the older Debussy'.[50]

All this talk of airships and aeroplanes strongly evokes futurism, especially when we take the date of the action (1920) into account. It seems quite likely that Diaghilev had at least heard of the futurists, given the intensive coverage of their first international exhibition at the Bernheim Gallery in Paris on 5 February 1912. Kessler had been there and had heard the leader of the movement, Filippo Marinetti, speak. Marinetti had said that 'bombs and petrol were hardly an inappropriate remedy for museums' and that 'all those who love old art [were] imbeciles'.[51] The evening ended in style with an old-fashioned brawl, which had to be broken up by the police. The futurist exhibition then moved on to London, Berlin, Brussels, The Hague, Amsterdam and Munich, generating interest and controversy wherever it went. It is not certain if Diaghilev caught up with the exhibition on any of its stops, but the excitement that followed in its wake could not have passed him by. Yet at that point the futurists were still too marginal a movement to exert a major influence on the creation of *Jeux*. Rather, the ballet appears to be a typical example of that mysterious phenomenon whereby a single idea germinates in several minds at once. If nothing else, the makers of the ballet had grand ambitions for their new dance: according to Karsavina, Diaghilev was attempting nothing less than a 'synthesis of the twentieth century'.[52]

Although the blimps and aeroplane were eventually cut from the final version of the ballet, *Jeux* nevertheless represented the introduction of modernism to the Ballets Russes and a break with the aesthetics of the fin de siècle, particularly as represented by the designs of Bakst, which had defined the company's look for so long. Emblematic of this transition was the conflict over the costumes that arose between Diaghilev and Bakst six months later, during the last few rehearsals. In a sport-themed ballet, Bakst had little scope for indulging his predilection for luxuriant, exotic and colourful costumes, though he still tried to set his own stamp on the proceedings. As Marie Rambert later wrote, 'Nijinsky leapt on to the stage wearing Bakst's idea of the sports costume for a tennis-player: hideous long shorts almost down to his knees and making his legs look very thick (we were used to tights which softened the line), thick socks half way up his legs, and to top it all ... a red wig.'[53]

Bakst's outfits would lead to an altercation with Diaghilev, who was unimpressed by his designer's experiments with a new aesthetic approach, and Bakst's abortive attempts to keep up with the times would ultimately be doomed to failure.

In November, Diaghilev again visited Hellerau in Dresden, accompanied by Nijinsky, Bronya and a number of others. Diaghilev had pinned his hopes to Dalcroze's eurhythmics as a way of teaching his dancers the complex rhythms of *Sacre*, which Stravinsky had recently completed. Nijinsky suspended preparations for *Jeux* in order to devote himself fully to this challenging new work. Rehearsals did not go smoothly: the dancers were bored by the eurhythmic exercises (led by Marie Rambert) and irritated by Nijinsky's wilfulness. This general dissatisfaction was reinforced by the fact that Nijinsky danced the leading roles in almost all the ballets, which often left him too tired to work.

In the summer of 1912 Stravinsky and Roerich had continued to work on *Sacre* on the estate of Maria Tenisheva, the latter's main patron. In early September, when Stravinsky and Diaghilev were on vacation for a week in Venice with Misia Sert, the composer played the nearly complete work all the way through. Diaghilev expressed surprise at the many repetitions in the piece, asking if it would go on 'this way' for much longer, to which Stravinsky replied, 'Till the end, my dear!'[54] The authenticity of this anecdote is debatable. Stravinsky had already played a number of excerpts to Diaghilev, without incident. Together with Debussy, Stravinsky had played the four-hand reduction of the piece to Diaghilev at Laloy's home in Paris.

Debussy later wrote to Stravinsky: 'I can still remember the performance of your *Sacre du printemps* at Laloy's ... It haunts me like a beautiful night-mare, and I've been trying in vain to recapture something of that terrible impression.'[55]

Sacre is probably the most talked-about and revered piece of music of the last century. Even though contemporary scholars have increasingly questioned its 'revolutionary' character (especially over the last fifteen years), it remains the most significant musical milestone since *Tristan und Isolde*, if for no other reason than its profound influence on the composer's contemporaries. Stravinsky's chief innovation was his focus on rhythm, particularly irregular metres, which had rarely been heard in Western music up to that point. Indeed, the metre changes so frequently that the composer himself often had a hard time deciding where to put the bar lines.[56] In taking 'the primitive' as a source for new artistic impulse, Stravinsky was very much a child of his time; equally characteristic of the age was the ballet's acceptance of violence as an amoral fact of life. But the piece's origins are too intricate and its roots in Western and Russian musical history too complex to interpret it in purely ideological terms. In the end, *Le Sacre*'s improbable power, beauty and musical richness transcend moral questions, and its status as the most important musical work of the twentieth century is as secure as ever.

The score was completed on 17 November 1912, and even then, Diaghi-lev knew it would cause a sensation. He summoned Pierre Monteux, who had since become the company's regular conductor, to hear the music, and Stravinsky played the piece from start to finish. Monteux recalled:

The old upright piano quivered and shook as Stravinsky tried to give us an idea of his new work for ballet. I remember vividly his dynamism and his sort of ruthless impetuosity as he attacked the score. By the time he had reached the second tableau, his face was so completely covered with sweat that I thought, 'He will surely burst, or have a syncope.' My own head ached badly, and I decided then and there that the symphonies of Beethoven and Brahms were the only music for me, not the music of this crazy Russian! I must admit I did not understand one note of *Le Sacre du printemps*. My one desire was to flee that room and find a quiet corner in which to rest my aching head. Then my Director turned to me and with a smile said, 'This is a masterpiece, Monteux, which will completely revolutionise music and make you famous, because you are going to conduct it.' And of course, I did.[57]

As with *L'Après-midi*, Diaghilev grew anxious about the revolutionary course that his company was pursuing. His apparent self-confidence was as ever shaky and liable to evaporate at any moment, leaving him wracked with doubt. Nijinsky's unpredictability was a complicating factor. The relationship between the two men was strained, and Nijinsky's increasingly prominent role in the company made him harder to dominate. What was more, he made no secret of being attracted to other people, not infrequently – to Diaghilev's horror – women. In his diary Nijinsky later wrote that he regularly used the services of prostitutes while in Paris, although the reliability of anything in that tragic document is questionable.[58]

Diaghilev's jealousy of his ex-lover was legendary and open conflicts became more and more common. One of Diaghilev's aristocratic English friends, Lady Juliet Duff (Lady Ripon's daughter), remembered an incident with Nijinsky: '[Diaghilev] was an odd mixture of ruthlessness and vulnerability. He could make others cry, but he could cry himself, and I remember a day at my mother's house ... when he had had a disagreement with Nijinsky, who had refused to come, and he sat in the garden with tears dripping down his face and would not be comforted.'[59]

With so much uncertainty hanging over the new season, Diaghilev longed for the return of Alexandre Benois, perhaps because the latter could counterbalance his own artistic radicalism. In the spring of 1913 he made fresh attempts to get Benois involved in the company. Initially he categorically refused, but Diaghilev was persistent, and after a time Benois hinted that he might be willing to consider returning – under very specific conditions. Diaghilev wrote to him:

> I always saw you at my side and as being of one mind with me. In my thoughts you were always *organically* connected with my every movement, and so I don't think 'certain conditions' exist which could part us for good. In particular I think that this year in the theatre is going to be especially difficult, as it's a year of *risky experiments*, and I especially value the intimacy of those few people who until now have been one with me.[60]

And although Benois had responded to one of Diaghilev's earlier over-tures by saying, 'I'm parting with you, categorically refusing to work with you. It's just as much a blow for me as it is for you, we're a kind of Siamese twins … But now a parting is essential – it's the only salvation,'[61] by the late spring of 1913 Benois was willing to consider collaborating with his old friend again. The two talked over a number of possible projects, including the Strauss–Hofmannsthal–Kessler ballet, as well as a new Stravinsky project. The latter was the opera *Le Rossignol*, which Stravinsky had begun before *Firebird* and for which Benois would indeed design the costumes and sets.

The 1914 season, which Diaghilev was in the midst of preparing, would be more conservative than the programme that was to premiere in Paris in 1913, as if the impresario wanted to give his audiences a respite after the furore that *Jeux* and *Sacre* were expected to unleash. The reaction to *Petrushka* in Vienna was a clear indicator that Europe was not entirely ready for the new ballet. Having no patience for Stravinsky's '*Schweinerei*', the Vienna Philharmonic put off rehearsals of this '*schmutzige*' music.[62] The presence of the composer made no impression on the musicians. In the end Diaghilev himself had to restore order. According to Monteux, Diaghilev came forward and,

> knowing very well their inability to understand fluent French spoken quickly, he strode forward … and really proceeded to insult them in an extraordinary mixture of French and Russian, calling them loggerheads, narrow-minded nincompoops, and other most uncomplimentary and even obscene names. They obviously did not comprehend … as he was a good actor and covered his fury and anger with restrained gestures and facial expressions …[63]

Bronislava gives a bowdlerised account of the incident. According to her Diaghilev merely called them 'some shoemakers who do not know a thing about music', going on to say: 'Stravinsky is a musical genius, the greatest contemporary musician, and you are refusing to play his music? … There was a time when Vienna accused Beethoven of violating the rules of harmony. Do not show yourselves to be as ignorant again.'[64] After the speech the musicians went back to work, but few were impressed by the quality of the eventual performance.

After Vienna, Diaghilev went back to St Petersburg for a short period, probably to make arrangements for the upcoming opera performances. While there, he gave two interviews in which he again expressed a desire to tour Russia with his company. In Moscow he discussed renting the Theatre on Bolshaya Dmitrovka (today the Moscow Operetta Theatre), and the Russian tour was planned for January or February of 1914.[65] The only difficulty was, as always, finding a theatre in St Petersburg.

Diaghilev also began to worry whether the Ballets Russes would appeal to the conservative audiences of the imperial capital: 'I think that I must rely on the middle class, i.e. the intelligentsia, the same people who brought success to the Moscow Art Theatre. At all events I don't expect any success with our *beau monde*. The difference between our own snobs and foreign ones is that in Paris they are hungry for new trends in art and are happy to welcome any experiment in that direction, but our snobs obstinately defend defunct traditions.'[66]

But Diaghilev overestimated the Parisian snobs' appetite for the avant-garde. The dress rehearsal of *Jeux* on 14 May gave little cause for optimism. Over the past few months Nijinsky had devoted all his energies to *Sacre*, to the detriment of *Jeux*. The last few minutes of the choreography were completed in great haste and had an improvised character. This was a drawback, as Nijinsky's choreography depended on the precise execution of his 'stylised gestures'. It is difficult to reconstruct his choreography, but Nijinsky's meticulous notes in his copy of the score tell us much about the dramatic structure he had envisioned and about the theme of the ballet, in which sexuality again played a dominant role. As rehearsals proceeded, the futuristic elements of the design gradually fell by the wayside and the plot came to the fore: a seduction scene involving two girls and a young man. In one of the most famous passages of his diary Nijinsky makes clear that the heterosexual trio in *Jeux* was a homosexual trio in disguise:

> I am very pleased if Diaghilev says it is he who has thought up these stories, that is, 'The Faun' and 'Jeux', for these ballets were composed by me under the influence of my life with Diaghilev. 'The Faun' is me, and 'Jeux' is the kind of life Diaghilev dreamt of ... Diaghilev wanted to make love to two boys at the same time and wanted these boys to make love to him. The two boys are two young girls, and Diaghilev is the young man. I camouflaged these personalities on purpose because I didn't want people to feel disgust.[67]

The accuracy of this memory appears to be borne out by his notes for the ballet. In his copy of the piano score, above measures 635 and 654, as the music reaches its dramatic climax and the three dancers are united in a triple kiss, Nijinsky wrote the word 'sin'.[68] Similar ideas would seem to be expressed in Diaghilev's explanation of the ballet in the above-quoted letter to Debussy. In it, he stresses that the three dancers would be made up to look as identical as possible and that the man would dance *en pointe* (a practice that had previously been the exclusive preserve of women) – all of which suggests that the boundaries of sexual identity were being kept deliberately vague.

'The audience was restive during the dress rehearsal,' wrote Kessler. 'Debussy felt the movements were "indecent" and resolved to write a letter of protest to the papers. Astruc wanted changes. Diaghilev grew agitated. Stravinsky yelled to Astruc from the stalls ... "You Parisians have got dirty minds if you think that's indecent."' Even Kessler, always willing to hail Nijinsky's every movement as a stroke of genius, found the work 'more or less a failure, and boring to boot'.

There was a consensus that Nijinsky's costume, which Kessler described as 'white shorts trimmed with black velvet, with green braces, by [the fashion designer] Paquin', was less than masculine if not downright ludicrous.[69] Marie Rambert recalled that

> Diaghilev was appalled, and started shouting at Bakst, 'He can't go on like that, Lyovushka!'
> And Bakst shouted back, 'How dare you say he can't go on, Seryozha? It's designed, and it's made, and it's going to go on.'
> And so they went on slanging one another; yet, funnily enough, however angry they got, they still called each other by their pet names.
> 'I won't alter a stitch, Seryozha,' yelled Bakst.
> 'All right, Lyovushka,' replied Diaghilev. 'But they are not going to appear in these costumes.'[70]

Ultimately it was decided, at the urging of both Cocteau and Kessler, to go out early the next morning and buy a regular tennis outfit for Nijinsky. The shorts were replaced by long white trousers; Bakst's shirt and tie remained.[71]

The first performance was not a success. The audience sniggered at the dancers' wooden movements, and the next day's reviews were withering.[72] The

Bakst, by Cocteau

harshest critic of '*le terroriste* Nijinsky', to quote Debussy, may have been the composer himself, who felt that Nijinsky's 'cruel and barbarous choreography ... had trampled all over my poor rhythms like so many weeds'.[73] Later that year, *Jeux* would be danced a few times in London, after which it would vanish from the repertoire.

Whatever its strengths and weaknesses, *Jeux* was the most progressive ballet Diaghilev produced before the war, in every respect but the music. Even without futurist trappings like aeroplanes and Zeppelins, the ballet contains so many novel elements, from its choice of subject (sport) to its costumes (everyday leisurewear) and its theme (the transgression of sexual identity), that it anticipated many twentieth-century trends.

The fact that *Jeux* was forgotten for decades was largely thanks to *Sacre*, which premiered two weeks later and thoroughly overshadowed the earlier work. Ironically, the events of that historic night were, in a sense, the result of the ambivalence and resistance that greeted *Jeux*. The deeply divided Parisian public was on edge, and the open attacks by the leading critics had created a precedent.

On 28 May, the evening before the premiere of *Sacre*, there was a surprisingly sedate dress rehearsal. Nevertheless the whole company (Diaghilev, Nijinsky, Stravinsky, Gide, Bakst, Kessler, Misia, Ravel), who met up afterwards at Larue, were convinced that 'there would be a scandal the following night at the premiere'.[74] It is unclear why. Later commentators have claimed that Diaghilev had handed out free tickets among groups of young aesthetes and artists who greeted every Ballets Russes production with enthusiastic applause, so that they could come to the defence of the dancers should a riot break out, but there are no sources to support this assertion.[75] Later on, Cocteau made an issue of the fact that Astruc's new theatre, decorated in austere late art-nouveau style, was too functional and had too little atmosphere for a public that was used to opulent auditoriums, where they could sit 'amidst the warmth of much red plush and gold,'[76] and that *Sacre* would have been given a better reception in less pretentious surroundings.

Pretension may just be a key word in this regard. In previous years audiences had tolerated Diaghilev's musical and choreographic experiments because doing so meant being treated to exoticism, eroticism and glamour. Now, however, theatre-goers were being served up a work with serious pretensions, which made no attempts to ingratiate itself with the public. Nijinsky's movements were devoid of any eroticism, as were Roerich's prehistoric tent dresses, which completely covered the dancers' bodies, showing no skin and obscuring bodily forms. There were no plunging necklines or sheer fabrics to ogle. The riot that broke out – and it was a riot, all sources are in agreement on that point – seems in retrospect to have been a revolt of the snobs; snobs who worried they had suddenly lost their claim on being the most progressive, the most daring. The same people who flew into raptures at the sight of Mata Hari's glorified stripteases or Nijinsky's masturbating faun were now confronted with a work of art which did not exist merely to affirm the superiority of their refined decadence, but which had the audacity to be taken seriously. And that was a bridge too far.

There are innumerable accounts of that evening, but of Diaghilev's inner circle, Kessler is the only one to have noted down his impressions the very next day. In what follows, his account is supplemented by well-known descriptions by Rambert, Monteux and Stravinsky.

Kessler, for his part, was completely bowled over by the performance, which he called a 'grandiose and absolutely new art of rhythmic mass movement' in a letter to Hugo von Hofmannsthal five days after the premiere. 'What N[ijinsky] has achieved here is as different from Fokine's choreography as a Gauguin is from a Bouguereau.'[77] That evening he wrote in his diary:

Suddenly an utterly new vision has arisen, something never before seen, gripping, persuasive. A new type of savagery in art and anti-art at once: all form is destroyed, and a new form suddenly emerges from the chaos. The audience, the most dazzling house I've ever seen in Paris, aristocracy, diplomats, the demi-monde, was restless from the start, laughing, whispering, making jokes. Here and there a few got up to leave. Stravinsky, who was sitting behind us with his wife, dashed out like a madman after just five minutes.[78]

Here Stravinsky takes up the story:

… I left the auditorium at the first bars of the prelude, which had at once evoked derisive laughter. I was disgusted. These demonstrations, at first isolated, soon became general, provoking counter-demonstrations and very quickly developing into a terrific uproar. During the whole performance I was at Nijinsky's side in the wings. He was standing on a chair, screaming 'sixteen, seventeen, eighteen' – they had their own method of counting to keep time. Naturally the poor dancers could hear nothing by reason of the row in the auditorium and the sound of their own dance steps.[79]

Monteux:

One of my bass players who from his stand at the end of the pit had a partial view of the stalls, told me that many a gentleman's shiny top hat or soft fedora was ignominiously pulled by an opponent down over his eyes and ears, and canes were brandished like menacing implements of combat all over the theatre.[80]

Rambert:

A shout went up in the gallery:
    '*Un docteur!*'
    Somebody else shouted louder:
    '*Un dentiste!*'

Then someone else screamed:
'*Deux dentistes!*'[81]

Stravinsky:

Diaghilev kept ordering the electricians to turn the lights on or off, hoping
in that way to put a stop to the noise.[82]

According to Monteux the police were eventually called to restore some
semblance of order. But if this was the case, Kessler fails to mention it in his
diary:

At the end of the performance ... a frenetic burst of applause prevailed, so
that Stravinsky and Nijinsky could come out and take their curtain calls,
bowing again and again.[83]

Stravinsky:

After the 'performance' we were excited, angry, disgusted, and ... happy.
I went with Diaghilev and Nijinsky to a restaurant ... Diaghilev's only
comment was: 'Exactly what I wanted.'[84]

Kessler continues:

Around three o'clock Diaghilev, Nijinsky, Bakst, Cocteau and I took a taxi
and went off on a wild ride through the virtually deserted, moonlit streets
of Paris – Bakst with a handkerchief tied to his walking stick which he
waved like a flag, Cocteau and I perched on the roof of the cab, Nijinsky
in a dress coat and top hat, quietly contented, smiling to himself. The first
light of morning was already starting to creep over the horizon, when the
wild, gay company dropped me off at my Tour d'Argent.[85]

Marie Rambert also recalled a night-time ride, though according to her
memoirs there were several cabs. In all likelihood the car was for Diaghilev and his closest associates, while the rest followed in ordinary carriages.
Rambert writes that a group of them rode to the Bois de Boulogne, where
they 'walked, and ran about, and played games on the grass and among the

trees for most of the night ... And so went on eating and drinking and whiling away time in the park until morning.'[86]

Jean Cocteau, who was sitting with Kessler on the roof of the cab (according to the latter's diary), also remembered the ride to the Bois de Boulogne:

When we came to the lakes, Diaghilev, muffled in his opossum coat, began to mutter to himself in Russian. I sensed that Stravinsky and Nijinsky were paying close attention, and when the coachman lit his lantern I saw tears on the impresario's face. He kept muttering, slowly and persistently.

'What is it?' I asked.

'It's Pushkin.'

... We returned at dawn. You cannot imagine the sweetness and nostalgia of those men, and whatever Diaghilev may have done since then, I will never forget there in that cab, his huge face, wet with tears, reciting Pushkin in the Bois de Boulogne.[87]

· 20 ·

Time of Troubles
1913–1914

IN CONTRAST to *Le Sacre du printemps*, the premiere of *Khovanshchina* featuring Chaliapin on 5 June was an unqualified success. Subsequent performances of *Sacre* on 2, 4, 6 and 13 June were more sedate than the opening night had been. While preparations for the grand tour of South America went ahead, the company got ready for the annual season in London, which for the first time would include an ambitious opera programme: *Boris Godunov*, *Ivan the Terrible* and *Khovanshchina*. London's audiences loved Chaliapin. The company mainly performed older works, saving *Jeux* and *Le Sacre* for the end of the season.

The commotion sparked by the latter was by now world news. In Russia, there was fierce debate, partly about Stravinsky's music, but chiefly about Nijinsky's choreography. The controversy became so heated that Diaghilev felt it necessary to wire his stepmother: 'Forgive me, my dearest one. Am very weary. Have been toiling away. Don't believe the papers, everything's going excellently. Will send three hundred [francs] tomorrow.'[1] An isolated scandal might have been 'exactly what he wanted', but interminable protests about an expensive ballet that could not be presented very often were a headache he could do without. He had to rethink his approach. One of the options he considered was rehiring Mikhail Fokine.

That wouldn't be easy: Fokine had been deeply hurt by the conflict with Diaghilev and would certainly demand satisfaction. And it was impossible to imagine the two rivals, Fokine and Nijinsky, ever working together again. Just when Diaghilev first tried to contact Fokine is unclear. Bronislava writes that the two entered into talks immediately after Paris, reaching agreement on two points: Nijinsky would no longer dance in Fokine's ballets, and Fokine would be given the Strauss ballet *La Légende de Joseph*, which had initially been promised to Nijinsky.[2] Nijinska's account is contradicted by both Fokine and Grigoriev, who stress that it was not until later, after his split with Nijinsky, that Diaghilev officially began negotiations with Fokine. That Diaghilev was seriously considering asking Fokine to come back before the dramatic developments of September is evident from an entry in Kessler's diary dated 6 August, concerning a meeting about *Joseph* at which Strauss and Nijinsky were present: 'Diagh. asked me whether it wouldn't be better to have Fokine choreograph the work.'[3] Kessler adds in a letter to Hofmannsthal that this would of course be with 'the obvious proviso' that Nijinsky danced the title role.[4]

Bronislava also states that Diaghilev was having trouble with the management of his regular theatres, particularly the Théâtre de Monte Carlo, the Paris Grand Opéra and Covent Garden, who refused to programme any Nijinsky ballets because they did not 'want to risk their box-office receipts' and couldn't 'afford to be "sponsors" for Nijinsky's researches'.[5] This seems to be borne out by a report published in the *Peterburgskaya gazeta* in September, which stated that: 'Diaghilev began to fear for his enterprise, began to fear that these failures [*Jeux* and *Sacre*] would have a disastrous effect on invitations to his company to European and American centres. The managements of the biggest theatres started to make it a condition that Nijinsky's productions didn't appear in the Diaghilev ballet's repertoire.'[6]

While Diaghilev may have already contacted Fokine before the row with Nijinsky, it seems implausible that the two had already reached full agreement, as Nijinska suggests. One thing was sure, however. In the wake of *Le Sacre*'s turbulent premiere Diaghilev had had his fill of daring experiments for a while. He had more than enough on his plate as it was. His star dancer scandalised the public as a choreographer. His star composer, Stravinsky, wrote music that had orchestras up in arms, and his star designer, Bakst, was refusing to produce Nijinsky's ballets. The controversy provoked by *Sacre* was now tearing Diaghilev's entourage apart.

Problems came to a head when Diaghilev considered making cuts to the ballet. The work was unpopular with the London orchestra, who made no effort to disguise their displeasure during rehearsals. Stravinsky, who was in a French sanatorium recovering from typhoid fever, got wind of this, probably from the composer Maurice Delage. Whether Diaghilev really intended to cut *Sacre* remains unclear, but he did of course have something of a reputation in that area. Stravinsky was not taking any risks and instructed Monteux from his sickbed not to allow the work to be touched under any circumstances. Monteux made a scene in front of the whole company, and Diaghilev was forced to back down. He had lost face in front of his musicians and dancers, and there was nothing that he hated more.

Misia Sert leapt into the breach and wrote a letter to Stravinsky shortly before the premiere:

> I think that Delage, if he were the person responsible, might have done better than to trouble you with intentions about which he does not know the truth …
>
> The truth is something that you must keep to yourself: Diaghilev is experiencing a terrible time, with financial difficulties that threaten to end in court or in civil war. He has broken with Bakst, perhaps for ever, over *Le Sacre* … In spite of the success of *The Firebird* and *Petrushka*, the orchestra made a big scandal at a *Sacre* rehearsal and Monteux lost his temper … Serge always has your best interests at heart, and, in keeping such things from you, simply did not want to worry you … You must understand that he is risking a great deal, and that, at the moment, *Le Sacre* is the justification of his life … My dear Igor, I am sorry that you cannot come here and quash the gossip … Be Russian and stay Russian … Serge has a Russian soul …[7]

However much Misia tried to convince Stravinsky of Diaghilev's noble intentions, the absence of an outright denial that he'd sought to cut *Sacre* can hardly have inspired confidence. Stravinsky reacted impassively to her emotional invocation of Russian brotherhood, sending a one-line telegram to Diaghilev: 'Sorry to have caused trouble but did not understand your diplomatic position.'[8] These were not the affectionate words of reconciliation that Misia (and presumably Diaghilev) had hoped for. So she fired off another appeal to Stravinsky:

I left Serge overwhelmed with troubles, defeated, exhausted … Nijinsky is intolerable and *mal élevé*, and Bakst no longer speaks to Serge. Only Nouvel remains faithful, though even he left for three days …

I must tell you what happened after Monteux's revelation. He said publicly, during a rehearsal, in front of Nijinsky and the whole ballet, on the day of the first performance: 'I am Stravinsky's representative and he has written to me: "Monsieur Diaghilev has the audacity to want to make cuts in my work. You are responsible."' [Monteux] then said, 'Now you can dismiss me and sue me.' Serge answered that he really saw the possibility of a suit and trial … But the worst effect of the incident was that it deprived Serge of all authority. The dancers did not want to continue rehearsing, and Nijinsky spoke to Serge as if he were a dog. The unhappy man left the theatre alone, and spent the day in a park …. I do not want to continue on the subject of the unhappiness that you, dear friend, have caused him.[9]

It would appear that Stravinsky was mollified by this letter – or perhaps by Diaghilev's offer to pay his large hospital bill. In any case, four weeks later, Stravinsky wrote to Benois: 'I'm just as convinced of Diaghilev's brotherly affections as I am of the total indifference of all my ballet and opera colleagues. This last hasn't depressed me very much as I didn't expect anything from them.'[10]

While Diaghilev's dealings with Stravinsky entered a rare phase of tranquillity, his relationship with Nijinsky was deteriorating. There has been endless speculation about the end of this storied affair, but there are almost no reliable, impartial accounts. The most well-known document, Nijinsky's 'diary', was written while he was in the grip of a psychosis that would rob him of his reason. The other two accounts, by Romola de Pulzsky and Bronislava Nijinska, are clearly biased. Both sought to salvage Nijinsky's reputation, while Romola tried to put a positive spin on her own role.

Nijinsky wrote in his diary about several alleged conflicts with Diaghilev:

I began to hate him quite openly, and once I pushed him on a street in Paris. I pushed him because I wanted to show him that I was not afraid of him. Diaghilev hit me with his cane because I wanted to leave him. He felt that I wanted to go away, and therefore he ran after me. I half ran, half walked. I was afraid of being noticed.[11]

Nijinsky's affection for Diaghilev was a thing of the past. He was now repelled by the ageing impresario:

Diaghilev dyes his hair so as not to be old. Diaghilev's hair is grey. Diaghilev buys black hair creams and rubs them in. I noticed this cream on Diaghilev's pillows, which have black pillowcases. I do not like dirty pillowcases and therefore felt disgusted when I saw them. Diaghilev has two false front teeth. I noticed this because when he is nervous he touches them with his tongue. They move, and I can see them. Diaghilev reminds me of a wicked old woman when he moves his two front teeth.[12]

Some time before, the two men had ceased to share a hotel room, and Nijinsky claimed that he locked his door to keep Diaghilev out. Diaghilev tried desperately to prevent him from being alone with women, making his manservant Vasily act as Nijinsky's bodyguard. The breakdown of their relationship was a tragic and at times embarrassing spectacle. However hard Diaghilev tried to hide the fact from the outside world, it was plain to friends like Benois that their affair had ended by the summer of 1913.[13]

On 15 August 1913 the company left for Buenos Aires, without Diaghilev. Not only was he terrified of sea voyages, he also still had his hands full organising the next season. So his business partner, Dmitri de Gunzburg, who had been quietly active since the 1909 season, was sent in his stead. It has been speculated that Diaghilev would never have let Nijinsky out of his sight if his infatuation had not cooled; as it was, Vasily went along to keep an eye on him.

The passenger list included the Hungarian millionaire's daughter Romola de Pulzsky. According to dancer and fellow passenger Marie Rambert, who was one of the few who enjoyed Nijinsky's confidence, the dancer fell in love with Romola, and witnesses confirm that they were seen together on a number of occasions, engaged in animated conversation.[14] Yet everyone dismissed it as a fleeting shipboard romance, aware that he was Diaghilev's lover. According to Romola, Nijinsky's proposal, somewhere in the second week of the voyage, came as a complete surprise.[15] On 10 September 1913 they were married in the Iglesia San Miguel, a few days after landing at Buenos Aires. Both the engagement and the wedding took place without the knowledge of his mother, his sister, or Diaghilev.

Bronislava Nijinska and her mother Eleonora were both in St Petersburg during the first few weeks of September. They learned of Nijinsky's marriage from the papers. His mother was deeply upset that her son had neither sought her permission nor informed her of his engagement by telegram. Romola later admitted to Bronislava that they had deliberately kept both the family and Diaghilev in the dark, for fear that they would prevent the marriage.

Diaghilev heard the news in Venice, where he was staying with the Serts. Misia vividly recalled the moment when the fateful telegram arrived. Diaghilev was in high spirits. He had just received a score, and asked her to play it for him.

> I can see myself entering his room, dangling a parasol, in a dress of white muslin. He was still in his nightshirt, with slippers on his feet … Performing elephantine capers across the room, in his enthusiasm he seized my parasol and opened it. I stopped playing with a start, and told him to shut it, as it brought bad luck to open it indoors and he was madly superstitious. Barely had I time to utter my warning when somebody knocked at the door. A telegram …
>
> Diaghilev turned livid …
>
> Serge, overcome with a sort of hysteria, ready to go to any extreme, sobbing and shouting, gathered everybody around – Sert, Bakst etc.… . We immediately took Diaghilev, drunk with grief and rage, to Naples, where he launched himself on a frantic bacchanalia.[16]

On the way south, the party stopped in Florence, where Diaghilev engaged a young Italian, Beppe Potetti, to serve him in Vasily's absence. He may have been angry that Vasily hadn't managed to prevent the marriage – or at least give his employer some warning.

By the end of September Diaghilev was back in Venice, where he immediately took steps to eject Nijinsky from his company. He and Hofmannsthal lost no time in agreeing that Fokine should choreograph the Strauss ballet *La Légende de Joseph*. What Diaghilev didn't tell Hofmannsthal was that this would prevent Nijinsky from dancing the leading role, since Fokine flatly refused to work with him. The next hurdle to be tackled was Stravinsky: if Nijinsky left the company and Fokine was put in charge of choreography, there wouldn't be any more performances of *Sacre*. What's more, not only was Stravinsky very happy with Nijinsky's choreography, the two men had also become friends. On 29 September Diaghilev wired Stravinsky, who was working in Clarens, that he would visit him the following day.[17]

He stayed for a few days with Stravinsky, who found the bad news hard to take. When Anna Fyodorova, a dancer from his company, happened upon Diaghilev at a Montreux café, she could scarcely conceal her fright at his appearance: 'He was sitting alone, at a cafe table on the terrace of the hotel on the shore of the lake. The table in front of him was empty. Diaghilev appeared deep in thought, his chin resting on his hands folded on top of his cane. I approached to greet him, he lifted his head and I was frightened to see his face so distorted by grief ... he did not say a word, he did not answer me.'[18]

When the news became known, more and more friends started to speculate about what had happened. Benois wrote to Stravinsky: 'Not a word's been heard from him. He's gone missing – so that I'm even prepared to believe these charming rumours (they've clearly also reached you) that Vatslav has married a Hungarian lady – nice, really, and Seryozha (in a rage?) "has sold his company to some entrepreneur". Do you know anything of our inconsolable [illegible]?'[19]

It is clear from Stravinsky's answer that he regarded Nijinsky's marriage as a calamity, but the letter also reveals that his quarrel with Diaghilev went deeper than this temporary crisis:

I didn't know anything about Nijinsky's marriage because I haven't been reading the newspapers recently and I only heard this from Seryozha ... Of course, this turns everything upside down – literally everything we've been doing – and you yourself can foresee all the consequences: for him it's all over, I too may long be deprived of the possibility of doing something valuable in choreography, and, even more important, of seeing my creation which had been made flesh, choreographically speaking, with such incredible efforts. Ah, my friend, this last creation gives me not a minute's rest. It's surrounded by a dreadful din, like devils gnashing their teeth. Seryozha tells me the facts of the betrayal – which pain me – by people who had responded to my earlier works with great enthusiasm or firm sympathy. So what, I say – or rather, think – this was bound to be – but why was Seryozha in two minds about *Sacre* – a work which at rehearsals he invariably listened to with exclamations of 'Divine!' He even said (which in truth one might look on as a compliment) that this work should be left to mature after composition, for the public wasn't yet ready for it – but

LE THÉÂTRE

M. WAZLAW NIJINSKY, PREMIER DANSEUR. — Mlle ANNA PAVLOVA, PRIMA BALLERINA DU THÉATRE IMPÉRIAL MARIE (PÉTERSBOURG)
LE PAVILLON D'ARMIDE

ÉDITEURS : *Manzi, Joyant & Cie*, 24, *Boulevard des Capucines, Paris.* — PRIX NET : **2** fr.; Étranger, **2** fr. **50**

1. *Nijinsky and Pavlova (wearing Benois' costumes) in* Le Pavillon d'Armide, *1909: cover of* Le Théâtre *advertising the first season of the Ballets Russes in Paris.*

2. Design for stage curtain for Schéhérazade *by Valentin Serov, 1910. The rest of the sets and costumes were from Bakst's sumptuous Orientalist designs.*

THE THEATRE

3. The exotic Ida Rubinstein as the favoured harem slave Zobéïde in Schéhérazade, *1911: cover of* The Theatre *advertising the Ballets Russes' English tour.*

4. Aleksandr Golovin's backdrop design 'The Realm of Kashchey' for The Firebird, *Paris Opéra, 1910: a highpoint of Russian stage design.*

5. *Bakst's costume design for two Boeotian women in* Narcisse, *1911, which had some of the most eye-catching designs he ever committed to paper.*

6. *Curtain design for Act II of* Chout *(1921) by Mikhail Larionov: in Buckle's words 'Abramtsevo … after an earthquake'.*

7. *Backcloth design for the finale of the 1926 revival of* The Firebird *by Natalia Goncharova: it very precisely fulfils Diaghilev's vision of the set.*

8. *A scale model (by Lesley-Anne Sayers, 1999) of Georgy Yakulov's astonishing Constructivist set for* Le Pas d'Acier, *1927.*

why did he never mention that kind of approach before – either in the *Mir iskusstva* period or later. Very simply, I fear he has come under bad influences, ones that I think are strong in a material rather than a moral sense. Actually, summing up my impressions of his attitude to *Sacre*, I come to the conclusion that he isn't encouraging me in this direction – that means I am deprived of my sole and truest support for the promotion of my artistic ideas – as you yourself will agree, that completely knocks my legs out from under me, for I can't, you must understand, I can't compose what they want from me – i.e. repeat myself – repeat anyone else but not yourself – that's how people expend themselves. But that's enough about *Sacre*, I'm feeling very low.[20]

Stravinsky had good cause to be disappointed in Diaghilev. In the contract for the next Stravinsky production (the opera *Le Rossignol*, planned for 1914), Diaghilev had included a clause stipulating that 'if the premiere in Paris creates a scandal like *Sacre*, then maybe he won't need to repeat *Le Rossignol* in view of the fact that this time the performances will be in the Grand Opéra'.[21]

That suggests that theatre managers were attaching conditions to productions of new works by Stravinsky. Whatever the case, the hard-pressed Diaghilev had little choice but to adopt a conservative programme for 1914.

It is unclear whether he had already discussed Fokine's possible return with Stravinsky. The doubts Diaghilev expressed about *Sacre* may have just been a way of preparing Stravinsky for the reappearance of a man whose dismissal he had openly encouraged, a man who would certainly not allow any work by Nijinsky – whose foray into choreography Stravinsky had promoted – to be performed next season.

Stravinsky was in a bad mood after his visit from Diaghilev, but it seemed he would toe the party line. The biggest challenge was to persuade Fokine to recommit to the company, so that they would at least be able to present new ballets in the coming season. Diaghilev left for Russia in December. His main purpose was to talk to Fokine, but he was also looking for a dancer who could replace Nijinsky. This would be a delicate mission, because neither Kessler nor Strauss was prepared even to consider the possibility of staging their ballet without Nijinsky.

On 8 November Diaghilev was in Berlin.[22] He probably then went straight to Moscow, rather than St Petersburg, to recruit singers for his opera pro-gramme. In the latter half of November he was back in St Petersburg, where he broke the Fokine plan to Grigoriev, just returned from South America. The latter was astonished at the notion, but Diaghilev was obdurate. Before ringing Fokine he wiped the receiver with his handkerchief as he always did, fearful as he was of infection.

> There was then a to me ominous pause before a conversation started. It lasted no less than five hours. I could not hear what Fokine said, but it was evident enough that Diaghilev was having no easy time with him ... But Diaghilev was not deterred. He let him say all he wished, biding his time, and then protested at Fokine's accusations, defended his own standpoint and embarked on persuasion as only he knew how ... As he replaced the receiver Diaghilev heaved a sigh of relief. 'Well, that's settled, I think,' he said. 'He was a tough nut to crack, though, all the same!'[23]

According to Grigoriev this conversation took place in 1914, but a letter from Bakst to Stravinsky shows that Fokine and Diaghilev had already reached agreement by the second half of November 1913.[24]

Only when he was sure that Fokine was on board did Diaghilev take the step of officially firing Nijinsky. He called Grigoriev over and handed him a telegram from Nijinsky, which had arrived around the end of November. In it he asked 'when rehearsals were to start and when he was to begin work on a new ballet, and requested Diaghilev to see that during rehearsals the company should not be employed on anything else'. Grigoriev continues:

> When I had read the telegram Diaghilev put it on the table and covered it with the palm of his hand. This was what he always did with any communication that annoyed him. Then, looking at me sideways with his ironical smile, he said, 'I should like you, as my *régisseur*, to sign the telegram I propose sending in reply to this.' He then took up a telegraph form from the table, and screwing his monocle into his eye and biting his tongue (as he would when worked up) he wrote his answer.[25]

This was the telegram informing Nijinsky that the Ballets Russes no longer had need of his services.

Much surprise has been expressed at Diaghilev's callousness in ending a partnership of several years with a telegram signed by an assistant. Indeed, his actions were even more reprehensible given that Nijinsky always worked without a contract and hadn't drawn a salary in years. That did not matter as long as he was with the Ballets Russes. As Diaghilev's partner he had wanted for nothing, and the company had even looked after his family. But now he was left without a cent. In his innocence Nijinsky was amazed at the vehemence of Diaghilev's reaction to his marriage and the cold-blooded way in which he had severed all contact. And Nijinsky was not alone in wondering how the Ballets Russes could carry on without its star performer. He turned to Stravinsky, begging the composer to intercede for him:

> You know that I went to South America and haven't been in Europe for four months. These months have cost me a lot of money and my health. I was paying 150 francs a day for my room and food. I wasn't being paid that money by Seryozha and I had to make it up from my own resources.
>
> I didn't know what Seryozha was doing during the time we were in America. I wrote to him a lot and didn't get a single letter in return. But I needed an answer because I was working on new ballets, Strauss's *Légende de Joseph* and another to the music of Bach …
>
> I didn't send you an invitation to my wedding because I knew you wouldn't come. I didn't write to you because I was very busy. Please forgive me.
>
> My wife and I went to her parents in Budapest and I sent Seryozha a telegram asking where and when we could meet. I received a reply to my telegram from Grigoriev, saying that this season no ballet productions are being given to me and that I am not needed as a dancer either. Please write to me – is this true or not? I can't believe that Seryozha could behave so badly to me. Seryozha owes me a lot of money. For two years I wasn't paid anything at all for my dancing or for the new productions of *Faune* and *Jeux* and *Sacre*. I was working without a contract. If it's true that Seryozha doesn't want to work with me any more, I have lost everything. You see what situation I'm in now.
>
> I can't understand why Seryozha's behaved like this. Ask him what the matter is, and write to me.
>
> All the magazines in Germany, Paris, London etc. write that I'm no longer working with Diaghilev and the whole of the press is producing satirical pieces against him. Besides saying that I won't be working with

Seryozha, they are writing that I'm putting a company together. I am being made all kinds of proposals from all sides. The most important proposal comes from a rich German who is offering something like a million francs to set up a new company like Diaghilev's Ballets Russes and I'm being offered the whole artistic direction of the company and a great deal of money. The sets and costumes, the music would be commissioned by me. But I'm not giving him a definite answer until I get news from you.[26]

A few days earlier, on 5 December 1913, Nijinsky had already told Astruc, 'Please inform the newspapers that I shall not be working any longer with Diaghilev.'[27] It was an unusually canny move on Nijinsky's part to break the news of his 'departure' from the Ballets Russes to the world's press, thus saving face. His appeal to Stravinsky seems to have fallen on deaf ears, though, and Diaghilev continued to act as if he did not exist. There was no returning to the Ballets Russes.

Even in the gossip and scandal-ridden history of the Russian ballet in Paris, the split-up of Diaghilev and Nijinsky has proved an inexhaustible mine of speculation and conspiracy theories. It has often been claimed that Diaghilev deliberately engineered the break-up by bringing Nijinsky and Romola together, because he was tired of Nijinsky and had lost faith in his abilities as a choreographer. Some maintain that Gunzburg exploited Diaghilev's absence to bring Nijinsky into contact with Romola because he wanted to set up his own company with Nijinsky as the star.[28] Not only are both these theories completely unsubstantiated, they rest on the assumption that Nijinsky would meekly allow himself to be manoeuvred into marriage. And that is where they lose all credence. Nijinsky was no cipher; his legendary stubbornness caused Diaghilev countless headaches.

Nijinsky's exit and Fokine's reappearance of course affected the next year's programme. *La Légende de Joseph*, destined to be the flagship production for 1914, could go ahead. Indeed, that was the ballet which had lured Fokine back into the team. But other works which were to have been entrusted to Nijinsky, like a Bach ballet, had to be postponed. New productions had to be completed in haste. Fortunately there was still the opera *Le Rossignol*, which Stravinsky had begun working on before *Firebird* and was now finalising. Benois was entrusted with the sets. From November, Diaghilev focused all his efforts on securing the premiere of Stravinsky's new work. His interest in the opera seems to have escalated on hearing that the management of Moscow's Svobodny Teatr (Free Theatre) was also interested in presenting it, and was already in negotiation with the composer.

Work also resumed on another long-dormant project, provisionally entitled *Metamorphoses*, to music by Stravinsky's old fellow student and close friend Maximilian Steinberg, a pupil and devotee of Rimsky-Korsakov's. Diaghilev was unimpressed by Steinberg and gave him a chance only at Stravinsky's insistence. When Bakst expressed enthusiasm about Steinberg's work, Diaghilev lambasted him for his 'lack of musical understanding'.[29] Eventually, it was decided to reduce the ballet to a single act, entitled *Midas*. The indifference to this production is witnessed by the scanty preparation time allotted to it: work on the sets, costumes and choreography started a mere twelve days before the premiere. The last stitches were being put into the costumes fifteen minutes before the curtain rose.[30] That *Midas* was put on at all was a result of diplomatic rather than musical considerations. Steinberg was married to Rimsky-Korsakov's daughter, and Diaghilev presumably hoped to placate Rimsky's widow (who still hadn't forgiven him for his cuts to *Schéhérazade* and *Khovanshchina*) by programming a work by her beloved son-in-law. It was important to get in her good graces, because he hoped to include in the 1914 programme Rimsky's last opera, *Le Coq d'or*, completed shortly before the composer's death in 1908. The design of *Midas* was entrusted to Mstislav Dobuzhinsky, an old friend from the *Mir iskusstva* days, who had made a name for himself as a set designer for Stanislavsky. 'Bakst was completely exhausted and had been left a nervous wreck, apparently by a recent row with Diaghilev,' recalled Dobuzhinsky. 'Both he and Benois had advised Diaghilev to contact me.'[31] Dobuzhinsky also designed the sets for another Fokine project, *Les Papillons*, a kind of follow-up to *Carnaval*, which had premiered in the Mariinsky Theatre in St Petersburg on 10 March 1912. Since 1910 Diaghilev had programmed only ballets he had produced himself, so this was in many ways a retrograde step.

Despite all this, Diaghilev was in high spirits that winter of 1913–14, after having apparently closed the Nijinsky chapter for good. According to Grigoriev, 'Diaghilev seemed like someone who has shed a load and can at last breathe freely.'[32] His good mood probably had a lot to do with his discovery

Massine, by Bakst

of a youth who could not only dance Joseph in *Légende*, but who had the potential to eclipse even Nijinsky. His name was Leonid Myasin.

The facts about Diaghilev's first encounter with Myasin (who would soon change his name to Léonide Massine) are a matter for conjecture, because Massine's memoirs are highly unreliable. He writes that Diaghilev saw him dance the tarantella in *Swan Lake* in December 1913, after which he was immediately summoned to Diaghilev's hotel room and offered the role of Joseph. He was told to come back the next day with his decision. Massine conferred with his friends and concluded that he would reject Diaghilev's offer. Yet when he returned to the hotel and Diaghilev looked him in the eye, he heard himself – to his own considerable surprise – say 'yes'. The next day they were on the train to St Petersburg, where the young dancer was to audition with Fokine. A few days later they headed for Cologne, where Diaghilev was to rejoin his company.[33]

But *Swan Lake* was not performed in December of that year, nor could Massine's departure from Russia have been arranged within a few days. Diaghilev may have seen him dance at the end of October, when *Swan Lake* was performed in Moscow.[34] If so, and he did ask the boy to join the company, it would still have taken months before Massine would have been available. Leave had to be granted by the Imperial Theatres, and a passport had to be obtained – lengthy procedures involving a great deal of red tape.[35] Diaghilev may have been alerted to Massine by one of his informants in Moscow and St Petersburg, possibly the choreographer Alexander Gorsky (in whose ballets the boy had danced a few minor roles).[36] On 22 January 1914 Diaghilev wrote to Gorsky extending initial agreements with Massine and contracting him up to 1 August 1916.[37] At that point the dancer was definitely still in Russia.

The mystery of his discovery is deepened by the fact that he was by no means an obvious choice. For one thing, the boy did not appear to be particularly gifted. Whereas Nijinsky's exceptional talent had been spotted by the time he was sixteen, the eighteen-year-old Massine had danced few solo roles and was moreover uncertain about his vocation: he was even thinking of giving up dancing and trying his fortune as an actor. Though strikingly handsome, he was very short and slightly bow-legged – two flaws that would typically rule out a career in ballet. In the winter of 1913 there was nothing to indicate that he would attain worldwide fame not only as a solo dancer, but also as one of the greatest choreographers of the twentieth century.

Just what did Diaghilev see in him? Was it his 'piercing eyes and Byzantine looks', as Massine's biographer García-Márquez claims?[38] His appearance obviously played a part: Diaghilev had only to send a couple of photographs to Hugo von Hofmannsthal to convince the librettist of *Légende* that he could safely forget Nijinsky.[39] But the boy's intellectual gifts must have appealed as well. He was interested in art, discussing with his friends the work of Gauguin and Toulouse-Lautrec, which they knew through mediocre reproductions in magazines (the would-be heirs to *Mir iskusstva*).[40] He was also keen on literature and apparently wrote poetry (the journal *Teatr* reported in early June that Diaghilev was planning to publish a book of poems by Massine, though nothing came of this).[41] Massine was undoubtedly much more cultivated and communicative than Nijinsky had been at his age. To Diaghilev, who was looking for a new pupil to mould and educate, these qualities may have outweighed the boy's imperfect mastery of classical dance techniques.

That winter in Moscow also saw other great changes to Diaghilev's company. A designer needed to be found for *Coq d'or*. It appears that Diaghilev was by now rather disenchanted with Bakst and did not believe, after the failure of *Jeux*, that he was capable of reinventing his visual style. He was even less pleased with Benois, who always felt manipulated (perhaps not without justification) and was therefore invariably at loggerheads with everyone. But Benois at least had a valuable tip for Diaghilev: he urged him to visit a large exhibition of work by Natalia Goncharova which he had just seen in Moscow.[42]

Diaghilev had met Goncharova back in 1906, when he was putting together his Russian exhibition for the Salon d'automne, but her art had undergone some dramatic changes since then. Her partner Larionov had become the leader of a group of young artists who were making a big noise in Russia, spreading the modernist gospel that true art lay in experimentation and unrelenting innovation. In recent years they had dabbled in cubism, futurism and abstractionism, in performances and film. They painted their faces, arms and chests with abstract compositions, and gave chaotic 'lectures' in which they threw jugs of water at the audience. If Larionov was the driving force behind this new movement, later to be classified as the Russian avant-garde, then Goncharova was its first true star, not only because she was a more discerning and imaginative artist, but also because she was much more productive.

Goncharova, by Larionov

Goncharova and Larionov brought artistic modernism to the design of Diaghilev's productions, just as Stravinsky had introduced musical modernism with *Sacre*. Their presence deepened the rift between Diaghilev and his old associates Bakst and Benois, who had loathed Larionov ever since the latter had dismissed Benois, in an article in *Zolotoye runo* (Golden fleece), as 'a grey nonentity' whose work was 'one disappointment after another'.[43] Diaghilev, by contrast, delighted in his association with the two artists, who reawakened his passion for innovation – a passion that had been smothered by the failure of *Jeux* and *Sacre*.

Benois could be noble, however: in the October 1913 issue of *Rech* he lavished praise on Goncharova's exhibition, calling her 'exceptionally gifted' and staunchly defending her against those who accused her of charlatanism.[44] Many years later Benois maintained that he personally gave Goncharova the commission for *Coq d'or*, and that the entire concept behind the production had been his idea.[45] Neither claim is true. Both Goncharova and Diaghilev independently state that Diaghilev was both the initiator and spiritual father of *Coq d'or*.[46] Yet Benois's article must have influenced Diaghilev, and Goncharova owed more to Benois at the start of her career than she was later prepared to admit.

Shortly after Diaghilev had approved a provisional design by Goncharova, he took her along to the home of his old friend Ilya Ostroukhov, where the opera (heavily cut by Diaghilev, of course) was played on the grand piano.[47] Right afterwards, Goncharova started work on the sets. Diaghilev had such confidence in his new designer that he had her paint the sets without ever once looking at them.[48]

On 6 January 1914 Diaghilev was back in Paris, where his team were working feverishly to prepare the new season. He summoned Stravinsky to the capital, and on 22 January the composer played the first two acts of *Le Rossignol* in Misia Sert's house, to a company that included André Gide, Maurice Ravel, Jean Cocteau and Erik Satie.[49] Stravinsky was struck by Diaghilev's change of heart, and delighted that he had recovered his faith in the most avant-garde art: 'Seryozha is in seventh heaven,' he wrote to his wife, 'and has completely changed his opinion about my work.'[50]

Not long afterwards Diaghilev was back in St Petersburg to contract singers for *Le Rossignol* and collect Massine. He soon heard rumours that Nijinsky was setting up a small ballet company of his own, with which he intended to perform Ballets Russes productions in Europe. He had already approached the music publishers Jurgenson and Struve, requesting permission to use music for various ballets. There was open speculation in St Petersburg as to whether Nijinsky would be able to compete with Diaghilev.[51] The latter pulled out all the stops in an effort to sabotage Nijinsky's season. He wired Stravinsky: 'Vestris [Nijinsky] asked Jurgenson for rights to perform *Narcisse*. Tcherepnin refused. I hope Struve [who owned the rights to *Petrushka*] will too. Take steps.'[52] Struve also owned the rights to *Le Rossignol*, and in an effort to get in his good books Diaghilev took the highly unusual step of paying him 3,000 marks up front for the right to perform the opera.[53]

Diaghilev then contacted Bronislava Nijinska in a bid to talk her out of joining her brother's venture. Nijinska was under contract to Diaghilev to perform during the upcoming German tour (starting in Prague), but he knew all too well that she could easily shed her obligations if so inclined.

Bronislava had not gone on the South American tour, being heavily pregnant with her first child. Diaghilev invited her to dinner at the Hotel Astoria, where he was staying. The meeting with his former lover's sister must have been difficult for the impresario, who was still nursing his emotional wounds. In her account of the charged meeting, Nijinska shows surprising warmth towards Diaghilev and admiration for the deadly weapon of his charm:

> Never in all the years I worked with Diaghilev … did I see him display so strongly his legendary irresistible charm … All during dinner Sergey Pavlovich continued to assure me that I had always been very dear to him, that he loved me as if I were his daughter, and that I was equally dear to him as an artist. I felt that Diaghilev's feelings were stronger towards me now than in the past, as though he saw in me a part of Vaslav. I could also feel how painful for him had been the break with Vaslav. He told me how hurt he had been, how insulted he had felt: 'He did not find it necessary to inform me of his marriage.' …
>
> The remaining time at dinner Sergey Pavlovich used to try to persuade me to remain with his ballet. 'Bronya, will you promise me that you will come to Prague for the beginning of our 1914 season?' However often he asked me this, he never once reminded me that I was bound by a contract that I had signed with him.
>
> When we parted he embraced me several times, and as he helped me on with my fur coat he looked deep into my eyes. Suddenly he took my *botiki* [felt overboots] from the hall porter, and as gallantly as a youth he bent on one knee to help me put them on. That was too much for me. I took my *botiki* from him and gave them to Sasha [her husband]. I hugged Sergey Pavlovich and said, 'All right, I shall come to Prague!' And so we parted that evening.[54]

But Bronislava broke her promise as soon as her brother managed to arrange a booking at London's Palace Theatre that March.[55] The two performed there, in what was billed as the 'saison Nijinsky', with a hastily assembled group of dancers. Nijinsky might not have obtained the right to use music by Tcherepnin and Stravinsky, but there was, of course, nothing to stop him performing *Les Sylphides* (Chopin), *Carnaval* (Schumann) and *Le Spectre de la rose* (Weber).

Whether Diaghilev was aware of this in late January is unclear. He had been occupied with Massine's training and rehearsals, and he had also arranged a meeting with a young, ambitious composer whose name had been circulating around Diaghilev's entourage for some time. Sergey Prokofiev, for it was he, knew Walter Nouvel well and had met Bakst, and he was desperate to broaden his horizons. Though still only twenty-three, he had already made a name for himself as a virtuoso pianist and groundbreaking composer. Indeed, he had few rivals in St Petersburg, though his gifts were not widely recognised at the time. In his diary Prokofiev is disarmingly open about his wish to break into Diaghilev's circle, though he had little idea what he would be getting himself into. When, on 26 January, he heard from Alfred Nurok that Diaghilev had already left the city without meeting him as arranged, Prokofiev was disappointed. 'This is a blow,' he wrote in his diary, 'because I had already built up in my mind all kinds of fantasies about creating a ballet for Paris and the European fame that would follow.'[56] Accompanied by Massine, Diaghilev was by now on a train to Cologne, where he was to join his company. He was already on intimate terms with the youth. The tradition whereby young dancers would confer sexual favours in return for patronage was as strong as it had been in 1908, and Massine apparently accepted this situation as natural – or at least inevitable.

In Germany Massine was placed under the wing of Enrico Cecchetti, whom Diaghilev had once again hired to train his dancers. He danced a few minor roles at first, starting with the night watchman in *Petrushka*. On 16 March Diaghilev made another brief trip to St Petersburg, probably to engage Boris Romanov as choreographer for *Le Rossignol*, because Fokine had his hands full. He must also have seen Benois, who was beavering away at the sets, and talked to him about the difficulties in producing Stravinsky's work. Diaghilev feared that they would not make the Paris premiere that summer. As usual, there were huge financial problems. And as usual, Benois was up in arms:

This will be a disgrace – that much is certain, given the way things are and Diaghilev's persistence in sacrificing his friends and most loyal colleagues to greedy thieves and charlatans ... I could simply quote Diaghilev's non-fulfilment of our contract and take away my designs, but I'm just not capable of taking that decision: in spite of everything, Diaghilev is 'Seryozha' and I take him to court. But this is what I can do: if the sets and costumes for *Le Rossignol* end up a terrible mess, then I'll simply demand that my name be taken off the poster. From now on I cannot work under these conditions and so I decline any further active involvement in this matter. If Diaghilev doesn't want to listen to my (our) advice, let him work out a way himself to rescue the situation. I am not going to deal with the production of sets until I first get the money I've already earned.[57]

On the evening of 21 March Diaghilev was back in Berlin. Grigoriev thought that the impresario would never again set foot in his fatherland.[58] Indeed, who was to say what the future held?

· 21 ·

'Let us be resolute and energetic'
1914–1915

IN THE MARGINS of the Berlin performances, the team worked hard to finish the dances that would premiere in Paris. Fokine and Kessler polished up *La Légende de Joseph* under the watchful eye of Richard Strauss, who was on hand to oversee the proceedings.

By this stage, the Ballets Russes were making regular appearances in Berlin. Yet from a historical perspective it seems strange that a company born of the Franco-Russian entente should be treading the boards in the German capital at that time. A bellicose frenzy had seized Europe, and artists on both sides of the divide were fiercely patriotic. According to Misia Sert 'there was hardly a Frenchman who did not ardently desire to teach our neighbours on the other side of the Rhine a severe lesson'.[1]

Kessler, still irked by Nijinsky's departure, put pressure on Diaghilev to rehire his former lover and ditch Massine. He claimed that both Lady Ripon and Misia Sert shared his doubts about the young man's qualities. Even Diaghilev, 'seemed decidedly uncertain' and 'somewhat disappointed in the boy wonder'.[2] The Count's first encounter with Massine did not fill him with confidence: '[He is] not especially good looking, but not especially ugly either: a decidedly nondescript personage … If Diaghilev, who is putting his future in the balance, wants to ruin himself for love of this unfortunate youth, we must stoically accept our lot.'³ But ten days later, when Massine first took the part of Joseph in a rehearsal, Kessler was immediately won over:

> Massine is indeed very special. At any rate, he is the complete opposite of Nijinsky. Not a trace of showiness or sensuality: he is all profundity and mysticism. His interpretation of the metaphysical, inner world is deeply moving … He is Russian to the core (whereas Nijinsky was a Pole), a Russian folksong that moves one to the depths of one's soul. Or to put it another way: Nijinsky was a Greek god, Massine a small, wild, graceful creature of the Steppes.⁴

Bakst was also in Berlin to help with the costumes and staging; fortunately he, too, appreciated Massine's qualities. Possibly at Diaghilev's behest, he waxed lyrical about the dancer in a telegram to Misia: 'Massine marvellous and astonishing with sincerity, fluency of movement, fantastic figure, great art.'⁵

The company remained in Germany until the beginning of April. Meanwhile, the brief 'saison Nijinsky' had opened in March at London's Palace Theatre. Nijinsky's company was inexperienced, poorly prepared and much too tiny to do justice to ensemble works like *Les Sylphides*. To make matters worse, Nijinsky lacked the communication skills necessary for a manager, and he was by then a nervous wreck. During the first performance, Bronislava was struck by something in the audience as she danced:

> Usually I never pay any attention to the audience, but this evening as I looked towards the conductor to watch for his signal to the musicians my eyes were drawn to a white spot in the front row, illuminated by the conductor's light; it was the white evening shirt of a man seated immediately to the left of the conductor. Diaghilev was in the Theatre. He was seated … nonchalantly sprawled in his seat, his large head leaning to the right, his lower lip protruding with great self-assurance in a sardonic smile … From time to time I would tear my eyes from Vaslav and glance at Diaghilev, who was intently following Vaslav in his dance, his eyes never leaving him. I could feel an inner battle being waged between them, a personal struggle that I knew Vaslav must win, by his dance and his creative genius.⁶

Bronislava may have been spinning yarns here: Nijinsky's wife Romola did not comment on the impresario's presence, nor was he spotted by Cyril Beaumont, the dance critic, who would certainly have recognised him. It seems unlikely that Diaghilev would have made that hated Channel crossing between performances in Germany and Monte Carlo just to see his ex-lover perform – though the possibility cannot be ruled out. Whatever the truth of the matter, the 'saison Nijinsky' was nothing short of a disaster. Nijinsky got into blazing rows with the theatre management and was given to ungovernable fits of rage. After two performances he withdrew, pleading illness, and his contract was terminated shortly afterwards.

Meanwhile, Diaghilev's company left for Monte Carlo to prepare the Paris premiere. Diaghilev must have been relieved that Massine was living up to his promise; yet his mind was not easy. The failures of the previous season haunted him, and he was conscious of the relentless scrutiny of theatre managements, determined to ensure a scandal-free season. On Easter Sunday Diaghilev cabled Stravinsky from Monte Carlo, giving him the traditional Russian Easter greeting: '*Khristos Voskrese* [Christ is risen], but will we, too, rise in Paris? I'm terrified.'[7]

On 29 April Diaghilev preceded his troupe to Paris to oversee the first orchestra rehearsals of *Légende de Joseph*, *Rossignol*, *Coq d'or* and *Midas*, which were all to premiere at the Opéra. The star of the season was Richard Strauss, who was to conduct his own ballet. Only a few years earlier it would have been quite unthinkable for a composer of his stature to stoop to participating in something as frivolous as ballet; yet now, Strauss was proud to be associated with Diaghilev's company. He threw himself into the preparations with gusto. During a rehearsal in Monte Carlo he suddenly whipped off his tailcoat and ran about the stage in his shirtsleeves to demonstrate his choreographic theories to Massine and Fokine, much to the latter's annoyance.[8] When Diaghilev decided that a particular passage was too lengthy, Strauss – clearly under the impresario's spell – meekly scrapped ten pages of the orchestral score.[9]

Yet *Légende de Joseph* was not the great hit they had hoped for. The ballet was well-received, but Strauss' score was deemed uninspiring, and the staging (lavish costumes by Bakst, with a black and gold decor by José Maria Sert), failed to cohere in the manner of, say, *Schéhérazade* or even *Sacre*. It would be up to that season's two operas to save the day.

Although backers and audiences could always be found for operas, Diaghilev's entourage had radically changed their stance on this genre. Diaghilev himself believed that opera was not the art form it had been,[10] and as far back as 1911, Stravinsky wrote that ballet meant more to him 'than any opera performance whatever'.[11] In an interview given a year later, he added, 'Generally speaking, I am not drawn to opera. I'm interested in choreographic drama, the only form in which I see movement forward, without guessing at what the future may bring. Opera is a lie, aspiring to truth, but I want a lie, aspiring to a lie. Opera is a battle against nature.'[12]

This view, a radicalisation of the anti-mimetic stance of the Miriskusniki, would remain the guiding principle of Diaghilev's shows, and its effect would, for obvious reasons, be most visible in his operatic productions. Since the company intended to go on staging operas, despite that art form's incompatibility with their artistic theories, their productions increasingly took the form of 'choreographic dramas'. This was the case with *Rossignol*, where the dancers and singers appeared simultaneously or successively, but more noticeably so in *Coq d'or*, where the singers were no longer part of the dramatic action, but simply sang in the wings while dancers portrayed the various roles. *Rossignol*, in particular, was something of a hybrid production. For one thing, Stravinsky's score had been composed partly before *Firebird* and partly after *Sacre*. The breakneck pace of his musical development in those years left a decidedly visible join. And although *Rossignol* was well received, the piece was by no means a great success.

The only real hit of the season was *Coq d'or*. Its appeal lay to a degree in the neat replacement of acting singers with a combination of dance and mime. Yet it was Goncharova's brilliant designs that stole the show. The artist's palette, inspired in part by Russian folk art, featured bright combinations of red, orange and yellow, and blended primitive and naïve patterns of flowers and leaves with abstract motifs and decorations. Goncharova's take on Slavic exoticism appeared much more authentic than that of designers of the *Mir iskusstva* school such as Golovin, Bakst and Roerich, while her abstract approach was unusually progressive. In their decorative splendour her designs were well matched to the idiom of the Ballets Russes, yet at the same time they heralded an entirely new aesthetic, thus marking the zenith as well as the end of an era.

This production boosted the prestige of the Ballets Russes among avant-garde artists. Guillaume Apollinaire, one of the movement's leaders in Paris, devoted two articles to Goncharova and Larionov, in which he described their work in glowing terms and proclaimed that their 'genuine aesthetic discoveries' would come to occupy a prominent place in contemporary art.[13] An exhibition of their work was held at the Galerie Paul Guillaume. It featured over a hundred items, including many neo-primitivist and abstract (Rayist) pieces. The opening was attended not only by Ballets Russes faithfuls like the Serts, Cocteau and Paul Poiret, but also by poets, artists and couturiers who were not yet part of Diaghilev's circle, such as Max Jacob, Blaise Cendrars, Coco Chanel, Brancusi, Delaunay, Braque, Picasso, Derain, Duchamp, Gris, Léger and Modigliani. That day, the crème de la crème of the modern art world turned out to marvel at the work of two completely unknown Russians; among the throng were designers who would become the face of the post-war Ballets Russes.

The fact that *Coq d'or* did not become a classic of the Diaghilev repertoire was mainly due to the ongoing feud with the Rimsky-Korsakov family following the cuts he made to *Schéhérazade* and *Khovanshchina*. Russia and France had recently signed a copyright convention and the Rimsky-Korsakovs seized upon this new legal instrument in their war with Diaghilev. Their attempts to prevent *Coq d'or* from being performed in Paris failed, though the impresario was ordered to pay them 3,000 francs in compensation. Diaghilev stumped up, but quailed at the prospect of further dunning demands from Rimsky's widow. *Coq d'or* was expensive enough as it was. After the 1914 season, therefore, it was permanently shelved. Never has a widow done a greater disservice to her late husband's reputation. The success of the work would certainly have made it part of Diaghilev's repertoire, guaranteeing it a place in the canon of European opera. Today, Rimsky-Korsakov has all but lost his European reputation as a composer of opera; of his instrumental pieces, only the fairly atypical *Schéhérazade* is still regularly performed.

Members of Diaghilev's circle were surprised to spot Nijinsky in the audience during the dress rehearsal of *Légende de Joseph*. He visited Misia in her box, but was given a cool reception, particularly by Cocteau.[14] A few days later he went to Cecchetti for a class, and Diaghilev sent Massine over to see him dance. Massine later claimed to have enjoyed the experience, though the encounter between the ex-favourite and his replacement must surely have been awkward.

After a short break the company opened in London, with roughly the same programme as in Paris, supplemented by the operas *Prince Igor* and *May Night*, which Diaghilev had imported almost wholesale from Russia and in which he had little artistic involvement. The premieres were received much as they had been in Paris; audiences were divided on *Légende de Joseph* but loved *Coq d'or*. This was Diaghilev's fourth London season; by now he had both the public and financial backers eating out of his hand.

The twenty-three-year-old Sergey Prokofiev was also in London. Ostensibly in the capital to see music publishers and concert organisers, he spent much of his time splashing out on brightly coloured socks, watching boxing matches where prizefighters spat teeth into buckets and spying on couples spooning in Hyde Park.

Prokofiev wanted to meet Diaghilev and resolved to ask Nouvel, whom he knew well, for an introduction. But by that time, the impresario had heard that he was in London and had invited him over for a chat. Prokofiev was to present himself behind the scenes after a performance, where Diaghilev would shake his hand. In his diary Prokofiev confessed to having felt 'nervous about the imminent meeting. I was most interested in Diaghilev the personality, and had heard of his legendary charm'.[15]

As so often, Diaghilev failed to turn up, but the next day, after a performance of *Rossignol*, Prokofiev finally found himself face to face with the impresario: 'He was awfully elegant, in tails and a top hat, and gave me his hand in a white glove, saying that he was very pleased to meet me and had wanted to do so for a long time ... and that one day soon he had to have a serious talk with me and listen to my works, which we could set up through Nouvel. On that we parted.'[16]

A few days later Prokofiev played Diaghilev several of his works, including his Second Piano Concerto. Delighted by the latter piece, which took aggressive modernism to new heights,[17] Diaghilev promptly asked the composer to write a ballet for the next season. Prokofiev's counter-proposal, to write an opera based on Dostoyevsky's novel *The Gambler*, was brushed aside by the impresario. As Prokofiev later recorded, 'He objected that opera as an art form was dying out, whereas ballet on the other hand was flourishing and hence I must write a ballet.'[18] There was also talk of another project, a ballet set to orchestral versions of some of his piano pieces, to be choreographed by, of all people, Nijinsky. Given the events of the previous year, it seems a remarkable choice on Diaghilev's part. But as Prokofiev wrote in his diary, 'At the mention of Nijinsky's name, his eyes took on an unnatural glow.'[19] It would seem that the impresario had not yet quite got over his old flame. Perhaps the spectacular failure of Nijinsky's own season in London had reassured him that the young man could never be a serious competitor; perhaps it had even sparked a certain pity.

Prokofiev played his Second Piano Concerto a few more times, on one occasion to Pierre Monteux and José Maria Sert, who exclaimed, 'My God, this man's a wild animal!'[20] Diaghilev was again madly enthusiastic. A bit too enthusiastic for Prokofiev's liking: 'Heaping praise on something before drawing up a contract seems a trifle naïve.'[21] Diaghilev suggested that Prokofiev get in touch with Sergey Gorodetsky, a poet often to be seen at Mikhail Kuzmin's, with a view to working with him on a libretto for a ballet with a Russian fairytale or 'prehistoric' theme.[22] It seemed that in the wake of the London season Diaghilev was firmly back on the modernist/primitivist path.

The London season lasted almost two months and was, according to Grigoriev, one of the most brilliant in the history of the Ballets Russes. Political storm clouds were gathering, but the German, French, English and Russian beau monde continued to attend garden parties, luncheons and receptions, where they prattled away over the canapés, blithely unaware of what was going on outside their bubble of privilege.

On 28 June in Sarajevo a student member of the conspiratorial Young Bosnia movement shot and killed the Archduke Franz Ferdinand, heir to the Austro-Hungarian throne, and his wife. The chain of events unleashed by this deed led, seemingly inexorably, to the outbreak of the Great War in little more than a month, a war which would bring down much of old Europe, not least imperial Russia. But when she heard of Franz Ferdinand's assassination all Misia Sert could say was, 'What luck! Oh God, if only there really is a war!'[23]

The international tensions had surprisingly little effect on the Ballets Russes' planned itinerary. Grigoriev's claim that Kessler wired Diaghilev from Berlin during the London premiere of *Légende de Joseph*, informing him that there would be a war and that German performances would have to be cancelled, is a fiction.[24] Kessler was actually in London at the time and on 23 July, a mere eight days before the outbreak of war, he had discussed with

Diaghilev details of the coming German tour. Kessler did vaguely think there might be a war, but it never occurred to him that it would disrupt the performances. He breakfasted with the British prime minister Herbert Asquith on 22 July, where the mood was exceptionally jovial.

As half Europe mobilised, there was some consternation when the Lord Chamberlain, who was responsible for theatre censorship, banned further performances by Maria Carmi in *Légende de Joseph* (she and Maria Kuznetsova took turns dancing the part of Potiphar's wife) on the grounds that her interpretation was 'too realistic'.[25] Diaghilev asked Kessler to intervene, and the matter appears to have died a quiet death. The London season ended triumphantly on 25 July. 'The ovation seemed endless,' wrote Grigoriev. 'Old Sir Joseph Beecham [Thomas's father] was led on to the stage and made a speech, in which he thanked the public for its support and promised another season with Diaghilev the next year ...'[26]

The Russians split up for their annual holiday, resolving to meet in Berlin on 1 October. On 1 August 1914 Germany declared war on Russia and, two days later, on France. On 4 August Great Britain declared war on Germany. The Europe in which Diaghilev had risen to stardom was on the verge of falling apart.

Misia Sert's description of the euphoria that swept Europe when war broke out is a classic of its kind:

> On the 2nd of August, 1914, on the Grands Boulevards, among a crowd delirious with joy, I suddenly found myself perched on a white horse riding before a *cuirassier* in gala uniform, round whose neck I had wound a wreath of flowers. The general excitement was such that this situation did not for a moment strike me as being strange. The *cuirassier*, the horse and the crowd were not astonished either, for the same spectacle could be seen throughout Paris. Flowers in wreaths, bunches, bouquets and loose, were being sold on every street corner, and a moment later you found them on the *képis* of the soldiers, on the end of their bayonets or behind their ears. Everybody kissed, sang, cried, laughed, trampled each other, hugged each other; we were filled with compassion, generosity, noble feelings, ready for any sacrifice, and, as a result of it all, wonderfully, unbelievably happy.[27]

Misia was not the only one to feel 'unbelievably happy' at the prospect of war. This enthusiasm was shared by many, and artists, writers, musicians and dancers were by no means immune to it. Many celebrated artists entered military service, though few fought at the front. Most joined army nursing corps or signed up with the Red Cross. Misia managed to persuade her couturier friends to provide a number of vans, which she converted into ambulances. Manned by artists and socialites, they sped to the aid of troops in northern France. Her nursing staff included Cocteau, sporting a natty little uniform designed by the couturier Poiret. Maurice Ravel also drove an ambulance, though in a regular army unit. Ida Rubinstein, too, worked as a nurse, though her uniform was designed by Bakst.[28]

Diaghilev wisely managed to avoid getting caught up in the madness; playing at soldiers or nurses was not for him. He left London for Italy, to relax and to work on Massine's artistic education. The Italian trip is hard to reconstruct; Diaghilev seems not to have contacted anyone during this period. 'Not a peep out of the old monocled conductor or the little boy Massine,'[29] Stravinsky complained to Benois as early as 24 July, and Diaghilev's silence was to continue until 5 September.[30] Massine wrote about the trip, but his memories are clearly confused, and the itinerary he gives there does not match that of the surviving telegrams.

Stravinsky was not the only one hoping for a sign of life. Of late, Diaghilev had communicated only sparsely with his stepmother and other relatives. His stepmother received a few telegrams a year, along with gifts of money. Though these donations usually only amounted to a few hundred francs, they may well have constituted his parents' chief income. By now both his half-brothers, Valentin and Yury, were high-ranking army officers and had families of their own. Valentin's youngest son, born in February 1911, had been named Sergey after his famous uncle. Contact was at any rate so limited that Diaghilev's family did not know how to reach him when his father's health took a sudden turn for the worse. On 2 August General Pavel Pavlovich breathed his last. His widow had no idea of her stepson's whereabouts.

On 10 August, by which time his father had already been buried, Diaghilev received the following two-word telegram in Venice: *Умер отец* (Father is dead).[31] He immediately wired back the following message (in transcribed Russian, rather than the usual French): 'My own dear Mama, your two words [only just] reached me. My dearest, you taught me to believe, and only faith can save [me] now as I grieve for my father. Seryozha Diaghilev.'[32]

Two days later, not having heard anything, he sent another cable, this time to the whole family. 'I got the news, didn't you get my telegrams? Tell me, where's Mama? How is she? How is everybody? Dear Lord, what a sad blow!'[33]

Exactly what Diaghilev did next is unclear. He doesn't seem to have told Massine, Misia or any of his other confidants about his father's death. As always, he kept his grief to himself. According to the family, he attended the funeral, but that is contradicted by the telegrams from Venice, the second of which was sent ten days after his father's death, long after the funeral. Yet there is a strong indication that Diaghilev did subsequently travel to Russia for the last time. Many years later Sergey Valentinovich, Valentin's youngest son, recalled that his uncle Sergey had been at the funeral, had brought a vast number of suitcases and had fed him strawberries.[34] Though he was only three and a half at the time, there may well be an element of truth in these memories. Diaghilev might, for instance, have attended a memorial service two weeks after the funeral, when the whole family visited the grave. Massine writes in his memoirs that he spent some time travelling solo around Italy that summer. Would Diaghilev have abandoned his eighteen-year-old lover in August without good cause?[35] All his business partners and friends were getting their affairs in order as war took hold, or were taking time off. Apart from the two above-mentioned telegrams from Venice, Diaghilev appears to have communicated with no one that month.

If he did travel to Russia, the rapid spread of hostilities would have affected his movements. The borders would probably not yet have closed entirely, allowing him to travel to Russia via Switzerland, Romania or Bulgaria. It must have been a dramatic reunion in St Petersburg, especially for Yelena Diaghileva. Her husband had just died; her two youngest sons were preparing to leave for the front and her beloved stepson would be heading back to Europe, perhaps never to return. Her fears were to prove well founded, though when Diaghilev got back to Italy at the end of August he could not have known that he would never see Russia again.

Sergey broke his silence on 5 September, during his stay in the smart resort of Cernobbio on the banks of Lake Como, when he wired Stravinsky (then in Switzerland) asking him to come to Italy at the earliest possible opportunity. By then it was, of course, clear that the German tour in October would not be going ahead. So Diaghilev prepared for a long stay in Italy, surrounding himself with as many friends as he could muster.

Stravinsky, by contrast, was working himself up into a terrible state about the war. He wrote to Bakst in September, 'I am not one of those fortunate men who can throw themselves into the fray without a second thought. How I envy them. My hatred of the Germans grows not by the day but by the hour, and I'm consumed with jealousy when I think that our friends Ravel, Delage, Schmitt are all in the thick of the action – every man jack of them!'[36] In this frame of mind, Stravinsky was clearly in no mood for a pleasant little tour of Italy's Renaissance art treasures with Diaghilev and Massine.

The impresario and the dancer travelled to Milan and then on to Florence. Massine relates that they also visited Pisa, San Gimignano and Siena. From late September to early November they based themselves in Florence, visiting Ravenna, Pistoia, Pescia and Lucca. There is something almost mythical about this journey: the man who shaped European artistic taste sallying forth with his young protégé to view the cradle of European civilisation, just as the rest of Europe was tumbling into the most destructive conflict of its history.

Massine was a bright and apt pupil, with an eye for the visual arts; presumably a much more satisfactory acolyte than Nijinsky. In Tuscany they sought out the works of early Renaissance and late medieval artists like Filippo Lippi and the Sienese master Simone Martini, whose glorious painting of the Annunciation (which hangs in the Uffizi) inspired the following bold prediction from Massine:

> One afternoon in the Uffizi, while I was looking up at Fra Filippo Lippi's Madonna and Child, Diaghilev said to me: 'Do you think you could compose [i.e. choreograph] a ballet?' 'No,' I answered, without thinking, 'I'm sure I never could.' Then, as we passed into another room, I was suddenly aware of the luminous colours of Simone Martini's Annunciation. As I looked at the delicate postures of Gabriel and the Virgin Mary, I felt as if everything I had seen in Florence had finally culminated in this painting. It seemed to be offering me the key to an unknown world, beckoning me along a path which I knew I must follow to the end. 'Yes,' I said to Diaghilev, 'I think I can create a ballet. Not only one, but a hundred, I promise you.'[37]

However satisfactory, Massine's intellectual (and presumably romantic) companionship was not enough for Diaghilev, who pined for his other friends. Nouvel and Benois were both in Russia, apparently intending to remain there until the end of the war. Grigoriev, too, was in St Petersburg, as were Prokofiev, Larionov and Goncharova. Misia did not intend to interrupt her rescue work for a trip to Italy. So Diaghilev's hopes centred on Stravinsky. War or no war, he was going to plan the 1915 season as if it were any other.

Besides the ballet that Diaghilev had commissioned from Prokofiev, plans included a new ballet by Stravinsky provisionally entitled *Svadba* (The Wedding) or *Svadebka* (The Little Wedding). The idea dated back to 1912, when Stravinsky was still busy with *Sacre*.[38] It was to be a choreographic and musical recreation of ancient Russian peasant wedding rituals, and Diaghilev had high hopes for the project. By the autumn of 1914, however, Stravinsky had not yet written a note of it; he was still collecting musical material. It was unclear who would choreograph the two ballets. Inexperienced as he was, Massine could not take on this task unaided, so Diaghilev's thoughts turned once more to Nijinsky. Meanwhile, the company needed a wartime income, and arrangements were made to tour the United States. On 10 October Diaghilev signed a contract with Giulio Gatti-Casazza, the manager of the Metropolitan Opera. He even managed to squeeze out a $45,000 advance, which gave him considerable artistic freedom to prepare the next season.[39]

Diaghilev, eager for the new ballet, wanted to keep Stravinsky's nose to the grindstone. He fired off telegram after telegram, each more impatient than the last, urging the composer to come and join him in Italy. Stravinsky, for his part, was reluctant to leave Switzerland. His wife and children were there, as was his new friend Ernest Ansermet, a professor of mathematics and self-taught conductor. Stravinsky found it hard to tear himself away from Ansermet, whose accomplishments and dedication to contemporary music made him something of a mainstay to the composer. He finally made a brief trip to Florence after Diaghilev sent him money at the end of September to cover his travel expenses, but this flying visit did not satisfy the impresario.[40] When he wired Stravinsky in mid-November that the contract for the American tour had been signed and he did not get an immediate reply, Diaghilev sent him a mock angry letter:

You're a frightful swine! I telegraph you that the American contract is signed, that I've had a reply from Meštrović, that I'm expected in Rome in November – and not a word from you! You force this old man to take up his pen.

We're stopping here till 10 November, then we're going to Rome. We were in Ravenna and were in complete ecstasy from that divine cemetery. I had a mad telegram from Misia that she won't leave Paris, for that is now the most beautiful city in the world! I had a missive from Nijinsky that he now can't come as for the time being (?) he doesn't have an exit permit! Prokofiev is working with Gorodetsky and apparently is finishing his piano reduction. Koussevitzky is conducting in Rome and I'll see him. I had a friendly enquiry from Mr Fokine asking how are things going. They are in Biarritz. And what about you – which scene of *Svadebka* are you doing?[41]

Diaghilev had another reason for wanting to see Stravinsky. During his odyssey through centuries of religious art he had conceived the notion of a ballet on the theme of the Passion of Christ, to be choreographed by Massine. It had been prompted by insights into the origins of Russian religious traditions that he gained from the Byzantine art in Ravenna, and presumably partly by pious sentiments in the aftermath of his father's death. Clearly, Diaghilev hoped to persuade Stravinsky to write the score, once he had finished *Svadebka*.[42]

The cunning impresario had devised the perfect lure to tempt Stravinsky: a concert of his music in the Teatro Augusteo in Rome, to be conducted by the composer – a first. Diaghilev had already arranged things with the theatre's director Enrico San Martino. Stravinsky trembled at the thought of conducting, though he could not resist the offer. To Diaghilev's great irritation, though, the concert was cancelled at the eleventh hour, allowing Stravinsky to slip through his fingers once again.

He made another attempt from Rome, telling Stravinsky that in order to work on both ballets for the next season (*Svadebka* and the as-yet unnamed Passion ballet) it was 'imperative' that they see one another. A designer had already been found, the Croatian sculptor Ivan Meštrović, who lived in Rome; Massine would be assigned the choreography. Diaghilev's letter to Stravinsky was full of practical details:

The best time would be about 20 December – that way you'll spend the holiday abroad with us. There's a small room in our little flat and the food isn't bad ...

And this is why you need to come: our plans with Meštrović are moving fast ... I am working with him and Massine, and I want to give Massine my blessing to produce this ballet ...

Even if Massine is too young, every day he is becoming more one of us, and that's very important.

I won't tell you the plot in detail – I'll just say that it's a sacred spectacle, an ecstatic Mass, 6–7 short scenes. Set roughly in the Byzantine period ... The music is a series of *a capella* choruses – purely religious, inspired perhaps by Gregorian themes ...

You know, the Roman underground churches of the first centuries AD with their frescoes and vaults really make a very special impression.

That's all for the moment. I hope you'll approve and, most important, that you come.[43]

But the composer was still playing hard to get. Diaghilev, who had been trying to organise a trip to Africa with Massine, was constantly having to shelve his plans. But he also had other irons in the fire. He was in touch with Goncharova, from whom he had commissioned sets and costumes for *Svadebka*. Larionov had been severely injured in the war and was recovering in hospital; it seemed likely that he would be discharged from the army. Diaghilev regularly wrote to Nouvel in St Petersburg to find out how Prokofiev was progressing. He hoped that the young composer would be able to come to Italy, to play him the first sketches of his new ballet. On 11 December he wrote to Nouvel:

I am very glad Prokofiev is working, and fruitfully. I rely on your keeping an eye on things ... I'd very much like to see Prokofiev. Couldn't he make up his mind to come as far as Savoy by sea, and from there take the direct express to Rome? I could arrange both his concerts with big symphony orchestras in the Augusteo if he came during January, February or even March (by the French calendar). I think it would be extremely useful for him (of course I'd pay for his journey). They are very good concerts; Debussy and Stravinsky are taking part and Stravinsky will now be conducting. The hall is huge, the orchestra is good, the audience curious but unlikely to pose any threats for him ...

I am most interested in putting on his ballet. Send me by a Foreign
Ministry courier the libretto if not the music, preferably both … After the
war I'll definitely come and have some fun in Russia.[44]

That final aspiration continued to torment Diaghilev. It was the first year
since the beginning of his European exile that he had not spent part of the
winter in Russia, and he must have felt the pangs of homesickness. He shared
the universal belief that the war would be over shortly, however, and consoled
himself with the thought that he would soon be able to return to his home
country. Grigoriev, one of his regular correspondents, was instructed to corral
the scattered company and bring everyone back for rehearsals in the spring.

In Rome, Diaghilev was seeing a lot of the futurists and gaining artistic
inspiration. By February 1915 he finally seemed to be making progress on the
Prokofiev-Stravinsky front. Prokofiev promised to make the risky journey
from Russia to Italy. Diaghilev had had to cancel his planned trip to Africa
due to Stravinsky's vacillations, though it appeared that the composer would
finally be coming in early February. When Stravinsky once again threatened
not to show, Diaghilev sent him a firm missive: 'I insist that you come for a
few days. Your presence is necessary for the talks with Meštrović, for the alliance with Marinetti and for decisions on many other important issues. Let
us be resolute and energetic.'[45]

Stravinsky finally capitulated, promising to come to Rome, where Diaghilev had arranged the concert for him in the Augusteo and a private concert
at the Grand Hotel, featuring a version of *Sacre* arranged as a piano duet. At
long last it was time to get back to work.

· 22 ·

A Parade of Revolutions
1915–1917

THE $45,000 ADVANCE from the Metropolitan Opera freed Diaghilev from the ever-looming threat of financial ruin. Since 1914 he had been forced to be conservative; now he was again free to indulge his passion for artistic innovation. Stravinsky came to Rome for the planned concert performance of *Petrushka*. Sometime in the second week of February the composer also played his first sketches of *Svadebka*, and Diaghilev was deeply moved by what he heard.

During the previous months, Diaghilev had seen a lot of the futurists, who were keen to work with him. Despite having spent the past half year rediscovering Italian art, he seemed untroubled by the futurists' lofty dismissal of all who clung to old art as 'imbeciles'.[1] And Marinetti and Diaghilev had much in common: they loathed naturalism and moralism; they championed the earthy and concrete, and they relished rows and provocation. If ever a group was receptive to Diaghilev's 'psychology of the hectic', then it was the futurists.

Diaghilev and Massine went to some futurist meetings in Rome, where they handed out invitations to a private concert given by Stravinsky on 13 February at the Grand Hotel. Marinetti came to Rome specially for the occasion, and the futurists 'gave Stravinsky a noisy welcome'.[2]

As so often when encountering a new visual language, Diaghilev was at first deeply impressed by the ideas of the futurists. This was most evident in his plans for the Passion ballet, which now bore the name *Liturgy*. He and Massine had spent thirty-two sessions developing the concept and the choreography, but he still didn't have any fitting music. He briefly toyed with the idea of Gregorian plainchant as an artistic evocation of Russian religiosity. Dancing the ballet in total silence was also considered – and similarly dismissed. 'We concluded that absolute silence is death, and that in our atmosphere there is no such thing as absolute silence – it is an impossibility.'[3] In the end, it was the futurists with their bizarre instruments who gave Diaghilev the idea of a musical background constructed of all kinds of music-making objects like 'bells with thickly swaddled clappers, an Aeolian harp, gusli [a kind of Russian zither], sirens, humming tops'.[4] Diaghilev invited Marinetti to come to Milan to see their instruments.

On 3 March, a few days before Stravinsky's departure, Prokofiev arrived – after an eighteen-day journey via Romania, Bulgaria and Greece – to play the music for the planned ballet to the Gorodetsky libretto, now christened *Ala and Lolli*. It was set in the prehistoric and semi-mythological world of the Scythians, and its heavily symbolic Wagnerian plot of warring gods was ill chosen: in 1915 people wanted something a bit more cheerful and diverting. Nouvel, who had already heard parts in St Petersburg, had written to Diaghilev that 'Prokofiev was turning out some weird stuff on a weird subject'.[5] Diaghilev may have had his doubts about the theme, but he was determined to make Prokofiev one of the team, with or without *Ala and Lolli*.

Prokofiev was soon introduced to the network that Diaghilev had built up among the Roman beau monde. The Second Piano Concerto was rehearsed and played in the Augusteo concert hall, with Prokofiev as soloist – his first appearance on an international stage. Diaghilev's publicity machine had done its work: 2,000 people came to hear the unknown Russian. However, the concert was by no means a sell-out, and the critics were more impressed by Prokofiev's keyboard pyrotechnics than his music.[6]

Shortly afterwards, Prokofiev played Diaghilev the music for his prehistoric ballet. Diaghilev's response must have taken Prokofiev by surprise: 'What's this?! A Russian composer, writing international music to a Russian theme? That's just not on.'[7] He told him that he 'must write a new ballet,'[8] adding, 'After Stravinsky there's just one composer left in Russia – you.

There's no one else there ... In your Petrograd [the new anti-German name for St Petersburg] no one appreciates anything that's Russian, it's a swamp from which we've got to pull you out, otherwise it's going to suck you down.'[9]

The famously headstrong Prokofiev was amazed to find himself giving in to almost all the impresario's demands. 'He was so convincing that I immediately agreed to scrap half the music of the ballet. Diaghilev's next command was "and change the story completely".'[10]

It was not only the music that needed reshaping, but Prokofiev too, Diaghilev thought, and he felt Stravinsky was the man to do it:

> There's a lot of news, but first about Prokofiev. He played yesterday in the Augusteo concert hall, and with unquestioned success, but that's not why I am writing. The fact is that he has brought me about a third of the music of his new ballet. The scenario is a piece of Petersburg frippery: it would have been suitable for the Mariinsky Theatre ten years ago but is no good for us. As he says, he makes no claim to write 'Russian' compositions. He 'just writes music'. Indeed, it is just music, and very poor music. Now we must start right from the beginning and so we must be nice to him and keep him with us for two or three months. I am counting on your help. He is gifted, but what can one expect from him if the most cultivated person he sees is Tcherepnin, who impresses him with his avant-gardism? He is very easily influenced and is more sympathetic than his arrogant appearance would suggest. I'll bring him to see you. He needs to change completely. Otherwise we'll lose him for good.[11]

Diaghilev suggested to Prokofiev that he go to Switzerland a few weeks later and find a place near Stravinsky's. The company could assemble there, and they could work jointly on a ballet. But Prokofiev wasn't particularly keen to prolong his stay abroad. Not only did he have a fiancée waiting for him in St Petersburg, he might also have been nervous at the idea of spending months under the Svengali-like influence of Diaghilev.

Prokofiev, Diaghilev and Massine travelled around southern Italy for a few days, taking in Naples, Pompeii, the Amalfi coast and Capri. During the trip Diaghilev managed to talk Prokofiev into abandoning *Ala and Lolli* entirely and writing a whole new ballet based on a Russian fairytale, for which Stravinsky was to provide the material. Prokofiev observed Diaghilev very closely, noting that he and Massine behaved like a couple of lovebirds, even as Diaghilev, who loved Italian food, had become so fat he had started to waddle.[12]

The impresario often talked to him about ballet as an art form, revealing a remarkable line of reasoning: 'Diaghilev and I spoke three or four times about ballet, passionately and at length – not so much about my ballet as about current trends in general. Diaghilev always spoke with enthusiasm and conviction and sometimes spoke truths that seemed absurd, but there was no chance to object to them because he immediately brought up a mass of the most logical arguments which substantiated the absurdity with extreme clarity.'[13]

On one occasion Diaghilev rebuked Prokofiev for his eclectic musical taste:

'In art, you must know how to hate – otherwise your music will lose all individuality.'

'But surely,' Prokofiev objected, 'that will lead to narrowness.'

'The cannon shoots far because it doesn't scatter its fire,' retorted Diaghilev.[14]

Once again they spent nearly a fortnight in Rome. Stravinsky sent them Afanasyev's famous collection of folktales, and they picked through the material looking for a theme. Previously, Stravinsky had suggested the story of the buffoon (*chout* or *shut* in Russian) as a possible ballet plot to Diaghilev, and Prokofiev now also saw potential in the subject.

At the beginning of March Diaghilev, Massine and Prokofiev left for Milan, to meet up with Stravinsky and see what the futurists had been getting up to. Prokofiev was delighted by Marinetti and the whole movement, and he also got the impression that Marinetti and Diaghilev had become 'very close friends'. It was, moreover, quite plain to him that the futurists 'cling on desperately to Diaghilev, because he is a colossal advertisement for them'.[15] The Russians were treated to an extensive show; Stravinsky and Diaghilev were as enthralled by the various instruments (mostly percussion) as they were by Luigi Russolo's noise machines. According to the poet Francesco Cangiullo, who was also present, Diaghilev trotted around like 'a vertical hippopotamus ... eccentrically rouged, with an enormous chrysanthemum in his buttonhole'.[16] Plans were conceived for two joint productions: a ballet to *Fireworks*, an early work by Stravinsky, and the staging of a Neapolitan popular festival, though the latter never made it past the drawing board.[17] *Liturgy* was still a serious project. All in all, the futurists' influence on Diaghilev and his circle was considerable at the time. Many years later Stravinsky played down the role of the strident Italians, but only in deference to the post-war political landscape, when tolerance for the political puerility of the futurists had understandably waned.[18] And as for Diaghilev, his remark to Prokofiev that 'pathos, inspiration and internationalism were … out of style'[19] shows that he was by no means indifferent to the movement's ideas.

It was a time of opportune personal alliances. The notion of bringing together Stravinsky and Prokofiev had been a happy one. Stravinsky was impressed by Prokofiev, heaping praise on his work. Prokofiev, for his part, experienced an epiphany when he and Stravinsky performed *Sacre* as a piano duet. Although he had heard the music once before in St Petersburg he had, as he himself admitted, understood little of the work. Now that he was one of the performers of this formidably difficult piano piece in a huge hall full of futurists and their fans, he was suddenly overwhelmed by its brilliance and beauty. Stravinsky was exceedingly conceited, but he was probably right when he said that it took Prokofiev years to recover from the experience.[20]

The next day was Holy Saturday, the day before Easter, but the Russians didn't exactly observe the usual fast. In fact Stravinsky got blind drunk, having solemnly resolved to knock back bottles of Asti until he keeled over. The next day he returned to Switzerland, and Diaghilev, Massine and Prokofiev to Rome. Prokofiev was anxious to get back to Russia, but not before hammering out a contract with Diaghilev. A canny businessman, he succeeded in extracting a fee that Diaghilev claimed was more than those of Debussy and Ravel combined. The fierce negotiations almost cost Prokofiev his amicable relationship with the impresario. There was a lot of stamping and shouting, but eventually, at three o'clock in the morning, the contract was signed.[21] Prokofiev went back to Russia the following day.

It was now high time to organise the tour of the United States, and Diaghilev had to rally the troops. This time, though, it was not just a matter of reassembling the company, which was by then scattered across Europe. What was really needed was a new troupe, and with that in mind Diaghilev called in the indispensable Grigoriev. In recent seasons, only a few Ballets Russes dancers had come from the Petersburg Imperial Theatres; the rest came from Moscow and private academies. Indeed, an increasing number weren't Russian at all.

The group was joined by a number of Polish dancers, including Léon Woizikovski and Stanislav Idzikovski, as well as a handful of English ballerinas that Grigoriev had picked up in London. One of them, Hilda Munnings, had been dancing with the company since 1913, first under the rather unfortunate soubriquet of Munningsova, and later, from mid-1915, as Lydia Sokolova – the name under which she became famous. 'Forget from now on that you have ever been anything but Russian,' Diaghilev decreed after this last name change.[22] 'Internationalism' was indeed out of style, at least as far as his company was concerned, because the Ballets Russes owed much of its appeal to its exotic Eastern roots.

Diaghilev had rented a villa called 'Belle Rive' in the hamlet of Ouchy, near Lausanne on the banks of Lake Geneva, and it was there the company gathered. The house became the epicentre of an international artistic colony at the height of its creative powers. Diaghilev had chosen Switzerland for practical reasons. It was neutral and, unlike Italy, planned to remain so. Plus, transport connections with France were good. Perhaps most importantly, Stravinsky was in Switzerland and, since he refused to go to Diaghilev, Diaghilev would have to go to him. Stravinsky and his family lived in Morges, two hours by bike (the composer's preferred mode of transport) from Ouchy.

On arriving in Switzerland, Diaghilev first went to Montreux, where he met Stravinsky on the evening of 25 April. The next day they learned of the sudden death of Alexander Scriabin, who had succumbed to blood poisoning at the age of forty-three. Although Diaghilev and Stravinsky had never enjoyed very cordial relations with the composer, the two were saddened by the news and sent a telegram to the family expressing their condolences.[23] Diaghilev, who was only two months younger than Scriabin, may have had intimations of his own mortality. Shortly afterwards he was moved to tears when Stravinsky played his latest version of *Svadebka*, proclaiming that this would be the most beautiful and purest Russian creation of the ballet.[24]

Diaghilev settled in Ouchy in early May. Grigoriev arrived after a two-week journey via Scandinavia, Britain and France, stayed for a week and was then sent back to Russia to contract more dancers. Karsavina got pregnant, ruling her out of the American tour. A dancer from Moscow, Ksenia Makletsova, was engaged to replace her, though she proved a poor substitute. Fokine threw another spanner in the works by refusing to leave Russia. Meanwhile, Diaghilev's attempts to summon Goncharova and Larionov (first to Rome, to

Ouchy: Stravinsky, the wife of a Russian diplomat, Diaghilev and Bakst

work with Marinetti, and now to Switzerland) were falling on stony ground. The war had left Larionov not only wounded but also shell-shocked; he was presumably unfit to travel. Diaghilev, nothing daunted, fired off a barrage of telegrams demanding that they 'depart immediately', whereupon the two artists capitulated.[25] Bakst also came over from Paris, but only briefly; the presence of modernists in the Ballets Russes camp must have brought home Diaghilev's change of artistic direction.

The two artists were quickly at home in the team. Larionov was interested in all kinds of theatrical innovation and worked better in a dynamic group than in his studio. It may have been true, as some claim, that his artistic powers were never the same after his war trauma,[26] but he certainly found his niche in Switzerland, where he could experiment to his heart's content. Perhaps even more importantly, Goncharova and Larionov both adored Diaghilev, which must have been balm to a man constantly smarting from conflicts with Bakst and Benois. Not that it affected his business practices: he only paid the two when he felt like it.

The dancers were something of a motley crew, with very different backgrounds and abilities. To mould them into a fit, unified group, Enrico Cecchetti and his wife were also brought over to Switzerland. Studios were set up in Diaghilev's villa, where sets, costumes and choreographies could be produced.

Massine continued to work on the choreography for *Liturgy*, while Goncharova tackled the costumes. (After she died, dozens of finished costume designs were found among her effects, along with an extensive, seventeen-scene libretto.) A brief experiment dispensed with music entirely, using only the sounds of the dancers' footfalls. It involved constructing a double floor on which the stage acted as a soundbox, reverberating like a giant drum. Diaghilev suggested a set designed to look like the interior of an early medieval church (presumably inspired by the churches they had seen in Ravenna).[27] But music remained a big problem. Stravinsky was busy with *Svadebka* and couldn't get away, though he did make some effort to find suitable music for *Liturgy*.[28] The fact that the ballet was not produced in 1915 should not be attributed to a lack of ambition, as Grigoriev seems to suggest. The reverse is true: the project sank under the weight of its creators' aspirations.[29] As late as January 1916 Diaghilev refers to *Liturgy* as a 'great enterprise, on which Stravinsky and Massine are working together'.[30]

It didn't look as if *Svadebka*, which now bore the French title *Les Noces villageoises* (The Village Wedding), would be ready in time for the American tour. By mid-August 1915 it was only half done. Around that time Stravinsky did play the work to Misia Sert, who wrote to Jean Cocteau: 'Imagine the most beautiful work of our greatest musician, with the quality of *Petrushka* as seen through *The Rite* ... He has opened yet another door, and there everything is permitted, everything is sonorous, joyous, and each note takes you by surprise, just as you would wish – and overwhelms you.'[31]

Misia was extremely impressed by the progress being made in Switzerland, especially by Massine: 'Last night, a dress rehearsal for us of what has been done these past months. [Presumably extracts from *Liturgy*.] Something completely new, very beautiful, in which Massine proves that he really is someone. And how prejudiced we were against him, Sert and I!! Serge fatter and fatter, his clothes tighter and his hat smaller, rather "circus director", as Igor says, has again found a way to surprise us.'[32]

Since neither *Liturgy* nor *Svadebka* was ready, and Prokofiev was not going to complete *Chout* by August, as his contract stipulated, an alternative had to be thought up. Desperate to present at least one new work, Diaghilev resolved to create a ballet to music from Rimsky-Korsakov's opera *Snow Maiden*, with sets and costumes by Larionov and choreography by Massine (aided by Larionov). This ballet, which had no libretto, was finished quite soon. Larionov wanted very much to extend the scenery – traditionally confined to a painted backdrop – to include objects on stage around which performers would dance. The idea was vetoed because of the difficulty of transporting such sets to America, but it shows how Larionov anticipated developments that would later become standard practice for the Ballets Russes.[33] Nevertheless, the ballet's design went a step further than *Coq d'or*. The lavish, whimsical costumes were earthier than in the previous Rimsky adaptation. The grotesquely oversize hats, necklaces and shoes heightened the fantasy element of the show. In fact, the gigantic costumes turned it into a tableau of moving objects rather than a traditional dance performance – much to the annoyance of the dancers, who, encumbered as they were, could demonstrate almost nothing of their skills.

Meanwhile, preparations for the tour were not going smoothly. The Americans had demanded to see Nijinsky, and Diaghilev had agreed. But when war broke out, Nijinsky was with his wife in Austria – a Russian in enemy territory – and he was placed under house arrest by the authorities. Diaghilev failed to tackle this difficulty with his usual energy, and it was still unresolved by the end of December.

And, of course, there were the inevitable money problems. The American advance was insufficient to maintain the entire company for six months, so Diaghilev had to shuttle back and forth to Paris, cap in hand. They didn't even have enough greasepaint, ballet shoes or fabric for costumes. Lydia Sokolova wrote that 'we always knew when Diaghilev had been successful after one of his Paris trips, because Massine would be wearing another sapphire ring on his little finger'.[34] But the financial difficulties remained, and Diaghilev wasn't able to send money to Russia.

On 20 December the Ballets Russes performed in Geneva for the first time in nearly sixteen months, at a Red Cross benefit show where they presented three ballets, including *Soleil de nuit*. Ansermet conducted the orchestra, except for the orchestral suite from *Firebird*, in which Stravinsky made his debut with the baton. Four days later the company was back in Paris to perform in another Red Cross show at the Grand Opéra. Massine's first ballet was very well received, and Diaghilev was as proud as Punch. Massine was much more his personal discovery than Stravinsky or Prokofiev had been, and there had been considerable scepticism when Diaghilev announced that he intended to turn the boy into his next star choreographer.

On New Year's Day 1916 Diaghilev and his company left Bordeaux for New York. For Diaghilev, who was terrified of crossing even the Channel, it was a hellish voyage. He made sure that he was always in grasping range of a lifebelt and left his cabin only when absolutely necessary. On 11 January they finally spied the Statue of Liberty. The first telegraph Diaghilev sent from the Plaza Hotel, where he and Massine were staying, was to his stepmother: 'We have arrived. Praise God.'[35]

Despite harbouring a modish anti-Americanism, Diaghilev must have been impressed by his first encounter with the New World, and – even allowing for diplomatic courtesy – this is borne out by one of the first interviews he gave. When asked what he thought of American art and its future prospects Diaghilev responded: 'When I told people how amazed I was by Broadway, its energy and joie de vivre, its inexhaustible variety and brilliance, they were amused. They thought I was joking. But I was absolutely serious. One day the American people will understand themselves. Broadway is authentic and exerts a powerful influence on American art …'[36]

The tour was to start at New York's Century Theater, travelling on to seventeen other cities, taking in such far-flung places as Milwaukee, St Paul and Kansas City. The repertoire would largely consist of Fokine's ballets from the first three seasons, with the principal exception of Nijinsky's *L'Après-midi d'un faune* and Massine's *Soleil de nuit*. The absence of its big stars – Karsavina and (for several months) Nijinsky – turned Diaghilev into the company's celebrity, and it seems as if the Metropolitan Opera's publicity machine made a concerted effort to put him in the spotlight. After all, it was the Met's directors who had insisted that Diaghilev join the tour, even demanding that he take out a costly life-assurance policy for the purpose.[37] In an interview with the *St Paul Pioneer Press*, Bakst too was suddenly full of praise for the old friend he referred to in letters as 'that fat spider' and 'that bastard'.[38]

But the lack of stars did present certain problems. Makletsova turned out to be a poor substitute for Karsavina, so Diaghilev called in Lydia Lopokova, who had been dancing in America for several years since performing in Diaghilev's 1910 season (when she also stood in for Karsavina). Though one of the most charming dancers ever to work for Diaghilev, Lopokova's novelty had by then somewhat worn off in the States. Almost every reviewer noted the relative weakness of the leads.[39] Makletsova, who was singled out for particular criticism, grew increasingly weary of the unfavourable comparisons with Lopokova. When she demanded a raise, Diaghilev fired her. Makletsova responded by suing Diaghilev and trying to get him arrested.[40]

The tour sparked one culture clash after another as the Old World collided with the New. There were puritan objections to the 'immoral scenes' in *Schéhérazade* and *L'Après-midi*. It was not the sexually explicit nature of the dance that caused revulsion so much as the spectacle of blacked-up men embracing white women, as Lynn Garafola convincingly postulated: 'America's ultimate racial taboo had been broken and that could not go unpunished.'[41] Diaghilev protested vociferously. ('These ballets have been performed in Europe in front of the kings of England and Belgium, the German court and Parisian society, and I've never had any complaints'),[42] but after police intervention he was forced to make cuts to both ballets. And Diaghilev's imperious style didn't go down well with theatre staff. As a Met employee put it, 'He detested our democratic ways.' Backstage personnel, in particular, found his arrogance hard to stomach. When a stage manager demurred at carrying out an assignment, Diaghilev struck him with his walking stick and was very nearly beaten up by angry stagehands. Later that night, a metal object crashed down from a 27-metre high stage tower, slicing a chunk out of Diaghilev's bowler hat and missing his head by a whisker. This 'accident' was never cleared up.[43]

Meanwhile, pressure was being placed on the Austrian authorities to free Nijinsky and allow him to travel to America. These efforts eventually succeeded, not through the intervention of the King of Spain and the Pope, as Nijinsky's wife claimed, but rather with the help of the American ambassador in Vienna and the US Secretary of State.[44]

But Nijinsky's arrival on 4 April 1916 only created fresh problems. He refused to perform until Diaghilev paid him his outstanding wages. New lawsuits followed, and Diaghilev was eventually forced to pay the dancer the very considerable sum of $24,000.[45] It is hardly surprising that Diaghilev's subsequent memories of his time in America were not particularly happy ones. His hope that the tour would make him financially independent proved illusory.

Misia Sert later described how Diaghilev talked about America, citing an anecdote that Diaghilev told her on his return:

It's inconceivable! [A] country where there are no beggars. Not one! It can't have any atmosphere, any local colour. What would Italy be without her beggars! I hunted for them in New York – hunted very conscientiously. At last, at the corner of a street, I almost cried with joy: a man was walking towards me, very decently dressed, but with that unmistakable air, that glance, half humble, half hopeful – presuming that you will put your hand in your pocket. I hastened to do so with such readiness that I gathered in my hand all that I had in coins and small notes. This man well deserved to receive all the money that the indecent absence of his colleagues had prevented me from distributing for days. When I handed him my offering, a broad smile illuminated his face, showing all his teeth … Alas, they were made of gold![46]

Despite the fact that the tour was not a financial success, the Ballets Russes proved popular in the United States, and the prospect of an autumn 'coast to coast' tour was discussed. The Americans had had enough of Diaghilev himself, though; it was proposed that he remain in Europe and that Nijinsky be made artistic director. Diaghilev was quite taken by the idea, since it would allow the company to keep earning while he and his artists and composers stayed put and worked on a new repertoire. The tour ended back in New York, with a nearly month-long season at the Met. On 6 May the entire company, with the exception of Nijinsky, set sail for Europe.

Diaghilev was even more frightened on the return voyage than he had been on the outward crossing. Shortly before he embarked, a fortune teller had told him that he would die 'on the water'. The story goes that Diaghilev had his manservant Vasily pray for their safety on deck, while the impresario cowered in his cabin. His fears were hardly imaginary: Europe's coastal waters were crawling with German U-boats; only the previous year the liner *Lusitania* had been sunk off the coast of Ireland, with the loss of over a thousand lives.

Instead of returning to France, the company travelled to Spain, where Diaghilev had arranged a brief tour. From Cadiz they went on to Madrid, where they were to perform at the Teatro Real from 26 May to 9 June. A week before the Madrid premiere Diaghilev cabled his stepmother: 'God be praised am back in Europe.'[47] Meanwhile the war raged on. Russia was proving a match for the Central Powers, but at a huge cost in terms of human life. Fifteen million Russians had been drafted, hundreds of thousands of soldiers had already fallen, and by the end of the war the death toll would be over a million. Life got harder and harder for the civilian population. In the summer of 1916 Diaghilev sent Vasily to his stepmother in St Petersburg, presumably with money. His two half-brothers had been caught up in the war by now, and could no longer look after their mother.

Diaghilev, for his part, was having a whale of a time in Madrid. The company had performed for King Alfonso, a fervent admirer who was fast becoming their main European patron. The local society at the time was a Bohemian mix; Spain's neutrality made the country a magnet for all kinds of odd figures: artists, adventurers, political refugees and spies. Diaghilev and his group were accompanied by the composer Manuel de Falla, who had met the impresario in Paris and become close friends with him and Massine. In Seville, Granada and Cordoba, de Falla introduced them to Spanish folk music and dance, which deeply impressed the two Russians.

Goncharova and Larionov also came to Spain, as did Stravinsky, and

The company in Seville: Diaghilev and Massine standing centre left

both he and Diaghilev were received in audience by the king. Over the previous six months the relationship between Diaghilev and Stravinsky had been
stretched to breaking point by bitter rows about money. The war had left
both men in extremely straitened circumstances. Diaghilev, ever the hard-
boiled businessman, always paid at the very last minute – if at all. He was
constantly robbing Peter to pay Paul. Advances for future tours were used to
settle old debts and to develop ballets that often never saw the light of day.
Ernest Ansermet, now the company's regular conductor and a faithful ally
of Stravinsky, frequently acted as middleman to prevent discussions about
money from flaring into acrimonious conflicts.

During the summer Diaghilev spent some time in Paris, where he saw a
lot of the Serts. After the summer he had scheduled a brief season in Spain,
for which he wanted to create a new ballet inspired by Velázquez's famous
painting *Las Meninas*. The music would be Gabriel Fauré's immortal *Pavane*.
Diaghilev asked José-Maria Sert to make the sets and costumes, but this
proved to be a bad move. Ansermet wrote to Stravinsky that 'Diaghilev was

depressed, on returning from Paris, to find that Sert had made a mess of the sets for *Pavane* but wouldn't let him change a thing.'[48]

There were rows with the Serts, and violent recriminations. But Misia had other irons in the fire. During the war she had grown very close to Jean Cocteau, and the young poet had now turned to her for help with a plan for a ballet. On 30 May 1916 she attended a musical soirée organised by Picasso and Matisse, among others, at which works by Satie and the Spanish composer Enrique Granados were performed. This was probably the first time the three creators of *Parade* (Cocteau, Picasso and Satie, with Massine as choreographer) had the opportunity to talk shop. By the second week of May Misia had already spoken to Satie about 'a theme for the Ballets Russes'.[49] A week later Diaghilev visited Picasso in his studio. Thus Cocteau's brainchild first saw the light of day in Paris, taking final shape in May 1916, without Diaghilev's direct involvement. But by 9 July he was in the picture and had given Satie the go-ahead.[50] Satie initially expressed distrust of Diaghilev ('Will he try to screw me? Probably. He'd better watch out!') but over the next few years his attitude evolved from astonishment ('Diaghilev's friendly, but he's an awful person') through appreciation (Diaghilev is variously described as 'charming', 'nice' and 'full of good ideas')[51] to open admiration.

By 24 August, Cocteau had got Picasso onto the team, and the three men started work in earnest.[52] Cocteau had staked all his hopes on the success of *Parade*, believing it would establish him as a serious, progressive artist. He was also driven by his obsession with Diaghilev, whom he both feared and admired. But his hero was a hard man to impress. One of the most famous anecdotes about the Ballets Russes centres on a conversation the two men had while walking home together across the Place de la Concorde in 1912:

> I [Cocteau] was at the absurd age when one thinks oneself a poet, and I sensed in Diaghilev a polite resistance. I questioned him about this, and he answered, 'Astound me! I'll wait for you to astound me.' That phrase saved me from a flashy career. I was quick to realise that one doesn't astound a Diaghilev in a week or two. From that moment I decided to die and be born again. The labour was long and agonising. That break with spiritual frivolity … I owe, as do so many others, to that ogre, that sacred monster, to the desire to astound that Russian prince to whom life was tolerable only to the extent to which he could summon up marvels.[53]

Picasso, by Cocteau

Parade seemed to be the perfect opportunity for Cocteau to summon up some marvels of his own. But it was clear that Diaghilev's interest in the project stemmed from his admiration for the headstrong, eccentric Satie, and for Picasso, who was already the most famous modernist painter in Paris. It was to be an inspiring partnership – at least for the artist and the composer. That autumn saw a meeting of the minds between Satie and Picasso which left poor Cocteau sidelined and presumably deeply frustrated.

At the end of August the brief season continued with performances in San Sebastian and Bilbao. Two very short ballets choreographed by Massine premiered in San Sebastian: *Las Meninas* and *Kikimora* ('the house spirit'). The latter, to pre-existing music by Lyadov, was also designed by Larionov, who stuck to his neo-primitivist approach, conceiving it as a grotesque, violent fairytale.

After the Spanish performances the company began to prepare for the second tour of the United States, this time without Diaghilev, Massine, Grigoriev and various dancers. Diaghilev had arranged to keep a small entourage in Europe, while the corps and a number of soloists travelled to America.

Financially speaking, the new tour started on an apparently excellent footing. Diaghilev received an advance of $20,000, with the prospect of $9,000 for every week they performed, plus half the net profits, to be paid at the end of the tour. Never shy about spending money – even money he didn't yet have – Diaghilev immediately used this sum to commission new ballets and shore up existing projects. Thus, the autumn and winter of 1916 saw eleven ballets go into production or pre-production. In production were *Parade*; *Russkiye Skazki* (later *Contes russes*) by Larionov to an existing score by Lyadov; *Feria*, a Spanish ballet to pre-composed music by Ravel, with sets to be designed by Bakst; *Le Chant du rossignol* (a reworking of Stravinsky's opera) with sets by the futurist Fortunato Depero; *Feux d'artifice* by Stravinsky, with a light show by Giacomo Balla; *Triana* by Goncharova and Albeniz; and *Les Femmes de bonne humeur*, a ballet to music by Domenico Scarlatti, reorchestrated by Vincenzo Tommasini. Meanwhile, Manuel de Falla was toiling away on the music for a work that would become *The Three-Cornered Hat*, Stravinsky still hadn't finished either *Les Noces* or *Liturgy*, and in Petrograd, Prokofiev was busy with *Chout*. Of all these works, only the first two would be performed in the 1917 season, and three (*Feria*, *Triana* and *Liturgy*) would never be staged at all. Diaghilev was juggling more artistic and financial risks than ever before, and at that chaotic period it was only a matter of time before he dropped a ball or two.

The biggest financial blow came from America, where the company lost its way without Diaghilev's leadership. Nijinsky proved a complete failure as artistic director, and the American organisers were at a loss to deal with either his whims or the everyday problems of a troupe of foreign dancers, almost none of whom spoke English. Not to put too fine a point on it, the tour was a disaster. The dancers performed in fifty-three towns and cities, including Los Angeles and San Francisco, but mostly smallish places like Worcester, Wichita, Tacoma, Grand Rapids, Toledo, Omaha, Tallahassee, Syracuse, Spokane and Des Moines. The provincial audiences of the time were simply not ready for a company like the Ballets Russes, especially one in organisational meltdown. By the time they reached the west coast at the end of December, things had got so bad that the dancers were actually going hungry. Nijinsky had sent Diaghilev three desperate telegrams, begging him to come to America.[54] Diaghilev, meanwhile, had dispatched Vasily to the States to assist the troupe, but he was powerless to avert disaster. The Metropolitan Opera incurred a loss of $25,000 on the tour, and Diaghilev received $75,000 less than agreed.[55]

This left him in a huge predicament. A whole army of dancers, designers and crew members needed to be paid. Where was the money to come from? Relations deteriorated, especially with Stravinsky, who was less and less inclined to tolerate Diaghilev's devil-may-care attitude toward financial matters. Moreover, Diaghilev had wanted to set aside money for a return to Russia, but he no longer had any reserves to draw on.

When he and Stravinsky failed to come to terms about renewing the contract for the rights to performances of *Firebird* and *Petrushka*, Diaghilev was for once entirely open with the composer:

> The war which is suffocating us all has interrupted my plans and now I must make a decision – either pay an intolerable sum of money or abandon my journey to Russia, which has been my dream. Haven't I earned the right to that journey by the agonies of ten years abroad? ... But you're wrong when you think that I've 'come back from America' and so ...
>
> So what? I am drawing my last breath, as one says, because of the war and also because of that very America which was meant to allow me to breathe. The whole of the last week I've spent in a frightening trance.[56]

After seeing in the New Year of 1917, he cabled his stepmother. 'My hugs to everyone, hope this year will find us together and finally bring prosperity.'[57]

Diaghilev had once again settled in Rome to prepare a short season there, after which the Ballets Russes hoped to make a triumphant return to Paris in April and May. His official residence was the Grand Hotel de Russie, but he spent nearly all his time in a palazzo on via Cordo, where Massine was staying. Massine had refused to sleep under the same roof as Diaghilev, wanting to avoid the impression that he was Diaghilev's lover. Firmly heterosexual, he presumably did not wish to ruin his chances with the Roman women. As Massine saw it, any intimacy with Diaghilev was simply the price he had to pay for climbing the artistic ladder.

Diaghilev had summoned Picasso and Cocteau to Italy, and the two arrived on 19 February. Satie had finished the music a week earlier, after making a few last changes suggested by Diaghilev.[58]

Diaghilev had fixed up one of the Patrizi studios off the via Margutta for Picasso, where he continued to work on the designs he had conceived in Paris. But the two Frenchmen were first made to see the sights of Rome. For a couple of days Diaghilev acted as their tour guide, taking in both highbrow art and culture of a rather less elevated sort: at a visit to the circus he fell asleep and woke with a start when an elephant put its feet on his knees.[59] He made a tense, worried impression. According to Cocteau, he ate and drank incessantly.[60]

He certainly had good reason to be worried. Besides his never-ending financial difficulties, there was the situation in Russia to consider. In telegrams to his stepmother he repeatedly enquired after the welfare of his two half-brothers. He must have heard reports of the chaos in the Russian army, the murder of Rasputin on 29 December 1916 and the various protest movements. Town-dwellers were finding it hard to get food and fuel, and inflation was rampant. Demonstrations and riots became common.

The tsarist regime collapsed in the second week of March, amid violent protests and general unrest, and a provisional government led by Alexander Kerensky assumed power. On the whole, Russian artists in Europe were fairly positive about this first revolution. Diaghilev and Stravinsky were downright enthusiastic. 'All my thoughts are with you at this time, so joyous and memorable for our dear, liberated Russia,' Stravinsky wrote to his wife.[61]

Just a few days into the revolution, writers and intellectuals in St Petersburg formed a committee to protect Russia's art treasures and cultural life. At the same time they put their heads together to consider who should become the new Minister of Culture. Prominent candidates included Alexandre Benois and the writer Maxim Gorky. But by 17 March a meeting concluded, after heated debate, that Diaghilev was the man for the job. They decided to send him a telegram, asking him to oversee cultural life in the new Russia. The next day Benois visited Kerensky to discuss Diaghilev's nomination. Kerensky clearly hadn't slept for days, and the conversation put Benois in mind of 'a mad dialogue by Dostoyevsky'. Kerensky did, however, sanction Diaghilev's nomination.[62]

On 20 March Benois visited Diaghilev's stepmother to get his address. Yelena Diaghileva thought it entirely possible that Diaghilev would return to Russia. But Benois had his doubts, and wrote in his journal: 'I was afraid of bothering Seryozha and taking him away from his European activities just to offer him again the bitter cup of this Russian mess.'[63]

The situation was indeed still highly unstable, and the nobility and the upper echelons of the bourgeoisie were unsure of their position. A few weeks earlier the Nouvel family's residence had been besieged by an armed group of revolutionaries who demanded that both Walter and his brother Richard give themselves up for trial. Others called for their immediate execution. It is unclear what was behind this incident. Benois merely reports that 'these two members of the bourgeoisie with their foreign names were suspected of being up to something unsavoury',[64] perhaps a veiled reference to Nouvel's homosexuality. The brothers were taken away for questioning but released after an interview with Duma representatives. Soldiers again gathered outside the Nouvel residence the next day, but apart from some shouting and threats the incident passed off peacefully.

The telegram duly reached Diaghilev in Rome, but he politely turned down the appointment. According to Ansermet, with whom he discussed the matter, Diaghilev was honoured, but preferred to wait until something slightly more definite and less exalted came along. Ansermet had his own theory: 'I think the main reason is he's scared of travelling.'[65] This may well have been a factor, but it is debatable whether Diaghilev would have rejected the offer had he known this was possibly the last chance to see his native country. Benois was disappointed, of course, but understood Diaghilev's position. The situation was so chaotic and power structures so uncertain that it made good sense to adopt a wait-and-see approach. As one of the few to keep a firm grip on reality, Benois expressed extreme pessimism about the situation in Russia in his diary: 'Perhaps it's better for Seryozha to stay where he is, in those more fortunate countries that we, alas, will have to emigrate to when everything here […] sinks into the mire.'[66]

Diaghilev also had practical reasons for declining the job offer. He had a great many ballets in production and was immersed in preparations for seasons in France and Italy. He had also signed a contract for a new tour of South America, with which he hoped to recoup the losses he had suffered in the US. If he had returned to Russia at that point, his company in Europe would have gone bankrupt and a decade's work would have been lost for good. It was an exhilarating, exhausting time; his energies were wholly taken up with rehearsals and preparations for the performances in Rome and Paris. Should he give all this up for St Petersburg, where his old friend Valechka had nearly been lynched by revolutionary soldiers?

On the Rome front, the only work ready for production was *Les Femmes de bonne humeur*. This ballet, with scenography by Bakst, was one of the few non-modernist works in the offing. *Les Femmes* looked back, rather than forward, in an attempt to revive the old *Mir iskusstva* charm of the very first productions. Never before had Diaghilev produced a work so firmly rooted in the eighteenth century: it was based on a play by Goldoni and set to music by Scarlatti. As an exploration of eighteenth-century aesthetics it went much further than, say, *Pavillon d'Armide*, and heralded a new stage in Diaghilev's uncooled ardour for the culture of that era. He was exceptionally pleased with the ballet, writing to Stravinsky's wife: 'With my close involvement it's difficult for me to judge, but I think it a little masterpiece. It's full of joy and life from beginning to end.'[67]

That this of all ballets should have been the first to premiere at a time of such artistic and political upheaval says much about Diaghilev – as does the premiere of *Parade* a month later. Even when pursuing innovation, he sought to produce a broad range of works and preserve an element of continuity. Moreover, he saw nothing wrong with mixing historic and contemporary imagery. His instincts did not let him down: *Les Femmes* was the hit of 1917.

At the beginning of May the company left for Paris and eight performances at the Châtelet. It was a special homecoming, after an absence of nearly three years, to the city and the theatre where the Ballets Russes had experienced a baptism of fire. On the opening night Diaghilev presented the Parisian premiere of *Les Femmes* and the world premiere of *Contes russes*, a ballet by Larionov to music by Lyadov-Korsakov. (In actuality, *Contes* was an expanded version of the previous year's *Kikimora*, to which three scenes had been added). It was the Parisians' first encounter with Larionov's coarse neo-primitivist style (*Soleil de nuit* had never been staged in Paris), and it went down very well. But the biggest surprise of the evening came at the end of *Firebird*. Diaghilev had replaced Tsarevich Ivan with a Russian *muzhik* wearing a cap of liberty and brandishing a red flag. Fearing a riot, he went so far as to post a detachment of Russian soldiers (apparently stationed in Paris) outside the artists' entrance.

Protests were made at this exhibition of Diaghilev's revolutionary fervour, and he was forced to defend his actions in a letter to *Le Figaro*:

After the premiere of the Russian Ballet people wrote to me asking what the red flag at the end of *Firebird* signifies.

In the Russia of today the red flag is the emblem of those who consider that the well-being of the whole world depends on the freedom of its peoples, which can only be achieved by a victorious struggle ...[68]

The red flag did not appear in subsequent performances; the one outing was enough for Diaghilev to achieve his aim. He had caused a stir in the press and taken a public stance. He was well aware that *Figaro* was also read in St Petersburg.

The premiere of *Parade* followed on 18 May. Picasso and his assistants had painted a spectacular stage curtain, almost devoid of cubist elements. Portraying a group of artists assembled on the stage of an old theatre, it was inspired by a similar curtain Picasso had seen in a theatre in Naples on his travels with Diaghilev. Some believed that the figures represented members of the company's entourage – the Moor was supposed to be Stravinsky and the Neapolitan sailor Diaghilev: a little joke of Picasso's, prompted by the impresario's mortal dread of the sea.

When the outer curtain rose to reveal Picasso's inner curtain, the audience gave an audible sigh of relief. Apparently this scary cubist was also capable of producing something quite tasteful.[69] Satie's music for *Parade* is heard much less frequently than his piano music of the 1880s and 1890s, and with its added 'concrete' sounds (sirens, the clatter of typewriters, pistol shots and a wheel of fortune) it now seems more of a historical curiosity than a glimpse of the musical future. But in 1917 it naturally came as a shock. An eclectic mix of music-hall tunes, ragtime, a fugue and a waltz, the score was remarkable for its studied anti-aestheticism and its subtle frivolity, which placed it just as far away from the music of Rimsky-Korsakov and Debussy as it was from Stravinsky and Schoenberg. Picasso's decor was a cubist cityscape featuring blocks of flats. Most of the dancers (representing acrobats and jugglers) wore fairly conventional costumes that allowed them sufficient freedom to dance, but two figures, the French Manager and the American Manager, were reduced to tottering cubist sculptures. The work's design was by no means wildly unconventional, but it nevertheless marked a significant moment – for the first time modernism was literally centre stage.

The public was raucous, though there was no scandal on the level of *Sacre*. If anything, people were upset because they expected a wartime programme to feature patriotic, self-affirming works, not frivolous unconventional experiments. Descriptions of its reception vary greatly. Grigoriev saw nothing out of the ordinary, while many years later Cocteau described an all-out riot featuring women brandishing hat pins. Writer and journalist Ilya Ehrenburg was present, and his account lies somewhere in between. According to him, people stormed out of the pit towards the stage, yelling for the curtain to be brought down. 'Then a horse came out on the stage wearing a cubist mask and began to perform circus tricks – it knelt down, danced and bowed. The audience clearly thought the dancers were mocking their protests and completely lost their heads; they yelled "Death to the Russians!" "Picasso's a Boche!" "The Russians are Boches!"'[70]

The premiere of *Parade* has gone down in history as the moment when the avant-garde elbowed its way into mainstream European elite culture, and the ballet's reputation is therefore perhaps greater than it might otherwise deserve. Around the same time Diaghilev had a number of avant-garde ballets waiting in the wings, such as *Liturgy*, which, from a conceptual standpoint, was more progressive. And Depero's decor for Stravinsky's *Chant du rossignol*, the ballet version of his opera, went much further in its exploration of avant-garde elements, to judge by the sole surviving photo of the maquette. But, for one reason or another, these works lost out in the avant-garde sweepstakes. They were pipped at the post by *Parade*, perhaps thanks to financial support from Misia Sert. *Parade* also happened to be the company's least Russian ballet to date – only the choreography was of Russian origin – and thus heralded the metamorphosis of the Ballets Russes into an international production company which brought together composers and artists of every stripe. This was in a sense an entirely new and different company, connected to the pre-war Ballets Russes only by historical ties. It was a reinvention, born not of artistic choice but of necessity.

Everyone assumed that, once the war was over, the company would revert to its old approach. Few in Diaghilev's Parisian entourage anticipated yet another Russian revolution, this time led not by a broad protest movement but by a small group of radicals under the revolutionary Vladimir Lenin. At the time the Bolshevik coup was widely viewed as a temporary hiccup. But the new movement proved unstoppable. Soon immensely powerful, it would bring about a bloody end to Diaghilev's Russia and turn the new state into a superpower.

In Petrograd, on 11 November 1917, Lenin asked Alexandre Benois to take on the portfolio of Minister of Fine Arts, but he refused.[71] Anatoly

Lunacharsky was then pushed forward. Three weeks later Benois was already regretting his decision, though he conceded that he would not have been capable of leading Russia's cultural world:

> Now if Seryozha Diaghilev had been there, things would have gone differently. He wouldn't have been scared of the public, and I would have taught him how to act as I always did. And he would have sorted out all those bungling idiots, and wouldn't have shrunk from getting rid of a few of them. The machine would have got going and there'd have been a really good performance. But Seryozha, who in March turned down the honour we offered him of coming to head the arts in a renewed Russia, is hardly going to want to come back to us. The sly old sage – his time clearly hasn't come yet; let's hope he's not too late.[72]

But he would be. For the first time in his life, Sergey Diaghilev, the eternal forerunner, was too late.

· 23 ·

A Letter from Nouvel
1917–1919

THE RUSSIAN REVOLUTION would soon change Diaghilev's company irrevocably, but initially, in the second half of 1917, it seemed as if the Ballets Russes would eventually be able to ease back into its pre-war routine.

Shortly after the premiere of *Parade* the troupe was again the talk of the town and its managing director the king of artistic Paris. 'As I was leaving the theatre after the performance by the Ballets Russes last Wednesday, I tried in vain to find you,' Claude Debussy wrote to Diaghilev. 'I phoned the Châtelet, but I think I would've had more luck calling God.'[1]

Parade brought the Ballets Russes in close contact with a new group of artists, who would gradually replace the pre-war entourage of fin-de-siècle greats. The poet Guillaume Apollinaire, who contributed an essay for the programme, attended the premiere, as did the painters Juan Gris and Joan Miró, and the composers Francis Poulenc and Georges Auric. This avant-garde public would also come to define the Ballets Russes's image behind the scenes. But in 1917 this was by no means a foregone conclusion. With its decidedly non-Russian air, *Parade* appeared to be a brief foray into unfamiliar aesthetic territory, rather than a prelude to a new trend. After the Paris shows, the company prepared for a series of performances in Madrid and Barcelona and a new tour of South America.

*Apollinaire and Diaghilev, by
Larionov*

Diaghilev had signed the contract for the overseas tour more than a year earlier, and the set-up was roughly the same as the disastrous second tour of the United States. That is to say, there would be no Diaghilev, and Nijinsky would be the star. Although he would not be in charge of day-to-day operations (that was Grigoriev's job), Nijinsky would be the public face of the company and their biggest draw. But first, the dancer had to come to Spain, for an engagement of several weeks.

Even with the benefit of hindsight, it is impossible to say when the first signs of Nijinsky's ultimate mental collapse began to appear. As far back as the first American tour his behaviour could be highly peculiar, to say the least. In Spain he proved unpredictable and irrational: without warning, he reneged on the agreement to go to South America and suddenly refused to dance in Barcelona. Diaghilev went so far as to have him arrested, in order to force him to fulfil his contractual obligations.

King Alfonso of Spain did not miss a single performance during the company's stint in Madrid and even invited the dancers to give a few private performances at the royal palace's theatre. Diaghilev again saw Manuel de Falla, who played him a first version of the Spanish-themed ballet that had been in the works for some time. While in Spain, Diaghilev also met up with Sonia and Robert Delaunay, married artists (he French, she Russian) who would collaborate closely with the company throughout its Spanish period. After the day's work the group would throw themselves into the local nightlife, with Diaghilev, Massine and some of the dancers dropping in on dimly lit dancehalls to observe the flamenco dancers. Apart from the incident with Nijinsky the mood was exuberant and the air electric with new ideas.

By now, Picasso was closely involved with the company, playing an ever expanding role in Diaghilev's plans for the future. The painter's presence was not only due to the lure of future commissions; he had also fallen for one of the company's dancers, Olga Khokhlova, who had joined the Ballets Russes only a few years before. No great star, she had danced a number of larger roles in various productions (for example in *Las Meninas*, which had been dusted off for the Spanish tour). Picasso had first noticed Khokhlova in Italy, but much to his surprise, the dancer initially resisted his overtures. She refused to sleep with him before marriage, an implicit ultimatum that only inflamed his desire and soon prompted a rash proposal. Diaghilev was by no means opposed to the union: he would not be losing a 'daughter' (Khokhlova was no more than a middling talent anyway); he would be gaining a 'son' (who just happened to be the greatest artist in Europe).

Picasso, for his part, was not blind to the benefits of marrying into Diaghilev's company. The artist had begun to cultivate a more refined appearance and manners under the influence of the great impresario. The coarse Bohemian from Montmartre traded in his overalls and espadrilles for plus-fours and ties, relishing the official dinners and receptions that Diaghilev took him to. Picasso now had the chance to show off his art to a larger, richer, more international and diverse public than would have ever been possible in the flashy but still decidedly marginal world of the Parisian avant-garde. Diaghilev even introduced him to King Alfonso, for whom they gave a command performance of *Parade* in Madrid. Picasso got along particularly well with one member of the company who secretly shared his fondness for chasing girls and frequenting brothels: Léonide Massine.

When the company (including Nijinsky) left for South America, Diaghilev, Massine, Khokhlova and Picasso remained behind in Spain. Everyone knew that a tour without Diaghilev was doomed to failure, and it was not long before the most pessimistic expectations came to pass. Transport problems,

Picasso, by Bakst

the ever-present danger of U-boat attacks, a fire that destroyed the sets for *Le Spectre de la rose* and *Cléopâtre* – these things were small beer compared to the tour's greatest problem: Nijinsky's mental deterioration. Grigoriev was finding it increasingly difficult to deal with the dancer's erratic behaviour, anxieties and delusions. In some instances Nijinsky refused to perform at all, and it was around this time that he began to exhibit signs of full-blown schizophrenia. He hired bodyguards, believing certain people, including Grigoriev, were out to kill him. In mid-September Nijinsky sank into an all-consuming psychosis, which would end his performing career for good and destroy his mind. On 26 December in Buenos Aires, Nijinsky danced with the Ballets Russes for the last time, in two of his most popular roles: *Le Spectre de la rose* and *Petrushka*. After the company set sail for Spain, Nijinsky danced in Buenos Aires one last time, in a shambolic benefit performance for the Red Cross. *Le Dieu de la danse* would never set foot on stage again.

In October 1917 Diaghilev was desperately on the lookout for new contracts that would keep his company afloat. He managed to arrange a number of performances in Barcelona, Madrid and Lisbon; this would at least get them through the winter. But these shows, too, were plagued by difficulties. Spain was in the grip of a flu epidemic (the first wave of what would become known as the Spanish flu), which felled some of the dancers and kept audiences at home. And in Lisbon the company was caught up in a revolution, which brought the whole country to a standstill. After calm had returned, the Ballets Russes danced a few times at the Coliseu dos Recreios and the

Teatro São Carlos. Then Diaghilev was stuck in Lisbon, down on his luck and with no prospects of new income. From there he sent his stepmother a New Year telegram.

Over the course of the hectic preceding year, Diaghilev had been in touch with his family in St Petersburg a few times, in the hope of receiving news of his half-brothers. In the winter of 1917–18 the situation was unstable, and nobody could predict what the new Bolshevik government would do. For the first time in his adult life Diaghilev had no informants in inner government circles who could give him the advance word on events. It is uncertain if Yelena was still replying to his telegrams at that point.

On 3 March 1918 Lenin signed the hated Peace of Brest-Litovsk, which ended Russia's involvement in the war in exchange for major territorial con-cessions to Germany. With one stroke of the pen, Russia became an inter-national pariah. Moreover, Diaghilev, Massine and most of the dancers of the company with their Russian imperial passports had now been rendered stateless. It is impossible to say whether rumours about the imminent peace found their way to Diaghilev, but a day before the signing he wrote to his stepmother, '[I'm] terribly worried, send news.' This was the very last tele-gram she would receive from him.[2]

In early 1918 Diaghilev managed, with the help of de Falla, to arrange another tour of provincial Spain. It began in Valladolid on 31 March and would take them to Salamanca and Bilbao in the north, and to Malaga and Granada in the south. Audiences in these provincial towns and cities were completely unprepared for what they saw, even though the company was dancing its most conservative repertory. To make matters worse, the decrepit old theatres in which they performed were unequipped to handle a group that up until the war had played only in the largest cities in Europe, for elite audiences. One of the dancers broke his foot when he crashed through a rotten plank.

It was impossible to pay everyone's salaries; most were given only pocket money, to cover their most basic expenses. Footwear and clothes could not be replaced, and the dancers took to wearing costumes and shoes from shows that were not being danced as their everyday apparel. When Sokolova's baby Natasha fell ill, Diaghilev dipped into his last remaining funds, copper and silver coins from various countries, to fetch a doctor.[3] Even as the war was drawing to a close, it seemed as if Diaghilev's company was on its last legs.

Diaghilev doggedly tried to cobble together a new contract in London, where theatres continued to draw crowds. He had been to London briefly the year before in the hope of organising a series of performances, but his negotiations with Thomas Beecham fell through. Diaghilev played Scarlatti's music (for *Les Femmes de bonne humeur*), and the music from *Parade*, and even though the first ballet was well received, the idea of putting on a show with sets by that wild Spaniard Picasso was too much for the British. In the end Beecham opted for an all-English season, which left the Russians out in the cold.[4] Now, in the wake of Brest-Litovsk, a Russian season was out of the question. In pure desperation Diaghilev accepted an offer to bring the Ballets Russes to the London Coliseum, a music hall. Diaghilev had always turned up his nose at music halls (unlike, for example, Pavlova), where the Russians had to share the bill with conjurors, acrobats and dog acts, but now he had no choice. He signed a contract for a series of performances which would last for several months, thus saving his company. The rest of the group gave him a hero's welcome on his return to Spain.

But new problems arose. The French authorities refused to grant the Russians permission to travel through their territory on the way to the Channel. The alternative, sailing to England from Spain, was far too dangerous on account of U-boats, but even if the waters hadn't been filled with marauding German submarines, Diaghilev's mortal fear of the sea would have made that option unpalatable. From Barcelona, Diaghilev consulted with French diplomats in Madrid. He was at the end of his tether. The burden of the previous year – the relentless poverty, the fall of Nijinsky, the existential uncertainty – weighed heavily on him as he fought to persuade the French to reconsider their decision. But there was something else on his mind, too: over the past year his relationship with Massine had begun to deteriorate. Having matured as both a dancer and choreographer, Massine could demand more independence; needless to say, this brought him into conflict with Diaghilev.

When it seemed that the French had finally relented, Diaghilev went to Madrid on his own to make a few final arrangements, but once there he faced new obstacles thrown up by the French authorities. He did everything he could, but he could expect little help from the Russian diplomats, who didn't even know what government they represented. Only the Spanish king was unwavering in his support. When Diaghilev finally had some good news to wire to Barcelona, but received no response from Massine, something snapped. Given the circumstances, there is no reason to doubt the sincerity of Diaghilev's emotional outburst. Of course, this doesn't mean he was above using emotional blackmail to get what he wanted from Massine:

> I begged the King three times to let us through and finally obtained the authorisation. As soon as I did, my nerves cracked and my whole system collapsed ...
>
> At times it's probably necessary to explain oneself, given that you don't want to understand or to feel ... I sent you a cable thinking that I was victorious, and received only a cable from the Lopokovs. From you not one word of tenderness, not one word of joy in return for my warmth. I asked frequently whether there was a note from you ...
>
> It is very hard for me to be without my family, my dear ones, without friends, without a drop of tenderness ...
>
> Someday you will understand all this and someday a ray of light will illuminate your heart of glass ... Can it be that it is not my destiny to infuse you with the warmth of a Russian spring sun?[5]

Diaghilev quickly recovered from this crisis and led his company over the Pyrenees to Paris, and then on to the Channel and London.

The long period in Spain was not simply a time of grinding poverty and struggle; it was also a time of rare artistic discovery, rooted in Spain's rich culture of folk music and folk dancing. At that point, Spain was perhaps the only country in Europe with an active folk dancing tradition, which was regularly practised in cafés and dancehalls. It had even developed its own schools, where masters passed on traditional techniques to pupils. Diaghilev's and Massine's most important guide and teacher in this new world was Félix Fernández García, an exceptionally gifted flamenco dancer, whom the impresario had first met in Granada. Fernández García had developed a system of notation for the *zapateado*, the complex steps characteristic of flamenco, and he had also taught himself to sing *seguidilla* and *alegría* songs while dancing. Diaghilev hired him to teach Massine Spanish dancing, and considered him for a role in the planned de Falla ballet.

In Russia, Spain enjoyed something of a minor cult following, thanks to a popular notion that the two nations were in some sense parallel cultures. Both were ancient civilisations that were starting to emerge from a long period of dormancy to claim their rightful place in the European mainstream. Both nations were defined by their resistance to foreign rule, whether in the guise of the Tatars or the Moors, and both had a special connection to the Orient. Diaghilev transformed this cult into a theory of a 'Latino-Slavic culture' in a bid to challenge the dominance of German culture in Europe. By presenting himself as the champion of an artistic alliance between Slavic and Latin countries, he tried to infuse new significance into his company, which was rapidly losing its ties to Mother Russia. Indeed, the ranks of the Ballets Russes had been so thinned out during the war that Diaghilev had to bring in a whole crew of English dancers (with transparently Russified names) to keep the company afloat. The Russian ballet was growing less Russian by the day.

In a series of interviews with the *Daily Mail* Diaghilev uncharacteristically vented his opinion on political matters, excoriating the whole German tradition in European culture:

> The soldiers are coming back to London to find the old German idols being worshipped here just as stupidly and uncritically as ever … Brahms is nothing but a putrefying corpse … Beethoven has been imposed on you by German propaganda. Beethoven, my dear Englishmen, is a mummy …
>
> *The War was nothing else but a struggle between two cultures*, and this struggle is not concluded by the victory of arms … But if we are invited during a whole year to funeral services such as a Beethoven festival or a grand Wagner concert, we can no longer breathe, work, or create.[6]

Never before had Diaghilev so unequivocally repudiated the great hero of his youth, Wagner, though even then it sounded as if he were arguing with himself rather than with the English critics, whom Diaghilev claimed were 'Bochified'.[7] Such aggressive outbursts, which did little to help his cause, suggest the release of pent-up frustration on the part of a man who had formerly taken great care to avoid making political statements in the press.

Despite the dog acts and the jugglers, the season at the London Coliseum was a resounding success. The Ballets Russes were welcomed as prodigal sons, drawing a more varied public than ever before. A new intellectual, bourgeois, avant-garde audience, which had previously avoided Covent Garden, flocked to the performances, eager to observe new trends in ballet. Unlike Thomas

Massine, by Picasso

Beecham, they were enthralled by the news that Picasso was now working for Diaghilev. The impresario now had all the more reason to step up his collaboration with the artist, and he hoped they would be able to stage not only *Parade* and de Falla's Spanish ballet in London, but also a new project centred on Pulcinella, the key figure of the commedia dell'arte.

Diaghilev used all his cunning to lure 'cher Pica' to London. First he prevailed upon his lover to write the artist a letter – he knew Picasso's affection for Massine – and when that failed to have the desired effect, he wrote to the Spaniard himself a few days later. In that letter he lambasted Picasso for not answering his telegrams and stressed the need for his presence, given that the premiere of *Parade* was just round the corner. Diaghilev wanted to get started on *Pulcinella* as well. He added that he had set aside 10,000 francs for a large portrait of Massine in the role of Pulcinella and tried to paint a rosy picture of life in London, to excite Picasso's curiosity:

> Things are very lively here. We want for nothing, and we manage to keep warm and well-fed. London is full of people. The theatres are doing better than ever, and we are working like blacks. And Olga? Has she given up dancing for good? That's really a pity. Massine regrets [her departure] as a choreographer and I as an 'old flame' … I hope to see you two again as soon as possible. I look forward to hearing all your news. Kisses to you both.[8]

The letter took a long time to arrive (Diaghilev had sent it to Biarritz, while Picasso was in Paris), and Picasso would not come to London until the spring of 1919, nor would he end up painting a portrait of Massine. He would, however, design both ballets, and that was the main thing, at least for the time being.

On 11 November 1918 the armistice was signed and the war was officially over. In London the company gave its thousandth performance on 18 November, a fact that Diaghilev did not want to celebrate for fear that it would bring bad luck. Neither of the Picasso ballets was performed during the long winter season, though there were two London premieres, designed by Larionov: on 21 November, *Le Soleil de minuit*, and on 23 December, *Contes russes*. The latter, which was presented under the name *Children's Tales*, was particularly successful; indeed, according to Sokolova it was the most popular ballet of that London season.[9] The public appreciation for Larionov's neo-primitivist designs strengthened Diaghilev's conviction that audiences were ready for Picasso. Attention now turned to the de Falla ballet, *The Three-Cornered Hat*, and the London premiere of *Parade*.

With preparations for these productions in full swing, 1918 came to a close. It had been the hardest year in the history of the company, but it seemed as if they had finally turned a corner. In London they tapped into a new and curious public, which was more receptive than pre-war audiences to avant-garde ballet. Diaghilev worked hard to revitalise his company and to realise the new ideas that had taken shape in 1915 and 1916. But the impresario's private life was still fraught with tension and uncertainty. His relationship with Massine lurched from one crisis to another. He had no idea how his family was faring, and he hadn't seen his closest friends for years. There must have been times when Diaghilev was beset by a sense of abandonment and despair. According to Ansermet, who met him in the spring of 1919, the Russian 'had aged a great deal [and] ... had shrunken everywhere, the poor man'.[10]

The preparations for *Three-Cornered Hat* went into high gear in April 1919 when Diaghilev went to Paris to negotiate a contract with Picasso, who still hadn't managed to find his way to London. The eventual agreement, which was signed on the fifteenth, stipulated that Picasso would receive 10,000 francs for his designs, but it also required him to join the company in London from 20 May until the premiere, which was scheduled for 22 July.[11] Starting then, Picasso got serious about the new ballet.

Another dormant project that had recently been revived was *Le Boutique fantasque*, a reworking of the classic *Die Puppenfee*, the first ballet Diaghilev ever saw during his earliest grand tour of Europe. The music consisted of various pieces by Rossini selected by Diaghilev and orchestrated by Ottorino Respighi. In 1917 Diaghilev had talked informally with Bakst about designing the sets and costumes for this ballet, but no contract was ever signed, an oversight that Bakst would come to regret. Bakst had worked on the ballet throughout 1918 and sent Diaghilev some of his costume designs, probably in early 1919. Diaghilev was unimpressed and decided to take another tack. He sent Massine to Paris to enter into negotiations with André Derain, the Fauvist painter whom he had known since his exhibition of Russian art at the Salon d'automne in 1906.[12] Derain's star was in the ascendant, and in the intervening years he had become one of the most famous artists in France. It seemed that it was Derain himself who expressed an interest in working with the Ballets Russes, and Diaghilev was certainly not going to let this opportunity pass him by.[13] An agreement was reached, in which Derain also pledged to report to London no later than the third week of May. From that point on there were two artists working independently on the same project. That was one too many, and Bakst would have to be cut loose. Instead of coming clean about his underhanded tactics, Diaghilev decided to make an impossible request. Sometime in mid-May he suddenly wrote that he needed the designs at very short notice, anticipating that Bakst would refuse to finish the job.

This is precisely what happened. Bakst wrote back a furious letter, full of accusations and underlining: 'This is utterly cheap and outrageous. For a whole year, you've been as silent as the grave and couldn't be bothered to answer a single one of my letters; not <u>one</u> word to let me know you're preparing a new production <u>now</u>, and then out of the blue I get this letter.'[14] A natural reaction, but of course what Bakst did not know was that Derain was in London at that very moment, working out his own ideas for the ballet. When Bakst found out he had been passed over in favour of Derain, he was understandably livid, and the old friendship, which had been volatile even in the best of times, suffered another blow.

According to Massine, Diaghilev 'was ruthless in anything that affected the work of the company. The artistic perfection of his productions was the most important thing in his life and he would allow nothing, not even a longstanding friendship, to stand in the way of it.'[15] That may be true, but the flare-ups that such working methods inevitably entailed did not always enhance the quality of his productions, and as he grew older these rows took an ever greater toll on his psychological well-being.

It was not Diaghilev, however, but a relative stranger to the company who crumbled under the pressure. Diaghilev had offered Félix Fernández García a contract to dance with the company, primarily with a view to the de Falla ballet. Fernández García had accompanied the troupe to London, where he continued to teach Massine the secrets of flamenco and *cante jondo*. Félix, the planned star of *Three-Cornered Hat*, was suddenly faced with the unfamiliar challenge of having to dance to a preset choreography, and this proved to be too much for him. His dancing was entirely improvised and could not be integrated into a fixed structure. Massine tried to get Félix to work with a metronome, but that backfired: the Spaniard became frustrated and nervous, and the prospects of his involvement in *Three-Cornered Hat* looked increasingly dim. In the meantime Massine continued to develop by leaps and bounds, absorbing Fernández García's techniques and innovations and winning praise for what was, at least in part, the other man's work. This frustrated Fernández García even more.

Even when he was still living in Spain, his mental health had been shaky (his friends called him '*el loco*'),[16] and under the pressure of the impending premiere, and perhaps the loneliness of living in a strange city, Félix had a nervous breakdown. Years later, Diaghilev told Harry Kessler how Félix had gone to the Church of St Martin in the Fields one night. When he saw a red lantern in the window, he asked a beggar woman if it was a brothel. He then gave her all his money, lamenting that even the Lord was reduced to living in a whorehouse. Then he forced his way into the locked church. When he didn't turn up that evening, Diaghilev called the police, who found Félix on the altar, naked. He was taken to an insane asylum in London, where he remained until his death in 1941.[17]

Diaghilev was deeply shocked. For some time he had hoped that Félix could become 'the new Nijinsky'.[18] It was a bizarre coincidence that within a few years, two great dancers in his circle would suffer mental breakdowns, but in Diaghilev's superstitious universe there was no such thing as coincidence. His anxiety about what such an inauspicious event could portend might explain his strange decision, a few years later, to tell acquaintances that Félix had died in an institution, more than twenty years before the fact (this is described independently by both Sokolova and Kessler).[19]

Despite the loss of Félix, preparations for the new premieres continued apace. Derain and Picasso worked on the designs, while Massine crafted his first choreographic masterpieces. Artistically, the collaboration with the French and Spanish painters was a great success, but that did not mean that conflicts were less common than in the days of Bakst and Benois. Derain and Picasso naturally saw themselves as more independent of the impresario, especially the strong-willed Picasso, who refused to allow himself to be manipulated. He needled Diaghilev by telling Massine that 'Diaghilev does the same thing they do at the Folies Bergère; only they do it better there'. Massine, who saw his chance to hit Diaghilev where it hurt, accused him of allowing his tastes and standards to decline.[20] Picasso's barbs were well chosen, undermining the confidence of his host and employer and breaking his power monopoly by encouraging the independence of his headstrong lover. Diaghilev did not show up to one of the last dress rehearsals and wrote Picasso a long letter in which he turned on all his charm: 'You know how much I love you, and how much I believe in your friendship. This is why I am writing to you in all candour.'

Massine, by Picasso

When he wanted to, Diaghilev could open up and show his vulnerable side:

> The thing that really bothers me is having to take direction from my own
> pupil: that discourages me … I freely admit that I'm old and weary …
> I'm disappointed, and I feel useless. Tonight will be a triumph, and the
> rehearsal will go very well if you and Derain will support me and be there.
> Massine will follow your instructions and will better understand Derain's
> intentions. If you don't have any other plans, it would be a pleasure to lunch
> with you and Massine as always at the Savoy from 11 to 2. Tell me what you
> think.[21]

The premieres would indeed be triumphs, every bit as spectacular as the
successes of the pre-war seasons. According to Sokolova, the reception given
to *Boutique fantasque* on 5 June 'must have been one of the most rapturous in theatre history. The applause was deafening and continuous, and the
stage was piled with flowers'.[22] Six weeks later *Three-Cornered Hat* repeated
this feat, on 22 July. In a sense it was the first modernist ballet to attain the

same level of artistic unity as the Ballets Russes's great pre-war successes, like *Schéhérazade* and *Petrushka*. This ballet was proof positive that Diaghilev's (sometimes wavering) commitment to modernism had been worthwhile. Picasso's designs were less cubist than in *Parade*, and de Falla's music was less preoccupied with the fads of the day than Satie's cakewalks and typewriters. *Hat* went beyond avant-garde provocation. It was a sign that modernist ballet had finally grown up, and in that respect it marked a new start in the ten-year history of the Ballets Russes.

Perhaps it was Massine even more than Picasso who was responsible for the production's success. As a choreographer he broke new ground by integrating the language of classical and folk dance in a way that had never been seen before. As a soloist he ascended to new heights, and as a coach he managed to bring out the best in his fellow dancers, members of the Ballets Russes who were much older than he – in some cases (Cecchetti and Grigoriev, for example, who both danced mime roles) decades older. According to Ansermet, who could be stingy with compliments, Massine danced 'with astonishing agility' and he was now fully ready to take on all of Nijinsky's old roles, even Petrushka. His achievement in *The Three-Cornered Hat* was, in Ansermet's view, 'unforgettable': Massine had been completely transformed into 'a Spanish dancer'.[23]

But however great his undoubted delight at the artistic rebirth of his company, Diaghilev remained preoccupied by the situation in Russia. That spring he had received a visit from Albert Coates, a Franco-Russian conductor who had just returned from Petrograd with 'some very bad news' about the general state of the city.[24] There was still no news about Diaghilev's family.

Sometime in the second half of July 1919, Diaghilev received a letter from his old friend Walter Nouvel, who was writing from Helsinki. Nouvel had fled from Petrograd to Finland, leaving behind his brother and his elderly, sick mother. From there he tried to contact his friends in Paris, and he wrote to both Bakst and Diaghilev. The latter epistle begins on an ominous note: 'I hope you will spare me the painful task of painting you a picture of the dreadful nightmare which all of us in Petersburg were living in and which those who are still there continue to suffer through.'[25] Nouvel saves the worst for the end, after giving Diaghilev the latest on his closest friends and family:

I'm sorry to have to tell you that your mother is gravely ill. When I left, she was in hospital, where she had undergone a fairly successful operation, but I heard from Kartsoff or Dima (I can't remember which) that she has a sarcoma, and her condition is quite serious. Your brother Yury is in the countryside with his wife, after having spent some time fighting on the Don. As for your brother Valentin, I couldn't say where he is at the moment.

Things were going no better for their friends. Nouvel himself had to burn all his furniture to stay warm during the winter. Dima Filosofov was still living with the Merezhkovskys in a 'state of profound moral depression', and they too were in great financial distress. Things were going slightly better for Benois, who was working as a curator at the Hermitage, where he had managed to maintain his independence and protect the museum's priceless collection from predatory Bolsheviks. Benois also had a little money and could occasionally send some to Nouvel, if he was running low on food. Nouvel had been in Finland for a few months without much human contact, and the loneliness was starting to wear him down. Obviously, his main priority was getting to Paris, and he hoped Diaghilev would use his good offices to arrange a visa for him:

> I need hardly tell you how happy I would be to see you again. I can imagine how hard these last few years have been for you! It would take your energy and your strength of character to endure all this and emerge unscathed. I wrote to Bakst in Paris. If he isn't there, I hope someone can forward the letter. Well, it's been more than five years since I've seen you all, my dear friends. Unfortunately, there's little hope of seeing you in the near future! …
>
> It's pointless to ask you to write. You never do. So at least send me a cable to let me know you've received my letter.

It is unclear how Diaghilev reacted to Nouvel's news. He certainly didn't talk to anybody about the letter, and if he responded to it, whether by post or telegram, the reply has not survived. By the time he got the letter, his stepmother was already dead. It's unlikely he knew that, but Diaghilev was no fool: he must have been able to read between the lines and realise that she was dying when Nouvel left for Finland.

A few days later Ansermet found Diaghilev in the throes of a deep crisis, which had undoubtedly been triggered by the news from Petrograd, although Diaghilev kept that to himself.

> I had a long and deeply distressing conversation with Diagh. He is very depressed and exhausted and cried a great deal. He told me it was time to shut up shop because he felt he was at loggerheads with everyone. Material difficulties were unimportant when he at least knew where he was headed, but now, he didn't even know that any more and the ballet's foundations were unsound. He disavowed being a Bolshevist, but that didn't mean he supported the tsar. He loved Russia, he said, but could do nothing for her. He wanted to work for the cause of Russian art but instead made shows like *Boutique* and *Le Corregidor* [*The Three-Cornered Hat*]. He said that Picasso was working with the ballet but when push came to shove he didn't give a damn about it, and neither did Derain. He lamented that Massine had lost his direction, and he mourned Stravinsky's departure. He complained he was living in a dream world and not in reality, in an empty bubble of prosperity and success. It was all just masturbation, and he didn't want any part in it any more.[26]

The profound doubts Diaghilev expressed about his artistic principles are surprising, given the success of the two premieres and the widespread appreciation for their artistic accomplishments. Of course he was concerned about his company's changing identity, and in these trying times he must have had to dig deep for the motivation he needed to press on. But, as so often, personal problems took their toll on his self-confidence; in this case they eroded what had always been the basis of his artistic success: an unshakeable faith in his chosen course and ultimate destination. It was inevitable that, in a situation like this, he was preoccupied by thoughts of the past and a desire to return to the company's roots (and those of Russian ballet in general).

After the summer, which he spent in Venice and Stresa, Diaghilev paid a brief visit to Paris, where the Ballets Russes would perform that winter after an absence of more than two and a half years. While there, Diaghilev saw Stravinsky again, and, despite the many professional conflicts that had clouded their friendship, they greeted each other as brothers. Diaghilev gave his friend a stack of music, attributed to the eighteenth-century Italian composer Giovanni Pergolesi, which he had unearthed in various Italian music libraries and in the library of the British Museum. Stravinsky was hired to orchestrate this music for a ballet à la Scarlatti's *Femmes de bonne humeur*. Diaghilev had already commissioned Picasso to design this new Pergolesi ballet. Along with that, he hired Ottorino Respighi to orchestrate a forgotten opera by Domenico Cimarosa. Like Pergolesi, Cimarosa was an obscure eighteenth-century composer, though he had the added distinction of serving for many years as court composer to Catherine the Great. As the year drew to a close with the London premiere of *Parade* on 14 November, at least two 'retrospective' ballets were in the works for the next season. And an even grander attempt to recreate the court culture of imperial St Petersburg began to ferment in the impresario's head.

In 1919 Diaghilev lost his stepmother and was separated from the rest of his family for good. His half-brother Valentin had joined the Red Army, but Valentin's two oldest sons fought together with General Yudenich against the Bolsheviks. Alyosha, Valentin's second born, died that year in Finland. His eldest son, Pavel, probably died in 1921 in one of the Baltic states. The fact that part of the Diaghilev family fought on the White side in the Russian Civil War certainly did not help their situation in St Petersburg. Diaghilev later learned of the death of his two nephews and must have realised that the name Diaghilev did not necessarily have positive connotations within the new regime.[27] As always, he kept family matters completely secret, even from his closest colleagues and confidants. In the Diaghilev archives there is not a single letter or telegram from his stepmother, father or half-brothers. He must have destroyed them long before his death.

As always, he swallowed his sorrow and frustration and threw himself into his work. Much of the next year and a half would be spent reconstructing the glory days of an imperial court culture that was now a distant memory.

· 24 ·

To the Brink of Catastrophe
1919–1922

THAT SEPTEMBER, Diaghilev and Stravinsky dropped in unannounced on Henri Matisse at his home in Issy-les-Moulineaux, just outside Paris. Diaghilev had made several previous attempts to involve Matisse in one of his projects, but to no avail. Now he decided to catch the painter unawares, hoping that the presence of Europe's foremost modern composer might tip the balance in his favour. The next season Diaghilev wanted to present three ballets designed by Picasso, Derain and Matisse, but France's greatest modern artist didn't want to be seen as treading in anyone's footsteps, least of all those of Picasso, his main rival. The project that Diaghilev was offering Matisse was *Le Chant du rossignol*, the ballet version of Stravinsky's opera (based on the fairytale by Hans Christian Andersen), on which he had set Fortunato Depero to work back in 1917, but which had never got as far as a premiere.

Once inside the artist's studio, Diaghilev brought all his charm to bear on the hapless Matisse. He proposed a sumptuous gold and black decor, while Stravinsky played extracts from the ballet on Matisse's grand piano. Rather against his will, the artist found all kinds of ideas welling up. He envisaged the work as a myth about reincarnation and renewal, 'spring-like, very fresh and youthful, and I couldn't see what on earth that had to do with black-and-gold sumptuosity', he commented later. His vision was of 'simple shapes, clear light and pure colour'. "'Well, that's it," cried Diaghilev, when the painter outlined his idea. "There's your décor all settled ... It's absolutely essential you do it ... there's no one but you who could.""[1] Although Matisse was dubious about working with the Russian and did not immediately accept the commission, he was, according to his biographer Hilary Spurling, 'haunted over the next few weeks by his vision of the life-giving Nightingale, and grew increasingly impatient to hear again from Diaghilev'.[2]

Diaghilev let him sweat for a fortnight before imperiously summoning him to London. On 12 October 1919 Matisse reluctantly crossed the Channel. He ended up staying much longer than he had intended, having been bull-dozed into producing all the costumes and sets on site. It was a painful experience for him. 'Diaghilev is Louis XIV,' he later remarked. 'You've no idea what he's like, that man ... He's charming and maddening at the same time – he's a real snake – he slips through your fingers – at bottom the only thing that counts is himself and his affairs.'[3] In Diaghilev, Matisse had finally encountered an individual as obstinate as himself but, as Spurling theorises, 'he also recognised a creative will that, like his own, acknowledged no limits to the power of imagination'.[4]

Matisse traipsed about the Victoria and Albert Museum in search of inspiration, made a maquette of his design, ordered textiles and called in the help of Parisian couturiers (Paul Poiret and his assistants). He developed a grudging admiration for the Russian work ethic: 'You can't imagine what it's like, the Ballets Russes,' he wrote to his wife. 'There's absolutely no fooling around here – it's an organisation where no one thinks of anything but his or her work – I'd never have guessed this is how it would be.'[5] When Matisse returned to France at the beginning of November, the designs were finished and the materials had been tested under the stage lights. The premiere took place on 2 February 1920 in Paris; die-hard Ballets Russes fans such as Laloy and the composer/critic Alexis Roland-Manuel were charmed.

The ballet score was a boiled-down, twenty-minute symphonic version of Stravinsky's opera, written entirely to Diaghilev's specifications. He had com-missioned it back in 1916, indicating precisely which extracts Stravinsky was to use and how they were to be altered. The letter containing these instruc-tions is important, because it shows how closely the two worked together, and how faithfully Stravinsky carried out Diaghilev's intentions. With the

Massine, by Matisse

exception of point 10, where the composer permitted himself a deviation, he carried out Diaghilev's instructions to the letter.

Rewrites for *Le Chant du rossignol*

1. Write a song for the nightingale, reducing a number of bars on p. 49.
2. p. 51 – cut the first three bars in the last line.
3. p. 60 – cut the first five bars.
4. p. 62 – create a transition from the last bar to p. 40. The repeat continues to p. 49.
5. p. 49 – after the first bar and transition go to bar four on p. 67; cut pp. 63–6 and the first three bars of p. 67.
6. p. 67 – transpose the whole of the rest of the page (the last four lines).
7. p. 70 – cut also the first four bars of p. 71; rewrite the next six bars.
8. pp. 78–9 – cut.
9. p. 80 – the first three bars need to be written, backing the tremolo in the accompaniment. Cut bars seven and eight.
10. p. 82 – write a good accompaniment from bar three to bar eight.
11. p. 83 – cut bars five and six. Rewrite bars seven, eight and nine; from bar nine transition to p. 90.
12. p. 93 – combine bars three and four.

In both songs of the nightingale the number of bars must be reduced (i.e. by complete separate bars), otherwise there will be a *deadly longueur* in the choreography. And there's no point in grumbling at me about this! I'm a man of the theatre and, thank God, not yet a composer.[6]

Despite the favourable reviews in Paris, *Chant du rossignol* was not a lasting success, and it has not been restaged much since. Stravinsky's score for the Andersen fairytale was never going to cause the kind of frisson audiences now expected from the Russian modernist, but according to the largely unfavourable London reviews it was the choreography that was lacking. After 1920, the Massine version was never produced again.

Meanwhile, *Pulcinella* was beginning to take shape. Diaghilev and Massine had conceived the idea for this ballet during trips to southern Italy, where they had been charmed by the region's traditional puppet theatres. Of course, dolls and puppets figured in a number of their ballets, from *The Nutcracker* to *Petrushka*.

Stravinsky was not an obvious candidate to orchestrate Pergolesi's score. Diaghilev's two previous reworkings of eighteenth-century Italian music had been entrusted to workaday composers like Tomassini (*Les Femmes de bonne humeur*) and Respighi (*Boutique fantasque*). Why should an iconoclast like Stravinsky do a favour for a dead composer, when he had so many urgent projects on his plate (like the still-unfinished *Les Noces*)? Simply put, the Stravinsky of 1919 was no longer the modernist trailblazer of 1913. He had mellowed in the intervening years, and gave in quite readily to Diaghilev's demands.

Picasso had agreed to design the ballet, and Stravinsky was enchanted by the idea of collaborating with the artist. As he later explained, he started work on the score almost immediately, 'composing on the Pergolesi manuscripts themselves, as though I were correcting an old work of my own'.[7] As it happened, only part of the music had been written by Pergolesi, but neither Diaghilev nor Stravinsky was aware of that.[8]

The composer made rapid progress, completing the music on 24 April 1920. Picasso was also working on the ballet by then, but not to everyone's satisfaction. Diaghilev envisioned an abstract version of commedia dell'arte, but Picasso's first costume designs were more redolent of an Offenbach operetta, featuring mutton-chop whiskers rather than masks.[9] An angry Diaghilev demanded that he start afresh. The evening concluded with Diaghilev actually throwing the drawings on the floor, stamping on them, and slamming the door as he left. The next day all of Diaghilev's charm was needed to reconcile the deeply insulted Picasso.[10]

Shortly afterwards, Picasso produced new, abstract designs that were received with great enthusiasm. The ballet critic Cyril Beaumont described the decor as a 'cubist study in black, blue-grey and white, admirably conveying with a remarkable economy of means a moonlit street overlooking the Bay of Naples'.[11]

Prior to the Paris premiere, the company went on a brief tour, taking in Rome, Milan and Monaco. In Rome, Diaghilev and Massine continued to rework Cimarosa's opera *Le Astuzie femminili* (Feminine Wiles), conceived as an opera-ballet along the lines of *Le Coq d'or*. Cimarosa composed the work in 1794, following a four-year stay at the court of Catherine the Great. It ended with a lively *ballo russo*, and Diaghilev erroneously assumed that the opera had been made for the Empress, prompting 'the inspired idea of staging [it] in the style of a St Petersburg court spectacle'.[12]

Diaghilev, by Picasso

The whole production was a thinly veiled plaudit for pre-revolutionary aristocratic Russia with its Westernised elite. As Taruskin put it, 'Diaghilev would show Europe that Russia was large and contained multitudes: multitudes of social classes and occupations, and multitudes of indigenous musical styles, not all of them "Asiatic" or peasant […]. Having bided his time and established himself as a tastemaker nonpareil, he could now, he felt, unveil such a Russia and such a music to the eyes and ears of Europe.'[13]

The sets and costumes were made by José-Maria Sert, who had already tried his hand at a ballet inspired by court culture (*Las Meninas*), but Sert was no Bakst and certainly no Picasso, and Cimarosa–Respighi–Sert was not the winning team Diaghilev had hoped it would be. However, the final part of the production, the *ballo russo*, reworked into a *grand divertissement*, did remain in the Ballets Russes repertoire under the title *Cimarosiana*.

Khokhlova and Massine, by Picasso

In Rome, Diaghilev was accompanied by his Italian servant Beppe and his wife Margherita. Diaghilev was fond of Margherita, and was terribly distressed when, in late February, she suddenly died. In an uncharacteristic show of public emotion, he wept bitter tears at the funeral, which was attended by the whole company.[14]

By the end of April the troupe was back in Paris, preparing for an ambitious new season in the Grand Opéra, with the premieres of *Pulcinella*, *Le Astuzie femminili*, a new version of *Sacre* (choreographed by Massine) and the Parisian premiere of *The Three-Cornered Hat*. On 4 May the company took part in a benefit show for Russian refugees, with performances by Sarah Bernhardt and Ida Rubinstein (dancing her famous role in *Schéhérazade* for the last time). Three years earlier, on the very same spot, Diaghilev had incorporated a revolutionary flag into the finale of *The Firebird*, but now he openly took up his place amidst the White refugees and Romanov loyalists thronging Paris.

More seasoned expatriates clustered round the Russian émigrés. Diaghilev was particularly happy to see one such newcomer: 'Seryozha Prokofiev has arrived!' he shouted when the young composer announced himself at the Hôtel Scribe, where the impresario was staying.[15] Prokofiev was roundly kissed by Diaghilev and Massine, and dragged off to a series of dinners and rehearsals. The composer was rather surprised to see Diaghilev himself directing the rehearsals for *Le Astuzie femminili* 'with boundless passion and consummate skill. He drilled the singers in every note and every word.'[16] Talk immediately turned to the unfortunate *Chout*, which had been waiting so long to be performed that it now seemed out of step with the company's new direction. However, Diaghilev still wanted to stage it – he had paid for it, after all, and Larionov had finished the designs – and he promised Prokofiev to see what could be achieved with a few amendments and (presumably) cuts.

Pulcinella and *Le Astuzie femminili* premiered on 15 May and 27 May, respectively. The former was much better received. Stravinsky later put it about that *Pulcinella* had attracted the ire of critics, who accused him of being a 'pasticheur' and of 'deserting modernism',[17] but in truth the work elicited little surprise and even less criticism. Stravinsky for his part saw the ballet as a key work in his oeuvre: '*Pulcinella* was my discovery of the past, the epiphany through which the whole of my late work became possible. It was a backward look, of course – the first of many love affairs in that direction – but it was a look in the mirror, too.'[18]

The same applied to Picasso, who regarded the ballet as the best he had ever made.[19]

Pulcinella's birth had been a typically difficult one. Prokofiev gave a glimpse of this after the ballet's second performance on 17 May. The scene he describes ties in with an observation by Stephen Walsh, who held that, 'like cartoon Russians, Diaghilev and Stravinsky could hug and get drunk together by night and still wrangle bitterly over money and contracts by day'.[20]

After the performance, dinner at Mme Edwards's, where Stravinsky and Diaghilev almost came to blows. Stravinsky said that the curtain came down too slowly at the end of *Pulcinella*, to which Diaghilev responded, 'That's because you made a mess of the end.' Stravinsky went for Diaghilev and said that *Pulcinella* was a work of genius and that Diaghilev understood nothing about music. Diaghilev responded that all composers had been saying he understood nothing about music for the last twenty years; likewise all artists that he understood nothing about painting; meanwhile, thank God, everything kept going ... Eventually they were separated and in five minutes they were peacefully drinking champagne.[21]

Ultimately, however, almost all of Diaghilev's greatest ballets were born of strife and *Pulcinella* was no exception. In many respects it defined the entire course of the Ballets Russes, with its mix of innovation and retrospection: at last Diaghilev could look back and forward at the same time. It also presented an entirely new aesthetic, a call for order and clarity in the arts after the chaos of modernist experimentation and the disillusionment of the war.

Artistically speaking, the Ballets Russes were now poised for the 1920s. As usual, however, the company was beset by problems. Rows with Massine were getting worse, and Diaghilev was so strapped for cash that he had to leave Picasso's curtain for *Pulcinella* behind in the Opéra, where it was forever to remain.[22] The mood was cheerful, nevertheless; Paris was a lively city, and one was forever running into old friends. Princess Violette Murat, a descendant of the last King of Naples, gave a party which everyone attended: Picasso, Cocteau, Larionov, Stravinsky, émigré grand dukes (including Dmitry Pavlovich, one of the murderers of Rasputin), and a sprinkling of young French composers to liven up the company. There was a lot of noise and horseplay, and by 'three in the morning Stravinsky was sitting at the piano with his enemy Cocteau, while on top of the piano a gramophone was screeching and someone else was banging the keys, and Diaghilev I think was dancing the Lancers with the lady of the house'.[23]

In London, their next destination, *Pulcinella* was even more warmly received, being rightly described as 'the quintessence of Diaghilevism'.[24] Perhaps the most important event in London, however, was the arrival in late June of Walter Nouvel, who had finally escaped from Russia via Finland. At the station Diaghilev and Prokofiev welcomed him with open arms and promptly installed him in the Savoy, where the three friends talked for hours, trying to catch up after six years of separation. Diaghilev urged Nouvel to come and work as his manager – a proposal that was hesitantly accepted. Now that the company was more or less back together again, European tours needed to be arranged, a job Grigoriev couldn't manage alone.

Diaghilev and Prokofiev continued to work on *Chout*. Over a period of three days they went over the whole score together, with Diaghilev indicating

Massine, Bakst and Diaghilev, by Picasso

which parts were to be fleshed out and which were to be cut. His general view was that the music was too illustrative, too much the servant of the action. He felt it should be more symphonic and that 'plastic' elements should be more independent of the music.[25] These new, neoclassicist convictions were, in a sense, a more radical take on the old *Mir iskusstva* position, which rejected art that aimed to be representative and instrumental. Prokofiev put up no objections and, as the manuscript of *Chout* shows, closely followed the suggestions he described in his diary in the latter half of June 1920.

Chout would not, however, be ready in time for the new summer season in Paris, which meant that Diaghilev still needed a production for the coming winter season in London. He decided on a new version of *Sacre*, choreographed by Massine. Stravinsky's music had been packing concert halls for some years now, so the time seemed right to restage the work. Roerich was also in London. A keen disciple of Madame Blavatsky, he held spiritualist séances featuring table rapping and piano chords played by unseen hands (Prokofiev was called upon to note down the chords 'from the Other Side').[26]

Meanwhile an argument about money arose between Diaghilev and the management of Covent Garden Theatre. Diaghilev cancelled the last performance at the advice of his lawyer; an unfortunate step, as it was already sold out. The public was upset, Diaghilev's reputation suffered and he received only a quarter of the contracted fee.[27] He could not pay his staff and had to borrow money from the famous couturière Gabrielle 'Coco' Chanel, a new member of his entourage (perhaps introduced by Grand Duke Dmitry, whose mistress she had been), to fund his holiday in Venice.

After so many years, however, problems of this kind were par for the course to him and his associates. En route for London, Diaghilev ran into Prokofiev in Paris: 'In his usual way he rose again from the ashes, found money, had engagements in hand, listened to *Chout*, praised the rewriting, paid me three thousand, made me play it on the pianola for the rehearsal and generally was splendid.'[28]

In autumn the company toured a number of English cities, while Massine continued to work on his version of *Sacre*. It premiered on 14 December in Paris. Stravinsky was quoted in the press as preferring it to the Nijinsky version. He also propounded ideas on the relationship between dance and music similar to those expressed by Diaghilev to Prokofiev:

> The music of *Le Sacre du printemps* shuns any form of illustration. It's more an objective construct … I must say that Massine has not only grasped the essence of my work with remarkable perception, but has also devised a new form of dance for *Le Sacre* … I believe that the time has come to jettison the notion that dance should completely adhere to quavers, semiquavers, beats, etc. In our new conception, dance need only follow broader musical lines.[29]

The synthetic approach that had informed the Russian ballet in the Fokine years, rooted in the theories of the Wagnerian *Gesamtkunstwerk*, was no more. This new, analytic take on the relationship between dance and music would shape the aesthetic of the Ballets Russes for the rest of the company's days and was to have a lasting influence on the future of classical dance in Europe and America.

Not everybody thought that Nijinsky's version was inferior. Grigoriev, for

Massine, by Cocteau

instance, deemed Massine's choreography too abstract and mechanical, an opinion shared by not a few critics (including André Levinson).[30] The 1913 premiere was on Diaghilev's mind too, but for completely different reasons. It was then that his relationship with Nijinsky began to fall apart; the same thing now appeared to be happening with Massine.

Diaghilev had learned from his mistakes with Nijinsky, and he had tried not to suffocate Massine. Their old intimacy might have been over, but the two men remained close, and their creative partnership was as strong as it had ever been. Massine had been a much more receptive pupil than Nijinsky, drinking in the impresario's teachings on art, music and dance; he was the instrument with which Diaghilev shaped his artistic ideas, and together they had weathered many Ballets Russes storms. In the space of five years Massine had blossomed into one of the world's leading choreographers, combining a unique style with a gift for innovation, while at the same time dancing almost all the male leads.

Nevertheless, the tension between the two men had been building up for a long time, and Massine wanted to break free. Quite how the crisis began has been lost to history, though Grigoriev believed it was during rehearsals for *Sacre*. Matters came to a head when the company left Paris for a short Italian tour.

Although Diaghilev had kept Massine on a looser leash than Nijinsky, allowing him the odd fling, he had made it plain to both Massine and the ballerinas as far back as the 1916 American tour that he would not tolerate a relationship between his choreographer and any of his dancers. During the *Sacre* rehearsals, however, it was bruited about that Massine was having an affair with one of the ballerinas. Diaghilev first suspected Sokolova, but the guilty party turned out to be an attractive English girl, Vera Savina, a promising dancer who had only lately joined the company. Unable to speak Russian, she did not understand how matters stood and failed to grasp what a heinous crime she had committed by responding to Massine's advances.

Diaghilev was by then so distraught that he lost all self-control. He hired private detectives to shadow Massine and Savina around Roman hotels in an attempt to catch them out in an assignation. He is even said to have invited Savina to his hotel room, where he got her drunk and forced her to strip. He then dragged her to the adjoining room and threw her on the bed where Massine was sleeping, exclaiming, 'Behold your beau ideal!'[31] According to Marinetti, who describes the incident in his diary, Massine immediately left the hotel and broke off contact with Diaghilev. Grigoriev relates that Diaghilev fired Massine and banished Savina to the corps de ballet.[32]

The impresario suffered a breakdown after the loss of Massine. 'It was as if Diaghilev had gone crazy,' said one of the dancers, Mikhail Semyonov.[33] He did not appear in public for several days. Only Nouvel and his two servants Vasily and Beppe were allowed to enter his room. 'For a time his friends feared for his health, and even for his reason, and they watched him anxiously day and night.'[34] 'When he emerged, he had such black rings under his eyes that he was barely recognisable.'[35]

Although Diaghilev pulled himself together again, the break-up with Massine seemed to hit him much harder than the end of the affair with Filosofov, or even Nijinsky. No one had caused him so much joy – or suffering. Many years later Diaghilev was to say that Massine had 'the most brilliant mind [he had] ever met with in a dancer'.[36]

There was another huge difficulty: Diaghilev could no longer return to Russia to look for a new choreographer, and without Russian choreography, the Ballets Russes would lose their raison d'être. Diaghilev might have been fond of observing that 'there is nobody indispensable in this world',[37] but where was Massine's replacement to come from? It was the spring of 1921; on

17 May a new season was starting in Paris for which premieres were needed. The most urgent problem was *Chout*, which so far only had a score and sets. Parisian critics had lately been claiming that Diaghilev had lost his fabled talent-spotting ability. Diaghilev hoped, through *Chout*, to launch Prokofiev as his latest discovery and silence these naysayers. He had no time to waste. Prokofiev's score was already several years old, and his sell-by date as young talent was fast approaching.[38]

Diaghilev eventually assigned *Chout*'s choreography to Tadeusz Slavinsky, a young Polish dancer. Worried that the complex score might prove too much for him, Diaghilev asked Larionov to help out – an odd choice, as the latter had no musical training and, though brilliant, was famously pig-headed and scatterbrained. It was on these choppy seas that *Chout*'s barque was launched.

The ballet *Cuadro Flamenco* was born of desperation. For this piece, Diaghilev brought in a group of Spanish folk dancers and musicians and asked Picasso to paint a backcloth. It was the first and last time that Diaghilev acted like a conventional impresario, simply hiring artists and delegating most of the artistic decisions to others. The quality of the dancers in *Cuadro Flamenco* was certainly high, and the soloist, Maria Dalbaicin, was by all accounts a great beauty (she was billed as 'the prettiest girl in the world'), but there was no getting away from the fact that the performance was not a Diaghilev ballet and certainly no 'Ballet Russe'.

There were production problems too. The company could not perform in any of the prestigious theatres in Paris, and they were forced to make do with the Gaîté Lyrique. London's main theatres were similarly unavailable; their venue there was the ill-starred Prince's Theatre, managed by the showman Charles Cochran. He was so impressed by Diaghilev ('a man whose charm could revive a corpse')[39] that he cheerfully incurred a loss of over £5,000 on the Ballets Russes later that year.

Yet one good thing did come of that troubled spring, in the form of a new young lover and pupil who was brought to Diaghilev by a strange chain of events. Boris Kochno was a Russian youth who had been carried along on the wave of Russian immigrants, washing up on the shores of Paris with empty pockets and no prospects. He and his mother had been refugees for several years, first fleeing south and then travelling to France via Constantinople. A homosexual who preferred older men, Kochno had been a lover of the Polish composer Karol Szymanowski when only fifteen. In Paris he met Sergey

Sudeykin, an artist who had been part of the *Mir iskusstva* circle and who in 1913 had designed sets and costumes for Diaghilev's (not terribly successful) production of Florent Schmitt's *Tragédie de Salomé*. Kuzmin was the link that bound Diaghilev and Sudeykin. A colourful figure, Sudeykin was one of Kuzmin's regular lovers, but he spread his favours far and wide, having affairs with men and women alike. Post-revolutionary Russia was not a safe place for Sudeykin: his father had been head of the St Petersburg secret service, and he was a marked man.

He was also the third husband of the actress Vera de Bosset, who was later to marry Stravinsky. Still charming and attractive in television appearances in the 1980s, she must have been irresistible when she arrived in Paris at the age of twenty-one.

The Sudeykins had an open marriage. The couple happily discussed Sergey's various lovers, and even welcomed some of them into their home. When Sudeykin met Boris Kochno in Paris and started an affair with him, Vera and Boris became good friends.

Sudeykin was keen to revive his old friendship with Diaghilev. He, of course, hoped for new commissions for the Ballets Russes, but even if they did not materialise it was crucial for any unknown Russian artist trying to establish himself in Paris to be on good terms with the impresario. Kochno offered a way of pleasing Diaghilev (whom Sudeykin always called 'the monster' when talking to his wife).[40] So Sudeykin decided to make him a present of the boy.

In the St Petersburg homosexual artistic clique it was not uncommon for lovers to circulate. Diaghilev had had quite a few youths passed on to him in Kuzmin's circle, and, of course, Nijinsky had come to him via Prince Lvov. At the end of February 1921 Kochno was sent to Diaghilev by Sudeykin. He was then seventeen years old. Kochno may have heard of Diaghilev as a boy, but it seems more likely that his knowledge of the impresario came from listening to tall tales from Sudeykin.[41] When Kochno caught a glimpse of Diaghilev in the foyer of the Théâtre des Champs Élysées, the sight of his commanding presence almost caused the boy to swoon.

Kochno and Diaghilev talked for a while. Diaghilev was taken by the good-looking youngster who wrote poetry and took an interest in the arts, announcing, before he sent him home, 'We shall meet again.' The very next day Kochno was offered the job of Diaghilev's secretary. When he asked

Kochno, by Picasso

what the duties entailed, Diaghilev replied, 'A secretary must be able to make himself indispensable.'[42] Kochno did just that, and at the beginning of March he went on tour with Diaghilev to Spain.

There, Diaghilev assembled the dancers and musicians for *Cuadro Flamenco*, and the rehearsals for *Chout* got under way. In mid-April the company left for Monte Carlo, where work on *Chout* continued. When Prokofiev arrived in Monaco to oversee the rehearsals, he found a state of pandemonium. The hired pianist Zemskaya couldn't follow the music, Larionov couldn't keep discipline and Slavinsky was 'a nincompoop'. Prokofiev immediately took charge, entering into an 'unspoken pact' with Larionov: 'He did everything I wanted, and I relied on his huge resourcefulness and good taste.' Larionov had a fat notebook full of poses and movements, which they used as a basis. 'We took Slavinsky in hand. Diaghilev often attended rehearsals; a great boon, because he always had valuable advice.'[43]

On 17 April the Ballets Russes opened in Paris, immediately presenting that season's two novelties. *Cuadro Flamenco* was well received, as was *Chout*, albeit mainly because of Prokofiev's score and Larionov's sets (brilliantly likened by Buckle to 'Abramtsevo … after an earthquake').[44] Roland-Manuel wrote that *Chout* was, 'at least musically, the most important work that the Russians have shown us since the War',[45] thus surpassing both Falla's *Three-Cornered Hat* and Stravinsky's *Pulcinella*. And the periodical *Bonsoir* wrote of Prokofiev, 'Tomorrow this young man with the shaved head, myopic eyes and hesitant manner will be as well known as Stravinsky.'[46]

Larionov's designs suffered slightly from Diaghilev's straitened circumstances. The quality of the materials used was far inferior to that of pre-war productions, and with such convoluted, eccentric costumes this presented a real difficulty. The dancers complained bitterly about the difficulty of dancing in them, and the awkward choreography did not make matters any easier. Nevertheless, Larionov's work was also very well received. Cyril Beaumont recalled that 'the colour contrasts were so vivid and dazzling that it was almost painful to look at the stage'.[47] In its use of futurist and neo-primitivist principles, *Chout* went further than any ballet Diaghilev had produced, including *Parade*. The fact that productions by Picasso and others have relegated it to the sidelines of European music theatre history is mainly due to its deficient choreography. Had Massine been in charge, its reputation might have exceeded that of *The Three-Cornered Hat*, and it would certainly have been revived more. As it was, *Chout* disappeared from the repertoire after 1923, and thereafter fell into obscurity.

The London performances enjoyed a similar reception, though British audiences and critics were even more enthusiastic about *Cuadro Flamenco*.

Diaghilev was nonetheless in a predicament. Slavinsky had not been a success, and yet no other choreographer was forthcoming. There was no question of lowering standards. Diaghilev would not countenance becoming a mere ten-a-penny showman with a portfolio of performers. So he returned to an idea that he had been mulling over for some time.

As far back as the wartime tour of America, Diaghilev had wanted to split his company into a commercial troupe that would provide a steady income and a smaller group with which he could make new, challenging productions. According to Grigoriev, the unparalleled success of the musical comedy *Chu Chin Chow*, which had been packing in London audiences for over four years, made him think that he could achieve something similar. One day he told Grigoriev 'half jokingly how much he wished he could discover a ballet that would run for ever – that would be happiness!' Grigoriev replied that 'not only was such a thing quite impossible, but it would bore him to death'. 'Not at all,' Diaghilev retorted, 'You'd run it and I'd do something else.'[48]

Concluding that the path to financial security lay in producing a retrospective work (like the Cimarosa opera of the previous season), Diaghilev eventually settled on a new production of *Sleeping Beauty* (the full-length Tchaikovsky-Petipa version), which he redubbed *The Sleeping Princess* for the English market. He drew up a contract with the impresario Sir Oswald Stoll for nightly performances throughout the winter at the Alhambra Theatre.

It was an uncharacteristic move. Admittedly, Diaghilev had produced full-length ballets before, notably *Giselle* in 1910 and a heavily cut *Swan Lake* in 1911, but these were largely Russian imports, designed to showcase the soloists Pavlova and Kshesinskaya. He himself had never presented ambitious productions of the kind that big, professional companies needed months, if not years, to prepare. Moreover, Diaghilev was well aware that Tchaikovsky's music had never been very popular in Europe, being regarded by many as derivative and insufficiently Russian. Up to then he had feared that staging work by the composer might be more than his reputation was worth.

Petipa was an even more surprising choice. It will be remembered that Diaghilev had built his ballet empire on a rejection of Petipa's notions of dance, and that in the *Mir iskusstva* years, Diaghilev and his friends had always been disdainful of the ballet master. As late as 1902 Benois had written, 'Mr Petipa is a long way off from real art. It is very decently executed academic drawing, devoid of all soul, devoid of all artistic temperament.'[49]

But after the war, everything changed. When Diaghilev and Stravinsky had been in Spain in 1920, they played the music of *Sleeping Beauty* constantly. It was then that they conceived the idea of a grand European revival of this work, the pinnacle of Petersburg classical ballet culture. The project was the antithesis of everything on which Diaghilev's fame rested – and that may have held a paradoxical appeal. But it was the political implications of this production that made it so significant. To present a ballet epitomising Petersburg court culture just after the Bolsheviks' victory was an act of political defiance. *The Sleeping Princess* was an ambitious celebration of pre-revolutionary tsarist art, performed by decidedly unproletarian political refugees, presented in the capital of the anti-Bolshevist coalition's main ally.

Diaghilev engaged the Mariinsky ballet master Nikolay Sergeyev, who by then was living in Paris. Sergeyev still had Petipa's notes for *Sleeping*

Beauty and could remember the choreography from the old days. The lead was assigned to Olga Spessivtseva. Having previously danced with the Ballets Russes during the second American tour of 1916, she now found herself in very reduced circumstances in Riga. Another refugee, with much more extensive Ballets Russes credentials, had arrived from Kiev: Bronislava Nijinska. Nouvel looked her up in Paris and asked about her plans. She had by then established herself as a choreographer, and as such her reappearance came as a godsend to Diaghilev. Not only was she a talented dancer with a mastery of classical technique, she could also choreograph in the spirit of Petipa.

Nijinska, who had not seen Diaghilev for over seven years, was shocked at his new artistic course. To her, 'the revival of *The Sleeping Princess* seemed … an absurdity, a dropping into the past, mere nonentity. [It] seemed the negation of the fundamental "religion" of the ballet as [Diaghilev] conceived it, and of his searching towards the creation of a new ballet.'[50] But she didn't have much choice. There simply were no other top-level companies and she did not have the means to finance her own projects.

Many were surprised by, or even opposed to, Diaghilev's plans, but he had at least one staunch ally: Stravinsky. Politically speaking, Stravinsky was probably as anti-Bolshevist as Diaghilev, and just as keen to distance himself from progressive movements in art. He assisted in various ways, for instance by orchestrating an entr'acte from some ballet music by Tchaikovsky that had never been previously performed – according to Diaghilev because the tsar found it too boring.[51] (Diaghilev's claim to present Tchaikovsky's music in an authentic setting did not prevent him from making savage cuts and slipping in the famous Dance of the Sugar Plum Fairy from *Nutcracker*). Stravinsky, moreover, published a long open letter to Diaghilev in *The Times* of 18 October in which he passionately defended Tchaikovsky in an attempt, as Diaghilev put it, 'to protect Tchaikovsky's talent from a universal lack of understanding'.[52]

Bakst was ultimately chosen to design the ballet, but not before Diaghilev had considered two alternatives. He had at first tried hard to secure André Derain, but the artist was not interested.[53] Diaghilev then toyed with the idea of asking Benois. His extensive knowledge of the eighteenth century made him an ideal candidate, but he could not leave St Petersburg, having committed himself to saving the Hermitage collections from post-revolutionary looters. It was only then that Bakst entered the picture.

Bakst was professional enough to foresee the great difficulties of such a production, but he realised that Diaghilev needed him desperately. In the previous seven years he had designed only one ballet for Diaghilev (*Les Femmes de bonne humeur* in 1917), and now his old friend was turning up shortly before the premiere of his largest and most expensive production ever with an order for over a hundred costumes and complete sets for three acts. Bakst was both suspicious and reluctant: suspicious, because he had not forgotten the affair of *Le Boutique fantasque* (when he was replaced at the last minute by Derain); reluctant, because modernism was then all the rage, and he feared being associated with something so old-fashioned as *The Sleeping Princess*. He therefore demanded that he also be involved in the next new Stravinsky project, which was to be called *Mavra*. Stravinsky equalled avant-garde, reasoned Bakst, and association with a project like that could restore his waning reputation. As it happened, *Mavra* was anything but avant-garde, but all this was academic, since Bakst would never be awarded the commission anyway.

Diaghilev had to hire a great many new dancers, more than he had ever contracted before. Daily performances meant that all the bigger roles had to be filled by three dancers; the lead even required five: Olga Spessivtseva, Vera Trefilova, Lyubov Egorova, Lydia Lopokova and a very young Vera Nemchinova.[54] For the role of Fairy Carabosse, Diaghilev hired Carlotta Brianza, who had danced the role of Princess Aurora in the world premiere in St Petersburg in 1890 – yet another nod to a tradition that had seemed so passé to Diaghilev in his early years.

For the role of Queen, Diaghilev needed a tall, handsome actress with a feel for the atmosphere of the ballet. She was found close to home in the person of Vera Sudeykina, who was both beautiful and had the right Petersburg background. Stravinsky may well have had a hand in her recruitment, as he and Vera had been intimate for some time. This was rather hard on Sudeykin, who in a short space of time lost not only his young lover but also his wife to Diaghilev's entourage. Even such an ardent exponent of free love had to draw the line somewhere, and Diaghilev soon found himself on the end of emotional, even threatening letters:

I am very sorry to trouble you, someone I love and appreciate so much …
    Vera Arturovna is the only one who can bring equilibrium to my life. I implore you to release her quickly …

I think that during this time you have come to know Vera. She's an exceptionally strong and honest character. Think of the choice confronting her now – either she has to leave you without your agreement or live with the knowledge that my work and health are suffering. You have to see, her position is desperate!

I gave you Boris (if you are tired of him, I'll gladly take him back) and Vera too. With that I showed my love for you …

You probably know or have heard that I sometimes have attacks of rage (it's the result of my illness) and I wouldn't want to cause a moment's pain to my wife, whom I worship … Igor, whom I saw and had lunch with, experienced my rage first hand and is of the view that Vera has to quickly come to me …[55]

It is clear from the letter that Sudeykin was aware of the passionate affair between Stravinsky and his wife, and perhaps suspected Diaghilev had a hand in it. Diaghilev ignored this plea, and another letter soon followed, in which Sudeykin brought up his delicate health, claiming that his doctor had warned him that any shock might be fatal. He continued,

I showed you how I felt by letting go the wife I adore for fifty days.

I am sure you'll understand me and give me back the life that is most precious to me.

It would be delightful if you could reduce the period of my waiting by even a few hours and answer me with a telegram saying when I'll see her.

My doctor joins my request.[56]

Diaghilev was more than prepared to release Vera from her contract, having realised that her affair with Stravinsky was becoming serious, and not wishing her marriage to be imperilled.[57] By the end of the year Vera was back with her husband, and the couple wrote a letter to Diaghilev in which Vera thanked him for 'freeing' her.[58]

By then *The Sleeping Princess* had premiered, and Diaghilev had much greater worries than orchestrating the sexual escapades of his entourage.

Well before that premiere, Bakst had warned him that the preparation time budgeted for the production was absurdly short. In the space of two months, he grumbled, 'I've had to make, with my own hands, more than two hundred maquettes, costumes and sets, not to mention the accessories, the wigs, the shoes, the jewellery … at the Imperial Theatres they allocated a year and a half to staging a ballet.'[59]

Even under these constraints, Diaghilev would not compromise on quality, and a few days before the performance he reduced the seamstresses to tears by demanding alterations to the extravagant costumes. As always he directed the lighting rehearsals personally.

> Those who had never been present at one of Diaghilev's lighting rehearsals did not know what they were in for. The rehearsals went on half the night if need be. At such times he cared nothing for the mounting cost of overtime, the passing of the hours, or the fact that he had not eaten for a long period. If the men showed signs of revolt, he would grant a ten or fifteen minutes' rest interval. As soon as the interval was up, he would utter a curt, '*Continuez, s'il vous plaît.*' The men would glare and curse under their breath, but they did his bidding.[60]

But for all their efforts, they were simply not equipped to produce such an extravagant performance. The risk was enormous: this time there would be no falling back on the old repertoire in the event of failure. Never before had a season depended so completely on a single new production, and up to now Diaghilev's guardian angel had always warded off disasters. But his luck had run out with *The Sleeping Princess*.

Things went wrong straight away. On the first night, the Alhambra's stage machinery failed, and parts of the sets collapsed on top of one another. Repairs had to be hastily made in the first interval, and Diaghilev ordered Tchaikovsky's Fifth Symphony to be played to fill the time. 'That night,' Stravinsky later wrote, 'probably because he had worked so hard and used so much vitality, he had a nervous breakdown. He sobbed like a child, and all around him had difficulty calming him. With his usual superstition he saw in this incident [i.e. the mechanical failure] a bad omen and seemed to lose confidence in his new creation, to which he had given so much of his soul and energy.'[61]

The Sleeping Princess had 105 performances in London, at first seven, and later eight a week, but business gradually fell off and the Alhambra's management decided to close the season in February 1922. Diaghilev still owed Stoll £11,000. Leaving Nouvel in charge of the company, he fled England before the last performance, sailing across the Channel to evade his creditors. Only a few months earlier he had welcomed King George V into his box; now he risked being arrested. Never before had he been in such dire straits. It looked as if the curtain were about to fall on the Diaghilev ballet for good.

· 25 ·

A Lifeline from Monte Carlo
1922–1924

DURING JANUARY AND FEBRUARY 1922, after returning to Paris, Diaghilev was consigned to a state of poverty that he had not known since the last year of the war. He took his meals in dingy restaurants frequented by taxi drivers. All he had was £500, and that he had borrowed from the mother of one of his British dancers, Hilda Bewicke.[1] For the time being he could forget about any further performances in London, the city that had always generated the lion's share of his annual income. He still had the sets from earlier productions, and at least some of his dancers were willing to go back to him, despite the fact that he had run out on the company and deprived them of a substantial proportion of their salaries. Years later he wrote that he 'realised that [the debacle] was a sign (and what is life if not a series of signs?) that this was not my destiny and that it ill befitted me to occupy myself resurrecting old glories'.[2] Be that as it may, he showed no inclination to rethink his aesthetic position. Although Diaghilev spent much of 1922 licking his wounds and trying to save his company, he remained preoccupied by the idea of recreating an idealised form of aristocratic Russian culture.

His plan to bring the London production of *The Sleeping Princess* to the Paris Opéra had to be scrapped, and so he decided to dust off the old costumes from *Pavillon d'Armide* and assemble a suite from the music of that evening-length work. He called the new piece *Le Mariage de la Belle au Bois Dormant*. There was also *Mavra*, which Stravinsky had been working on since the autumn of the previous year.

Stravinsky had not yet been paid for this new work, at least not in full, and so he took a lively interest in Diaghilev's cash-strapped state: 'I realise you're having a hard time of it at the moment,' Stravinsky wrote to him '... I only wish I could help you. But how? If the music can't help you, what can? I worry about you all the time and what you're going through, although I've heard, all told, not a single word from you.'[3]

Diaghilev's biggest problem was the presentation of premieres. The Opéra would never accept a Russian season without premieres, but where was the money for new ballets to come from? Eventually, help came from one of his oldest Parisian friends: Winnaretta Singer, Princesse de Polignac. The fabulously wealthy Singer had supported Diaghilev when he was just starting out, though the two had never been close. For one thing, she did not care for Misia Sert, the mother hen of Diaghilev's Parisian coterie. For another, she was more interested in music than dance. A few years before, Singer had commissioned a piece from Stravinsky to be presented at her salon. Diaghilev had always ignored the existence of the work, *Le Renard*, as was his custom when 'his' composers went to work for outsiders. But now he had no other options, and so he sent Stravinsky to obtain Singer's permission for the Ballets Russes to use *Renard* as the basis for a new work in the upcoming season.

Singer agreed, and the company was able to begin work on this ballet with vocal parts that Stravinsky had completed back in 1916. Although the music was only six years old, it seemed rooted in another era. When writing *Renard*, Stravinsky had still been immersed in his experimental phase. A modernist reworking of Slavic folk tunes, the piece was imbued with the neo-nationalistic spirit that animated *Sacre* and the (still incomplete) *Noces*. Initially, Diaghilev had entrusted the design to Sudeykin, perhaps as a thank-you for Kochno. But he quickly concluded that this particular work needed somebody with the right earthy, Slavic credentials, and that could only be Larionov. This meant that Diaghilev had to drop Sudeykin, and during the negotiations the latter gave him ample opportunity to do so by playing the big shot and making impossible demands. For one thing, he insisted on designing an entire evening's worth of shows, not just a single ballet. This was the proverbial red rag to the bull, and Diaghilev obligingly rose to the provocation:

I think that if I were now to insist, then out of your friendship for me you would agree to take the commission. However, that conflicts with my principles – every artist must work with me for the joy of what he does, not from mere good intentions, or even friendship! You maintain that your situation has changed during the last year, that you have become the premier set designer in Paris and are snowed under with work. Knowing you tell the honest truth and being receptive to your arguments, I gave *Renard* to another artist while waiting for something more important to come along.[4]

That was the end of poor Sudeykin, and a fresh opportunity for Larionov, who had again bested an old Miriskusnik.

Once more, Diaghilev had confirmed his reputation for untrustworthiness, though from an artistic standpoint his actions were justified. Larionov was the right man for the job, and many scholars regard the ballet as his most successful theatrical work. Nevertheless, there may have been another reason that Diaghilev suddenly wanted to get rid of Sudeykin, who was an outspoken opponent of the new communist regime. Stories had begun trickling in about the growing repressiveness of the new Soviet empire, and Diaghilev had to consider the precarious position of his family in St Petersburg, who were already in a bad odour with the authorities on account of his nephews' enlistment in the White Army. If he had any hope of returning to Russia (and he certainly hadn't given up on the dream), he had to give a wide berth to tainted individuals like Sudeykin.

With *Renard* and *Le Mariage de la Belle au Bois Dormant*, Diaghilev had now managed to throw together two premieres for the new Paris season. All that remained was to tie up arrangements for *Mavra*, which had been promised to Bakst as compensation for helping out with *The Sleeping Princess*. But in one of his trademark changes of heart, Diaghilev decided that the unknown Russian artist Léopold Survage would be a better choice for *Mavra*. Survage, who shared a studio with Modigliani, had made a minor name for himself as an avant-garde artist who experimented with abstraction and film. That may have piqued Diaghilev's interest, but it certainly doesn't explain why the impresario was willing to fall foul of Bakst to acquire the services of the then obscure Survage. According to Kochno, he had been goaded into it by Larionov, while Bakst claimed that Stravinsky was to blame.[5] A furious Bakst sent

Bakst, by Picasso

his lawyer to Diaghilev to demand 10,000 francs in compensation for lost income. 'I'd like to take the opportunity,' Bakst wrote, 'to suggest you deduct the amount from his [Stravinsky's] fee. But that's just some friendly advice.'[6] The conflict eventually resulted in a lawsuit, which Bakst won. One of the reasons the parties ended up in court was, of course, Diaghilev's depleted treasury: he couldn't have paid Bakst even if he had wanted to.

It must have been a sorry sight: two friends of over thirty years, who had shared their greatest triumphs, now on opposite sides of a courtroom. Bakst vowed he would never work for Diaghilev again. Perhaps the impresario thought that after a cooling-off period of a year or two, the artist could be coaxed back into the fold, but that was not to be. Bakst had 'broken with Diaghilev for good' and even refused to acknowledge him when they ran into each other on the street.[7] What neither man knew was that Bakst had just a year and a half to live – not enough time for these wounds to heal.

Bakst's resentment was so great that he could not help sending a sarcastic note to Diaghilev after the premiere of *Mavra*, which did not go well. In it he again vented his spleen about Stravinsky's 'betrayal', even though the latter probably had nothing to do with the whole situation: 'I wasn't at all surprised when I learned of the failure of the new work from Yankel Shtravinsky; [illegible] told me of the pomposity and tedium of the fiasco; musicians (and what musicians!) condescendingly nodded their heads: "*Assez pittoresque, mais insupportablement long* [quite picturesque but intolerably long]".'[8]

Mavra was a failure with audiences and critics alike. This came as a surprise to both Diaghilev and Stravinsky, who were equally convinced that the new work perfectly captured the zeitgeist. Stravinsky wrote to Diaghilev that he felt that '*Mavra* was the best thing I've ever done',[9] and to Kochno that he had 'managed to achieve such a clarity and simplicity as I have not been able to do before'.[10] For the composer and the impresario, *Mavra*, which deftly evoked the musical language of Tchaikovsky, Dargomizhky and even Glinka, was the next step in their project to recreate the culture of old St Petersburg. The opera, based on a long poem by Pushkin, contained all the elements that the two considered to be characteristic of that age: irony, clarity, grace, style (with an emphasis on storytelling, rather than the story itself) but with a bittersweet aftertaste that came from the opera's 'hidden theme': the decline and fall of tsarist Russia. *Mavra* was a sepia-toned slice of nostalgia, a recreation of a musical world that had gone for good, with anachronistic dissonances that were like the craquelure on the surface of an old painting. But French audiences missed the point, and although subsequent musicologists came to regard the opera as a pivotal work in Stravinsky's oeuvre, it never became part of the repertoire.

Fortunately for Diaghilev, and Stravinsky too, the rest of the season at the Opéra *was* a success, especially *Le Mariage de la Belle au Bois Dormant*, which was performed in Paris twelve times, as opposed to only seven performances of *Mavra* and a mere five of *Renard*, which was also well received. The rest of the programme was conservative; *Chout* was the only avant-garde work to be danced, and even that was aired on just a few occasions.

Diaghilev now had a bit more breathing room and the money he needed to pay his dancers. He also managed to book engagements elsewhere in Europe, in Liège, Bordeaux, Bayonne, San Sebastian and Ostend, places that probably would have been beneath him in less penurious circumstances. This modicum of financial security presumably enabled him to pay back the 10,000 francs he owed Bakst.

Of course, this was only a stop-gap solution. His debts still prevented him from travelling to Britain, putting an end to those London seasons that had always been the lifeblood of his company. Germany was still recovering from the war, and a tour of that country was out of the question. Diaghilev's hope of splitting the Ballets Russes into a repertory group that would provide a steady income and an avant-garde ensemble that would produce innovative premieres seemed to have faded after the *Sleeping Princess* fiasco. He needed a more radical solution for his company's chronic shortage of money. Somewhere he had to find a source of steady income that could provide the Ballets Russes with a degree of security, while simultaneously covering the risks associated with experimental new productions.

Just at that moment a golden opportunity fell into his lap. In Monte Carlo, Prince Louis II had inherited the throne. His only daughter, Charlotte, was married to Pierre de Polignac, a nephew of Winnaretta Singer and a good friend of Diaghilev's. Pierre, who cultivated a reputation as a lover of culture, took up the role of Diaghilev's guardian angel. Monaco would become the Ballets Russes's base of operations, and during the winter months the company would play the principality's theatre. This deal would give Monaco the world's most prestigious dance company and end the company's money woes for good. According to Grigoriev and Kochno, the plan had been concocted by Diaghilev;[11] according to Polignac, the idea came from his aunt, who wanted to extricate herself from the ever-impecunious Russian.[12] Whatever the case, a contract was signed and, starting in the winter of 1923, Diaghilev's Ballets Russes would have a permanent home at the Grand Théâtre at the Monte Carlo Casino.

The next summer season would mark a transitional phase, with a brief stint in Monaco in the spring followed by performances in Lyon and Switzerland. After that, the company would head to Paris for a week, where it would perform at the Gaîté Lyrique.

In late 1922 Diaghilev paid his first visit to Berlin since the war, where he and Kochno met not only Stravinsky and Prokofiev, but also the poet Vladimir Mayakovsky, the conductor Sergey Koussevitzky, the musicologist Pyotr Suvchinsky and the young artist Pavel Tchelitchew – all of whom (save Stravinsky) had just come from the Soviet Union. The meeting with Mayakovsky was particularly important to Diaghilev because the poet represented the Soviet avant-garde, and the impresario was keen to keep abreast of the latest artistic trends in Russia. According to Prokofiev, Diaghilev and Mayakovsky spent every evening together,

> arguing furiously, mainly about contemporary artists. Mayakovsky, who of course acknowledges nothing except his own group of Futurists ... sought to declare to the world that it had got left behind and that the future would be in the hands of the Moscow artists. Their exhibition had just opened in Berlin. But here he found in Diaghilev a dangerous opponent, for Diaghilev had dealt with new art all his life and knew what had recently been done abroad; all these last years Mayakovsky had been sitting in Moscow and so none of his high-handed arguments could get the better of Diaghilev's weighty reasoning. Eventually Diaghilev was banging his fists on the table as he laid into Mayakovsky ...
>
> He [Mayakovsky] was clearly fond of me and for some reason had an *a priori* dislike of Stravinsky. His attempts to prove to Diaghilev that I was a real composer but Stravinsky was no good were also unconvincing, as here too Mayakovsky was inadequately armed for the dispute. However where Mayakovsky won a real victory was with his poetry, which he read out in his own style, crudely, expressively, with a cigarette in his mouth. This enraptured Stravinsky, Suvchinsky and Diaghilev ...[13]

Diaghilev helped Mayakovsky obtain a visa, enabling the poet to pay a famous seven-day visit to Paris. Furnished with introductions from the impresario, he visited the studios of Picasso, Léger, Braque and Delaunay. Mayakovsky also attended Proust's funeral and dropped in on Stravinsky at his Pleyel studio. After that, the poet organised a grand banquet, which Diaghilev attended and at which Goncharova spoke.

It would not be the last meeting between the two men: they had already discussed the possibility that Diaghilev might come to the Soviet Union. When Mayakovsky sent Diaghilev a thank-you note a few months later, he mentioned that he had already spoken to various friends and officials about the idea. 'The conversation about a possible artistic presentation by my Parisian friends was received with great interest … I'm prepared to offer my services in any way possible.'[14] In the brief pamphlet that Mayakovsky wrote about his time in Paris, he thanked Diaghilev fulsomely: 'I feel obliged to express my gratitude to Sergey Pavlovich Diaghilev, whose knowledge of Parisian painting and whose exceptional loyalty to the RSFSR [Russian Socialist Federative Soviet Republic], made my research possible.'[15] This would seem a transparent attempt on Mayakovsky's part to sell Diaghilev to the hardliners within the new establishment, and pave the way for the Ballets Russes to travel to Moscow.

As these tentative overtures were being made toward the Soviet Union, Stravinsky and Diaghilev were continuing to hone *Les Noces*, which had been postponed so many times. Stravinsky had never laboured for so long on a single score; the first ideas for the work dated all the way back to 1912. By now the music was a throwback to an earlier stage in his artistic development: Slavic neo-nationalism. Yet the piece remained dear to the composer, as it did to Diaghilev. He had stood behind the work from the outset, and the sessions at which Stravinsky had played excerpts from it had been high points of their long friendship. The ballet reminded both men of the happy period in Switzerland and Rome in 1915, when their days were filled with artistic experiments and Russia's political future was still an open question. Stravinsky's devotion to *Noces* bordered on the obsessive: he simply could not put it down. No work of his has such a complex structure and at the same time, as Richard Taruskin put it, 'a degree of global coherence greater than that exhibited by the other masterpieces of the Russian period'.[16]

Diaghilev wanted to premiere the work in 1921 and hired Goncharova to make the sets and costumes, but the project failed to get off the ground, either that year or the next. Paradoxically, the repeated postponements were actually a sign of Diaghilev's attachment to the ballet. He was doing everything in his power to ensure that the work, which had caused Stravinsky so many headaches, was given the premiere it deserved.

During its long gestation *Noces* grew ever more radical. The ensemble Stravinsky envisioned for the ballet is as advanced now as it was eighty-five years ago: a choir, four soloists, four pianos and assorted percussion. Goncharova's brown-and-white costumes were extreme in their simplicity, and her sets were assembled mainly from large, sparsely ornamented, monochromatic planes – a sharp break with her earlier theatre designs. Diaghilev's willingness to programme such a radical work at such a sensitive time, so soon after his company had finally emerged from its financial worries, shows that he hadn't lost his faith in Stravinsky's musical gifts. It may even be possible to interpret *Mavra*'s lacklustre reception as similar loyalty on the part of Parisian audiences: perhaps the public also wanted to see Stravinsky as a true progressive, not a peddler of old music in modern dress. Diaghilev's encounter with Mayakovsky was another signal that the younger generation was unyielding in its commitment to artistic innovation – for good or for ill – and that if he wanted to continue playing the role of a pioneer, he could not continue looking to the past. Perhaps the most important reason that Diaghilev chose to revel in the work's radicalism was the arrival of Alexander Tairov's theatrical company in Paris in March 1923. Diaghilev saw his performances in the company of Cocteau and Nijinska, and Tairov's success with the Parisian avant-garde must have got the impresario thinking.[17]

Diaghilev was also aware of the need for artistic balance, and in his first season in Monte Carlo he hoped to stage a number of operas that would appeal to a more conservative public (and his own nostalgic leanings). In his desire to make Monte Carlo a centre of Franco-Russian musical culture, he sought to revive a series of forgotten French operas. They would be presented in modified form, that is to say reorchestrated, reorganised, redesigned and judiciously cut – the time-honoured Diaghilev formula. The operas in question were by Gounod, one of his father's favourite composers, and Chabrier, the old French defender of Wagner, with whom he had hoped to study in a distant past. The ideal partner for this enormous project (the production of four new operas, all of which would premiere in January 1924) had been warming up in the wings for some time: Alexandre Benois.

For the past few years Benois had been working non-stop to rescue the priceless collections of the Hermitage, but lately he had grown weary and lost his motivation. 'I feel like I'm wasting away,' he wrote to Argutinsky-Dolgorukov in December 1922 from Petrograd. 'I need to find something fresh and new.' He then asked Arguntinsky if he would mind making overtures to Diaghilev, because he was convinced that it was 'hopeless to expect a reply if I write to him myself'.[18] On 9 June 1923, six months later, Benois received a package from Diaghilev containing a score to Gounod's opera *Le Médecin malgré lui*, and a proposal that he design the sets for a fee of 6,000 francs.

Benois wrote back the very same day: 'After eight years, you and I are connected; I hope the connection is a long one this time, unbroken and only ending at the grave.' Benois was 'enthusiastic' and got right to business, discussing the various aspects of the opera. He ended his letter on a cheerful note:

> And so, my dear, it appears that in the very near future I shall again see that grey streak (I hope it still stands out against the rest of your black hair), that I shall see your tantalising toothy smile and get from you that charge of energy which has always had such a beneficial effect on me. In turn I'll try not to fall on my face, and refrain from comment about my age – my almost completely grey hairs and generally venerable appearance.
>
> P.S. Have you heard anything about your brother Linchik's boys? I've asked Vladimir … about this but haven't had a reply. Pavka too is said to be intending to come to Paris.[19]

The last line suggests that by 1923 Diaghilev still didn't know about the deaths of his brother's two sons, who had enlisted in the White Army. It seems that Diaghilev asked Benois, who was relatively close to the centres of power, to keep his ear to the ground. For Lenin's Cheka, the forerunner of the KGB, any family with ties to the White Army was tainted. And although no one knew exactly what the ultimate consequences would be, it made sense to keep tabs on events in Russia. In the few sources that have survived from

Lopokova, by Picasso

this period, there are no references to the matter. It is clear, however, that Diaghilev's family situation was still on his mind and impeding the personal rapprochement with the Soviet Union that he was trying to facilitate through Mayakovsky.

In early June 1923 Diaghilev was hard at work on the premiere of *Noces*, which took place on the 13th in Paris. Lydia Lopokova, who had not danced for Diaghilev since *Sleeping Beauty*, was in the audience that night, and went back to pay her respects to 'Big Serge' (as she called him) before the curtain went up. She described the encounter in a letter to her lover, John Maynard Keynes, in her charmingly imperfect English:

> Big Serge gave me outwardly affectionate embrace, then Boris [Kochno], then Picasso, then [Ida] Rubinstein, then most tragic of all Serge said: 'Nijinsky is [in] the box', to verify I went into the box and there I saw indeed Nijinsky but he did not know me, nor anybody, he does not recognise anyone, but being in a quiet state the doctors want to give him a

thrill, so as to move him, and then perhaps he might be cured. His wife is with him. Who is so cruel to him? Terrible, terrible …[20]

It must have been heart-rending to see Nijinsky sitting there, watching the work that had once been meant for him and had now been entrusted to his sister. After the intermission, the company performed *Petrushka*, one of his signature roles, but apparently nothing could rouse him from his mental torpor.

Bronislava Nijinska's choreography, which proved to be no less progressive than Stravinsky's music or Goncharova's designs, had a polarising effect on audiences. André Levinson, the most influential ballet critic of his generation and an arch conservative, went so far as to call the ballet 'Marxist' because of the absence of solo roles and the absorption of the individual into the collective drama.[21] But in Paris, at least, his was a lone voice. Grigoriev wrote that the work called to mind the triumphs of 1909.[22] The evening after the premiere, the group celebrated on a grand scale, just like in the old days. Gerald and Sara Murphy, an affluent American couple who were the archetypal expatriates of the 'Lost Generation', threw a swanky party for the whole company on a boat on the Seine, and this, too, seemed to hark back to old times. Everyone was there: the Serts, Goncharova and Larionov, Picasso, Cocteau, Tristan Tzara, Kochno, Stravinsky and every one of the group of composers known as 'Les Six': Georges Auric, Louis Durey, Arthur Honneger, Darius Milhaud, Francis Poulenc and Germaine Tailleferre. As it was a Sunday, all the florists were closed, and so Sara Murphy decided to decorate the tables with pyramids of toys, which she had picked up at the little markets in Montparnasse.

> Picasso was enchanted and rearranged the toys into a 'fantastic accident topped by a cow perched on a fireman's ladder' … Stravinsky switched the place cards; Goncharova read palms; … and, as usual, Cocteau tried to steal the show – at first refusing to go on board for fear of seasickness, and then rushing round with a lantern, dressed up as the captain, proclaiming, '*On coule*' (We're sinking). As dawn broke, Kochno and Ansermet … took down the gigantic laurel wreath, inscribed '*Les Noces – Hommages*', which Sara had put up in the main saloon, and held it like a hoop for Stravinsky to make a running jump through.[23]

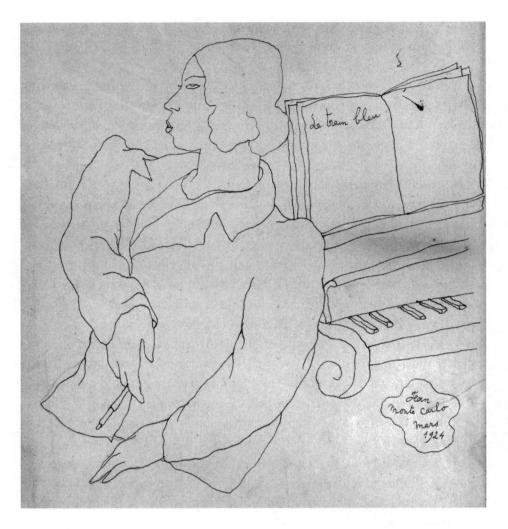

Bronislava Nijinska, by Cocteau

This initial success was not just a flash in the pan, and the status of the ballet has only grown since its premiere. *Les Noces* would certainly appear on any list of Diaghilev's most important productions.

The work's enduring status is as much the result of Nijinska's choreography as of Stravinsky's music. The many striking architectural ensemble positions in the ballet seem unusual even today and reinforce the ritualistic and primitive nature of the dance. In that sense *Noces* bears a strong resemblance to the last ballet her brother made for Diaghilev, *Le Sacre du printemps*. Yet

Nijinska's language of movement differed from her brother's in that it was rooted in the classics, albeit in an altered form and with inverted gender roles. Men and women danced the same steps in *Noces*, and here the proliferation of *pointe* work (an instrument for idealising 'the feminine' in the language of classical dance) conveyed masculine violence. In the words of Lynn Garafola, the entire ballet speaks of 'male power and female pain'.[24]

In the short season in Paris, the company performed *Noces* every day, alongside the Picasso ballets *Parade* and *Pulcinella*, and other modernist productions such as *Chout*, *Contes Russes* and *Sacre*. The character of the season was entirely different from that of the previous year, and it would seem that Diaghilev had now elevated the lesson of the *Sleeping Princess* disaster – stop trying to resurrect old triumphs – to general policy.

The situation was, however, more complicated than that. At the same time that Paris was enjoying daring modernist fare, preparations continued apace for an opera season in Monaco comprising a number of nineteenth-century French works. It would appear that Diaghilev's earlier attempts to tailor his company's programming to the audience's expectations were now coming to fruition. He hoped this new arrangement would allow him to present a wide variety of musical productions that would offset the risks of his artistically progressive premieres in Paris. The more conservative productions would first be performed in Monaco and then taken on tour through the provincial towns and cities of Europe. Yet this did not mean that those more conservative works were of any less concern to Diaghilev. The operas they began to rehearse in November were produced with old-fashioned care and energy. After a brief holiday in Venice, Diaghilev went to Milan to cast singers. There were a great many roles to be filled, and Diaghilev, with his love of bel canto, felt that the most suitable candidates would be found in Italy. In Milan he reviewed a seemingly endless parade of singers, and at times his perfectionism seemed to verge on the grotesque. 'Diaghilev is still in Milan, listening to his 200th tenor,' Ansermet remarked dryly to Stravinsky.[25]

While still up to his neck in auditions, Diaghilev heard that Benois had arrived in Paris. He wrote to him straight away:

> If only you knew how glad I am you've come and how much I want to see you and Atya [Benois' wife]. So much cursed work keeps me back – I've

now been stuck in exhausting Milan for over three weeks, putting together my opera company. There's masses of work and it's very difficult. I dream of our collaboration which we must start right away …

Are you working on *Le Médecin malgré lui* and have you got to know the score? Are you preparing the costumers and the sketches for the sets? …

My [white] streak has grown a lot and is very obvious.[26]

To all appearances, Diaghilev was genuinely happy at the prospect of seeing his old friend again, but it is unclear if his expectations were the same as Benois's. The impresario was probably in Paris to welcome Benois, and perhaps his cousin Pavka as well, who had arrived there around the same time. Pavka soon settled in Monaco, where he went to work for Diaghilev as a sort of factotum. Despite the many differences between the two men, Diaghilev's reunion with his cousin was an emotional experience: at that point he didn't have much family left.

In Paris, Diaghilev spent most of his time getting ready for the Monaco season, which would include at least three new ballets in addition to the operas. One of his main artistic advisers was Jean Cocteau, whose creative impulses Diaghilev hoped to profit from and who got along well with Boris Kochno, an increasingly influential figure in the company. Somewhat more in the shadows was Erik Satie, who had built up a formidable reputation over the previous ten years among younger artists as the 'spiritual' guide of Les Six. Three of the six – Poulenc, Auric and Milhaud – would play a major role in the coming season. Satie campaigned hard for his disciples, especially Milhaud, whose gifts he talked up relentlessly to Diaghilev. Satie's nonconformist stance was a great source of inspiration for the young French composers. Speaking of Satie, Milhaud said that 'the purity of his art, his horror of all concessions, his contempt for money, and his ruthless attitude toward the critics were a marvellous example for us all'.[27]

Diaghilev had asked Satie to write some new music for the recitative sections of Gounod's *Le Médecin malgré lui*, and Poulenc to do the same for *La Colombe*, also by Gounod. Milhaud would ultimately compose the recitatives for *Une Éducation manquée*, a Diaghilev favourite by Emmanuel Chabrier. By giving this assignment to young composers, Diaghilev achieved a number of objectives. First of all, he made the operas his own by reworking them, while cultivating the loyalty of a fresh crop of musicians. In the absence of any young Russian talent, he hoped to groom them as members of his new musical stable. It is not entirely clear if Diaghilev was really as enthusiastic as he appeared about this generation of French composers, but he had few alternatives. Around this time competitors had begun popping up, first and foremost Rolf de Maré's Ballets Suédois, which employed many of the same artists and composers, staking a claim to artistic territory over which Diaghilev had previously held a monopoly. They could not compete in terms of overall quality, but conceptually, their performances were alarmingly similar. Undoubtedly, the rise of this fearsome competitor was a reason to welcome so many French composers and painters with open arms, if only to undercut the Swedes.

Along with the operas there were also new ballets, again with music by young Frenchmen, in this case Poulenc and Auric. These two works, *Les Biches* and *Les Faucheux*, would form the core of the Paris season. Another two ballets were in preparation, one to an eighteenth-century score by Michel de Monteclair, *Les Tentations de la bergère*, and the other to Mussorgsky's *Night on Bald Mountain*. That made a total of eight new productions, more than they had produced since 1909. It was clear that Diaghilev was looking to make a fresh start.

Since splitting with Massine, Diaghilev had no major male stars in his company, but that problem, too, seemed to be on the way to resolving itself. Part of the magic of the Ballets Russes had always been the prominence of male dancers and the aura of sexual transgression projected by their forceful but sexually ambiguous choreographies. The solution came from Serafima Astafieva, a former dancer, whose London dance academy had become a major supplier of fresh talent to the company. Diaghilev received word about the rapid development of an English dancer named Patrick Healy-Kay, who had previously danced a small role in *The Sleeping Princess* under the rather ludicrous *nom de danse* of 'Patrikief'. Now known as Anton Dolin, he was brought to Monaco to fill leading roles in Diaghilev's company. Dolin was young and good looking, and soon became Diaghilev's lover. Prior to that, Diaghilev's partners had always been Russians, and perhaps some of the tolerance of his homosexuality stemmed from that fact: strange behaviour could be accepted more readily from exotic foreigners. But standards were different for an Englishman like Dolin, and moralistic mutterings could soon be heard.

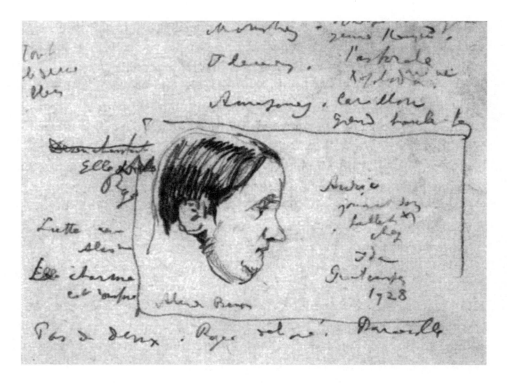

Auric, by Benois

According to Lydia Lopokova it was 'dangerous for Serge to be in sexual rela-tions with a Britt [sic]. Shadow of Oscar Wilde'.[28]

But Diaghilev was not one to be bothered by insinuations or finger-wagging, and enjoyed his new love in the few free hours that he had. He also made an effort to tutor Dolin, as he had done before with Nijinsky and Massine, but his new protégé proved to be a less apt pupil. Another dancer was already waiting in the wings, ready to do whatever it took to win Diaghi-lev's favour. This was Serge Lifar, who had come from Kiev with Bronislava Nijinska, and what he lacked in talent and technique he more than made up for with ambition. Lifar simply bided his time, never losing sight of the object of his desire and aspiration.

While Nijinska made the choreographies for the ballet performances, Benois was largely responsible for directing the four operas. He worked tire-lessly, knowing how much was at stake for him. In addition to his directing duties he also made sets for Gounod's *Le Médecin malgré lui* and *Philémon et Baucis*. (The other two operas, *La Colombe* and Chabrier's *Une Éducation manquée*, were designed by Juan Gris, who had been suggested by Picasso.)

The four operas premiered in the course of the first two weeks of January 1924. According to Grigoriev they were well received, but Milhaud claimed that audiences reacted badly: 'As nearly always happens, the public proved to be lacking in imagination and spurned the unexpected. It felt itself cheated, and clamoured: "Bring on the ballets!" so noisily that *L'Éducation* had to be withdrawn from the programme.'[29]

Whatever the truth of the matter, Diaghilev decided never to present another season of opera. And although the negative public response surely influenced his decision, it couldn't have been the only reason. In the past he had kept poorly received pieces on the programme if he believed in them. It is more likely that he was disenchanted by the end result and had lost the desire to transform older operas into a vital new brand of theatre. Most disappointed of all, however, was Benois, whom Diaghilev had finished with for good. Given the energy that Diaghilev devoted to these opera productions, their failure must have struck a personal nerve, and it is not impossible that he associated this failure, rightly or wrongly, with Benois.

On the other hand, the ballets were a great success, especially *Les Biches*. Poulenc's music was charming and melodious, and Nijinska's choreography contained everything that had always attracted audiences to the Ballets Russes: subtle sexual transgressions in the dance, playing with gender stereotypes, androgyny and homosexuality, though in this case it was the female roles that were endowed with masculine characteristics and not the other way round.[30] In its open exploration of sexual perversity (or what was taken for it), this ballet went further than any other work Diaghilev ever produced. But thanks to the frothiness of the music and the apparent innocence of Marie Laurencin's designs, it seemed less provocative than, say, *L'Après-midi d'un faune*. The ballet was the ideal vehicle for the new zeitgeist of the 1920s, with its graceful hedonism, cult of youth and glamorous neoclassicism.

This may have been even truer for *Le Train bleu*, the only ballet to premiere in Paris that summer. It was Diaghilev's first production with a contemporary, realistic and recognisable setting, evoking the leisure activities of the Parisian *beau monde* on the Côte d'Azur. With its costumes by Chanel, flimsy 'plot' – the depiction of various forms of sport on the beach – and featherweight music by Darius Milhaud (Diaghilev called it an 'operette dansée'), it was the

Picasso, self-portrait

company's trendiest ballet. The stage curtain by Picasso was so successful that the artist formally dedicated it to Diaghilev, who continued to use it as the official curtain of the Ballets Russes for many years after. Despite the success of the curtain, and the tremendous publicity it generated for Picasso, it would be the last time the artist accepted a direct commission from Diaghilev.[31]

The company toured throughout the season, as it had during its salad days. In the spring it paid its first visit to Holland, playing in Rotterdam, The Hague and Amsterdam, before returning to Barcelona. After the summer the Ballets Russes embarked on their first major post-war tour of Germany, visiting Berlin, Hanover, Hamburg and Munich. Their schedule was full, the money was rolling in, and it seemed like they were poised for new European triumphs. But to a certain extent, that financial success masked deeper problems with the company's artistic direction. Virtually no Russian works had been performed the previous season. French composers were dominant; the sets and costumes were largely the work of French and Spanish artists, and the leading male dancer was British. The only artistic element over which the Russians still held sway was the choreography.

At the same time they stubbornly clung to the myth that they were a Russian company. A wholly Russian company would always exert a unique exotic appeal. An international company with an exotic veneer, however, was more susceptible to imitation. It was no coincidence that Diaghilev was facing increasing competition from groups who were bent on repeating his success; the Ballets Suédois was just one example. The only real question was how long Diaghilev would continue to believe in and devote his energies to a cosmopolitan company. His intimate circle still consisted exclusively of Russians. His relationship with his French composers and designers was very different from the one he maintained with his Russian staff. The atmosphere within the company became more professional, more distant, and the relationship between producer and artist was 'normalised'. But Diaghilev was not interested in businesslike relations in a harmonious workplace. It is clear that this kind of set-up could never be a source of ongoing inspiration to him.

Understandably, he looked to his homeland to find inspiration and to heal old wounds. When Diaghilev bought a first edition of the novel *The Tarantas* by Vladimir Sollogub, he wrote in it: 'A *tarantas* [carriage] in which to return to Russia. S.D. Paris, 1923.'[32] His homesickness seemed to be as powerful as ever. In Berlin he hosted Mayakovsky again, with whom he talked regularly. This new meeting was preceded by correspondence, and plans for a tour of the Soviet Union, projected in all likelihood for the following year, were eagerly discussed at great length. In Moscow a few theatres had already been reserved for his arrival. That November, Diaghilev received a visa for the Soviet Union, probably for the purpose of visiting Russia in the winter and making the final preparations for the tour. Mayakovsky wrote to Osip Brik to ask him to act as a guide for Diaghilev and to introduce him to the country's new artistic leaders: 'Be Sergey Pavlovich's guiding star – show him everything one should see in Moscow … If S.P doesn't like Rodchenko, Lavinsky, Eisenstein etc., then sweeten him with some caviare … if he doesn't like that, then nothing can be done.'[33]

A letter was also sent to Anatol Lunacharsky, the man who became Minister of Culture after Diaghilev had declined the job. Mayakovsky specifically asked Lunacharsky to help Diaghilev upon his arrival. Not everyone was charmed by the impending visit of the émigré impresario with his aristocratic manners, but the Russians plainly anticipated that Diaghilev would come. They knew very well how badly he wanted to return (they also knew that Stravinsky, for example, was far less interested), and they understood what a boost it would mean to their reputation if Diaghilev, who was still the implicit leader of the European artistic avant-garde, were to come back to the Soviet Union.

> This 'letter of introduction' is more or less superfluous. You know Sergey Pavlovich Diaghilev as well as I do, and S.P. doesn't need any introductions. I am only writing these lines so that S.P. can speed through the bureaucracy, which can on occasion be excessively defensive. Of course the Parisified 'former' Russians have been scaring S.P. a lot about Moscow. However, his desire to come won out in the end, and also my assertions that we can beat the French at tact and grace, and the Americans at efficiency.
>
> I hope that with your help S.P. will also be convinced of this fact, especially since the main thing is for S.P. to come away with a good opinion of us.[34]

Mayakovsky was right: Diaghilev was afraid to go to the Soviet Union. And for once, the ever superstitious impresario's fears were well founded.

· 26 ·

The Soviet Union Strikes Back
1924–1927

THE MAIN STUMBLING BLOCK to a tour of the USSR was the author-
ities' refusal to guarantee that Boris Kochno, whose age made him liable for
military service, would be allowed to return to France. This suggested that the
Soviet establishment was split as to the desirability of Diaghilev's presence.
What would happen when his whole company travelled to Moscow? Many
of the young men would be in the same boat as Kochno, including Serge
Lifar, who had begun to edge out Anton Dolin as the director's favourite.
Diaghilev's closest friends warned him not to get into bed with the Bolshe-
viks. Cousin Pavka and Nouvel flatly refused to return to the Soviet Union.

Russian émigrés were pouring into Europe, and few had anything heartening to say about the situation back home. A troupe of dancers, some of
them from the Mariinsky Theatre, had ended up in Berlin, where they gave
the occasional performance in local fleapits. Although the press took little
notice, Diaghilev got wind of their activities and sent Pavka to Germany to
cast an eye over them. They had gone by the time he arrived, but he caught
up with the group in London and invited them to come to Paris.[1] The
meeting place was Misia Sert's apartment, where Diaghilev found himself
face to face with the man who held the future of classical ballet in his hands:
Giorgi Balanchivadze. Later to become famous as George Balanchine, the

twenty-year-old from Petersburg was already a talented dancer, with a passion for choreography. He worshipped Kasyan Goleyzovsky, a modernist choreographer 'whose main aim was the achievement of sculptural effects, for which he was wont almost to denude his dancers of all clothing'.[2] Having given up on the idea of a Soviet tour, Diaghilev keenly listened to Balanchine's news from the home front. After a preliminary audition, he engaged the dancers that Balanchine had brought with him: Alexandra Danilova, Tamara Gevergeva and Nicholas Efimov. Both Danilova and Gevergeva (who later shortened her surname to Geva) were soon to dance leading roles with the Ballets Russes.

At the end of 1924 the company was once again in London – Diaghilev having managed to pay off part of his debt to Stoll the previous year – and the new dancers were immediately pressed into service. Diaghilev worked almost exclusively with one particular manager in the British capital, Eric Wollheim, whose dedication did much to restore the impresario's reputation there. A conventional, rather bourgeois man, who had little affinity with Diaghilev's coterie of the great and glamorous, Wollheim nevertheless held the Russian in high esteem and showed a willingness to make sacrifices that others would not. His son Richard offers a striking description of the relationship between the two men, as well as a perceptive portrait of Diaghilev:

> My father deeply admired Diaghilev, and he was, I feel, much drawn
> into his way of thinking and feeling. He was very sympathetic to the
> perfectionism, and I believe that he found the fury and the scenes of rage
> and jealousy very vital … [He] was intrigued by Diaghilev's superstition
> and by his fear of water, and no small part of the special prerogatives with
> which he was credited came from the fact, magical in my father's eyes, that
> he was Russian. A journalist once asked my father in what way Diaghilev
> was so Russian, and my father, who had no great belief in national
> characteristics, said that to see this you had to watch the great man in a
> hurry, because the more worried he was about time, the shorter and shorter
> steps he took, so that, in the end, he was at a standstill.[3]

On 27 December 1924, Diaghilev learnt of the sudden death of Leon Bakst. Devastated, he wept bitterly in the arms of his manservant Vasily. He wired the Serts in Paris, urging them to convey to Bakst's family 'my deep sympathy at the loss of a friend. I have many moving memories from the long period of our working together and a thirty-five-year-old friendship.'[4]

It was the end of a friendship and artistic collaboration that had shaped the artistic face of pre-war Europe. As the French press put it, Bakst's demise marked 'the passing of an epoch of European cultural history'.[5] That epoch had actually ended a decade earlier, when modernism in all its forms began to dominate European artistic culture, partly through Diaghilev's own influence. As of that time Diaghilev had distanced himself from Bakst, feeling that the latter's work had lost its artistic authority. For his part, Bakst was taken aback by the emergence of modernism, which he came to loathe with a passion. He simply couldn't comprehend how Diaghilev, of all people, had become Europe's most powerful prophet of the new art. In Bakst's view, his friend was not only terribly wrong, but guilty of rank treachery.

When the last performance of the London season ended on 12 January, the reviews were effusive. The magazine *People* reported that it had been 'one of the most remarkable farewells ever given in a variety theatre … The leading ladies and men were snowed under with bouquets, floral wreaths and other floral tributes. The applause lasted for a solid twenty minutes and continued long after the final curtain had been lowered.'[6] Diaghilev once again reigned supreme in London's theatrical world, and his company suddenly found itself on a more secure financial footing.

The new season in Monaco was much more modest than the previous one. There were no opera premieres, and most of the ballets were no more than suites, old-fashioned 'salades Russes', with little new material. Diaghilev's contract with the Monaco Opera required his company to provide balletic interludes for in-house operas. It was for such divertissements that Balanchine produced his first choreographies.

The two main premieres of the year were *Zéphire et Flore* and *Les Matelots*. The former was set to music by a very young Ukrainian called Vladimir Dukelsky. Dukelsky's symphonic works are all but forgotten, but the music he composed under the name Vernon Duke – classic songs like 'April in Paris' and 'Autumn in New York' – can still be heard all over the world. Dukelsky's autobiography, *Passport to Paris*, is a witty, engaging sketch of the jazz era, easily one of the most readable of the myriad memoirs produced by the members of Diaghilev's entourage. The composer was only twenty years old when he arrived in Europe with a few changes of clothes and a freshly composed piano concerto under his arm. He hoped to present his work to Diaghilev, and to this end he contacted Walter Nouvel, whom he describes in a perceptive, touching portrait:

> Dear Valechka was, in reality, one of the sweetest of God's creatures, but also a frustrated composer (like his friend Diaghilev), frustrated lover, frustrated sybarite – he loved luxury and could not afford it – and I think was genuinely angry at himself for possessing so kind a heart. He was fond of cutting and artfully insulting remarks, which he made often between puffs on his eternal cigarette … In a perpetual rage at himself, he covered it up by being ingeniously unpleasant to people – especially if he liked them … Valechka … turned to me: 'I hear you write music – *must* you?' … No answer was expected, obviously, and Nouvel went on: 'Don't be scared by me; nobody is scared by Valechka any longer; they took out my fangs and they won't let me talk. Seryozha occasionally listens to me, but never agrees with me.'[7]

Dukelsky played his unpolished pieces to Nouvel, who promised to show them to Diaghilev. At their first meeting in the latter's box, the impresario fell for Dukelsky's charms: "'Ah, a good-looking boy," he drawled. "That in itself is most unusual. Composers are seldom good-looking; neither Stravinsky nor Prokofiev ever won any beauty prizes. How old are you?" I told him I was twenty. "That's encouraging, too. I don't like young men over twenty-five."'[8]

Needing Russian music and wanting to impress the public with his eye for talent, Diaghilev lost no time in commissioning a ballet from the young man, even though Dukelsky had not yet matured as a composer (and his real talents did not lie in symphonic music). He had promise, however, according to Prokofiev and Stravinsky, who had both taken a shine to him. Dukelsky immediately started work, and the ballet that was to become *Zéphire et Flore* premiered on 28 April in Monte Carlo. The sets were by Georges Braque, the costumes by Coco Chanel,[9] and the choreography by the returned prodigal, Léonide Massine.

Bronislava Nijinska had left Diaghilev at the end of the previous season, partly because she wanted to set up her own company and partly because she felt sidelined by Balanchine. This was a blow for Diaghilev, as Nijinska was a unique choreographer who had invigorated the language of classical dance as no one had done since Fokine. On the other hand, she was also headstrong and independent, qualities that Diaghilev found hard to appreciate in a woman. Massine was quick to offer his services when he heard of her departure, and Diaghilev took him on, fearing that the inexperienced Balanchine could not manage alone. He made the appointment reluctantly, though, remarking to Dukelsky that 'Léonide had no soul, no heart and no taste and was only interested in money.'[10]

Zéphire et Flore was well received, but it was yet another slick, lightweight product churned out by the Diaghilev factory, destined for great success and instant obscurity. The most striking feature of the ballet was Kochno's libretto. *Zéphire et Flore* sought to recreate the kind of dances performed by serfs on Russian estates, and in that respect it was another veiled ode to the lost empire. There have been many ballets of the same name, the most famous being a Russian production from 1808 featuring dances by the legendary choreographer Charles Didelot and music by Catterino Cavos, Alexandre Benois's grandfather.[11] Diaghilev told Dukelsky that his family (in point of fact his stepmother's family) had once had its own serf theatre. In short, *Zéphire* was a work full of historical and personal associations, though these were probably lost on the Monaco audiences, who were chiefly interested in spotting new fashions among Chanel's creations.

The next big premiere of that year, *Les Matelots*, with music by Georges Auric and sets by Pedro Pruna, tried to recapture the success of *Le Train bleu*, with jolly Jack tars tripping nimbly to Auric's tuneful score. The ballet was a big hit everywhere, particularly in London, where it became an annual fixture.

Diaghilev's new lover, Serge Lifar, danced leading roles in both ballets. Lifar was no Nijinsky – in his early days in Diaghilev's entourage he was conspicuous mainly for his clumsiness – but he was a quick learner. He lacked Massine's acute intelligence and artistic sensitivity, but made up for it with pathos and ambition. Diaghilev sent him to Cecchetti in Milan to improve his technique, instructing him, in a letter, to learn more about Italian art:

I spent three days in Florence and was convinced once again that no cultivated artist can do without a knowledge of that place, which is sacred to art. It is truly God's abode …

I'm sending you a small present from here – ten little books – the

Diaghilev watching Lifar in rehearsal, by Larionov

works of the greatest masters: the blessed Raphael's portraits – the greatest things he created, Botticelli, Mantegna (do you remember the Christ?), Piero della Francesca, Donatello, Filippo Lippi, Francesca Francia, Masaccio, Michelangelo and our Milanese Luini. I think it your duty to get to know all these photographs by heart, to understand the difference between the masters and to commit all this to memory ... Write to let me know that you got them, and also the ballet shoes. I am very pleased you're going to the Maestro's [Cecchetti's] and helping him dig in his vegetable plot and little garden – that's very good, really praiseworthy ...[12]

Lifar had few admirers among Diaghilev's entourage. Indeed, he inspired almost universal antipathy, unlike any of the impresario's previous premier danseurs and lovers. Yet despite the boy's undeniable shortcomings and scepticism on the part of Nijinska and others, Diaghilev did succeed in turning him into a great dancer. Lifar, for his part, was fiercely devoted to the impresario.

When *Zéphire* was almost ready, Lifar dislocated both ankles, and the premiere had to be postponed to 28 April 1925. The dancer, still troubled by his injuries, put on a brave show. Though it didn't equal the success of *Les Matelots* in Paris two months later, the work was well received. Diaghilev, never satisfied with crowd-pleasing potboilers, desperately needed fresh artistic input. He also wanted to infuse some Russian influence into his shows to preserve the company's identity. By now, Russian fairytales and neo-nationalism were passé; something novel was required. Diaghilev approached Prokofiev, who was in Monaco that May.

For years after the London debacle he hadn't been able to commission works by established composers (Stravinsky's *Noces* had been paid for much earlier). Young talents like Poulenc, Auric and Dukelsky were a bargain; Diaghilev could get three ballets by Auric for the price of one by Prokofiev. This was another reason he loved composers in their early twenties.[13]

Prokofiev was worried that Kochno, whom he loathed, would be asked to devise a theme and write the libretto, but Diaghilev already had a very clear notion of the ballet's subject.

'If I needed a foreign ballet I'd ask Auric,' he told Prokofiev. 'No one's interested in a Russian ballet based on Afanasyev's fairytales or the life of Ivan the Terrible. You, Seryozha, must write a ballet about today's Russia.'

'A Bolshevist ballet?'

'Yes.'[14]

Diaghilev wanted Ilya Ehrenburg, a Russian writer with close ties to the Soviet authorities, to write the libretto, presumably to forestall criticism that a Bolshevist ballet was being produced in Monaco by decadent émigrés who had not set foot in Russia for over a decade. Ehrenburg, however, had delusions of grandeur. He asked a fee of 5,000 francs (over three times what Prokofiev was being paid for his music), whereupon Diaghilev angrily dropped him. A libretto was then assembled with the help of Grigory Yakulov, who had been engaged early on as the ballet's designer, and Prokofiev was able to start work. A setting was soon devised: a new factory, with the dancers playing the part of workers.

Right from the outset, the politically sensitive theme sparked heated debate. The Russian community in France – a significant portion of the theatre-going public – would not, it was feared, appreciate a ballet with a Bolshevist theme. Pavka and Nouvel urgently sought to dissuade Diaghilev from his plan, 'arguing that [he] would alienate not only the emigrants, but their aristocratic patrons'.[15] Even Prokofiev, who was fairly well disposed to

Yakulov, by Mayakovsky

the Soviet Union, warned that the ballet should not degenerate into an 'apotheosis of Bolshevism'.[16] Most of the composer's income derived from tours of the US, so he too had to tread carefully when it came to matters of politics. Besides the predictable criticism from Europe and America, the group was worried about the Soviet response. Diaghilev talked at length with the Soviet ambassador in London, Christian Rakovsky, and also Platon Kerzhentsev, the ambassador in Rome.[17] 'We've got nothing to do with politics', Diaghilev claimed, as if producing a ballet of this kind were not in itself a highly political statement.

He still sought to connect a well-known Soviet artist to the project – if not Ehrenburg, then someone else. That problem could be solved later, however. Yakulov and Prokofiev would produce a joint libretto, after which Prokofiev would start on the score. Agreement had been reached on the main issues as early as 16 August 1925: 'I think that we've devised exactly what's needed: something apolitical, typical of the time (love in a factory), with the parts of the heroes accentuated as you wanted, and finally in the finale the whole factory (including the hammers) comes into motion as an accompaniment to the dance of the two main characters.'[18]

The caution with which Diaghilev set to work, his contact with the ambassadors and his considerable efforts to give the work Soviet credentials show that the Russian response to his ballet was uppermost in his mind. He had to be very careful of his status in the Soviet Union if he was ever to return to his homeland. The ballet's working title, *Ursignol* – a portmanteau word made up of URSS (USSR *en français*) and *guignol* – was felt to be insufficiently politically correct and was ultimately scrapped.[19]

Prokofiev had already made great progress with the score, which he described as, 'Russian, often impetuous, almost always diatonic, using the white keys. In short, white music to a red theme.'[20] On 7 October he gave a preliminary recital to Diaghilev and Nouvel, who were largely enthusiastic: Diaghilev pronounced nine of the twelve parts good. On 16 October Prokofiev played the piece once more, apparently after having made changes, at Coco Chanel's home to a gathering that included Kochno, Larionov and Yakulov.[21] A fortnight later Prokofiev left on a long tour of Sweden, the Netherlands and the United States. As a result, work ground to a halt for many months, despite the fact that *Ursignol* was scheduled to premiere in the spring or summer of 1926.

By the time Prokofiev left Paris, the company was already in London for the long annual season. Then it was off to Berlin from 21 December to 6 January. Harry Kessler was in town, and at the end of their run there he joined Diaghilev, Kochno, Nouvel, Lifar and the director Max Reinhardt for supper.

On tour: Lifar (holding the coconut from Petrushka?*), flanked by Diaghilev and Kochno on a station platform*

The company went straight from Germany to Monaco to perform and prepare the premieres for the next season. Officially, *Ursignol* was still on the spring programme, but Diaghilev was once again strapped for cash. He requested Yakulov, who was then in Moscow, to ask Meyerhold to direct the ballet. The latter was well acquainted with the impresario: almost twenty years earlier, in 1906, Diaghilev had been instrumental in Meyerhold's efforts to develop 'impressionist theatre', and Meyerhold had attended a number of premieres in the early years of the Ballets Russes.[22] However, the great director wanted nothing to do with a Monaco-produced Soviet show, and in a note to Yakulov he firmly distanced himself from the project. He wrote that he could not, 'for a variety of reasons', accede to Diaghilev's proposal to direct 'his enterprise'.[23]

On receiving this news, Diaghilev decided to postpone the premiere. He asked Nouvel to write a note to Yakulov, parodying Meyerhold's wording: 'S. P. Diaghilev has requested me to inform you that, for a variety of reasons, he is unfortunately compelled to postpone performance of the ballet until the autumn.'[24] This decision was prompted not just by Diaghilev's failure to recruit Meyerhold (or someone of similar standing),[25] but also by his intention to celebrate the twentieth anniversary of his theatrical activities in Europe in 1927 with an all-Russian season, featuring works by Stravinsky, Prokofiev and Dukelsky. As usual, his big problem was money. 'Find me eight hundred francs,' he told Prokofiev, 'and I will start rehearsing your ballet tomorrow.'[26]

Financial difficulties continued to dog Diaghilev's company, and he remained dependent on contributions from sponsors. Besides old faithfuls like Coco Chanel, Princesse de Polignac and Lady Juliet Duff, there were new donors such as the fabulously wealthy newspaper baron Lord Rothermere and the American songwriter Cole Porter. As usual, personal affairs spilled over into professional ones. Diaghilev used Sokolova's charms to wheedle funding out of Rothermere. Porter stumped up large sums of money as well, having fallen head over heels for Boris Kochno. This did not sit well with Diaghilev, who was capable of feeling jealous even long after the end of a relationship.[27]

Despite the many donations, they still struggled to make ends meet. Diaghilev economised on the materials for sets and costumes, and (having already cut costs on composers) engaged cheaper conductors. Many of the shows in Monte Carlo and Paris were conducted by such lesser lights as Marc-César Scotto, Edouard Flament, Henri Defosse and the charmingly named René-Emmanuel Baton.

Diaghilev would never allow quality to suffer, though. For challenging pieces by Stravinsky and Prokofiev he hired big-name talents, for example Ernest Ansermet, Eugene Goossens, Roger Désormière. Yet even they did not escape the impresario's criticism: 'Diaghilev has not let my slightest mistake pass unremarked,' Ansermet said later, 'and I have not conducted many ballets without having him pursue me with criticisms. Nevertheless, his exaggerated and unjust attitude is for the best; thanks to his perpetual criticisms, he maintains control.'[28]

This led to many walkouts, since Diaghilev treated conductors no differently from designers and dancers. He retained his hold on them, though, something Ansermet ascribed to the fact that, 'in spite of everything, he is the only impresario who does interesting things, and one is always obliged to return to him'.[29]

Ursignol was on the back burner, but four new premieres were being prepared for the coming season. They included *La Pastorale*, a ballet by Georges Auric, which, like *Les Matelots*, was designed by Pedro Pruna. Then there were two ballets with music by English composers, a first for the company: *Romeo and Juliet* by Constant Lambert and *The Triumph of Neptune* by Lord Berners. None of these productions entered the repertoire, nor did the music survive independently. *La Pastorale* did, however, mark an important moment in dance history, because it was the first premiere choreographed by Balanchine (after he had been allowed to re-choreograph Stravinsky's *Le Chant du rossignol* the previous year).

Diaghilev had not asked Stravinsky to produce any new works since the war (*Les Noces* dated back to 1913 and *Le Renard* had been commissioned not by Diaghilev but by Princesse de Polignac). This was not due only to lack of money. The relationship between the two men was a complex one, with each constantly jockeying for power. Yet there was no question that Diaghilev deeply admired the composer's music: he always sought to turn a Stravinsky premiere into an event. For the previous season he had asked Balanchine to do the choreography, and for the 1926 season he had commissioned new sets for *The Firebird* from Natalia Goncharova. The latter responded with a sweet note: 'I accept the conditions you give me for *Firebird* in your letter, not because the production is a Russian one, or something else, but because it's yours and the music is Igor's ... I embrace you, as does Misha [Larionov].'[30]

The closeness of the bond between Diaghilev and Stravinsky is evident from a letter from the composer that Diaghilev received in Monaco on 7 April:

> I am writing to you in the firm conviction that you'll take what I say for what it really is.
>
> It's been twenty years since I fasted before taking communion and I'm doing it now out of sheer mental and spiritual need – in a few days I will make my confession and before I do so I will ask those I can to forgive me. Dear Seryozha, I am asking you, with whom I've worked so much over the years that have gone by without my repenting before God, to forgive my transgressions with as much heartfelt sincerity as I feel in asking you.
>
> Answer me, I beg you, just with one word, I'll still get it in time.

I ask you not to tell anyone about this letter – and it would be best if you destroyed it.

In my thoughts I give you a brotherly kiss.[31]

Stravinsky had his own demons to grapple with. Just like Diaghilev, he suffered under life in exile and the separation from his family back home. His marriage was also on shaky ground as a result of his affair with Vera Sudeykin. Pangs of guilt over his sick, dependent wife left him anxious and depressed. Stravinsky's unbosomings touched Diaghilev deeply:

> I read your letter with tears as I have never, not for one minute, ceased to think of you as a brother, and so I feel radiantly happy that in your letter you give me 'a brotherly kiss'. I remember the letter you wrote me after the death of your brother Gury; I also remember a letter which long ago I began writing to you in which I said that when I am greatly depressed and think of God, you are there by me and that cheers me up.
>
> I think only God can forgive because only He can judge. When we quarrel and when we repent we, poor little lost souls, must have enough strength to greet one another as brothers and to forget all that wants forgiveness. If I want it, it's because it concerns me too, and although I am not preparing for communion I still ask you to forgive me all my conscious and unconscious sins towards you and only to keep in your heart that feeling of brotherly love I feel for you.[32]

Diaghilev had never been particularly devout, and there is no indication that he ever attended mass after he left home. (This did not prevent him from being, like Stravinsky, extraordinarily superstitious, forever interpreting omens and seeking to placate malign influences. His pockets were stuffed with amulets to ward off the evil eye, and he adopted all kinds of peasant beliefs from his Italian manservant.) France, like many other countries at the time, was in the grip of new spiritual movements and religious fads, but Diaghilev was immune to them. He had had enough of that kind of thing in the final years of his relationship with Filosofov, and though he seemed to be genuinely touched by Stravinsky's 'conversion', his own attitude to religion was not affected.

Diaghilev and Stravinsky met again in May at the beginning of the Paris season, when Stravinsky attended the first performance of his revamped

Stravinsky, by Picasso

Firebird. The most striking premiere was undoubtedly *Romeo and Juliet*. Diaghilev, now in a surrealist phase, had asked Max Ernst and Juan Miró to make sets and costumes for the Lambert ballet. Diaghilev was particularly taken with Ernst and spent many evenings with him while the ballet was being produced in Monaco. Meanwhile, the hardcore surrealists were up in arms. The idea that art could have a utilitarian function was anathema to them, and a theatrical production was considered downright sacrilegious. They resolved to disrupt the Paris premiere (the ballet had already been performed once in Monaco). After the first interval, just before *Romeo and Juliet* was due to start, a group of fifty demonstrators poured into the concert hall and, when the orchestra struck up, began to whistle and yell, drowning out the music. Diaghilev had been prepared for this and had instructed the conductor to carry on regardless. He had also alerted the police, who soon arrived at the scene. English members of the audience interpreted the protest as an attack on their national music and launched a spirited assault on the demonstrators.

Prokofiev, who was in Diaghilev's box, described the spectacle: 'From my balcony seat I saw incredible dandies in evening tails coming into action and giving fearsome blows, proper pugilistic punches, to the unfortunate demonstrators. One of them, who'd been hit on the cheekbone, sat on the ground covering his head with his hands, when a lady all décolletée rushed up to him and hit him several times with her programme.'[33] The police eventually managed to eject all the demonstrators, and the rest of the evening – indeed, the rest of the season – passed off without a hitch.

As always, everyone who was anyone flocked to Diaghilev's Paris shows, but there was one person in particular he wished to see: the great director Vsevolod Meyerhold, who happened to be in town. The impresario had not yet abandoned his plan to ask him to contribute to *Ursignol*. Perhaps some compromise might yet be reached. Diaghilev was, however, painfully aware that he had not as yet answered the two letters that Meyerhold had written to him from Moscow. On 27 May Meyerhold (who spoke not a word of French) was given a grand reception, organised by Milhaud, at which Diaghilev was not present. Two days later Meyerhold turned up at a Ballets Russes rehearsal with Prokofiev, to talk to Diaghilev. When Meyerhold entered the auditorium Prokofiev

> went up to him [Diaghilev] and said that Meyerhold was here. Diaghilev became agitated and rushed over to him. They embraced. Diaghilev at once began to apologise for not having answered his letters. 'You must understand, I was so insanely busy now with the first nights ... Like now,

you mustn't look, there's a performance tonight and nothing's working properly yet ... But I carry around your letters in my pocket all the time to answer them ...' Here he started to take all sorts of letters and papers out of his pocket, but by ill luck not a single one was from Meyerhold.[34]

Diaghilev was called away on other business, but he invited Meyerhold to sit in his box every night: an honour extended only to the favoured few. (Prokofiev was not among them, a fact the composer noted with great displeasure.) Later that week Diaghilev and Meyerhold spoke again, but that encounter resulted in nothing more than a vague agreement to meet in Paris the following year.

After the Paris season, the company went to London and Ostend, subsequently travelling to Italy. They performed in Turin over Christmas and on 10, 12 and 16 January at La Scala in Milan. It meant a lot to Diaghilev to appear at the world-famous venue, though their shows were not a great success.

From then on, all attention turned to the main premieres of the coming season. It was Diaghilev's twentieth Paris season, starting with his 1906 exhibition (in 1918 there were no performances in the French capital). Such an important anniversary had to be celebrated in style. Besides *Ursignol* there were two other premieres: *Le Mercure* and *La Chatte*. The former ballet, with music by Satie and sets and costumes by Picasso, had been premiered by Les Soirées de Paris, a competing company run by Étienne de Beaumont. Diaghilev now included it in the programme as a tribute to Satie, who had died the previous year. Despite the impressive team of artists involved in *Mercure* (Satie, Picasso and Massine, with Cocteau – the same four that had produced *Parade* almost a decade earlier) it was a weak production that played only four times in Paris and was never restaged by Diaghilev.

La Chatte was of an altogether different calibre. It ranks among the most important of Diaghilev's late productions, thanks to the constructivist sets and costumes by the Russian sculptor Naum Gabo and Balanchine's choreography. (The music, by Henri Sauguet, was decidedly less groundbreaking.)

Diaghilev had met Gabo (né Pevsner) and his brother Antoine in Paris back in 1924, at an exhibition in Galerie Percier. Naum Gabo had made a name for himself with his constructivist sculptures of translucent plastic and technical installations that he called kinetic constructions. He was also an architect, an industrial designer and a prominent thinker. In the late 1920s, a time when European art was marked by diversity, innovation and experimentation with new forms, theories and materials, he was possibly the most advanced artist on the Continent. When Gabo expressed interest in designing for Diaghilev in late 1926, the impresario was quick to sign him up.[35] In February 1927, talks with Gabo and his brother Antoine led to the commission for *Chatte*. The brothers understood what Diaghilev wanted. 'In Paris, in two and a half months' time they will celebrate the twentieth anniversary of the Diaghilev Ballet. Naturally, for this occasion he wants to make the ultimate splash.' They also realised what was in it for them, 'This of course will create a colossal amount of publicity and noise for us.'[36]

Scenographically speaking, *La Chatte* ranks with Bakst's *Schéhérazade* and Picasso's *Parade* as one of Diaghilev's most significant ballets. It was not the first theatrical work to use constructivist installations as sets, but it was certainly the first ballet to do so, thrusting the work of avant-garde artists like Gabo into the cultural mainstream. *Chatte*'s success was also due to its brilliant choreography: ballet audiences were electrified by their first true encounter with Balanchine's talent.

Indeed, *La Chatte* would become a perennial favourite, being repeated every year up until Diaghilev's death.

Of course, an anniversary season had to feature a new work by Stravinsky. It had been four years since Diaghilev had premiered a piece by the composer – partly because he was extremely expensive, and partly because of the risk element: the *Mavra* fiasco had shown that he did not always produce hits. Meanwhile, Stravinsky had secretly started work on a highly experimental project, an opera-oratorio without dramatic action, to a Latin text based on Sophocles' Oedipus plays. Stravinsky later claimed that he wanted to make Diaghilev a present of this work for his anniversary, though he only divulged this plan to Diaghilev when his efforts to secure funding elsewhere fell through.[37]

The two men were extremely close at that time. Stravinsky's wife Katya was gravely ill and needed an operation, and Diaghilev rose splendidly to the occasion. He assumed the care of Stravinsky's children in Monaco during Katya's operation and convalescence, and sent the composer a string of heartening letters.[38] When Katya had recovered somewhat, Stravinsky wrote, 'Tomorrow Katya is already being discharged from the clinic and is coming

Prokoviev, by Matisse

back home to the joy of everyone. I am writing to you to tell you this, for I know how much you took to heart the operation, which had been worrying me greatly, and I thank you, dear friend, for your concern.'[39]

Still in the dark about Stravinsky's secret plan, Diaghilev travelled to Paris on 25 March. Around the same time, Prokofiev was due to return from a winter tour of the Soviet Union. It had proved surprisingly straight-forward for him to enter (and leave) the country, and he found it to be an inspiring place, with very receptive audiences. When he arrived in Monaco to prepare his ballet, Diaghilev questioned him eagerly about his trip: 'Diaghilev moved on to questions about Russia, where he very much wants to go. I said that in Russia people are most afraid that he'll be snaring their male and female dancers. So before he goes he should solemnly state, maybe even in writing, that he is just going to look; then they'll be very pleased with him.'[40]

Prokofiev was not naïve about the Soviet regime, though. Writing of a sudden phone call from the Comintern, he remarked, 'You have to be careful when dealing with them – they're a dangerous lot.'[41] The exchange between Prokofiev and Diaghilev reveals that by then the latter had abandoned his plan to tour the Soviet Union. He only wanted to visit the country as a private citizen. Prokofiev's tales seem to have given him hope that this might be possible in the near future.

It was on 11 April that Diaghilev first heard his 'present' from Stravinsky, *Oedipus Rex*. According to Prokofiev, Stravinsky sat at the piano, flanked by both his sons, 'and they all sang'.[42] It must have been a curious spectacle: a father and his sons playing a piece about one of the most famous patricides in literature.

There was also another factor which presumably did not escape Diaghilev. Stravinsky's biographer Stephen Walsh, usually wary of psychological speculation, saw in the work a reflection of the relationship between the impresario and the composer: 'Was there not in fact something almost deliberately anti-Diaghilev about the whole opera, as if the old tyrant had been cast in Stravinsky's mind as Laius himself, murdered at the parting of the ways and usurped by his own composer "son"?' It was not for nothing that Diaghilev referred to the opera-oratorio as 'a very macabre gift'.[43]

Another distinguished visitor arrived shortly before the Paris season started: Anatoly Lunacharsky, the Soviet People's Commissar of Enlightenment, responsible for culture and education. Lunacharsky knew Diaghilev and his company well, because in 1913 and 1914 he had worked as French correspondent for a couple of left-wing periodicals in Paris and had reviewed their performances. Before the revolution Lunacharsky had written in mainly positive terms about Diaghilev. He must have been aware that the latter had been the first choice for his job, but he claimed never to have met him personally. His current visit bore all the hallmarks of an audience.

A breakfast had been laid on; present were not only Lunacharsky and Diaghilev but also Prokofiev, Larionov and an inebriated Yakulov. Prokofiev described the event in his diary:

Lunacharsky bowed and scraped in front of Diaghilev and at the end of the conversation his wife summed things up by saying that if she had been blind and present at this conversation, she would have said without any doubt that the Soviet minister was Diaghilev and the representative of bourgeois art Lunacharsky. But there was one remark of Lunacharsky's that really bowled Diaghilev over. He said, 'You know, we recently had a big success with Russian art in Vienna. I took an exhibition of old icons there, and it made a huge impression.' 'When I heard that remark,' said Diaghilev, 'coming from the lips of a Soviet minister and official atheist, I didn't know where to look!'[44]

On his return to Moscow, Lunacharsky wrote a long newspaper article about his meeting with Diaghilev. Its tone jarred sharply with that of the convivial gathering described by Prokofiev. The People's Commissar praised Diaghilev's taste and energy, but criticised his elitism. Painting Diaghilev as the victim of his own delusions and of his public, he ended on an ominous note, accusing him of being an 'Ahasuerus', a rootless cosmopolitan: a damning piece of Soviet parlance that often heralded a denunciation.

> I think Diaghilev an outstanding organiser, a man of great taste and great artistic culture. His lively energy, his exceptional education and his unusual powers of invention could have made him a truly great, maybe even historically creative innovator in the sphere of the arts.
>
> Unfortunately fate decreed otherwise: his first successes at the time of the Parisian '*grands saisons*' chained Diaghilev as it were to a rootless idle crowd wandering the world in search of fresh entertainments. It's that gilded mob which all great artists have always deeply loathed. That mob can pay big money, it can provide great celebrity in the press, but it's greedy. It constantly demands of its 'entertainer' new sensations, in fresh combinations ...
>
> Of course he despises his great public. He is shielded from it by the illusion that he is serving thirty or forty connoisseur Croesuses and that the rest will follow that leadership like a thread through a needle ... The trouble is that not only these lords but Diaghilev himself only cherish form and novelty. In our conversation he said something to the effect of, 'You in Soviet Russia have so much important work that of course you have no time to worry about art, but here, I assure you, a very great deal is done for it' ...

But tell me, how can someone speak otherwise, when he is driven by the whirlwind of his public's desires for innovation, like Paolo and Francesca carried eternally onward by the whirlwind of flame in Dante's hell. In Diaghilev's ears, as in Ahasuerus's, there rings the constant command, 'Go forth!' And he goes forth, leaving a country that is often beautiful and fertile, and goes into the desert searching for shadowy mirages.[45]

The precise effect of Lunacharsky's article cannot be known, but it would seem that after such a vitriolic critique from the most powerful man in the Russian art world, there was little prospect that Diaghilev would ever be welcome in Russia, let alone be allowed to tour with the Ballets Russes. We do not know whether Diaghilev ever read the article, but it seems unlikely that it could have escaped his notice. However, when the twentieth Parisian season opened, Lunacharsky's piece had not yet been published, and Diaghilev once again had his hands full with premieres.

On 29 May a preview performance of *Oedipus Rex* was held at the home of Princesse de Polignac. According to Prokofiev, there was 'a colossal gathering; crowds queued on the street'.[46] The premiere took place the following day in the Théâtre Sarah Bernhardt. It was not a great success. Exactly a week later, *Le Pas d'acier* was performed for the first time, after a sleepless, busy night for Diaghilev and Yakulov.[47] It was a tremendous hit, with both the public and the critics. In the run-up to the premiere the papers had devoted a lot of space to the controversial new ballet. Diaghilev gave various interviews in which he defended his new production, dwelling on its music and design, while sidestepping politically sensitive issues.

He saw it as his company's most significant production since *Les Noces*. Prokofiev, he said, stood beside Stravinsky at the forefront of contemporary Russian music. While the latter was increasingly in touch with the divine, the former seemed to be taking the opposite route: his diabolic music was wont to frighten the public into their shells like so many snails.[48]

Diaghilev had feared protests from White Russian émigrés, indignant at a Bolshevist ballet. But the only hiccup came, not from them, but from Jean Cocteau, who reproached Massine (the ballet's choreographer) 'for having turned something as great as the Russian Revolution into a cotillion-like

Cocteau, by Picasso

spectacle within the intellectual grasp of ladies who pay six thousand francs for a box'.[49] Dukelsky, who loathed Cocteau, made a snide remark to Prokofiev about the decadent Parisian *musiquette*, alluding to the group of composers known as Les Six, who tended to follow in Cocteau's footsteps. A fight broke out, and Dukelsky challenged Cocteau to a duel. Diaghilev hauled the two young bantams apart, telling them exasperatedly, 'Don't you dare fight in my theatre, I have quite enough difficulties with the authorities as it is – don't you realise they could have us all deported?'[50] A remarkable comment, perhaps a slip of the tongue, but notable in the light of what was about to happen to his relatives in the Soviet Union.

In the late summer or early autumn of 1927, Valentin Pavlovich Diaghilev was dragged from his bed in Leningrad and taken away by the NKVD, the Soviet secret police. His family were not told where he was being held or what the charges were. Soon afterwards, Valentin was transported to Solovki, a monastery that had been turned into a prison camp. The first large concentration camp in the Soviet Union, Solovki would serve as a model for the Gulag system.[51]

Diaghilev was aware of his half-brother's disappearance by that autumn, though his reaction to the distressing news is not known. If nothing else, it hammered home the message that Diaghilev had no future in the Soviet Union and that his life would be at risk if he returned to his native country. In 1927 or 1928 his other half-brother Yury was also arrested and deported to central Asia. There is no indication that Diaghilev ever learned of the latter's disappearance.[52]

Usually extremely reticent about family affairs, Diaghilev resolved that unusual measures were called for. He decided to enlist aid in the hope of learning of Valentin's fate.

· 27 ·

The Final Curtain
1928–1929

DIAGHILEV WAITED for a time before making a serious effort to find out what had happened to his half-brother, but by the early autumn it became clear that Valentin's disappearance was not a temporary one. He contacted Philippe Berthelot, the secretary-general of the French foreign ministry. A veteran diplomat, Berthelot was probably more powerful than the minister himself, and since the war he had been the chief architect of French foreign policy. He was a well-known figure in artistic circles and a good friend of Paul Claudel and Jean Giraudoux; his connection to Diaghilev rested mainly on his close friendship with Misia Sert.

Berthelot took Diaghilev's request for help seriously, calling in the assistance of the French ambassador in Moscow (France had established diplomatic ties with the USSR in 1924) and asking him to pump Soviet foreign minister Maxim Litvinov for information. Berthelot used the full weight of his office to gather information from the highest authorities, making it clear that France took the matter very seriously.

The French ambassador, Jean Herbette, reported back on his meeting with Litvinov:

I spoke to M. Litvinov yesterday and reminded him of the fame and sympathy M. Serge de Diaghilev enjoys in France and of the regrettable effect that actions taken against his brother would have everywhere. I urged M. Litvinov in my private capacity to intervene, and I did not neglect to mention that the outcry over M. and Mme. Valentin de Diaghilev had already reached your ears. M. Litvinov could not make any promises because, as he told me, the GPU is not obliged to respond to requests for information about a Soviet citizen, even if coming from the Commissariat of the Foreign Ministry. But I am confident that M. Litvinov, without making any commitment, will do his utmost to avoid creating a bad impression abroad ...[1]

But Herbette had been overly optimistic. Nine days later he heard back from Litvinov, who stated that he had 'made enquiries and that the GPU had no record of the arrest of M. and Mme. Valentine de Diaghilev. M. Litvinov asked me to indicate where and how this was supposed to have taken place'.[2] Transcriptions of both letters in Kochno's hand can be found in the Diaghilev archive. Berthelot kept the originals. There is nothing further on this matter in the collection. This is not to say that Diaghilev simply forgot about his half-brother; indeed, as we shall see, there are indications that he made repeated efforts to support Valentin's family.

The fact that even the intercession of so important a man as Berthelot elicited no more than a blunt denial plainly shows that certain factions in the Soviet Union were a law unto themselves. For the first time it must have dawned on Diaghilev that he would never see his homeland again.

We can only guess at the effect these events had on his mental and emotional state. He did not share his feelings with anyone, and nobody in his inner circle spoke or wrote about the matter after his death. Stravinsky was seemingly unaware of it, as was Grigoriev; even Lifar, who was so close to him in those years, says nothing about it. It is virtually inconceivable that Nouvel and Pavka, the only two in Diaghilev's entourage who knew Valentin and Yury well, were kept in the dark, but they too were silent on the matter. The only person who certainly knew about the disappearance of Diaghilev's half-brothers was Kochno. But he too said nothing, either in his own writings or in subsequent interviews. It's possible that Diaghilev asked his friends not to mention it, fearing that imprudent talk about Valentin could endanger his remaining relatives in Russia.

OGPU photograph of Valentin Diaghilev in custody

According to Grigoriev, Diaghilev was 'gloomy and taciturn' throughout the spring of 1928, and his mind frequently strayed from company business.[3] Grigoriev and Kochno were given additional responsibilities for the new season, which would feature three premieres: *Ode*, *Apollon musagète* and *The Gods Go a-Begging*. The last of these, which was made exclusively for British audiences, used the music of Handel as arranged by Beecham. *Apollon* was a new work by Stravinsky, which, like *Renard* and *Oedipus Rex*, had not originally been commissioned by Diaghilev. Stravinsky had been asked to write the piece by the music department of the Library of Congress and was paid by the great patroness Elizabeth Sprague Coolidge. *Apollon* had its premiere in Washington, DC on 27 April 1928; by then the work had already been promised to Diaghilev. The latter had been ambivalent about showcasing a 'second-hand' work by Stravinsky until the composer cunningly suggested that *Apollon* could serve as a showpiece for Lifar.[4] It was some consolation to Diaghilev that a premiere in Washington meant no competition for him; over in Europe he could simply present the ballet as a new Stravinsky creation that had been made exclusively for him. He tried to put the composer in his place by making condescending remarks about Stravinsky's patroness ('This American woman is completely deaf'). But the composer's comeback was devastating: 'She may be deaf, but she pays.'[5] The fact that Diaghilev could no longer afford a composer of his stature and was thus forced to import 'foreign ballets' would become a growing source of frustration.

The third ballet, and the first premiere, had been written by a very young (and thus very cheap) Russian composer named Nicolas Nabokov, who arrived in France in mid-1924. Nabokov was certainly the least talented of all the Russian composers Diaghilev ever worked with, and it seems inconceivable that this would have escaped the impresario's notice. But Nabokov had other qualities: he was intelligent, cultured and articulate, but above all he had been a regular guest of Valentin's family in St Petersburg. He had played in an amateur orchestra with Pavel and Alyosha, the two nephews who had been killed in the Civil War; the conductor had been Valentin himself.[6] Perhaps this fact alone would have been reason to hire Nabokov. This personal connection did not prevent Diaghilev from entrusting Nabokov's creation to the inexperienced Kochno. He gave the commission for *Ode* to Nabokov some time in the first half of 1927. The young Russian artist Pavel Tchelitchew was brought in to design the sets.

The only work that Diaghilev expended any personal energy on that spring was *Apollon*, which Balanchine would choreograph and for which the 'naïve' painter Bauchant would make the sets and costumes. Stravinsky had finished the first part of the music the previous summer. Diaghilev took a day-trip to Nice, where Stravinsky was living, and it was there that he heard the music for the first time. He wrote to Lifar in glowing terms about Stravinsky's new creation: 'The work of course is amazing, unprecedentally quiet and clear; a contrapuntal piece of exceptional delicacy, featuring transparent noble themes, all in a major key, a music not of this earth but from somewhere on high.'[7]

Six months later they met again in Nice, now with Balanchine. This was the first direct collaboration between the composer and the young choreographer and the start of a long and fruitful relationship, which would endure until Stravinsky's death.

On 30 March in Nice, Diaghilev gave a charity gala arranged by Grand Duke Mikhail Mikhailovich, a Romanoff who had emigrated to western Europe long before the revolution. His wife, Countess Torby, was a direct descendant of Pushkin. She owned eleven of the great poet's letters and had inveigled the impresario into accepting the job by promising to leave him one in her will. This was reason enough to accept the assignment. Like so many others of his generation, Diaghilev revered Pushkin, but his admiration for the writer had become all the more fervent since the Revolution had cut him off from his homeland. It was not only the letters of Pushkin that interested him: he had recently become a passionate collector of antique Russian books in general. A great deal of his energy, and an increasing amount of his money, went to slake his thirst for old books, for which he scoured the whole of Europe, from Greece to Poland. He would spend entire days in antiquarian bookshops, and if he had no time to check out a hot tip himself, he would send Kochno to investigate or ask acquaintances who lived nearby to buy him the volumes in question.[8] Shortly after amending her will to include Diaghilev, Countess Torby died, and the impresario inherited the promised letter (to the poet's mother-in-law). In the meantime the impresario was busily raising money to acquire the remaining ten letters, which were even more appealing, being addressed to his fiancée Natalia Goncharova. This lay behind his decision to sell the original curtain to Picasso's *Three-Cornered Hat* for the considerable sum of 175,000 francs, with the help of the artist himself and his dealer Rosenberg.[9]

The rest of May was spent preparing for the premieres. Kochno the tyro producer had not been equal to the task entrusted to him. This was hardly surprising, as Diaghilev had thrown him in at the deep end with this assignment. Indeed, nobody working on *Ode* had any experience with a show of that scale (with the exception of Massine, who was only responsible for the choreography). Nabokov was twenty-five, Tchelitchew twenty-nine and Kochno, who was officially in charge, was a mere twenty-four. When Diaghilev arrived in Paris with the company in late May, ten days before the season was scheduled to open, *Ode* was still in embryonic form and the impresario had to pull out all the stops to save the production.

Nabokov described how Diaghilev took control in early June, rapidly whipping the half-complete ballet into shape:

> He supervised the dyeing, cutting, and sewing of costumes. He was
> present at every orchestra and choral rehearsal and made the conductor,
> Désormière, the soloists, and the chorus repeat sections of the music over

and over again until they blended well with the choreographic motions and the light-play of Tchelitchew's scenery. He encouraged the leisurely and sluggish stagehands of the Théâtre Sarah Bernhardt by bribes and flattery. He helped all of us paint the props and the scenery.

But above all else he spent two whole nights directing the complicated lighting rehearsals, shouting at Tchelitchew and at his technical aides when the delicate lighting machinery went wrong, at me when my piano playing slackened and became uneven, and at Lifar when his steps ceased following the rhythm of the music and the changes of lighting.[10]

Thanks to Diaghilev's last-minute intervention, *Ode* was saved. Nevertheless, the reviews were tepid. It couldn't have helped matters that the ballet was sandwiched between *Le Pas d'acier* and *Les Noces*, two of the best things the Ballets Russes had done since the war. *Ode* must have seemed especially weak in such august company. The premiere of *Apollon* proved to be Balanchine's second triumph in the space of a year (after *La Chatte*).

Diaghilev took little pleasure in the success, however. Despite his avowed appreciation for the music, the production bore little of his own personal stamp. Stravinsky had worked mostly on his own, as had the young Balanchine, who was now eager to set off down his own path. The impresario felt that the only thing that really interested him – the creative moment, his own artistic contribution – was being taken from him.

After the brief season in Paris there was, as always, a longer season in London, from 25 June to 28 July, after which the company ended the summer in Ostend with performances on 29 and 30 July. In London, Diaghilev had lost the exclusive support of Lord Rothermere, who had financed the last few London seasons, but thanks to the intervention of the tireless Wollheim, Diaghilev found new backers, and their time in England proved much more lucrative than in recent years. 'The first week was packed,' Diaghilev wrote to Prince Argutinsky, 'and the success was outstanding. The dancers were covered with flowers. The press was stupid as always, but kind. The King of Spain went almost directly from the railway station to the theatre.'[11] This financial success set off a frenzy of book buying, including a rare edition of Pushkin for which he shelled out 3,500 francs.[12] This was followed a few weeks later by the purchase of the remaining ten letters from the estate of the Countess Torby, for 30,000 francs.[13]

Diaghilev and Kochno

The acquisition of the Pushkin letters was hugely significant to Diaghilev, who devotes several pages to the topic in his very brief 'memoirs'.[14] By way of comparison, the only subject that occupies more space in that work was the historic production of *Boris Godunov* in Paris in 1908. In those few years of bibliomania, Diaghilev would assemble a collection of antique Russian books that was, according to Zilbershteyn, unrivalled outside Russia. Besides the above-mentioned letters, he also acquired a handwritten poem by Pushkin, two manuscripts and four letters by Lermontov, and manuscripts by such writers as Gogol, Glinka and Turgenev.[15] He kept a catalogue and compiled extensive notecards, full of bibliographic and historical information for the most important books. For the first time in his life he rented an apartment in Paris, mainly to have a place to keep his ever expanding collection. His insatiable desire for costly books and manuscripts had the unexpected effect of making him more disciplined in his personal spending habits. He decided to publish the Pushkin letters in October 1929, but this was to be a vain hope, as Diaghilev's days were already numbered.

*

In 1921 Diaghilev had been diagnosed with diabetes, but he made little effort to modify his diet. His frenetic lifestyle, with recurring bouts of intense stress, also took its toll on his health. Strict diets alternated with periods of unbridled gluttony. His weight fluctuated wildly, which exacerbated his diabetes. Starting around 1927, he began to suffer from furunculosis (regular outbreaks of boils and carbuncles), which in turn led to major infections and attacks of fever.[16] In a world without penicillin, such infections could be life-threatening, a fact that Diaghilev knew all too well. All his life he had been terrified of germs and infections, and now it would seem that his worst fears were finally coming true.

Yet by August Diaghilev was back in Venice again, undeterred by its unwholesome damps and ready to plan a new season. He went to Warsaw to try out dancers and look for books, and while there he took the opportunity to drop in on an old friend. Dima Filosofov was still living in the Polish capital, publishing the anti-Bolshevik newspaper *Za Svobodu* (For Freedom). Diaghilev wrote to Lifar that Poland made him think of 'our Mother Russia' but that Warsaw itself was 'a pleasant little German town that I unfortunately saw too little of on account of the frightful cold'. He cheerfully added that he had a large boil under his arm which had burst during one of his first nights in the city. Somewhere in the middle of the letter he writes, 'tell Pavka I'm going to see Dima and tell him all about it in great detail'.[17]

Diaghilev did see Dima, but the latter was apparently not in the mood to reminisce about the good old days. According to Lifar, the two men 'had nothing in common any more, and Diaghilev was taken aback to be hectored by the fanatical journalist, who attacked [him] for wasting his time with utterly trivial, futile matters at a time when …'[18] Lifar's account ends here, but it is not difficult to fill in the gaps. Filosofov had evolved into a major political commentator in Warsaw and become one of the leaders of the anti-communist resistance in exile. There is a good chance that he had heard the rumours about their family, and now took Diaghilev to task for his preoccupation with frivolous things like premieres and old books after all that had happened. The fact that Filosofov had adopted his mother's point of view ('political action is far more exalted than artistic expression'), against which the two men had so vigorously rebelled in their youth, must have struck Diaghilev as a cruel irony. The distance between the two former friends had become unbridgeable, and this would be their last meeting.

Diaghilev had lengthy conversations with Prokofiev about the new ballet he envisioned. There was already a synopsis, a quarter of which was by Kochno and three-quarters by Diaghilev, according to Prokofiev. The subject was the parable of the prodigal son, 'transplanted to Russian soil', as Diaghilev put it.[19] We know from Prokofiev's diary how personally invested Diaghilev was in this ballet, more than any other production in his final years. Although Prokofiev was unhappy about working with Kochno, who would be credited as the official librettist, he found the subject matter sufficiently inspiring, and after more tortuous financial negotiations, he agreed to undertake the project on 9 November 1928. The contract for *Le Fils prodigue* was signed, and only two weeks later Prokofiev had already composed a substantial amount of the score, which was remarkably fast even for him. On 23 November Prokofiev played his music to Diaghilev in the company of a guest from the Soviet Union, Vsevolod Meyerhold, who had come to Paris, primarily to confer with the impresario. The piece was received with great enthusiasm. Diaghilev advised Prokofiev to cut a specific dance number, but otherwise he praised him profusely for the serenity and clarity of music, which was unlike almost anything he had written before.

His enthusiasm for Prokofiev's music came at a time when his relationship with Stravinsky had reached its nadir. This was largely due to Stravinsky's decision to accept a commission from a new company under the artistic leadership of Diaghilev's old star Ida Rubinstein. Of course this was not the first time Diaghilev had had to deal with competing companies, but they had not been Russian, and they had never struck at the heart of his own entourage. But the ambitious productions Rubinstein wanted to make in 1928 were evocative of the kinds of ballets Diaghilev had put on before the war. This was a clever move on her part: there was a strong nostalgia for those years and those shows among Diaghilev's audiences, as well as among members of his own company. All the performances would take place at the Paris Opéra, which was still the heart of Parisian musical life and a theatre that Diaghilev himself had not played since 1922 (with the exception of two shows in the winter of 1927).

Rubinstein's financial resources were unmatched. It was said that she spent five million francs on her venture, many times more than Diaghilev's annual investments.[20] She had asked Maurice Ravel and Darius Milhaud to write new music for her, and Bronislava Nijinska to do the choreography.

Benois would design the Ravel production, and maybe some other shows too. Even though Diaghilev had written off Benois as a designer, it must have pained him to see him working for the competition. But the greatest blow was the fact that Rubinstein had managed to snare Stravinsky, whom she had hired to write a major new ballet exclusively for her company. The work would be based on themes of Tchaikovsky, with sets by Benois. This was too much for Diaghilev.

Prokofiev remarked that Diaghilev 'spoke with extraordinary venom about Ida Rubinstein's premiere',[21] which he had made the point of crossing the Channel to attend, as the Ballets Russes were touring England and Scotland at the time. That venom also permeates two letters that Diaghilev wrote to Lifar during his short stay in Paris, in which he described the Ravel work (*Boléro*) and the first performance of the Stravinsky ballet *Le Baiser de la fée*. The performances were a great event in Paris, an occasion to see and be seen. Besides the regular entourage, Mayakovsky was also present; like Meyerhold, he was in the midst of another tour of France.

The first letter was written on 23 November:

> Paris is a terrible city. One hasn't five minutes to write a couple of words. Everyone has come and there's terrible confusion. I'll start with Ida – the house was packed, but the crowds had been planted by her. However she didn't send any of us a ticket … The performance was nothing but provincial boredom. Everything was interminably long, even the Ravel which went on for a whole fourteen minutes. The worst of all was Ida herself … She appeared with [the dancer Anatole] Vilzak but no one in the theatre, not even I, recognised her. Hunched, with dishevelled red hair, hatless, in ballet shoes (all the others were in helmets, feathers and high heels) – in order to appear shorter. She was a total failure. She can't dance at all. She stands on her toes with bent knees and Vilzak keeps moving her along … All that's left of her face is a huge open mouth and a mass of clenched teeth that represents a smile. Pure horror …
>
> Bronya hasn't a single new idea, it's all just a lot of running about, sloppiness and completely unremarkable choreography …[22]

In the next letter he had some choice words for Stravinsky:

> I just got back from the theatre with a headache from the whole miserable

spectacle, but most of all from Stravinsky … Exactly what it is is difficult to determine. An ill-judged choice of music by Tchaikovsky, tiresome and lachrymose, allegedly brilliantly orchestrated by Igor. I say 'allegedly' because to me it sounds grey, and the whole style is moribund.

Diaghilev concluded with a lament, which referred to his own situation and which was unusually morbid even given his present circumstances:

I'm constantly asking myself the same question – what's the point of this? No, it doesn't matter if it's the Bolsheviks who come or Napoleon, let them. If only someone would blow up all these old barracks, with their audiences and their red-headed … who fancy themselves dancers, with their squandered millions and their bought composers.[23]

Diaghilev was not afraid to voice such opinions publicly either. In an interview with the émigré magazine *Vozrozhdeniye*, Diaghilev again aimed his poison darts at Rubinstein:

Rubinstein herself doesn't realise that the art of dance is the most difficult, the most delicate and the most cruel art. It doesn't forgive mistakes. The hunched figure of poor Rubinstein with her feebly bent knees, the complete confusion of her classical spasms, made a second-ranking but trained dancer in her company seem like the heroine of old-fashioned adagio dances devised half a century ago.[24]

Yet Diaghilev's enthusiasm for dance was less dimmed than he sometimes led his closest friends and associates to believe. In that same interview he also made a few thoughtful observations on his own productions. He responded to a conservative article in another émigré magazine, in which he was portrayed as an out-and-out classicist. That was too much to take, and in the interview, Diaghilev tried to elucidate his own brand of neoclassicism:

Duncan and Dalcroze and Laban and Wigman were splendid forerunners in the search for a new school. Their work on the development of the human body, that most perfect choreographic instrument, deserves universal approval. But their battle with 'obsolete' classical dance led Germany up a blind alley from which she couldn't extricate herself.

However, it absolutely does not follow from all of this that the future of modern choreography lies in a passion for preserving classical uniformity. The proponents of this view should join a society for the protection of ancient monuments, but must absolutely not give advice to modern architects.

The creators of the marvellous American skyscrapers could easily have turned their hands to the Venus of Milo since they had received a complete classical education. But if anything does offend our eye in New York, it's the Greek porticos of the Carnegie Library and the Doric columns of the railway stations. The skyscrapers have their own kind of classicism, i.e. our kind. Their lines, scale, proportions are the formula of our classical achievements, they are the true palaces of the modern age. It's the same with choreography. Our plastic and dynamic structure must have the same foundation as the classical work which enables us to seek new forms. It too has to be well proportioned and harmonious, but that doesn't mean propounding a compulsory 'cult' of classicism in the creative work of the modern choreographer. Classicism is a means, not an end.[25]

To hear Diaghilev talk so rhapsodically about the art of dance makes it hard to believe that he had lost all interest in his company and ballet in general, as many would later claim. Kochno went the furthest in this regard, when he wrote that Diaghilev 'avoided talking about the world of this ballet company, peopled with unconscious and rebellious subjects whom, in the last years of his life, he ruled wearily and, it seemed, out of obligation'.[26]

The truth was more complicated. Diaghilev was getting old; in 1929 he would turn fifty-seven. Unquestionably, managing the company had become more of a routine, and he devoted more of his time to other matters than he had in the first twenty years of his career outside Russia. But he continued to work enthusiastically on new productions and to speak passionately about his output. To his not inconsiderable satisfaction, Diaghilev signed a contract in late November 1928 with the Italian artist Giorgio de Chirico, who was then at the height of his fame. De Chirico was to design a new ballet, *Le Bal*, with music by the Italian neoclassicist Vittore Rieti, who had already worked with Diaghilev in 1925. On 26 November Diaghilev breakfasted with Prokofiev and Meyerhold, and spoke to the latter about a joint season in Paris, in which they would present their performances on alternate days. Serious preparations were made (Diaghilev spoke to Prokofiev about the project and described it to Lifar).[27] The idea of touring the Soviet Union had understandably been dropped, but Diaghilev was still very keen to work with avant-garde artists from his homeland. He wrote to Lifar:

> For his part, all traces of political expression will be completely eliminated. I think this could be a very interesting and significant partnership for both of us. I am convinced that he is talented and we need him right now; tomorrow will perhaps be too late. The only one who is indignant is of course Valechka, who roars and rages against it – but it can't be helped! – people like him and Pavka are sweet, but if one listens to them – one might as well go straight to the cemetery.[28]

In late 1928 Diaghilev was anything but world-weary and had certainly not stopped discussing future plans. He was, however, increasingly moody and often shut himself off from even his closest friends.

Maybe he was in one of these petulant moods when a thoughtless, or vengeful, action on his part ended up alienating the most highly regarded artist in his circle. Sometime between the autumn of 1928 and the spring of 1929 he suddenly decided to cut part of Stravinsky's *Apollon* (the 'Terpsichore variation', to be precise). Diaghilev was, of course, well known for 'improving' other people's intellectual property, but in the past he had always done so with existing scores, generally by dead composers (with Rimsky-Korsakov as a notable exception). Stravinsky had provoked him by going to work for Rubinstein and asserting his independence. The fact that Diaghilev had not played a creative role in one of Stravinsky's ballets since *Les Noces* was also a source of irritation. He surely knew that Stravinsky would soon find out about the cuts, and that he would be furious, but that did not seem to bother him. Or perhaps it had been his plan all along to provoke a conflict and bring matters to a head. Certainly, this would fit into a pattern we have seen before in his relations with his close friends and associates.

It would seem, however, that by the start of 1929 Stravinsky was still unaware of what had happened. Diaghilev gave a few performances in Paris at the Opéra, and had the insane Nijinsky brought to see *Petrushka* there on 27 December. He had done the same five years before, and it was just as heart-rending on this occasion. Karsavina, now forty-five and no longer at the top

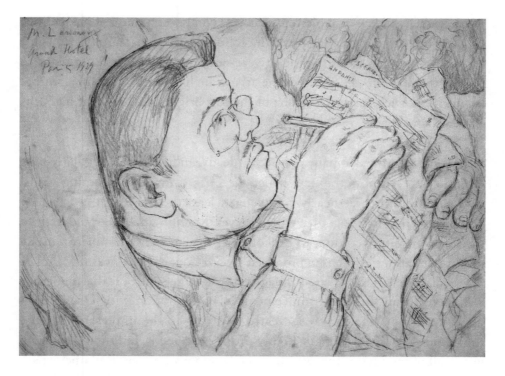

Diaghilev, by Larionov

of her game, once more played the female lead. In the audience was Harry Kessler, who was again in negotiations with Diaghilev about a new ballet, to music by Kurt Weill.

At first, Kessler could not believe it was really Nijinsky that Diaghilev was supporting on his arm. Diaghilev asked Kessler to help him: 'Diaghilev had taken him by the arm. To get down the three flights of stairs, he asked me to take the other arm, as [Nijinsky], who had once seemed capable of leaping over houses, felt his way – hesitantly, anxiously – from one step to the next … With his big eyes, like a sick animal, he gave me a look that was uncomprehending and yet deeply moving.'[29]

According to Diaghilev, Nijinsky did not want to leave the theatre. That night the regulars dined at the Café de la Paix, as they had in the good old days. Karsavina, Misia Sert, Gordon Craig and Kessler put in an appearance, but the mood was sombre.

That evening there was a new addition to Diaghilev's entourage: Igor

Markevich, a sixteen-year-old musician and composer, a pupil of Nadia Bou-
langer, who had probably been introduced to Diaghilev that autumn. Diaghilev was in love for the first time in years and was already making plans to
initiate the boy into the world of the arts, as he had done with all his former
lovers. Markevich's arrival was one of the few bright spots in what had otherwise been a dismal year.

In January 1929 the company played Bordeaux, and Diaghilev regularly rang
Prokofiev to see how the new ballet, *Le Fils prodigue*, was coming along.
By then, the work was nearly complete, at least the music. On 6 February
he visited Prokofiev, together with Nouvel, Kochno and Lifar, to listen to
the final version. According to Prokofiev, Diaghilev had 'a number of useful
recommendations', which he promised to carry out. By the next day Prokofiev had made 'all the changes Diaghilev had suggested'; all that remained
was to 'chop up the fourth movement, in collaboration with Diaghilev'.[30]
Their musical partnership was greatly satisfying to the impresario because
the composer clearly thought highly of his judgement, faithfully following
nearly all of his advice. This was not merely opportunism on Prokofiev's part.
As he writes many times in his diary, he had great respect for Diaghilev's
musicality, and in all the years they worked together there were only a few
occasions on which the composer did not follow his suggestions. The one fly
in the ointment was Prokofiev's fraught relationship with Kochno, whom the
composer tolerated out of necessity. Prokofiev took no account of the librettist and composed when the spirit moved him, forcing Kochno to dream up
a plot to a pre-existing score. As a result Kochno's contribution was utterly
insubstantial. Diaghilev nevertheless insisted that he had been responsible
for one-third of the ballet, as stipulated in the contract. This was the impresario's way of securing his protégé's financial future: as co-author, he would
be entitled to royalties for every performance of *Le Fils*.

On 16 March, Prokofiev presented Diaghilev with the complete piano
score. When Prokofiev told him that the ballet was dedicated to him, 'He was
visibly flattered (much more than by the dedication of the other two ballets)
and said that this was especially pleasing to him as *The Prodigal Son* was his
favourite of my ballets. He kissed me and we bade each other farewell until
Monte Carlo.'[31]

To anyone who has followed the development of *Le Fils* in Prokofiev's

Ansermet, by Picasso

diary, this will come as no surprise. There was hardly any other production in the previous two or three years that had filled Diaghilev with so much enthusiasm. It also seems safe to assume that he identified with the title character and perceived a dramatic link between the biblical parable and his own exile. His predilection for theatrical gestures in the creation of his personal mythology and his obsession with 'signs' and 'connections' undoubtedly contributed to this.

To the outside world it seemed that Diaghilev was his old self again, and he appeared to throw himself into the new season with renewed energy. But his worries persisted. Ernest Ansermet had been invited to conduct several concerts in Leningrad and Moscow, and Diaghilev had asked him to 'run some errands' for him in Leningrad. Nouvel wrote to Diaghilev that Ansermet had agreed and requested that 'everything be brought to Geneva'. The nature of these 'errands' remains a mystery. Maybe Diaghilev kept them secret from Nouvel; maybe Nouvel left out any details in his letter for fear of Soviet spies. Yet it seems highly probable that the errands had something to do with Diaghilev's family. We know for certain that Ansermet visited Valentin's two surviving children, Sergey and Vasily, in Leningrad.[32] By then, their mother had also been deported. The children still had no information about their parents, and relatives of 'disappeared' persons faced a highly uncertain future. The Soviet Union under Stalin was in the midst of its first five-year plan, and the regime was becoming increasingly brutal. Assuming that Diaghilev had asked Ansermet to bring him news of his family, the reports he brought back could not have been encouraging.

Nor was all well on other fronts. Stravinsky had since found out about the cuts Diaghilev had made to *Apollon*, and he had put his agent, the shrewd music publisher Gavril Paichadze, on the case. And then there was Benois. The two old friends no longer saw much of each other, but neither wanted to give up on a relationship of so many years, however taxing it had become. Benois's hope that his involvement in Rubinstein's season would bring him new celebrity, or at least appreciation, proved vain. After the performance of *Petrushka* that Nijinsky attended, Benois wrote a gloomy, peevish letter to Diaghilev in which he blamed him for the failure of his own artistic career and bitterly lamented the parting of their ways. Benois, like so many other artists in exile, found it hard to accept his newly marginal status in western

Europe. For a man of so many talents, who had commanded such respect in his homeland, this pill was a hard one to swallow. We do not know if Diaghilev replied to the letter. However, we do know that when Benois opened a small exhibition of his work in the spring of 1929, Diaghilev did not come to the viewing. Benois then wrote him a short note, undoubtedly meant as an attempt at reconciliation:

> Don't be a swine; come visit your old friend's exhibition. I think the odd thing will even please you, if only for nostalgic reasons. Oh, Seryozha, why does this life … arrange things so that people who love each other tenderly are so different? (I continue to think that you're not completely without feelings for me, while it's not worth expanding on mine for you) … Well, in a word, come![33]

This olive branch marks the end of the long and rich correspondence between Diaghilev and Benois, and its melancholy is still palpable. We do not know if Diaghilev took Benois up on his invitation.

It was a busy time. The company was booked in Monte Carlo until 12 May; on 21 May the new season in Paris would begin, featuring the premiere of *Le Fils* and a new version of Stravinsky's *Renard*. Diaghilev was again plagued by boils, which grew into abscesses and forced him to take a break from his busy lifestyle. By the end of April he and Kochno had gone to Paris, where Prokofiev's ballet was being rehearsed. (*Le Bal*, on the other hand, would be premiered in Monte Carlo.) Around this time Diaghilev received a letter from Paichadze, who threatened to treat the cut to *Apollon* as a breach of contract and to deny him the right to stage any further performances. Paichadze was already in negotiations with Ida Rubinstein over the possibility of transferring the performance rights to her. Diaghilev responded angrily to the letter, saying that the publisher had no reason to suspect that he would 'renege on his earlier promise to undo the cut'.[34]

The premiere of *Le Fils* was a great success, thanks to Prokofiev's brilliant music and, to a lesser degree, Balanchine's equally brilliant choreography. The press complained about Balanchine, claiming that the dances were cold and self-consciously modern. (Prokofiev himself shared this opinion.) From a twenty-first century standpoint this is hard to understand, since the ballet has remained in the repertoire, and three-quarters of a century later still

Stravinsky, by Larionov

has the power to astonish and move audiences. The last scene, in which the prodigal son is embraced by his father and carried off stage like a little boy, has an iconic power that rivals Rembrandt's famous depiction of the scene, a painting that Diaghilev and Balanchine knew so well from their visits to the Hermitage.

In Paris, Diaghilev visited a doctor, who prescribed him rest and a special diet, accompanied by a stern warning.[35] After that Diaghilev left for Berlin.

Shortly before his departure, on 10 June, another conflict broke out. Prokofiev, who also used the services of Paichadze, published the score of *Le Fils prodigue* without crediting Boris Kochno as the librettist. Kochno responded by suing both Prokofiev and Paichadze and seeking to have the score withdrawn.[36] Prokofiev was furious at Kochno's reaction, which seemed extreme, given the paucity of his contribution. The next day the composer went to see his lawyer, where to his surprise he bumped into Stravinsky, who had been sent there by Paichadze. The composer believed that Kochno was getting back at him for his response to the cuts to *Apollon*. 'I came here especially for this,' said Stravinsky to Prokofiev. 'It's not Kochno, but Diaghilev. Kochno wouldn't dare do something like this without Diaghilev.'[37]

He might well have been right. At the lawyer's office Stravinsky monopolised the conversation, pleading what he saw as their common cause. Stravinsky's parting shot was, 'I am very interested in this business, and not just out of love for you but out of hatred for Kochno. But it's not just Kochno here, it's Diaghilev too, and it's not just against you but against the publisher. Paichadze and I are raising the rates [for sheet music]. You'll see, he'll be paying for our lawyer too.'[38]

In many respects the conflict resembled Diaghilev's earlier courtroom battle with Bakst, and, as before, the opposing parties allowed matters to get completely out of hand. But despite everything, the ties between the two men were still strong. Strange as it may seem, just a few days later Stravinsky asked Ansermet to tell Diaghilev that he would be in London for a few weeks at the same time as the impresario. Moreover, the composer expressed surprise at the fact that Diaghilev 'seemed to be avoiding [him] for reasons that only he knows'.[39] Perhaps this was not just Stravinsky's imagination. We do know that the two were in Berlin at the same time without making contact.

In Berlin Ansermet conducted performances by the Ballets Russes, and it was probably then that Diaghilev first heard about the situation in Leningrad, though, as was his custom, he spoke to no one about such private matters. A bright spot in these troubled times was the performance of *Le Sacre du printemps*, the first time the work was danced in the German capital. It received an unexpectedly rapturous reception: in the past Berlin had always been resistant to the charms of the Ballets Russes.

Doctor's orders forgotten, Diaghilev was constantly on the go. After Berlin the company went to Paris via Cologne, and then travelled on to London. On 24 June Diaghilev was waiting for a train with Kochno and Markevich at the Gare du Nord when he caught sight of Stravinsky. 'I suddenly felt a hand on my shoulder,' Stravinsky later told Prokofiev. 'It was Diaghilev, who said, in a somewhat forced way, "Are you going to London? Me too. This will give us a chance to catch up."'[40] But when the train arrived, each man went to his own carriage and neither took the initiative to call on the other. In London they both stayed at Albert Court, in adjacent apartments. The walls were so thin that they could hear each other's conversations, but they still managed to avoid each other. The two would never meet again.

If Diaghilev had been more open – about the fate of his family and his failing health –Stravinsky might not have been so standoffish. But Diaghilev was obsessed with keeping up appearances; the slightest hint of vulnerability had to be avoided at all costs, and it was this feature of his personality that so antagonised his friends and associates. Incidentally, the conflict did not in any way dim his love of Stravinsky's music. A few months earlier, he had stated in an interview, 'Stravinsky ... is the living incarnation of true passion, of true love of art and a never-ending quest ... Stravinsky is always raging, seeking, and with every step forward, he rejects himself as it were, rejects what he was in his earlier works.'[41] And in London, in his room, where he could hear Stravinsky talking to Vera, he wrote to Markevich, expressing his joy at Stravinsky's great success there:

> Yesterday *Le Sacre* was a real triumph. The imbeciles finally grasped it. *The Times* says that *Le Sacre* is for the twentieth century what Beethoven's Ninth Symphony was for the nineteenth! At last! In life one must have patience and be somewhat philosophical, so as to look down from on high at the obstacles which small and limited people put up against any attempt to overcome mediocrity. My God, it's all so vulgar, like good weather, but it can't be helped – one can't live without the hope of seeing again at dawn the rays of the rising sun.[42]

But in England, Diaghilev's health continued to decline. He again consulted a doctor, who advised him to hire a nurse to look after his boils, but Diaghilev characteristically refused. Instead he had Kochno drain them every day and bind the wounds.[43] According to Nouvel, Diaghilev had a 'whole crop of boils on his stomach'.[44] His physical deterioration shocked his London friends, but he continued to give interviews, attend social functions and drink champagne. After another triumphant season, the company went to Ostend for two performances, and from there via Paris to Vichy, where four performances were given. On 4 August the Ballets Russes performed for the last time.

During the brief stop in Paris, Diaghilev's personal physician urgently advised him to rest and take a cure in Vichy. Diaghilev disregarded this advice, instead taking Markevich on a tour along the Rhine, to acquaint his young pupil with the musical culture of Germany. In Baden-Baden they spoke to Paul Hindemith about the new ballet, and they heard his *Lehrstücke* to a text by Bertolt Brecht. Darius Milhaud was also in Baden-Baden, as

Pavka Koribut, by Picasso

were Princesse de Polignac and Nicolas Nabokov. 'Despite his appearance, his mood seemed happy,' Nabokov later wrote, 'He talked gaily about his plans for the rest of the summer and for the autumn season.'[45]

In Munich they saw *Die Zauberflöte* (The Magic Flute) conducted by Richard Strauss. On 1 August Diaghilev also attended a performance of *Tristan und Isolde*. It had been almost forty years since he and Dima had taken their grand tour of the European capitals and he had seen his first Wagner opera in Vienna. 'Today, while watching *Tristan*, I shed bitter tears,' he wrote to Lifar.[46] When Markevich asked him what the matter was, he simply said, 'It's the same as with [my] cousin Dima.'[47]

The next day they saw *Così fan tutte* and *Die Meistersinger*. After that they left for Salzburg, where they saw *Don Giovanni*. Throughout the trip Diaghilev had succeeded in concealing his health problems from Markevich.[48] He wrote to Pavka, urging him to come to Venice, and then travelled to Vevey in Switzerland, where he bid an emotional farewell to his last protégé.

On 7 August the dying impresario dragged himself to his beloved Venice. The next evening he checked into the Grand Hotel des Bains de Mer. Later that night Lifar arrived, surprised that Diaghilev had not come to meet him at the pier. By then Diaghilev was suffering from blood poisoning, as a result of the abscesses, and his fever was soaring. By the 12th he was too sick to leave his bed, and Lifar took on the role of nurse. Neither man knew that Diaghilev was dying. In his lucid moments he spoke of the upcoming season and of his most recent travels. Lying in bed, he sang part of *Tristan* and the 'Pathétique' Symphony: Wagner and Tchaikovsky, the two heroes of his youth. Kochno arrived on the 16th, after receiving a telegram with the words: 'Am sick, come quickly'. Two days later Misia Sert and Coco Chanel came too. Misia was dressed in white, and after the women had left, Diaghilev said to Kochno, 'They looked so young … They were all in white. They were *so white*!'[49]

On the 18th his fever climbed to forty degrees. They received a telegram from Pavka which said, 'Looking forward to getting in on Monday the 18th. Get well soon!'[50] Diaghilev laughed and said, 'Of course, Pavka will be late again and get here after I'm dead.' That evening a priest was sent for to give the dying man absolution.[51] In the early hours of 19 August 1929, Diaghilev's fever rose to forty-one degrees and he lost consciousness. He died at daybreak, as the first rays of the sun fell on his face.

Diaghilev died as impecuniously as he had lived, and Misia and Coco paid for the funeral. A brief *panikhida* (requiem service) was held at his bed, as was customary in the Orthodox Church, and then the body was taken to San Michele, where it was buried in the Greek section. The next day the world learned of the great impresario's passing, and it was front-page news.

Stravinsky heard the news on 21 August. He and his sons had been visiting Prokofiev, who lived in the neighbourhood, and when he got home his wife was waiting at the door for him with a telegram saying that Diaghilev had 'died without suffering'.[52] Stravinsky was shocked; he hadn't seen it coming, and he was tormented by the thought that their final months had been marred by quarrels. Vera wrote to him:

> My friendship with you is linked to my friendship with Diaghilev. I cannot separate our relationship from that period. All morning I cried and cried.
>
> What will happen to the Ballets Russes now? Does this mean that everything is finished, all of the Russian seasons? Will there be no more performances?
>
> I feel sorry for the old fellows, Valechka, who was Diaghilev's oldest

friend, and Pavka – who will now be thrown out into the street. All this is terribly sad.[53]

Vera's letter was followed by one from Ansermet, who seemed to divine Stravinsky's feelings:

I was devastated to hear of Sergey Pavlovich's death, and … despite everything that has happened (and perhaps because of it), I thought that this news must have affected you deeply as well. A piece of our lives is now gone … I feel as if I am taking part in the family mourning, since I was brought into the circle by you. Poor Serge died on bad terms with those who should have been his best friends, and alone – in short, like a vagabond. I think with great sympathy of his last moments.[54]

It was left to Nouvel to sort out the estate. The official heir was not Pavka but Diaghilev's elderly aunt Yulia Parensova-Diaghileva, one of his father's sisters, who lived in Sofia. But Aunt Yulia wrote a kind note to Nouvel in which she renounced the entire inheritance and entrusted it to Nouvel and Lifar.[55] Nouvel organised a service of remembrance for Diaghilev at the Russian Cathedral of St Alexander Nevsky in Paris. A meeting was held to decide the future of the Ballets Russes. It was agreed to at least honour outstanding contracts, but even that proved unfeasible. Nouvel was seen by most as the obvious representative of the impresario's surviving friends and next of kin. Prokofiev wrote to him on 25 August:

What a terrible thing Sergey Pavlovich's death is. He was such a lively, vital human being and the impression he made was always so vivid that for me, who wasn't near him at the time of his death, it's impossible to believe that Diaghilev is no more!
   I'd like to ask you about many things: how did the illness come about, could one have saved him, what were his last moments like – but you probably haven't the time for that now. News gets to my provincial abode only through the newspapers, and I learn the odd thing from Stravinsky, who is sixty kilometres away.[56]

A few days later Prokofiev added that Diaghilev was a 'giant, undoubtedly the only one whose dimensions increase the more he recedes into the distance'.[57]

Also on the 25th, Benois wrote an emotional letter to his old school friend Valechka:

A part of me has been cut off and I feel I've become a cripple. And it's weird, since in these last years Seryozha didn't play a big part in my life: our paths went in different directions and I didn't feel that I needed him, either purely for my work or in a spiritual sense. And now, suddenly, it seems as if I'm still to a very great extent 'filled with him'; he occupies a unique place in my spirit, in my mind and in my heart; he continues to be there and by old habit I continue to turn to him constantly, to ask his opinion and at the same time to worry about him and to live for his interests … the passage of time will … show the true significance of this elemental being, one of the most curious and characteristic figures of our country, who brought together in his person all the fabulous beauty and all the inexhaustible might of Russian culture.[58]

It was not until the twenty-sixth that Stravinsky found the courage to write to Nouvel:

Although it's difficult for me to write these lines as I prefer silence to a letter, which expresses what one feels so feebly, all the same I decided to overcome my feelings, thinking you too would feel some relief, seeing (although you know this yourself) and feeling the keen pain which I carry at the sudden loss of my dearly loved Seryozha, and of which this letter is testimony!

When I came to from the terrible news (which I only received two days after Seryozha's death), my first thoughts were of you and Pavka, and this letter is therefore also addressed to him. In spite of the bitterness of your bereavement, I felt relief in the knowledge that besides me there are other people whom he loved very much and who mourn him bitterly in their heart. Know, my friends, that I share your sorrow with all my heart and I pray to our Lord … that He in his mercy give rest to his soul which possessed such richness and such sensitivity.[59]

The reply that Nouvel wrote to Stravinsky a few days later is a powerful monument to a friendship of many years and perhaps the most apt portrait ever made of Diaghilev:

Nouvel, by Bakst

I am sincerely touched by your heartfelt letter. I can see we feel exactly the same sorrow. I have lost a man to whom I was tied by a forty-year friendship, and I am happy that I never betrayed that friendship.

Many things united us, many things kept us apart. I often suffered because of him, I often got angry. But now, when he is in the grave, all is forgotten, all is forgiven, and I understood that one can't apply the normal measure of human relationships to this exceptional man.

He lived and died 'a favourite of the gods'. For he was a pagan, and a Dionysian pagan – not an Apollonian. He loved everything earthly – earthly love, earthly passions, earthly beauty. Heaven for him was just a lovely dome above the lovely earth. That doesn't mean he had no religious feeling. But that feeling was pagan rather than Christian.

Instead of faith he had superstition, instead of the fear of God terror of the universe and its secrets, instead of Christian meekness a delicate, almost childlike tenderness.

And his death was lovely – like a pagan's. He died in love and beauty, under the tender smile of those gods whom all his life he passionately served and worshipped.

And I think Christ cannot but love such a man.[60]

Less than three weeks after Nouvel sent his letter, Valentin Diaghilev was executed at the Solovki prison camp, together with about forty other prisoners. His family never knew his fate; even the news that he had been arrested and imprisoned was kept from them until after his death. Of course, the authorities had been keeping a close eye on Valentin because of the French government's great interest in him, and it is inconceivable he would have been killed if his half-brother had still been alive. The Soviets must have calculated that the French would have little interest in the prisoner after the impresario's death.

Sergey's two cousins, Pavka and Dima, both died in 1940, Pavka in Monte Carlo, Dima in Warsaw. Benois died in Paris in 1960, aged nearly ninety. He remained active as a critic and writer almost up to the end. Nouvel receded into the shadows, working as an adviser to various ballet and opera companies. He wrote the first biography of Diaghilev, which was never published, but which served as a basis for Arnold Haskell's book. He became Stravinsky's ghost-writer and wrote, among other texts, his 'autobiography' *Chronique de ma vie*. Of course, Stravinsky himself went on to have a brilliant career, becoming the most celebrated composer of his generation. Prokofiev returned to the Soviet Union, where his death in 1953 went almost unnoticed, as the composer had the misfortune to die on the same day as Stalin. Nijinsky died in the spring of 1950 in a psychiatric institution in London. Massine travelled the world as a choreographer, leading various companies that modelled themselves on Diaghilev's example. After the war, Balanchine spearheaded the great flowering of American ballet, redefining classical ballet for the twentieth century.

Diaghilev's family in the Soviet Union continued to be subjected to persecution. Valentin's son was arrested in 1937 and sent to the mines of Norilsk as an enemy of the people. Four years after Stalin's death he was rehabilitated and permitted to return to Leningrad, where he conducted a local orchestra. When Stravinsky visited the Soviet Union in 1967, he met this Sergey Diaghilev briefly. Sergey's daughter Yelena was an important source of both information and inspiration for this book. After a childhood in which she was shunted from one place of exile to another, in the late 1950s she and her father returned to Leningrad, where she taught English and French. She lived long enough to see the city's name changed back to St Petersburg. Her son, Sergey, still works there as a composer and conductor.

NOTES

Introduction: Death in Venice

1. Picasso once said that 'Diaghilev had done more to disseminate his fame internationally than Rosenberg's Paris shows'. Richardson, 2007, p. 379. It is safe to say that this observation could be applied to the avant-garde as a whole.

2. Benois to Nouvel, 25 August 1929. Karasik, 1995, p. 242.

3. Diaghilev is either joking or he has made a mistake. Chopin did not die in the Canary Islands but in Paris. Perhaps he was thinking of the time when the composer fell seriously ill while staying on the island of Mallorca in the Balearics.

4. Diaghilev to Diaghileva, 22 August 1902. IRLi, fond 102, ed. khr. 84, l.406–7.

5. See Dobuzhinsky, 1987, p. 200.

6. Diaghilev to Diaghileva, [October] 1902. IRLi, fond 102, ed. khr. 86, l.478–9.

7. Diaghilev to von Meck, 9 January 1900. '*Pis'ma S.P. Dyagileva V.V. fon Mekky*', in Belyaeva et al., 1989, p. 131.

8. Zilbershteyn and Samkov, 1982, ii, pp. 463–4.

1 A Big Head, 1872–1880

1. The poet Mikhail Lermontov served at the same barracks for several years.

2. Haskell and Nouvel, 1935, p. 10.

3. Lifar, 1994, p. 17.

4. Buckle, 1979, p. 6.

5. Bronislava Nijinska wrote about this in her *Early Memoirs*: 'Sergey Pavlovich told me sometime later that his big head had been the cause of his mother's death.' In Nijinska, 1982, p. 255.

6. Haskell and Nouvel, 1935.

7. Bowlt, 1979, p. 151.

8. For a description of Yevgenia Diaghileva's pregnancy, delivery and final illness, see Dyagileva, 1998, pp. 52–5.

9. Pavel Diaghilev to Anna Diaghileva, 29 March 1872. Ibid., p. 53.

10. Diagnosis and historical information from Dr N. E. van Trommel and Dr N. I. Grebensjikov, Radboud Ziekenhuis Nijmegen, on the basis of information ibid.

11. Ibid., p. 253.

12. Subbotin and Dyldin, 2003, p. 29. I am grateful to Oleg Brezgin for bringing this work to my attention.

13. Ibid., p. 30.

14. Ibid., pp. 19–20, n. 2.

15. Retold without irony in Haskell and Nouvel, 1935, p. 6.

16. Subbotin and Dyldin, 2003, p. 18.

17. For more about the history of vodka production, the licensing system and the reforms of 1863, see Pokhlyobkin, 1994, p. 197. I am grateful to Erwin Trommelen for drawing my attention to this information.

18. For biographies of Pavel Dmitriyevich and his children, see 'Rodoslovnaya Dyagilevykh' in Dyagileva, 1998, pp. 250–53.

19. Ibid., p. 57.

20. Ibid., p. 73.

21. Ibid., pp. 90, 91; cited in Scheijen, *Sergei Diaghilev*, 2004, pp. 19–20.

22. Dyagileva, 1998, pp. 91, 98.

23. Walter Nouvel, unpublished memoirs. Zilbershteyn and Samkov, 1982, ii, p. 335.

24. Dyagileva, 1998, p. 124.

25. Ibid., p. 125.

26. Ibid., p. 183.

27. See D. V. Filosofov, 'Pogovorim o Starine', in *Za Svobodu*, Warsaw, 1929.

28. Dyagileva, 1998, p. 189.

29. Ibid., pp. 189–90.

2 The Fruits of Enlightenment, 1879–1890

1. Dyagileva, 1998, p. 23.

2. Valentin Diaghilev drew a plan of the house at the age of thirteen. It clearly shows the twenty rooms. See ibid., p. 285. Pavel Koribut mistakenly speaks of thirty rooms in Lifar, 1994.

3. Aunt Tatusha was also supposed to have known Anton Rubinstein, Fyodor Dostoyevsky and Fyodor Stravinsky, the most celebrated bass of the Imperial Theatres (but mainly remembered as the father of the composer). Dyagileva, 1998, p. 260.

4. Diaghilev's account of his meeting with Tchaikovsky comes from Lifar (and not from Dima Filosofov, as Richard Buckle claims). See Lifar, 1994, p. 21.

5. This is made clear in such sources as the memoirs of Bronislava Nijinska. Nijinska, 1982, pp. 396–403.

6. Varunts (ed.), *Muzykal'naya Akademiya*, 2001, no. 3, p. 155.

7. Dyagileva, 1998, p. 171.

8. With Fyodor Stravinsky as Mephistopheles. See Walsh, 2000, p. 9.

9. Diaghilev's love of Tchaikovsky is generally known. Stravinsky mentioned his fondness for Gounod in his article 'Dyagilev, kotorogo ya znal'. In Varunts, 1988, p. 165.

10. O. Vasilyev, 'Seryozha Dyagilev. Iz dali let'. In *Vozrozhdeniya*, no. 1547, 27 August 1929, Paris.

11. Dyagileva, 1998, p. 13.

12. Diaghilev to Diaghileva, undated. IRLi, fond 102, ed. khr. 76, l.16.

13. Diaghilev to Diaghileva, [1884]. Scheijen, *Sergei Diaghilev*, 2004, pp. 13–14.

14. Dyagileva, 1998, p. 157.

15. Diaghilev to Diaghileva, [1884]. Scheijen, *Sergei Diaghilev*, 2004, p. 13.

16. Ibid., pp. 15–18.

17. E. P. Subbotin, 'Sergey Dyagilev – gimnazist', in Belyaeva et al., 1989, p. 12.

18. Vasiliyev, 'Seryozha Dyagilev. Iz dali let', n. 13.

19. Walter Nouvel, unpublished memoirs. Zilbershteyn and Samkov, 1982, ii, p. 339.

20. *Permskiye gubernskiye vedomosti*, no. 12, Thursday, 10 February 1890, Perm.

21. Diaghilev to Diaghileva, undated. IRLi, fond 102, ed. khr. 80, l.151–2.

22. Benois [Benua], 1980, i, p. 383.

23. See Stites, 1978, p. 80.

24. Extract from the third letter concerning *The Precipice*, undated, probably late 1880s. IRLi, fond 102, ed. khr. 79, l.93–5.

25. Diaghileva to Diaghilev, 29 October 1886. Dyagileva, 1998, p. 90.

26. Haskell and Nouvel, 1935, p. 10.

27. Nicolas Nabokov once related this to Elmer Schönberger. See Schönberger, 2005, p. 354.

28. The story comes from Lifar, 1994, p. 33, including the detail about the venereal disease.

29. Dyagileva, 1998, p. 195.

30. Ibid., p. 200.

31. Ibid., p. 201.

32. *Permskiye gubernskiye vedomosti*, no. 11, 8 February 1884, Perm, p. 55.

33. Reports of the murders can be found in the *Permskiye gubernskiye vedomosti*, nos. 13, 15, 19.

34. *Permskiye gubernskiye vedomosti*, no. 26, 22 March 1884, p. 137.

35. Subbotin and Dyldin, 2003, p. 27, n. 2.

36. Dyagileva, 1998, p. 203.

3 Rise and Fall, 1890–1891

1. Benois [Benua], 1980, i, p. 505.

2. A good description of Dima can be found in Haskell and Nouvel, 1935, p. 22.

3. This character sketch is from the poet Vasily Rozanov, quoted in Filosofov, 2004, p. 5.

4. Ibid., p. 657. For more about Stanislavsky and the Meiningen Theatre, see Magarshack, 1986, pp. 40–43, 75.

5. Diaghilev to Diaghileva, 17 July 1890. IRLi, fond 102, ed. khr. 79, l.106.

6. Over the years it has been taken for granted that Diaghilev and Filosofov were lovers, but there is actually little concrete evidence to support the premise beyond a conversation between Diaghilev and Igor Markevich about the intimate side of his relationship with Filosofov (see Buckle, 1979, p. 545, n. 33) and Benois asserting on one occasion that Filosofov and Diaghilev were more than just friends (see Benois [Benua], 1980, ii, p. 364).

7. Benois [Benua], 1980, i, p. 497.

8. IRLi, Zapiski D. V. Filosofova, tetr. 1, l.91–2.

9. Benois [Benua], 1980, i, p. 640.

10. Cocteau quoted in Spencer, 1978, p. 75.

11. IRLi, Zapiski D. V. Filosofova, tetr. 1, l.91–2.

12. In Dima's diary. Ibid.

13. Diaghilev to Diaghileva, undated. IRLi, fond 102, ed. khr. 80, l.120.

14. Diaghilev to Diaghileva, undated. IRLi, fond 102, ed. khr. 79, l.109.

15. Ibid., l.110.

16. Ibid., l.111.

17. The baritone Antonio Cotogni (1831–1918) was one of the greatest Italian singers of the golden age of bel canto. He sang in premieres of operas by Donizetti and Bellini, but he chiefly found fame as an interpreter of Verdi, with whom he worked closely to develop his roles. In his later years he became a well-known vocal coach who counted Beniamino Gigli and Giacomo Lauri-Volpi among his pupils.

18. Diaghilev to Diaghileva, undated. IRLi, fond 102, ed. khr. 79, l.112–13.

19. According to Pavel Koribut-Kubitovich, quoted in Lifar, 1994, p. 24.

20. Diaghilev to Diaghileva, 7 August 1890. IRLi, fond 102, ed. khr. 79, l.107ob.–108.

21. IRLi, Zapiski D. V. Filosofova, tetr. 4, l.92–3.

22. Diaghilev to Diaghileva, 28 August 1890. IRLi, fond 102, ed. khr. 80, l.131.

23. *Permskiye gubernskiye vedomosti*, no. 76, 7 October 1890. The first to discuss the Diaghilevs' bankruptcy and the auction of their property is Ilya Zilbershteyn (see following note).

24. Zilbershteyn and Samkov, 1982, ii, p. 338, n. 22.

25. Subbotin and Dyldin, 2003, pp. 29–30.

26. Diaghilev to Diaghileva, autumn 1890. IRLi, fond 102, ed. khr. 80, l.132.

27. None of Diaghilev's biographers mention his family's bankruptcy. Serge Lifar, who may have known about it, says nothing on the subject. Alexandre Benois and Walter Nouvel, both of whom were surely aware of it, are equally silent. It seems virtually impossible that such a secret could be concealed in the midst of such a tight circle of friends. As is clear from Diaghilev's letter about his visit to Tolstoy (chapter 4), even the elderly writer was aware of his family's financial difficulties.

28. Diaghilev to Diaghileva. IRLi, fond 102, ed. khr. 80, l.180.

29. Diaghilev to Diaghileva, 18 July 1891. IRLi, fond 102, ed. khr. 82, l.99–204.

4 Student Years: A Visit to Tolstoy, 1891–1893

1. See Benois [Benua], 1980, i, p. 640.

2. Diaghilev's comparative lack of contact with his late mother's family is described by Walter Nouvel in a letter to Haskell of 15 January 1935. Fondation Custodia, inv. 1993-A.1328.

3. Diaghilev to Diaghileva, 1892. IRLi, fond 102, ed. khr. 84, l.367.

4. Yury Diaghilev to Diaghileva, quoted in Laskin, 2002, p. 74.

5. For Diaghilev's complaints about Pavka, see IRLi, fond 102, ed. khr. 81, l.254–5, 144–5. For more about his habit of appearing at parties uninvited: ed. khr. 82, l.236.

6. Benois [Benua], 1980, i, p. 506.

7. Diaghilev to Diaghileva, IRLi, fond 102, ed. khr. 81, l.286–7; Diaghilev to Diaghileva, IRLi, fond 102, ed. khr. 80, l.142–3; Diaghilev to Diaghileva, IRLi, fond 102, ed. khr. 82, l.213.

8. Gippius, 2002, p. 248.

9. Diaghilev to Diaghileva, IRLi, fond 102, ed. khr. 81, l.254.

10. Ibid., l.267–8.

11. Diaghilev wrote a number of letters to Tolstoy on this subject. They are apparently held by the Tolstoy archive in Moscow, but are currently untraceable. Ilya Zilbershteyn, who was able to locate them, did not include them in his collection. However, he discusses them in a few sentences. The comment that Diaghilev turned to Tolstoy with existential questions comes from Zilbershteyn and Samkov, 1982, ii, p. 334.

12. There is, however, no doubt that Diaghilev wrote this letter. For a discussion of its authorship see ibid., pp. 335–6, n. 3.

13. Diaghilev to Diaghileva, 14 February 1892. Scheijen, *Sergei Diaghilev*, 2004, pp. 21–35. Zilbershteyn was the first to publish the letter, but he, too, made cuts. Zilbershteyn and Samkov, 1982, ii, pp. 7–16. The original is to be found at IRLi, fond 102.

14. Diaghilev to Tolstoy, 15 April 1892. Zilbershteyn and Samkov, 1982, ii, p. 334.

15. Ibid. The commentary is Zilbershteyn's.

16. Diaghilev to Tolstoy, 19 March 1893. Zilbershteyn and Samkov, 1982, i, p. 10.

5 Student Years: Alexandre Benois, 1890–1894

1. See Kennedy, 1977, p. 243.

2. Bowlt, 1976, p. 59.

3. Aleksandr Benua, *Vystavka Braka*, in Benois [Benua], 1968, p. 452.

4. Bowlt, 1979, p. 172.

5. Benois [Benua], 1980, ii, p. 640.

6. Ibid., pp. 640–41.

7. Filosofov, 2004, p. 665.

8. Benois [Benua], 'Konstantin Somov', in Podkopayeva and Sveshnikova, 1979, p. 476.

9. See Muravyova, 2004, ii, p. 71.

10. Diaghilev to Diaghileva. IRLi, fond 102, ed. khr. 81, l.147–8. There is some doubt about the exact nature of these lecture evenings. In his memoirs

Benois suggests that they continued for years, naturally evolving into the activities of *Mir iskusstva*. But Benois would seem to be overstating the case. In Diaghilev's correspondence after 1891 there is scarcely any mention of the lectures. Benois refers to a number of lecture titles in his memoirs. These lectures had already been delivered by the end of 1890, because they are the same ones Diaghilev tells his stepmother about. Could this mean that after that point hardly any lectures were given? Did the group's activities grind to a halt once all the members had given a lecture or two? See Benois [Benua], 1998, p. 9.

11. Benois [Benua], 1980, i, p. 641.

12. Ibid.

13. Diaghilev to Diaghileva. IRLi, fond 102, ed. khr. 80, l.179–80.

14. Ibid., l.182.

15. Diaghilev to Diaghileva, 14 October 1892. IRLi, fond 102, ed. khr. 86, l.84–5.

16. Diaghilev to Diaghileva, 28 August 1894, in Laskin, 2002, pp. 93–4.

17. We know that Diaghilev was taught by Solovyov from a letter he wrote to his stepmother in August 1892. See Israel Nestyev, 'Diaghilev's Musical Education', in Garafola and Van Norman Baer, 1999, pp. 38–9. Diaghilev himself only mentioned Nikolay Sokolov and Anatoly Lyadov when discussing his teachers. See Kochno, 1970, p. 280. Pavka Koribut also described Sokolov as one of Diaghilev's teachers, making the claim more credible. See Zilbershteyn and Samkov, 1982, ii, p. 414. As to the other names that have been mooted over the years as possible teachers of Diaghilev (Kalifati, Rimsky-Korsakov, Akimenko, Lyadov), there is no reliable historical evidence.

18. Diaghilev to Diaghileva, 17 December 1892(?). IRLi, fond 102, ed. khr. 81, l.294–5.

19. Diaghilev to Diaghileva, 11 November 1893. IRLi, fond 102, ed. khr. 87, l.17 (426).

20. For a broad description and analysis of Wagner's reception in Russia, see Bartlett, 1995.

21. 'I am a music fanatic and Wagner fanatic.' Diaghilev to Diaghileva, 18 February 1892. In Nestyev, 1978, p. 118.

22. IRLi, fond 102, ed. khr. 83, l.358.

23. Diaghilev to Diaghileva, Nuremberg, 14 July 1892. Scheijen, *Sergei Diaghilev*, 2004, pp. 36–7.

24. Ibid., p. 38.

25. Ibid., pp. 39–40.

26. Diaghilev to Diaghileva, 14 October 1892. IRLi, fond 102, ed. khr. 84, l.24ob.–25.

27. Diaghilev to Diaghileva, 27 July 1892. IRLi, fond 102, ed. khr. 83, l.66–7.

28. Diaghilev to Diaghileva, 14 October 1892. IRLi, fond 102, ed. khr. 84, l.23–4.

29. Diaghilev to Diaghileva, 11 November 1893. IRLi, fond 102, ed. khr. 87, l.17 (426) ob.

30. Diaghilev to Diaghileva, [1894]. IRLi, fond 102, ed. khr. 88, l.40b.–5.

31. Yury Diaghilev to Diaghileva, 18 September 1894. Nestyev, 1994, p. 32.

6 'The Serge Diaguileff Museum': St Petersburg, Rome, Genoa, Paris, 1894–1896

1. See I. P. Lapshina, 'Mir iskusstva', in Alekseyev et al., 1969, p. 133.

2. Diaghilev to Diaghileva, 11 August 1892. Scheijen, *Sergei Diaghilev*, 2004, p. 41.

3. Diaghilev to Diaghileva, 13 October 1893. IRLi, fond 102, ed. khr. 87, l.18 (427). Tchaikovsky's biographer Alexander Poznansky writes that 'the front doors remained open from the early morning, and a steady stream of students, colleagues and admirers made their way to Modest's apartment [Modest was Tchaikovsky's brother]'. Poznansky, 1991, p. 591. It is entirely possible that Diaghilev was among them.

4. Varunts (ed.), *Muzykal'naya Akademiya*, 2001, no. 1, p. 147.

5. In *Syn otechestva*, 26 October 1893. Quoted ibid, p. 149, n. 14.

6. Diaghilev to Diaghileva, 11 November 1893. IRLi, fond 102, ed. khr. 87, l.18 (427).

7. Diaghilev to Diaghileva. ibid., l.19 (428) ob.

8. Diaghilev to Diaghileva, cited in Nestyev, 1994, p. 29.

9. Diaghilev to Diaghileva, 17 January 1894. Quoted ibid., p. 28.

10. Dyagileva, 1998, p. 139.

11. Diaghilev to Diaghileva, 28 August 1894. IRLi, fond 102, ed. khr. 87, l.33 (442)–33 (442) ob.

12. Yastrebtsev, 1985, pp. 90–91.

13. Zilbershteyn and Samkov, 1982, ii, p. 414.

14. As evident from documents in the St Petersburg historical archives. Lichnoye Delo: S. P. Dyagileva, TsGIA SPb, fond 14, delo 27819. See Laskin, 2002, p. 57.

15. Diaghilev to Diaghileva. IRLi, fond 102, ed. khr. 85, l.1.

16. Diaghilev to Diaghileva, 11 December 1894. Ibid., l.22–3.

17. Ibid.

18. See Benois [Benua], 1998, p. 17.

19. Diaghilev to Benois, 15 June 1895. Zilbershteyn and Samkov, 1982, ii, p. 17.

20. Benois [Benua], 1980, ii, p. 68.

7 Charlatan and Charmer, 1895–1898

1. Dyagileva, 1998, p. 208.

2. Diaghilev to Diaghileva, October 1895. Scheijen, *Sergei Diaghilev*, 2004, pp. 45–6.

3. Sergey Dyagilev, 'Evropeyskiye vystavki i russky khudozhniki', in Zilbershteyn and Samkov, 1982, i, p. 57.

4. Ibid., p. 56.

5. Sergey Dyagilev, 'Akvarel'naya vystavka', ibid., p. 50.

6. 'Seryozha was then thoroughly inexperienced in writing   … His rough draft was usually entirely remodelled by me.' Benois, 1941, p. 177.

7. Diaghilev to Diaghileva, 23 July 1896. IRLi, fond 102, ed. khr. 90.

8. Tenisheva, 2002, p. 224.

9. Zilbershteyn and Samkov, 1982, ii, p. 447.

10. Sergey Dyagilev, 'Po povodu dvukh akvarel'nykh vystavok', in Zilbershteyn and Samkov, 1982, i, p. 67.

11. Diaghilev to Tenisheva, 4 February 1897. Zilbershteyn and Samkov, 1982, ii, pp. 18–19.

12. For more about the exhibition see Diaghilev's correspondence with the journalist Vaksel ibid., pp. 19–20.

13. See Laskin, 2002, p. 126.

14. Benois to Somov, 18/30 September 1896. Podkopayeva and Sveshnikova, 1979, pp. 441–2.

15. Diaghilev to Benois, 11 March 1897. Scheijen, *Sergei Diaghilev*, 2004, pp. 51–2.

16. Diaghilev to Benois, Sunday, April 1897. Zilbershteyn and Samkov, 1982, ii, pp. 21–3.

17. Benois to Somov, 8/20 August 1897. Podkopayeva and Sveshnikova, 1979, p. 444.

18. Benois to Nouvel, 3 November 1897. Benois [Benua], 2003, p. 24, n. 2.

19. Somov to A. A. Somov, 21 April/3 May. Podkopayeva and Sveshnikova, 1979, p. 62.

20. Benois [Benua], 1980, ii, p. 263.

21. Diaghilev to Diaghileva, IRLi, fond 102, ed. khr. 85, l.13.

22. IRLi, fond 102, ed. khr. 88, l.9.

23. Benois to Filosofov and Diaghilev, 4 December 1898. Benois [Benua], 2003, p. 45.

24. Ibid., p. 47.

25. Wilde to Smithers, 4 May 1898. Wilde, 1962, p. 734.

26. Interview with Boris Kochno by Richard Buckle, paraphrased by the author. In Buckle, 1979, p. 38.

8 'I'm full of big plans!', 1897–1898

1. Zilbershteyn and Samkov, 1982, ii, p. 345.

2. Diaghilev to Benois, 29 October 1896. Ibid., p. 18.

3. Diaghilev to Benois, 8 October 1897. Scheijen, *Sergei Diaghilev*, 2004, pp. 57–8.

4. Diaghilev to various recipients, 20 May 1897. Zilbershteyn and Samkov, 1982, ii, p. 24.

5. Ibid.

6. Diaghilev to Benois, early May 1897. Scheijen, *Sergei Diaghilev*, 2004, pp. 13–14.

7. Benois [Benua], 1998, p. 25.

8. Diaghilev to Benois, 8 October 1897. Zilbershteyn and Samkov, 1982, ii, p. 28.

9. Benois [Benua], 1998, p. 29.

10. Review in *Zhizn'*, no. 6 (1898). Zilbershteyn and Samkov, 1971, i, p. 77. For an assortment of press reactions to the exhibition, see pp. 76–8.

11. Stasov, 1952, iii, p. 238.

12. Craft and Stravinsky, *Expositions*, 1981, p. 21.

13. Tyrkova, 1915, i, p. 390.

14. Stasov to Polenova, 31 May/12 June. Zilbershteyn and Samkov, 1982, ii, pp. 156–7.

15. Zilbershteyn and Samkov, 1982, i, pp. 296–7.

16. Sergey Dyagilev, 'Otvet V. V. Stasovu'. Ibid., pp. 73–6.

17. Diaghilev to Stasov, 2 February 1898. Ibid., p. 297.

18. Stasov to Polenova, 31 May/12 June 1898. Zilbershteyn and Samkov, 1982, ii, p. 157.

19. Ibid.

20. Ibid.

21. Stasov, cited in Volkov, 1997, p. 131.

22. See Valkenier, 2001, p. 67.

23. Filosofov to Benois, 30 March 1898. Filosofov, 2004, p. 673.

24. Benois, 1941, p. 193; Dobuzhinsky, 1987, p. 202.

25. Craft and Stravinsky, *Expositions*, 1981, p. 25.

26. See Repin to Kurennom, 13 September 1898. Repin, 1969, ii, pp. 141–2. Zilbershteyn also cites the letter, but gives the date as 13 October. Zilbershteyn and Samkov, 1982, ii, p. 159.

27. See Lapshina, 1977, pp. 41–5.

28. Diaghilev to Benois, 2 June 1898. Scheijen, *Sergei Diaghilev*, 2004, pp. 62–3.

29. Filosofov, 2004, p. 672.

30. Ibid.

31. Nouvel to Benois, 15 June 1898. Benois [Benua], 2003, p. 43.

9 The World of Art, 1898–1900

1. For a more in-depth discussion of neo-nationalism see Bowlt, 1979, pp. 15–46.

2. Interview in *Peterburgskaya gazeta* of May 1898 with Diaghilev, Mamontov and an unidentified 'young artist', quoted in Zilbershteyn and Samkov, 1971, i, p. 452.

3. Nouvel, 'Diaghileff' (photocopy of an unpublished manuscript). RGALi, fond 2712, op. 1, ed. khr. 104, l.72.

4. Another piece of evidence that points to Diaghilev's authorship was the fact that Benois never questioned that it was his friend's own work; either when he offered a personal reaction shortly after its appearance (see Benois [Benua] and Dyagilev, 2003, p. 46), or when he reviewed the article in his own *Vozniknoveniye Mira iskusstva*, which was far from pro-Diaghilev (see Benois [Benua], 1998, p. 46). He did, however, assert that Filosofov's influence on the piece was substantial. Grabar does not doubt Diaghilev's authorship either (see Grabar, 1975, p. 118). The style of the essay is plainly Diaghilev's. His impassioned, stentorian grandiosity is a far cry from Filosofov's restrained prose. Finally, the total absence of religious themes, which so preoccupied Filosofov even then, is proof that Diaghilev set the agenda for the text. On the basis of Nouvel's claims, Ilya Zilbershteyn concludes that Filosofov was the actual author of the *entire* essay (see Zilbershteyn and Samkov, 1982, i, p. 16) and for that reason elected not to include it in his *Sergey Dyagilev i russkoye iskusstvo*. The reason for Zilbershteyn's hasty conclusion may well have been political: Diaghilev's essay was very pro-Western and anti-Chernyshevsky, and might have therefore been unacceptable to the Soviet censors.

5. Sergey Dyagilev, 'Slozhnye voprosy', in *Mir iskusstva*, vol. I (1899), nos. 1–4. For an exhaustive analysis of Diaghilev's essay, see Kennedy, 1977, pp. 63–113. This quotation from it and the next three are taken from the English online translation by Alexey Makhrov and Robert Russell to be found at www.hrionline.ac.uk/rva/texts/diaghilev/diagbib.html (accessed 15 April 2009).

6. The Frits Lugt collection (Paris, Fondation Custodia) contains the annual accounts for *Mir iskusstva*'s first year of operation (*Otchet po pervomu godu izdaniya zhurnala 'Mir iskusstva'*), which Diaghilev sent to Tenisheva. The payments to the various suppliers are itemised. Fondation Custodia, 2004-A.620.

7. Ibid.

8. Benois [Benua], 1998, p. 36.

9. Pertsov, 1933, pp. 290–91.

10. Dobuzhinsky, 1987, p. 199.

11. Haskell and Nouvel, 1935, p. 206.

12. There is some disagreement about the nanny's real name. I cite the name used in the *Semeynaya Zapis' Dyagilevych*. Pertsov calls her Arina Rodionova.

13. Pertsov, 1933, pp. 300–301.

14. Gippius and others, in Gippius, 2003, p. 48.

15. Somov to his brother Alexander, 1 January 1899. Podkopayeva and Sveshnikova, 1979, p. 67.

16. Gippius, 2003, p. 49.

17. Ibid., p. 48.

18. *Mir iskusstva*, vol. I (1899), nos. 1–2.

19. Zilbershteyn and Samkov, 1982, i, p. 312.

20. Benois [Benua], 1980, i, p. 690.

21. Pertsov, 1933, pp. 302–3.

22. Annual accounts for *Mir iskusstva*, Fondation Custodia, 2004-A.620.

23. Zilbershteyn and Samkov, 1990, p. 58.

24. Grabar, 2001, p. 164.

25. Pertsov, 1933, p. 294.

26. Diaghilev wired Benois about this on 6 June. See Zilbershteyn and Samkov, 1982, ii, p. 53.

27. Zilbershteyn and Samkov, 1971, i, p. 675.

28. Filosofov to Rozanov, 13 June 1900. Ibid.

29. Nesterov to Sredin, 8 July 1900. Ibid.

30. Haskell and Nouvel, 1935, pp. 110–11.

31. This song is mentioned in one of Filosofov's letters to Benois, 20 August 1893, quoted in Lapshina, 'Mir iskusstva', in Alekseyev et al., 1969, p. 133.

32. In the end Volkonsky would contribute just one article to *Mir iskusstva*, in vol. I (1899), nos. 3–4.

33. Telyakovsky, 1998, p. 336.

10 The *Sylvia* Debacle, 1900–1902

1. For Diaghilev's ideas on this theatrical journal, see Zilbershteyn and Samkov, 1982, ii, pp. 45–7. For more on Somov's involvement in this scheme see Podkopayeva and Sveshnikova, 1979, p. 71.

2. Diaghilev to Nouvel, undated, in Nestyev, 1994, p. 50.

3. Volkonsky, 1923, p. 135.

4. Benois [Benua], 1980, ii, p. 305.

5. Benois, 1964, p. 103.

6. See Zilbershteyn and Samkov, 1982, i, p. 350, n. 4.

7. For an extensive historical description see Benois [Benua], 1980, ii, pp. 342–6.

8. Nouvel to Somov, 14 September 1897, in Podkopayeva and Sveshnikova, 1979, pp. 457–8.

9. Tenisheva, 2002, p. 212.

10. Diaghilev to Benois, 29 October 1896, in Scheijen, *Sergei Diaghilev*, 2004, pp. 49–50. Although Benois claims in his memoirs that he was already fanatical about ballet in the mid-1890s, this remark by Diaghilev clearly suggests that he saw Benois as a potential ally who would also scoff at Nouvel's balletomania. There is nothing in Benois's published correspondence that resembled Nouvel's avowed passion for ballet as expressed in his letter to Somov (n. 8 above). One may therefore safely conclude that, of the group of friends, it was Nouvel and not Benois who was driving the growing interest in ballet as an art form.

11. Telyakovsky, 1998, p. 512.

12. Ibid., pp. 514–15, 520 for this and the foregoing.

13. See Zilbershteyn and Samkov, 1982, ii, p. 36.

14. Telyakovsky, 1998, p. 524.

15. See Benois [Benua], 1980, ii, p. 345.

16. For the details of this 'third category' see Zilbershteyn and Samkov, 1985, p. 335.

17. Benois [Benua], 1980, ii, p. 345.

18. In that application for dismissal, Volkonsky merely requests permission to relieve him of his function as editor of the annual. Zilbershteyn and Samkov, 1982, ii, p. 169.

19. Diaghilev to Telyakovsky, 10 March 1901. Ibid, p. 64.

20. Benois [Benua], 1980, ii, p. 346.

21. Dyagilev, 1902, p. 2 (actually published in October 1901).

22. Diaghilev to Diaghileva, 23 October 1901. IRLi, fond 102, ed. khr. 83.

23. This was preceded by the founding of 'Glavnoye' (The Main Thing), a kind of religious love triangle between Merezhkovsky, Gippius and Filosofov. It came into being on Maunday Thursday, 29 March 1901. See Filosofov, 2004, p. 3.

24. As is very clear from Diaghilev's letter to Anton Chekhov of 23 December 1902. See Zilbershteyn and Samkov, 1982, ii, p. 80.

25. Filosofov, 2004, p. 3.

26. Diaghilev to Rozanov, 29 November 1901. Scheijen, *Sergei Diaghilev*, 2004, pp. 93–4.

27. The whole affair bears all the hallmarks of a lovers' tiff, though Gippius maintains in her diary that no real intimacy had yet taken place between her, her husband and Filosofov in 1902. The most detailed account of the affair between the three has been written by Vladimir Zlobin. Zlobin, 'Gippius i Filosofov', in Gippius, 2003, pp. 471–503.

28. See Zilbershteyn and Samkov, 1982, ii, p. 386.

29. Diaghilev to W. Propert, 17 February 1926, cited in Lifar, 1940, p. 98. Diaghilev's account of events is exceptionally careless, not to say dishonest. It is, for instance, quite impossible that he obtained a position in the chancery 'within a week of his dismissal'. According to Benois, he got this job a year or two after being sacked by the Imperial Theatres.

30. Benois [Benua], 1980, ii, pp. 345–6.

31. Diaghilev to Benois, 9 September 1902. Zilbershteyn and Samkov, 1982, ii, p. 76.

32. Diaghilev to Diaghileva, Warsaw 1902. IRLi, fond 102, ed. khr. 86, l.3–4.

33. Stravinsky's performance is mentioned in *Russkaya muzikal'naya gazeta*, no. 51/52 (1901), a fact that was unearthed by the indefatigable and prolific Stravinsky expert Viktor Varunts. See Varunts, 1998, p. 110. The fact that Stravinsky performed at these evenings was overlooked by his biographer Stephen Walsh.

34. See Kutateladze, 1972, p. 203.

35. See I. V. Nestyev, 'Muzikal'nye kruzhki', in Alekseyev et al., 1977, pp. 474–82.

11 The Hour of Reckoning, 1902–1905

1. Muravyova, 2004, i, p. 146.

2. Ibid., p. 147.

3. Serov to Diaghilev, late December 1901. Zilbershteyn and Samkov, 1985, p. 330.

4. For the full protocol of the *Mir iskusstva* exhibition association, see Zilbershteyn and Samkov, 1982, ii, pp. 369–71.

5. Bakst to L. P. Gritsenko, Petersburg, 16 February 1903, in Zilbershteyn and Samkov, 1971, i, p. 590.

6. Zilbershteyn and Samkov, 1985, p. 370.

7. Grabar, 2001, pp. 173–4.

8. Ibid., p. 174.

9. Zilbershteyn and Samkov, 1982, ii, p. 88.

10. This is according to Diaghilev himself; not all the letters have survived. See ibid., p. 403.

11. Ibid., pp. 84–5.

12. Ibid., p. 403.

13. Dyagileva, 1998, p. 243.

14. There may also have been problems with the payment of subsidies to *Mir iskusstva*, but the reason was not, as Benois maintained, that 'Diaghilev had become a *bête noire* in imperial circles'. Other projects of Diaghilev received generous support from the imperial court for years beyond that. See Benois [Benua], 1998, p. 52.

15. His pacifist theories and diplomatic initiatives to promote world peace attracted sympathy at the highest levels (Franklin Roosevelt's vice president, Henry Wallace, was an admirer).

16. Under the terms of the compromise, neither Benois nor Roerich would become editor, and Diaghilev would again be in a position to call the shots. Obviously, Tenisheva rejected the arrangement.

17. However, that issue would appear after the 'Bloody Sunday' of 9/22 January 1905.

18. According to Zilbershteyn it was principally financial problems that doomed *Mir iskusstva*, but this is contradicted by some of his own sources. See Zilbershteyn and Samkov, 1982, ii, p. 469.

19. Ibid., p. 93.

20. Different numbers have been suggested over the years: the figure 2,500 (or 3,000) has been mentioned by several scholars, including Buckle. See Buckle, 1979, p. 83. Grabar (2001, p. 146) claims there were actually 6,000 paintings on show. The correct number, however, is 4,000. For more on this point, the reader is referred to Bowlt, 'Diaghilev and the Eighteenth Century', in Sjeng Scheijen, *In Dienst van Diaghilev* (catalogue of an exhibition held at the Groninger Museum, 11 December 2004–28 March 2005) (Groningen, 2004), p. 47.

21. Zilbershteyn and Samkov, 1982, ii, p. 299.

22. Grabar, 2001, pp. 146–7.

23. See Diaghilev, 1904. The copy I consulted is held by the Library of Congress, Washington, DC.

24. Zilbershteyn and Samkov, 1982, i, pp. 193–4, quoting *Vesy*, no. 4 (1905), pp. 45–6.

25. Filosofov to Filosofova, 2 August 1905, quoted in Vladimir Zlobin, 'Gippius i Filosofov', in Gippius, 2003, pp. 480–81.

26. Benois to Nouvel, 16 August 1905. RGALi, fond 938, op. 1, ed. khr. 48, l.156.

27. Ibid., l.159.

28. Diaghilev to Benois, 16 October 1905. Zilbershteyn and Samkov, 1982, ii, p. 95.

29. Lifar, 1994, p. 139.

30. Nouvel to Benois, 25 December 1905. RGALi, fond 938, op. 1, ed. khr. 48, l.213.

31. Filosofov to Gippius. Zlobin, in Gippius, 2003, p. 484.

12 The 'Homosexual Clique', 1906–1907

1. Gippius, 2003, p. 49.

2. See Lifar, 1994, pp. 139–40, where the date is given erroneously as January 1905.

3. Cited in a letter from Filosofov to Gippius, quoted by Zlobin in Gippius, 2003, p. 484.

4. Filosofov to Gippius. Ibid., p. 485.

5. Ibid.

6. See Garafola, 1989, p. 3.

7. Nouvel, unpublished memoirs. RGALi, fond. 2712, op. 1, ed. khr. 104, l.167.

8. See Karsavina, 1950, pp. 125–6, and Krasovskaya, 1971, pp. 81–2.

9. In Zilbershteyn and Samkov, 1982, i, p. 198.

10. Ibid.

11. For the reactions to Diaghilev's article, see ibid., pp. 394–5.

12. To be precise, Diaghilev approached Count Ivan Tolstoy, vice president of the art academy. For more on this subject see Dobuzhinsky's letter to Grabar of 27 January 1906, ibid., p. 176. See also Dobuzhinsky's letter to Bilibin of 28 January 1906, in Dobuzhinsky, 2001, p. 73.

13. For more information on the legal status of homosexuality in Russia before the Revolution, see Healy, 2001, pp. 77–99.

14. Ibid., p. 95.

15. Ibid., p. 89.

16. Alexander Blok, diary entry of 12 March 1913, cited in Pyman, 1980, ii, p. 185.

17. The meeting with Nouvel was linked to the 'contemporary music soirees' regularly attended by Kuzmin. Kuzmin, 2000, p. 273.

18. Kuzmin, diary entry of 10 June 1906. Ibid., p. 168.

19. Kuzmin, diary entry of 1 September 1907. Ibid., p. 397.

20. See ibid., p. 591.

21. Ibid.

22. Kuzmin, diary entry of 5 September 1907. Ibid., p. 399.

23. Kuzmin, diary entry of 31 October 1907. Ibid., p. 420.

24. Zilbershteyn and Samkov, 1982, ii, p. 96.

25. Benois, diary entries of 23 May and 6 June 1906. Benois [Benua], 2003, p. 64.

26. Benois's diary entry of 4 June 1906 speaks of ten rooms. Ibid.

27. The words of Maria Tenisheva, cited in Zilbershteyn and Samkov, 1982, i, p. 204.

28. Benois, diary entry of 26 September 1906. Benois [Benua], 2003, p. 66.

29. See Zlobin in Gippius, 2003, p. 489.

30. Diaghilev to Diaghileva, [December?] 1906. IRLi, fond 102, ed. khr. 86, l.21.

31. Bakst to Serov, 1 December 1906. Zilbershteyn and Samkov, 1989, p. 80.

32. Parton, 1993, p. 9.

33. For the reactions in France, see Zilbershteyn and Samkov, 1982, i, p. 406.

34. Diaghilev to Nouvel, 1 December 1916. Ibid., p. 407.

35. See Acocella, 1984, p. 31, n. 34.

13 Tsar Boris and Tsar Sergey, 1907–1908

1. The first reference to this can be found in a letter from V. P. Loboykov to Ilya Ostroukhov. See Zilbershteyn and Samkov, 1982, i, p. 409.

2. Greffulhe told this story to Lifar. She claimed that Diaghilev told her of his plans to produce a series of Russian concerts during his very first visit. If that is the case (and it doesn't seem terribly likely), the initiative for the concert series goes back to the first week of June 1906. See Lifar, 1994,

p. 143 (for Greffulhe's comments) and Benois [Benua], 2003, p. 64 (for the exact date of Diaghilev's first meeting with Greffulhe).

3. Gilse van der Pals is discussed in Haskell and Nouvel, 1935, p. 150, n. 2. For the notice announcing his arrival in St Petersburg, see Holtrop, 2005, p. 61. Another son, Leopold, became a composer and wrote music for Rudolf Steiner, among others.

4. See Garafola, 1989, p. 161 and p. 440, n. 39.

5. See Zilbershteyn and Samkov, 1982, i, p. 409.

6. See Dyagileva, 1998, p. 212.

7. Ibid., p. 211.

8. Repin to Ostroukhov, 25 November 1901: 'Yes, the Good Lord neglected to give Diaghilev the gift of tact. He wreaks havoc wherever he goes. He is obsessed with power to an unnatural degree. He is making frantic efforts to become Minister of Culture.' In Repin, 1969, ii, p. 167.

9. 'He greatly admired Witte ... for his daring and his willpower.' Nouvel, RGALi, fond 2712, op. 1, ed. khr. 104, l.167. Hopes of intercession: ibid., l.168–9.

10. Ivan Lazarevsky in *Slovo*, 3 August 1907. Quoted in Zilbershteyn and Samkov, 1982, ii, p. 473.

11. Benois to Serov, 1 May 1907. Zilbershteyn and Samkov, 1989, p. 96.

12. See Benois [Benua], 1980, ii, pp. 455–6.

13. Scriabin to Morozova, 10 April 1907. Zilbershteyn and Samkov, 1982, i, p. 410.

14. Ibid., p. 409.

15. As recalled by Bakst. See Zilbershteyn and Samkov, 1982, ii, p. 414.

16. Diaghilev to Rimsky-Korsakov, spring 1907. Scheijen, *Sergei Diaghilev*, 2004, p. 133.

17. Varunts (ed.), *Muzykal'naya Akademiya*, 2001, no. 3, p. 153.

18. Both quotes are from Telyakovsky's diary, cited in Zilbershteyn and Samkov, 1982, i, p. 450. For more about Diaghilev and Astruc, see pp. 449–50. For more about Scriabin and Astruc, see Bowers, 1969, p. 27. And for more about Astruc and Mata Hari, see Waagenaar, 1994, pp. 65 and 69ff.

19. A detailed description of that evening's audience can be found in Buckle, 1979, p. 99.

20. Varunts (ed.), *Muzykal'naya Akademiya*, 2001, no. 3, p. 153.

21. Scriabin to Altshuler, 2 June 1907, in Zilbershteyn and Samkov, 1982, i, p. 412. It is quite possible that the concerts ran at a loss and that in the end the organisers had to appeal to the tsar, even though Diaghilev later claimed that, apart from the 1909 season, he had never received a cent from Nicholas.

22. See Zlobin in Gippius, 2003, p. 489.

23. Ibid.

24. Review by Ninov, 16 April 1906, in *Teatr i iskusstvo*, quoted in Krasovskaya, 1971, p. 388.

25. Review by L. L. Kozlyaninov, 17 April 1907, in *Novoye vremya*, quoted ibid., p. 389.

26. Review by Valerian Svetlov, 29 October 1907, in *Birzhevye vedomosti*, quoted ibid., p. 390.

27. Buckle, 1998, p. 65.

28. Nouvel wrote about their meeting in his unpublished manuscript, intended for Haskell. But in the sections about Nijinsky he explicitly says, 'Here I must touch on matters of an intimate nature which are not meant for publication, but which are necessary in order to understand the origins of D.'s relationship with Nijinsky.' In Nouvel, RGALi, fond. 2712, op. 1, ed. khr. 104, l.202.

29. See Buckle, 1998, p. 61.

30. Quotations here and in the following two paragraphs are from Nouvel, RGALi, fond. 2712, op. 1, ed. khr. 104, l.202–5.

31. This is the version propagated by Buckle. See Buckle, 1998, p. 62. Nouvel speculated that Lvov may have been interested in a threesome, but that Diaghilev was put off by the idea. Nouvel, RGALi, fond. 2712, op. 1, ed. khr. 104, l.204.

32. These adjectives are from Krasovskaya, 1979, p. 97, who has done even more than Buckle to perpetuate the myth of Nijinsky as victim.

33. Kuzmin, diary entry of 25 December 1907. Kuzmin, 2000, p. 437.

34. Diaghilev to Rimsky-Korsakov, 5 June 1907. Zilbershteyn and Samkov, 1982, ii, pp. 100–101.

35. Ibid., p. 135.

36. Diaghilev to Rimsky-Korsakov, 11 August 1907. Ibid., pp. 137–8.

37. Rimsky-Korsakov to Diaghilev, 26 August 1907. Ibid., p. 141.

38. Diaghilev to Rimsky-Korsakov, 26 August 1907. Ibid., p. 142.

39. Zilbershteyn and Samkov, 1982, ii, p. 417.

40. A French newspaper article from 28 November 1907, in which the management of the Opéra discusses the planned production of *Sadko* at some length, proves that Diaghilev was not bluffing about having reached an agreement with the Opéra. ibid., pp. 417–18.

41. In 1911 Diaghilev did produce a ballet, *Sadko*, based on the sixth scene of the opera.

42. Money, 1982, p. 95.

43. See Benois [Benua], 1980, ii, p. 488.

44. Valts, 1928, p. 216.

45. To execute their designs and paint the backdrops and scenery, Diaghilev did not hire professional stage painters but rather young Miriskusniki such as Yevgeny Lansere and Stepan Yaremich.

46. Varunts (ed.), *Muzykal'naya Akademiya*, 2001, no. 3, p. 153.

47. Benois [Benua], 1980, ii, p. 485. Benois's account is not completely reliable. Diaghilev says nothing in his memoirs about scouring the markets with Benois, who was in Brittany almost continuously from 1907 to 1908.

48. Namely Diaghilev, Benois and the conductor Blumenfeld. See ibid., p. 486.

49. Ibid., p. 487. Varunts (ed.), *Muzykal'naya Akademiya*, 2001, no. 3, pp. 153–4.

50. Benois claims that this all happened a day before the premiere. Diaghilev wrote in his memoirs that it was actually three days before, which seems more likely.

51. Benois [Benua], 1980, ii, p. 488.

52. Ibid.

53. Varunts (ed.), *Muzykal'naya Akademiya*, 2001, no. 3, p. 154.

54. Sert, 1953, p. 112. The remark that they had already met in 1899 is from Benois. Benois [Benua], 1980, ii, p. 491, n. 7.

55. Benois [Benua], 1980, ii, p. 491.

56. Nouvel, RGALi, fond 2712, op. 1, ed. khr. 104, l.206.

14 The Rise of the Ballets Russes, 1908–1909

1. Aleksandr Benua, 'Beseda o balete', in *Teatr: kniga o novom teatre* (St Petersburg, 1908), cited in Krasovskaya, 1971, p. 214.

2. Telyakovsky, diary entry of 10 November 1905. Telyakovsky, 2002, p. 560.

3. V. P. Loboykov, a senior official at the art academy, wrote to Ilya Ostroukhov in September 1906, 'He [Diaghilev] is now here [with Grand Duke Vladimir Alexandrovich] and is planning performances for Paris (*Prince Igor*, *Maid of Pskov*, *Raymonda*, *Pavillon d'Armide*, and a new ballet).' Cited in Zilbershteyn and Samkov, 1982, ii, p. 409.

4. Brussel writes this in his article 'Avant la Féerie', published in *La revue musicale*, December 1930. Cited in Buckle, 1979, p. 550, n. 1.

5. The premiere of *Pavillon d'Armide* was preceded by a performance of a single scene from the ballet, danced by students of the Imperial Ballet School. Entitled *The Tapestry That Came to Life*, it premiered on 15 April 1907 at the Mariinsky Theatre.

6. Garafola, 1989, p. 7.

7. See Money, 1982, p. 52. Money posits that this happened during Duncan's first visit in 1905, and I take my lead from him. However, it is not impossible that he errs on this point, and that the said dinner took place during Duncan's second visit in 1907.

8. Nouvel. RGALi, fond. 2712, op. 1, ed. khr. 104, l.202.

9. Interview with Diaghilev in *Utro Rossii*, 24 August 1910, in Zilbershteyn and Samkov, 1982, ii, p. 214.

10. Benois, 1941, p. 257.

11. Valerian Svetlov, cited by Lifar, 1994, pp. 154–5.

12. Benois does not mention Gilse van der Pals by name, but speaks of 'a salesman of galoshes'. Benois moreover claims that the Dutchman proposed to donate the vast sum of 100,000 gold roubles if Diaghilev would use his influence to secure him (or one of the other rubber barons)

a knighthood (Benois, 1941, pp. 279–80). This 'salesman of galoshes' must be the same as the *galoshisty* mentioned by Ziloti, who uses the term to refer to Gilse van der Pals and his group. See Ziloti, 1963, p. 399, n. 2, letter 54. The sum in question seems quite incredible; had he received such an amount, Diaghilev would never have had any financial problems.

13. See Baron Frederiks' letter to Nicholas II in Zilbershteyn and Samkov, 1982, ii, pp. 182–3.

14. Ibid.

15. Ibid., p. 476, n. 2.

16. Grigoriev, 1960, p. 18.

17. Ibid., p. 19.

18. Benois [Benua], 1980, ii, p. 476.

19. Varunts (ed.), *Muzykal'naya Akademiya*, 2001, no. 3, p. 155.

20. Lifar, 1994, p. 156.

21. See Zilbershteyn and Samkov, 1982, ii, p. 418.

22. Andrey Vladimirovich to Nicholas II, 18 March 1909. Lifar, 1994, p. 157.

23. Diaghilev to Frederiks, 20 March 1909. Zilbershteyn and Samkov, 1982, ii, p. 419.

24. Buckle, 1998, p. 135.

25. Ibid., pp. 135–6.

26. Benois, 1941, p. 282.

27. Andrey Vladimirovich to Boris Vladimirovich, 19 March 1909. Zilbershteyn and Samkov, 1982, ii, 418.

28. Diaghilev to Kochubey, 25 February 1910. Ibid., p. 419.

29. Grigoriev, 1960, pp. 25–6.

30. Benois, 1941, pp. 282–3.

31. These claims are cited by V. Svetlov in his article 'Russkiy sezon v Parizhe', quoted in Zilbershteyn and Samkov, 1982, ii, p. 419.

32. Nijinska, 1982, pp. 261–2.

33. The figure of 250 is in a telegram from Diaghilev to Astruc of 31 March 1909 (Buckle, 1979, p. 135). The size of the orchestra is given in an article

in the *Peterburgskaya gazeta* of 10 May 1909, cited in Zilbershteyn and Samkov, 1982, i, p. 420.

34. Valts, 1928, p. 217.

35. Astruc, cited in Steegmuller, 1970, p. 68.

36. The first performance, a dress rehearsal open to the public, had been held the day before.

37. Anna de Noailles, cited in Acocella, 1984, p. 1. In the first and fifth chapters of her dissertation Acocella gives detailed consideration to the reception of the Ballets Russes in Paris.

38. Shortly after the performances, Kessler met Benois, who tried (unsuccessfully) to introduce him to Diaghilev. See Benois's letter to Argutinsky of 2 July 1909, in Zilbershteyn and Samkov, 1982, ii, p. 185.

39. Kessler to Hofmannsthal, 28 May 1909, in Hofmannsthal and Kessler, 1968, p. 234.

40. Kessler, diary entry of 4 June 1909, Kessler, 2005, p. 574.

41. Kessler to Hofmannsthal, 5 June 1909. Hofmannsthal and Kessler, 1968, pp. 239–40.

42. Interview with Diaghilev and Bakst, in the Moscow paper *Utro Rossii*, 24 August 1910. Zilbershteyn and Samkov, 1982, i, p. 430.

43. Ibid.

44. Wagner postulated his theory of the *Gesamtkunstwerk* in *Kunst und Revolution*, 1849.

45. According to Karsavina, Diaghilev stated, 'We're all living in the witchery of Armida's groves. The very air round the Russian season is intoxicated.' Karsavina, 1950, p. 243.

46. Remark by Jean Cocteau, cited in Steegmuller, 1970, p. 69.

47. Benois [Benua], 1980, ii, p. 505.

48. Ibid.

49. Lifar, 1994, p. 73.

50. See Nijinska, 1982, p. 277.

51. Ibid., p. 279.

52. Diaghilev to Benois, 12 June. Zilbershteyn and Samkov, 1982, ii, p. 109.

15 Bakst and the Art of Seduction, 1909–1910

1. Diaghilev to Benois, September 1909. Zilbershteyn and Samkov, 1982, ii, pp. 110–11.

2. Debussy to Durand, 18 July 1909. Debussy, 2005, p. 1196.

3. Debussy to Laloy, 30 July 1909. Ibid., p. 1200.

4. Diaghilev to Benois, 12 June 1909. Zilbershteyn and Samkov, 1982, ii, pp. 108–9.

5. Ravel to De Saint-Merceaux, June 1909. Orenstein, 1975, p. 60.

6. We know this from a letter from Diaghilev to Benois, 12 June 1909, in Zilbershteyn and Samkov, 1982, ii, p. 108. Akimenko's name is first mentioned in connection with a possible ballet in 1908, in a letter from Bakst to his wife of 24 July 1908, ibid., p. 181.

7. For more on Akimenko and the Contemporary Music Evenings see Nestyev, 'Muzikalnye kruzhki', in Alekseyev et al., 1977, p. 477. For more on Akimenko and Kuzmin, see Kuzmin, 2000, p. 418.

8. Diaghilev to Benois, 12 September 1909. Zilbershteyn and Samkov, 1982, ii, p. 111.

9. Benois writes this in his article in *Rech*, 18 July 1910, on the genesis of *The Firebird*, quoted in Lapshina, 1977, pp. 233–4. Benois states that Tcherepnin took himself out of the running, being completely uninterested in ballet. This sounds implausible because at that very moment Tcherepnin was working on *Le Masque Rouge*, a ballet based on Poe's 'The Masque of the Red Death', which would not, in the end, be staged by Diaghilev.

10. Diaghilev to Lyadov, 4 September 1909. Zilbershteyn and Samkov, 1982, ii, p. 109.

11. Debussy to Laloy, 2 August 1909. Debussy, 2005, pp. 1200–1201.

12. Nijinska, 1982, p. 279.

13. Diaghilev to Benois, September 1909. Zilbershteyn and Samkov, 1982, ii, p. 111.

14. Fokine, 1981, p. 139. Fokine writes that 'months' had passed, but that seems like an exaggeration. Stravinsky started work on *The Firebird* in the autumn of 1909. The story about the music paper has taken on a life of its own. According to Lifar it was Benois who ran into Lyadov. Lifar, 1994, p. 205.

15. See chapter 10, n. 33.

16. Grigoriev, 1960, p. 39.

17. Drummond, 1997, p. 21. Stravinsky does not say whether this meeting took place before or after he was hired to do the Chopin orchestration. It seems a safe assumption that Diaghilev would have wanted to meet a composer before giving him a commission, and thus in all likelihood the two got together before the offer was made. However, both Grigoriev and Fokine suggest that the invitation to score *The Firebird* was made right after the concert featuring *Fireworks*. In that case, Diaghilev must have invited Stravinsky to do the Chopin ballet in a letter that has not survived. We can only assume that Diaghilev had heard Stravinsky's music at that point, either at one of the Evenings, or at another concert, such as the Siloti concert, where *Fireworks* was played. Here I have basically followed Stephen Walsh's reconstruction. Walsh, 2000, pp. 121–3.

18. Craft and Stravinsky, *Expositions*, 1981, p. 127.

19. Garafola, 1989, p. 178.

20. Gheusi to Sert, 27 June 1909. Gold and Fizdale, 1980, pp. 137–8.

21. See Garafola, 1989, p. 178.

22. Astruc to Enoch, 14 December 1909. Lincoln Center, Astruc Papers, ga 15–12.

23. See chapter 10, nn. 29 and 30.

24. 'Rapport Confidentiel sur la Saison Russe'. Lincoln Center, Astruc Papers, ga 25–17.

25. Garafola, 1989, p. 178.

26. Benois to Argutinsky, 2/15 July 1909. Zilbershteyn and Samkov, 1982, ii, p. 185.

27. Diaghilev to Nicholas II, 25 February 1910. Zilbershteyn and Samkov, 1982, i, p. 425.

28. Kokovtsev (Minister of Finance) to Kochubey, 12 April 1910. Ibid., p. 425.

29. Nicholas II to the Ministry of Finance. Ibid., p. 425. Peter Lieven mentions the tsar's subsidy, but his account is muddled. See Lieven, 1973, pp. 115–16.

30. Benois to José Maria Sert, 2 December 1909. Gold and Fizdale, 1980, p. 139.

31. Garafola, 1989, p. 179.

32. Diaghilev to Petrenko, [16 April? 1910]. Zilbershteyn and Samkov, 1982, i, p. 426.

33. *Carnaval* had had its premiere on 20 February 1910.

34. See Grigoriev, 1960, p. 38.

35. Ibid., p. 42.

36. Ibid.

37. Ibid.

38. Nijinska, 1982, pp. 293–4.

39. Kochno, 1970, p. 37.

40. Grigoriev, 1960, p. 44.

41. See Walsh, 2000, p. 138.

42. Karsavina, 1950, p. 164.

43. Debussy to Jacques Durand, 8 July 1910. Debussy, 2005, pp. 1297–8.

44. Spencer, 1978, p. 69.

45. See Diaghilev's remarks on the subject in his memoirs. Varunts (ed.), *Muzykal'naya Akademiya*, 2001, no. 3, p. 155.

46. Interview with Diaghilev in *Utro Rossii*, 23 August 1910. Zilbershteyn and Samkov, 1982, i, p. 214.

47. Bakst to Bakst-Gritsenko, 31 May 1910. Ibid., p. 438.

48. This comes from Benois. Benois [Benua], 1980, i, p. 618.

49. Ibid.

50. Bakst to Bakst-Gritsenko, 27 June. Zilbershteyn and Samkov, 1989, p. 217, n. 7.

51. McBrien, 1998, p. 71.

52. Benois [Benua], 1980, ii, p. 519.

53. For a discussion of *Giselle*'s authorship, see Zilbershteyn and Samkov, 1971, pp. 607–8 and 622–3, n. 58. In his memoirs Benois says nothing about the disputed authorship of *Giselle*, though his correspondence suggests that for some reason it was a more important issue for him than the related question of who should be given credit for *Schéhérazade*.

16 Emergence of a Genius, 1910–1911

1. Cited by Davenport-Hines, 2006, pp. 36–7.

2. Kessler, diary entry of 9 June 1910. Kessler, 2005, p. 595.

3. Sert, 1953, p. 115.

4. Benois's stay at Casa Camuzzi is mentioned in a letter from Stravinsky to Benois, 30 June/13 July 1911. Varunts, 1998, p. 287.

5. Benois to Diaghilev, 27 June 1910. Zilbershteyn and Samkov, 1982, ii, pp. 112–13.

6. Bakst to Benois, July 1910. Zilbershteyn and Samkov, 1971, pp. 607–8.

7. According to Benois it was Nijinsky who accompanied Diaghilev, not Bakst. But given that Bakst was responsible for the changes to *Giselle*, it would have been logical for him to go along to the 'peace talks' in Switzerland. See also chapter 15, n. 53.

8. Grigoriev, 1960, p. 56; Nijinska, 1982, p. 305; Benois, 1941, p. 323.

9. Nijinska, 1982, p. 305.

10. Ibid., p. 307.

11. Zilbershteyn and Samkov, 1982, i, p. 433.

12. Diaghilev, letter to the editor, *Peterburgskaya gazeta*, 28 August 1910. Zilbershteyn and Samkov, 1982, i, pp. 215–17.

13. Zilbershteyn and Samkov, 1982, ii, p. 187.

14. Zilbershteyn and Samkov, 1982, i, pp. 435–6.

15. Ibid., p. 219.

16. Ibid., p. 427.

17. Diaghilev to Rimskaya-Korsakova, 10 September 1910. Ibid., pp. 220–22.

18. Krasovskaya, 1971, p. 267.

19. Walsh, 2000, p. 137.

20. Stravinsky, 1962, p. 31.

21. The two interviews were published in the *Peterburgskaya gazeta*, 28 February 1910, and *Obozreniye teatrov*, 30 September 1910.

22. Walsh is less certain than Varunts, although he uses the same sources. See Walsh, 2000, pp. 138ff. and Varunts, 1998, p. 239, n. 10.

23. Stravinsky to Roerich, 19 June 1910. Varunts, 1998, p. 225.

24. The letter has not survived. This paraphrased version comes from Lieven (1973, p. 134), whose monograph on the Ballets Russes was mainly based on information provided by Benois, who is thought by some to have ghost-written the book. Benois's own version is more or less identical. Benois [Benua], 1980, ii, p. 521.

25. Diaghilev to Roerich, 9 October 1910. Zilbershteyn and Samkov, 1982, ii, pp. 166–7.

26. Quoted from an article by Benois in *Poslednye novosti* of 21 and 22 March 1930, cited in Varunts, 1998, p. 244, n. 2. Stravinsky's response was unambiguous: 'What an insolent and shameless lie.' In his memoirs Benois tones this claim down a bit, but still creates the impression that he immediately sprang into action. See Benois, 1941, pp. 324–7 and Benois [Benua], 1980, ii, pp. 520–22.

27. Stravinsky to Benois, 3 November 1910 and Benois to Stravinsky, 22 December 1910. Varunts, 1998, pp. 242, 252.

28. Benois to Diaghilev, 31 January/13 February 1911. Zilbershteyn and Samkov, 1982, ii, p. 114.

29. This is shown by a letter from Aleksey Neklyudov, an employee of the Russian embassy in Paris, to the director of the French Philharmonic Association. Ibid., p. 186 and commentary, p. 478.

30. Karsavina, 1950, p. 167.

31. Ibid., p. 165.

32. Ibid., p. 171.

33. Telyakovsky, diary entry of 24 January 1911, cited in Krasovskaya, 1971, pp. 402–3. Walter Nouvel also names Sergey Alexandrovich as the one who inspected Nijinsky's costume: Haskell and Nouvel, 1935, p. 212. Nijinska, by contrast, claimed that it was Grand Duke Andrey Vladimirovich who questioned her brother: Nijinska, 1982, p. 322.

34. Nijinska, 1982, p. 323.

35. Telyakovsky, diary entry of 24 February(?) 1911, cited in Krasovskaya, 1971, p. 403.

36. Nijinska, 1982, p. 320.

37. Ibid.

38. Diaghilev to Astruc, 10/23 February(?) 1911, in Buckle, 1979, p. 187.

39. Stravinsky to Benois, 2/15 February 1911. Varunts, 1998, p. 267.

40. Nijinska, 1982, p. 313.

41. Telyakovsky, diary entry of 23 March 1910, cited in Zilbershteyn and Samkov, 1989, pp. 311–12, n. 1.

42. This is largely Buckle's stance: 'It is almost impossible to believe that Diaghilev had not engineered this dismissal.' Buckle, 1979, p. 187.

43. Benois, 1941, p. 318.

44. Krasovskaya, 1971, p. 402.

45. Ibid., p. 404.

17 *Petrushka*, 1911–1912

1. Kessler, diary entry of 10 August 1911. Kessler, 2005, p. 717.

2. De Cossart, 1987, p. 46.

3. Grigoriev, 1960, p. 56.

4. Bakst to Bakst-Gritsenko, 23 May 1911. Zilbershteyn and Samkov, 1982, ii, p. 189.

5. Grigoriev, 1960, pp. 61–2.

6. Stravinsky to Vladimir Rimsky-Korsakov [son of Nikolay], 21 June 1911. Varunts, 1998, p. 294.

7. Benois, 1941, pp. 332–3.

8. Published on 14 May 1911 in *La Tribuna*.

9. Nijinska, 1982, p. 360.

10. Article in *Obozreny teatrov*, 3 May 1911. Zilbershteyn and Samkov, 1982, i, p. 445.

11. Benois, 1941, pp. 331–2.

12. Karsavina, 1950, p. 182.

13. Nijinska, 1982, p. 361.

14. Grigoriev, 1960, p. 62.

15. Serov to Ostroukhov, 11 May 1911. Zilbershteyn and Samkov, 1989, p. 285.

16. Gury Stravinsky [brother of Igor] to Vladimir Rimsky-Korsakov, 10 June 1911. Varunts, 1998, p. 278.

17. Grigoriev, 1960, p. 63.

18. Monteux, 1965, pp. 75–6.

19. Sert, 1953, pp. 128–9.

20. See Nijinska, 1982, p. 363.

21. Grigoriev, 1960, p. 62.

22. Benois, 1941, pp. 194, 338.

23. Serov to Ostroukhov, 26 June 1911. Zilbershteyn and Samkov, 1989, pp. 298–9. Over the past twenty years, research surrounding the Ballets Russes has tended to focus on the sources and background of Stravinsky's music. This is largely the doing of Richard Taruskin, whose *Stravinsky and the Russian Traditions* is a monument to this giant of twentieth-century music. An entire book has been devoted to *Petrushka* alone: Andrew Wachtel's compilation *Petrushka: Sources and Contexts* (Evanston, IL, 1998).

24. Tcherepnin, 1976, p. 30.

25. Stravinsky to Vladimir Rimsky-Korsakov, 16/29 June 1911. Varunts, 1998, p. 283.

26. Stravinsky attributes the criticism of some journalists to the fact that Diaghilev had declined to stage Reynaldo Hahn's new ballet that season. See ibid.

27. Debussy to Robert Godet, 18 December 1911. Debussy, 2005, p. 1470.

28. Debussy to Stravinsky, 13 April 1912. Ibid., p. 1503.

29. Craft and Stravinsky, *Expositions*, 1981, p. 137.

30. Ibid.

31. Benois, 1941, p. 334.

32. Quoted in a letter from Serov to Benois, 18 June 1911. Zilbershteyn and Samkov, 1989, p. 297.

33. Serov to his wife, 18 June 1911. Ibid., p. 296.

34. Benois to Diaghilev, June 1911. Zilbershteyn and Samkov, 1982, ii, p. 117.

35. Serov to Benois, 18 June 1911. Zilbershteyn and Samkov, 1989, pp. 296–7.

36. Benois, 1941, p. 335.

37. Benois to Serov, [late June] 1911. Zilbershteyn and Samkov, 1989, pp. 301–2.

38. A month later Serov informed Nouvel that he had yet to receive a letter from Benois and had little hope he ever would. Serov to Nouvel, 29 July 1911. Ibid., p. 305.

39. Ibid.

40. Grigoriev, 1960, p. 67.

41. Nijinska, 1982, p. 380.

42. Buckle, 1979, p. 209.

43. Diaghilev to Astruc, 23 June 1911. Ibid.

44. Karsavina, 1950, p. 225.

45. Cited in Scheijen, 2009, p. 297.

46. Stravinsky to his wife, 17 March 1912. Varunts, 1998, pp. 319–20.

18 Prelude to a Scandal, 1911–1912

1. Kessler, diary entry of 8 August 1911. Kessler, 2005, p. 715.

2. See Easton, 2002, p. 202.

3. To some extent this was due to the machinations of one of Rilke's advisers, Pavel Ettinger (who was hostile to Diaghilev). For the full Rilke–Diaghilev story, see Asadowski, 1986, pp. 191–6, 203–4, 265, 315.

4. Kessler, diary entry of 9 August 1911. Kessler, 2005, p. 715.

5. Kessler, diary entry of 12 August 1911. Ibid., p. 719.

6. The various sources disagree on this point. Nijinska claims that Nijinsky was sent directly to Venice (from London; she forgets the visit to Paris) (Nijinska, 1982, p. 383). Kessler claims in his diary that Nijinsky went along to Marienbad (Kessler, 2005, p. 715). Since Nijinsky's presence is not mentioned in the correspondence from Germany (see n. 7), I assume he was not there.

7. Ostroukhov to Tretyakovskaya-Botkina, 16/29 August 1911. Varunts, 1998, p. 297.

8. I have paraphrased Stravinsky's biographer Walsh here. Walsh, 2000, p. 175.

9. It was Ilya Zilbershteyn who first made the connection between Diaghilev's planned season in St Petersburg and the hiring of Kshesinskaya. Zilbershteyn and Samkov, 1982, ii, p. 428.

10. Nijinska, 1982, p. 391.

11. According to Karsavina, Vasily seriously proposed having Kshesinskaya poisoned at the time of the conflict surrounding Nijinsky. Karsavina, 1950, p. 167.

12. Serov to Nouvel, 10 September 1911. Zilbershteyn and Samkov, 1989, p. 311.

13. Telyakovsky, diary entry of 24 October 1911, cited in Zilbershteyn and Samkov, 1982, ii, p. 428.

14. Nijinska, 1982, p. 390.

15. Diaghilev to Kshesinskaya, 19 October/1 November 1911. Zilbershteyn and Samkov, 1982, ii, p. 117.

16. Bronislava claims that the Petersburg season took place in January and February. Nijinska, 1982, p. 391. Grigoriev maintains that it was December and January. Grigoriev, 1960, p. 69.

17. Cited in Buckle, 1979, p. 211.

18. Craft and Stravinsky, *Expositions*, 1981, p. 65.

19. Kessler, diary entry of 30 October 1911. Kessler, 2005, pp. 734–5.

20. Kuzmin, diary entries of 17 and 23 September 1911. Kuzmin, 2005, pp. 300, 301 and p. 703, n. 9.

21. Kuzmin, diary entry of 24 September 1911. Ibid., p. 302.

22. Diaghilev to Diaghileva, 23 November/6 December 1911. IRLi, fond 102, ed. khr. 91, l.39.

23. Stravinsky to Benois, 2/15 February 1912. Varunts, 1998, p. 309.

24. Grigoriev, 1960, p. 72.

25. The average duration of Debussy's composition. In an article for *Figaro* about the dress rehearsal Jacques-Emile Blanche speaks of 'eight minutes of beauty' (J.-E. Blanche, 'L'antiquité en 1912', *Le Figaro*, 29 May 1912). If Blanche is right, *L'après-midi* is played much more slowly nowadays.

26. Craig and Kessler, 1995, p. 77.

27. Stravinsky to Andrey Rimsky-Korsakov [son of Nikolay], 24 September/7 October 1911. Varunts, 1998, pp. 300–301.

28. Tyrkova, 1915, ii, p. 105.

29. Ibid., p. 112.

30. Nijinska, 1982, p. 427. Rambert, 1972, p. 61.

31. Nijinska, 1982, p. 430.

32. Ibid., p. 431.

33. Ibid.

34. Stravinsky to Benois, 13 March 1912. Varunts, 1998, p. 322.

35. Diaghilev to Astruc, 14 and 16 January 1912, Astruc Papers, Lincoln Center, ga 74–3, 74–4.

36. Waagenaar, 1994, p. 94.

37. Ibid.

38. Ibid., p. 95.

39. Grigoriev, 1960, p. 78.

40. Sert, 1953, p. 116.

41. Ibid., p. 115.

42. Ibid.

43. Ibid.

44. Ibid., pp. 115–16.

45. Craft and Stravinsky, *Memories*, 1981, p. 36.

46. Kessler, diary entry of 23 May 1912. Kessler, 2005, p. 826.

47. Kessler, diary entry of 29 May 1912. Ibid., p. 834.

48. Kessler, diary entry of 28 May 1912. Ibid. Fokine (1981) also describes the dress rehearsal, but his account diverges from Kessler's on several points.

49. Kessler, diary entry of 29 May 1912. Kessler, 2005, pp. 834–5.

50. Grigoriev, 1960, p. 79.

51. Buckle, 1979, p. 226.

52. Ibid., p. 227.

53. Kessler, diary entry of 31 May 1912. Kessler, 2005, p. 837.

54. Ibid., p. 838.

55. Kessler, diary entry of 5 June 1912. Ibid., p. 844.

56. Ibid., pp. 844–5.

19 A Year of Risky Experiments, 1912–1913

1. Zilbershteyn and Samkov, 1982, i, p. 453.

2. Grigoriev, 1960, p. 77.

3. Nijinska, 1982, p. 434.

4. Kessler, diary entry of 12 July 1912. Kessler, 2005, p. 850.

5. Ibid.

6. Kessler, diary entry of 13 July 1912. Ibid., p. 851.

7. The evening is described in another context by Polignac's biographer Sylvia Kahan. Kahan, 2003, p. 176.

8. Kessler, diary entry of 15 July 1912. Kessler, 2005, p. 851.

9. Kessler, diary entry of 17 July 1912. Ibid., p. 852.

10. Craft and Stravinsky, *Memories*, 1981, pp. 36–7. According to Stravinsky the party took place before the premiere of *Sacre*, which strongly suggests that it was the same one described by Kessler.

11. Quoted in Krasovskaya, 1979, p. 220 (no source given).

12. As quoted by Andrey Rimsky-Korsakov. A. H. Rimsky-Korsakov to N. N. Rimsky-Korsakov, 24 June/7 July 1910. Varunts, 1998, p. 229.

13. Moss, 2005, p. 95.

14. Bakst to Stravinsky, 17 November 1912. Varunts, 1998, pp. 375–6, n. 10.

15. Interview with Diaghilev in the *Peterburgskaya gazeta*, 1 October 1912. Zilbershteyn and Samkov, 1982, ii, p. 429.

16. Diaghilev to Diaghileva, 26 September 1912. IRLi, fond 102, ed. khr. 91, l.33.

17. Diaghilev to Diaghileva, 2 October 1912. IRLi, fond 102, ed. khr. 86, l.40.

18. See Karsavina, 1950, p. 226.

19. Thomas Beecham, quoted in Schouvaloff, 1997, p. 201.

20. Only one of the three operas, *The Maid of Pskov*, was performed in its entirety.

21. Haskell and Nouvel, 1935, p. 220. Astruc quotes this exchange in a slightly altered form: Astruc, 1929, p. 286.

22. Maes, 2006, p. 137.

23. Interview with Diaghilev for the *Peterburgskaya gazeta*, 11 February 1910. Zilbershteyn and Samkov, 1982, i, p. 212.

24. Ibid.

25. Kessler, diary entry of 8 August 1912. Kessler, 2005, pp. 855–6.

26. Ibid.

27. Stravinsky, 1962, pp. 38–9. See also Walsh, 2000, p. 183.

28. *Berliner Tageblatt*, 5 December 1912. Varunts, 1998, p. 373.

29. Stravinsky is hazy about this point in his memoirs. In *Conversations* he writes that Schoenberg attended both *Firebird* and *Petrushka* (Craft and Stravinsky, 1979, p. 69). In *Dialogues* Stravinsky mentions Schoenberg's presence only at the latter concert (Craft and Stravinsky, 1982, p. 104).

30. Craft and Stravinsky, 1979, p. 69.

31. On 8 December in Berlin's Choralion-Saal. See Craft and Stravinsky, 1982, p. 104.

32. Ibid.

33. Bakst to Ziloti, 8 March 1913. Ziloti, 1963, p. 287.

34. Stravinsky to Schmitt, 21 January 1913. Walsh, 2000, p. 190.

35. Interview with Stravinsky. *Daily Mail*, 13 February 1913.

36. Prokofiev, diary entry of 19 June 1911. Prokofiev, 2002, i, p. 159.

37. Kessler, diary entry of 17 February 1913. Kessler, 2005, p. 866.

38. Kessler to Craig, 17 February 1913. Craig and Kessler, 1995, p. 104.

39. Ibid., p. 78.

40. Kessler, diary entry of 19 February 1913. Kessler, 2005, p. 867.

41. '*Contrat avec Serge de Diaghilev*', 18 June 1912. Debussy, 2005, p. 1521.

42. The talk of aeroplanes and Zeppelins is echoed strangely in Nijinsky's diary, where he goes on at some length about the difference between them. See Nijinsky, 1999, pp. 215–16.

43. Diaghilev to Debussy, 18 July 1912. Debussy, 2005, pp. 1530–31.

44. Debussy to Durand, 9 August 1912. Ibid., p. 1536.

45. Debussy to Durand, 1 September 1912. Ibid., p. 1542.

46. Ibid.

47. Debussy to Durand, 5 September 1912. Ibid., p. 1543.

48. Diaghilev, interview in *Peterburgskaya gazeta*, 1 October 1912. Zilbershteyn and Samkov, 1982, i, p. 229.

49. Stravinsky to Derzhanovsky, 23 December 1912. Varunts, 1998, p. 393.

50. Stravinsky to Steynberg, 13 November 1912. Ibid., p. 373.

51. Kessler, diary entry of 15 February 1912. Kessler, 2005, p. 790.

52. Karsavina, 1950, p. 183. Karsavina also mentions the association with futurism, recalling a meeting with Marinetti, though she doesn't say if it took place at the time of *Jeux*.

53. Rambert, 1972, p. 70.

54. This exchange was recounted by Stravinsky in a radio interview, 'Stravinsky in his own words'. *Igor Stravinsky: Symphonies & Rehearsals and Talks*. Sony Classical. CD: SM2K 46294.

55. Debussy to Stravinsky, 7 November 1912. Debussy, 2005, pp. 1554–5.

56. See Walsh, 2002, p. 13.

57. Monteux, 1965, pp. 88–9. According to Monteux, this scene took place in the summer of 1912, but he would seem to be mistaken, since at that point the music was not yet complete, even in a draft version.

58. See Nijinsky, 1999, pp. 18–21.

59. Buckle, 1979, p. 235.

60. Diaghilev to Benois, Wednesday [1913], Zilbershteyn and Samkov, 1982, ii, p. 122.

61. Benois to Diaghilev, 4 February 1912. Ibid., pp. 117–18.

62. See Walsh, 2000, p. 194. See also Stravinsky to Schmitt, 17 January 1913. Craft, 1984, p. 106.

63. Monteux, 1965, p. 82.

64. Nijinska, 1982, p. 456.

65. See interviews with Diaghilev in the *Peterburgskaya gazeta*, 16 and 30 January 1913. Zilbershteyn and Samkov, 1982, i, pp. 229–30, 231–2.

66. Ibid., p. 232.

67. Nijinsky, 1999, pp. 206–7.

68. See McGinness, 2005, pp. 559ff.

69. Kessler, diary entry of 15 May 1913. Kessler, 2005, pp. 879–80.

70. Rambert, 1972, p. 70.

71. See Kessler, 2005, p. 880.

72. For more on the critics' response, see Buckle, 1998, pp. 344–6.

73. Debussy to Gabriel Pierné, 8 and 4 February 1914, respectively. Debussy, 2005, pp. 1759–60, 1758.

74. Kessler, diary entry of 28 May 1913. Kessler, 2005, pp. 885–6. This flatly contradicts Stravinsky's claim (many years later) that he did not expect an outburst. Stravinsky, 1962, p. 47.

75. This story is told by Buckle (and others). Buckle, 1979, p. 253.

76. Steegmuller, 1970, p. 85.

77. Kessler to Hofmannsthal, 4 June 1913. Hofmannsthal and Kessler, 1968, p. 361.

78. Kessler, diary entry of 29 May 1913. Kessler, 2005, pp. 886–7.

79. Stravinsky, 1962, p. 47.

80. Monteux, 1965, p. 90.

81. Rambert, 1972, pp. 64–5.

82. Stravinsky, 1962, p. 47.

83. Kessler, diary entry of 29 May 1913. Kessler, 2005, pp. 886–7.

84. Craft and Stravinsky, 1979, p. 46. The fact that Diaghilev was initially delighted by the scandal is confirmed by Roerich in an interview with *Teatr i Zhizn'*, 31 May 1913. See Varunts, 2000, p. 565.

85. Kessler, diary entry of 29 May 1913. Kessler, 2005, pp. 886–7.

86. Rambert, 1972, p. 65.

87. Steegmuller, 1970, p. 89. Stravinsky later dismissed this anecdote of Cocteau's, subsequently denying (or at least ignoring) many other stories associated with that legendary night, including the wild taxi ride, which is confirmed by two other sources (Rambert and Kessler, in addition to Cocteau). This makes Stravinsky's denials suspect, particularly in view of the deeply anti-sentimentalist position the composer adopted from the early 1930s, a position that was at odds with an anecdote like this one. See Craft and Stravinsky, 1979, pp. 46–7.

20 Time of Troubles, 1913–1914

1. Diaghilev to Diaghileva, 8 June 1913. IRLi, fond. 102, ed. khr. 91, l.31.

2. Nijinska, 1982, pp. 472–3.

3. Kessler, diary entry of 6 August 1913. Kessler, 2005, p. 905.

4. Kessler to Hofmannsthal, 10 October 1913. Hofmannsthal and Kessler, 1968, p. 366.

5. Nijinska, 1982, p. 473.

6. *Peterburgskaya gazeta*, 3/16 September 1913. Zilbershteyn and Samkov, 1982, i, p. 463.

7. Misia Sert to Stravinsky, 7–11 July 1913. Craft, 1978, p. 516.

8. Stravinsky to Diaghilev, 12 July 1913. Ibid., p. 517.

9. Misia Sert to Stravinsky, 15 July 1913. Ibid.

10. Stravinsky to Benois, 30 July 1913. Varunts, 2000, pp. 121–3.

11. Nijinsky, 1999, p. 110.

12. Ibid.

13. See Benois to Stravinsky, 22 September 1913. Varunts, 2000, p. 148.

14. See Rambert, 1972, p. 74; Buckle, 1998, p. 381.

15. Nijinsky, 1934, p. 236.

16. Sert, 1953, pp. 120–21.

17. Diaghilev to Stravinsky, 16 and 17 September 1913. Varunts, 2000, p. 143.

18. Nijinska, 1982, p. 489.

19. Benois to Stravinsky, 17 September 1913. Varunts, 2000, pp. 144–5.

20. Stravinsky to Benois, 20 September 1913. Ibid., pp. 146–7.

21. Struve to Stravinsky, 28 October 1913. Ibid., p. 166.

22. See ibid. Struve's letter states that Diaghilev was still in Berlin on 26 October.

23. Grigoriev, 1960, pp. 102–3. Fokine's account of the negotiations with Diaghilev does not mention the telephone conversation, only the ensuing meeting. Fokine, 1981, p. 396.

24. 'We've got Fokine at last.' Bakst to Stravinsky, 21 November/4 December 1913. Varunts, 2000, pp. 179–80. That the meeting took place in late 1913

is also evident from a letter from Fokine to Diaghilev, dated 'late 1913'. Zilbershteyn and Samkov, 1982, ii, p. 123.

25. Grigoriev, 1960, p. 100.

26. Nijinsky to Stravinsky, 9 December 1913. Varunts, 2000, pp. 181–2. Craft's translation in the second volume of *Selected Correspondence* differs considerably on a number of points from the Russian original, including dates. Craft gives 1 December as the date of the letter. See Stravinsky, 1984, pp. 47–8. The original of the letter is in the archive of the Paul Sacher Stiftung in Basel.

27. Nijinsky to Astruc, 5 December 1913. NYPL, Lincoln Center, Dance Collection, ga 92–2. Quoted in Buckle, 1979, p. 264.

28. Benois is the author of the latter theory (Benois, 1941, p. 352), Nijinska of the former. She suggests that it was Diaghilev himself who masterminded the wedding, abetted by Gunzburg. Nijinska, 1982, p. 484.

29. Bakst to Stravinsky, 17 November 1912. Varunts, 1998, p. 375.

30. See Dobuzhinsky to Stanislavsky, 26 July 1914. Quoted in Chugunov, 1984, p. 103.

31. Dobuzhinsky, 1987, p. 285.

32. Grigoriev, 1960, p. 105.

33. See Massine, 1968, pp. 41–5.

34. See Souritz, 2005, p. 111.

35. See ibid. and García-Márquez, 1996, p. 34.

36. At the time, Diaghilev was negotiating with Gorsky about his possible involvement in Tcherepnin's Poe ballet (never performed).

37. See García-Márquez, 1996, p. 34.

38. Ibid., p. 31.

39. Ibid., p. 34.

40. Ibid., pp. 20–21.

41. *Teatr*, 1–2 June 1914, p. 6.

42. See Chamot, 1979, p. 13.

43. Larionov in *Zolotoye runo*, nos. 2–3, 1909; quoted in Zilbershteyn and Samkov, 1989, p. 176.

44. Alexandre Benois [A. N. Benua], 'Iz dnevnika khudozhnika', *Rech*, 21 October 1913. Petrova, 2002, p. 341.

45. Benois, 1941, p. 356.

46. Goncharova is particularly convincing. She responded angrily to Benois's claims when he first wrote in 1934 that he was the 'spiritual father' of *Coq d'or*. See Goncharova to Benois, 1934, in Ilyukhina and Shumanova, 1997, p. 114.

47. Ibid.

48. Ibid.

49. Stravinsky, 1982, p. 74.

50. Stravinsky to Stravinskaya, 22 January 1914. Varunts, 2000, pp. 200–201.

51. See Vera Ziloti to A. P. Tretyakova, 20 December 1913: 'How will Nijinsky finance his ballet in Paris? Interesting, don't you think? Might he compete with Diaghilev?' In Ziloti, 1963, p. 392.

52. Diaghilev to Stravinsky, 25 January/5 February 1914. Varunts, 2000, p. 207.

53. Ibid.

54. Nijinska, 1982, pp. 489–91.

55. According to Romola Nijinsky, Diaghilev sued Bronislava for breach of contract and lost. See Nijinsky, 1934, p. 265. Bronislava doesn't mention a lawsuit, and there is no reason to assume that Diaghilev would have lost such a case, because Bronislava was contracted to him to the end of March.

56. Prokofiev, diary entry of 26 January 1914. Prokofiev, 2006, p. 591.

57. Benois to Svetlov, 13 March 1914. Zilbershteyn and Samkov, 1982, ii, pp. 199–200.

58. Grigoriev, 1960, p. 107.

21 'Let us be resolute and energetic', 1914–1915

1. Sert, 1953, p. 140.

2. Kessler to Hofmannsthal, 15 March 1914. Hofmannsthal and Kessler, 1968, p. 375.

3. Kessler to Hofmannsthal, 19 March 1914. Ibid., pp. 376–7.

4. Kessler to Hofmannsthal, 29 March 1914. Ibid., pp. 377–8.

5. Bakst to Misia Sert. García-Márquez, 1996, p. 37.

6. Nijinska, 1982, p. 501.

7. Diaghilev to Stravinsky, 21 April 1914. Varunts, 2000, p. 243.

8. See Kessler, diary entry of 25 March 1914. Kessler, 2005, p. 912.

9. See García-Márquez, 1996, p. 38.

10. See Nice, 2003, pp. 116, 188.

11. Stravinsky to V. N. Rimsky-Korsakov, 8 July 1911. Varunts, 1998, pp. 290–94.

12. Interview with Stravinsky, *Peterburgskaya gazeta*, 27 September 1912. Ibid., p. 294.

13. Parton, 1993, pp. 143–4.

14. Nijinsky, 1934, p. 272.

15. Prokofiev, diary entry of 9 June–7 July 1914. Prokofiev, 2002, i, p. 479.

16. Ibid.

17. This at least is the view of Francis Maes: Maes, 2006, p. 249.

18. Prokofiev, *Autobiography*, in Prokofiev, 1992, p. 249.

19. Prokofiev, diary entry of 9 June–7 July, 1914. Prokofiev, 2002, i, p. 480.

20. Ibid.

21. Ibid., p. 481.

22. Prokofiev, *Autobiography*, in Prokofiev, 1992, p. 250.

23. Sert, 1953, p. 140.

24. See Grigoriev, 1960, p. 111; Kessler, 2005, pp. 913–15. Many years later Kessler maintained he had not been aware of the German war plans until the very last minute. Kessler, diary entry of 6 January 1923. Kessler, 1996, p. 375.

25. Kessler, 2005, p. 915.

26. Grigoriev, 1960, p. 111.

27. Sert, 1953, p. 141.

28. See Gold and Fizdale, 1980, pp. 162–6; Cossart, 1987, p. 64.

29. Stravinsky to Benois, 11 July 1914. Varunts, 2000, p. 281.

30. On 5 September Stravinsky received a telegram from Cernobbio. Ibid., p. 289.

31. This telegram has not come down to us, but in a subsequent cable Diaghilev alludes to the 'two words' she wrote to him. In this context those words could only be '*umer otets*'.

32. Diaghilev to Diaghileva, 10 August 1914. IRLi, fond 102, ed. khr. 91, l.24.

33. Diaghilev to Diaghileva, 12 August 1914. Ibid., l.25.

34. See Dyagileva, 1998, p. 233, n. 58. In conversations with the author, Elena Sergeyevna Dyagileva confirmed her father's memory of Sergey Pavlovich's last journey to St Petersburg.

35. Massine's biographer García-Márquez suggests that Massine falsely claimed that he occasionally travelled alone, as a way of emphasising his independence from Diaghilev, but García-Márquez apparently did not know about the death of Diaghilev's father. See García-Márquez, 1996, p. 393, n. 1.

36. Stravinsky to Bakst, 20 September 1914. Varunts, 2000, p. 290.

37. Massine, 1968, p. 70.

38. See Varunts, 2000, pp. 36, 38, n. 9.

39. See Lynn Garafola, 'The Ballets Russes in America', in Van Norman Baer, 1988, pp. 122–37 at p. 122.

40. See Diaghilev to Stravinsky, 29 September 1914. Varunts, 2000, p. 292. There is some doubt about whether this trip to Florence actually occurred (Varunts questions it, and Walsh follows his lead: Walsh, 2000, p. 246). Stravinsky mentions the trip to Florence in his autobiography (Stravinsky, 1962, p. 56).

41. Diaghilev to Stravinsky, 1 November 1914. Scheijen, *Sergei Diaghilev*, 2004, p. 168. Diaghilev mentions a '*kladbishcheh*', a cemetery in Ravenna. I assume he is referring to one of the two Byzantine mausoleums in that city.

42. The ballet would eventually be titled *Liturgy*. For more on Stravinsky's involvement see Taruskin, 1996, ii, p. 1379, n. 64.

43. Diaghilev to Stravinsky, 25 November 1914. Varunts, 2000, p. 296.

44. Diaghilev to Nouvel, 28 November [1914]. RGALi, fond 781, ed. khr. 6, l.24–5.

45. Diaghilev to Stravinsky, [early February] 1915. Varunts, 2000, p. 308.

22 A Parade of Revolutions, 1915–1917

1. See chapter 19, n. 51.
2. See Stravinsky to Stravinskaya, 18 February 1915. Varunts, 2000, p. 310.
3. Diaghilev to Stravinsky, 8 March 1915. Ibid., p. 315.
4. Ibid.
5. The letter, apparently Nouvel's reply to Diaghilev's letter of 28 November (chapter 21, n. 44), has not been preserved. Prokofiev quotes this one sentence in his short autobiography. Prokofiev, 1992, p. 250.
6. Prokofiev, diary entry of 18 February 1915. Prokofiev, 2002, i, p. 551.
7. Prokofiev, diary entry of 18 February 1915 (slightly paraphrased). Ibid.
8. Prokofiev, 1992, p. 251.
9. Prokofiev, diary entry of 18 February 1915. Prokofiev, 2002, i, pp. 551–2.
10. Ibid.
11. Diaghilev to Stravinsky, 8 March 1915. Scheijen, *Sergei Diaghilev*, 2004, pp. 172–4.
12. Prokofiev, diary entry of 25 February–10 March 1915. Prokofiev, 2002, i, pp. 553–4.
13. Ibid.
14. Prokofiev, 1992, pp. 251–2.
15. Prokofiev, diary entry of 20–22 March 1915. Prokofiev, 2002, i, p. 555.
16. Francesco Cangiullo, quoted in Walsh, 2000, p. 252.
17. See Taruskin, 1996, ii, p. 1320, n. 2.
18. See Craft and Stravinsky, 1979, p. 94.
19. Prokofiev quotes Diaghilev in a letter to Myaskovsky. Quoted in Robinson, 2002, p. 111.
20. Craft and Stravinsky, *Memories*, 1981, pp. 66–7.
21. Prokofiev, diary entry of 20–22 March 1915. Prokofiev, 2002, i, pp. 556–7.
22. Sokolova, 1960, p. 69.
23. See Varunts, 2000, p. 328.

24. Craft and Stravinsky, *Expositions*, 1981, p. 118. Stravinsky's memory fails him here. When he played the piece to Diaghilev in Montreux (Clarens) – not Ouchy, as Stravinsky claims – Diaghilev had already heard it at least twice. See also Walsh, 2000, p. 253.

25. Diaghilev and Stravinsky to Goncharova and Larionov, 22 May 1915. Zilbershteyn and Samkov, 1982, ii, p. 125.

26. See Parton, 1993, p. 148.

27. The most detailed information about Goncharova's involvement with *Liturgy* is in Ilyukhina and Shumanova, 1997, pp. 94–5, 115–16. The book also includes a libretto and a long list of characters.

28. See Taruskin, 1996, ii, p. 1379, n. 64.

29. See Grigoriev, 1960, p. 114. Also Sokolova, 1960, p. 69.

30. Diaghilev in the *New York Post*, 24 January 1916, cited in Taruskin, 1996, ii, p. 1321, n. 5.

31. Misia Sert to Cocteau. Gold and Fizdale, 1980, p. 172.

32. Ibid., p. 173.

33. See Ilyukhina and Shumanova, 1997, p. 115.

34. Sokolova, 1960, pp. 70–71.

35. Diaghilev to Diaghileva, 11(?) January 1916. IRLi, fond 102, ed. khr. 91, l.19.

36. Interview with Diaghilev in the *New York Times*, 23 January 1916.

37. The subject of life assurance is mentioned by Prokofiev. Prokofiev, diary entry of 6 March. Prokofiev, 2002, i, p. 554.

38. For instance Bakst to Stravinsky, 20 December 1914 and 24 January 1915. Varunts, 2000, pp. 300, 307–8.

39. For a detailed description of the reception of the Ballets Russes in America see Lynn Garafola, 'The Ballets Russes in America', in Van Norman Baer, 1988, pp. 122–37.

40. See ibid., p. 129, and Zilbershteyn and Samkov, 1982, ii, p. 435, n. 1.

41. Garafola, 'Ballets Russes in America', p. 126.

42. Interview with Diaghilev in the *New York Evening Post*, 25 January 1916.

43. Garafola, 'Ballets Russes in America', p. 129.

44. Nijinsky, 1934, p. 301; Garafola, 'Ballets Russes in America', p. 129.

45. Garafola, 'Ballets Russes in America', p. 130.

46. Sert, 1953, pp. 121–2.

47. Diaghilev to Diaghileva, 19 May 1916. IRLi, fond 102, ed. khr. 91, l.15.

48. Ansermet to Stravinsky, 12 August 1916. Ansermet and Stravinsky, 1990, i, pp. 52–3.

49. Satie to Misia Sert, 15 May 1916. Satie, 2003, p. 242.

50. On 9 July, Satie wrote to Misia Sert: 'Diaghilev won't go back on his word, will he?' Ibid., p. 247.

51. Satie to Valentine Gros, 13 July 1916; to Jean-Aubry, 6 November 1916; and to others. Ibid., pp. 248–9, 265, 275, 276, 363.

52. Steegmuller, 1970, p. 164.

53. Ibid., p. 82.

54. Diaghilev refers to Nijinsky's telegrams in his letter to Stravinsky of 3 December 1916. Varunts, 2000, p. 390.

55. At least this is what Diaghilev claimed. Garafola, 'Ballets Russes in America', p. 136.

56. Diaghilev to Stravinsky, 3 December 1916. Varunts, 2000, p. 390.

57. Diaghilev to Diaghileva, 3 January 1917. IRLi, fond 102, ed. khr. 91, l.6.

58. See Satie, 2003, pp. 276, 278.

59. Richardson, 2007, p. 4.

60. Cocteau to his mother, 20 February 1917. Clair, 1998, p. 326.

61. Stravinsky to Stravinskaya, 20 March 1917. Varunts, 2000, p. 398.

62. Benois, diary entry of 5 March 1917, Benois [Benua] and Dyagilev, 2003, pp. 94–5. There are two versions of Benois's diary. The volume just cited consists of fairly brief daily entries; extracts were incorporated into a second version (Benois [Benua], 2003), which is a 'composed diary', intended for publication, and which contains much more detailed notes. The two versions differ substantially on certain crucial points. In such cases I have deliberately opted for the first, unedited, version.

63. Benois, diary entry of 7 March 1917. Benois [Benua] and Dyagilev, 2003, p. 95.

64. Benois, diary entry of 2 March 1917. Benois [Benua], 2003, p. 128.

65. Ansermet to Stravinsky, 26 March 1917. Ansermet and Stravinsky, 1990, i. p. 60.

66. Benois, diary entry of 18 March 1917. Benois [Benua], 2003, p. 96.

67. Diaghilev to Stravinskaya, 17 December 1916. Varunts, 2000, pp. 392–3.

68. Diaghilev in *Le Figaro*, 14 May 1917. Quoted in Zilbershteyn and Samkov, 1982, i, p. 239.

69. See Norton, 2004, p. 45.

70. Ilya Ehrenburg, quoted in Zilbershteyn and Samkov, 1982, ii, p. 489.

71. Benois, diary entry of 29 October 1917. Benois [Benua] and Dyagilev, 2003, pp. 97–8.

72. Benois, diary entry of 20 November 1917. Ibid., p. 98.

23 A Letter from Nouvel, 1917–1919

1. Debussy to Diaghilev, 20 May 1917. Debussy, 2005, p. 2113.

2. Diaghilev to Diaghileva, 2 March 1918. IRLi, fond 102, ed. khr. 91, l.1. It is, at any rate, the last telegram in the family archives.

3. The most complete account of this tour of Spain is in Sokolova, 1960.

4. See Buckle, 1979, pp. 338–9.

5. Diaghilev to Massine, [before 29 July 1918]. García-Márquez, 1996, pp. 117–18.

6. Passages from two interviews with the *Daily Mail* quoted in Haskell and Nouvel, 1935, pp. 280–81.

7. Ibid., p. 281.

8. Diaghilev to Picasso, 18 October 1918. Archives of the Musée Picasso, Ap.cs 756.

9. Sokolova, 1960, pp. 131–2.

10. Ansermet to Stravinsky, 4 May 1919. Ansermet and Stravinsky, 1990, i, p. 88.

11. Diaghilev to Picasso, 15 April 1919. Richardson, 2007, p. 111.

12. For the lead-up to the conflict over *Boutique fantasque*, see Spencer, 1979, pp. 123–5.

13. The source for this is Massine, quoted ibid., p. 125.

14. Bakst to Diaghilev, 24 May 1919. Fonds Kochno (Musée de l'Opéra, Paris), pièce 4, 2.

15. Massine, 1968, p. 133.

16. Haskell and Nouvel, 1935, p. 282.

17. Kessler, diary entry of 28 December 1925. Kessler, 1996, p. 467.

18. Ibid. Others, including John Richardson in his biography of Picasso, have assumed for no particularly good reason that Félix's exploitation at the hands of Diaghilev and Massine was the source of his madness. See Richardson, 2007, pp. 113–17. Yet this claim doesn't hold water: Félix was already known as '*el loco*' before he left Spain. See n. 16 above.

19. Sokolova, 1960, p. 221; Kessler, 1996, p. 467.

20. Diaghilev to Picasso, May–June 1919. Laurence, 2003, p. 159.

21. Ibid.

22. Sokolova, 1960, p. 139.

23. Ansermet to Stravinsky, 4 May 1919. Ansermet and Stravinsky, 1990, i, p. 88; Ansermet to Stravinsky, 18 July 1919. Ibid., p. 136.

24. Ansermet to Stravinsky, 4 May 1919. Ibid., p. 88.

25. Nouvel to Diaghilev, 16 July 1919. Harvard Theatre Collection, bMS Thr 466(1).

26. Ansermet to Stravinsky, 28 July [1919]. Ansermet and Stravinsky, 1990, i, p. 143.

27. Nabokov confirms that Diaghilev was aware of the death of his two nephews. Nabokov, 1951, p. 67.

24 To the Brink of Catastrophe, 1919–1922

1. Matisse in an interview, quoted in Spurling, 2005, p. 229. According to Spurling the meeting took place in the early summer, but the fact that Stravinsky was present means it must have been September.

2. Ibid.

3. Ibid., p. 230.

4. Ibid.

5. Matisse to his wife, 22 October 1919. Quoted ibid., p. 232.

6. Diaghilev to Stravinsky, November 1916. Scheijen, *Sergei Diaghilev*, 2004, p. 176.

7. Craft and Stravinsky, *Expositions*, 1981, p. 112.

8. The musical material for *Pulcinella* was actually assembled from the work of four composers: Pergolesi, Domenico Galli, Carlo Monza and the Dutchman Unico Wilhelm van Wassenaer. A complete list of the various sources can be found in Varunts, 2000, p. 461.

9. Diaghilev's preference for an abstract interpretation comes from Massine. See García-Márquez, 1996, pp. 147–8.

10. Craft and Stravinsky, 1979, p. 105.

11. Beaumont, quoted in García-Márquez, 1996, p. 148.

12. See Taruskin, 1996, ii, p. 1508.

13. Ibid.

14. Diaghilev's shocked reaction to Margherita's death is documented by both Grigoriev and Sokolova. Grigoriev, 1960, p. 162; Sokolova, 1960, p. 149.

15. Prokofiev, diary entry of 7 May 1920. Prokofiev, 2002, ii, p. 98.

16. Prokofiev, diary entry of 10 May 1920. Ibid., p. 100.

17. Craft and Stravinsky, *Expositions*, 1981, p. 113.

18. Walsh, 2000, pp. 113–14.

19. Richardson, 2007, p. 154.

20. Walsh, 2000, p. 307.

21. Prokofiev, diary entry of 17 May 1920. Prokofiev, 2002, ii, p. 103.

22. See Craft and Stravinsky, 1979, p. 104.

23. Prokofiev, diary entry of 19 May 1920. Prokofiev, 2002, ii, p. 104.

24. Edward Dent, quoted in Norton, 2004, p. 78.

25. See Prokofiev, diary entry of 13 June–30 July 1920. Prokofiev, 2002, ii, p. 111.

26. See Prokofiev, diary entry of 29 May 1920. Ibid., p. 107.

27. See Grigoriev, 1960, p. 165; Prokofiev, 2002, ii, p. 115.

28. Prokofiev, diary entry of October 1920. Prokofiev, 2002, ii, p. 118.

29. Stravinsky in *Comœdia Illustré*, 14 and 20 December 1920. Reprinted for the first time in Varunts, 1988, pp. 30–32.

30. See Grigoriev, 1960, p. 67. For an overview of the reviews see Norton, 2004, p. 89.

31. This story comes from three different sources. Marinetti described it in his journal, and Kochno related it many years later to Massine's biographer García-Márquez. Buckle has it from Sokolova and Vera Stravinskaya. Marinetti, 1987, p. 474; García-Márquez, 1996, p. 161; Buckle, 1979, p. 371.

32. Grigoriev, 1960, p. 170.

33. Noted by Marinetti, 1987, p. 474.

34. Haskell and Nouvel, 1935, p. 289.

35. Sokolova, quoted in Buckle, 1979, p. 371.

36. Haskell and Nouvel, 1935, p. 272.

37. Sokolova, 1960, p. 173.

38. Prokofiev, diary entry of 13 June–30 July 1920. Prokofiev, 2002, ii, p. 112.

39. Spurling, 2005, p. 229.

40. 'The monster – that's what Seryozha [Sudeykin] always calls D. [Diaghilev].' Sudeykina to Stravinsky, July 1921. Varunts, 2000, p. 489.

41. Kochno later told Buckle that he had 'frequently cut [Diaghilev's picture] out of newspapers in Russia', plainly in an effort to convince the author that he was already a fan of Diaghilev before he met Sudeykin. (Buckle, 1979, p. 376). The story is dubious, however: when Kochno left Russia he was only fourteen. And how many photos of Diaghilev would have appeared in wartime newspapers? It wasn't until 1916 that Diaghilev first circulated a publicity photo of himself. Moreover, it was published in periodicals, not newspapers, and it certainly would not have reached Russia by 1917.

42. Both quotations ibid.

43. Prokofiev, diary entry of 1–30 April 1921. Prokofiev, 2002, ii, p. 156.

44. Buckle, 1979, p. 385.

45. Roland-Manuel, quoted in Robinson, 2002, p. 162.

46. Ibid.

47. Beaumont, quoted in Press, 2006, p. 51.

48. Grigoriev, 1960, p. 176.

49. Benois, quoted in Taruskin, 1996, ii, p. 1509.

50. Nijinska, quoted in Garafola, 1989, p. 124.

51. Varunts (ed.), *Muzykal'naya Akademiya*, 2001, no. 1, p. 142.

52. Ibid.

53. This information comes from Nouvel. Zilbershteyn and Samkov, 1982, ii, p. 491.

54. This list comes from Diaghilev himself. Varunts (ed.), *Muzykal'naya Akademiya*, 2001, no. 1, p. 142.

55. Sudeykin to Diaghilev, early December 1921. Varunts, 2000, p. 513.

56. Sudeykin to Diaghilev, 20(?) December 1921. Ibid., pp. 513–14.

57. See also Walsh, 2000, pp. 343–5.

58. Sudeykin and Sudeykina to Diaghilev, 29 December 1921. Varunts, 2000, pp. 514–15.

59. Bakst to Diaghilev, 4 October 1921. Quoted in Walsh, 2000, p. 342.

60. Beaumont, 1945, pp. 195–6.

61. Stravinsky, 'The Diaghilev I Knew', quoted in Buckle, 1979, p. 393. See also Varunts, 1988.

25 A Lifeline from Monte Carlo, 1922–1924

1. Garafola, 1989, p. 223.

2. Varunts (ed.), *Muzykal'naya Akademiya*, 2001, no. 1, p. 142.

3. Stravinsky to Diaghilev, 11 February 1922. Zilbershteyn and Samkov, 1982, ii, p. 135.

4. Diaghilev to Sudeykin, March 1922. Varunts, 2000, p. 518.

5. Kochno as quoted by Buckle, 1979, p. 401. The more likely culprit is Larionov, considering that he was a childhood friend of Survage. See Parton, 1993, p. 3.

6. Bakst to Diaghilev, 26 April 1922. Varunts, 2000, p. 521.

7. Bakst to Dobuzhinsky, 15 June 1923. H. L. Dunayeva, 'Ya uzhe navsegda porval s nim' (a letter from Bakst to Dobuzhinsky), unpublished manuscript in possession of author, p. 114.

8. Bakst to Diaghilev, [after 3 June 1922]. Varunts, 2000, pp. 523–4.

9. Stravinsky to Diaghilev, 11 January 1922. Ibid., pp. 515–16.

10. Stravinsky to Kochno, undated. Quoted in Walsh, 2000, p. 346.

11. Grigoriev, 1960, p. 187. For Kochno, see Buckle, 1979, p. 403.

12. See Kahan, 2003, p. 230.

13. Prokofiev, diary entry of 25 February–23 November 1922. Prokofiev, 2002, ii, pp. 205–6.

14. Mayakovski to Diaghilev, 15 February 1923. Varunts, 2000, pp. 533–4.

15. See Nestyev, 1994, p. 182.

16. Taruskin, 1996, ii, pp. 1419–21.

17. See Garafola, 1989, pp. 435–6, n. 66.

18. Benois to Argutinsky-Dolgorukov, 24 December 1922. Benois [Benua], 2003, p. 105.

19. Benois to Diaghilev, 9 June 1923. Fonds Kochno (Musée de l'Opéra, Paris), pièce 11. The published version of this letter (Benois [Benua], 2003, pp. 41–2) differs in a number of respects from the version at the Kochno archive. The former version is based on Benois's copy of the letter, which is now part of the Benois archive at the Russian Museum in St Petersburg (fond 137, op. 1, ed. khr. 358). The main difference is the postscript about Valentin's two sons. In the Parisian original the postscript is partly illegible. It appears to say that Benois made enquiries with Vladimir. It is unclear what is meant by this.

20. Lopokova to Keynes, 15 June 1923. Hill and Keynes, 1989, p. 95.

21. See Garafola, 1989, p. 126.

22. Grigoriev, 1960, pp. 192–3.

23. Richardson, 2007, pp. 228–9.

24. Garafola, 1989, p. 128.

25. Ansermet to Stravinsky, 17 September 1923. Ansermet and Stravinsky, 1990, ii, p. 75.

26. Diaghilev to Benois, 3 September 1923. Zilbershteyn and Samkov, 1982, ii, p. 135.

27. Milhaud, 1957, p. 98.

28. Lopokova to Keynes, 14 January 1924. Hill and Keynes, 1989, p. 141.

29. Milhaud, 1957, p. 156.

30. See Garafola, 1989, p. 129.

31. Picasso would later make sketches for programmes on a few occasions.

32. Zilbershteyn and Samkov, 1982, ii, p. 442.

33. Mayakovsky to Osip Brik, 20 November 1924. Ibid.

34. Mayakovsky to Lunacharsky, 20 November 1924. Ibid., p. 205.

26 The Soviet Union Strikes Back, 1924–1927

1. This information comes from Danilova, 1986, p. 65.

2. Grigoriev, 1960, p. 208.

3. Wollheim, 2004, pp. 166–7.

4. Diaghilev to José Maria Sert, 29 December 1924. Zilbershteyn and Samkov, 1982, ii, p. 138.

5. Ibid., p. 440.

6. Buckle, 1979, p. 448.

7. Duke, 1955, pp. 110–11.

8. Ibid., p. 114.

9. Most sources do not mention Chanel in this context, but in his memoirs Dukelsky refers to her as the costume designer. Ibid., p. 136.

10. Ibid., p. 137.

11. There are many ballets entitled *Zéphire et Flore*, but the Didelot and Cavos version is the one that made history. See Krasovskaya, 2008, p. 111.

12. Diaghilev to Lifar, summer 1924. Scheijen, *Sergei Diaghilev*, 2004, p. 199.

13. Prokofiev describes the negotiations in his diary. He was given 1,500 francs for a ballet, whereas Auric got 500. Prokofiev, 2002, ii, pp. 319–20, 331–2.

14. Prokofiev, diary entry of 22 June 1925. Ibid., p. 331.

15. See Lifar, 1940, p. 389.

16. Prokofiev to Diaghilev, 4 February 1926. Varunts (ed.), *Muzykal'naya Akademiya*, 2000, no. 2, p. 198.

17. Diaghilev mentioned the talk with Rakovsky to Prokofiev. Prokofiev, diary entry of 18 June 1925. Prokofiev, 2002, ii, p. 340. Kerzhentsev mediated between Diaghilev and Meyerhold. See Varunts (ed.), Muzykal'naya Akademiya, 2000, no. 2, p. 197 (n. 11, letter 5).

18. Prokofiev to Diaghilev, 16 August 1925. Varunts (ed.), Muzykal'naya Akademiya, 2000, no. 2, p. 196.

19. This theory of the name's origin comes from Varunts. See ibid.

20. Ibid.

21. Prokofiev, diary entries, 7 and 16 October. Prokofiev, 2002, ii, pp. 349–50.

22. On the subject of this virtually unknown connection between Meyerhold and Diaghilev, see Volkov, 1929, e.g. i, pp. 202, 231, 233.

23. Meyerhold to Yakulov, April 1926. Ibid., p. 199.

24. Nouvel to Yakulov, 14 April 1926. Ibid., p. 200.

25. See Prokofiev, diary entry of 23 March 1926. Prokofiev, 2002, ii, p. 384.

26. Ibid.

27. For more on the relationship between Rothermere, Diaghilev and Sokolova, see Buckle, 1979, pp. 464–5. For more on the relationship between Diaghilev, Porter and Kochno, and the sums of money that Diaghilev received from Porter, see McBrien, 1998, pp. 101–2.

28. Ansermet quoted in Craft, 1984, p. 154.

29. Ibid., p. 153.

30. Goncharova to Diaghilev, 30 August 1926. Varunts, 2003, pp. 202–3.

31. Stravinsky to Diaghilev, 6 April 1926. Ibid., p. 184.

32. Diaghilev to Stravinsky, 7 April 1926. Ibid., p. 186.

33. Prokofiev, diary entry of 18 May 1926. Prokofiev, 2002, ii, p. 403.

34. Prokofiev, diary entry of 29 May 1926. Ibid., p. 408.

35. A detailed history of the run-up to the collaboration can be found in Hammer and Lodder, 2000, pp. 155–6.

36. Both quotations are from a letter from Pevsner to Gabo, 11 February 1927. Ibid., p. 156.

37. There are two lengthy reconstructions of the genesis of *Oedipus* and the question of its being a 'present' for Diaghilev. See Walsh, 2000, pp. 442–6.

38. Diaghilev's letters to Stravinsky from this period have been lost, but Stravinsky's surviving letters suggest that the impresario was a regular correspondent. See Varunts, 2003, pp. 222–3.

39. Stravinsky to Diaghilev, 31 January 1927. Ibid.

40. Prokofiev, diary entry of 9 April 1927. Prokofiev, 2002, ii, p. 557.

41. Prokofiev, diary entry of 22 March 1927. Ibid., p. 551.

42. Prokofiev, diary entry of 11 April 1927. Ibid., p. 558.

43. Walsh, 2000, p. 443. Craft and Stravinsky, 1982, pp. 24–5.

44. Prokofiev, diary entry of 21 May 1927. Prokofiev, 2002, ii, p. 561.

45. Lunacharsky in *Vechernyaya Moskva*, 25 June 1927. In Zilbershteyn and Samkov, 1982, ii, pp. 215–17.

46. Prokofiev, diary entry of 29 May 1927. Prokofiev, 2002, ii, p. 563.

47. See ibid., p. 565.

48. Interview with Diaghilev in the *Observer*, 3 July 1927. In Varunts, 1991, p. 70.

49. Kochno, 1970, p. 265.

50. Vladimir Dukelsky, 'Ob odnoy prervannoy druzhbe', in Rakhmanova, 2007, pp. 89–90.

51. The main source here is Dyagileva, 1998, pp. 253–4. Additional information comes from the author's conversations with Valentin's granddaughter, Yelena Sergeyevna Diaghileva, and the document referred to in chapter 27, n. 1.

52. See Dyagileva, 1998, p. 254.

27 The Final Curtain, 1928–1929

1. Jean Hervette to Berthelot, 15 January 1928. Lincoln Center, Dance Collection, Diaghilev papers, C-20–16.2. It was Lynn Garafola who unearthed this invaluable source, and I am deeply grateful to her for making this information available to me.

2. Hervette to Berthelot, 24 January 1928. Ibid.

3. Grigoriev, 1960, p. 246.

4. This obvious suggestion is from Walsh. Walsh, 2000, p. 453.

5. Craft and Stravinsky, 1982, p. 32.

6. Nabokov is very careless with facts in his memoirs. He calls Valentin's youngest son Kolya, even though his name was Sergey. He has Diaghilev mention Valentin's imprisonment in 1924; in reality, Valentin was not arrested till 1927. Incidentally, this allusion to Valentin's detention is the

only reference we have to the tragic events of 1927. See Nabokov, 1951, pp. 58–67.

7. Diaghilev to Lifar, 13 July 1927. Zilbershteyn and Samkov, 1982, ii, p. 139.

8. See ibid., pp. 441–2.

9. See Buckle, 1979, p. 496.

10. Nabokov, 1951, p. 125.

11. Diaghilev to Argutinsky, 1 July 1928. Zilbershteyn and Samkov, 1982, ii, p. 141.

12. Ibid.

13. Lifar, 1994, p. 404. Varunts mentions an amount of 50,000 francs but offers no source. See Varunts (ed.), *Muzykal'naya Akademiya*, 2001, no. 2, p. 125 n. 27.

14. Published in Varunts (ed.), *Muzykal'naya Akademiya*, 2001, nos. 1–3.

15. Zilbershteyn claimed that Diaghilev had 'the best collection of Russian cultural artefacts abroad'. Zilbershteyn and Samkov, 1982, ii, p. 442.

16. On 26 March 1927 Prokofiev noted in his diary that Diaghilev was bedridden with a chest abscess. Prokofiev, 2002, ii, p. 554. This is probably the first mention of Diaghilev's furunculosis.

17. Diaghilev to Lifar, 3 October 1928. Lifar, 1994, p. 408.

18. Ibid., p. 409.

19. Prokofiev, diary entry of 8–28 October 1928. Prokofiev, 2002, ii, p. 644.

20. The amount of five million is mentioned in a letter from Kostya Somov, who attended the Parisian premiere. Somov to Mikhailova, 26 November 1928. Podkopayeva and Sveshnikova, 1979, p. 346.

21. Prokofiev, diary entry of 23 November 1928. Prokofiev, 2002, ii, p. 648.

22. Diaghilev to Lifar, 25 November 1928. Scheijen, *Sergei Diaghilev*, 2004, pp. 212–13.

23. Diaghilev to Lifar, [28 November 1928]. Lifar, 1994, p. 413. This passage was partly cut in the US version. In the Russian original there is an ellipsis after 'red-headed'. I'm assuming that the ellipsis stood for something derogatory that Lifar preferred to omit.

24. Sergey Diaghilev, interview in *Vozrozhdeniye*, 18 December 1928. Zilbershteyn and Samkov, 1982, i, pp. 250–52. The article to which

Diaghilev was reacting, 'Diaghilev and Classicism' by A. V. Bundikov, had appeared the week before in the same magazine. Ibid., p. 480.

25. Ibid., pp. 250–52.

26. This quote is from Kochno, in Walsh, 2000, p. 477. Lifar says much the same. See Lifar, 1994, p. 416.

27. See Prokofiev, 2002, ii, p. 650. Lifar, 1994, p. 412.

28. Diaghilev to Lifar, [late November 1928]. Lifar, 1994, p. 412.

29. Kessler, diary entry of 27 December 1928. Kessler, 1996, p. 613.

30. Prokofiev, diary entry of 7 February 1929. Prokofiev, 2002, ii, p. 654.

31. Prokofiev diary entry of 16 March 1929. Ibid., p. 685.

32. Yelena Sergeyevna Diaghileva (Sergey Valentinovich's daughter) told me that Ansermet had visited her grandmother and grandfather in the spring of 1929. A year later I found the remarks about 'commissions for Ansermet' in Leningrad in a letter from Nouvel to Diaghilev, at the Harvard Theatre Library, which would appear to confirm Yelena Sergeyevna's story. Nouvel's letter to Diaghilev is from 23 March 1929 (Harvard Theatre Library, bMS Thr 466(8)).

33. Benois to Diaghilev, between January and April 1929. Scheijen, *Sergei Diaghilev*, 2004, pp. 218–19.

34. Stravinsky referred to the letter to Diaghilev and Diaghilev's response in a letter to Ansermet of 11 June 1929. Ansermet and Stravinsky, 1990, ii, pp. 183–4. The fact that Paichadze was already in negotiations with Rubinstein was clear from the former's letter to Stravinsky of 10 April 1929. Varunts, 2003, pp. 344–5.

35. See Buckle, 1979, p. 524.

36. Prokofiev, diary entry of 4–10 June 1929. Prokofiev, 2002, ii, p. 710.

37. Ibid.

38. Ibid.

39. Stravinsky to Ansermet, 19 June 1929. Ansermet and Stravinsky, 1990, ii, pp. 187–8.

40. Prokofiev, diary entry of August 1929. Prokofiev, 2002, ii, p. 721. Stravinsky described this incident many years later in Craft and Stravinsky, *Expositions*, 1981, p. 85. This version differs from the account Prokofiev

gives in his diary. In *Expositions* Diaghilev does not clasp Stravinsky on the shoulder; they merely catch sight of each other, making a meeting inevitable. In Prokofiev's version it is clear that Diaghilev took the initiative to talk to Stravinsky. We know the exact date (24 June) thanks to Vera Sudeykina's diary, quoted in Varunts, 2003, p. 351.

41. Interview with L. B. Bernstein, 'Iz besedy s S. P. Dyagilevym', in Zilbershteyn and Samkov, 1982, i, p. 259.

42. Diaghilev to Markevich, 23 July 1929. Zilbershteyn and Samkov, 1982, ii, pp. 147–8.

43. See Buckle, 1979, p. 528.

44. Nouvel quoted in a letter from Somov to Mikhailova, 10 September 1929. Podkopayeva and Sveshnikova, 1979, p. 358.

45. Buckle, 1979, p. 536.

46. Lifar, 1994, p. 438.

47. Buckle, 1979, p. 537.

48. Ibid.

49. Ibid., p. 540.

50. Lifar, 1994, p. 444.

51. Misia Sert wrote that they called for a Catholic priest, who initially refused to administer the last rites. Sert, 1953, pp. 162–3. According to Lifar it was an Orthodox priest. Lifar, 1994, p. 446.

52. See Prokofiev, 2002, ii, p. 722.

53. Craft, 1985, pp. 43–4.

54. Ansermet to Stravinsky, 21 August 1929. Ansermet and Stravinsky, 1990, ii, p. 193.

55. The note from Aunt Yulia is in the Frits Lugt Collection, Fondation Custodia, 2002-A.1267.

56. Prokofiev to Nouvel, 25 August 1929. Zilbershteyn and Samkov, 1982, ii, p. 211.

57. Prokofiev to Asafiev, 29 August 1929. Varunts, 2003, p. 359.

58. Benois to Nouvel, 25 August 1929. Karasik, 1995, p. 242.

59. Stravinsky to Nouvel, 26 August 1929. Varunts, 2003, pp. 358–9.

60. Nouvel to Stravinsky, 30 August 1929. Ibid., p. 360.

BIBLIOGRAPHY

Archives

Archives Picasso, Musée Picasso, Paris

Bibliothèque Nationale de France, Musée de l'Opéra, Paris

Centre Nationale de la Dance, Pantin

Fondation Custodia, Paris

Gabriel Astruc papers, Jerome Robbins Dance Division, Lincoln Center, New
York Public Library

Harvard Theatre Collection, Cambridge, MA

Institut Russkoy Literatury (IRLi), St Petersburg

Music Division, Library of Congress, Washington, DC

Rossiysky gosudarstvenny arkhiv Literatura i Iskusstvo (RGALi), Moscow

Serge Diaghilev (correspondence), Jerome Robbins Dance Division, Lincoln
Center, New York Public Library

Serge Diaghilev (papers), Jerome Robbins Dance Division, Lincoln Center,
New York Public Library

Tsentralny gosudarstvenny istorichesky arkhiv (TsGIA SPb), St Petersburg

Primary sources: letters, diaries, memoirs and autobiographical writings

Ernest Ansermet and Igor Stravinsky, *Correspondance, édition complète (1914–
1967)*, ed. Claude Tappolet, 3 vols. (Geneva, 1990)

Konstantin Asadowski (ed.), *Rilke und Russland: Briefe, Erinnerungen, Gedichte*, trans. Ulrike Hirschberg (Frankfurt, 1986)

Gabriel Astruc, *Le Pavillon des fantômes: Souvenirs* (Paris, 1929)

Cyril Beaumont, *The Diaghilev Ballet in London: A Personal Record* (London, 1945)

Andrey Beli, *Mezhdu dvukh revolutsiy* (Moscow, 1990)

——, *Nachalo veka* (Moscow, 1990)

Alexandre Benois, *Reminiscences of the Russian Ballet* (London, 1941)

——, *Memoirs*, 2 vols. (London, 1960, 1964)

—— [A. N. Benua], *Aleksandr Benua razmyshlyayet* (Moscow, 1968)

—— [A. N. Benua], *Moi vospominaniya*, 2 vols. (Moscow, 1980)

—— [A. N. Benua], *Vozniknoveniya Mira iskusstva, reprintnoye izdaniye* (Moscow, 1998)

—— [A. N. Benua], *Moy dnevnik, 1916–1917–1918* (Moscow, 2003)

Alexandre Benois [A. N. Benua] and M. V. Dobuzhinsky, *Perepiska (1903–1957)* (St Petersburg, 2003)

Alexandre Benois [A. N. Benua] and S. P. Dyagilev, *Perepiska (1893–1928)* (St Petersburg, 2003)

Valery Bryusov, *The Diary of Valery Bryusov (1893–1905)*, trans. and ed. Joan Delaney Grossman (Berkeley and Los Angeles, 1980)

Charles B. Cochran, *The Secrets of a Showman* (London, 1925)

——, *Showman Looks On* (London, 1945)

Jean Cocteau, *Dessins* (Paris, 1923)

Robert Craft, *An Improbable Life* (Nashville, 2002)

Robert Craft (ed.), *Stravinsky in Pictures and Documents* (New York, 1978)

——, *Dearest Bubushkin: The Correspondence of Vera and Igor Stravinsky, 1921–1954, with Excerpts from Vera Stravinsky's Diaries, 1922–1971* (London, 1985)

Robert Craft and Igor Stravinsky, *Conversations with Igor Stravinsky* (London, 1979)

——, *Expositions and Developments* (Los Angeles, 1981)

——, *Memories and Commentaries* (Berkeley and Los Angeles, 1981)

——, *Dialogues* (London, 1982)

Edward Gordon Craig and Harry Kessler, *The Correspondence of Edward Gordon Craig and Count Harry Kessler, 1903–1937*, ed. L. M. Newman (London, 1995)

Alexandra Danilova, *Choura: The Memoirs of Alexandra Danilova* (New York, 1986)

Claude Debussy, *Correspondance, 1872–1918*, ed. François Lesure and Denis Herlin (Paris, 2005)

Sergey Diaghilev [S. P. Dyagilev], *Russkya zhivopis' v XVIII veke*, vol. i, *D. G. Levitsky, 1735–1822* (St Petersburg, 1902)

——, *Sostoyavshaya pod vysochayshim yego velichestva gosudarya imperatora pokrovitel'stvom', istoriko-khudozhestvennaya vystavka russkikh portretov, 1905. Predpolagayemy spisok eksponentov, ostavlenny S. Dyagilevym. Izdaniye tret'e* (St Petersburg, 1904)

Sergey Diaghilev [S. P. Dyagilev] (ed.), *Ezhegodnik imperatorskikh teatrov, Sezon' 1899–1900* (St Petersburg, 1900)

M. V. Dobuzhinsky, *Vospominaniya* (Moscow, 1987)

——, *Pis'ma*, ed. G. I. Chugunov (St Petersburg, 2001)

Anton Dolin, *Autobiography* (London, 1960)

John Drummond, *Speaking of Diaghilev* (London, 1997)

Vernon Duke, *Passport to Paris* (New York, 1955)

E. V. Dyagileva, *Semeynaya zapis' o Dyagilevykh* (St Petersburg, 1998)

D. V. Filosofov, *Zagadki russkoy kul'tury* (Moscow, 2004)

Mikhail Fokine, *Protiv techeniya: Vospominaniya baletmeystera. Stsenarii i zamysly baletov. Stat'i, interv'yu i pis'ma* (Leningrad, 1981)

A. Fyodorova-Davydova, *I. I. Levitan: Pis'ma, Dokumenty, Vospominaniya* (Moscow, 1956)

Tamara Geva, *Split Seconds* (New York, 1972)

Zinaida Gippius, *Sobrannye sochineniya*, 10 vols. (Moscow, 2001–6). Quoted in this volume: vol. vi, *Zhivye litsa* (2002); vol. viii, *Dnevniki, 1893–1919* (2003)

E. P. Gomberg-Verzhbinskoy and Y. N. Podkopayeva (eds.), *Vrubel', perepiska, vospominaniya, o khudozhnike* (Leningrad, 1963)

Edmond de Goncourt, *Mémoires de la vie littéraire*, vol. vi, *1878–1884* (Paris, 1892)

Igor Grabar, *Pis'ma, 1891–1917* (Moscow, 1975)

——, *Pis'ma, 1917–1941* (Moscow, 1977)

——, *Moya zhizn', avtomonografiya, etyudi o khudozhnikakh* (Moscow, 2001)

S. L. Grigoriev, *The Diaghilev Ballet, 1909–1929* (Harmondsworth, 1960)

E. A. Grosheva (ed.), *Fyodor Ivanovich Shalyapin*, vol. i, *Literaturnoye nasledstvo, pis'ma* (Moscow, 1976)

——, *Fyodor Ivanovich Shalyapin*, vol. ii, *Vospominaniya o F. I. Shalyapine* (Moscow, 1977)

Polly Hill and Richard Keynes (eds.), *Lydia and Maynard: The Letters of Lydia Lopokova and John Maynard Keynes* (London, 1989)

Zinaida Hippius [Gippius], *De schittering van woorden* (Amsterdam, 1984)

Hugo von Hofmannsthal and Harry Graf Kessler, *Briefwechsel* (Frankfurt, 1968)

E. A. Ilyukhina and I. V. Shumanova, *M. Larionov. N. Goncharova: Parizhskoye naslediye v Tret'yakovskoy galereye* (Moscow, 1997)

I. N. Karasik (ed.), *Iz istorii muzeya* (St Petersburg, 1995)

Tamara Karsavina, *Theatre Street: The Reminiscences of Tamara Karsavina* (London, 1950)

Harry Graf Kessler, *Tagebücher, 1918 bis 1937* (Frankfurt, 1996)

——, *Das Tagebuch*, vol. iv, *1906–1914* (Stuttgart, 2005)

Aga Khan, *Die Memoiren des Aga Khan: Welten und Zeiten* (Vienna, 1954)

Mikhail Kuzmin, *Dnevniki, 1905–1906–1907*, ed. N. Bogomolov and S. Shumikhin (St Petersburg, 2000)

——, *Dnevniki, 1908–1915*, ed. N. Bogomolov and S. Shumikhin (St Petersburg, 2005)

Michel Larionov, *Diaghilev et les Ballets Russes* (Paris, 1970)

Madeline Laurence (ed.), *Les Archives de Picasso, 'On est ce que l'on garde!'* (catalogue to an exhibition) (Paris, 2003)

Prince Peter Lieven, *The Birth of the Ballets Russes* (New York, 1973)

Serge Lifar, *Serge Diaghilev: His Life, His Work, His Legend* (New York, 1940)

——, *Dyagilev i s Dyagilevym* (Moscow, 1994)

Sergey Makovsky, *Portrety Sovremenikov* (New York, 1955)

Filippo Tommaso Marinetti, *Taccuini, 1915–1921* (Bologna, 1987)

Alicia Markova, *Markova Remembers* (Boston, 1986)

Léonide Massine, *My Life in Ballet*, ed. Phyllis Hartnoll and Robert Rubens (London, 1968)

Darius Milhaud, *Notes without Music: An Autobiography* (New York, 1957)

Doris Monteux, *It's All in the Music: The Life and Work of Pierre Monteux* (New York, 1965)

Nicolas Nabokov, *Old Friends and New Music* (London, 1951)

Bronislava Nijinska, *Early Memoirs*, trans. and ed. Irina Nijinska and Jean Rawlinson (London, 1982)

Romola Nijinsky, *Nijinsky* (New York, 1934)

Vaslav Nijinsky, *The Diary of Vaslav Nijnsky, Unexpurgated Edition*, ed. Joan Acocella; trans. Kyril Fitzlyon (New York, 1999)

Alice Nikitina, *Nikitina by Herself*, trans. Baroness Budberg (London, 1959)

P. Pertsov, *Literaturnye vospominaniya, 1890–1902* (Moscow, 1933)

Y. N. Podkopayeva and A. N. Sveshnikova (eds.), *Konstantin Andreyevich Somov: Pis'ma. Dnevniki. Suzhdeniya sovremennikov* (Moscow, 1979)

Vladimir Polunin, *The Continental Method of Scene Painting*, ed. Cyril Beaumont (London, 1980)

Francis Poulenc, *My Friends and Myself*, ed. Stéphane Audel and trans. James Harding (London, 1978)

Sergei Prokofiev, *Soviet Diary (1927) and Other Writings*, trans. and ed. Oleg Prokofiev with Christopher Palmer (Boston, 1992)

——, *Dnevnik*, vol. i, *1907–1918*; vol. ii, *1919–1933* (Paris, 2002)

——, *Diaries, 1907–1914: Prodigious Youth*, trans. and ed. Anthony Phillips (London, 2006)

M. P. Rakhmanova, *Sergey Prokof'yev, pis'ma, vospominaniya, stat'i* (Moscow, 2007)

Marie Rambert, *Quicksilver: An Autobiography* (London, 1972)

Ilya Repin, *Izbrannye pis'ma, 1867–1930*, 2 vols. (Moscow, 1969)

Nikolay Andreyevich Rimsky-Korsakoff, *My Musical Life*, trans. Carl van Vechten and Judah A. Joffe; ed. Carl van Vechten (New York, 1935)

Arthur Rubinstein, *My Young Years* (London, 1973)

——, *My Many Years* (New York, 1980)

A. A. Rusakova (ed.), *M. B. Nesterov, Pis'ma, izbrannoye* (Leningrad, 1988)

Erik Satie, *Correspondance presque complete*, ed. Ornella Volta (Paris, 2003)

Sjeng Scheijen (ed.), *Sergei Diaghilev: Ik zit vol grootse plannen: brieven* (Amsterdam, 2004)

Misia Sert, *Two or Three Muses: The Memoirs of Misia Sert*, trans. Moura Budberg (London, 1953)

Lydia Sokolova, *Dancing for Diaghilev: The Memoirs of Lydia Sokolova*, ed. Richard Buckle (London, 1960)

V. V. Stasov, *Izbrannye Sotsineniya*, 3 vols. (Moscow, 1952)

Igor Stravinsky, *An Autobiography* (New York, 1962)

——, *Selected Correspondence*, ed. Robert Craft, 3 vols. (New York, 1982, 1984, 1985)

——, 'Stravinsky in His Own Words', on the recording *Igor Stravinsky: Symphonies & Rehearsals and Talks*, Sony Classical CD: SM2K 46294

N. Tcherepnin, *Vospominaniya muzykanta* (Leningrad, 1976)

V. A. Telyakovsky, *Vospominaniya* (Leningrad, 1965)

——, *Dnevniki direktora imperatorskikh teatrov, 1898–1901* (Moscow, 1998)

Mariya Tenisheva, *Vpechatleniya Moyey Zhizni* (Moscow, 2002)

K. F. Valts, *Shestdeshat pyat' Let v Teatre* (Leningrad, 1928)

Viktor Varunts (ed.), *I. Stravinsky: Publitsist i sobesednik* (Moscow, 1988)

——, *Prokof'yev o Prokof'yeve* (Moscow, 1991)

——, *I. F. Stravinsky: Perepiska c Russkimi Korespondentami, Materiali k biografii*, vol. i, *1882–1912*; vol. ii, *1913–1922*; vol. iii, *1923–1939* (Moscow, 1998, 2000, 2003)

S. M. Volkonsky, *Moi Vospominaniya. Rodina* (Munich, 1923)

I. I. Vydrin and V. P. Tretyakov (eds.), *Stepan Petrovich Yaremich* (St Petersburg, 2004)

Oscar Wilde, *The Letters of Oscar Wilde*, ed. Rupert Hart-Davis (London, 1962)

Richard Wollheim, *Germs: A Memoir of Childhood* (London, 2004)

V. V. Yastrebtsev, *Reminiscences of Rimsky-Korsakov*, ed. and trans. Florence Jonas (New York, 1985)

I. S. Zilbershteyn and V. A. Samkov (eds.), *Valentin Serov v vospominaniyakh, dnevnikakh, i perepiske sovremenikov*, 2 vols. (Leningrad, 1971)

——, *Sergey Dyagilev i russkoye iskusstvo, stat'i, otkrytye pis'ma, interv'yu. Perepiska. Sovremeniki o Dyagileve*, 2 vols. (Moscow, 1982)

——, *Valentin Serov v perepiske, dokumentakh i interv'yu*, 2 vols. (Leningrad, 1985, 1989)

——, *Konstantin Korovin ospominayet* (Moscow, 1990)

Aleksandr Ilyich Ziloti, *1863–1945, Vospominaniya i pis'ma* (Leningrad, 1963)

Secondary sources

Joan Acocella, 'The Reception of Diaghilev's Ballets Russes by Artists and Intellectuals in Paris and London, 1909–1914', PhD thesis, Rutgers University, 1984

A. D. Alekseyev, et al. (eds.), *Russkaya khudozhestvennaya kul'tura kontsa XIX–nachala XX veka*, vol. ii, *1895–1907*; vol. iii, *1908–1917* (Moscow, 1969, 1977)

Stijn Alsteens, 'L'inconstance de Maria Tenicheva', in *L'Art russe dans la seconde moitié du XIXe siècle: En quête d'identité* (catalogue to an exhibition) (Paris, 2005)

——, *Mélange russe: Dessins, estampes et lettres russes de la Collection Frits Lugt* (catalogue to an exhibition) (Paris, 2005)

Louis Andriessen and Elmer Schönberger, *Het Apollinisch uurwerk: Over Stravinsky* (Amsterdam, 1983)

Susan Au, *Ballet and Modern Dance* (London, 1988)

N. B. Avtonomova and A. G. Lukanova (eds.), *Parizhskiye nakhodki, k 100-letiyu so dnya rozhdeniya I. S. Zil'bershteyna* (Moscow, 2005)

Charles Barber, *Lost in the Stars: The Forgotten Musical Life of Alexander Siloti* (Lanham, MD, 2002)

Rosamund Bartlett, *Wagner and Russia* (Cambridge, 1995)

Cyril W. Beaumont, *Five Centuries of Ballet Design* (London, n.d.)

N. V. Belyaeva, et al. (eds.), *Sergey Dyagilev i khudozhestvennaya kul'tura XIX–XX vv.* (Perm, 1989)

Brian Blackwood, 'The Black Notebook of Serge Diaghilev', Jerome Robbins dance division, Lincoln Center, New York Public Library

Faubion Bowers, *Scriabin: A Biography of the Russian Composer, 1871–1915* (Tokyo, 1969)

John Bowlt, *Russian Art, 1875–1975: A Collection of Essays* (New York, 1976)

——, *The Silver Age: Russian Art of the Early Twentieth Century and the 'World of Art' Group* (Newtonville, 1979)

——, *Russian Stage Design: Scenic Innovation, 1900–1930*, from the collection of Mr & Mrs Nikita D. Lobanov-Rostovsky (catalogue to an exhibition) (Jackson, MS, 1982)

——, *Khudozhniki russkogo teatra, 1880–1930, katalog-rezone, sobraniye Nikity i Niny Lobanovykh-Rostovskikh* (Moscow, 1994)

Oleg Brezgin, *Persona Dyagileva v khudozhestvennoy kul'ture Rossii, zapadnoy Yevropy i Ameriki (bibliografiya)* (Perm, 2007)

Richard Buckle, *Diaghilev* (London, 1979)

——, *George Balanchine, Ballet Master* (New York, 1988)

——, *Nijinsky* (London, 1998)

Mary Chamot, *Goncharova: Stage Designs and Painting* (London, 1979)

G. Chugunov, *Mstislav Valeryanovich Dobuzhinsky* (Leningrad, 1984)

Jean Clair (ed.), *Picasso: Le Voyage d'Italie, 1917–1924* (catalogue to an exhibition) (Venice, 1998)

Michael de Cossart, *Ida Rubinstein (1885–1960): A Theatrical Life* (Liverpool, 1987)

Robert Craft, *Prejudices in Disguise: Articles, Essays, Reviews* (New York, 1974)

——, *Present Perspectives* (New York, 1984)

——, *Stravinsky: Glimpses of a Life* (New York, 1992)

Richard Davenport-Hines, *A Night at the Majestic: Proust and the Great Modernist Dinner Party of 1922* (London, 2006)

Anton Dolin, *The Sleeping Ballerina: The Story of Olga Spessivtzeva* (London, 1966)

Laird M. Easton, *The Red Count: The Life and Times of Harry Kessler* (Berkeley, 2002)

Modris Eksteins, *Lenteriten: De Eerste Wereldoorlog en het ontstaan van de nieuwe tijd* (Antwerp, 2003)

Mark Etkind, *Aleksandr Nikolayevich Benua, 1870–1960* (Leningrad, 1965)

——, *A. N. Benua i russkaya khudozhestvennaya kul'tura* (Leningrad, 1989)

A. H. Franks, *Pavlova: A Biography* (London, 1956)

Joseph Gale, *I Sang for Diaghilev* (Brooklyn, 1982)

Lynn Garafola, *Diaghilev's Ballets Russes* (New York, 1989)

——, *Legacies of Twentieth-Century Dance* (Middletown, 2005)

Lynn Garafola and Nancy Van Norman Baer (eds.), *The Ballets Russes and Its World* (New Haven, 1999)

Vicente García-Márquez, *Massine: A Biography* (London, 1996)

Arthur Gold and Robert Fizdale, *Misia: The Life of Misia Sert* (London, 1980)

S. V. Golynets, *Lev Bakst, zhivopis', grafika, teatral'no-dekoratsionnoye iskusstvo* (Moscow, 1992)

Martin Hammer and Christina Lodder, *Constructing Modernity: The Art and Career of Naum Gabo* (New Haven and London, 2000)

Arnold L. Haskell and Walter Nouvel, *Diaghileff, His Artistic and Private Life* (New York, 1935)

Dan Healy, *Homosexual Desire in Revolutionary Russia: The Regulation of Sexual and Gender Dissent* (Chicago, 2001)

Carol A. Hess, *Sacred Passions: The Life and Music of Manuel de Falla* (Oxford, 2005)

P. N. Holtrop, *De Hollandse Hervormde Kerk in Sint-Petersburg*, vol. ii, *1713–1927* (Kampen, 2005)

Paul Horgan, *Encounters with Stravinsky: A Personal Record* (London, 1972)

Charles M. Joseph, *Stravinsky Inside Out* (New Haven, 2001)

——, *Stravinsky and Balanchine: A Journey of Invention* (New Haven, 2002)

Sylvia Kahan, *Music's Modern Muse: A Life of Winnaretta Singer, Princesse de Polignac* (Rochester, NY, 2003)

Martine Kahane, *Les Ballets Russes à l'Opéra* (Paris, 1992)

Janet Kennedy, *The 'Mir Iskusstva' Group and Russian Art, 1898–1912* (New York, 1977)

Boris Kochno, *Diaghilev and the Ballets Russes* (New York, 1970)

Ann Kodicek (ed.), *Diaghilev, Creator of the Ballets Russes* (catalogue to an exhibition) (London, 1996)

Vera Krasovskaya, *Russky baletny teatr nachala XX veka*, vol. i, *Khoreografy*; vol. ii, *Tantsovshchiki* (Leningrad, 1971, 1972)

——, *Nijinsky*, trans. John E. Bowlt (New York, 1979)

——, *Russky baletny teatr, ot vozniknoveniya do serediny XIX veka* (St Petersburg, 2008)

L. Kutateladze (ed.), *F. Stravinsky, stat'i, pis'ma, vospominaniya* (Leningrad, 1972)

N. Lapshina, *'Mir iskusstva': Ocherki istorii i tvorcheskoy praktiki* (Moscow, 1977)

A. S. Laskin, *Russky period deyatel'nosti S. P. Dyagileva: Formirovaniye novatorskikh khudozhestvennykh printsipov* (St Petersburg, 2002)

——, *Dolgoye puteshestviye s Djagilevym* (Yekaterinburg, 2003)

Edward Lockspeiser, *Debussy: His Life and Mind*, 2 vols. (London, 1965)

Nesta Macdonald, *Diaghilev Observed by Critics in England and the United States, 1911–1929* (London, 1975)

Francis Maes, *Geschiedenis van de Russische muziek, van Glinka tot Sjostakovitsj* (Amsterdam, 2006)

David Magarshack, *Stanislavsky: A Life* (London, 1986)

John E. Malmstad and Nikolay Bogmolov, *Mikhail Kuzmin: A Life in Art* (Cambridge, 1999)

Steven G. Marks, *How Russia Shaped the Modern World: From Art to Anti-Semitism, Ballet to Bolshevism* (Princeton, 2003)

William McBrien, *Cole Porter: A Biography* (New York, 1998)

Konstantin Mokhulsky, *Aleksandr Blok*, trans. Doris V. Johnson (Detroit, 1983)

Keith Money, *Anna Pavlova: Her Life in Art* (New York, 1982)

Walter G. Moss, *A History of Russia*, vol. ii, *Since 1855* (n.p., 2005)

I. A. Muravyova, *Vek moderna*, 2 vols. (St Petersburg, 2004)

I. V. Nestyev, *Dyagilev i muzykal'ny teatr XX veka* (Moscow, 1994)

David Nice, *Prokofiev: From Russia to the West, 1891–1935* (New Haven, 2003)

Leslie Norton, *Léonide Massine and the 20th Century Ballet* (Jefferson, NC, 2004)

Arbie Orenstein, *Ravel, Man and Musician* (New York, 1975)

Peter Ostwald, *Nijinsky: A Leap into Madness* (New York, 1991)

Dominique Païni (ed.), *Cocteau* (catalogue to an exhibition) (Paris, 2003)

Anthony Parton, *Mikhail Larionov and the Russian Avant-Garde* (Princeton, 1993)

Eleonora Paston, *Abramtsevo, iskusstvo i zhizn'* (Moscow, 2003)

E. Petrova (ed.), *Natalya Goncharova, gody v Rossii* (St Petersburg, 2002)

Vilyam Pokhlyobkin, *Istoriya vodki* (Novosibirsk, 1994)

M. N. Pozharskaya, *Russkiye sezony v Parizhe, eskizy dekoratsiy i kostyumov, 1908–1929* (Moscow, 1988)

Alexander Poznansky, *Tchaikovsky: The Quest for the Inner Man* (New York, 1991)

Walter Archibald Propert, *The Russian Ballet, 1921–1929* (London, 1931)

Stephen Press, *Prokofiev's Ballets for Diaghilev* (Aldershot, 2006)

I. N. Pruzhan, *Lev Samoylovich Bakst* (Leningrad, 1975)

Avril Pyman, *The Life of Alexander Blok*, vol. i, *The Distant Thunder*; vol. ii, *The Release of Harmony* (Oxford, 1980)

John Richardson, *A Life of Picasso*, vol. iii, *Triumphant Years* (New York, 2007)

Harlow Robinson, *Sergei Prokofiev: A Biography* (Boston, 2002)

Larissa Salmina-Haskell, *Catalogue of Russian Drawings, Victoria and Albert Museum* (London, 1972)

Sjeng Scheijen, *In dienst van Diaghilev* (Groningen, 2004)

——, *Sergej Diaghilev: Een leven voor de kunst* (Amsterdam, 2009)

Sjeng Scheijen and Henk van Os, *Ilja Repin, het geheim van Rusland* (Zwolle, 2001)

Elmer Schönberger, *Het gebroken oor* (Amsterdam, 2005)

Alexander Schouvaloff, *Léon Bakst: The Theatre Art* (London, 1991)

——, *The Art of Ballets Russes* (New Haven, 1997)

Charles Spencer, *Leon Bakst* (London, 1978)

——, *The World of Serge Diaghilev* (Harmondsworth, 1979)

Hilary Spurling, *Matisse the Master: A Life of Henri Matisse. The Conquest of Colour, 1909–1954* (New York, 2005)

Francis Steegmuller, *Cocteau* (London, 1970)

G. J. Sternin, *Khudozhestvennaya zhizn' Rossii na rubezhe XIX–XX vekov* (Moscow, 1970)

——, *Khudozhestvennaya zhizn' Rossii 1900–1910 godov* (Moscow, 1988)

Richard Stites, *The Women's Liberation Movement in Russia: Feminism, Nihilism and Bolshevism* (Princeton, 1978)

Peter Stoneley, *A Queer History of the Ballet* (London, 2007)

E. P. Subbotin and V. A. Dyldin, *Dyagilevy v Permi: Pamyatnye mesta* (Perm, 2003)

Richard Taruskin, *Stravinsky and the Russian Tradition: A Biography of the Works through 'Mavra'*, 2 vols. (Oxford, 1996)

V. P. Tretyakov, *Otkrytye pis'ma serebryanogo veka* (St Petersburg, 2000)

A. V. Tyrkova, *Anna Pavlovna Filosofova i eya vremeni*, 2 vols. (Petrograd, 1915)

Elizabeth Kridl Valkenier, *Ilya Repin and the World of Russian Art* (New York, 1990)

——, *Valentin Serov, Portraits of Russia's Silver Age* (Evanston, IL, 2001)

Nancy Van Norman Baer (ed.), *The Art of Enchantment: Diaghilev's Ballets Russes, 1909–1929* (San Francisco, 1988)

——, *Russian Avant-Garde Stage Design, 1913–1935* (New York, 1991)

Hugo Vickers, *Cecil Beaton: The Authorized Biography* (London, 1985)

R. I. Vlasova, *Russkoye teatralno-dekoratsionnoye iskusstvo, nachalo xx-veka* (Leningrad, 1984)

N. D. Volkov, *Meyerkhold*, 2 vols. (Moscow, 1929)

Solomon Volkov, *St. Petersburg: A Cultural History*, trans. Antonina W. Bouis (New York, 1997)

Sam Waagenaar, *Mata Hari: Geslepen spionne of onschuldige schoonheid* (Baarn, 1994)

Stephen Walsh, *Igor Stravinsky, a Creative Spring: Russia and France, 1882–1934* (London, 2000)

——, *The New Grove Stravinsky* (London, 2002)

Eric Walter White, *Stravinsky: The Composer and His Works* (Berkeley and Los Angeles, 1979)

Vicky Woolf, *Dancing in the Vortex: The Story of Ida Rubinstein* (Amsterdam, 2000)

Vladimir Zlobin, 'Gippius i Filosofov', in Zinaida Gippius, *Sobrannye sochineniya*, vol. viii, *Dnevniki, 1893–1919* (Moscow, 2003)

Articles

V. Khodashevich, 'Vstrechi', *Novy Mir*, 7 (1969), pp. 180–215

John McGinness, 'Vaslav Nijinsky's Notes for *Jeux*', *Musical Quarterly*, 88 (2005), pp. 556–89

I. Nestyev, 'Sergey Dyagilev – Russkii Muzikant', *Sovetskaya muzyka*, 10 (1978), pp. 111–26

E. Y. Souritz, 'Myassin nachinalsha tak', in *S. Dyagilev i russkoye iskusstvo XIX–XX vv.*, vol. i (Perm, 2005)

Viktor Varunts (ed.), 'Novye materialy iz zarubezhnikh arkhivov', *Muzykal'naya Akademiya*, 2000, no. 2

——, 'S. P. Dyagilev: Nesostoyavshchiyesya memuary', *Muzykal'naya Akademiya*, 2001, nos. 1–3

ILLUSTRATION CREDITS

Colour illustrations

1. Nijinsky and Pavlova in *Le Pavillon d'Armide*, 1909: cover of *Le Théâtre* (Bibliothèque Nationale, Paris. Photo: Archives Charmet/The Bridgeman Art Library).

2. Design for stage curtain for *Schéhérazade* by Serov, 1910: gouache (A. A. Bakhrushin Museum, Moscow. Photo: akg-images).

3. Ida Rubinstein in *Schéhérazade*, 1911: cover of *The Theatre*: lithograph (Private Collection. Photo: Archives Charmet/The Bridgeman Art Library).

4. Aleksandr Golovin's backdrop design 'The Realm of Kashchey' for *The Firebird*, 1910 (Tretyakov Gallery, Moscow. Photo: akg-images).

5. Bakst's costume design for two Boeotian women in *Narcisse*, 1911: watercolour (Theatre Museum, St Petersburg. Photo: akg-images).

6. Curtain design for Act II of *Chout* by Mikhail Larionov: watercolour (Howard D. Rothschild Collection, The Harvard Theatre Collection, Houghton Library. © ADAGP, Paris & DACS, London 2009).

7. Backcloth design for the finale of the 1926 revival of *The Firebird* by Natalia Goncharova (V & A Images/Victoria & Albert Museum; © ADAGP, Paris & DACS, London 2009).

8. A scale model (reconstructed by Lesley-Anne Sayers, 1999) of Georgy Yakulov's set for *Le Pas d'Acier*, 1927. (Project funded by the Arts and Humanities Research Council UK. Photo: Peter Sayers).

Black and white illustrations

(the numbers given are those of the pages on which the illustrations occur):

Stravinsky-Diaghilev Foundation Collection, The Harvard Theatre Collection, Houghton Library: 322

I. S. Zilbershteyn and V. A. Samkov (eds.), *Sergey Dyagilev i russkoye iskusstvo* ...: (1982), vol. 1: 102, 131, 164; vol 2: 181, 190 (© Pictoright, Amsterdam 2009), 336, 402, 412 (© Succession Henri Matisse / Pictoright, Amsterdam 2009)

AUTHOR'S ACKNOWLEDGEMENTS

MANY PEOPLE HELPED make this book possible, and I would like to thank a few of them by name: Yelena Diaghileva, John Bowlt, Nina Lobanov-Rostovsky, Oleg Brezgin, Wilbert Bank, Stijn Alsteens, Eva van Schaik, Michaela van Wassenaer, Willem Korthals Altes, Christiane and Arne Hosmann-Bürgers, Claire Weeda, Otto Boele, Job Lisman, Willem van Maanen, Pieter van Os, Natasha Nikolaevna, Olga van Beijeren, Nienke van Trommel, Hugo van der Velden, Maria Kager, Steve Leinbach, Jane Hedley-Prôle and Thera Giezen. And finally, Wendel ten Arve, for everything.

Without the extraordinary confidence and generous help of Kees ter Horst, this book never would have seen the light of day. I am also deeply grateful to Lynn Garafola of Columbia University, to whom I owe some of the most important archival finds in this book.

I would also like to thank the staff of the Pushkinsky Dom in St Petersburg and the Staatsbibliothek in Berlin. And of course, my thesis supervisor, the reading committee and all my sponsors.

INDEX